PLATO

II

LACHES   PROTAGORAS
MENO   EUTHYDEMUS

PLATO

IN TWELVE VOLUMES

II

LACHES PROTAGORAS MENO
EUTHYDEMUS

WITH AN ENGLISH TRANSLATION BY

W. R. M. LAMB, M.A.

SOMETIME FELLOW OF TRINITY COLLEGE, CAMBRIDGE

CAMBRIDGE, MASSACHUSETTS
HARVARD UNIVERSITY PRESS
LONDON
WILLIAM HEINEMANN LTD
MCMLXVII

First printed 1924
Reprinted 1937, 1952, 1962, 1967

Printed in Great Britain

CONTENTS

PREFACE

THE Greek text in this volume is based on the recension of Schanz: a certain number of emendations by other scholars have been adopted, and these are noted as they occur.

The special introductions are intended merely to prepare the reader for the general character and purpose of each dialogue.

W. R. M. LAMB.

GENERAL INTRODUCTION

PLATO was born in 427 B.C. of Athenian parents who could provide him with the best education of the day, and ample means and leisure throughout his life. He came to manhood in the dismal close of the Peloponnesian War, when Aristophanes was at the height of his success, and Sophocles and Euripides had produced their last plays. As a boy he doubtless heard the lectures of Gorgias, Protagoras, and other sophists, and his early bent seems to have been towards poetry. But his intelligence was too progressive to rest in the agnostic position on which the sophistic culture was based. A century before, Heracleitus had declared knowledge to be impossible, because the objects of sense are continually changing; yet now a certain Cratylus was trying to build a theory of knowledge over the assertion of flux, by developing some hints let fall by its oracular author about the truth contained in names. From this influence Plato passed into contact with Socrates, whose character and gifts have left a singular impress on the thought of mankind. This effect is almost wholly due to Plato's applications and extensions of

A 2

his master's thought ; since, fortunately for us, the pupil not only became a teacher in his turn, but brought his artistic genius into play, and composed the memorials of philosophic talk which we know as the Dialogues. Xenophon, Antisthenes, and Aeschines were other disciples of Socrates who drew similar sketches of his teaching : the suggestion came from the " mimes " of the Syracusan Sophron, —realistic studies of conversation between ordinary types of character. As Plato became more engrossed in the Socratic speculations, this artistic impulse was strengthened by the desire of recording each definite stage of thought as a basis for new discussion and advance.

When Plato was twenty years old, Socrates was over sixty, and had long been notorious in Athens for his peculiar kind of sophistry. In the *Phaedo* he tells how he tried, in his youth, the current scientific explanations of the universe, and found them full of puzzles. He then met with the theory of Anaxagoras,—that the cause of everything is " mind." This was more promising : but it led nowhere after all, since it failed to rise above the conception of physical energy ; this " mind " showed no intelligent aim. Disappointed of an assurance that the universe works for the best, Socrates betook himself to the plan of making *definitions* of " beautiful," " good," " large," and so on, as qualities observed in the several classes of beautiful, good and large material things, and then employing these propositions, if they

x

appeared to be sound, for the erection of higher hypotheses. The point is that he made a new science out of a recognized theory of " ideas " or " forms," which had come of reflecting on the quality predicated when we say " this man is good," and which postulates some sure reality behind the fleeting objects of sense. His " hypothetical " method, familiar to mathematicians, attains its full reach and significance in the *Republic*.

The Pythagoreans who appear in the intimate scene of the *Phaedo* were accustomed to the theory of ideas, and were a fit audience for the highest reasonings of Socrates on the true nature of life and the soul. For some years before the master's death (399 B.C.) Plato, if not a member of their circle, was often a spell-bound hearer of the " satyr." But ordinary Athenians had other views of Socrates, which varied according to their age and the extent of their acquaintance with him. Aristophanes' burlesque in the *Clouds* (423 B.C.) had left a common impression not unlike what we have of the King of Laputa. Yet the young men who had any frequent speech with him in his later years, while they felt there was something uncanny about him, found an irresistible attraction in his simple manner, his humorous insight into their ways and thoughts, and his fervent eloquence on the principles of their actions and careers. He kept no school, and took no fees ; he distrusted the pretensions of the regular sophists, with whom he was carelessly confounded ; moreover, he professed to have no knowledge himself, except so far as to know that he was ignorant. The earliest Dialogues, such as the *Apology*, *Crito*, *Euthyphro*, *Charmides*, *Laches* and *Lysis*, show the manner in which he performed his ministry. In rousing men, especially those whose minds were fresh, to the need of knowing themselves, he promoted the authority of the intellect, the law of definite individual knowledge, above all reason of state or tie of party ; and it is not surprising that his city, in the effort of recovering her political strength, decided to hush such an inconvenient voice. He must have foreseen his fate, but he continued his work undeterred.

Though he seems, in his usual talk, to have professed no positive doctrine, there were one or two beliefs which he frequently declared. Virtue, he said, is knowledge ; for each man's good is his happiness, and once he knows it clearly, he needs must choose to ensue it. Further, this knowledge is innate in our minds, and we only need to have it awakened and exercised by " dialectic," or a systematic course of question and answer. He also believed his mission to be divinely ordained, and asserted that his own actions were guided at times by the prohibitions of a " spiritual sign." He was capable, as we find in the *Symposium*, of standing in rapt meditation at any moment for some time, and once for as long as twenty-four hours.

It is clear that, if he claimed no comprehensive theory of existence, and although his ethical reliance on knowledge, if he never analysed it, leaves him in a very crude stage of psychology, his logical and mystical suggestions must have led his favourite pupils a good way towards a new system of metaphysics. These intimates learnt, as they steeped their minds in his, and felt the growth of a unique affection amid the glow of enlightenment, that happiness may be elsewhere than in our dealings with the material world, and that the mind has prerogatives and duties far above the sphere of civic life.

After the death of Socrates in 399, Plato spent some twelve years in study and travel. For the first part of this time he was perhaps at Megara, where Eucleides, his fellow-student and friend, was forming a school of dialectic. Here he may have composed some of the six Dialogues already mentioned as recording Socrates' activity in Athens. Towards and probably beyond the end of this period, in order to present the Socratic method in bolder conflict with sophistic education, he wrote the *Protagoras*, *Meno*, *Euthydemus*, and *Gorgias*. [These works show a much greater command of dramatic and literary art, and a deeper interest in logic.] The last of them may well be later than 387, the year in which, after an all but disastrous attempt to better the mind of Dionysius of Syracuse, he returned to Athens, and, now forty years of age, founded the Academy; where the memory of his master was to be perpetuated by continuing and expanding the

Socratic discussions among the elect of the new generation. The rivalry of this private college with the professional school of Isocrates is discernible in the subject and tone of the *Gorgias*. Plato carried on the direction of the Academy till his death, at eighty-one, in 346; save that half-way through this period (367) he accepted the invitation of his friend Dion to undertake the instruction of the younger Dionysius at Syracuse. The elder tyrant had been annoyed by the Socratic freedom of Plato's talk : now it was a wayward youth who refused the yoke of a systematic training. What that training was like we see in the *Republic*, where true political wisdom is approached by an arduous ascent through mathematics, logic, and metaphysics. Plato returned, with less hopes of obtaining the ideal ruler, to make wonderful conquests in the realm of thought.

The *Meno* and *Gorgias* set forth the doctrine that knowledge of right is latent in our minds : dialectic, not the rhetoric of the schools, is the means of eliciting it. The method, as Plato soon perceived, must be long and difficult : but he felt a mystical rapture over its certainty, which led him to picture the immutable " forms " as existing in a world of their own. This feeling, and the conviction whence it springs—that knowledge is somehow possible, had come to the front of his mind when he began to know Socrates. Two brilliant compositions, the *Cratylus* and *Symposium*, display the strength of the conviction, and then, the noble fervour of the feeling. In the latter of these works, the highest powers of imaginative sympathy and eloquence are summoned to unveil the sacred vision of absolute beauty. The *Phaedo* turns the logical theory upon the soul, which is seen to enjoy, when freed from the body, familiar cognition of the eternal types of being. Here Orphic dogma lends its aid to the Socratic search for knowledge, while we behold an inspiring picture of the philosopher in his hour of death.

With increasing confidence in himself as the successor of Socrates, Plato next undertook, in the *Republic*, to show the master meeting his own unsatisfied queries on education and politics. We read now of a " form " of good to which all thought and action aspire, and which, contemplated in itself, will explain not merely why justice is better than injustice, but the meaning and aim of everything. In order that man may be fully understood, we are to view him " writ large " in the organization of an ideal state. The scheme of description opens out into many subsidiary topics, including three great proposals already known to Greece,—the abolition of private property, the community of women and children, and the civic equality of the sexes. But the central subject is the preparation of the philosopher, through a series of ancillary sciences, for dialectic ; so that, once possessed of the supreme truth, he may have light for directing his fellow-men. As in the *Phaedo*, the spell of mythical revelation is brought to enhance the discourse of reason. The *Phaedrus* takes up the subject of rhetoric, to lead us allegorically into the realm of " ideas," and thence to point out a new rhetoric, worthy of the well-trained dialectician. We get also a glimpse of the philosopher's duty of investigating the mutual relations of the " forms " to which his study of particular things has led him.

A closer interest in logical method, appearing through his delight in imaginative construction, is one distinctive mark of this middle stage in Plato's teaching. As he passes to the next two Dialogues, the *Theaetetus* and *Parmenides*, he puts off the aesthetic rapture, and considers the ideas as categories of thought which require co-ordination. The discussion of knowledge in the former makes it evident that the Academy was now the meeting-place of vigorous minds, some of which were eager to urge or hear refuted the doctrines they had learnt from other schools of thought ; while the arguments are conducted with a critical caution very different from the brilliant and often hasty zeal of Socrates. The *Parmenides* corrects an actual or possible misconception of the theory of ideas in the domain of logic, showing perhaps how Aristotle, now a youthful disciple of Plato, found fault with the theory as he understood it. The forms are viewed in the light of the necessities of thought : knowledge is to be attained by a careful practice which will raise our minds to the vision of all particulars in their rightly distinguished and connected classes.

Plato is here at work on his own great problem :—If what we know is a single permanent law under which a multitude of things are ranged, what is the link between the one and the many ? The *Sophist* contains some of his ripest thought on this increasingly urgent question : his confident advance beyond Socratic teaching is indicated by the literary form, which hardly disguises the continuous exposition of a lecture. We observe an attention to physical science, the association of soul, motion, and existence, and the comparative study of being and not-being. The *Politicus* returns to the topic of state-government, and carries on the process of acquiring perfect notions of reality by the classification of things. Perhaps we should see in the absolute " mean " which is posited as the standard of all arts, business, and conduct, a contribution from Aristotle. The *Philebus*, in dealing with pleasure and knowledge, dwells further on the correct division and classification required if our reason, as it surely must, is to apprehend truth. The method is becoming more thorough and more complex, and Plato's hope of bringing it to completion is more remote. But he is gaining a clearer insight into the problem of unity and plurality.

The magnificent myth of the *Timaeus*, related by a Pythagorean, describes the structure of the universe, so as to show how the One manifests itself as the Many. We have here the latest reflections of Plato on space, time, soul, and many physical matters. In the lengthy treatise of the *Laws*, he addresses himself to the final duty of the philosopher as announced in the *Republic* : a long habituation to abstract thought will qualify rather than disqualify him for the practical regulation of public and private affairs. Attention is fixed once more on soul, as the energy of the world and the vehicle of our sovereign reason.

Thus Plato maintains the fixity of the objects of knowledge in a great variety of studies, which enlarge the compass of Socrates' teaching till it embraces enough material for complete systems of logic and metaphysics. How far these systems were actually worked out in the discussions of the Academy we can only surmise from the Dialogues themselves and a careful comparison of Aristotle ; whose writings, however, have come down to us in a much less perfect state. But it seems probable that, to the end, Plato was too fertile in thought to rest content with one authoritative body of doctrine. We may be able to detect in the *Timaeus* a tendency to view numbers as the real principles of things ; and we may conjecture a late-found interest in the physical complexion of the world. As a true artist, with a keen sense of the beauty and stir of life, Plato had this interest, in a notable degree, throughout : but in speaking of his enthusiasm for science we must regard him rather as a great inventor of sciences than as what we should now call a scientist. This is giving him a splendid name, which few men have earned. Some of his inventions may be unrealizable, but it is hard to find one that is certainly futile. There are flaws in his arguments : to state them clearly and fairly is to win the privilege of taking part in a discussion at the Academy.

W. R. M. LAMB.

[NOTE.—*Each of the Dialogues is a self-contained whole. The order in which they have been mentioned in this Introduction is that which agrees best in the main with modern views of Plato's mental progress, though the succession in some instances is uncertain.*]

BIBLIOGRAPHY

The following give useful accounts of Socratic and Platonic thought :—

T. Gomperz: *The Greek Thinkers*, vols. ii. and iii. Murray, 1901–5.

W. Lutoslawski: *The Origin and Growth of Plato's Logic.* Longmans, 1897.

R. L. Nettleship: *Philosophic Lectures and Remains.* 2 vols. Macmillan, 2nd ed., 1901.

D. G. Ritchie: *Plato.* T. and T. Clark, 1902.

J. A. Stewart: *The Myths of Plato.* Macmillan, 1905.

    ,,   ,,   *Plato's Doctrine of Ideas.* Clarendon Press, 1909.

A. E. Taylor: *Plato.* Constable, 1911.

A. M. Adam: *Plato : Moral and Political Ideals.* Camb. Univ. Press, 1913.

H. Jackson: *Presocratics, Socrates and the Minor Socratics, Plato and the Old Academy* (Cambridge Companion to Greek Studies). Camb. Univ. Press, 1905.

J. Burnet: *Greek Philosophy : Thales to Plato.* Macmillan, 1914.

F. M. Cornford: *Before and after Socrates.* Camb. Univ. Press, 1932.

The following are important editions :—

J. Adam : *The Republic.* 2 vols. Camb. Univ. Press, 1902.

W. H. Thompson : *The Phaedrus.* Bell, 1868.

    ,,   ,,   *The Gorgias.* Bell, 1871.

R. D. Archer-Hind : *The Phaedo.* Macmillan, 2nd ed., 1894.

    ,,   ,,   *The Timaeus.* Macmillan, 1888.

J. Burnet: *The Phaedo.* Clarendon Press, 1911.

L. Campbell : *The Theaetetus.* Clarendon Press, 1883.

    ,,   ,,   *The Sophistes and Politicus.* Clarendon Press, 1867.

E. S. Thompson : *The Meno.* Macmillan, 1901.

E. B. England : *The Laws.* 2 vols. Manchester Univ. Press, 1921.

LIST OF PLATO'S WORKS

LACHES

INTRODUCTION TO THE *LACHES*

THIS dialogue is so simple and clear that it requires but little preparatory comment, and indeed is in itself an excellent introduction to the Socratic method of probing the primary difficulties of any moral question. Two eminent generals, Nicias and Laches, are consulted by two old men, Lysimachus and Melesias, who, though their own fathers were Aristeides the Just and the elder Thucydides,[1] are at a loss to know what is the best education for their sons. The four friends have just witnessed an exhibition of fighting in armour, and the immediate question is whether the boys ought to learn this new accomplishment. Socrates, now about fifty years old, is invited to join in the discussion ; and after modestly disclaiming, in his usual manner, any knowledge of the subject, he turns the talk into an investigation of the nature of courage (190). Henceforward the argument is between Nicias, Laches, and Socrates : it soon passes from military to moral courage (192) ; and Nicias, working from a definition which he has previously heard from Socrates, suggests that courage is knowledge of what is to be dreaded (194). But this excludes animals and children, and Socrates points out that what is required

[1] The aristocratic opponent of Pericles: see *Meno* 94 c (note).

is a knowledge of good and evil alike in the past, the present, and the future,—in fact, an equivalent of all the moral virtues together (199). Thus they find themselves as far as ever from knowing what courage may be, and there is nothing for it but to go to school themselves with the boys.

The supposed time of the conversation is about 420 B.C., and Plato's main purpose in composing the piece seems to have been to show Socrates' manner of dealing with distinguished men who are older than himself, and who soon recognize in him an intellectual acuteness at least equal to the steadfast courage that has already won the admiration of Laches. The characters of the two generals are lightly but firmly drawn : Nicias is interested in the military possibilities of the new mode of fighting, and wishes to have some reasoned discussion upon it ; Laches is less intelligent, and bluntly dismisses it as a fashion evidently rejected by the Lacedae-monians. His gradual conversion from this state of impatient prejudice to a more philosophic attitude is admirably presented. On the artistic side we may also notice the charming dramatic touches by which Lysimachus's recognition of Socrates as a friend of his family is contrived (180–1) ; the humorous story told by Laches of the sad plight of Stesilaus in a naval engagement (183–4) ; and Nicias's friendly sketch of Socrates' artful way of conducting an argument (187–8). Philosophically, the result of the discussion appears to be *nil* ; but the emphasis throughout is rather on the *process* of the Socratic " midwifery " or assistance in bringing correct notions to birth. In particular we should observe the care bestowed on evolving the general notion of a quality, as distinct from its various concrete instances (191–2), and the insistence on the universality of knowledge, which must somehow embrace all the virtues, and can suffer no limitation in point of time. The way is thus prepared for the doctrine of the permanence and invariability of the true objects of knowledge.

ΛΑΧΗΣ

[Η ΠΕΡΙ ΑΝΔΡΕΙΑΣ· ΜΑΙΕΥΤΙΚΟΣ]

ΤΑ ΤΟΥ ΔΙΑΛΟΓΟΥ ΠΡΟΣΩΠΑ

ΛΥΣΙΜΑΧΟΣ, ΜΕΛΗΣΙΑΣ, ΝΙΚΙΑΣ, ΛΑΧΗΣ, ΠΑΙΔΕΣ ΛΥΣΙΜΑΧΟΥ ΚΑΙ ΜΕΛΗΣΙΟΥ, ΣΩΚΡΑΤΗΣ

ΛΥ. Τεθέασθε μὲν τὸν ἄνδρα μαχόμενον ἐν ὅπλοις,
ὦ Νικία τε καὶ Λάχης· οὗ δ' ἕνεκα ὑμᾶς ἐκελεύ-
σαμεν συνθεάσασθαι ἐγώ τε καὶ Μελησίας ὅδε,
τότε μὲν οὐκ εἴπομεν, νῦν δ' ἐροῦμεν. ἡγούμεθα
γὰρ χρῆναι πρός γε ὑμᾶς παρρησιάζεσθαι. εἰσὶ
γάρ τινες οἳ τῶν τοιούτων καταγελῶσι, καὶ ἐάν τις
αὐτοῖς συμβουλεύσηται, οὐκ ἂν εἴποιεν ἃ νοοῦσιν,
B ἀλλὰ στοχαζόμενοι τοῦ συμβουλευομένου ἄλλα
λέγουσι παρὰ τὴν αὐτῶν δόξαν· ὑμᾶς δὲ ἡμεῖς
ἡγησάμενοι καὶ ἱκανοὺς γνῶναι καὶ γνόντας ἁπλῶς
ἂν εἰπεῖν ἃ δοκεῖ ὑμῖν, οὕτω παρελάβομεν ἐπὶ
τὴν συμβουλὴν περὶ ὧν μέλλομεν ἀνακοινοῦσθαι.
ἔστιν οὖν τοῦτο, περὶ οὗ πάλαι τοσαῦτα προοι-
179 μιάζομαι, τόδε. ἡμῖν εἰσὶν υἱεῖς οὑτοί, ὅδε μὲν
τοῦδε, πάππου ἔχων ὄνομα Θουκυδίδης, ἐμὸς δὲ
αὖ ὅδε· παππῷον δὲ καὶ οὗτος ὄνομ' ἔχει τοὐμοῦ

6

LACHES

[or ON COURAGE: "obstetric"]

CHARACTERS

Lysimachus, Melesias, Nicias, Laches, Sons of
Lysimachus and Melesias, Socrates

lys. You have seen the performance of the man
fighting in armour, Nicias and Laches; but my friend
Melesias and I did not tell you at the time our reason
for requesting you to come and see it with us. However, we will tell you now; for we think we should
speak our minds freely to friends like you. Some
people, of course, pour ridicule on such appeals, and
when consulted for their advice will not say what
they think, but something different, making the
inquirer's wishes their aim, and speaking against
their own judgement. But you, we consider, not
merely have the necessary discernment but will give
us the benefit of it in telling us just what is in your
minds; and hence we have enlisted your counsel
on the question which we are about to lay before
you. Now the matter about which I have made all
this long preamble is this: we have two sons here,
my friend that one, called Thucydides after his
grandfather, and I this one; he also is named in

7

πατρός· Ἀριστείδην γὰρ αὐτὸν καλοῦμεν. ἡμῖν
οὖν τούτων δέδοκται ἐπιμεληθῆναι ὡς οἷόν τε
μάλιστα, καὶ μὴ ποιῆσαι ὅπερ οἱ πολλοί, ἐπειδὴ
μειράκια γέγονεν, ἀνεῖναι αὐτοὺς ὅ τι βούλονται
ποιεῖν, ἀλλὰ νῦν δὴ καὶ ἄρχεσθαι αὐτῶν ἐπιμε-
B λεῖσθαι καθ' ὅσον οἷοί τ' ἐσμέν· εἰδότες οὖν καὶ
ὑμῖν υἱεῖς ὄντας ἡγησάμεθα μεμεληκέναι περὶ
αὐτῶν, εἴπερ τισὶν ἄλλοις, πῶς ἂν θεραπευθέντες
γένοιντο ἄριστοι· εἰ δ' ἄρα πολλάκις μὴ προσ-
εσχήκατε τὸν νοῦν τῷ τοιούτῳ, ὑπομνήσοντες ὅτι
οὐ χρὴ αὐτοῦ ἀμελεῖν, καὶ παρακαλοῦντες ὑμᾶς
ἐπὶ τὸ ἐπιμέλειάν τινα ποιήσασθαι τῶν υἱέων
κοινῇ μεθ' ἡμῶν.

Ὅθεν δὲ ἡμῖν ταῦτ' ἔδοξεν, ὦ Νικία τε καὶ
Λάχης, χρὴ ἀκοῦσαι, κἂν ᾖ ὀλίγῳ μακρότερα.
συσσιτοῦμεν γὰρ δὴ ἐγώ τε καὶ Μελησίας ὅδε,
C καὶ ἡμῖν τὰ μειράκια παρασιτεῖ. ὅπερ οὖν καὶ
ἀρχόμενος εἶπον τοῦ λόγου, παρρησιασόμεθα πρὸς
ὑμᾶς. ἡμῶν γὰρ ἑκάτερος περὶ τοῦ ἑαυτοῦ πατρὸς
πολλὰ καὶ καλὰ ἔργα ἔχει λέγειν πρὸς τοὺς νεανίσκους, καὶ ὅσα ἐν πολέμῳ εἰργάσαντο καὶ ὅσα ἐν
εἰρήνῃ, διοικοῦντες τά τε τῶν συμμάχων καὶ τὰ
τῆσδε τῆς πόλεως· ἡμέτερα δ' αὐτῶν ἔργα οὐδέτερος ἔχει λέγειν. ταῦτα δὴ ὑπαισχυνόμεθά τε
τούσδε καὶ αἰτιώμεθα τοὺς πατέρας ἡμῶν, ὅτι
D ἡμᾶς μὲν εἴων τρυφᾶν, ἐπειδὴ μειράκια ἐγενόμεθα,
τὰ δὲ τῶν ἄλλων πράγματα ἔπραττον· καὶ τοῖσδε
τοῖς νεανίσκοις αὐτὰ ταῦτα ἐνδεικνύμεθα, λέγοντες
ὅτι, εἰ μὲν ἀμελήσουσιν ἑαυτῶν καὶ μὴ πείσονται
ἡμῖν, ἀκλεεῖς γενήσονται, εἰ δ' ἐπιμελήσονται,

the same way, after my father; we call him Aristeides. Well, we have resolved to give them our most constant care, and not—as most fathers do when their boys begin to be young men [1]—let them run loose as their fancy leads them, but begin forthwith taking every possible care of them. Now, knowing that you too have sons, we thought that you above all men must have concerned yourselves with the question of the kind of upbringing that would make the best of them; and if by any chance you have not given your attention to the subject, we would remind you that it ought not to be neglected, and we invite you to join us in arranging some way of taking care of our sons.

How we formed this resolve, Nicias and Laches, is worth hearing, even though the story be somewhat long. My friend Melesias and I take our meals together, and our boys share our table. Now, as I said at the beginning of my remarks, we are going to speak quite freely to you. Each of us has many noble deeds of his own father to relate to these young fellows—their numerous achievements both in war and in peace, when they were managing the affairs either of the allies or of this city; but neither of us has any deeds of his own to tell. We cannot help feeling ashamed that our boys should observe this, and we blame our fathers for leaving us to indulge ourselves when we began to be young men, while they looked after other folks' affairs; and we point the moral of it all to these young people, telling them that if they are careless of themselves and will not take our advice they will win no reputation, but if they take due pains they may very likely

[1] μειράκιον is applied to youths from 15 to 21.

τάχ' ἂν τῶν ὀνομάτων ἄξιοι γένοιντο ἃ ἔχουσιν.
οὗτοι μὲν οὖν φασὶ πείσεσθαι· ἡμεῖς δὲ δὴ τοῦτο
σκοποῦμεν, τί ἂν οὗτοι μαθόντες ἢ ἐπιτηδεύσαντες
ὅτι ἄριστοι γένοιντο. εἰσηγήσατο οὖν τις ἡμῖν
E καὶ τοῦτο τὸ μάθημα, ὅτι καλὸν εἴη τῷ νέῳ μαθεῖν
ἐν ὅπλοις μάχεσθαι· καὶ ἐπῄνει τοῦτον ὃν νῦν
ὑμεῖς ἐθεάσασθε ἐπιδεικνύμενον, κᾆτ' ἐκέλευε
θεάσασθαι. ἔδοξε δὴ χρῆναι αὐτούς τε ἐλθεῖν
ἐπὶ θέαν τἀνδρὸς καὶ ὑμᾶς συμπαραλαβεῖν ἅμα μὲν
συνθεατάς, ἅμα δὲ συμβούλους τε καὶ κοινωνούς,
ἐὰν βούλησθε, περὶ τῆς τῶν υἱέων ἐπιμελείας.
180 ταῦτ' ἐστὶν ἃ ἐβουλόμεθα ὑμῖν ἀνακοινώσασθαι.
ἤδη οὖν ὑμέτερον μέρος συμβουλεύειν καὶ περὶ
τούτου τοῦ μαθήματος, εἴτε δοκεῖ χρῆναι μανθάνειν εἴτε μή, καὶ περὶ τῶν ἄλλων, εἴ τι ἔχετε
ἐπαινέσαι μάθημα νέῳ ἀνδρὶ ἢ ἐπιτήδευμα, καὶ
περὶ τῆς κοινωνίας λέγειν ὁποῖόν τι ποιήσετε.

ΝΙ. Ἐγὼ μέν, ὦ Λυσίμαχε καὶ Μελησία, ἐπαινῶ τε ὑμῶν τὴν διάνοιαν καὶ κοινωνεῖν ἕτοιμος,
οἶμαι δὲ καὶ Λάχητα τόνδε.

B ΛΑ. Ἀληθῆ γὰρ οἴει, ὦ Νικία. ὡς ὅ γε ἔλεγεν
ὁ Λυσίμαχος ἄρτι περὶ τοῦ πατρὸς τοῦ αὑτοῦ τε
καὶ τοῦ Μελησίου, πάνυ μοι δοκεῖ εὖ εἰρῆσθαι καὶ
εἰς ἐκείνους καὶ εἰς ἡμᾶς καὶ εἰς ἅπαντας ὅσοι τὰ
τῶν πόλεων πράττουσιν, ὅτι αὐτοῖς σχεδόν τι ταῦτα
συμβαίνει, ἃ οὗτος λέγει, καὶ περὶ παῖδας καὶ περὶ
τἆλλα, τὰ ἴδια ὀλιγωρεῖσθαί τε καὶ ἀμελῶς δια-
τίθεσθαι. ταῦτα μὲν οὖν καλῶς λέγεις, ὦ Λυσί-
C μαχε· ὅτι δ' ἡμᾶς μὲν συμβούλους παρακαλεῖς

come to be worthy of the names they bear. Now they, for their part, say they will do as we bid ; so we are now considering what lessons or pursuits will lead them to the highest attainable excellence. Someone directed us to this particular accomplishment of fighting in armour, as being an admirable one for a young man to learn ; and he praised that man whose performance you were just watching, and then urged us to go and see him. So we decided that it would be well to go and see the man ourselves, and to take you along with us not merely as companions at the show, but also as counsellors and co-partners, if you will be so good, in the matter of looking after our sons. That is the question which we wanted to discuss with you. And we look to you now, on your part, to give us your advice, first as to whether you think this accomplishment should be learnt or not, and then as to any other such art or pursuit that you can recommend for a young man ; and also, how you feel inclined as regards our partnership.

NIC. For myself, Lysimachus and Melesias, I highly approve of your purpose, and am ready to lend a hand ; and I may say the same, I think, for Laches here.

LACH. Yes, you think truly, Nicias. For that remark which Lysimachus made just now about his father and the father of Melesias was very apposite, in my opinion, not only to them but to us and to all who deal with public affairs : it is practically the rule with them, as he says, to treat their private concerns, whether connected with children or anything else, in a slighting, careless spirit. You are quite right in saying that, Lysimachus ; but to invite

180

ἐπὶ τὴν τῶν νεανίσκων παιδείαν, Σωκράτη δὲ
τόνδε οὐ παρακαλεῖς, θαυμάζω, πρῶτον μὲν ὄντα
δημότην, ἔπειτα ἐνταῦθα ἀεὶ τὰς διατριβὰς ποιού-
μενον, ὅπου τί ἐστι τῶν τοιούτων ὧν σὺ ζητεῖς
περὶ τοὺς νέους ἢ μάθημα ἢ ἐπιτήδευμα καλόν.

ΛΥ. Πῶς λέγεις, ὦ Λάχης; Σωκράτης γὰρ ὅδε
τινὸς τῶν τοιούτων ἐπιμέλειαν πεποίηται;

ΛΑ. Πάνυ μὲν οὖν, ὦ Λυσίμαχε.

ΝΙ. Τοῦτο μέν σοι κἂν ἐγὼ ἔχοιμι εἰπεῖν οὐ
χεῖρον Λάχητος· καὶ γὰρ αὐτῷ μοι ἔναγχος
D ἄνδρα προὐξένησε τῷ υἱεῖ διδάσκαλον μουσικῆς,
Ἀγαθοκλέους μαθητὴν Δάμωνα, ἀνδρῶν χαριέ-
στατον οὐ μόνον τὴν μουσικήν, ἀλλὰ καὶ τἆλλα
ὁπόσου βούλει ἄξιον συνδιατρίβειν τηλικούτοις
νεανίσκοις.

ΛΥ. Οὗτοι, ὦ Σώκρατές τε καὶ Νικία καὶ
Λάχης, οἱ ἡλίκοι ἐγὼ ἔτι γιγνώσκομεν τοὺς
νεωτέρους, ἅτε κατ᾽ οἰκίαν τὰ πολλὰ διατρίβοντες
ὑπὸ τῆς ἡλικίας· ἀλλ᾽ εἴ τι καὶ σύ, ὦ παῖ Σωφρονίσκου, ἔχεις τῷδε τῷ σαυτοῦ δημότῃ ἀγαθὸν
E συμβουλεῦσαι, χρὴ συμβουλεύειν. δίκαιος δ᾽ εἶ·
καὶ γὰρ πατρικὸς ἡμῖν φίλος τυγχάνεις ὤν· ἀεὶ
γὰρ ἐγὼ καὶ ὁ σὸς πατὴρ ἑταίρω τε καὶ φίλω
ἦμεν, καὶ πρότερον ἐκεῖνος ἐτελεύτησε, πρίν τι
ἐμοὶ διενεχθῆναι. περιφέρει δέ τίς με καὶ μνήμη
ἄρτι τῶνδε λεγόντων· τὰ γὰρ μειράκια τάδε πρὸς
ἀλλήλους οἴκοι διαλεγόμενοι θαμὰ ἐπιμέμνηνται
Σωκράτους καὶ σφόδρα ἐπαινοῦσιν· οὐ μέντοι
πώποτε αὐτοὺς ἀνηρώτησα, εἰ τὸν Σωφρονίσκου
181 λέγοιεν. ἀλλ᾽, ὦ παῖδες, λέγετέ μοι, ὅδ᾽ ἐστὶ
Σωκράτης, περὶ οὗ ἑκάστοτε μέμνησθε;

ΠΑΙΣ. Πάνυ μὲν οὖν, ὦ πάτερ, οὗτος.

12

us to be your advisers for the education of your boys, and not to invite Socrates here, is to me very strange, when, to begin with, he is of your district, and then he is always spending his time wherever there is any such excellent study or pursuit for young men as you are seeking.

LYS. How do you mean, Laches? Has Socrates here given his attention to anything of this sort?

LACH. To be sure he has, Lysimachus.

NIC. I too might perhaps be in as good a position as Laches to inform you about that; for quite recently he introduced to myself a music-teacher for my son—Damon, pupil of Agathocles, who is not only the most exquisitely skilled of musicians, but in every other way as profitable a companion as you could wish for young men of that age.

LYS. It is not possible, Socrates, Nicias, and Laches, for men of my years to continue to know our juniors, because old age makes us spend most of our time at home; but if you, son of Sophroniscus, have any good advice for our friend, who belongs to your own district, you ought to let him have it. And it is only right that you should: for you happen to be our friend through your father; he and I were constant companions and friends, and he died without ever having a single difference with me. And a certain recollection comes back to me on hearing what has just been said: for these boys, in talking with each other at home, frequently mention Socrates in terms of high praise; but I have never asked them whether they meant the son of Sophroniscus. Now tell me, my boys, is this the Socrates whose name you have mentioned so often?

SON. To be sure, father, it is he.

ΛΥ. Εὖ γε νὴ τὴν Ἥραν, ὦ Σώκρατες, ὅτι
ὀρθοῖς τὸν πατέρα, ἄριστον ἀνδρῶν ὄντα, καὶ
ἄλλως καὶ δὴ καὶ ὅτι οἰκεῖα τά τε σὰ ἡμῖν ὑπάρξει
καὶ σοὶ τὰ ἡμέτερα.

ΛΑ. Καὶ μήν, ὦ Λυσίμαχε, μὴ ἀφίεσό γε τἀνδρός·
ὡς ἐγὼ καὶ ἄλλοθί γε αὐτὸν ἐθεασάμην οὐ μόνον
B τὸν πατέρα ἀλλὰ καὶ τὴν πατρίδα ὀρθοῦντα· ἐν
γὰρ τῇ ἀπὸ Δηλίου φυγῇ μετ' ἐμοῦ συνανεχώρει,
κἀγώ σοι λέγω ὅτι εἰ οἱ ἄλλοι ἤθελον τοιοῦτοι
εἶναι, ὀρθὴ ἂν ἡμῶν ἡ πόλις ἦν καὶ οὐκ ἂν ἔπεσε
τότε τοιοῦτον πτῶμα.

ΛΥ. Ὦ Σώκρατες, οὗτος μέντοι ὁ ἔπαινός ἐστι
καλός, ὃν σὺ νῦν ἐπαινῇ ὑπ' ἀνδρῶν ἀξίων πιστεύε-
σθαι καὶ εἰς ταῦτα εἰς ἃ οὗτοι ἐπαινοῦσιν. εὖ
οὖν ἴσθι ὅτι ἐγὼ ταῦτα ἀκούων χαίρω ὅτι εὐδο-
κιμεῖς, καὶ σὺ δὲ ἡγοῦ με ἐν τοῖς γ' εὐνούστατόν
C σοι εἶναι. χρῆν μὲν οὖν καὶ πρότερόν γε φοιτᾶν
αὐτὸν παρ' ἡμᾶς καὶ οἰκείους ἡγεῖσθαι, ὥσπερ τὸ
δίκαιον· νῦν δ' οὖν ἀπὸ τῆσδε τῆς ἡμέρας, ἐπειδὴ
ἀνεγνωρίσαμεν ἀλλήλους, μὴ ἄλλως ποίει, ἀλλὰ
σύνισθί τε καὶ γνώριζε καὶ ἡμᾶς καὶ τούσδε τοὺς
νεωτέρους, ὅπως ἂν διασώζητε καὶ ὑμεῖς τὴν
ἡμετέραν φιλίαν. ταῦτα μὲν οὖν καὶ σὺ ποιήσεις
καὶ ἡμεῖς σε καὶ αὖθις ὑπομνήσομεν· περὶ δὲ ὧν
ἠρξάμεθα τί φατε; τί δοκεῖ; τὸ μάθημα τοῖς
μειρακίοις ἐπιτήδειον εἶναι ἢ οὔ, τὸ μαθεῖν ἐν
ὅπλοις μάχεσθαι;

D ΣΩ. Ἀλλὰ καὶ τούτων πέρι, ὦ Λυσίμαχε, ἔγωγε
πειράσομαι συμβουλεύειν ἄν τι δύνωμαι, καὶ αὖ

---

[1] On the coast just north of Attica, where the Athenians
were severely defeated by the Boeotians in 424 B.C.

LACHES

LYS. On my soul, Socrates, it is good to know that you keep up your father's name, which was a most honourable one, both on general grounds and particularly because of the intimate relation in which you and we shall equally feel ourselves to be.

LACH. Indeed, Lysimachus, he is a person you must not lose hold of; for I have observed him elsewhere too keeping up not merely his father's but his country's name. He accompanied me in the retreat from Delium,[1] and I assure you that if the rest had chosen to be like him, our city would be holding up her head and would not then have had such a terrible fall.

LYS. Socrates, this is indeed splendid praise which you are now receiving from men whose word is of great weight, and for such conduct as wins their praise. So let me tell you that I rejoice to hear this and to know you have such a good reputation; and you in return must count me as one of your warmest well-wishers. You ought indeed, on your own part, to have visited us before, and treated us on intimate terms, as you have a right to do: now, however, that we have discovered each other, from to-day onwards you must make a point of sharing our thoughts and getting to know us and our young people also, that you and they may in your turn preserve the friendship of our houses. That, however, you will do yourself, and we will remind you of it another time : but what do you say of the matter on which we began to speak ? What is your view ? Is the accomplishment of fighting in armour a suitable one for our boys to learn or not ?

SOC. On that matter, Lysimachus, I will do my best to advise you, so far as I can, and also to do all

ἃ προκαλῇ πάντα ποιεῖν. δικαιότατον μέντοι μοι
δοκεῖ εἶναι, ἐμὲ νεώτερον ὄντα τῶνδε καὶ ἀπει-
ρότερον τούτων ἀκούειν πρότερον τί λέγουσι καὶ
μανθάνειν παρ' αὐτῶν· ἐὰν δ' ἔχω τι ἄλλο παρὰ τὰ
ὑπὸ τούτων λεγόμενα, τότ' ἤδη διδάσκειν καὶ
πείθειν καὶ σὲ καὶ τούτους. ἀλλ', ὦ Νικία,
τί οὐ λέγει πότερος ὑμῶν;

ΝΙ. Ἀλλ' οὐδὲν κωλύει, ὦ Σώκρατες. δοκεῖ
E γὰρ καὶ ἐμοὶ τοῦτο τὸ μάθημα τοῖς νέοις ὠφέλιμον
εἶναι ἐπίστασθαι πολλαχῇ. καὶ γὰρ τὸ μὴ ἄλλοθι
διατρίβειν ἐν οἷς δὴ φιλοῦσιν οἱ νέοι τὰς διατριβὰς
ποιεῖσθαι, ὅταν σχολὴν ἄγωσιν, ἀλλ' ἐν τούτῳ,
εὖ ἔχει, ὅθεν καὶ τὸ σῶμα βέλτιον ἴσχειν ἀνάγκη
182 —οὐδενὸς γὰρ τῶν γυμνασίων φαυλότερον οὐδ'
ἐλάττω πόνον ἔχει—καὶ ἅμα προσήκει μάλιστ'
ἐλευθέρῳ τοῦτό τε τὸ γυμνάσιον καὶ ἡ ἱππική·
οὗ γὰρ ἀγῶνος ἀθληταί ἐσμεν καὶ ἐν οἷς ἡμῖν ὁ
ἀγὼν πρόκειται, μόνοι οὗτοι γυμνάζονται οἱ ἐν
τούτοις τοῖς περὶ τὸν πόλεμον ὀργάνοις γυμνα-
ζόμενοι. ἔπειτα ὀνήσει μέν τι τοῦτο τὸ μάθημα
καὶ ἐν τῇ μάχῃ αὐτῇ, ὅταν ἐν τάξει δέῃ μάχεσθαι
μετὰ πολλῶν ἄλλων· μέγιστον μέντοι αὐτοῦ
ὄφελος, ὅταν λυθῶσιν αἱ τάξεις καὶ ἤδη τι δέῃ
μόνον πρὸς μόνον ἢ διώκοντα ἀμυνομένῳ τινὶ ἐπι-
B θέσθαι ἢ καὶ ἐν φυγῇ ἐπιτιθεμένου ἄλλου ἀμύνασθαι
αὐτόν· οὔτ' ἂν ὑπό γε ἑνὸς εἷς ὁ τοῦτ' ἐπιστάμενος
οὐδὲν ἂν πάθοι, ἴσως δ' οὐδὲ ὑπὸ πλειόνων, ἀλλὰ
πανταχῇ ἂν ταύτῃ πλεονεκτοῖ. ἔτι δὲ καὶ εἰς
ἄλλου καλοῦ μαθήματος ἐπιθυμίαν παρακαλεῖ τὸ

---

[1] *i.e.* in regular warfare.

the rest that you so kindly ask. It seems to me, however, most proper that I, being so much younger and less experienced than you and your friends, should first hear what they have to say, and learn of them ; and then, if I have anything else to suggest as against their remarks, I might try to explain it and persuade you and them to take my view. Come, Nicias, let one or other of you speak.

NIC. There is no difficulty about that, Socrates. For in my opinion this accomplishment is in many ways a useful thing for young men to possess. It is good for them, instead of spending their time on the ordinary things to which young men usually give their hours of leisure, to spend it on this, which not only has the necessary effect of improving their bodily health—since it is as good and strenuous as any physical exercise—but is also a form of exercise which, with riding, is particularly fitting for a free citizen ; for only the men trained in the use of these warlike implements can claim to be trained in the contest whereof we are athletes and in the affairs wherein we are called upon to contend.[1] Further, this accomplishment will be of some benefit also in actual battle, when it comes to fighting in line with a number of other men ; but its greatest advantage will be felt when the ranks are broken, and you find you must fight man to man, either in pursuing some-one who is trying to beat off your attack, or in retreating yourself and beating off the attack of another. Whoever possessed this accomplishment could come to no harm so long as he had but one to deal with, nor yet, perhaps, if he had several ; it would give him an advantage in any situation. Moreover, it is a thing which impels one to desire

τοιοῦτον· πᾶς γὰρ ἂν μαθὼν ἐν ὅπλοις μάχεσθαι
ἐπιθυμήσειε καὶ τοῦ ἑξῆς μαθήματος τοῦ περὶ
τὰς τάξεις, καὶ ταῦτα λαβὼν καὶ φιλοτιμηθεὶς
C ἐν αὐτοῖς ἐπὶ πᾶν ἂν τὸ περὶ τὰς στρατηγίας ὁρμή-
σειε· καὶ ἤδη δῆλον ὅτι τὰ τούτων ἐχόμενα καὶ
μαθήματα πάντα καὶ ἐπιτηδεύματα καὶ καλὰ καὶ
πολλοῦ ἄξια ἀνδρὶ μαθεῖν τε καὶ ἐπιτηδεῦσαι, ὧν
καθηγήσαιτ' ἂν τοῦτο τὸ μάθημα. προσθήσομεν
δ' αὐτῷ οὐ σμικρὰν προσθήκην, ὅτι πάντα ἄνδρα
ἐν πολέμῳ καὶ θαρραλεώτερον καὶ ἀνδρειότερον
ἂν ποιήσειεν αὐτὸν αὑτοῦ οὐκ ὀλίγῳ αὕτη ἡ ἐπιστήμη. μὴ ἀτιμάσωμεν δὲ εἰπεῖν, εἰ καί τῳ
σμικρότερον δοκεῖ εἶναι, ὅτι καὶ εὐσχημονέστερον
D ἐνταῦθα οὗ χρὴ τὸν ἄνδρα εὐσχημονέστερον φαίνεσθαι, οὗ ἅμα καὶ δεινότερος τοῖς ἐχθροῖς φανεῖται
διὰ τὴν εὐσχημοσύνην. ἐμοὶ μὲν οὖν, ὦ Λυσίμαχε, ὥσπερ λέγω, δοκεῖ τε χρῆναι διδάσκειν τοὺς
νεανίσκους ταῦτα καὶ δι' ἃ δοκεῖ εἴρηκα· Λάχητος
δ', εἴ τι παρὰ ταῦτα λέγει, κἂν αὐτὸς ἡδέως ἀκούσαιμι.

ΛΑ. Ἀλλ' ἔστι μέν, ὦ Νικία, χαλεπὸν λέγειν
περὶ ὁτουοῦν μαθήματος, ὡς οὐ χρὴ μανθάνειν·
πάντα γὰρ ἐπίστασθαι ἀγαθὸν δοκεῖ εἶναι. καὶ
E δὴ καὶ τὸ ὁπλιτικὸν τοῦτο, εἰ μέν ἐστι μάθημα,
ὅπερ φασὶν οἱ διδάσκοντες, καὶ οἷον Νικίας λέγει,
χρὴ αὐτὸ μανθάνειν· εἰ δ' ἔστι μὲν μὴ μάθημα,
ἀλλ' ἐξαπατῶσιν οἱ ὑπισχνούμενοι, ἢ μάθημα μὲν
τυγχάνει ὄν, μὴ μέντοι πάνυ σπουδαῖον, τί καὶ
δέοι ἂν αὐτὸ μανθάνειν; λέγω δὲ ταῦτα περὶ αὐτοῦ
εἰς τάδε ἀποβλέψας, ὅτι οἶμαι ἐγὼ τοῦτο, εἰ τὶ ἦν,

another noble accomplishment; for everyone who
has learnt how to fight in armour will desire to learn
the accomplishment which comes next, the management of troops; and when he has got that and once
taken a pride in his work he will push on to attain
the whole art of generalship. It is evident already
that all accomplishments and pursuits in the military
sphere are both honourable and valuable to a man,
either in acquisition or in practice; and this particular one may well be an introduction to them.
And we can make this addition—no slight one—to
its claims, that this science will make any man individually a great deal bolder and braver in war.
Nor let us disdain to mention, even though some
may think it a rather slight matter, that it will give
him a smarter appearance in the place where a man
should look smartest, and where at the same time
he will appear more terrible to the enemy because
of his smartness. So my opinion is, Lysimachus, as
I say, that we ought to teach this skill to our young
men, and I have told you my reasons for so thinking.
But if Laches has a different view to state, I shall
be as glad as anyone to hear it.

LACH. Well, Nicias, I am loth to say of any sort of
accomplishment that it ought not to be learnt; for
it seems good to know all things. And besides, if
this skill in arms is an accomplishment, as they say
who teach it, and as Nicias terms it, it ought to be
learnt; while if it is not an accomplishment, and
those who promise to give it are deceiving us, or if
it is an accomplishment, but not a very important
one, what can be the good of learning it? I speak
of it in this way from the following point of view:
I conceive that if there were anything in it, it would

B 2

182

οὐκ ἂν λεληθέναι Λακεδαιμονίους, οἷς οὐδὲν ἄλλο
μέλει ἐν τῷ βίῳ ἢ τοῦτο ζητεῖν καὶ ἐπιτηδεύειν,
183 ὅ τι ἂν μαθόντες καὶ ἐπιτηδεύσαντες πλεονεκτοῖεν
τῶν ἄλλων περὶ τὸν πόλεμον. εἰ δ' ἐκείνους
ἐλελήθει, ἀλλ' οὐ τούτους γε τοὺς διδασκάλους
αὐτοῦ λέληθεν αὐτὸ τοῦτο, ὅτι ἐκεῖνοι μάλιστα τῶν
Ἑλλήνων σπουδάζουσιν ἐπὶ τοῖς τοιούτοις καὶ
ὅτι παρ' ἐκείνοις ἄν τις τιμηθεὶς εἰς ταῦτα καὶ
παρὰ τῶν ἄλλων πλεῖστ' ἂν ἐργάζοιτο χρήματα,
ὥσπερ γε καὶ τραγῳδίας ποιητὴς παρ' ἡμῖν τιμη-
θείς. τοιγάρτοι ὃς ἂν οἴηται τραγῳδίαν καλῶς
B ποιεῖν, οὐκ ἔξωθεν κύκλῳ περὶ τὴν Ἀττικὴν κατὰ
τὰς ἄλλας πόλεις ἐπιδεικνύμενος περιέρχεται, ἀλλ'
εὐθὺς δεῦρο φέρεται καὶ τοῖσδ' ἐπιδείκνυσιν εἰκότως.
τοὺς δὲ ἐν ὅπλοις μαχομένους ἐγὼ τούτους ὁρῶ
τὴν μὲν Λακεδαίμονα ἡγουμένους εἶναι ἄβατον
ἱερὸν καὶ οὐδὲ ἄκρῳ ποδὶ ἐπιβαίνοντας, κύκλῳ
δὲ περιόντας αὐτὴν καὶ πᾶσι μᾶλλον ἐπιδεικνυ-
μένους, καὶ μάλιστα τούτοις οἳ κἂν αὐτοὶ ὁμολογή-
σειαν πολλοὺς σφῶν προτέρους εἶναι πρὸς τὰ τοῦ
πολέμου. ἔπειτα, ὦ Λυσίμαχε, οὐ πάνυ ὀλίγοις ἐγὼ
C τούτων παραγέγονα ἐν αὐτῷ τῷ ἔργῳ, καὶ ὁρῶ οἷοί
εἰσιν. ἔξεστι δὲ καὶ αὐτόθεν ἡμῖν σκέψασθαι.
ὥσπερ γὰρ ἐπίτηδες οὐδεὶς πώποτ' εὐδόκιμος γέγονεν ἐν τῷ πολέμῳ ἀνὴρ τῶν τὰ ὁπλιτικὰ ἐπιτηδευσάντων. καίτοι εἴς γε τἆλλα πάντα ἐκ τούτων
οἱ ὀνομαστοὶ γίγνονται, ἐκ τῶν ἐπιτηδευσάντων
ἕκαστα· οὗτοι δ', ὡς ἔοικε, παρὰ τοὺς ἄλλους
οὕτω σφόδρα εἰς τοῦτο δεδυστυχήκασιν. ἐπεὶ
καὶ τοῦτον τὸν Στησίλεων, ὃν ὑμεῖς μετ' ἐμοῦ ἐν
τοσούτῳ ὄχλῳ ἐθεάσασθε ἐπιδεικνύμενον καὶ τὰ

not have been overlooked by the Lacedaemonians, whose only concern in life is to seek out and practise whatever study or pursuit will give them an advantage over others in war. And if they have overlooked it, at any rate these teachers of it cannot have overlooked the obvious fact that the Lacedaemonians are more intent on such matters than any of the Greeks, and that anybody who won honour among them for this art would amass great riches elsewhere, just as a tragic poet does who has won honour among us. And for this reason he who thinks himself a good writer of tragedy does not tour round with his show in a circuit of the outlying Attic towns, but makes a straight line for this place and exhibits to our people, as one might expect. But I notice that these fighters in armour regard Lacedaemon as holy ground where none may tread, and do not step on it even with the tips of their toes, but circle round it and prefer to exhibit to any other people, especially to those who would themselves admit that they were inferior to many in the arts of war. Furthermore, Lysimachus, I have come across more than a few of these persons in actual operations, and I can see their quality. Indeed, we can estimate it offhand : for, as though it were of set purpose, not one of these experts in arms has ever yet distinguished himself in war. And yet in all the other arts, the men who have made a name are to be found among those who have specially pursued one or other of them ; while these persons, apparently, stand out from the rest in this particularly hapless fate of their profession. Why, this man Stesilaus, whom you watched with me in that great crowd as he gave his performance and spoke in

183

D μεγάλα περὶ αὐτοῦ λέγοντα ἃ ἔλεγεν, ἑτέρωθι ἐγὼ
κάλλιον ἐθεασάμην [ἐν τῇ ἀληθείᾳ]¹ ὡς ἀληθῶς
ἐπιδεικνύμενον οὐχ ἑκόντα. προσβαλούσης γὰρ
τῆς νεὼς ἐφ᾽ ᾗ ἐπεβάτευε πρὸς ὁλκάδα τινά, ἐμάχετο
ἔχων δορυδρέπανον, διαφέρον δὴ ὅπλον ἅτε καὶ
αὐτὸς τῶν ἄλλων διαφέρων. τὰ μὲν οὖν ἄλλα
οὐκ ἄξια λέγειν περὶ τἀνδρός, τὸ δὲ σόφισμα τὸ
τοῦ δρεπάνου τοῦ πρὸς τῇ λόγχῃ οἷον ἀπέβη.

E μαχομένου γὰρ αὐτοῦ ἐνέσχετό που ἐν τοῖς τῆς
νεὼς σκεύεσι καὶ ἀντελάβετο· εἷλκεν οὖν ὁ Στησί-
λεως βουλόμενος ἀπολῦσαι, καὶ οὐχ οἷός τ᾽ ἦν·
ἡ δὲ ναῦς τὴν ναῦν παρῄει. τέως μὲν οὖν παρ-
έθει ἐν τῇ νηὶ ἀντεχόμενος τοῦ δόρατος· ἐπεὶ δὲ
δὴ παρημείβετο ἡ ναῦς τὴν ναῦν καὶ ἐπέσπα αὐτὸν
τοῦ δόρατος ἐχόμενον, ἐφίει τὸ δόρυ διὰ τῆς χειρός,

184 ἕως ἄκρου τοῦ στύρακος ἀντελάβετο. ἦν δὲ
γέλως καὶ κρότος ὑπὸ τῶν ἐκ τῆς ὁλκάδος ἐπί τε
τῷ σχήματι αὐτοῦ, καὶ ἐπειδὴ βαλόντος τινὸς
λίθῳ παρὰ τοὺς πόδας αὐτοῦ ἐπὶ τὸ κατάστρωμα
ἀφίεται τοῦ δόρατος, τότ᾽ ἤδη καὶ οἱ ἐκ τῆς τριή-
ρους οὐκέτι οἷοί τ᾽ ἦσαν τὸν γέλωτα κατέχειν,
ὁρῶντες αἰωρούμενον ἐκ τῆς ὁλκάδος τὸ δορυδρέπανον ἐκεῖνο. ἴσως μὲν οὖν εἴη ἂν τὶ ταῦτα,
ὥσπερ Νικίας λέγει· οἷς δ᾽ οὖν ἐγὼ ἐντετύχηκα,
τοιαῦτ᾽ ἄττα ἐστίν. ὃ οὖν καὶ ἐξ ἀρχῆς εἶπον, ὅτι

B εἴτε οὕτω σμικρᾶς ὠφελείας ἔχει μάθημα ὄν, εἴτε μὴ
ὂν φασὶ καὶ προσποιοῦνται αὐτὸ εἶναι μάθημα, οὐκ
ἄξιον ἐπιχειρεῖν μανθάνειν· καὶ γὰρ οὖν μοι δοκεῖ, εἰ
μὲν δειλός τις ὢν οἴοιτο αὐτὸ² ἐπίστασθαι, θρασύ-
τερος ἂν δι᾽ αὐτὸ γενόμενος ἐπιφανέστερος γένοιτο

---

¹ ἐν τῇ ἀληθείᾳ secl. Schanz.
² αὐτὸ Burnet : αὐτὸν, αὑτὸν δεῖν mss.

22

those high terms of himself before us, I have watched elsewhere giving a finer entertainment in the form of a very real display that he made against his will. The ship on which he was serving struck a transport vessel, and he was using in the fight a combination of a scythe and a spear—a remarkable weapon that suited so remarkable a man. Well, the story of this fellow's doings is hardly of enough interest in the main, but you must hear the upshot of his device of a scythe fixed to a spear. As he was fighting, it stuck somehow in the other ship's rigging, and held fast ; so Stesilaus pulled at it in the hope of getting it free, but he could not, and the ships were passing by each other. For the first moments he ran along in his ship holding on to his spear ; but as the other ship sheered off from his and drew him after, still holding the spear, he let it slip through his hand until he gripped the butt-end of the shaft. From the crew of the transport there came laughter and clapping at his posture, and when someone aimed a stone at him which hit the deck near his feet, and he let go the spear, the troops on the warship in their turn could no longer restrain their laughter, as they saw the notable scythe-spear dangling from the transport. Now, there may perhaps be something in this art of theirs, as Nicias argues, but at any rate that is my impression of it, in the cases I have met with. Hence, as I said at the beginning, whether it be an accomplishment, and one of but little use, or not an accomplishment, but only supposed and pretended to be such, it is not worth the trouble of learning it. For indeed I hold that if a man who was a coward believed that he possessed it, his only gain would be in rashness, which would make his

οἷος ἦν· εἰ δὲ ἀνδρεῖος, φυλαττόμενος ἂν ὑπὸ
τῶν ἀνθρώπων, εἰ καὶ σμικρὸν ἐξαμάρτοι, μεγάλας
ἂν διαβολὰς ἴσχειν· ἐπίφθονος γὰρ ἡ προσποίησις
C τῆς τοιαύτης ἐπιστήμης, ὥστ' εἰ μή τι θαυμαστὸν
ὅσον διαφέρει τῇ ἀρετῇ τῶν ἄλλων, οὐκ ἔσθ' ὅπως
ἄν τις φύγοι τὸ καταγέλαστος γενέσθαι, φάσκων
ἔχειν ταύτην τὴν ἐπιστήμην. τοιαύτη τις ἔμοιγε
δοκεῖ, ὦ Λυσίμαχε, ἡ περὶ τοῦτο τὸ μάθημα εἶναι
σπουδή· χρὴ δ' ὅπερ σοι ἐξ ἀρχῆς ἔλεγον, καὶ
Σωκράτη τόνδε μὴ ἀφιέναι, ἀλλὰ δεῖσθαι συμβουλεύειν ὅπῃ δοκεῖ αὐτῷ περὶ τοῦ προκειμένου.

ΛΥ. Ἀλλὰ δέομαι ἔγωγε, ὦ Σώκρατες· καὶ
γὰρ ὥσπερ [ἐπὶ]¹ τοῦ διακρινοῦντος δοκεῖ μοι
D δεῖν ἡμῖν ἡ βουλή. εἰ μὲν γὰρ συνεφερέσθην τώδε,
ἧττον ἂν τοῦ τοιούτου ἔδει· νῦν δέ—τὴν ἐναντίαν
γάρ, ὡς ὁρᾷς, Λάχης Νικίᾳ ἔθετο—εὖ δὴ ἔχει
ἀκοῦσαι καὶ σοῦ, ποτέρῳ τοῖν ἀνδροῖν σύμψηφος εἶ.

ΣΩ. Τί δαί, ὦ Λυσίμαχε; ὁπότερ' ἂν οἱ πλείους
ἐπαινῶσιν ἡμῶν, τούτοις μέλλεις χρῆσθαι;

ΛΥ. Τί γὰρ ἄν τις καὶ ποιοῖ, ὦ Σώκρατες;

ΣΩ. Ἦ καὶ σύ, ὦ Μελησία, οὕτως ἂν ποιοῖς;
E κἂν εἴ τις περὶ ἀγωνίας τοῦ υἱέος σοι βουλὴ εἴη
τί χρὴ ἀσκεῖν, ἆρα τοῖς πλείοσιν ἂν ἡμῶν πείθοιο,
ἢ ἐκείνῳ ὅστις τυγχάνοι² ὑπὸ παιδοτρίβῃ ἀγαθῷ
πεπαιδευμένος καὶ ἠσκηκώς;

ΜΕΛ. Ἐκείνῳ εἰκός γε, ὦ Σώκρατες.

ΣΩ. Αὐτῷ ἄρ' ἂν μᾶλλον πείθοιο ἢ τέτταρσιν
οὖσιν ἡμῖν;

¹ ἐπὶ secl. Ast : ἔτι Heindorf.
² τυγχάνοι Bekker : τυγχάνει MSS.

true nature the more conspicuous; while if he were brave, people would be on the look-out for even the slightest mistake on his part, and he would incur much grievous slander; for the pretension to such skill arouses jealousy, so that unless a man be prodigiously superior to the rest in valour he cannot by any means escape being made a laughing-stock through professing to be so skilled. Such is my opinion, Lysimachus, of the interest taken in this accomplishment; but do as I told you at the beginning; you are not to let our friend Socrates go, but must request him to advise us according to his judgement on the matter in hand.

LYS. Well, I ask it of you, Socrates: for indeed our members of council, as it were, seem to me to need someone who will decide between them. Had these two agreed, we should not have required this help so much; but as it is—for Laches, you see, has voted on the opposite side to Nicias—it is as well that we should hear your view and see on which side you cast your vote.

SOC. What, Lysimachus? Are you going to join the side which gets the approval of the majority of us?

LYS. Why, what can one do, Socrates?

SOC. And you too, Melesias, would do the same? Suppose you had a consultation as to what your son's exercise should be for a coming contest, would you be guided by the majority of us, or by the one who happened to have trained and exercised under a good master?

MEL. By the latter, naturally, Socrates.

SOC. Would you be guided by him alone rather than the four of us?

ΜΕΛ. Ἴσως.

ΣΩ. Ἐπιστήμῃ γάρ, οἶμαι, δεῖ κρίνεσθαι ἀλλ' οὐ πλήθει τὸ μέλλον καλῶς κριθήσεσθαι.

ΜΕΛ. Πῶς γὰρ οὔ;

ΣΩ. Οὐκοῦν καὶ νῦν χρὴ πρῶτον αὐτὸ τοῦτο σκέ-
185 ψασθαι, εἰ ἔστι τις ἡμῶν τεχνικὸς περὶ οὗ βουλευόμεθα, ἢ οὔ· καὶ εἰ μὲν ἔστιν, ἐκείνῳ πείθεσθαι
ἑνὶ ὄντι, τοὺς δ' ἄλλους ἐᾶν· εἰ δὲ μή, ἄλλον τινὰ
ζητεῖν. ἢ περὶ σμικροῦ οἴεσθε νυνὶ κινδυνεύειν
καὶ σὺ καὶ Λυσίμαχος, ἀλλ' οὐ περὶ τούτου τοῦ
κτήματος, ὃ τῶν ὑμετέρων μέγιστον ὂν τυγχάνει;
υἱέων γάρ που ἢ χρηστῶν ἢ τἀναντία γενομένων
καὶ πᾶς ὁ οἶκος ὁ τοῦ πατρὸς οὕτως οἰκήσεται,
ὁποῖοι ἄν τινες οἱ παῖδες γένωνται.

ΜΕΛ. Ἀληθῆ λέγεις.

ΣΩ. Πολλὴν ἄρα δεῖ προμηθίαν αὐτοῦ ἔχειν.

ΜΕΛ. Πάνυ γε.

B ΣΩ. Πῶς οὖν, ὃ ἐγὼ ἄρτι ἔλεγον, ἐσκοποῦμεν ἄν,
εἰ ἐβουλόμεθα σκέψασθαι τίς ἡμῶν περὶ ἀγωνίαν
τεχνικώτατος; ἆρ' οὐχ ὁ μαθὼν καὶ ἐπιτηδεύσας,
ᾧ καὶ διδάσκαλοι ἀγαθοὶ γεγονότες ἦσαν αὐτοῦ
τούτου;

ΜΕΛ. Ἔμοιγε δοκεῖ.

ΣΩ. Οὐκοῦν ἔτι πρότερον, τίνος ὄντος τούτου [οὗ]¹
ζητοῦμεν τοὺς διδασκάλους;

ΜΕΛ. Πῶς λέγεις;

ΣΩ. Ὧδε ἴσως μᾶλλον κατάδηλον ἔσται. οὔ μοι
δοκεῖ ἐξ ἀρχῆς ἡμῖν ὡμολογῆσθαι, τί ποτ' ἔστι
περὶ οὗ βουλευόμεθα [καὶ σκεπτόμεθα],² ὅστις ἡμῶν

---

¹ οὗ secl. Jacobs.
² καὶ σκεπτόμεθα secl. Ast.

MEL. Very likely.

SOC. Yes, for a question must be decided by knowledge, and not by numbers, if it is to have a right decision.

MEL. To be sure.

SOC. Then in this case also we must first consider, in particular, whether anyone among us has expert skill in the subject of our consultation, or not; and if here is one who has, we must be guided by him, though he be but one, and pass over the rest; while if there is not, we must look for somebody else. Or do you think it a slight matter that you and Lysimachus have now at stake, and not that which is really your greatest possession? For I take it that according as the sons turn out well or the opposite will the whole life of their father's house be affected, depending for better or worse on their character.

MEL. Truly spoken.

SOC. So it demands much forethought from us.

MEL. Certainly.

SOC. How then—to take the case I suggested just now—should we set to work if we wanted to consider which of us was the most expert in regard to a contest? Should we not pick him who had learnt and practised, and had also had good teachers of this particular skill?

MEL. I think so.

SOC. And even before that, we should ask what was this skill of which we are looking for the teachers?

MEL. How do you mean?

SOC. Perhaps it will be more easily grasped in this form. I think we have not started with an agreement between us as to what the thing is about which we are consulting, in this question of who

185

τεχνικὸς καὶ τούτου ἕνεκα διδασκάλους ἐκτήσατο,
C καὶ ὅστις μή.

ΝΙ. Οὐ γάρ, ὦ Σώκρατες, περὶ τοῦ ἐν ὅπλοις μάχεσθαι σκοποῦμεν, εἴτε χρὴ αὐτὸ τοὺς νεανίσκους
μανθάνειν εἴτε μή;

ΣΩ. Πάνυ μὲν οὖν, ὦ Νικία. ἀλλ' ὅταν περὶ
φαρμάκου τίς του πρὸς ὀφθαλμοὺς σκοπῆται, εἴτε
χρὴ αὐτὸ ὑπαλείφεσθαι εἴτε μή, πότερον οἴει τότε
εἶναι τὴν βουλὴν περὶ τοῦ φαρμάκου ἢ περὶ τῶν
ὀφθαλμῶν;

ΝΙ. Περὶ τῶν ὀφθαλμῶν.

D ΣΩ. Οὐκοῦν καὶ ὅταν ἵππῳ χαλινὸν σκοπῆταί τις
εἰ προσοιστέον ἢ μή, καὶ ὁπότε, τότε που περὶ τοῦ
ἵππου βουλεύεται ἀλλ' οὐ περὶ τοῦ χαλινοῦ;

ΝΙ. Ἀληθῆ.

ΣΩ. Οὐκοῦν ἑνὶ λόγῳ, ὅταν τίς τι ἕνεκά του
σκοπῇ, περὶ ἐκείνου ἡ βουλὴ τυγχάνει οὖσα οὗ
ἕνεκα ἐσκόπει, ἀλλ' οὐ περὶ τοῦ ὃ ἕνεκα ἄλλου
ἐζήτει.

ΝΙ. Ἀνάγκη.

ΣΩ. Δεῖ ἄρα καὶ τὸν σύμβουλον σκοπεῖν, ἆρα
τεχνικός ἐστιν εἰς ἐκείνου θεραπείαν, οὗ ἕνεκα
σκοποῦμεν ὃ[1] σκοποῦμεν.

ΝΙ. Πάνυ γε.

ΣΩ. Οὐκοῦν νῦν φαμὲν περὶ μαθήματος σκοπεῖν
E τῆς ψυχῆς ἕνεκα τῆς τῶν νεανίσκων;

ΝΙ. Ναί.

ΣΩ. Εἴ τις ἄρα ἡμῶν τεχνικὸς περὶ ψυχῆς θεραπείαν καὶ οἷός τε καλῶς τοῦτο θεραπεῦσαι, καὶ
ὅτῳ διδάσκαλοι ἀγαθοὶ γεγόνασι, τοῦτο σκεπτέον.

ΛΑ. Τί δέ, ὦ Σώκρατες; οὔπω ἑώρακας ἄνευ

---

[1] σκοποῦμεν ὃ Cron: σκοπούμενοι MSS.

28

among us is an expert and to this end has resorted to teachers, and who not.

NIC. Why, Socrates, is it not fighting in armour that we are considering, and whether it is a thing to be learnt by young men or not?

SOC. Of course, Nicias; but when someone considers whether a medicine is to be used as an eye-salve or not, do you think that this consultation is about the medicine or about the eyes?

NIC. About the eyes.

SOC. And when one considers whether a horse is to be bridled or not, and at what time, I presume one takes counsel about the horse, and not about the bridle?

NIC. True.

SOC. And in a word, when one considers a thing for any purpose, the consulting is in fact about the end one had in view to start with, and not about the means to be used for such end.

NIC. Necessarily.

SOC. So we must consider our adviser too, and ask ourselves whether he is a skilled expert in the treatment required for the end which is the subject of our consideration.

NIC. Certainly.

SOC. And we say that our present subject is an accomplishment studied for the sake of young men's souls?

NIC. Yes.

SOC. So what we have to consider is whether one of us is skilled in treatment of the soul, and is able to treat it rightly, and which of us has had good teachers.

LACH. But I say, Socrates, have you never noticed

διδασκάλων τεχνικωτέρους γεγονότας εἰς ἔνια ἢ
μετὰ διδασκάλων;

ΣΩ. Ἔγωγε, ὦ Λάχης· οἷς γε σὺ οὐκ ἂν ἐθέλοις
πιστεῦσαι, εἰ φαῖεν ἀγαθοὶ εἶναι δημιουργοί, εἰ μή
τί σοι τῆς αὑτῶν τέχνης ἔργον ἔχοιεν ἐπιδεῖξαι εὖ
186 εἰργασμένον, καὶ ἓν καὶ πλείω.

ΛΑ. Τοῦτο μὲν ἀληθῆ λέγεις.

ΣΩ. Καὶ ἡμᾶς ἄρα δεῖ, ὦ Λάχης τε καὶ Νικία,
ἐπειδὴ Λυσίμαχος καὶ Μελησίας εἰς συμβουλὴν
παρεκαλεσάτην ἡμᾶς περὶ τοῖν υἱέοιν, προθυμού-
μενοι αὐτοῖν ὅτι ἀρίστας γενέσθαι τὰς ψυχάς, εἰ
μέν φαμεν ἔχειν, ἐπιδεῖξαι αὐτοῖς καὶ διδασκάλους
οἵτινες ἡμῶν γεγόνασιν, ⟨οἳ⟩[1] αὐτοὶ πρῶτον[2] ἀγαθοὶ
ὄντες καὶ πολλῶν νέων τεθεραπευκότες ψυχὰς
B ἔπειτα καὶ ἡμᾶς διδάξαντες φαίνονται· ἢ εἴ τις
ἡμῶν αὐτῶν ἑαυτῷ διδάσκαλον μὲν οὔ φησι γεγονέναι, ἀλλ' οὖν ἔργα αὐτὸς αὑτοῦ ἔχει εἰπεῖν καὶ
ἐπιδεῖξαι, τίνες Ἀθηναίων ἢ τῶν ξένων, ἢ δοῦλοι
ἢ ἐλεύθεροι, δι' ἐκεῖνον ὁμολογουμένως ἀγαθοὶ
γεγόνασιν· εἰ δὲ μηδὲν ἡμῖν τούτων ὑπάρχει,
ἄλλους κελεύειν ζητεῖν καὶ μὴ ἐν ἑταίρων ἀνδρῶν
υἱέσι κινδυνεύειν διαφθείροντας τὴν μεγίστην αἰτίαν
ἔχειν ὑπὸ τῶν οἰκειοτάτων. ἐγὼ μὲν οὖν, ὦ
Λυσίμαχέ τε καὶ Μελησία, πρῶτος περὶ ἐμαυτοῦ
C λέγω ὅτι διδάσκαλός μοι οὐ γέγονε τούτου πέρι.
καίτοι ἐπιθυμῶ γε τοῦ πράγματος ἐκ νέου ἀρξάμε-
νος. ἀλλὰ τοῖς μὲν σοφισταῖς οὐκ ἔχω τελεῖν
μισθούς, οἵπερ μόνοι ἐπηγγέλλοντό με οἷοί τ'
εἶναι ποιῆσαι καλόν τε κἀγαθόν· αὐτὸς δ' αὖ

---

[1] οἳ add. Bekker.
[2] πρῶτον Stephanus : πρῶτοι MSS.

how some people have become more skilled in certain
things without teachers than others with them ?

soc. Yes, I have, Laches ; people, that is, whom
you would not care to trust on their mere statement
that they were good practitioners, unless they could
put forward some example of their personal skill—
some work well carried out—not in one only, but
several cases.

LACH. That is truly spoken.

soc. We also, therefore, Laches and Nicias—since
Lysimachus and Melesias have invited us to a consultation on their sons, whose souls they are anxious
to have as good as possible—should bring to their
notice what teachers we have had, if we say that we
have any to mention, who being themselves good to
begin with, and having treated the souls of many
young people, taught us also in due course and are
known to have done so. Or if any of ourselves says
he has had no teacher, but has however some works
of his own to speak of, and can point out to us what
Athenians or strangers, either slaves or freemen, are
acknowledged to owe their goodness to him, let him
do so. But if there is nothing of the sort to be found
amongst us, let us bid them look elsewhere ; for we
cannot run a risk with our good friends' children
where we may ruin them, and so bring upon us the
most grievous of accusations from our nearest and
dearest. Now I, Lysimachus and Melesias, am the
first to avow that I have had no teacher in this
respect ; and yet I have longed for such lessons
from my youth up. But I have not the means to
pay fees to the sophists, who were the only persons
that professed to be able to make me a complete
gentleman ; and to this moment I remain powerless

εὑρεῖν τὴν τέχνην ἀδυνατῶ ἔτι νυνί. εἰ δὲ Νικίας
ἢ Λάχης εὕρηκεν ἢ μεμάθηκεν, οὐκ ἂν θαυμάσαιμι·
καὶ γὰρ χρήμασιν ἐμοῦ δυνατώτεροι, ὥστε μαθεῖν
παρ᾽ ἄλλων, καὶ ἅμα πρεσβύτεροι, ὥστε ἤδη
εὑρηκέναι. δοκοῦσι δή μοι δυνατοὶ εἶναι παιδεῦσαι
D ἄνθρωπον· οὐ γὰρ ἄν ποτε ἀδεῶς ἀπεφαίνοντο
περὶ ἐπιτηδευμάτων νέῳ χρηστῶν τε καὶ πονηρῶν,
εἰ μὴ αὑτοῖς ἐπίστευον ἱκανῶς εἰδέναι. τὰ μὲν
οὖν ἄλλα ἔγωγε τούτοις πιστεύω· ὅτι δὲ δια-
φέρεσθον ἀλλήλοιν, ἐθαύμασα. τοῦτο οὖν σου ἐγὼ
ἀντιδέομαι, ὦ Λυσίμαχε, καθάπερ ἄρτι Λάχης μὴ
ἀφίεσθαί σε ἐμοῦ διεκελεύετο ἀλλὰ ἐρωτᾶν, καὶ
ἐγὼ νῦν παρακελεύομαί σοι μὴ ἀφίεσθαι Λάχητος
μηδὲ Νικίου, ἀλλ᾽ ἐρωτᾶν λέγοντα, ὅτι ὁ μὲν Σω-
E κράτης οὔ φησιν ἐπαΐειν περὶ τοῦ πράγματος, οὐδ᾽
ἱκανὸς εἶναι διακρῖναι ὁπότερος ὑμῶν ἀληθῆ λέγει·
οὔτε γὰρ εὑρετὴς οὔτε μαθητὴς οὐδενὸς περὶ τῶν
τοιούτων γεγονέναι· σὺ δ᾽, ὦ Λάχης καὶ Νικία,
εἴπετον ἡμῖν ἑκάτερος, τίνι δὴ δεινοτάτῳ συγ-
γεγόνατον περὶ τῆς τῶν νέων τροφῆς, καὶ πότερα
μαθόντε παρά του ἐπίστασθον ἢ αὐτὼ ἐξευρόντε,
καὶ εἰ μὲν μαθόντε, τίς ὁ διδάσκαλος ἑκατέρῳ καὶ
187 τίνες ἄλλοι ὁμότεχνοι αὐτοῖς, ἵν᾽, ἂν μὴ ὑμῖν
σχολὴ ᾖ ὑπὸ τῶν τῆς πόλεως πραγμάτων, ἐπ᾽
ἐκείνους ἴωμεν καὶ πείθωμεν ἢ δώροις ἢ χάρισιν ἢ
ἀμφότερα ἐπιμεληθῆναι καὶ τῶν ἡμετέρων καὶ τῶν
ὑμετέρων παίδων, ὅπως μὴ καταισχύνωσι τοὺς
αὑτῶν προγόνους φαῦλοι γενόμενοι· εἰ δ᾽ αὐτοὶ
εὑρεταὶ γεγονότε τοῦ τοιούτου, δότε παράδειγμα,

to discover the art myself. But I should not be surprised if Nicias or Laches has discovered or learnt it : for they have more means at their command to enable them to learn from others, and they are also older, and have had time to discover it. Indeed, I regard them as able to educate a man ; for they would never declare their minds so freely on pursuits that are beneficial or harmful to a youth unless they felt confident that they had the requisite knowledge. And I have entire confidence in them myself, except that I wondered at their differing from each other. I therefore make this counter-request of you, Lysimachus : just as Laches urged you a moment ago not to release me but to ask me questions, so I now call upon you not to release Laches or Nicias, but to question them in these terms : " Socrates says that he has no understanding of the matter, and that he is not competent to decide which of your statements is true ; that he has never been either a discoverer or a learner of anything of the sort. But you, Laches and Nicias, are each to tell us who is the cleverest person you have heard on the upbringing of youth ; whether you have knowledge of it by learning from someone or by discovering it yourselves ; and if you learnt it, who were your teachers respectively, and what other colleagues they had : in order that, if you are not at leisure through the demands of public business, we may go to them and induce them either with gifts or good turns or with both to undertake the care of our and your children together, and so prevent them from turning out knaves and disgracing their ancestors. But if you have made the grand discovery yourselves, give us an instance to show what other persons you have

33

τίνων ἤδη ἄλλων ἐπιμεληθέντες ἐκ φαύλων καλούς
τε κἀγαθοὺς ἐποιήσατε. εἰ γὰρ νῦν πρῶτον ἄρ-
B ξεσθε παιδεύειν, σκοπεῖν χρὴ μὴ οὐκ ἐν τῷ Καρὶ
ὑμῖν ὁ κίνδυνος κινδυνεύηται, ἀλλ' ἐν τοῖς υἱέσι τε
καὶ ἐν τοῖς τῶν φίλων παισί, καὶ ἀτεχνῶς τὸ λεγόμενον κατὰ τὴν παροιμίαν ὑμῖν συμβαίνῃ ἐν πίθῳ
ἡ κεραμεία γιγνομένη. λέγετε οὖν, τί τούτων ἢ
φατὲ ὑμῖν ὑπάρχειν τε καὶ προσήκειν, ἢ οὔ φατε.
ταῦτ', ὦ Λυσίμαχε, παρ' αὐτῶν πυνθάνου τε καὶ
μὴ μεθίει τοὺς ἄνδρας.

C ΛΤ. Καλῶς μὲν ἔμοιγε δοκεῖ, ὦ ἄνδρες, Σωκράτης λέγειν· εἰ δὲ βουλομένοις ὑμῖν ἐστι περὶ
τῶν τοιούτων ἐρωτᾶσθαί τε καὶ διδόναι λόγον,
αὐτοὺς δὴ χρὴ γιγνώσκειν, ὦ Νικία τε καὶ Λάχης.
ἐμοὶ μὲν γὰρ καὶ Μελησίᾳ τῷδε δῆλον ὅτι ἡδομένοις
ἂν εἴη, εἰ πάντα, ἃ Σωκράτης ἐρωτᾷ, ἐθέλοιτε
λόγῳ διεξιέναι· καὶ γὰρ ἐξ ἀρχῆς ἐντεῦθεν ἠρχόμην
λέγων, ὅτι εἰς συμβουλὴν διὰ ταῦτα ὑμᾶς παρακαλέ-
σαιμεν, ὅτι μεμεληκέναι ὑμῖν ἡγούμεθα, ὡς εἰκός,
περὶ τῶν τοιούτων, καὶ ἄλλως καὶ ἐπειδὴ οἱ παῖ-
D δες ὑμῖν ὀλίγου ὥσπερ οἱ ἡμέτεροι ἡλικίαν ἔχουσι
παιδεύεσθαι. εἰ οὖν ὑμῖν μή τι διαφέρει, εἴπατε
καὶ κοινῇ μετὰ Σωκράτους σκέψασθε, διδόντες τε
καὶ δεχόμενοι λόγον παρ' ἀλλήλων· εὖ γὰρ καὶ
τοῦτο λέγει ὅδε, ὅτι περὶ τοῦ μεγίστου νῦν βουλευόμεθα τῶν ἡμετέρων. ἀλλ' ὁρᾶτε εἰ δοκεῖ
χρῆναι οὕτω ποιεῖν.

ΝΙ. Ὦ Λυσίμαχε, δοκεῖς μοι ὡς ἀληθῶς Σωκράτη
E πατρόθεν γιγνώσκειν μόνον, αὐτῷ δ' οὐ συγγεγο-

---

[1] Lit. " on the Carian slave."
[2] *i.e.* on a large instead of a small piece of work, in

succeeded in changing, by your care of them, from knaves to honest gentlemen. For if you are now going to make your first attempt at educating, you must beware lest you try your experiment, not on a *corpus vile*,[1] but on your sons and the children of your friends, and you prove to be a mere case, as the proverbial saying has it, of starting pottery on a wine-jar.[2] So tell us what you claim, or do not claim, as your resources and acquirements in this kind." There, Lysimachus, demand that from these good persons, and do not let them off.

LYS. To my mind, good sirs, these remarks of Socrates are excellent : but it is for you, Nicias and Laches, to decide for yourselves whether it suits you to be questioned and offer some explanation on such points. For I and Melesias here would certainly be delighted if you would consent to expound in detail all that Socrates puts to you in his questions : as I began by saying at the outset, we invited you to consult with us just because we thought, very naturally, that you had given serious consideration to this kind of thing, especially as your boys, like ours, are almost of an age to be educated. Accordingly, if it is all the same to you, discuss it now by joint inquiry with Socrates, exchanging views with him in turn : for it is a particularly good remark of his that we are consulting now about the greatest of all our concerns. Come, see if you consider that this is the proper course to take.

NIC. Lysimachus, it looks to me, in very truth, as though you only knew Socrates at second hand— through his father—and had not conversed with him

which a beginner's mistake would be less costly. Cf. *Gorg.* 514 E.

νέναι ἀλλ' ἢ παιδὶ ὄντι, εἴ που ἐν τοῖς δημόταις
μετὰ τοῦ πατρὸς ἀκολουθῶν ἐπλησίασέ σοι ἢ ἐν
ἱερῷ ἢ ἐν ἄλλῳ τῳ συλλόγῳ τῶν δημοτῶν· ἐπειδὴ
δὲ πρεσβύτερος γέγονεν, οὐκ ἐντετυχηκὼς τῷ
ἀνδρὶ δῆλος εἶ.

ΛΥ. Τί μάλιστα, ὦ Νικία;

ΝΙ. Οὔ μοι δοκεῖς εἰδέναι ὅτι, ὃς ἂν ἐγγύτατα
Σωκράτους ᾖ [λόγῳ ὥσπερ γένει]¹ καὶ πλησιάζῃ
διαλεγόμενος, ἀνάγκη αὐτῷ, ἐὰν ἄρα καὶ περὶ
ἄλλου του πρότερον ἄρξηται διαλέγεσθαι, μὴ
παύεσθαι ὑπὸ τούτου περιαγόμενον τῷ λόγῳ, πρὶν
ἂν ἐμπέσῃ εἰς τὸ διδόναι περὶ αὑτοῦ λόγον, ὅντινα
188 τρόπον νῦν τε ζῇ καὶ ὅντινα τὸν παρεληλυθότα βίον
βεβίωκεν· ἐπειδὰν δ' ἐμπέσῃ, ὅτι οὐ πρότερον
αὐτὸν ἀφήσει Σωκράτης, πρὶν ἂν βασανίσῃ ταῦτα
εὖ τε καὶ καλῶς ἅπαντα. ἐγὼ δὲ συνήθης τέ
εἰμι τῷδε καὶ οἶδ' ὅτι ἀνάγκη ὑπὸ τούτου πάσχειν
ταῦτα, καὶ ἔτι γε αὐτὸς ὅτι πείσομαι ταῦτα εὖ
οἶδα· χαίρω γάρ, ὦ Λυσίμαχε, τῷ ἀνδρὶ πλησιάζων,
καὶ οὐδὲν οἶμαι κακὸν εἶναι τὸ ὑπομιμνήσκεσθαι
B ὅ τι μὴ καλῶς ἢ πεποιήκαμεν ἢ ποιοῦμεν, ἀλλ' εἰς
τὸν ἔπειτα βίον προμηθέστερον ἀνάγκη εἶναι τὸν
ταῦτα μὴ φεύγοντα, ἀλλ' ἐθέλοντα κατὰ τὸ τοῦ
Σόλωνος καὶ ἀξιοῦντα μανθάνειν ἕωσπερ ἂν ζῇ,
καὶ μὴ οἰόμενον αὐτῷ τὸ γῆρας νοῦν ἔχον προσ-
ιέναι. ἐμοὶ μὲν οὖν οὐδὲν ἄηθες οὐδ' αὖ ἀηδὲς
ὑπὸ Σωκράτους βασανίζεσθαι, ἀλλὰ καὶ πάλαι
σχεδόν τι ἠπιστάμην, ὅτι οὐ περὶ τῶν μειρακίων
ἡμῖν ὁ λόγος ἔσοιτο Σωκράτους παρόντος, ἀλλὰ

¹ λόγῳ ὥσπερ γένει secl. Cron.

personally except in his childhood, when you may have chanced to meet him among the people of his district, accompanying his father at the temple or at some local gathering. But you have evidently not yet had to do with him since he has reached maturer years.

LYS. How are you so sure of that, Nicias ?

NIC. You strike me as not being aware that, whoever comes into close contact with Socrates and has any talk with him face to face, is bound to be drawn round and round by him in the course of the argument—though it may have started at first on a quite different theme—and cannot stop until he is led into giving an account of himself, of the manner in which he now spends his days, and of the kind of life he has lived hitherto ; and when once he has been led into that, Socrates will never let him go until he has thoroughly and properly put all his ways to the test. Now I am accustomed to him, and so I know that one is bound to be thus treated by him, and further, that I myself shall certainly get the same treatment also. For I delight, Lysimachus, in conversing with the man, and see no harm in our being reminded of any past or present misdoing : nay, one must needs take more careful thought for the rest of one's life, if one does not fly from his words but is willing, as Solon said,[1] and zealous to learn as long as one lives, and does not expect to get good sense by the mere arrival of old age. So to me there is nothing unusual, or unpleasant either, in being tried and tested by Socrates ; in fact, I knew pretty well all the time that our argument would not be about the boys if

---

[1] Fr. 10 γηράσκω δ' αἰεὶ πολλὰ διδασκόμενος, " I grow old learning ever more and more " ; see below, 189 A.

C περὶ ἡμῶν αὐτῶν. ὅπερ οὖν λέγω, τὸ μὲν ἐμὸν
οὐδὲν κωλύει Σωκράτει συνδιατρίβειν ὅπως οὗτος
βούλεται· Λάχητα δὲ τόνδε ὅρα ὅπως ἔχει περὶ τοῦ
τοιούτου.

ΛΑ. Ἁπλοῦν τό γ᾽ ἐμόν, ὦ Νικία, περὶ λόγων
ἐστίν· εἰ δὲ βούλει, οὐχ ἁπλοῦν, ἀλλὰ διπλοῦν.
καὶ γὰρ ἂν δόξαιμί τῳ φιλόλογος εἶναι καὶ αὖ
μισόλογος. ὅταν μὲν γὰρ ἀκούω ἀνδρὸς περὶ
ἀρετῆς διαλεγομένου ἢ περί τινος σοφίας ὡς ἀληθῶς
ὄντος ἀνδρὸς καὶ ἀξίου τῶν λόγων ὧν λέγει, χαίρω
D ὑπερφυῶς, θεώμενος ἅμα τόν τε λέγοντα καὶ τὰ
λεγόμενα ὅτι πρέποντα ἀλλήλοις καὶ ἁρμόττοντά
ἐστι· καὶ κομιδῇ μοι δοκεῖ μουσικὸς ὁ τοιοῦτος
εἶναι, ἁρμονίαν καλλίστην ἡρμοσμένος οὐ λύραν
οὐδὲ παιδιᾶς ὄργανα, ἀλλὰ τῷ ὄντι [ζῆν ἡρμοσμένος
οὗ]¹ αὐτὸς αὑτοῦ τὸν βίον σύμφωνον τοῖς λόγοις
πρὸς τὰ ἔργα, ἀτεχνῶς δωριστὶ ἀλλ᾽ οὐκ ἰαστί,
οἴομαι δὲ οὐδὲ φρυγιστὶ οὐδὲ λυδιστί, ἀλλ᾽ ἥπερ
μόνη Ἑλληνική ἐστιν ἁρμονία. ὁ μὲν οὖν τοιοῦτος
E χαίρειν με ποιεῖ φθεγγόμενος καὶ δοκεῖν ὁτῳοῦν
φιλόλογον εἶναι· οὕτω σφόδρα ἀποδέχομαι παρ᾽
αὐτοῦ τὰ λεγόμενα· ὁ δὲ τἀναντία τούτου πράττων
λυπεῖ με, ὅσῳ ἂν δοκῇ ἄμεινον λέγειν, τοσούτῳ
μᾶλλον, καὶ ποιεῖ αὖ δοκεῖν εἶναι μισόλογον. Σωκράτους δ᾽ ἐγὼ τῶν μὲν λόγων οὐκ ἔμπειρός εἰμι,
ἀλλὰ πρότερον, ὡς ἔοικε, τῶν ἔργων ἐπειράθην,
καὶ ἐκεῖ αὐτὸν εὗρον ἄξιον ὄντα λόγων καλῶν καὶ

---

¹ ζῆν ἡρμοσμένος οὗ secl. Badham.

---

[1] Laches plays with the two meanings of ἁπλοῦν—" I am
single - minded (simple, straightforward) in such matters,
that is, I should rather say, double-minded."

[2] The different modes or scales in Greek music were

Socrates were present, but about ourselves. Let me therefore repeat that there is no objection on my part to holding a debate with Socrates after the fashion that he likes; but you must see how Laches here feels on the matter.

LACH. I have but a single mind,[1] Nicias, in regard to discussions, or if you like, a double rather than a single one. For you might think me a lover, and yet also a hater, of discussions : for when I hear a man discussing virtue or any kind of wisdom, one who is truly a man and worthy of his argument, I am exceedingly delighted; I take the speaker and his speech together, and observe how they sort and harmonize with each other. Such a man is exactly what I understand by " musical,"—he has tuned himself with the fairest harmony, not that of a lyre or other entertaining instrument, but has made a true concord of his own life between his words and his deeds, not in the Ionian, no, nor in the Phrygian nor in the Lydian, but simply in the Dorian mode,[2] which is the sole Hellenic harmony. Such a man makes me rejoice with his utterance, and anyone would judge me then a lover of discussion, so eagerly do I take in what he says : but a man who shows the opposite character gives me pain, and the better he seems to speak, the more I am pained, with the result, in this case, that I am judged a hater of discussion. Now of Socrates' words I have no experience, but formerly, I fancy, I have made trial of his deeds ; and there I found him living up to any

associated with different moral feelings. The Dorian was most favoured, as having a manly, stately character : the Ionian was more passionate and contentious. The Phrygian and Lydian were foreign modes, on the character of which there were various opinions. *Cf. Rep.* 398–99.

189 πάσης παρρησίας. εἰ οὖν καὶ τοῦτο ἔχει, συμ-
βούλομαι τἀνδρί, καὶ ἥδιστ᾽ ἂν ἐξεταζοίμην ὑπὸ
τοῦ τοιούτου, καὶ οὐκ ἂν ἀχθοίμην μανθάνων, ἀλλὰ
καὶ ἐγὼ τῷ Σόλωνι, ἓν μόνον προσλαβών, συγχωρῶ·
γηράσκων γὰρ πολλὰ διδάσκεσθαι ἐθέλω ὑπὸ χρηστῶν μόνον. τοῦτο γάρ μοι συγχωρείτω, ἀγαθὸν
καὶ αὐτὸν εἶναι τὸν διδάσκαλον, ἵνα μὴ δυσμαθὴς
φαίνωμαι ἀηδῶς μανθάνων· εἰ δὲ νεώτερος ὁ διδά-
B σκων ἔσται ἢ μήπω ἐν δόξῃ ὢν ἤ τι ἄλλο τῶν
τοιούτων ἔχων, οὐδέν μοι μέλει. σοὶ οὖν, ὦ
Σώκρατες, ἐγὼ ἐπαγγέλλομαι καὶ διδάσκειν καὶ
ἐλέγχειν ἐμὲ ὅ τι ἂν βούλῃ, καὶ μανθάνειν γε ὅ τι
αὖ ἐγὼ οἶδα· οὕτω σὺ παρ᾽ ἐμοὶ διάκεισαι ἀπ᾽
ἐκείνης τῆς ἡμέρας, ᾗ μετ᾽ ἐμοῦ συνδιεκινδύνευσας
καὶ ἔδωκας σαυτοῦ πεῖραν ἀρετῆς, ἣν χρὴ διδόναι
τὸν μέλλοντα δικαίως δώσειν. λέγ᾽ οὖν ὅ τί σοι
φίλον, μηδὲν τὴν ἡμετέραν ἡλικίαν ὑπόλογον
C ποιούμενος.

ΣΩ. Οὐ τὰ ὑμέτερα, ὡς ἔοικεν, αἰτιασόμεθα μὴ
οὐχ ἕτοιμα εἶναι καὶ συμβουλεύειν καὶ συσκοπεῖν.

ΛΥ. Ἀλλ᾽ ἡμέτερον δὴ ἔργον, ὦ Σώκρατες· ἕνα
γάρ σε ἔγωγε ἡμῶν τίθημι· σκόπει οὖν ἀντ᾽ ἐμοῦ
ὑπὲρ τῶν νεανίσκων, ὅ τι δεόμεθα παρὰ τῶνδε
πυνθάνεσθαι, καὶ συμβούλευε διαλεγόμενος τούτοις.
ἐγὼ μὲν γὰρ καὶ ἐπιλανθάνομαι ἤδη τὰ πολλὰ διὰ
τὴν ἡλικίαν ὧν ἂν διανοηθῶ ἐρέσθαι καὶ αὖ ἃ ἂν
ἀκούσω· ἐὰν δὲ μεταξὺ ἄλλοι λόγοι γένωνται, οὐ
πάνυ μέμνημαι. ὑμεῖς οὖν λέγετε καὶ διέξιτε
D πρὸς ὑμᾶς αὐτοὺς περὶ ὧν προυθέμεθα· ἐγὼ δ᾽

---

[1] This instance of Socrates' intrepidity (at Delium, *cf.*
above, 181 B) is more fully described by Alcibiades in the
Symposium (221).

fine words however freely spoken. So if he has that gift as well, his wish is mine, and I should be very glad to be cross-examined by such a man, and should not chafe at learning; but I too agree with Solon, while adding just one word to his saying : I should like, as I grow old, to learn more and more, but only from honest folk. Let him concede to me that my teacher is himself good—else I shall dislike my lessons and be judged a dunce—but if you say that my teacher is to be a younger man, or one who so far has no reputation, or anything of that sort, I care not a jot. I therefore invite you, Socrates, both to teach and to refute me as much as you please, and to learn too what I on my part know; such is the position you hold in my eyes since that day on which you came through the same danger with me,[1] and gave a proof of your own valour which is to be expected of anyone who hopes to justify his good name. So say whatever you like, leaving out of account the difference of our ages.

soc. You two, it seems, will give us no ground for complaint on the score of your not being ready to join both in advising and in inquiring.

lys. No, but the matter now rests with *us*, Socrates; for I venture to count you as one of us. So take my place in inquiring on behalf of the young men; make out what it is that we want our friends here to tell us, and be our adviser by discussing it with them. For I find that owing to my age I forget the questions I intend to put, and also the answers I receive; and if the discussion changes in the middle, my memory goes altogether. Do you therefore discuss and elucidate our problem among yourselves;

ἀκούσομαι καὶ ἀκούσας αὖ μετὰ Μελησίου τοῦδε
ποιήσω τοῦτο ὅ τι ἂν καὶ ὑμῖν δοκῇ.

ΣΩ. Πειστέον, ὦ Νικία τε καὶ Λάχης, Λυσιμάχῳ
καὶ Μελησίᾳ. ἃ μὲν οὖν νῦν δὴ ἐπεχειρήσαμεν
σκοπεῖν, τίνες οἱ διδάσκαλοι ἡμῖν τῆς τοιαύτης
παιδείας γεγόνασιν ἢ τίνας ἄλλους βελτίους πεποιήκαμεν, ἴσως μὲν οὐ κακῶς ἔχει ἐξετάζειν καὶ
E τὰ τοιαῦτα ἡμᾶς αὐτούς· ἀλλ᾽ οἶμαι καὶ ἡ τοιάδε
σκέψις εἰς ταὐτὸν φέρει, σχεδὸν δέ τι καὶ μᾶλλον
ἐξ ἀρχῆς εἴη ἄν. εἰ γὰρ τυγχάνομεν ἐπιστάμενοι
ὁτουοῦν πέρι, ὅτι παραγενόμενόν τῳ βέλτιον
ποιεῖ ἐκεῖνο ᾧ παρεγένετο, καὶ προσέτι οἷοί τέ
ἐσμεν αὐτὸ ποιεῖν παραγίγνεσθαι ἐκείνῳ, δῆλον
ὅτι αὐτό γε ἴσμεν τοῦτο, οὗ πέρι σύμβουλοι ἂν
γενοίμεθα ὡς ἄν τις αὐτὸ ῥᾷστα καὶ ἄριστ᾽ ἂν
κτήσαιτο. ἴσως οὖν οὐ μανθάνετέ μου ὅ τι λέγω,
ἀλλ᾽ ὧδε ῥᾷον μαθήσεσθε. εἰ τυγχάνομεν ἐπι-
190 στάμενοι, ὅτι ὄψις παραγενομένη ὀφθαλμοῖς βελτίους ποιεῖ ἐκείνους οἷς παρεγένετο, καὶ προσέτι
οἷοί τέ ἐσμεν ποιεῖν αὐτὴν παραγίγνεσθαι ὄμμασι,
δῆλον ὅτι ὄψιν γε ἴσμεν αὐτὴν ὅ τί ποτ᾽ ἔστιν, ἧς
πέρι σύμβουλοι ἂν γενοίμεθα ὡς ἄν τις αὐτὴν
ῥᾷστα καὶ ἄριστα κτήσαιτο. εἰ γὰρ μηδ᾽ αὐτὸ
τοῦτο εἰδεῖμεν, ὅ τί ποτ᾽ ἔστιν ὄψις ἢ ὅ τι ἔστιν
ἀκοή, σχολῇ ἂν σύμβουλοί γε ἄξιοι λόγου γενοίμεθα
καὶ ἰατροὶ ἢ περὶ ὀφθαλμῶν ἢ περὶ ὤτων, ὅντινα
B τρόπον ἀκοὴν ἢ ὄψιν κάλλιστ᾽ ἂν κτήσαιτό τις.

ΛΑ. Ἀληθῆ λέγεις, ὦ Σώκρατες.

ΣΩ. Οὐκοῦν, ὦ Λάχης, καὶ νῦν ἡμᾶς τώδε παρακα-
λεῖτον εἰς συμβουλήν, τίν᾽ ἂν τρόπον τοῖς υἱέσιν
αὐτῶν ἀρετὴ παραγενομένη ταῖς ψυχαῖς ἀμείνους
ποιήσειεν;

and I will listen, and then with my friend Melesias I will act at once upon whatever may be your decision.

soc. Let us do, Nicias and Laches, as Lysimachus and Melesias bid us. Now the questions that we attempted to consider a while ago—" Who have been our teachers in this sort of training ? What other persons have we made better ? "— are perhaps of a kind on which we might well examine ourselves : but I believe this other way of inquiring leads to the same thing, and will probably also start more from the beginning. For if we happen to know of such and such a thing that by being joined to another thing it makes this thing better, and further, if we are able to get the one joined to the other, we obviously know the thing itself on which we might be consulting as to how it might be best and most easily acquired. Now I daresay you do not grasp my meaning. Well, you will grasp it more easily in this way. If we happen to know that sight joined to eyes makes those eyes the better for it, and further if we are able to get it joined to eyes, we obviously know what this faculty of sight is, on which we might be consulting as to how it might be best and most easily acquired. For if we did not know first of all what sight or hearing is, we should hardly prove ourselves consultants or physicians of credit in the matter of eyes or ears, and the best way of acquiring sight or hearing.

lach. Truly spoken, Socrates.

soc. And you know, Laches, at this moment our two friends are inviting us to a consultation as to the way in which virtue may be joined to their sons' souls, and so make them better ?

ΛΑ. Πάνυ γε.

ΣΩ. Ἆρ᾽ οὖν τοῦτό γ᾽ ὑπάρχειν δεῖ, τὸ εἰδέναι ὅ τί ποτ᾽ ἔστιν ἀρετή; εἰ γάρ που μηδ᾽ ἀρετὴν εἰδεῖμεν τὸ παράπαν ὅ τί ποτε τυγχάνει ὄν, τίν᾽ ἂν
C τρόπον τούτου σύμβουλοι γενοίμεθα ὁτῳοῦν, ὅπως ἂν αὐτὸ κάλλιστα κτήσαιτο;

ΛΑ. Οὐδένα, ἔμοιγε δοκεῖ, ὦ Σώκρατες.

ΣΩ. Φαμὲν ἄρα, ὦ Λάχης, εἰδέναι αὐτὸ ὅ τι ἔστιν.

ΛΑ. Φαμὲν μέντοι.

ΣΩ. Οὐκοῦν ὅ γε ἴσμεν, κἂν εἴποιμεν δήπου τί ἔστιν.

ΛΑ. Πῶς γὰρ οὔ;

ΣΩ. Μὴ τοίνυν, ὦ ἄριστε, περὶ ὅλης ἀρετῆς εὐθέως σκοπώμεθα· πλέον γὰρ ἴσως ἔργον· ἀλλὰ μέρους τινὸς πέρι πρῶτον ἴδωμεν, εἰ ἱκανῶς ἔχομεν
D πρὸς τὸ εἰδέναι· καὶ ἡμῖν, ὡς τὸ εἰκός, ῥᾴων ἡ σκέψις ἔσται.

ΛΑ. Ἀλλ᾽ οὕτω ποιῶμεν, ὦ Σώκρατες, ὡς σὺ βούλει.

ΣΩ. Τί οὖν ἂν προελοίμεθα τῶν τῆς ἀρετῆς μερῶν; ἢ δῆλον δὴ ὅτι τοῦτο εἰς ὃ τείνειν δοκεῖ ἡ ἐν τοῖς ὅπλοις μάθησις; δοκεῖ δέ που τοῖς πολλοῖς εἰς ἀνδρείαν. ἦ γάρ;

ΛΑ. Καὶ μάλα δὴ οὕτω δοκεῖ.

ΣΩ. Τοῦτο τοίνυν πρῶτον ἐπιχειρήσωμεν, ὦ Λαχης, εἰπεῖν, ἀνδρεία τί ποτ᾽ ἐστίν· ἔπειτα μετὰ τοῦτο σκεψόμεθα καὶ ὅτῳ ἂν τρόπῳ τοῖς νεανίσκοις
E παραγένοιτο, καθ᾽ ὅσον οἷόν τε ἐξ ἐπιτηδευμάτων τε καὶ μαθημάτων παραγενέσθαι. ἀλλὰ πειρῶ εἰπεῖν ὃ λέγω, τί ἐστιν ἀνδρεία.

ΛΑ. Οὐ μὰ τὸν Δία, ὦ Σώκρατες, οὐ χαλεπὸν εἰπεῖν· εἰ γάρ τις ἐθέλοι ἐν τῇ τάξει μένων ἀμύνε-

44

LACHES

<small>LACH.</small> Yes, indeed.

<small>SOC.</small> Then our first requisite is to know what virtue [1] is ? For surely, if we had no idea at all what virtue actually is, we could not possibly consult with anyone as to how he might best acquire it ?

<small>LACH.</small> I certainly think not, Socrates.

<small>SOC.</small> Then we say, Laches, that we know what it is.

<small>LACH.</small> I suppose we must.

<small>SOC.</small> And of that which we know, I presume, we can also say what it is.

<small>LACH.</small> To be sure.

<small>SOC.</small> Let us not, therefore, my good friend, inquire forthwith about the whole of virtue, since that may well be too much for us ; but let us first see if we are sufficiently provided with knowledge about some part of it. In all likelihood this will make our inquiry easier.

<small>LACH.</small> Yes, let us do as you propose, Socrates.

<small>SOC.</small> Then which of the parts of virtue shall we choose ? Clearly, I think, that which the art of fighting in armour is supposed to promote ; and that, of course, is generally supposed to be courage, is it not ?

<small>LACH.</small> Yes, it generally is, to be sure.

<small>SOC.</small> Then let our first endeavour be, Laches, to say what courage is : after that we can proceed to inquire in what way our young men may obtain it, in so far as it is to be obtained by means of pursuits and studies. Come, try and tell me, as I suggest, what is courage.

<small>LACH.</small> On my word, Socrates, that is nothing difficult : anyone who is willing to stay at his post and

---

[1] Here, and in what follows, "virtue" embraces the accomplishments and excellences of a good citizen.

45

σθαι τοὺς πολεμίους καὶ μὴ φεύγοι, εὖ ἴσθι ὅτι ἀνδρεῖος ἂν εἴη.

ΣΩ. Εὖ μὲν λέγεις, ὦ Λάχης· ἀλλ᾽ ἴσως ἐγὼ αἴτιος, οὐ σαφῶς εἰπών, τὸ σὲ ἀποκρίνασθαι μὴ τοῦτο ὃ διανοούμενος ἠρόμην, ἀλλ᾽ ἕτερον.

ΛΑ. Πῶς τοῦτο λέγεις, ὦ Σώκρατες;

191   ΣΩ. Ἐγὼ φράσω, ἐὰν οἷός τε γένωμαι. ἀνδρεῖός που οὗτος, ὃν καὶ σὺ λέγεις, ὃς ἂν ἐν τῇ τάξει μένων μάχηται τοῖς πολεμίοις.

ΛΑ. Ἐγὼ γοῦν φημί.

ΣΩ. Καὶ γὰρ ἐγώ. ἀλλὰ τί αὖ ὅδε, ὃς ἂν φεύγων μάχηται τοῖς πολεμίοις, ἀλλὰ μὴ μένων;

ΛΑ. Πῶς φεύγων;

ΣΩ. Ὥσπερ που καὶ Σκύθαι λέγονται οὐχ ἧττον φεύγοντες ἢ διώκοντες μάχεσθαι, καὶ Ὅμηρός που ἐπαινῶν τοὺς τοῦ Αἰνείου ἵππους κραιπνὰ μάλ᾽
B ἔνθα καὶ ἔνθα ἔφη αὐτοὺς ἐπίστασθαι διώκειν ἠδὲ φέβεσθαι· καὶ αὐτὸν τὸν Αἰνείαν κατὰ τοῦτ᾽ ἐνεκωμίασε, κατὰ τὴν τοῦ φόβου ἐπιστήμην, καὶ εἶπεν αὐτὸν εἶναι μήστωρα φόβοιο.

ΛΑ. Καὶ καλῶς γε, ὦ Σώκρατες· περὶ ἁρμάτων γὰρ ἔλεγε· καὶ σὺ τὸ τῶν Σκυθῶν ἱππέων πέρι λέγεις. τὸ μὲν γὰρ ἱππικὸν [τὸ ἐκείνων] οὕτω μάχεται, τὸ δὲ ὁπλιτικὸν [τό γε τῶν Ἑλλήνων],[1] ὡς ἐγὼ λέγω.

ΣΩ. Πλήν γ᾽ ἴσως, ὦ Λάχης, τὸ Λακεδαιμονίων.
C Λακεδαιμονίους γάρ φασιν ἐν Πλαταιαῖς, ἐπειδὴ πρὸς τοῖς γερροφόροις ἐγένοντο, οὐκ ἐθέλειν μένον-

---

[1] τὸ ἐκείνων, τό γε τῶν Ἑλλήνων om. papyr. Arsin.

---

[1] *Il.* viii. 107-108. Socrates pretends to take the hero's epithet "prompter of fright" (in the enemy) as meaning

face the enemy, and does not run away, you may be
sure, is courageous.

soc. Rightly spoken, Laches; but I fear I am to
blame, by not putting it clearly, for your having
answered not the intention of my question, but
something else.

lach. What do you mean by that, Socrates?

soc. I will explain, so far as I can : let us take that
man to be courageous who, as you describe him
yourself, stays at his post and fights the enemy.

lach. I, for one, agree to that.

soc. Yes, and I do too. But what of this other
kind of man, who fights the enemy while fleeing,
and not staying?

lach. How fleeing?

soc. Well, as the Scythians are said to fight, as
much fleeing as pursuing ; and as you know Homer
says in praise of Aeneas' horses, that they knew
" how to pursue and to flee in fright full swiftly
this way and that way ; " and he glorifies Aeneas
himself for this very knowledge of fright, calling
him " prompter of fright." [1]

lach. And very properly too, Socrates ; for he
was speaking of chariots ; and so are you speaking
of the mode of the Scythian horsemen. That is the
way of cavalry fighting ; but with men-at-arms it is
as I state it. [2]

soc. Except, perhaps, Laches, in the case of the
Spartans. For they say that at Plataea, when the
Spartans came up to the men with wicker shields,

that he prompted fright in himself and his side, and so knew
all about the feeling.

[2] *i.e.* they stand fast at their posts in the ranks (above,
191 A).

τας πρὸς αὑτοὺς μάχεσθαι, ἀλλὰ φεύγειν, ἐπειδὴ
δ' ἐλύθησαν αἱ τάξεις τῶν Περσῶν, ἀναστρεφομένους
ὥσπερ ἱππέας μάχεσθαι καὶ οὕτω νικῆσαι τὴν
ἐκεῖ μάχην.

ΛΑ. Ἀληθῆ λέγεις.

ΣΩ. Τοῦτο τοίνυν ἄρτι ἔλεγον, ὅτι ἐγὼ αἴτιος
μὴ καλῶς σε ἀποκρίνασθαι, ὅτι οὐ καλῶς ἠρόμην.
D βουλόμενος γάρ σου πυθέσθαι μὴ μόνον τοὺς ἐν
τῷ ὁπλιτικῷ ἀνδρείους, ἀλλὰ καὶ τοὺς ἐν τῷ
ἱππικῷ καὶ ἐν σύμπαντι τῷ πολεμικῷ εἴδει, καὶ
μὴ μόνον τοὺς ἐν τῷ πολέμῳ, ἀλλὰ καὶ τοὺς ἐν
τοῖς πρὸς τὴν θάλατταν κινδύνοις ἀνδρείους ὄντας,
καὶ ὅσοι γε πρὸς νόσους καὶ ὅσοι πρὸς πενίας ἢ
καὶ πρὸς τὰ πολιτικὰ ἀνδρεῖοί εἰσι, καὶ ἔτι αὖ μὴ
μόνον ὅσοι πρὸς λύπας ἀνδρεῖοί εἰσιν ἢ φόβους,
ἀλλὰ καὶ πρὸς ἐπιθυμίας ἢ ἡδονὰς δεινοὶ μάχεσθαι,
E καὶ μένοντες ἢ ἀναστρέφοντες—εἰσὶ γάρ πού τινες,
ὦ Λάχης, καὶ ἐν τοῖς τοιούτοις ἀνδρεῖοι.

ΛΑ. Καὶ σφόδρα, ὦ Σώκρατες.

ΣΩ. Οὐκοῦν ἀνδρεῖοι μὲν πάντες οὗτοί εἰσιν,
ἀλλ' οἱ μὲν ἐν ἡδοναῖς, οἱ δ' ἐν λύπαις, οἱ δ' ἐν
ἐπιθυμίαις οἱ δ' ἐν φόβοις τὴν ἀνδρείαν κέκτηνται·
οἱ δέ γ', οἶμαι, δειλίαν ἐν τοῖς αὐτοῖς τούτοις.

ΛΑ. Πάνυ γε.

ΣΩ. Τί ποτε ὂν ἑκάτερον τούτων, τοῦτο ἐπυνθανόμην. πάλιν οὖν πειρῶ εἰπεῖν ἀνδρείαν πρῶτον,
τί ὂν ἐν πᾶσι τούτοις ταὐτόν ἐστιν· ἢ οὔπω κατα-
μανθάνεις ὃ λέγω;

ΛΑ. Οὐ πάνυ τι.

---

[1] In the final struggle at Plataea (479 B.C.) the Spartans
at first hesitated before the barrier of wicker shields opposed

they were not willing to stand and fight against these, but fled; when, however, the Persian ranks were broken, the Spartans kept turning round and fighting like cavalry, and so won that great battle.[1]

LACH. What you say is true.

SOC. And so this is what I meant just now by saying that I was to blame for your wrong answer, by putting my question wrongly. For I wanted to have your view not only of brave men-at-arms, but also of courage in cavalry and in the entire warrior class; and of the courageous not only in war but in the perils of the sea, and all who in disease and poverty, or again in public affairs, are courageous; and further, all who are not merely courageous against pain or fear, but doughty fighters against desires and pleasures, whether standing their ground or turning back upon the foe—for I take it, Laches, there are courageous people in all these kinds.

LACH. Very much so, Socrates.

SOC. Then all these are courageous, only some have acquired courage in pleasures, some in pains, some in desires and some in fears, while others, I conceive, have acquired cowardice in these same things.

LACH. To be sure.

SOC. What either of them[2] *is*—that is what I wanted to know. So try again, and tell me first what is this thing, courage, which is the same in all of these cases; or do you still not comprehend my meaning?

LACH. Not very well.

to them by the Persians; but by a supreme effort they broke through and defeated the Persians by turning on them in man-to-man combat. *Cf.* Herod. ix. 61–2.
[2] *i.e.* courage and cowardice.

192 ΣΩ. Ἀλλ' ὧδε λέγω, ὥσπερ ἂν εἰ τάχος ἠρώτων τί ποτ' ἐστίν, ὃ καὶ ἐν τῷ τρέχειν τυγχάνει ὂν
ἡμῖν καὶ ἐν τῷ κιθαρίζειν καὶ ἐν τῷ λέγειν καὶ ἐν
τῷ μανθάνειν καὶ ἐν ἄλλοις πολλοῖς, καὶ σχεδόν τι
αὐτὸ κεκτήμεθα, οὗ καὶ πέρι ἄξιον λέγειν, ἢ ἐν
ταῖς τῶν χειρῶν πράξεσιν ἢ σκελῶν ἢ στόματός
τε καὶ φωνῆς ἢ διανοίας· ἢ οὐχ οὕτω καὶ σὺ λέγεις;

ΛΑ. Πάνυ γε.

ΣΩ. Εἰ τοίνυν τίς με ἔροιτο· ὦ Σώκρατες, τί
λέγεις τοῦτο, ὃ ἐν πᾶσιν ὀνομάζεις ταχυτῆτα
Β εἶναι; εἴποιμ' ἂν αὐτῷ, ὅτι τὴν ἐν ὀλίγῳ χρόνῳ
πολλὰ διαπραττομένην δύναμιν ταχυτῆτα ἔγωγε
καλῶ καὶ περὶ φωνὴν καὶ περὶ δρόμον καὶ περὶ
τἆλλα πάντα.

ΛΑ. Ὀρθῶς γε σὺ λέγων.

ΣΩ. Πειρῶ δὴ καὶ σύ, ὦ Λάχης, τὴν ἀνδρείαν
οὕτως εἰπεῖν, τίς οὖσα δύναμις ἡ αὐτὴ ἐν ἡδονῇ
καὶ ἐν λύπῃ καὶ ἐν ἅπασιν οἷς νῦν δὴ ἐλέγομεν
αὐτὴν εἶναι, ἔπειτα ἀνδρεία κέκληται.

ΛΑ. Δοκεῖ τοίνυν μοι καρτερία τις εἶναι τῆς
ψυχῆς, εἰ τό γε διὰ πάντων [περὶ ἀνδρείας]¹ πεφυ-
κὸς δεῖ εἰπεῖν.

C ΣΩ. Ἀλλὰ μὴν δεῖ, εἴ γε τὸ ἐρωτώμενον ἀποκρινούμεθα ἡμῖν αὐτοῖς. τοῦτο τοίνυν ἔμοιγε φαίνεται, ὅτι οὔτι πᾶσά γε, ὡς ἐγῷμαι, καρτερία
ἀνδρεία σοι φαίνεται· τεκμαίρομαι δὲ ἐνθένδε· σχεδὸν γάρ τι οἶδα, ὦ Λάχης, ὅτι τῶν πάνυ καλῶν
πραγμάτων ἡγῇ σὺ ἀνδρείαν εἶναι.

¹ περὶ ἀνδρείας secl. Badham.

50

soc. I mean in this way : suppose, for instance, I were asking you what is quickness, as we find it in running and harping, in speaking and learning, and in many other activities, and as possessed by us practically in any action worth mentioning, whether of arms or legs, or mouth or voice, or mind : or do you not use the word so ?

lach. Yes, to be sure.

soc. Well then, suppose someone asked me : Socrates, what do you mean by this thing which in all cases you term quickness ? My reply would be : The faculty that gets a great deal done in a little time is what I call quickness, whether in a voice or in a race or in any of the other instances.

lach. Your statement would be quite correct.

soc. So now try and tell me on your part, Laches, about courage in the same way : what faculty is it, the same whether in pleasure or in pain or in any of the things in which we said just now it was to be found, that has been singled out by the name of courage ?

lach. Well then, I take it to be a certain endurance of the soul, if I am to speak of the natural quality that appears in them all.

soc. Why, of course we must, if we are each to answer the other's actual question. Now it appears to me that by no means *all* endurance, as I conceive it, can appear to you to be courage. And my grounds for thinking so are these : I am almost certain, Laches, that you rank courage among the nobler qualities.

ΛΑ. Εὖ μὲν οὖν ἴσθι ὅτι τῶν καλλίστων.

ΣΩ. Οὐκοῦν ἡ μὲν μετὰ φρονήσεως καρτερία καλὴ κἀγαθή;

ΛΑ. Πάνυ γε.

D ΣΩ. Τί δ᾽ ἡ μετ᾽ ἀφροσύνης; οὐ τοὐναντίον ταύτῃ βλαβερὰ καὶ κακοῦργος;

ΛΑ. Ναί.

ΣΩ. Καλὸν οὖν τι φήσεις σὺ εἶναι τὸ τοιοῦτον, ὂν κακοῦργόν τε καὶ βλαβερόν;

ΛΑ. Οὔκουν δίκαιόν γε, ὦ Σώκρατες.

ΣΩ. Οὐκ ἄρα τήν γε τοιαύτην καρτερίαν ἀνδρείαν ὁμολογήσεις εἶναι, ἐπειδήπερ οὐ καλή ἐστιν, ἡ δὲ ἀνδρεία καλόν ἐστιν.

ΛΑ. Ἀληθῆ λέγεις.

ΣΩ. Ἡ φρόνιμος ἄρα καρτερία κατὰ τὸν σὸν λόγον ἀνδρεία ἂν εἴη.

ΛΑ. Ἔοικεν.

E ΣΩ. Ἴδωμεν δή, ἡ εἰς τί φρόνιμος; ἢ ἡ εἰς ἅπαντα καὶ τὰ μεγάλα καὶ τὰ σμικρά; οἷον εἴ τις καρτερεῖ ἀναλίσκων ἀργύριον φρονίμως, εἰδὼς ὅτι ἀναλώσας πλέον ἐκτήσεται, τοῦτον ἀνδρεῖον καλοῖς ἄν;

ΛΑ. Μὰ Δί᾽ οὐκ ἔγωγε.

ΣΩ. Ἀλλ᾽ οἷον εἴ τις ἰατρὸς ὤν, περιπλευμονίᾳ τοῦ υἱέος ἐχομένου ἢ ἄλλου τινὸς καὶ δεομένου πιεῖν ἢ φαγεῖν δοῦναι, μὴ κάμπτοιτο ἀλλὰ καρτεροῖ;

193 ΛΑ. Οὐδ᾽ ὁπωστιοῦν οὐδ᾽ αὕτη.

ΣΩ. Ἀλλ᾽ ἐν πολέμῳ καρτεροῦντα ἄνδρα καὶ ἐθέλοντα μάχεσθαι, φρονίμως λογιζόμενον, εἰδότα μὲν ὅτι βοηθήσουσιν ἄλλοι αὐτῷ, πρὸς ἐλάττους δὲ

LACH. Nay, among the noblest, you may be quite certain.

SOC. And endurance joined with wisdom is noble and good ?

LACH. Very much so.

SOC. But what of it when joined with folly ? Is it not, on the contrary, hurtful and mischievous ?

LACH. Yes.

SOC. And can you say that such a thing is noble, when it is both mischievous and hurtful ?

LACH. Not with any justice, Socrates.

SOC. Then you will not admit that such an endurance is courage, seeing that it is not noble, whereas courage is a noble quality.

LACH. That is true.

SOC. So, by your account, wise endurance will be courage.

LACH. Apparently.

SOC. Now let us see *in what* it is wise. In all things, whether great or small ? For instance, if a man endures in spending money wisely, because he knows that by spending he will gain more, would you call him courageous ?

LACH. On my word, not I.

SOC. Or what do you call it in the case of a doctor who, when his son or anyone else is suffering from inflammation of the lungs and begs for something to drink or eat, inflexibly and enduringly refuses ?

LACH. That is no case of it, in any sense, either.

SOC. Well now, when a man endures in war, and is willing to fight, on a wise calculation whereby he knows that others will come to his aid, and that the forces

καὶ φαυλοτέρους μαχεῖται ἢ μεθ᾽ ὧν αὐτός ἐστιν,
ἔτι δὲ χωρία ἔχει κρείττω, τοῦτον τὸν μετὰ τῆς
τοιαύτης φρονήσεως καὶ παρασκευῆς καρτεροῦντα
ἀνδρειότερον ἂν φαίης ἢ τὸν ἐν τῷ ἐναντίῳ
στρατοπέδῳ ἐθέλοντα ὑπομένειν τε καὶ καρτερεῖν;

B   ΛΑ. Τὸν ἐν τῷ ἐναντίῳ, ἔμοιγε δοκεῖ, ὦ Σώκρατες.

ΣΩ. Ἀλλὰ μὴν ἀφρονεστέρα γε ἡ τούτου ἢ ἡ
τοῦ ἑτέρου καρτερία.

ΛΑ. Ἀληθῆ λέγεις.

ΣΩ. Καὶ τὸν μετ᾽ ἐπιστήμης ἄρα ἱππικῆς καρτεροῦντα ἐν ἱππομαχίᾳ ἧττον φήσεις ἀνδρεῖον εἶναι
ἢ τὸν ἄνευ ἐπιστήμης.

ΛΑ. Ἔμοιγε δοκεῖ.

C   ΣΩ. Καὶ τὸν μετὰ σφενδονητικῆς ἢ τοξικῆς ἢ
ἄλλης τινὸς τέχνης καρτεροῦντα.

ΛΑ. Πάνυ γε.

ΣΩ. Καὶ ὅσοι ἂν ἐθέλωσιν εἰς φρέαρ καταβαίνον-
τες καὶ κολυμβῶντες καρτερεῖν ἐν τούτῳ τῷ ἔργῳ,
μὴ ὄντες δεινοί, ἢ ἔν τινι ἄλλῳ τοιούτῳ, ἀνδρειοτέ-
ρους φήσεις τῶν ταῦτα δεινῶν.

ΛΑ. Τί γὰρ ἄν τις ἄλλο φαίη, ὦ Σώκρατες;

ΣΩ. Οὐδέν, εἴπερ οἴοιτό γε οὕτως.

ΛΑ. Ἀλλὰ μὴν οἶμαί γε.

ΣΩ. Καὶ μήν που ἀφρονεστέρως γε, ὦ Λάχης,
οἱ τοιοῦτοι κινδυνεύουσί τε καὶ καρτεροῦσιν ἢ οἱ
μετὰ τέχνης αὐτὸ πράττοντες.

ΛΑ. Φαίνονται.

D   ΣΩ. Οὐκοῦν αἰσχρὰ ἡ ἄφρων τόλμα τε καὶ
καρτέρησις ἐν τῷ πρόσθεν ἐφάνη ἡμῖν οὖσα καὶ
βλαβερά;

ΛΑ. Πάνυ γε.

against him will be fewer and feebler than those who are with him, and when he has besides the advantage of position,—would you say of this man, if he endures with such wisdom and preparation, that he, or a man in the opposing army who is willing to stand up against him and endure, is the more courageous?

LACH. The man opposed to him, I should say, Socrates.

soc. But yet his endurance is more foolish than that of the first man.

LACH. That is true.

soc. So you would say that he who in a cavalry fight endures with a knowledge of horsemanship is less courageous than he who endures without it.

LACH. Yes, I think so.

soc. And he who endures with a skill in slinging or shooting or other such art.

LACH. To be sure.

soc. And anyone who agrees to descend into a well, and to dive, and to endure in this or other such action, without being an adept in these things, you would say is more courageous than the adepts.

LACH. Yes, for what else can one say, Socrates?

soc. Nothing, provided one thinks so.

LACH. But I do think it.

soc. And you observe, I suppose, Laches, that persons of this sort are more foolish in their risks and endurances than those who do it with proper skill.

LACH. Evidently.

soc. Now, we found before that foolish boldness and endurance are base and hurtful?

LACH. Quite so.

ΣΩ. Ἡ δέ γε ἀνδρεία ὡμολογεῖτο καλόν τι εἶναι.

ΛΑ. Ὡμολογεῖτο γάρ.

ΣΩ. Νῦν δ' αὖ πάλιν φαμὲν ἐκεῖνο τὸ αἰσχρόν, τὴν ἄφρονα καρτέρησιν, ἀνδρείαν εἶναι.

ΛΑ. Ἐοίκαμεν.

ΣΩ. Καλῶς οὖν σοι δοκοῦμεν λέγειν;

ΛΑ. Μὰ τὸν Δί', ὦ Σώκρατες, ἐμοὶ μὲν οὔ.

ΣΩ. Οὐκ ἄρα που κατὰ τὸν σὸν λόγον δωριστὶ E ἡρμόσμεθα ἐγώ τε καὶ σύ, ὦ Λάχης· τὰ γὰρ ἔργα οὐ συμφωνεῖ ἡμῖν τοῖς λόγοις. ἔργῳ μὲν γάρ, ὡς ἔοικε, φαίη ἄν τις ἡμᾶς ἀνδρείας μετέχειν, λόγῳ δ', ὡς ἐγῷμαι, οὐκ ἄν, εἰ νῦν ἡμῶν ἀκούσειε διαλεγομένων.

ΛΑ. Ἀληθέστατα λέγεις.

ΣΩ. Τί οὖν; δοκεῖ καλὸν εἶναι οὕτως ἡμᾶς διακεῖσθαι;

ΛΑ. Οὐδ' ὁπωστιοῦν.

ΣΩ. Βούλει οὖν ᾧ λέγομεν πειθώμεθα τό γε τοσοῦτον;

ΛΑ. Τὸ ποῖον δὴ τοῦτο, καὶ τίνι τούτῳ;

194 ΣΩ. Τῷ λόγῳ ὃς καρτερεῖν κελεύει. εἰ οὖν βούλει, καὶ ἡμεῖς ἐπὶ τῇ ζητήσει ἐπιμείνωμέν τε καὶ καρτερήσωμεν, ἵνα καὶ μὴ ἡμῶν αὐτὴ ἡ ἀνδρεία καταγελάσῃ, ὅτι οὐκ ἀνδρείως αὐτὴν ζητοῦμεν, εἰ ἄρα πολλάκις αὐτὴ ἡ καρτέρησίς ἐστιν ἀνδρεία.

ΛΑ. Ἐγὼ μὲν ἕτοιμος, ὦ Σώκρατες, μὴ προαφίστασθαι· καίτοι ἀήθης γ' εἰμὶ τῶν τοιούτων λόγων· ἀλλά τίς με καὶ φιλονικία εἴληφε πρὸς τὰ εἰρημένα, B καὶ ὡς ἀληθῶς ἀγανακτῶ, εἰ οὑτωσὶ ἃ νοῶ μὴ

soc. But courage was admitted to be something noble.

lach. Yes, it was.

soc. Whereas now, on the contrary, we say that this base thing—foolish endurance—is courage.

lach. Apparently.

soc. Then do you think our statement is correct?

lach. On my word, Socrates, not I.

soc. Hence I presume that, on your showing, you and I, Laches, are not tuned to the Dorian harmony: for our deeds do not accord with our words. By our deeds, most likely, the world might judge us to have our share of courage, but not by our words, I fancy, if they should hear the way we are talking now.

lach. That is very true.

soc. Well now, does it seem right that we should be in such a condition?

lach. Not by any means.

soc. Then do you mind if we accept our statement to a certain point?

lach. To what point do you mean, and what statement?

soc. That which enjoins endurance. And, if you please, let us too be steadfast and enduring in our inquiry, so as not to be ridiculed by courage herself for failing to be courageous in our search for her, when we might perchance find after all that this very endurance is courage.

lach. For my part I am ready, Socrates, to continue without faltering ; and yet I am unaccustomed to discussions of this sort. But a certain ambitious ardour has got hold of me at hearing what has been said, and I am truly vexed at finding myself unable

PLATO

οἷός τ᾽ εἰμὶ εἰπεῖν. νοεῖν μὲν γὰρ ἔμοιγε δοκῶ περὶ ἀνδρείας ὅ τι ἔστιν, οὐκ οἶδα δ᾽ ὅπη με ἄρτι διέφυγεν, ὥστε μὴ συλλαβεῖν τῷ λόγῳ αὐτὴν καὶ εἰπεῖν ὅ τι ἔστιν.

ΣΩ. Οὐκοῦν, ὦ φίλε, τὸν ἀγαθὸν κυνηγέτην μεταθεῖν χρὴ καὶ μὴ ἀνιέναι.

ΛΑ. Παντάπασι μὲν οὖν.

ΣΩ. Βούλει οὖν καὶ Νικίαν τόνδε παρακαλῶμεν ἐπὶ τὸ κυνηγέσιον, εἴ τι ἡμῶν εὐπορώτερός ἐστιν;

C   ΛΑ. Βούλομαι· πῶς γὰρ οὔ;

ΣΩ. Ἴθι δή, ὦ Νικία, ἀνδράσι φίλοις χειμαζομένοις ἐν λόγῳ καὶ ἀποροῦσι βοήθησον, εἴ τινα ἔχεις δύναμιν. τὰ μὲν γὰρ δὴ ἡμέτερα ὁρᾷς ὡς ἄπορα· σὺ δ᾽ εἰπὼν ὅ τι ἡγῇ ἀνδρείαν εἶναι, ἡμᾶς τε τῆς ἀπορίας ἔκλυσαι καὶ αὐτὸς ἃ νοεῖς τῷ λόγῳ βεβαίωσαι.

ΝΙ. Δοκεῖτε τοίνυν μοι πάλαι οὐ καλῶς, ὦ Σώκρατες, ὁρίζεσθαι τὴν ἀνδρείαν· ὃ γὰρ ἐγὼ σοῦ ἤδη καλῶς λέγοντος ἀκήκοα, τούτῳ οὐ χρῆσθε.

ΣΩ. Ποίῳ δή, ὦ Νικία;

D   ΝΙ. Πολλάκις ἀκήκοά σου λέγοντος, ὅτι ταῦτα ἀγαθὸς ἕκαστος ἡμῶν, ἅπερ σοφός, ἃ δὲ ἀμαθής, ταῦτα δὲ κακός.

ΣΩ. Ἀληθῆ μέντοι νὴ Δία λέγεις, ὦ Νικία.

ΝΙ. Οὐκοῦν εἴπερ ὁ ἀνδρεῖος ἀγαθός, δῆλον ὅτι σοφός ἐστιν.

ΣΩ. Ἤκουσας, ὦ Λάχης;

ΛΑ. Ἔγωγε, καὶ οὐ σφόδρα γε μανθάνω ὃ λέγει.

to express offhand what I think. For I feel that I conceive in thought what courage is, but somehow or other she has given me the slip for the moment, so that I fail to lay hold of her in speech and state what she is.

soc. Well, my dear sir, the good huntsman must follow the hounds and not give up the chase.

lach. Yes, indeed, by all means.

soc. Then do you agree to our inviting Nicias here to join in our hunt? He may be more resourceful than we are.

lach. I agree, of course.

soc. Come now, Nicias, and use what powers you have to assist your friends, who are caught in a storm of argument and are quite perplexed. You see the perplexity of our case; you must now tell us what you think courage is, and so at once set us free from our perplexity and give your own thoughts the stability of speech.

nic. Well, for some time I have been thinking, Socrates, that you two are not defining courage in the right way; for you are not acting upon an admirable remark which I have formerly heard you make.

soc. What is that, Nicias?

nic. I have often heard you say that every man is good in that wherein he is wise, and bad in that wherein he is unlearned.

soc. Well, that is true, Nicias, I must say.

nic. And hence, if the brave man is good, clearly he must be wise.

soc. Do you hear him, Laches?

lach. I do, without understanding very well what he says.

ΣΩ. Ἀλλ' ἐγὼ δοκῶ μανθάνειν, καί μοι δοκεῖ
ἀνὴρ σοφίαν τινὰ τὴν ἀνδρείαν λέγειν.

ΛΑ. Ποίαν, ὦ Σώκρατες, σοφίαν;

ΣΩ. Οὐκοῦν τόνδε τοῦτο ἐρωτᾷς;

ΛΑ. Ἔγωγε.

ΣΩ. Ἴθι δή, αὐτῷ εἰπέ, ὦ Νικία, ποία σοφία
ἀνδρεία ἂν εἴη κατὰ τὸν σὸν λόγον. οὐ γάρ που ἥ
γε αὐλητική.

ΝΙ. Οὐδαμῶς.

ΣΩ. Οὐδὲ μὴν ἡ κιθαριστική.

ΝΙ. Οὐ δῆτα.

ΣΩ. Ἀλλὰ τίς δὴ αὕτη ἢ τίνος ἐπιστήμη;

ΛΑ. Πάνυ μὲν οὖν ὀρθῶς αὐτὸν ἐρωτᾷς, ὦ
Σώκρατες, καὶ εἰπέτω γε τίνα φησὶν αὐτὴν εἶναι.

ΝΙ. Ταύτην ἔγωγε, ὦ Λάχης, τὴν τῶν δεινῶν
195 καὶ θαρραλέων ἐπιστήμην καὶ ἐν πολέμῳ καὶ ἐν
τοῖς ἄλλοις ἅπασιν.

ΛΑ. Ὡς ἄτοπα λέγει, ὦ Σώκρατες.

ΣΩ. Πρὸς τί τοῦτ' εἶπες βλέψας, ὦ Λάχης;

ΛΑ. Πρὸς ὅ τι; χωρὶς δήπου σοφία ἐστὶν ἀνδρείας.

ΣΩ. Οὔκουν φησί γε Νικίας.

ΛΑ. Οὐ μέντοι μὰ Δία· ταῦτά τοι καὶ ληρεῖ.

ΣΩ. Οὐκοῦν διδάσκωμεν αὐτόν, ἀλλὰ μὴ λοιδο-
ρῶμεν.

ΝΙ. Οὔκ, ἀλλά μοι δοκεῖ, ὦ Σώκρατες, Λάχης
ἐπιθυμεῖν κἀμὲ φανῆναι μηδὲν λέγοντα, ὅτι καὶ
Β αὐτὸς ἄρτι τοιοῦτος ἐφάνη.

ΛΑ. Πάνυ μὲν οὖν, ὦ Νικία· καὶ πειράσομαί
γε ἀποφῆναι. οὐδὲν γὰρ λέγεις· ἐπεὶ αὐτίκα ἐν
ταῖς νόσοις οὐχ οἱ ἰατροὶ τὰ δεινὰ ἐπίστανται;

soc. But I think I understand it : our friend appears to me to mean that courage is a kind of wisdom.

lach. What kind of wisdom, Socrates ?

soc. Well, will you put that question to your friend here ?

lach. I do.

soc. Come now, tell him, Nicias, what kind of wisdom courage may be, by your account. Not that, I presume, of flute-playing.

nic. Not at all.

soc. Nor yet that of harping.

nic. Oh, no.

soc. But what is this knowledge then, or of what ?

lach. I must say you question him quite correctly, Socrates, so let him just tell us what he thinks it is.

nic. I say, Laches, that it is this—the knowledge of what is to be dreaded or dared, either in war or in anything else.

lach. How strangely he talks, Socrates !

soc. What is it that makes you say that, Laches ?

lach. What is it ? Why, surely wisdom is distinct from courage.

soc. Well, Nicias denies that.

lach. He does indeed, to be sure : that is where he just babbles.

soc. Then let us instruct and not abuse him.

nic. No, it seems to me, Socrates, that Laches wants to have it proved that I am talking nonsense, because he was proved a moment ago to be in the same case himself.

lach. Quite so, Nicias, and I will try to make it evident. You *are* talking nonsense : for instance, do not doctors know what is to be dreaded in dis-

61

ἢ οἱ ἀνδρεῖοι δοκοῦσί σοι ἐπίστασθαι; ἢ τοὺς
ἰατροὺς σὺ ἀνδρείους καλεῖς;

ΝΙ. Οὐδ' ὁπωστιοῦν.

ΛΑ. Οὐδέ γε τοὺς γεωργοὺς οἶμαι. καίτοι τά
γε ἐν τῇ γεωργίᾳ δεινὰ οὗτοι δήπου ἐπίστανται,
καὶ οἱ ἄλλοι δημιουργοὶ ἅπαντες τὰ ἐν ταῖς αὑτῶν
τέχναις δεινά τε καὶ θαρραλέα ἴσασιν· ἀλλ' οὐδέν
C τι μᾶλλον οὗτοι ἀνδρεῖοί εἰσιν.

ΣΩ. Τί δοκεῖ Λάχης λέγειν, ὦ Νικία; ἔοικε
μέντοι λέγειν τι.

ΝΙ. Καὶ γὰρ λέγει γέ τι, οὐ μέντοι ἀληθές γε.

ΣΩ. Πῶς δή;

ΝΙ. Ὅτι οἴεται τοὺς ἰατροὺς πλέον τι εἰδέναι
περὶ τοὺς κάμνοντας ἢ τὸ ὑγιεινὸν εἰπεῖν οἷόν τε
καὶ νοσῶδες. οἱ δὲ δήπου τοσοῦτον μόνον ἴσασιν·
εἰ δὲ δεινόν τῳ τοῦτό ἐστι τὸ ὑγιαίνειν μᾶλλον ἢ
τὸ κάμνειν, ἡγῇ σὺ τουτί, ὦ Λάχης, τοὺς ἰατροὺς
ἐπίστασθαι; ἢ οὐ πολλοῖς οἴει ἐκ τῆς νόσου ἄμεινον
D εἶναι μὴ ἀναστῆναι ἢ ἀναστῆναι; τοῦτο γὰρ εἰπέ·
σὺ πᾶσι φὴς ἄμεινον εἶναι ζῆν καὶ οὐ πολλοῖς
κρεῖττον τεθνάναι;

ΛΑ. Οἶμαι ἔγωγε τοῦτό γε.

ΝΙ. Οἷς οὖν τεθνάναι λυσιτελεῖ, ταῦτὰ οἴει δεινὰ
εἶναι καὶ οἷς ζῆν;

ΛΑ. Οὐκ ἔγωγε.

ΝΙ. Ἀλλὰ τοῦτο δὴ σὺ δίδως τοῖς ἰατροῖς γιγνώσκειν ἢ ἄλλῳ τινὶ δημιουργῷ πλὴν τῷ τῶν δεινῶν
καὶ μὴ δεινῶν ἐπιστήμονι, ὃν ἐγὼ ἀνδρεῖον καλῶ;

ΣΩ. Κατανοεῖς, ὦ Λάχης, ὅ τι λέγει;

ease ? Or do you suppose that the courageous know this ? Or do you call doctors courageous ?

NIC. No, not at all.

LACH. Nor, I fancy, farmers either. And yet they, I presume, know what is to be dreaded in farming, and every other skilled worker knows what is to be dreaded and dared in his own craft ; but they are none the more courageous for that.

SOC. What is Laches saying, in your opinion, Nicias ? There does seem to be something in it.

NIC. Yes, there is something, only it is not true.

SOC. How so ?

NIC. Because he thinks that doctors know something more, in treating sick persons, than how to tell what is healthy and what diseased. This, I imagine, is all that they know : but to tell whether health itself is to be dreaded by anyone rather than sickness, — do you suppose, Laches, that this is within a doctor's knowledge ? Do you not think that for many it is better that they should never arise from their bed of sickness ? Pray tell me, do you say that in every case it is better to live ? Is it not often preferable to be dead ?

LACH. I do think that is so.

NIC. And do you think that the same things are to be dreaded by those who were better dead, as by those who had better live ?

LACH. No, I do not.

NIC. Well, do you attribute the judgement of this matter to doctors or to any other skilled worker except him who has knowledge of what is to be dreaded and what is not—the man whom I call courageous ?

SOC. Do you comprehend his meaning, Laches ?

ΛΑ. Ἔγωγε, ὅτι γε τοὺς μάντεις καλεῖ τοὺς ἀνδρείους· τίς γὰρ δὴ ἄλλος εἴσεται ὅτῳ ἄμεινον ζῆν ἢ τεθνάναι; καίτοι σύ, ὦ Νικία, πότερον ὁμολογεῖς μάντις εἶναι ἢ οὔτε μάντις οὔτε ἀνδρεῖος;

ΝΙ. Τί δαί; μάντει αὖ οἴει προσήκει τὰ δεινὰ γιγνώσκειν καὶ τὰ θαρραλέα;

ΛΑ. Ἔγωγε· τίνι γὰρ ἄλλῳ;

ΝΙ. Ὧι ἐγὼ λέγω πολὺ μᾶλλον, ὦ βέλτιστε· ἐπεὶ μάντιν γε τὰ σημεῖα μόνον δεῖ γιγνώσκειν τῶν ἐσομένων, εἴτε τῳ θάνατος εἴτε νόσος εἴτε ἀποβολὴ 196 χρημάτων ἔσται, εἴτε νίκη εἴτε ἧττα ἢ πολέμου ἢ καὶ ἄλλης τινὸς ἀγωνίας· ὅ τι δέ τῳ ἄμεινον τούτων ἢ παθεῖν ἢ μὴ παθεῖν, τί μᾶλλον μάντει προσήκει κρῖναι ἢ ἄλλῳ ὁτῳοῦν;

ΛΑ. Ἀλλ’ ἐγὼ τούτου οὐ μανθάνω, ὦ Σώκρατες, ὅ τι βούλεται λέγειν· οὔτε γὰρ μάντιν οὔτε ἰατρὸν οὔτε ἄλλον οὐδένα δηλοῖ ὅντινα λέγει τὸν ἀνδρεῖον, εἰ μὴ εἰ θεόν τινα λέγει αὐτὸν εἶναι. ἐμοὶ μὲν B οὖν φαίνεται Νικίας οὐκ ἐθέλειν γενναίως ὁμολογεῖν ὅτι οὐδὲν λέγει, ἀλλὰ στρέφεται ἄνω καὶ κάτω ἐπικρυπτόμενος τὴν αὑτοῦ ἀπορίαν. καίτοι κἂν ἡμεῖς οἷοί τε ἦμεν ἄρτι ἐγώ τε καὶ σὺ τοιαῦτα στρέφεσθαι, εἰ ἐβουλόμεθα μὴ δοκεῖν ἐναντία ἡμῖν αὐτοῖς λέγειν. εἰ μὲν οὖν ἐν δικαστηρίῳ ἡμῖν οἱ λόγοι ἦσαν, εἶχεν ἄν τινα λόγον ταῦτα ποιεῖν· νῦν δὲ τί ἄν τις ἐν συνουσίᾳ τοιᾷδε μάτην κενοῖς λόγοις αὐτὸς αὑτὸν κοσμοῖ;

ΣΩ. Οὐδὲν οὐδ’ ἐμοὶ δοκεῖ, ὦ Λάχης· ἀλλ’

LACH. I do : it seems to be the seers whom he calls the courageous : for who else can know for which of us it is better to be alive than dead ? And yet, Nicias, do you avow yourself to be a seer, or to be neither a seer nor courageous ?

NIC. What ! Is it now a seer, think you, who has the gift of judging what is to be dreaded and what to be dared ?

LACH. That is my view : who else could it be ?

NIC. Much rather the man of whom I speak, my dear sir : for the seer's business is to judge only the signs of what is yet to come—whether a man is to meet with death or disease or loss of property, or victory or defeat in war or some other contest ; but what is better among these things for a man to suffer or avoid suffering, can surely be no more for a seer to decide than for anyone else in the world.

LACH. Well, I fail to follow him, Socrates, or to see what he is driving at ; for he points out that neither a seer nor a doctor nor anybody else is the man he refers to as the courageous, unless perchance he means it is some god. Now it appears to me that Nicias is unwilling to admit honestly that he has no meaning at all, but dodges this way and that in the hope of concealing his own perplexity. Why, you and I could have dodged in the same way just now, if we wished to avoid the appearance of contradicting ourselves. Of course, if we were arguing in a law-court, there would be some reason for so doing ; but here, in a meeting like this of ours, why waste time in adorning oneself with empty words ?

SOC. I agree that it is out of place, Laches : but let

C ὁρῶμεν μὴ Νικίας οἴεταί τι λέγειν καὶ οὐ λόγου
ἕνεκα ταῦτα λέγει. αὐτοῦ οὖν σαφέστερον πυθώ-
μεθα τί ποτε νοεῖ· καὶ ἐάν τι φαίνηται λέγων,
συγχωρησόμεθα, εἰ δὲ μή, διδάξομεν.

ΛΑ. Σὺ τοίνυν, ὦ Σώκρατες, εἰ βούλει πυνθάνεσθαι, πυνθάνου· ἐγὼ δ' ἴσως ἱκανῶς πέπυσμαι.

ΣΩ. 'Αλλ' οὐδέν με κωλύει· κοινὴ γὰρ ἔσται ἡ
πύστις ὑπὲρ ἐμοῦ τε καὶ σοῦ.

ΛΑ. Πάνυ μὲν οὖν.

ΣΩ. Λέγε δή μοι, ὦ Νικία, μᾶλλον δ' ἡμῖν· κοι-
νούμεθα γὰρ ἐγώ τε καὶ Λάχης τὸν λόγον· τὴν
D ἀνδρείαν ἐπιστήμην φῂς δεινῶν τε καὶ θαρραλέων
εἶναι;

ΝΙ. Ἔγωγε.

ΣΩ. Τοῦτο δὲ οὐ παντὸς δὴ εἶναι ἀνδρὸς γνῶναι,
ὁπότε γε μήτε ἰατρὸς μήτε μάντις αὐτὸ γνώσεται
μηδὲ ἀνδρεῖος ἔσται, ἐὰν μὴ αὐτὴν ταύτην τὴν
ἐπιστήμην προσλάβῃ· οὐχ οὕτως ἔλεγες;

ΝΙ. Οὕτω μὲν οὖν.

ΣΩ. Κατὰ τὴν παροιμίαν ἄρα τῷ ὄντι οὐκ ἂν πᾶσα
ὗς γνοίη οὐδ' ἂν ἀνδρεία γένοιτο.

ΝΙ. Οὔ μοι δοκεῖ.

E ΣΩ. Δῆλον δή, ὦ Νικία, ὅτι οὐδὲ τὴν Κρομμυω-
νίαν ὗν πιστεύεις σύ γε ἀνδρείαν γεγονέναι. τοῦτο
δὲ λέγω οὐ παίζων, ἀλλ' ἀναγκαῖον οἶμαι τῷ ταῦτα
λέγοντι μηδενὸς θηρίου ἀποδέχεσθαι ἀνδρείαν, ἢ
συγχωρεῖν θηρίον τι οὕτω σοφὸν εἶναι, ὥστε ἃ
ὀλίγοι ἀνθρώπων ἴσασι διὰ τὸ χαλεπὰ εἶναι γνῶναι,
ταῦτα λέοντα ἢ πάρδαλιν ἤ τινα κάπρον φάναι εἰδέ-

---

[1] The fierce monster slain by Theseus in the region between Corinth and Megara before he became the hero of
Attica.

us see : perhaps Nicias thinks he does mean something, and is not talking just for the sake of talking.
So let us ask him to explain more clearly what is in
his mind ; and if we find that he means something,
we will agree with him ; if not, we will instruct him.

LACH. Then, Socrates, if you would like to ask him,
please do so : I daresay I have done enough asking.

SOC. Well, I see no objection, since the question
will be on behalf of us both.

LACH. Very well, then.

SOC. Now tell me, Nicias, or rather, tell us—for
Laches and I are sharing the argument between us—
do you say that courage is knowledge of what is to
be dreaded or dared ?

NIC. I do.

SOC. And that it is not every man that knows it,
since neither a doctor nor a seer can know it, and
cannot be courageous unless he add this particular
knowledge to his own ? This was your statement,
was it not ?

NIC. Yes, it was.

SOC. And so in fact this is not a thing which, as
the proverb says, " any pig would know " ; and thus
a pig cannot be courageous.

NIC. I think not.

SOC. Indeed it is obvious, Nicias, that you at least
do not believe that even the Crommyonian sow [1]
could have been courageous. I say this not in jest,
but because I conceive it is necessary for him who
states this theory to refuse courage to any wild
beast, or else to admit that a beast like a lion or a
leopard or even a boar is so wise as to know what
only a few men know because it is so hard to perceive. Why, he who subscribes to your account of

ναι· ἀλλ' ἀνάγκη ὁμοίως λέοντα καὶ ἔλαφον καὶ
ταῦρον καὶ πίθηκον πρὸς ἀνδρείαν φάναι πεφυκέναι
τὸν τιθέμενον ἀνδρείαν τοῦθ' ὅπερ σὺ τίθεσαι.

197　ΛΑ. Νὴ τοὺς θεούς, καὶ εὖ γε λέγεις, ὦ Σώκρατες.
καὶ ἡμῖν ὡς ἀληθῶς τοῦτο ἀπόκριναι, ὦ Νικία,
πότερον σοφώτερα φῂς ἡμῶν ταῦτα εἶναι τὰ θηρία,
ἃ πάντες ὁμολογοῦμεν ἀνδρεῖα εἶναι, ἢ πᾶσιν ἐναν-
τιούμενος τολμᾷς μηδὲ ἀνδρεῖα αὐτὰ καλεῖν;

ΝΙ. Οὐ γάρ τι, ὦ Λάχης, ἔγωγε ἀνδρεῖα καλῶ
οὔτε θηρία οὔτε ἄλλο οὐδὲν τὸ τὰ δεινὰ ὑπὸ ἀνοίας
μὴ φοβούμενον, ἀλλ' ἄφοβον καὶ μωρόν· ἢ καὶ τὰ
B παιδία πάντα οἴει με ἀνδρεῖα καλεῖν, ἃ δι' ἄνοιαν
οὐδὲν δέδοικεν; ἀλλ' οἶμαι τὸ ἄφοβον καὶ τὸ
ἀνδρεῖον οὐ ταὐτόν ἐστιν. ἐγὼ δὲ ἀνδρείας μὲν
καὶ προμηθίας πάνυ τισὶν ὀλίγοις οἶμαι μετεῖναι,
θρασύτητος δὲ καὶ τόλμης καὶ τοῦ ἀφόβου μετὰ
ἀπρομηθίας πάνυ πολλοῖς καὶ ἀνδρῶν καὶ γυναικῶν
καὶ παίδων καὶ θηρίων. ταῦτ' οὖν ἃ σὺ καλεῖς
ἀνδρεῖα καὶ οἱ πολλοί, ἐγὼ θρασέα καλῶ, ἀνδρεῖα
C δὲ τὰ φρόνιμα περὶ ὧν λέγω.

ΛΑ. Θέασαι, ὦ Σώκρατες, ὡς εὖ ὅδε ἑαυτὸν
δή, ὡς οἴεται, κοσμεῖ τῷ λόγῳ· οὓς δὲ πάντες
ὁμολογοῦσιν ἀνδρείους εἶναι, τούτους ἀποστερεῖν
ἐπιχειρεῖ ταύτης τῆς τιμῆς.

ΝΙ. Οὔκουν σέ γε,[1] ὦ Λάχης, ἀλλὰ θάρρει· φημὶ γάρ
σε εἶναι σοφόν, καὶ Λάμαχόν γε, εἴπερ ἐστὲ ἀνδρεῖοι,
καὶ ἄλλους γε συχνοὺς Ἀθηναίων.

ΛΑ. Οὐδὲν ἐρῶ πρὸς ταῦτα, ἔχων εἰπεῖν, ἵνα
μή με φῇς ὡς ἀληθῶς Αἰξωνέα εἶναι.

---

[1] σέ γε papyr. Oxyr. : ἔγωγε mss.

---

[1] A deme or district of Attica, noted for the abusive
wit of its people.

courage must needs agree that a lion, a stag, a bull, and a monkey have all an equal share of courage in their nature.

LACH. Heavens, Socrates, how admirably you argue! Now answer us sincerely, Nicias, and say whether those animals, which we all admit to be courageous, are wiser than we are ; or whether you dare, in contradiction of everyone else, describe them as not even courageous.

NIC. No, Laches, I do not describe animals, or anything else that from thoughtlessness has no fear of the dreadful, as courageous, but rather as fearless and foolish. Or do you suppose I describe all children as courageous, that have no fear because they are thoughtless ? I rather hold that the fearless and the courageous are not the same thing. In my opinion very few people are endowed with courage and forethought, while rashness, boldness, and fearlessness, with no forethought to guide it, are found in a great number of men, women, children, and animals. So you see, the acts that you and most people call courageous, I call rash, and it is the prudent acts which I speak of that are courageous.

LACH. Mark you, Socrates, how finely, as he fancies, my friend decks himself out with his words ! And how he attempts to deprive of the distinction of courage those whom everyone admits to be courageous !

NIC. I am not referring to you, Laches, so do not be frightened : for I grant that you, and Lamachus also, are wise, since you are courageous, and I say the same of numerous other Athenians.

LACH. I will not say what I could say in answer to that, lest you call me a true son of Aexone.[1]

197

D ΣΩ. Μηδέ γε εἴπῃς, ὦ Λάχης· καὶ γάρ μοι δοκεῖς οὐδὲ [μὴ]¹ ᾐσθῆσθαι ὅτι ταύτην τὴν σοφίαν παρὰ Δάμωνος τοῦ ἡμετέρου ἑταίρου παρείληφεν, ὁ δὲ Δάμων τῷ Προδίκῳ πολλὰ πλησιάζει, ὃς δὴ δοκεῖ τῶν σοφιστῶν κάλλιστα τὰ τοιαῦτα ὀνόματα διαιρεῖν.

ΛΑ. Καὶ γὰρ πρέπει, ὦ Σώκρατες, σοφιστῇ τὰ τοιαῦτα μᾶλλον κομψεύεσθαι ἢ ἀνδρὶ ὃν ἡ πόλις ἀξιοῖ αὑτῆς προϊστάναι.

E ΣΩ. Πρέπει μέν που,² ὦ μακάριε, τῶν μεγίστων προστατοῦντι μεγίστης φρονήσεως μετέχειν· δοκεῖ δέ μοι Νικίας ἄξιος εἶναι ἐπισκέψεως, ὅποι ποτὲ βλέπων τοὔνομα τοῦτο τίθησι τὴν ἀνδρείαν.

ΛΑ. Αὐτὸς τοίνυν σκόπει, ὦ Σώκρατες.

ΣΩ. Τοῦτο μέλλω ποιεῖν, ὦ ἄριστε· μὴ μέντοι οἴου με ἀφήσειν σε τῆς κοινωνίας τοῦ λόγου, ἀλλὰ πρόσεχε τὸν νοῦν καὶ συσκόπει τὰ λεγόμενα.

ΛΑ. Ταῦτα δὴ ἔστω, εἰ δοκεῖ χρῆναι.

ΣΩ. Ἀλλὰ δοκεῖ. σὺ δέ, Νικία, λέγε ἡμῖν πάλιν 198 ἐξ ἀρχῆς· οἶσθ' ὅτι τὴν ἀνδρείαν κατ' ἀρχὰς τοῦ λόγου ἐσκοποῦμεν ὡς μέρος ἀρετῆς σκοποῦντες;

ΝΙ. Πάνυ γε.

ΣΩ. Οὐκοῦν καὶ σὺ τοῦτο ἀπεκρίνω ὡς μόριον, ὄντων δὴ καὶ ἄλλων μερῶν, ἃ σύμπαντα ἀρετὴ κέκληται;

ΝΙ. Πῶς γὰρ οὔ;

ΣΩ. Ἆρ' οὖν ἅπερ ἐγὼ καὶ σὺ ταῦτα λέγεις; ἐγὼ δὲ καλῶ πρὸς ἀνδρείᾳ σωφροσύνην καὶ δικαιοσύνην καὶ ἄλλ' ἄττα τοιαῦτα. οὐ καὶ σύ;

¹ μὴ om. papyr. Oxyr.
² που Stob.: τοι MSS.

¹ *Cf.* 190 c.

LACHES

soc. No, say nothing, Laches: for in fact you seem to me to have failed to perceive that he has acquired his wisdom from Damon, our good friend; and Damon constantly associates with Prodicus, who is supposed to be the cleverest of the sophists at distinguishing terms like these.

LACH. Yes, for it is more suitable, Socrates, for a sophist to make a show of such refinements than for a man whom the State thinks worthy to govern her.

soc. Indeed it is suitable, I presume, my amiable friend, for a man in the highest seat of government to be gifted with the highest degree of wisdom. But it seems to me that Nicias is worthy of further attention, so that we may learn in what connexion he uses this word " courage."

LACH. Then attend to him yourself, Socrates.

soc. That is what I propose to do, my good sir: still, you are not to think that I will release you from your due share of the argument. No, you must put your mind to it and join in weighing well what is said.

LACH. Well, so be it, if you think that I ought.

soc. Indeed I do. Now, Nicias, please go back to the beginning [1] and answer us: you know we started our discussion by considering courage as a part of virtue?

NIC. Quite so.

soc. And you joined in this answer,—that it is a part, there being also other parts, which taken all together have received the name of virtue?

NIC. Why, of course.

soc. Now, do you mean the same as I do by these? Besides courage, I refer to temperance, justice, and other similar qualities. And you also, do you not?

B ΝΙ. Πάνυ μὲν οὖν.

ΣΩ. Ἔχε δή· ταῦτα μὲν γὰρ ὁμολογοῦμεν,
περὶ δὲ τῶν δεινῶν καὶ θαρραλέων σκεψώμεθα,
ὅπως μὴ σὺ μὲν ἄλλ' ἄττα ἡγῇ, ἡμεῖς δὲ ἄλλα. ἃ
μὲν οὖν ἡμεῖς ἡγούμεθα, φράσομέν σοι· σὺ δὲ ἂν
μὴ ὁμολογῇς, διδάξεις. ἡγούμεθα δ' ἡμεῖς δεινὰ
μὲν εἶναι ἃ καὶ δέος παρέχει, θαρραλέα δὲ ἃ μὴ
δέος παρέχει· δέος δὲ παρέχει οὐ τὰ γεγονότα
οὐδὲ τὰ παρόντα τῶν κακῶν, ἀλλὰ τὰ προσδοκώ-
μενα· δέος γὰρ εἶναι προσδοκίαν μέλλοντος κακοῦ·
ἢ οὐχ οὕτω καὶ συνδοκεῖ,[1] ὦ Λάχης;

C ΛΑ. Πάνυ γε σφόδρα, ὦ Σώκρατες.

ΣΩ. Τὰ μὲν ἡμέτερα τοίνυν, ὦ Νικία, ἀκούεις,
ὅτι δεινὰ μὲν τὰ μέλλοντα κακὰ φαμεν εἶναι,
θαρραλέα δὲ τὰ μὴ κακὰ ἢ ἀγαθὰ μέλλοντα· σὺ
δὲ ταύτῃ ἢ ἄλλῃ περὶ τούτων λέγεις;

ΝΙ. Ταύτῃ ἔγωγε.

ΣΩ. Τούτων δέ γε τὴν ἐπιστήμην ἀνδρείαν προσαγορεύεις;

ΝΙ. Κομιδῇ γε.

ΣΩ. Ἔτι δὴ τὸ τρίτον σκεψώμεθα εἰ συνδοκεῖ
σοί τε καὶ ἡμῖν.

D ΝΙ. Τὸ ποῖον δὴ τοῦτο;

ΣΩ. Ἐγὼ δὴ φράσω. δοκεῖ γὰρ δὴ ἐμοί τε
καὶ τῷδε, περὶ ὅσων ἐστὶν ἐπιστήμη, οὐκ ἄλλη
μὲν εἶναι περὶ γεγονότος εἰδέναι ὅπῃ γέγονεν,
ἄλλη δὲ περὶ γιγνομένων ὅπῃ γίγνεται, ἄλλη δὲ
ὅπῃ ἂν κάλλιστα γένοιτο καὶ γενήσεται τὸ μήπω
γεγονός, ἀλλ' ἡ αὐτή. οἷον περὶ τὸ ὑγιεινὸν εἰς
ἅπαντας τοὺς χρόνους οὐκ ἄλλη τις ἢ ἰατρική,
μία οὖσα, ἐφορᾷ καὶ γιγνόμενα καὶ γεγονότα καὶ

---

[1] συνδοκεῖ Burnet: σὺ δοκεῖ, δοκεῖ καὶ σὺ MSS.

NIC. Certainly I do.

SOC. So much for that; thus far we agree: but let us pass on to what is to be dreaded and what to be dared, and make sure that you and we do not take two different views of these. Let me tell you our view of them, and if you do not agree with it, you shall instruct us. We hold that the dreadful are things that cause fear, and the safely ventured are those that do not; and fear is caused not by past or present, but by expected evils: for fear is expectation of coming evil. You are of the same mind with us in this, are you not, Laches?

LACH. Yes, entirely so, Socrates.

SOC. So there you have our view, Nicias,—that coming evils are to be dreaded, and things not evil, or good things, that are to come are to be safely dared. Would you describe them in this way, or in some other?

NIC. I would describe them in this way.

SOC. And the knowledge of these things is what you term courage?

NIC. Precisely.

SOC. There is still a third point on which we must see if you are in agreement with us.

NIC. What point is that?

SOC. I will tell you. It seems to your friend and me that, to take the various subjects of knowledge, there is not one knowledge of how a thing has happened in the past, another of how things are happening in the present, and another of how a thing that has not yet happened might or will happen most favourably in the future, but it is the same knowledge throughout. For example, in the case of health, it is medicine always and alone that

73

E γενησόμενα ὅπῃ γενήσεται· καὶ περὶ τὰ ἐκ τῆς
γῆς αὖ φυόμενα ἡ γεωργία ὡσαύτως ἔχει· καὶ
δήπου τὰ περὶ τὸν πόλεμον αὐτοὶ ἂν μαρτυρήσαιτε
ὅτι ἡ στρατηγία κάλλιστα προμηθεῖται τά τε ἄλλα
καὶ περὶ τὸ μέλλον ἔσεσθαι, οὐδὲ τῇ μαντικῇ οἴεται
δεῖν ὑπηρετεῖν ἀλλὰ ἄρχειν, ὡς εἰδυῖα κάλλιον τὰ
199 περὶ τὸν πόλεμον καὶ γιγνόμενα καὶ γενησόμενα·
καὶ ὁ νόμος οὕτω τάττει, μὴ τὸν μάντιν τοῦ στρατηγοῦ ἄρχειν, ἀλλὰ τὸν στρατηγὸν τοῦ μάντεως.
φήσομεν ταῦτα, ὦ Λάχης;

ΛΑ. Φήσομεν.

ΣΩ. Τί δέ; σὺ ἡμῖν, ὦ Νικία, σύμφης περὶ τῶν
αὐτῶν τὴν αὐτὴν ἐπιστήμην καὶ ἐσομένων καὶ
γιγνομένων καὶ γεγονότων ἐπαΐειν;

ΝΙ. Ἔγωγε· δοκεῖ γάρ μοι οὕτως, ὦ Σώκρατες.

ΣΩ. Οὐκοῦν, ὦ ἄριστε, καὶ ἡ ἀνδρεία τῶν δεινῶν
B ἐπιστήμη ἐστὶ καὶ θαρραλέων, ὡς φής· ἦ γάρ;

ΝΙ. Ναί.

ΣΩ. Τὰ δὲ δεινὰ ὡμολόγηται καὶ τὰ θαρραλέα τὰ
μὲν μέλλοντα ἀγαθά, τὰ δὲ μέλλοντα κακὰ εἶναι.

ΝΙ. Πάνυ γε.

ΣΩ. Ἡ δέ γ' αὐτὴ ἐπιστήμη τῶν αὐτῶν καὶ
μελλόντων καὶ πάντως ἐχόντων εἶναι.

ΝΙ. Ἔστι ταῦτα.

ΣΩ. Οὐ μόνον ἄρα τῶν δεινῶν καὶ θαρραλέων
ἡ ἀνδρεία ἐπιστήμη ἐστίν· οὐ γὰρ μελλόντων
μόνον πέρι τῶν ἀγαθῶν τε καὶ κακῶν ἐπαΐει, ἀλλὰ
C καὶ γιγνομένων καὶ γεγονότων καὶ πάντως ἐχόντων,
ὥσπερ αἱ ἄλλαι ἐπιστῆμαι.

surveys present, past, and future processes alike ;
and farming is in the same position as regards the
productions of the earth. And in matters of war I
am sure you yourselves will bear me out when I say
that here generalship makes the best forecasts on the
whole, and particularly of future results, and is the
mistress rather than the servant of the seer's art,
because it knows better what is happening or about
to happen in the operations of war ; whence the law
ordains that the general shall give orders to the seer,
and not the seer to the general. May we say this,
Laches ?

LACH. We may.

SOC. Well now, do you agree with us, Nicias, that
the same knowledge has comprehension of the same
things, whether future, present, or past ?

NIC. I do, for that is my own opinion, Socrates.

SOC. And courage, my good friend, is knowledge
of what is to be dreaded and dared, as you say, do
you not ?

NIC. Yes.

SOC. And things to be dreaded and things to be
dared have been admitted to be either future goods
or future evils ?

NIC. Certainly.

SOC. And the same knowledge is concerned with
the same things, whether in the future or in any
particular stage ?

NIC. That is so.

SOC. Then courage is knowledge not merely of
what is to be dreaded and what dared, for it com-
prehends goods and evils not merely in the future,
but also in the present and the past and in any stage,
like the other kinds of knowledge.

ΝΙ. Ἔοικέ γε.

ΣΩ. Μέρος ἄρα ἀνδρείας ἡμῖν, ὦ Νικία, ἀπεκρίνω σχεδόν τι τρίτον· καίτοι ἡμεῖς ἠρωτῶμεν
ὅλην ἀνδρείαν ὅ τι εἴη. καὶ νῦν δή, ὡς ἔοικε, κατὰ
τὸν σὸν λόγον οὐ μόνον δεινῶν τε καὶ θαρραλέων
ἐπιστήμη ἡ ἀνδρεία ἐστίν, ἀλλὰ σχεδόν τι ἡ περὶ
πάντων ἀγαθῶν τε καὶ κακῶν καὶ πάντως ἐχόντων,
D ὡς νῦν αὖ ὁ σὸς λόγος, ἀνδρεία ἂν εἴη· οὕτως αὖ
μετατίθεσθαι ἢ πῶς λέγεις, ὦ Νικία;

ΝΙ. Ἔμοιγε δοκεῖ, ὦ Σώκρατες.

ΣΩ. Δοκεῖ οὖν σοι, ὦ δαιμόνιε, ἀπολείπειν ἄν τι
ὁ τοιοῦτος ἀρετῆς, εἴπερ εἰδείη τά τε ἀγαθὰ πάντα
καὶ παντάπασιν ὡς γίγνεται καὶ γενήσεται καὶ
γέγονε, καὶ τὰ κακὰ ὡσαύτως; καὶ τοῦτον οἴει ἂν
σὺ ἐνδεᾶ εἶναι σωφροσύνης ἢ δικαιοσύνης τε καὶ
ὁσιότητος, ᾧ γε μόνῳ προσήκει καὶ περὶ θεοὺς
E καὶ περὶ ἀνθρώπους ἐξευλαβεῖσθαί τε τὰ δεινὰ καὶ
τὰ μή, καὶ τἀγαθὰ πορίζεσθαι, ἐπισταμένῳ ὀρθῶς
προσομιλεῖν;

ΝΙ. Λέγειν τὶ ὦ Σώκρατές μοι δοκεῖς.

ΣΩ. Οὐκ ἄρα, ὦ Νικία, μόριον ἀρετῆς ἂν εἴη τὸ
νῦν σοι λεγόμενον, ἀλλὰ σύμπασα ἀρετή.

ΝΙ. Ἔοικεν.

ΣΩ. Καὶ μὴν ἔφαμέν γε τὴν ἀνδρείαν μόριον εἶναι
ἓν τῶν τῆς ἀρετῆς.

ΝΙ. Ἔφαμεν γάρ.

ΣΩ. Τὸ δέ γε νῦν λεγόμενον οὐ φαίνεται.

ΝΙ. Οὐκ ἔοικεν.

NIC. Apparently.

SOC. So the answer that you gave us, Nicias, covers only about a third part of courage ; whereas our question was of what courage is as a whole. And now it appears, on your own showing, that courage is knowledge not merely of what is to be dreaded and what dared, but practically a knowledge concerning all goods and evils at every stage ; such is your present account of what courage must be. What do you say to this new version, Nicias ?

NIC. I accept it, Socrates.

SOC. Now do you think, my excellent friend, there could be anything wanting to the virtue of a man who knew all good things, and all about their production in the present, the future, and the past, and all about evil things likewise ? Do you suppose that such a man could be lacking in temperance, or justice, and holiness, when he alone has the gift of taking due precaution, in his dealings with gods and men, as regards what is to be dreaded and what is not, and of procuring good things, owing to his knowledge of the right behaviour towards them ?

NIC. I think, Socrates, there is something in what you say.

SOC. Hence what you now describe, Nicias, will be not a part but the whole of virtue.

NIC. Apparently.

SOC. But, you know, we said that courage is one of the parts of virtue.

NIC. Yes, we did.

SOC. And what we now describe is seen to be different.

NIC. So it seems.

ΣΩ. Οὐκ ἄρα ηὑρήκαμεν, ὦ Νικία, ἀνδρεία ὅ τι ἔστιν.

ΝΙ. Οὐ φαινόμεθα.

ΛΑ. Καὶ μὴν ἔγωγε, ὦ φίλε Νικία, ᾤμην σε 200 εὑρήσειν, ἐπειδὴ ἐμοῦ κατεφρόνησας Σωκράτει ἀποκριναμένου· πάνυ δὴ μεγάλην ἐλπίδα εἶχον, ὡς τῇ παρὰ τοῦ Δάμωνος σοφίᾳ αὐτὴν ἀνευρήσεις.

ΝΙ. Εὖ γε, ὦ Λάχης, ὅτι οὐδὲν οἴει σὺ ἔτι πρᾶγμα εἶναι, ὅτι αὐτὸς ἄρτι ἐφάνης ἀνδρείας πέρι οὐδὲν εἰδώς, ἀλλ' εἰ καὶ ἐγὼ ἕτερος τοιοῦτος ἀναφανήσομαι, πρὸς τοῦτο βλέπεις, καὶ οὐδὲν ἔτι διοίσει, ὡς ἔοικε, σοὶ μετ' ἐμοῦ μηδὲν εἰδέναι ὧν προσήκει ἐπιστήμην ἔχειν ἀνδρὶ οἰομένῳ τὶ εἶναι. σὺ μὲν B οὖν μοι δοκεῖς ὡς ἀληθῶς ἀνθρώπειον πρᾶγμα ἐργάζεσθαι, οὐδὲν πρὸς αὑτὸν βλέπειν ἀλλὰ πρὸς τοὺς ἄλλους· ἐγὼ δ' οἶμαι ἐμοὶ περὶ ὧν ἐλέγομεν νῦν τε ἐπιεικῶς εἰρῆσθαι, καὶ εἴ τι αὐτῶν μὴ ἱκανῶς εἴρηται, ὕστερον ἐπανορθώσεσθαι καὶ μετὰ Δάμωνος, οὗ σύ που οἴει καταγελᾶν, καὶ ταῦτα οὐδὲ ἰδὼν πώποτε τὸν Δάμωνα, καὶ μετ' ἄλλων· καὶ ἐπειδὰν βεβαιώσωμαι αὐτά, διδάξω καὶ σέ, C καὶ οὐ φθονήσω· δοκεῖς γάρ μοι καὶ μάλα σφόδρα δεῖσθαι μαθεῖν.

ΛΑ. Σοφὸς γάρ τοι σὺ εἶ, ὦ Νικία. ἀλλ' ὅμως ἐγὼ Λυσιμάχῳ τῷδε καὶ Μελησίᾳ συμβουλεύω, σὲ μὲν καὶ ἐμὲ περὶ τῆς παιδείας τῶν νεανίσκων χαίρειν ἐᾶν, Σωκράτη δὲ τουτονί, ὅπερ ἐξ ἀρχῆς ἔλεγον, μὴ ἀφιέναι· εἰ δὲ καὶ ἐμοὶ ἐν ἡλικίᾳ ἦσαν οἱ παῖδες, ταὐτὰ ἂν ταῦτ' ἐποίουν.

LACHES

soc. Thus we have failed to discover, Nicias, what courage really is.

NIC. Evidently.

LACH. And I, in fact, supposed, my dear Nicias, that you were going to discover it, when you showed such contempt for the answers I made to Socrates : indeed I had very great hopes that the wisdom you derived from Damon would avail you for the discovery.

NIC. That is all very fine, Laches ; you think you can now make light of the fact that you were yourself shown just now to know nothing about courage ; when my turn comes to be shown up in the same light, that is all you care, and now it will not matter to you at all, it seems, if I share your ignorance of things whereof any self-respecting man ought to have knowledge. You really strike me, indeed, as following the average man's practice of keeping an eye on others rather than on oneself : but I fancy that for the present I have said as much as could be expected on the subject of our discussion, and that later on I must make good any defects in my statement upon it with the help of Damon—whom I know you choose to ridicule, and that without ever having seen the actual Damon—and with others' help besides. And when I have settled the matter I will enlighten you, in no grudging spirit : for I think you are in very great need of instruction.

LACH. You are a man of wisdom, I know, Nicias. But still I advise Lysimachus here and Melesias to dismiss you and me, and to retain our friend Socrates as I said at first, for the education of your boys : were my own sons old enough, I should do the same thing too.

ΝΙ. Ταῦτα μὲν κἀγὼ συγχωρῶ, ἐάνπερ ἐθέλῃ
Σωκράτης τῶν μειρακίων ἐπιμελεῖσθαι, μηδένα
D ἄλλον ζητεῖν· ἐπεὶ κἂν ἐγὼ τὸν Νικήρατον τούτῳ
ἥδιστα ἐπιτρέποιμι, εἰ ἐθέλοι οὗτος· ἀλλὰ γὰρ
ἄλλους μοι ἑκάστοτε συνίστησιν, ὅταν τι αὐτῷ περὶ
τούτου μνησθῶ, αὐτὸς δὲ οὐκ ἐθέλει. ἀλλ᾽ ὅρα, ὦ
Λυσίμαχε, εἴ τι σοῦ ἂν μᾶλλον ὑπακούοι Σωκράτης.

ΛΥ. Δίκαιόν γέ τοι, ὦ Νικία, ἐπεὶ καὶ ἐγὼ τούτῳ
πολλὰ ἂν ἐθελήσαιμι ποιεῖν, ἃ οὐκ ἂν ἄλλοις πάνυ
πολλοῖς ἐθέλοιμι. πῶς οὖν φῄς, ὦ Σώκρατες;
ὑπακούσῃ τι καὶ συμπροθυμήσῃ ὡς βελτίστοις
γενέσθαι τοῖς μειρακίοις;

E ΣΩ. Καὶ γὰρ ἂν δεινὸν εἴη, ὦ Λυσίμαχε, τοῦτό
γε, μὴ ἐθέλειν τῳ συμπροθυμεῖσθαι ὡς βελτίστῳ
γενέσθαι. εἰ μὲν οὖν ἐν τοῖς διαλόγοις τοῖς ἄρτι
ἐγὼ μὲν ἐφάνην εἰδώς, τώδε δὲ μὴ εἰδότε, δίκαιον
ἂν ἦν ἐμὲ μάλιστα ἐπὶ τοῦτο τὸ ἔργον παρακαλεῖν·
νῦν δ᾽, ὁμοίως γὰρ πάντες ἐν ἀπορίᾳ ἐγενόμεθα·
τί οὖν ἄν τις ἡμῶν τινὰ προαιροῖτο; ἐμοὶ μὲν οὖν
δὴ αὐτῷ δοκεῖ οὐδένα· ἀλλ᾽ ἐπειδὴ ταῦτα οὕτως
201 ἔχει, σκέψασθε ἄν τι δόξω συμβουλεύειν ὑμῖν.
ἐγὼ γάρ φημι χρῆναι, ὦ ἄνδρες—οὐδεὶς γὰρ ἔκφορος
λόγος—κοινῇ πάντας ἡμᾶς ζητεῖν μάλιστα μὲν ἡμῖν
αὐτοῖς διδάσκαλον ὡς ἄριστον—δεόμεθα γάρ—
ἔπειτα καὶ τοῖς μειρακίοις, μήτε χρημάτων φειδο-
μένους μήτε ἄλλου μηδενός· ἐᾶν δὲ ἡμᾶς αὐτοὺς
ἔχειν, ὡς νῦν ἔχομεν, οὐ συμβουλεύω. εἰ δέ τις
ἡμῶν καταγελάσεται, ὅτι τηλικοίδε ὄντες εἰς διδα-
B σκάλων ἀξιοῦμεν φοιτᾶν, τὸν Ὅμηρον δοκεῖ μοι
χρῆναι προβάλλεσθαι, ὃς ἔφη οὐκ ἀγαθὴν εἶναι
αἰδῶ κεχρημένῳ ἀνδρὶ παρεῖναι. καὶ ἡμεῖς οὖν

---

[1] *Od.* xvii. 347.

NIC. For my part I agree ; if Socrates will consent to take charge of these young people, I will seek for no one else. I should be only too glad to entrust him with Niceratus, if he should consent : but when I begin to mention the matter to him, he always recommends other men to me and refuses himself. Just see, Lysimachus, if Socrates will give you a more favourable hearing.

LYS. It is only right that he should, Nicias, for indeed I would be willing to do many things for him which I would not do for a great many others. Well, what do you say, Socrates ? Will you comply, and lend your endeavours for the highest improvement of these boys ?

SOC. Why, how strange it would be, Lysimachus, to refuse to lend one's endeavours for the highest improvement of anybody ! Now if in the debates that we have just held I had been found to know what our two friends did not know, it would be right to make a point of inviting me to take up this work : but as it is, we have all got into the same difficulty, so why should one of us be preferred to another ? In my own opinion, none of us should ; and this being so, perhaps you will allow me to give you a piece of advice. I tell you, gentlemen—and this is confidential—that we ought all alike to seek out the best teacher we can find, first for ourselves—for we need one—and then for our boys, sparing neither expense nor anything else we can do : but to leave ourselves as we now are, this I do not advise. And if anyone makes fun of us for seeing fit to go to school at our time of life, I think we should appeal to Homer, who said that " shame is no good mate for a needy man." [1] So let us not mind what any-

ἐάσαντες χαίρειν εἴ τίς τι ἐρεῖ, κοινῇ ἡμῶν αὐτῶν καὶ τῶν μειρακίων ἐπιμέλειαν ποιησώμεθα.

ΛΥ. Ἐμοὶ μὲν ἀρέσκει, ὦ Σώκρατες, ἃ λέγεις· καὶ ἐθέλω, ὅσῳπερ γεραίτατός εἰμι, τοσούτῳ προθυμότατα μανθάνειν μετὰ τῶν νεανίσκων. ἀλλά C μοι οὑτωσὶ ποίησον· αὔριον ἕωθεν ἀφίκου οἴκαδε, καὶ μὴ ἄλλως ποιήσῃς, ἵνα βουλευσώμεθα περὶ αὐτῶν τούτων· τὸ δὲ νῦν εἶναι τὴν συνουσίαν διαλύσωμεν.

ΣΩ. Ἀλλὰ ποιήσω, ὦ Λυσίμαχε, ταῦτα, καὶ ἥξω παρὰ σὲ αὔριον, ἐὰν θεὸς ἐθέλῃ.

one may say, but join together in arranging for our own and the boys' tuition.

LYS. I gladly approve of your suggestion, Socrates ; and as I am the oldest, so I am the most eager to have lessons with the young ones. Now this is what I ask you to do : come to my house to-morrow at daybreak ; be sure not to fail, and then we shall consult on this very matter. For the present, let us break up our meeting.

SOC. I will not fail, Lysimachus, to come to you to-morrow, God willing.

PROTAGORAS

INTRODUCTION TO THE *PROTAGORAS*

THE masterly powers of description, characterization, rhetoric, and reasoning, which conspire in the *Protagoras* to produce, with such apparent ease, one rapid and luminous effect, have earned it a very high —with some judges the highest—place among Plato's achievements in philosophic drama. After an introductory scene, in which the excitement of ardent young spirits over the arrival of a great intellectual personage leads quickly to the setting of the stage for the main business of the plot, we are shown Socrates in respectful but keenly critical contact with the first and most eminent of the itinerant professors of a new culture or enlightenment. On the other side we see the old and celebrated teacher displaying his various abilities with weight and credit, but with limitations which increasingly suggest that his light is waning before the fresh and more searching flame of Socratic inquiry. The drama is philosophic in the fullest sense, not merely owing to this animated controversy and its development of a great moral theme,—the acquisition of virtue, but because we are made to feel that behind or above the actual human disputants are certain principles and modes of thought, which hold a high and shadowy debate, as it were, of their own in the dimness of what is as yet unexamined and unexplained. Of this larger argument the human

86

scene gives but fitful glimpses ; but in the end it is suggested and impressed in sufficiently definite outline to become the further object of our roused and refined curiosity.

This dialogue is, indeed, a work of profoundly suggestive art, and our first duty is to observe and comprehend as clearly as may be the persons in the play and the interaction of their salient thoughts and feelings. Protagoras was the founder of a popular culture which aimed at presenting the highest lessons of the poets, thinkers, and artists of the preceding age in a convenient form for the needs of the rising generation of Greek statesmen,—a form also that should be marketable, for he invented the trade of the professional educator, and was the first to charge a regular fee for the wisdom or skill that he imparted. His own chief accomplishment was impressive declamation on moral and political themes : he was prone, as we find in this interview, to a somewhat lengthy style of exposition, and correspondingly loth to undergo the mental strain of being cross-examined by Socrates. No attempt is made here to tease or bait him. It is clear enough, without the express statement made in the *Republic* (x. 600), that he had attained a most honourable position in Greece through his earnest zeal for educational progress. But he did not stop to think out the bases of his teaching ; and the immediate interest of the dialogue consists largely in watching the succession of strokes by which Socrates, a younger[1] and subtler advocate of the same cause,

---

[1] At the time of this meeting (just before the Peloponnesian War, in 432 B.C.) Socrates would be 36 years old, and Alcibiades 19.

exposes and undermines the fine but unsound fabric of his fame.

In the stately myth (320–328) by which Protagoras unfolds his theory of the origin of human society and morals, Plato gives us a carefully wrought imitation of the professor's favourite method and style. It is an eloquent substantiation of the common-sense view that virtue can be taught; and fidelity in characterization seems to have prompted Plato to attribute to the old sophist some principles which are more than ordinarily enlightened. In particular we may notice his account of the beginning of governments (322), and his appeal for the curative and preventive use of punishment (324). And later on, while he totters defenceless under the force and acuteness of Socrates' questions, we find him objecting—and it was soon to be Plato's own opinion—that it is rash to regard all pleasure as good (351). Plato, in fact, appears to be more intent on exhibiting the impetuous energy and superior skill with which Socrates could on occasion upset an experienced teacher and famous scholar, than on impressing us with the correctness of this or that theory which the younger man may snatch up and fling at the professor's head in the momentary sport or heat of the contest. The explanation which Socrates propounds of the poem of Simonides (343–347) is obviously a mocking satire on certain sophistic performances; but he is no less obviously serious, for the purpose in hand, when he makes his statement on the relation of virtue to pleasure. The unsatisfactory effect which this leaves upon our minds must be referred to the main object of the dialogue, which is to prove the power of the new science of dialectic in disturbing our settled habits of thought and in stimulating fresh inquiry into problems of the highest import to mankind.

Among the many minor interests attaching to this vivid picture of the intellectual life of Athens in the latter part of the fifth century, the appropriate style given in each case to the utterances of Protagoras, Prodicus, and Hippias deserves attention for the evidence thus afforded of a deliberate cultivation of prose-form at that time. Plato has left us a less sympathetic but similarly interesting study of Protagoras' manner of speech in his later work, the *Theaetetus.*

The following brief outline of the discussion may be useful:—

I. 309 A–316 A. Socrates tells his (unnamed) friend that he and Alcibiades have just been conversing with Protagoras, and describes how his young friend Hippocrates had announced to him the great sophist's arrival in Athens, and how, after questioning Hippocrates on his design of learning from the sophist, he proceeded with him to the house of Callias, with whom Protagoras was staying. They found there not only Protagoras but the learned Hippias and Prodicus also, and many followers and disciples who had assembled to hear their discourses.

II. 316 A–320 C. Protagoras explains the purpose of his teaching: he will educate Hippocrates in politics and citizenship. Socrates raises the question whether virtue can be taught.

III. 320 C–328 D. Protagoras delivers a characteristic speech, in which he relates a fable of the origin of man. It illustrates his doctrine that virtue can be taught, both by individuals and by the State.

IV. 328 D–334 C. Socrates cross-examines Protagoras: (1) Is each of the virtues a part of virtue, or only a different name for the same thing? (2) Protagoras replies that the several virtues differ like the parts of the face. (3) In answer to an objection from Socrates, Protagoras allows that justice and holiness must be like each other. (4) Socrates then urges that temperance and wisdom must be the same, and would argue likewise of temperance and justice; but (5) Protagoras, impatient of being questioned, reverts to his favourite method of declamation on the notions of "good" and "beneficial."

V. 334 C–338 E. Socrates makes as if to go: he will only stay if Protagoras will keep to the method of question and answer. At the request of Callias, Alcibiades, Critias, Prodicus and Hippias he agrees to stay and be questioned by Protagoras, after which Protagoras will be questioned by him.

VI. 338 E–347 A. Socrates is cross-examined by Protagoras on the meaning of a poem of Simonides, and tries to save the consistency of the poet, which Protagoras impugns, by distinguishing between "being good" and "becoming good"; he also suggests a peculiar significance of words in Ceos (the native place of the poet and of Prodicus, whose verbal learning he satirizes with some pedantic nonsense). He then gives his own explanation of the poem, which he holds to have been written to refute a saying of Pittacus (an Ionian sage of the latter part of the seventh century B.C.) that "it is hard to be good" : to *become* good, said the poet, is hard; to *be* good is impossible; he looked for no perfect virtue on earth.

VII. 347 A–360 E. Alcibiades and Callias prevail on Protagoras, rather against his will, to be questioned by Socrates as to whether wisdom, temperance, courage, justice and holiness are all the same thing, or different parts of virtue. Protagoras singles out courage as distinct from the rest. When Socrates argues that it is the same as wisdom, Protagoras objects to his reasoning, and Socrates starts on a new line: Is not pleasure, viewed apart from its consequences, the same as the good? To be overcome by pleasure is merely to choose the less instead of the greater good, through ignorance; and pleasure being good, every action must be good that has pleasure as its object. The coward who will not fight when he ought is suffering from an ignorant misconception of what lies before him, so that courage must be knowledge.

VIII. 360 E–362 A. It is shown, in conclusion, that Socrates and Protagoras have each been led into a position opposite to that which they held at the beginning: Socrates' identification of virtue with knowledge brings him to the view that virtue must be teachable, which he at first denied; while Protagoras, who held that it is teachable, now declares that it is not knowledge, thus denying it the sole means of being taught.

A good modern edition of the *Protagoras* is that by J. Adam, Cambridge University Press, 1905.

ΠΡΩΤΑΓΟΡΑΣ

[Η ΣΟΦΙΣΤΑΙ· ΕΝΔΕΙΚΤΙΚΟΣ]

ΤΑ ΤΟΥ ΔΙΑΛΟΓΟΥ ΠΡΟΣΩΠΑ

ΕΤΑΙΡΟΣ, ΣΩΚΡΑΤΗΣ, ΙΠΠΟΚΡΑΤΗΣ, ΠΡΩΤΑΓΟΡΑΣ,
ΑΛΚΙΒΙΑΔΗΣ, ΚΑΛΛΙΑΣ, ΚΡΙΤΙΑΣ, ΠΡΟΔΙΚΟΣ, ΙΠΠΙΑΣ

St. I.
p. 309

ΕΤ. Πόθεν, ὦ Σώκρατες, φαίνῃ; ἢ δῆλα δὴ ὅτι ἀπὸ κυνηγεσίου τοῦ περὶ τὴν Ἀλκιβιάδου ὥραν; καὶ μήν μοι καὶ πρῴην ἰδόντι καλὸς μὲν ἐφαίνετο ἀνὴρ ἔτι, ἀνὴρ μέντοι, ὦ Σώκρατες, ὥς γ᾽ ἐν αὐτοῖς ἡμῖν εἰρῆσθαι, καὶ πώγωνος ἤδη ὑποπιμπλάμενος.

ΣΩ. Εἶτα τί τοῦτο; οὐ σὺ μέντοι Ὁμήρου
B ἐπαινέτης εἶ, ὃς ἔφη χαριεστάτην ἥβην εἶναι τοῦ ὑπηνήτου, ἣν νῦν Ἀλκιβιάδης ἔχει;

ΕΤ. Τί οὖν τὰ νῦν; ἦ παρ᾽ ἐκείνου φαίνῃ; καὶ πῶς πρὸς σὲ ὁ νεανίας διάκειται;

ΣΩ. Εὖ, ἔμοιγε ἔδοξεν, οὐχ ἥκιστα δὲ καὶ τῇ νῦν ἡμέρᾳ· καὶ γὰρ πολλὰ ὑπὲρ ἐμοῦ εἶπε, βοηθῶν ἐμοί, καὶ οὖν καὶ ἄρτι ἀπ᾽ ἐκείνου ἔρχομαι. ἄτοπον μέντοι τί σοι ἐθέλω εἰπεῖν· παρόντος γὰρ

92

PROTAGORAS

[OR SOPHISTS : AN ARRAIGNMENT]

CHARACTERS

A FRIEND, SOCRATES, HIPPOCRATES, PROTAGORAS,
ALCIBIADES, CALLIAS, CRITIAS, PRODICUS, HIPPIAS

FR. Where have you been now, Socrates ? Ah, but
of course you have been in chase of Alcibiades and his
youthful beauty ! Well, only the other day, as I
looked at him, I thought him still handsome as a
man—for a man he is, Socrates, between you and
me, and with quite a growth of beard.

soc. And what of that ? Do you mean to say you
do not approve of Homer,[1] who said that youth has
highest grace in him whose beard is appearing, as
now in the case of Alcibiades ?

FR. Then how is the affair at present ? Have you
been with him just now ? And how is the young
man treating you ?

soc. Quite well, I considered, and especially so to-
day : for he spoke a good deal on my side, supporting
me in a discussion—in fact I have only just left him.
However, there is a strange thing I have to tell you :

---

[1] *Iliad*, xxiv. 348.

ἐκείνου, οὔτε προσεῖχον τὸν νοῦν, ἐπελανθανόμην τε αὐτοῦ θαμά.

C ΕΤ. Καὶ τί ἂν γεγονὸς εἴη περὶ σὲ κἀκεῖνον τοσοῦτον πρᾶγμα; οὐ γὰρ δήπου τινὶ καλλίονι ἐνέτυχες ἄλλῳ ἔν γε τῇδε τῇ πόλει.

ΣΩ. Καὶ πολύ γε.

ΕΤ. Τί φῄς; ἀστῷ ἢ ξένῳ;

ΣΩ. Ξένῳ.

ΕΤ. Ποδαπῷ;

ΣΩ. Ἀβδηρίτῃ.

ΕΤ. Καὶ οὕτω καλός τις ὁ ξένος ἔδοξέ σοι εἶναι, ὥστε τοῦ Κλεινίου υἱέος καλλίων σοι φανῆναι;

ΣΩ. Πῶς δ' οὐ μέλλει, ὦ μακάριε, τὸ σοφώτατον κάλλιον φαίνεσθαι;

ΕΤ. Ἀλλ' ἦ σοφῷ τινι ἡμῖν, ὦ Σώκρατες, ἐντυχὼν πάρει;

D ΣΩ. Σοφωτάτῳ μὲν οὖν δήπου τῶν γε νῦν, εἴ σοι δοκεῖ σοφώτατος εἶναι Πρωταγόρας.

ΕΤ. Ὢ τί λέγεις; Πρωταγόρας ἐπιδεδήμηκεν;

ΣΩ. Τρίτην γε ἤδη ἡμέραν.

ΕΤ. Καὶ ἄρτι ἄρα ἐκείνῳ συγγεγονὼς ἥκεις;

310 ΣΩ. Πάνυ γε πολλὰ καὶ εἰπὼν καὶ ἀκούσας.

ΕΤ. Τί οὖν οὐ διηγήσω ἡμῖν τὴν ξυνουσίαν, εἰ μή σέ τι κωλύει, καθιζόμενος ἐνταυθί, ἐξαναστήσας τὸν παῖδα τουτονί;

ΣΩ. Πάνυ μὲν οὖν· καὶ χάριν γε εἴσομαι, ἐὰν ἀκούητε.

---

[1] The Friend had an attendant who was sitting by him.

although he was present, I not merely paid him no attention, but at times forgot him altogether.

FR. Why, what can have happened between you and him? Something serious! For surely you did not find anyone else of greater beauty there,—no, not in our city.

soc. Yes, of far greater.

FR. What do you say? One of our people, or a foreigner?

soc. A foreigner.

FR. Of what city?

soc. Abdera.

FR. And you found this foreigner so beautiful that he appeared to you of greater beauty than the son of Cleinias?

soc. Why, my good sir, must not the wisest appear more beautiful?

FR. Do you mean it was some wise man that you met just now?

soc. Nay, rather the wisest of our generation, I may tell you, if " wisest " is what you agree to call Protagoras.

FR. Ah, what a piece of news! Protagoras come to town!

soc. Yes, two days ago.

FR. And it was his company that you left just now?

soc. Yes, and a great deal I said to him, and he to me.

FR. Then do let us hear your account of the conversation at once, if you are disengaged: take my boy's place,[1] and sit here.

soc. Very good; indeed, I shall be obliged to you, if you will listen.

ετ. Καὶ μὴν καὶ ἡμεῖς σοί, ἐὰν λέγῃς.

Σω. Διπλῆ ἂν εἴη ἡ χάρις. ἀλλ' οὖν ἀκούετε.
Τῆς παρελθούσης νυκτὸς ταυτησί, ἔτι βαθέος
ὄρθρου, Ἱπποκράτης ὁ Ἀπολλοδώρου υἱός, Φά-
σωνος δὲ ἀδελφός, τὴν θύραν τῇ βακτηρίᾳ πάνυ
B σφόδρα ἔκρουε, καὶ ἐπειδὴ αὐτῷ ἀνέῳξέ τις,
εὐθὺς εἴσω ᾔει ἐπειγόμενος, καὶ τῇ φωνῇ μέγα
λέγων, Ὦ Σώκρατες, ἔφη, ἐγρήγορας ἢ καθεύδεις;
καὶ ἐγὼ τὴν φωνὴν γνοὺς αὐτοῦ, Ἱπποκράτης,
ἔφην, οὗτος· μή τι νεώτερον ἀγγέλλεις; Οὐδέν
γ', ἦ δ' ὅς, εἰ μὴ ἀγαθά γε. Εὖ ἂν λέγοις, ἦν
δ' ἐγώ· ἔστι δὲ τί, καὶ τοῦ ἕνεκα τηνικάδε ἀφίκου;
Πρωταγόρας, ἔφη, ἥκει, στὰς παρ' ἐμοί. Πρῴην,
ἔφην ἐγώ· σὺ δὲ ἄρτι πέπυσαι; Νὴ τοὺς θεούς,
C ἔφη, ἑσπέρας γε. καὶ ἅμα ἐπιψηλαφήσας τοῦ
σκίμποδος ἐκαθέζετο παρὰ τοὺς πόδας μου, καὶ
εἶπεν· Ἑσπέρας δῆτα, μάλα γε ὀψὲ ἀφικόμενος
ἐξ Οἰνόης. ὁ γάρ τοι παῖς με ὁ Σάτυρος ἀπέδρα·
καὶ δῆτα μέλλων σοι φράζειν, ὅτι διωξοίμην
αὐτόν, ὑπό τινος ἄλλου ἐπελαθόμην· ἐπειδὴ δὲ
ἦλθον καὶ δεδειπνηκότες ἦμεν καὶ ἐμέλλομεν
ἀναπαύεσθαι, τότε μοι ἀδελφὸς λέγει, ὅτι ἥκει
Πρωταγόρας. καὶ ἔτι μὲν ἐνεχείρησα εὐθὺς
παρὰ σὲ ἰέναι, ἔπειτά μοι λίαν πόρρω ἔδοξε τῶν
D νυκτῶν εἶναι· ἐπειδὴ δὲ τάχιστά με ἐκ τοῦ κόπου
ὁ ὕπνος ἀνῆκεν, εὐθὺς ἀναστὰς οὕτω δεῦρο ἐπο-
ρευόμην. καὶ ἐγὼ γιγνώσκων αὐτοῦ τὴν ἀνδρείαν
καὶ τὴν πτοίησιν, Τί οὖν σοι, ἦν δ' ἐγώ, τοῦτο;
μῶν τί σε ἀδικεῖ Πρωταγόρας; καὶ ὃς γελάσας,
Νὴ τοὺς θεούς, ἔφη, ὦ Σώκρατες, ὅτι γε μόνος
ἐστὶ σοφός, ἐμὲ δὲ οὐ ποιεῖ. Ἀλλὰ ναὶ μὰ Δία,
ἔφην ἐγώ, ἂν αὐτῷ διδῷς ἀργύριον καὶ πείθῃς

FR. And we also to you, I assure you, if you will tell us.

soc. A twofold obligation. Well now, listen.

During this night just past, in the small hours, Hippocrates, son of Apollodorus and brother of Phason, knocked violently at my door with his stick, and when they opened to him he came hurrying in at once and calling to me in a loud voice : Socrates, are you awake, or sleeping ? Then I, recognizing his voice, said : Hippocrates, hallo ! Some news to break to me ? Only good news, he replied. Tell it, and welcome, I said : what is it, and what business brings you here at such an hour ? Protagoras has come, he said, standing at my side. Yes, two days ago, I said : have you only just heard ? Yes, by Heaven ! he replied, last evening. With this he groped about for the bedstead, and sitting down by my feet he said : It was in the evening, after I had got in very late from Oenoë. My boy Satyrus, you see, had run away : I meant to let you know I was going in chase of him, but some other matter put it out of my head. On my return, when we had finished dinner and were about to retire, my brother told me, only then, that Protagoras had come. I made an effort, even at that hour, to get to you at once, but came to the conclusion that it was too late at night. But as soon as I had slept off my fatigue I got up at once and made my way straight here. Then I, noting the man's gallant spirit and the flutter he was in, remarked : Well, what is that to you ? Has Protagoras wronged you ? At this he laughed and, Yes, by the gods ! he said, by being the only wise man, and not making me one. But, by Zeus ! I said, if you give him a fee and win him over he will

97

ἐκεῖνον, ποιήσει καὶ σὲ σοφόν. Εἰ γάρ, ἦ δ' ὅς,
E ὦ Ζεῦ καὶ θεοί, ἐν τούτῳ εἴη· ὡς οὔτ' ἂν τῶν
ἐμῶν ἐπιλίποιμι οὐδὲν οὔτε τῶν φίλων· ἀλλ'
αὐτὰ ταῦτα καὶ νῦν ἥκω παρὰ σέ, ἵνα ὑπὲρ ἐμοῦ
διαλεχθῇς αὐτῷ. ἐγὼ γὰρ ἅμα μὲν καὶ νεώτερός
εἰμι, ἅμα δὲ οὐδὲ ἑώρακα Πρωταγόραν πώποτε
οὐδ' ἀκήκοα οὐδέν· ἔτι γὰρ παῖς ἦ, ὅτε τὸ
πρότερον ἐπεδήμησεν. ἀλλὰ γάρ, ὦ Σώκρατες,
πάντες τὸν ἄνδρα ἐπαινοῦσι καί φασι σοφώτατον
εἶναι λέγειν· ἀλλὰ τί οὐ βαδίζομεν παρ' αὐτόν,
311 ἵνα ἔνδον καταλάβωμεν; καταλύει δ', ὡς ἐγὼ
ἤκουσα, παρὰ Καλλίᾳ τῷ Ἱππονίκου· ἀλλ' ἴωμεν.
καὶ ἐγὼ εἶπον· Μήπω, ὠγαθέ, ἐκεῖσε ἴωμεν, πρῲ
γάρ ἐστιν, ἀλλὰ δεῦρο ἐξαναστῶμεν εἰς τὴν αὐλήν,
καὶ περιιόντες αὐτοῦ διατρίψωμεν, ἕως ἂν φῶς
γένηται· εἶτα ἴωμεν. καὶ γὰρ τὰ πολλὰ Πρωταγόρας ἔνδον διατρίβει, ὥστε, θάρρει, καταληψό-
μεθα αὐτόν, ὡς τὸ εἰκός, ἔνδον.

Μετὰ ταῦτα ἀναστάντες εἰς τὴν αὐλὴν περιῇμεν·
B καὶ ἐγὼ ἀποπειρώμενος τοῦ Ἱπποκράτους τῆς
ῥώμης διεσκόπουν αὐτὸν καὶ ἠρώτων, Εἰπέ μοι,
ἔφην ἐγώ, ὦ Ἱππόκρατες, παρὰ Πρωταγόραν
νῦν ἐπιχειρεῖς ἰέναι, ἀργύριον τελῶν ἐκείνῳ μισθὸν
ὑπὲρ σεαυτοῦ, ὡς παρὰ τίνα ἀφιξόμενος καὶ τίς
γενησόμενος; ὥσπερ ἂν εἰ ἐπενόεις παρὰ τὸν
σαυτοῦ ὁμώνυμον ἐλθὼν Ἱπποκράτη τὸν Κῷον,
τὸν τῶν Ἀσκληπιαδῶν, ἀργύριον τελεῖν ὑπὲρ
σαυτοῦ μισθὸν ἐκείνῳ, εἴ τίς σε ἤρετο, Εἰπέ μοι,
C μέλλεις τελεῖν, ὦ Ἱππόκρατες, Ἱπποκράτει μισθὸν
ὡς τίνι ὄντι; τί ἂν ἀπεκρίνω; Εἶπον ἄν, ἔφη, ὅτι

make you wise too. Would to Zeus and all the
gods, he exclaimed, only that were needed! I
should not spare either my own pocket or those of
my friends. But it is on this very account I have
come to you now, to see if you will have a talk with
him on my behalf: for one thing, I am too young
to do it myself; and for another, I have never yet
seen Protagoras nor heard him speak a word—I was
but a child when he paid us his previous visit. You
know, Socrates, how everyone praises the man and
tells of his mastery of speech: let us step over to
him at once, to make sure of finding him in; he is
staying, so I was told, with Callias, son of Hipponicus.
Now, let us be going. To this I replied: We had
better not go there yet, my good friend, it is so
very early: let us rise and turn into the court here,
and spend the time strolling there till daylight
comes; after that we can go. Protagoras, you see,
spends most of his time indoors, so have no fear, we
shall find him in all right, most likely.

So then we got up and strolled in the court; and
I, to test Hippocrates' grit, began examining him
with a few questions. Tell me, Hippocrates, I said,
in your present design of going to Protagoras and
paying him money as a fee for his services to yourself, to whom do you consider you are resorting, and
what is it that you are to become? Suppose, for
example, you had taken it into your head to call on
your namesake Hippocrates of Cos, the Asclepiad,
and pay him money as your personal fee, and suppose
someone asked you—Tell me, Hippocrates, in pur-
posing to pay a fee to Hippocrates, what do you
consider him to be? How would you answer that?

A doctor, I would say.

311

ὡς ἰατρῷ. Ὡς τίς γενησόμενος; Ὡς ἰατρός,
ἔφη. Εἰ δὲ παρὰ Πολύκλειτον τὸν Ἀργεῖον ἢ
Φειδίαν τὸν Ἀθηναῖον ἐπενόεις ἀφικόμενος μισθὸν
ὑπὲρ σαυτοῦ τελεῖν ἐκείνοις, εἴ τίς σε ἤρετο·
τελεῖν τοῦτο τὸ ἀργύριον ὡς τίνι ὄντι ἐν νῷ ἔχεις
Πολυκλείτῳ τε καὶ Φειδίᾳ; τί ἂν ἀπεκρίνω;
Εἶπον ἂν ὡς ἀγαλματοποιοῖς. Ὡς τίς δὲ γενησόμενος αὐτός; Δῆλον ὅτι ἀγαλματοποιός. Εἶεν,
ἦν δ' ἐγώ· παρὰ δὲ δὴ Πρωταγόραν νῦν ἀφικό-
D μενοι ἐγώ τε καὶ σὺ ἀργύριον ἐκείνῳ μισθὸν ἕτοιμοι
ἐσόμεθα τελεῖν ὑπὲρ σοῦ, ἂν μὲν ἐξικνῆται τὰ
ἡμέτερα χρήματα καὶ τούτοις πείθωμεν αὐτόν,
εἰ δὲ μή, καὶ τὰ τῶν φίλων προσαναλίσκοντες.
εἰ οὖν τις ἡμᾶς περὶ ταῦτα οὕτω σφόδρα σπου-
δάζοντας ἔροιτο· εἰπέ μοι, ὦ Σώκρατές τε καὶ
Ἱππόκρατες, ὡς τίνι ὄντι τῷ Πρωταγόρᾳ ἐν νῷ
ἔχετε χρήματα τελεῖν; τί ἂν αὐτῷ ἀποκριναίμεθα;
E τί ὄνομα ἄλλο γε λεγόμενον περὶ Πρωταγόρου
ἀκούομεν; ὥσπερ περὶ Φειδίου ἀγαλματοποιὸν καὶ
περὶ Ὁμήρου ποιητήν, τί τοιοῦτον περὶ Πρωταγόρου ἀκούομεν; Σοφιστὴν δή τοι ὀνομάζουσί
γε, ὦ Σώκρατες, τὸν ἄνδρα εἶναι, ἔφη. Ὡς
σοφιστῇ ἄρα ἐρχόμεθα τελοῦντες τὰ χρήματα;
Μάλιστα. Εἰ οὖν καὶ τοῦτό τίς σε προσέροιτο·
312 αὐτὸς δὲ δὴ ὡς τίς γενησόμενος ἔρχῃ παρὰ τὸν
Πρωταγόραν; καὶ ὃς εἶπεν ἐρυθριάσας—ἤδη γὰρ
ὑπέφαινέ τι ἡμέρας, ὥστε καταφανῆ αὐτὸν γενέσθαι

And what would you intend to become ?

A doctor, he replied.

And suppose you had a mind to approach Polycleitus the Argive or Pheidias the Athenian and pay them a personal fee, and somebody asked you—What is it that you consider Polycleitus or Pheidias to be, that you are minded to pay them this money ? What would your answer be to that ?

Sculptors, I would reply.

And what would you intend to become ?

Obviously, a sculptor.

Very well then, I said ; you and I will go now to Protagoras, prepared to pay him money as your fee, from our own means if they are adequate for the purpose of prevailing on him, but if not, then drawing on our friends' resources to make up the sum. Now if anyone, observing our extreme earnestness in the matter, should ask us,—Pray, Socrates and Hippocrates, what is it that you take Protagoras to be, when you purpose to pay him money ? What should we reply to him ? What is the other name that we commonly hear attached to Protagoras ? They call Pheidias a sculptor and Homer a poet : what title do they give Protagoras ?

A sophist, to be sure, Socrates, is what they call him.

Then we go to him and pay him the money as a sophist ?

Certainly.

Now suppose someone asked you this further question : And what is it that you yourself hope to become when you go to Protagoras ?

To this he replied with a blush—for by then there was a glimmer of daylight by which I could see him

—Εἰ μέν τι τοῖς ἔμπροσθεν ἔοικε, δῆλον ὅτι σοφιστὴς γενησόμενος. Σὺ δέ, ἦν δ' ἐγώ, πρὸς
θεῶν, οὐκ ἂν αἰσχύνοιο εἰς τοὺς Ἕλληνας σαυτὸν
σοφιστὴν παρέχων; Νὴ τὸν Δία, ὦ Σώκρατες,
εἴπερ γε ἃ διανοοῦμαι χρὴ λέγειν. Ἀλλ' ἄρα, ὦ
Ἱππόκρατες, μὴ οὐ τοιαύτην ὑπολαμβάνεις σου τὴν
παρὰ Πρωταγόρου μάθησιν ἔσεσθαι, ἀλλ' οἵαπερ
B ἡ παρὰ τοῦ γραμματιστοῦ ἐγένετο καὶ κιθαριστοῦ
καὶ παιδοτρίβου; τούτων γὰρ σὺ ἑκάστην οὐκ
ἐπὶ τέχνῃ ἔμαθες, ὡς δημιουργὸς ἐσόμενος, ἀλλ'
ἐπὶ παιδείᾳ, ὡς τὸν ἰδιώτην καὶ τὸν ἐλεύθερον
πρέπει. Πάνυ μὲν οὖν μοι δοκεῖ, ἔφη, τοιαύτη
μᾶλλον εἶναι ἡ παρὰ Πρωταγόρου μάθησις.

Οἶσθα οὖν ὃ μέλλεις νῦν πράττειν, ἤ σε λαν-
θάνει; ἦν δ' ἐγώ. Τοῦ πέρι; Ὅτι μέλλεις τὴν
C ψυχὴν τὴν σαυτοῦ παρασχεῖν θεραπεῦσαι ἀνδρί,
ὡς φῄς, σοφιστῇ· ὅ τι δέ ποτε ὁ σοφιστής ἐστι,
θαυμάζοιμ' ἂν εἰ οἶσθα. καίτοι εἰ τοῦτ' ἀγνοεῖς,
οὐδὲ ὅτῳ παραδίδως τὴν ψυχὴν οἶσθα, οὔτ' εἰ
ἀγαθῷ οὔτ' εἰ κακῷ πράγματι. Οἶμαί γ', ἔφη,
εἰδέναι. Λέγε δή, τί ἡγῇ εἶναι τὸν σοφιστήν;
Ἐγὼ μέν, ἦ δ' ὅς, ὥσπερ τοὔνομα λέγει, τοῦτον
εἶναι τὸν τῶν σοφῶν ἐπιστήμονα. Οὐκοῦν, ἦν
δ' ἐγώ, τοῦτο μὲν ἔξεστι λέγειν καὶ περὶ ζωγράφων

quite clearly—If it is like the previous cases, obviously, to become a sophist.

In Heaven's name, I said, would you not be ashamed to present yourself before the Greeks as a sophist?

Yes, on my soul I should, Socrates, if I am to speak my real thoughts.

Yet after all, Hippocrates, perhaps it is not this sort of learning that you expect to get from Protagoras, but rather the sort you had from your language-master, your harp-teacher, and your sports-instructor; for when you took your lessons from each of these it was not in the technical way, with a view to becoming a professional, but for education, as befits a private gentleman.

I quite agree, he said; it is rather this kind of learning that one gets from Protagoras.

Then are you aware what you are now about to do, or is it not clear to you? I asked.

To what do you refer?

I mean your intention of submitting your soul to the treatment of a man who, as you say, is a sophist; and as to what a sophist really is, I shall be surprised if you can tell me. And yet, if you are ignorant of this, you cannot know to whom you are entrusting your soul,—whether it is to something good or to something evil.

I really think, he said, that I know.

Then tell me, please, what you consider a sophist to be.

I should say, he replied, from what the name implies, that he is one who has knowledge of wise matters.

Well, I went on, we are able to say this of painters

D καὶ περὶ τεκτόνων, ὅτι οὗτοί εἰσιν οἱ τῶν σοφῶν
ἐπιστήμονες· ἀλλ' εἴ τις ἔροιτο ἡμᾶς, τῶν τί
σοφῶν εἰσιν οἱ ζωγράφοι ἐπιστήμονες, εἴποιμεν
ἄν που αὐτῷ, ὅτι τῶν πρὸς τὴν ἀπεργασίαν τὴν
τῶν εἰκόνων, καὶ τἆλλα οὕτως. εἰ δέ τις ἐκεῖνο
ἔροιτο, ὁ δὲ σοφιστὴς τῶν τί σοφῶν ἐστί; τί ἂν
ἀποκρινοίμεθα αὐτῷ; ποίας ἐργασίας ἐπιστάτης;
Τί ἂν εἴποιμεν αὐτὸν εἶναι, ὦ Σώκρατες, ἢ ἐπιστάτην τοῦ ποιῆσαι δεινὸν λέγειν; Ἴσως ἄν, ἦν
δ' ἐγώ, ἀληθῆ λέγοιμεν, οὐ μέντοι ἱκανῶς γε·
ἐρωτήσεως γὰρ ἔτι ἡ ἀπόκρισις ἡμῖν δεῖται, περὶ
ὅτου ὁ σοφιστὴς δεινὸν ποιεῖ λέγειν· ὥσπερ ὁ
E κιθαριστὴς δεινὸν δήπου ποιεῖ λέγειν περὶ οὗπερ
καὶ ἐπιστήμονα, περὶ κιθαρίσεως· ἢ γάρ; Ναί.
Εἶεν· ὁ δὲ δὴ σοφιστὴς περὶ τίνος δεινὸν ποιεῖ
λέγειν; Δῆλον ὅτι περὶ οὗπερ καὶ ἐπίστασθαι[1];
Εἰκός γε. τί δή ἐστι τοῦτο, περὶ οὗ αὐτός τε
ἐπιστήμων ἐστὶν ὁ σοφιστὴς καὶ τὸν μαθητὴν
ποιεῖ; Μὰ Δί', ἔφη, οὐκέτι ἔχω σοι λέγειν.

313   Καὶ ἐγὼ εἶπον μετὰ τοῦτο· Τί οὖν; οἶσθα εἰς
οἷόν τινα κίνδυνον ἔρχῃ ὑποθήσων τὴν ψυχήν; ἢ εἰ
μὲν τὸ σῶμα ἐπιτρέπειν σε ἔδει τῳ, διακινδυνεύοντα
ἢ χρηστὸν αὐτὸ γενέσθαι ἢ πονηρόν, πολλὰ ἂν
περιεσκέψω, εἴτ' ἐπιτρεπτέον εἴτε οὔ, καὶ εἰς

---

[1] ἐπίστασθαι Stahl: ἐπίσταται MSS.

also, and of carpenters,—that they are the persons
who have knowledge of wise matters; and if someone asked us for what those matters are wise, of
which painters have knowledge, I suppose we should
tell him that they are wise for the production of
likenesses, and similarly with the rest. But if he
should ask for what the matters of the sophist are
wise, how should we answer him? What sort of
workmanship is he master of?

How should we describe him, Socrates,—as a
master of making one a clever speaker?

Perhaps, I replied, we should be speaking the
truth, but yet not all the truth; for our answer still
calls for a question, as to the subject on which the
sophist makes one a clever speaker: just as the harp-
player makes one clever, I presume, at speaking on
the matter of which he gives one knowledge, namely
harp-playing,—you agree to that?

Yes.

Well, about what does the sophist make one a
clever speaker?

Clearly it must be the same thing as that of which
he gives one knowledge.

So it would seem: now what is this thing, of which
the sophist himself has knowledge and gives knowledge to his pupil?

Ah, there, in good faith, he said, I fail to find
you an answer.

I then went on to say: Now tell me, are you
aware upon what sort of hazard you are going to
stake your soul? If you had to entrust your body to
someone, taking the risk of its being made better or
worse, you would first consider most carefully whether
you ought to entrust it or not, and would seek the

συμβουλὴν τούς τε φίλους ἂν παρεκάλεις καὶ τοὺς
οἰκείους, σκοπούμενος ἡμέρας συχνάς· ὃ δὲ περὶ
πλείονος τοῦ σώματος ἡγεῖ, τὴν ψυχήν, καὶ ἐν ᾧ
πάντ᾽ ἐστὶ τὰ σὰ ἢ εὖ ἢ κακῶς πράττειν, χρηστοῦ
ἢ πονηροῦ αὐτοῦ γενομένου, περὶ δὲ τούτου οὔτε
B τῷ πατρὶ οὔτε τῷ ἀδελφῷ ἐπεκοινώσω οὔτε ἡμῶν
τῶν ἑταίρων οὐδενί, εἴτ᾽ ἐπιτρεπτέον εἴτε καὶ οὐ
τῷ ἀφικομένῳ τούτῳ ξένῳ τὴν σὴν ψυχήν, ἀλλ᾽
ἑσπέρας ἀκούσας, ὡς φῄς, ὄρθριος ἥκων περὶ μὲν
τούτου οὐδένα λόγον οὐδὲ συμβουλὴν ποιῇ, εἴτε
χρὴ ἐπιτρέπειν σαυτὸν αὐτῷ εἴτε μή, ἕτοιμος δ᾽
εἶ ἀναλίσκειν τά τε σαυτοῦ καὶ τὰ τῶν φίλων
χρήματα, ὡς ἤδη διεγνωκώς, ὅτι πάντως συνεστέον
Πρωταγόρᾳ, ὃν οὔτε γιγνώσκεις, ὡς φῄς, οὔτε
C διείλεξαι οὐδεπώποτε, σοφιστὴν δ᾽ ὀνομάζεις, τὸν
δὲ σοφιστήν, ὅ τί ποτε ἔστι, φαίνει ἀγνοῶν, ᾧ
μέλλεις σαυτὸν ἐπιτρέπειν; καὶ ὃς ἀκούσας,
Ἔοικεν, ἔφη, ὦ Σώκρατες, ἐξ ὧν σὺ λέγεις.
Ἆρ᾽ οὖν, ὦ Ἱππόκρατες, ὁ σοφιστὴς τυγχάνει ὢν
ἔμπορός τις ἢ κάπηλος τῶν ἀγωγίμων, ἀφ᾽ ὧν
ψυχὴ τρέφεται; φαίνεται γὰρ ἔμοιγε τοιοῦτός τις.
Τρέφεται δέ, ὦ Σώκρατες, ψυχὴ τίνι; Μαθήμασι
δήπου, ἦν δ᾽ ἐγώ. καὶ ὅπως γε μή, ὦ ἑταῖρε, ὁ
σοφιστὴς ἐπαινῶν ἃ πωλεῖ ἐξαπατήσῃ ἡμᾶς,
ὥσπερ οἱ περὶ τὴν τοῦ σώματος τροφήν, ὁ ἔμπορός
D τε καὶ κάπηλος. καὶ γὰρ οὗτοί που ὧν ἄγουσιν
ἀγωγίμων οὔτε αὐτοὶ ἴσασιν ὅ τι χρηστὸν ἢ πονηρὸν περὶ τὸ σῶμα, ἐπαινοῦσι δὲ πάντα πωλοῦντες,

advice of your friends and relations and ponder it
for a number of days : but in the case of your soul,
which you value much more highly than your body,
and on which depends the good or ill condition of
all your affairs, according as it is made better or
worse, would you omit to consult first with either
your father or your brother or one of us your com-
rades,—as to whether or no you should entrust your
very soul to this newly-arrived foreigner ; but choose
rather, having heard of him in the evening, as you
say, and coming to me at dawn, to make no mention
of this question, and take no counsel upon it—
whether you ought to entrust yourself to him or not ;
and are ready to spend your own substance and that
of your friends, in the settled conviction that at all
costs you must converse with Protagoras, whom you
neither know, as you tell me, nor have ever met in
argument before, and whom you call " sophist," in
patent ignorance of what this sophist may be tc
whom you are about to entrust yourself ?

When he heard this he said : It seems so, Socrates,
by what you say.

Then can it be, Hippocrates, that the sophist is
really a sort of merchant or dealer in provisions on
which a soul is nourished ? For such is the view I
take of him.

With what, Socrates, is a soul nourished ?

With doctrines, presumably, I replied. And we
must take care, my good friend, that the sophist, in
commending his wares, does not deceive us, as both
merchant and dealer do in the case of our bodily
food. For among the provisions, you know, in which
these men deal, not only are they themselves ignorant
what is good or bad for the body, since in selling they

E   107

οὔτε οἱ ὠνούμενοι παρ' αὐτῶν, ἐὰν μή τις τύχῃ
γυμναστικὸς ἢ ἰατρὸς ὤν. οὕτω δὲ καὶ οἱ τὰ
μαθήματα περιάγοντες κατὰ τὰς πόλεις καὶ πωλοῦντες καὶ καπηλεύοντες τῷ ἀεὶ ἐπιθυμοῦντι
ἐπαινοῦσι μὲν πάντα ἃ πωλοῦσι, τάχα δ' ἄν τινες,
ὦ ἄριστε, καὶ τούτων ἀγνοοῖεν ὧν πωλοῦσιν ὅ τι
Ε χρηστὸν ἢ πονηρὸν πρὸς τὴν ψυχήν· ὡς δ' αὕτως
καὶ οἱ ὠνούμενοι παρ' αὐτῶν, ἐὰν μή τις τύχῃ
περὶ τὴν ψυχὴν αὖ ἰατρικὸς ὤν. εἰ μὲν οὖν σὺ
τυγχάνεις ἐπιστήμων τούτων τί χρηστὸν καὶ
πονηρόν, ἀσφαλές σοι ὠνεῖσθαι μαθήματα καὶ
παρὰ Πρωταγόρου καὶ παρ' ἄλλου ὁτουοῦν· εἰ δὲ
μή, ὅρα, ὦ μακάριε, μὴ περὶ τοῖς φιλτάτοις
314 κυβεύῃς τε καὶ κινδυνεύῃς. καὶ γὰρ δὴ καὶ πολὺ
μείζων κίνδυνος ἐν τῇ τῶν μαθημάτων ὠνῇ ἢ ἐν
τῇ τῶν σιτίων. σιτία μὲν γὰρ καὶ ποτὰ πριάμενον
παρὰ τοῦ καπήλου καὶ ἐμπόρου ἔξεστιν ἐν ἄλλοις
ἀγγείοις ἀποφέρειν, καὶ πρὶν δέξασθαι αὐτὰ εἰς
τὸ σῶμα πιόντα ἢ φαγόντα, καταθέμενον οἴκαδε
ἔξεστι συμβουλεύσασθαι, παρακαλέσαντα τὸν
ἐπαΐοντα, ὅ τι τε ἐδεστέον ἢ ποτέον καὶ ὅ τι μή,
καὶ ὁπόσον καὶ ὁπότε· ὥστε ἐν τῇ ὠνῇ οὐ μέγας
Β ὁ κίνδυνος. μαθήματα δὲ οὐκ ἔστιν ἐν ἄλλῳ
ἀγγείῳ ἀπενεγκεῖν, ἀλλ' ἀνάγκη, καταθέντα τὴν
τιμήν, τὸ μάθημα ἐν αὐτῇ τῇ ψυχῇ λαβόντα καὶ
μαθόντα ἀπιέναι ἢ βεβλαμμένον ἢ ὠφελημένον.
ταῦτα οὖν σκοπώμεθα καὶ μετὰ τῶν πρεσβυτέρων
ἡμῶν· ἡμεῖς γὰρ ἔτι νέοι ὥστε τοσοῦτον πρᾶγμα
διελέσθαι. νῦν μέντοι, ὥσπερ ὡρμήσαμεν, ἴωμεν

commend them all, but the people who buy from them are so too, unless one happens to be a trainer or a doctor. And in the same way, those who take their doctrines the round of our cities, hawking them about to any odd purchaser who desires them, commend everything that they sell, and there may well be some of these too, my good sir, who are ignorant which of their wares is good or bad for the soul ; and in just the same case are the people who buy from them, unless one happens to have a doctor's knowledge here also, but of the soul. So then, if you are well informed as to what is good or bad among these wares, it will be safe for you to buy doctrines from Protagoras or from anyone else you please : but if not, take care, my dear fellow, that you do not risk your greatest treasure on a toss of the dice. For I tell you there is far more serious risk in the purchase of doctrines than in that of eatables. When you buy victuals and liquors you can carry them off from the dealer or merchant in separate vessels, and before you take them into your body by drinking or eating you can lay them by in your house and take the advice of an expert whom you can call in, as to what is fit to eat or drink and what is not, and how much you should take and when ; so that in this purchase the risk is not serious. But you cannot carry away doctrines in a separate vessel : you are compelled, when you have handed over the price, to take the doctrine in your very soul by learning it, and so to depart either an injured or a benefited man. These, then, are questions which we have to consider with the aid of our elders, since we ourselves are still rather young to unravel so great a matter. For the moment, how-

καὶ ἀκούσωμεν τοῦ ἀνδρός, ἔπειτα ἀκούσαντες
καὶ ἄλλοις ἀνακοινωσώμεθα· καὶ γὰρ οὐ μόνος
Πρωταγόρας αὐτόθι ἐστίν, ἀλλὰ καὶ Ἱππίας ὁ
C Ἠλεῖος· οἶμαι δὲ καὶ Πρόδικον τὸν Κεῖον· καὶ
ἄλλοι πολλοὶ καὶ σοφοί.

Δόξαν ἡμῖν ταῦτα ἐπορευόμεθα· ἐπειδὴ δὲ ἐν
τῷ προθύρῳ ἐγενόμεθα, ἐπιστάντες περί τινος
λόγου διελεγόμεθα, ὃς ἡμῖν κατὰ τὴν ὁδὸν ἐνέπεσεν·
ἵν' οὖν μὴ ἀτελὴς γένοιτο, ἀλλὰ διαπερανάμενοι
οὕτως ἐσίοιμεν, στάντες ἐν τῷ προθύρῳ διελεγόμεθα, ἕως συνωμολογήσαμεν ἀλλήλοις. δοκεῖ οὖν
μοι, ὁ θυρωρός, εὐνοῦχός τις, κατήκουεν ἡμῶν, κιν-
D δυνεύει δὲ διὰ τὸ πλῆθος τῶν σοφιστῶν ἄχθεσθαι
τοῖς φοιτῶσιν εἰς τὴν οἰκίαν· ἐπειδὴ γοῦν ἐκρού-
σαμεν τὴν θύραν, ἀνοίξας καὶ ἰδὼν ἡμᾶς, Ἔα, ἔφη,
σοφισταί τινες· οὐ σχολὴ αὐτῷ· καὶ ἅμα ἀμφοῖν
τοῖν χεροῖν τὴν θύραν πάνυ προθύμως ὡς οἷός τ'
ἦν ἐπήραξε. καὶ ἡμεῖς πάλιν ἐκρούομεν, καὶ ὃς
ἐγκεκλημένης τῆς θύρας ἀποκρινόμενος εἶπεν,
Ὦ ἄνθρωποι, ἔφη, οὐκ ἀκηκόατε, ὅτι οὐ σχολὴ
αὐτῷ; Ἀλλ' ὦ 'γαθέ, ἔφην ἐγώ, οὔτε παρὰ Καλλίαν
E ἥκομεν οὔτε σοφισταί ἐσμεν· ἀλλὰ θάρρει· Πρωταγόραν γάρ τοι δεόμενοι ἰδεῖν ἤλθομεν· εἰσ-
άγγειλον οὖν. μόγις οὖν ποτὲ ἡμῖν ἄνθρωπος
ἀνέῳξε τὴν θύραν· ἐπειδὴ δὲ εἰσήλθομεν, κατελά-
βομεν Πρωταγόραν ἐν τῷ προστώῳ περιπατοῦντα,
ἑξῆς δ' αὐτῷ συμπεριεπάτουν ἐκ μὲν τοῦ ἐπὶ

ever, let us pursue our design and go and hear this person; and when we have heard him we shall proceed to consult others: for Protagoras is not the only one there; we shall find Hippias of Elis and, I believe, Prodicus of Ceos, and numerous other men of wisdom besides.

This we resolved on, and set forth; and when we arrived at the doorway, we stood discussing some question or other that had occurred to us by the way: so, not to leave it unfinished, but to get it settled before we went in, we stood there and discussed in front of the door, until we had come to an agreement with each other. Now, I fancy the door-keeper, who was a eunuch, overheard us; very likely the great number of sophists has made him annoyed with callers at the house: at any rate, when we had knocked on the door, he opened it and, on seeing us, —Hullo, he said, sophists there! Master is engaged. So saying, he seized the door with both hands and very smartly clapped it to with all his might. We tried knocking again, and then he spoke in answer through the closed door,—Sirs, have you not heard, he is engaged? But, my good fellow, I said, we have not come to see Callias, nor are we sophists. Have no fear: I tell you, we have come to ask if we may see Protagoras; so go and announce us. Then with much hesitation the fellow opened the door to us; and when we had entered, we came upon Protagoras as he was walking round in the cloister,[1] and close behind him two companies were walking round also; on the one side Callias, son of

[1] The passage from the front door led into a cloister which surrounded an open court and gave access to the various rooms of the house.

314

315 θάτερα Καλλίας ὁ Ἱππονίκου καὶ ὁ ἀδελφὸς
αὐτοῦ ὁ ὁμομήτριος, Πάραλος ὁ Περικλέους, καὶ
Χαρμίδης ὁ Γλαύκωνος, ἐκ δὲ τοῦ ἐπὶ θάτερα ὁ
ἕτερος τῶν Περικλέους Ξάνθιππος καὶ Φιλιππίδης
ὁ Φιλομήλου καὶ Ἀντίμοιρος ὁ Μενδαῖος, ὅσπερ
εὐδοκιμεῖ μάλιστα τῶν Πρωταγόρου μαθητῶν καὶ
ἐπὶ τέχνῃ μανθάνει, ὡς σοφιστὴς ἐσόμενος. τούτων δὲ οἳ ὄπισθεν ἠκολούθουν ἐπακούοντες τῶν
λεγομένων, τὸ μὲν πολὺ ξένοι ἐφαίνοντο, οὓς ἄγει
ἐξ ἑκάστων τῶν πόλεων ὁ Πρωταγόρας, δι' ὧν
διεξέρχεται, κηλῶν τῇ φωνῇ ὥσπερ Ὀρφεύς, οἱ
B δὲ κατὰ τὴν φωνὴν ἕπονται κεκηλημένοι· ἦσαν
δέ τινες καὶ τῶν ἐπιχωρίων ἐν τῷ χορῷ. τοῦτον
τὸν χορὸν μάλιστα ἔγωγε ἰδὼν ἥσθην, ὡς καλῶς
ηὐλαβοῦντο μηδέποτε ἐμποδὼν ἐν τῷ πρόσθεν
εἶναι Πρωταγόρου, ἀλλ' ἐπειδὴ αὐτὸς ἀναστρέφοι
καὶ οἱ μετ' ἐκείνου, εὖ πως καὶ ἐν κόσμῳ περι-
εσχίζοντο οὗτοι οἱ ἐπήκοοι ἔνθεν καὶ ἔνθεν, καὶ ἐν
κύκλῳ περιόντες ἀεὶ εἰς τὸ ὄπισθεν καθίσταντο
κάλλιστα.

Τὸν δὲ μετ' εἰσενόησα, ἔφη Ὅμηρος, Ἱππίαν
C τὸν Ἠλεῖον, καθήμενον ἐν τῷ κατ' ἀντικρὺ προ-
στῴῳ ἐν θρόνῳ· περὶ αὐτὸν δ' ἐκάθηντο ἐπὶ
βάθρων Ἐρυξίμαχός τε ὁ Ἀκουμενοῦ καὶ Φαῖδρος
ὁ Μυρρινούσιος καὶ Ἄνδρων ὁ Ἀνδροτίωνος καὶ
τῶν ξένων πολῖταί τε αὐτοῦ καὶ ἄλλοι τινές.
ἐφαίνοντο δὲ περὶ φύσεώς τε καὶ τῶν μετεώρων
ἀστρονομικὰ ἄττα διερωτᾶν τὸν Ἱππίαν, ὁ δ' ἐν
θρόνῳ καθήμενος ἑκάστοις αὐτῶν διέκρινε καὶ
διεξῄει τὰ ἐρωτώμενα. καὶ μὲν δὴ καὶ Τάνταλόν

---

[1] Od. xi. 601.

Hipponicus and his brother on the mother's side, Paralus, son of Pericles, and Charmides, son of Glaucon, while the other troop consisted of Pericles' other son Xanthippus, Philippides, son of Philomelus, and Antimoerus of Mende, who is the most highly reputed of Protagoras' disciples and is taking the course professionally with a view to becoming a sophist. The persons who followed in their rear, listening to what they could of the talk, seemed to be mostly strangers, brought by the great Protagoras from the several cities which he traverses, enchanting them with his voice like Orpheus, while they follow where the voice sounds, enchanted; and some of our own inhabitants were also dancing attendance. As for me, when I saw their evolutions I was delighted with the admirable care they took not to hinder Protagoras at any moment by getting in front; but whenever the master turned about and those with him, it was fine to see the orderly manner in which his train of listeners split up into two parties on this side and on that, and wheeling round formed up again each time in his rear most admirably.

" And next did I mark," as Homer[1] says, Hippias of Elis, seated high on a chair in the doorway opposite ; and sitting around him on benches were Eryximachus, son of Acumenus, Phaedrus of Myrrhinous, Andron son of Androtion and a number of strangers,— fellow-citizens of Hippias and some others. They seemed to be asking him a series of astronomical questions on nature and the heavenly bodies, while he, seated in his chair, was distinguishing and expounding to each in turn the subjects of their questions. " Nay more, Tantalus also did I there

γε εἰσεῖδον· ἐπεδήμει γὰρ ἄρα καὶ Πρόδικος ὁ
D Κεῖος· ἦν δὲ ἐν οἰκήματί τινι, ᾧ πρὸ τοῦ μὲν ὡς
ταμιείῳ ἐχρῆτο Ἱππόνικος, νῦν δὲ ὑπὸ τοῦ πλήθους
τῶν καταλυόντων ὁ Καλλίας καὶ τοῦτο ἐκκενώσας
ξένοις κατάλυσιν πεποίηκεν. ὁ μὲν οὖν Πρόδικος ἔτι κατέκειτο, ἐγκεκαλυμμένος ἐν κῳδίοις
τισὶ καὶ στρώμασι καὶ μάλα πολλοῖς, ὡς ἐφαίνετο·
παρεκάθηντο δὲ αὐτῷ ἐπὶ ταῖς πλησίον κλίναις
Παυσανίας τε ὁ ἐκ Κεραμέων καὶ μετὰ Παυσανίου
νέον τι ἔτι μειράκιον, ὡς μὲν ἐγᾦμαι, καλόν τε
E κἀγαθὸν τὴν φύσιν, τὴν δ᾽ οὖν ἰδέαν πάνυ καλός.
ἔδοξα ἀκοῦσαι ὄνομα αὐτῷ εἶναι Ἀγάθωνα, καὶ
οὐκ ἂν θαυμάζοιμι, εἰ παιδικὰ Παυσανίου τυγχάνει
ὤν. τοῦτό τ᾽ ἦν τὸ μειράκιον, καὶ τὼ Ἀδειμάντω
ἀμφοτέρω, ὅ τε Κήπιδος καὶ ὁ Λευκολοφίδου, καὶ
ἄλλοι τινὲς ἐφαίνοντο· περὶ δὲ ὧν διελέγοντο οὐκ
ἐδυνάμην ἔγωγε μαθεῖν ἔξωθεν, καίπερ λιπαρῶς
ἔχων ἀκούειν τοῦ Προδίκου· πάσσοφος γάρ μοι
316 δοκεῖ ἀνὴρ εἶναι καὶ θεῖος· ἀλλὰ διὰ τὴν βαρύτητα
τῆς φωνῆς βόμβος τις ἐν τῷ οἰκήματι γιγνόμενος
ἀσαφῆ ἐποίει τὰ λεγόμενα.

Καὶ ἡμεῖς μὲν ἄρτι εἰσεληλύθειμεν, κατόπιν δὲ
ἡμῶν ἐπεισῆλθον Ἀλκιβιάδης τε ὁ καλός, ὡς φὴς
σὺ καὶ ἐγὼ πείθομαι, καὶ Κριτίας ὁ Καλλαίσχρου.
ἡμεῖς οὖν ὡς εἰσήλθομεν, ἔτι σμίκρ᾽ ἄττα δια-
τρίψαντες καὶ ταῦτα διαθεασάμενοι προσῇμεν
B πρὸς τὸν Πρωταγόραν, καὶ ἐγὼ εἶπον· Ὦ Πρωταγόρα, πρὸς σέ τοι ἤλθομεν ἐγώ τε καὶ Ἱπποκράτης
οὗτος. Πότερον, ἔφη, μόνῳ βουλόμενοι διαλεχθῆναι ἢ καὶ μετὰ τῶν ἄλλων; Ἡμῖν μέν, ἦν δ᾽

---

[1] Od. xi. 582. A touch of epic dignity is humorously

behold," [1]—for you know Prodicus of Ceos is in Athens too: he was in a certain apartment formerly used by Hipponicus as a strong-room, but now cleared out by Callias to make more space for his numerous visitors, and turned into a guest-chamber. Well, Prodicus was still abed, wrapped up in sundry fleeces and rugs, and plenty of them too, it seemed; and near him on the beds hard by lay Pausanias from Cerames, and with Pausanias a lad who was still quite young,—of good birth and breeding, I should say, and at all events a very good-looking person. I fancied I heard his name was Agathon, and I should not be surprised to find he is Pausanias' favourite. Besides this youth there were the two Adeimantuses, sons of Cepis and Leucolophidas, and there seemed to be some others. The subjects of their conversation I was unable to gather from outside, despite my longing to hear Prodicus; for I regard the man as all-wise and divine: but owing to the depth of his voice the room was filled with a booming sound which made the talk indistinct.

We had only just come in, when close on our heels entered Alcibiades the good-looking, as you call him and I agree that he is, and Critias, son of Callaeschrus. So, when we had entered, after some more little delays over certain points we had to examine, we went up to Protagoras, and I said: Protagoras, you see we have come to you, Hippocrates and I.

Is it your wish, he asked, to converse with me alone, or in company with others?

It is all the same to us, I replied: let me first

given to the mention of the two famous sophists, Hippias and Prodicus.

ἐγώ, οὐδὲν διαφέρει· ἀκούσας δέ, οὗ ἕνεκα ἤλθομεν,
αὐτὸς σκέψαι. Τί οὖν δή ἐστιν, ἔφη, οὗ ἕνεκα
ἥκετε; Ἱπποκράτης ὅδε ἐστὶ μὲν τῶν ἐπιχωρίων,
Ἀπολλοδώρου υἱός, οἰκίας μεγάλης τε καὶ εὐδαί-
μονος, αὐτὸς δὲ τὴν φύσιν δοκεῖ ἐνάμιλλος εἶναι
C τοῖς ἡλικιώταις. ἐπιθυμεῖν δέ μοι δοκεῖ ἐλλόγιμος γενέσθαι ἐν τῇ πόλει, τοῦτο δὲ οἴεταί
οἱ μάλιστ᾽ ἂν γενέσθαι, εἰ σοὶ συγγένοιτο· ταῦτ᾽
οὖν ἤδη σὺ σκόπει, πότερον περὶ αὐτῶν μόνος οἴει
δεῖν διαλέγεσθαι πρὸς μόνους, ἢ μετ᾽ ἄλλων.
Ὀρθῶς, ἔφη, προμηθῇ, ὦ Σώκρατες, ὑπὲρ ἐμοῦ.
ξένον γὰρ ἄνδρα καὶ ἰόντα εἰς πόλεις μεγάλας, καὶ
ἐν ταύταις πείθοντα τῶν νέων τοὺς βελτίστους
ἀπολείποντας τὰς τῶν ἄλλων συνουσίας, καὶ
οἰκείων καὶ ὀθνείων, καὶ πρεσβυτέρων καὶ νεω-
τέρων, ἑαυτῷ συνεῖναι ὡς βελτίους ἐσομένους διὰ
D τὴν ἑαυτοῦ συνουσίαν, χρὴ εὐλαβεῖσθαι τὸν ταῦτα
πράττοντα· οὐ γὰρ σμικροὶ περὶ αὐτὰ φθόνοι τε
γίγνονται καὶ ἄλλαι δυσμένειαί τε καὶ ἐπιβουλαί.
ἐγὼ δὲ τὴν σοφιστικὴν τέχνην φημὶ μὲν εἶναι
παλαιάν, τοὺς δὲ μεταχειριζομένους αὐτὴν τῶν
παλαιῶν ἀνδρῶν, φοβουμένους τὸ ἐπαχθὲς αὐτῆς,
πρόσχημα ποιεῖσθαι καὶ προκαλύπτεσθαι, τοὺς
μὲν ποίησιν, οἷον Ὅμηρόν τε καὶ Ἡσίοδον καὶ
Σιμωνίδην, τοὺς δὲ αὖ τελετάς τε καὶ χρησμῳδίας,
τοὺς ἀμφί τε Ὀρφέα καὶ Μουσαῖον· ἐνίους δέ
τινας ᾔσθημαι καὶ γυμναστικήν, οἷον Ἴκκος τε ὁ
Ταραντῖνος καὶ ὁ νῦν ἔτι ὢν οὐδενὸς ἥττων σο-
E φιστὴς Ἡρόδικος ὁ Σηλυμβριανός, τὸ δὲ ἀρχαῖον
Μεγαρεύς· μουσικὴν δὲ Ἀγαθοκλῆς τε ὁ ὑμέτερος

tell you our object in coming, and then you must
decide.

Well, what is your object? he asked.

My friend Hippocrates is a native of the city, a
son of Apollodorus and one of a great and prosperous
family, while his own natural powers seem to make
him a match for anyone of his age. I fancy he is
anxious to gain consideration in our city, and he
believes he can best gain it by consorting with you.
So now it is for you to judge whether it will be
fittest for you to converse on this matter privately
with us alone, or in company with others.

You do right, Socrates, he said, to be so thoughtful
on my behalf. For when one goes as a stranger into
great cities, and there tries to persuade the best of
the young men to drop their other connexions, either
with their own folk or with foreigners, both old and
young, and to join one's own circle, with the promise
of improving them by this connexion with oneself,
such a proceeding requires great caution; since very
considerable jealousies are apt to ensue, and numerous enmities and intrigues. Now I tell you that
sophistry is an ancient art, and those men of ancient
times who practised it, fearing the odium it involved,
disguised it in a decent dress, sometimes of poetry, as
in the case of Homer, Hesiod, and Simonides; sometimes of mystic rites and soothsayings, as did Orpheus,
Musaeus and their sects; and sometimes too, I have
observed, of athletics, as with Iccus[1] of Tarentum
and another still living—as great a sophist as any
—Herodicus[2] of Selymbria, originally of Megara;
and music was the disguise employed by your own

[1] A famous athlete and trainer.
[2] A trainer who also practised medicine.

316

πρόσχημα ἐποιήσατο, μέγας ὢν σοφιστής, καὶ
Πυθοκλείδης ὁ Κεῖος καὶ ἄλλοι πολλοί. οὗτοι
πάντες, ὥσπερ λέγω, φοβηθέντες τὸν φθόνον ταῖς
317 τέχναις ταύταις παραπετάσμασιν ἐχρήσαντο· ἐγὼ
δὲ τούτοις ἅπασι κατὰ τοῦτο εἶναι οὐ ξυμφέρομαι·
ἡγοῦμαι γὰρ αὐτοὺς οὔ τι διαπράξασθαι ὃ ἐβουλή-
θησαν· οὐ γὰρ λαθεῖν τῶν ἀνθρώπων τοὺς δυνα-
μένους ἐν ταῖς πόλεσι πράττειν, ὧνπερ ἕνεκα ταῦτ᾽
ἐστὶ τὰ προσχήματα· ἐπεὶ οἵ γε πολλοὶ ὡς ἔπος
εἰπεῖν οὐδὲν αἰσθάνονται, ἀλλ᾽ ἅττ᾽ ἂν οὗτοι
διαγγέλλωσι, ταῦτα ὑμνοῦσι. τὸ οὖν ἀποδιδρά-
σκοντα μὴ δύνασθαι ἀποδρᾶναι, ἀλλὰ καταφανῆ
B εἶναι, πολλὴ μωρία καὶ τοῦ ἐπιχειρήματος, καὶ
πολὺ δυσμενεστέρους παρέχεσθαι ἀνάγκη τοὺς
ἀνθρώπους· ἡγοῦνται γὰρ τὸν τοιοῦτον πρὸς τοῖς
ἄλλοις καὶ πανοῦργον εἶναι. ἐγὼ οὖν τούτων τὴν
ἐναντίαν ἅπασαν ὁδὸν ἐλήλυθα, καὶ ὁμολογῶ τε
σοφιστὴς εἶναι καὶ παιδεύειν ἀνθρώπους, καὶ
εὐλάβειαν ταύτην οἶμαι βελτίω ἐκείνης εἶναι, τὸ
ὁμολογεῖν μᾶλλον ἢ ἔξαρνον εἶναι· καὶ ἄλλας
πρὸς ταύτῃ ἔσκεμμαι, ὥστε, σὺν θεῷ εἰπεῖν,
C μηδὲν δεινὸν πάσχειν διὰ τὸ ὁμολογεῖν σοφιστὴς
εἶναι. καίτοι πολλά γε ἔτη ἤδη εἰμὶ ἐν τῇ τέχνῃ·
καὶ γὰρ καὶ τὰ ξύμπαντα πολλά μοί ἐστιν· οὐδενὸς
ὅτου οὐ πάντων ἂν ὑμῶν καθ᾽ ἡλικίαν πατὴρ εἴην·
ὥστε πολύ μοι ἥδιστόν ἐστιν, εἴ τι βούλεσθε, περὶ
τούτων ἁπάντων ἐναντίον τῶν ἔνδον ὄντων τὸν
λόγον ποιεῖσθαι. καὶ ἐγώ—ὑπώπτευσα γὰρ βούλεσθαι αὐτὸν τῷ τε Προδίκῳ καὶ τῷ Ἱππίᾳ
ἐνδείξασθαι καὶ καλλωπίσασθαι, ὅτι ἐρασταὶ αὐτοῦ
D ἀφιγμένοι εἴημεν—Τί οὖν, ἔφην ἐγώ, οὐ καὶ Πρό-

Agathocles,[1] a great sophist, Pythocleides[1] of Ceos, and many more. All these, as I say, from fear of ill-will made use of these arts as outer coverings. But I do not conform to the method of all these persons, since I believe they did not accomplish any of their designs : for the purpose of all this disguise could not escape the able men of affairs in each city ; the multitude, of course, perceive practically nothing, but merely echo this or that pronouncement of their leaders. Now to try to run away, and to fail through being caught in the act, shows sad folly in the mere attempt, and must needs make people far more hostile ; for they regard such an one, whatever else he may be, as a rogue. Hence the road I have taken is one entirely opposite to theirs : I admit that I am a sophist and that I educate men ; and I consider this precaution, of admitting rather than denying, the better of the two. There are others besides that I have meditated, so as to avoid, under Heaven, any harm that may come of admitting that I am a sophist. And yet many long years have I now been in the profession, for many in total number are those that I have lived : not one of you all, but in age I might be his father.[2] Hence it suits me by far the best, in meeting your wishes, to make my discourse on these matters in the presence of all who are in the house.

On this, as I suspected that he wished to make a display before Prodicus and Hippias, and give himself airs on the personal attachment shown by our coming to him, I remarked : Then surely we must call

[1] A music-teacher.
[2] In the *Meno* (91 E) we are told that Protagoras lived nearly seventy years, forty of which he spent in teaching.

119

δικον καὶ Ἱππίαν ἐκαλέσαμεν καὶ τοὺς μετ'
αὐτῶν, ἵνα ἐπακούσωσιν ἡμῶν; Πάνυ μὲν οὖν,
ἔφη ὁ Πρωταγόρας. Βούλεσθε οὖν, ὁ Καλλίας
ἔφη, συνέδριον κατασκευάσωμεν, ἵνα καθεζόμενοι
διαλέγησθε; Ἐδόκει χρῆναι· ἄσμενοι δὲ πάντες
ἡμεῖς, ὡς ἀκουσόμενοι ἀνδρῶν σοφῶν, καὶ αὐτοί
τε ἀντιλαβόμενοι τῶν βάθρων καὶ τῶν κλινῶν
κατεσκευάζομεν παρὰ τῷ Ἱππίᾳ· ἐκεῖ γὰρ προ-
ὑπῆρχε τὰ βάθρα. ἐν δὲ τούτῳ Καλλίας τε καὶ
E Ἀλκιβιάδης ἡκέτην ἄγοντε τὸν Πρόδικον, ἀνα-
στήσαντες ἐκ τῆς κλίνης, καὶ τοὺς μετὰ τοῦ
Προδίκου.

Ἐπεὶ δὲ πάντες συνεκαθεζόμεθα, ὁ Πρωταγόρας,
Νῦν δὴ ἄν, ἔφη, λέγοις, ὦ Σώκρατες, ἐπειδὴ καὶ
οἵδε πάρεισι, περὶ ὧν ὀλίγον πρότερον μνείαν
ἐποιοῦ πρὸς ἐμὲ ὑπὲρ τοῦ νεανίσκου. καὶ ἐγὼ
318 εἶπον ὅτι Ἡ αὐτή μοι ἀρχή ἐστιν, ὦ Πρωταγόρα,
ἥπερ ἄρτι, περὶ ὧν ἀφικόμην. Ἱπποκράτης γὰρ
ὅδε τυγχάνει ἐν ἐπιθυμίᾳ ὢν τῆς σῆς συνουσίας·
ὅ τι οὖν αὐτῷ ἀποβήσεται, ἐάν σοι συνῇ, ἡδέως
ἄν φησι πυθέσθαι. τοσοῦτος ὅ γε ἡμέτερος λόγος.
ὑπολαβὼν οὖν ὁ Πρωταγόρας εἶπεν· Ὦ νεανίσκε,
ἔσται τοίνυν σοι, ἐὰν ἐμοὶ συνῇς, ᾗ ἂν ἡμέρᾳ ἐμοὶ
συγγένῃ, ἀπιέναι οἴκαδε βελτίονι γεγονότι, καὶ ἐν
τῇ ὑστεραίᾳ ταὐτὰ ταῦτα· καὶ ἑκάστης ἡμέρας
B ἀεὶ ἐπὶ τὸ βέλτιον ἐπιδιδόναι. καὶ ἐγὼ ἀκούσας
εἶπον· Ὦ Πρωταγόρα, τοῦτο μὲν οὐδὲν θαυμαστὸν
λέγεις, ἀλλὰ εἰκός, ἐπεὶ κἂν σύ, καίπερ τηλικοῦτος

Prodicus and Hippias and their followers to come and listen to us !

By all means, said Protagoras.

Then do you agree, said Callias, to our making a session of it, so that we may sit at ease for our conversation ?

The proposal was accepted ; and all of us, delighted at the prospect of listening to wise men, took hold of the benches and couches ourselves and arranged them where Hippias was, since the benches were there already. Meanwhile Callias and Alcibiades came, bringing with them Prodicus, whom they had induced to rise from his couch, and Prodicus' circle also.

When we had all taken our seats,—So now, Socrates, said Protagoras, since these gentlemen are also present, be so good as to tell what you were mentioning to me a little while before on the young man's behalf.

To which I replied : The same point, Protagoras, will serve me for a beginning as a moment ago, in regard to the object of my visit. My friend Hippocrates finds himself desirous of joining your classes ; and therefore he says he would be glad to know what result he will get from joining them. That is all the speech we have to make.

Then Protagoras answered at once, saying : Young man, you will gain this by coming to my classes, that on the day when you join them you will go home a better man, and on the day after it will be the same ; every day you will constantly improve more and more.

When I heard this I said : Protagoras, what you say is not at all surprising, but quite likely, since even

ὢν καὶ οὕτω σοφός, εἴ τίς σε διδάξειεν ὃ μὴ τυγ-
χάνοις ἐπιστάμενος, βελτίων ἂν γένοιο· ἀλλὰ μὴ
οὕτως, ἀλλ' ὥσπερ ἂν εἰ αὐτίκα μάλα μεταβαλὼν
τὴν ἐπιθυμίαν Ἱπποκράτης ὅδε ἐπιθυμήσειε τῆς
συνουσίας τούτου τοῦ νεανίσκου τοῦ νῦν νεωστὶ
ἐπιδημοῦντος, Ζευξίππου τοῦ Ἡρακλεώτου, καὶ
ἀφικόμενος παρ' αὐτόν, ὥσπερ παρὰ σὲ νῦν,
C ἀκούσειεν αὐτοῦ ταὐτὰ ταῦτα, ἅπερ σοῦ, ὅτι
ἑκάστης ἡμέρας ξυνὼν αὐτῷ βελτίων ἔσται καὶ
ἐπιδώσει· εἰ αὐτὸν ἐπανέροιτο· τί δὴ φῂς βελτίω
ἔσεσθαι καὶ εἰς τί ἐπιδώσειν; εἴποι ἂν αὐτῷ ὁ
Ζεύξιππος, ὅτι πρὸς γραφικήν· κἂν εἰ Ὀρθαγόρα
τῷ Θηβαίῳ συγγενόμενος, ἀκούσας ἐκείνου ταὐτὰ
ταῦτα, ἅπερ σοῦ, ἐπανέροιτο αὐτὸν εἰς ὅ τι βελτίων
καθ' ἡμέραν ἔσται συγγιγνόμενος ἐκείνῳ, εἴποι
ἄν, ὅτι εἰς αὔλησιν· οὕτω δὴ καὶ σὺ εἰπὲ τῷ νεανί-
D σκῳ καὶ ἐμοὶ ὑπὲρ τούτου ἐρωτῶντι, Ἱπποκράτης
ὅδε Πρωταγόρᾳ συγγενόμενος, ᾗ ἂν αὐτῷ ἡμέρᾳ
συγγένηται, βελτίων ἄπεισι γενόμενος καὶ τῶν
ἄλλων ἡμερῶν ἑκάστης οὕτως ἐπιδώσει εἰς τί, ὦ
Πρωταγόρα, καὶ περὶ τοῦ; καὶ ὁ Πρωταγόρας
ἐμοῦ ταῦτα ἀκούσας, Σύ τε καλῶς ἐρωτᾷς, ἔφη,
ὦ Σώκρατες, καὶ ἐγὼ τοῖς καλῶς ἐρωτῶσι χαίρω
ἀποκρινόμενος. Ἱπποκράτης γὰρ παρ' ἐμὲ ἀφικόμενος οὐ πείσεται, ἅπερ ἂν ἔπαθεν ἄλλῳ τῳ
συγγενόμενος τῶν σοφιστῶν· οἱ μὲν γὰρ ἄλλοι
λωβῶνται τοὺς νέους· τὰς γὰρ τέχνας αὐτοὺς
E πεφευγότας ἄκοντας πάλιν αὖ ἄγοντες ἐμβάλλουσιν
εἰς τέχνας, λογισμούς τε καὶ ἀστρονομίαν καὶ

you, though so old and so wise, would be made better if someone taught you what you happen not to know. But let me put it another way : suppose Hippocrates here should change his desire all at once, and become desirous of this young fellow's lessons who has just recently come to town, Zeuxippus of Heraclea, and should approach him, as he now does you, and should hear the very same thing from him as from you,—how on each day that he spent with him he would be better and make constant progress ; and suppose he were to question him on this and ask : In what shall I become better as you say, and to what will my progress be ? Zeuxippus's reply would be, to painting. Then suppose he came to the lessons of Orthagoras the Theban, and heard the same thing from him as from you, and then inquired of him for what he would be better each day through attending his classes, the answer would be, for fluting. In the same way you also must satisfy this youth and me on this point, and tell us for what, Protagoras, and in what connexion my friend Hippocrates, on any day of attendance at the classes of Protagoras, will go away a better man, and on each of the succeeding days will make a like advance.

When Protagoras heard my words,—You do right, he said, to ask that, while I am only too glad to answer those who ask the right question. For Hippocrates, if he comes to me, will not be treated as he would have been if he had joined the classes of an ordinary sophist. The generality of them maltreat the young ; for when they have escaped from the arts they bring them back against their will and force them into arts, teaching them

318

γεωμετρίαν καὶ μουσικὴν διδάσκοντες—καὶ ἅμα
εἰς τὸν Ἱππίαν ἀπέβλεψε—παρὰ δ' ἐμὲ ἀφικόμενος
μαθήσεται οὐ περὶ ἄλλου του ἢ περὶ οὗ ἥκει. τὸ
δὲ μάθημά ἐστιν εὐβουλία περί τε τῶν οἰκείων
ὅπως ἂν ἄριστα τὴν αὑτοῦ οἰκίαν διοικοῖ, καὶ περὶ
319 τῶν τῆς πόλεως, ὅπως τὰ τῆς πόλεως δυνατώτατος
ἂν εἴη καὶ πράττειν καὶ λέγειν.

Ἆρ', ἔφην ἐγώ, ἕπομαί σου τῷ λόγῳ; δοκεῖς γάρ
μοι λέγειν τὴν πολιτικὴν τέχνην καὶ ὑπισχνεῖσθαι
ποιεῖν ἄνδρας ἀγαθοὺς πολίτας.

Αὐτὸ μὲν οὖν τοῦτό ἐστιν, ἔφη, ὦ Σώκρατες, τὸ
ἐπάγγελμα, ὃ ἐπαγγέλλομαι.

Ἦ καλόν, ἦν δ' ἐγώ, τέχνημα ἄρα κέκτησαι,
εἴπερ κέκτησαι· οὐ γάρ τι ἄλλο πρός γε σὲ εἰρή-
σεται ἢ ἅπερ νοῶ. ἐγὼ γὰρ τοῦτο, ὦ Πρωταγόρα,
B οὐκ ᾤμην διδακτὸν εἶναι, σοὶ δὲ λέγοντι οὐκ ἔχω
ὅπως [ἂν]¹ ἀπιστῶ. ὅθεν δὲ αὐτὸ ἡγοῦμαι οὐ
διδακτὸν εἶναι μηδ' ὑπ' ἀνθρώπων παρασκευαστὸν
ἀνθρώποις, δίκαιός εἰμι εἰπεῖν. ἐγὼ γὰρ Ἀθηναίους, ὥσπερ καὶ οἱ ἄλλοι Ἕλληνες, φημὶ σοφοὺς εἶναι. ὁρῶ οὖν, ὅταν συλλεγῶμεν εἰς τὴν
ἐκκλησίαν, ἐπειδὰν μὲν περὶ οἰκοδομίας τι δέῃ
πρᾶξαι τὴν πόλιν, τοὺς οἰκοδόμους μεταπεμπο-
μένους συμβούλους περὶ τῶν οἰκοδομημάτων, ὅταν
δὲ περὶ ναυπηγίας, τοὺς ναυπηγούς, καὶ τἆλλα
C πάντα οὕτως, ὅσα ἡγοῦνται μαθητά τε καὶ διδακτὰ
εἶναι· ἐὰν δέ τις ἄλλος ἐπιχειρῇ αὐτοῖς συμβουλεύειν, ὃν ἐκεῖνοι μὴ οἴονται δημιουργὸν εἶναι,
κἂν πάνυ καλὸς ᾖ καὶ πλούσιος καὶ τῶν γενναίων,
οὐδέν τι μᾶλλον ἀποδέχονται, ἀλλὰ καταγελῶσι

¹ ἂν secl. Heindorf.

arithmetic and astronomy and geometry and music (and here he glanced at Hippias); whereas, if he applies to me, he will learn precisely and solely that for which he has come. That learning consists of good judgement in his own affairs, showing how best to order his own home; and in the affairs of his city, showing how he may have most influence on public affairs both in speech and in action.

I wonder, I said, whether I follow what you are saying; for you appear to be speaking of the civic science, and undertaking to make men good citizens.

That, Socrates, he replied, is exactly the purport of what I profess.

Then it is a goodly accomplishment that you have acquired, to be sure, I remarked, if indeed you have acquired it—to such a man as you I may say sincerely what I think. For this is a thing, Protagoras, that I did not suppose to be teachable; but when you say it is, I do not see how I am to disbelieve it. How I came to think that it cannot be taught, or provided by men for men, I may be allowed to explain. I say, in common with the rest of the Greeks, that the Athenians are wise. Now I observe, when we are collected for the Assembly, and the city has to deal with an affair of building, we send for builders to advise us on what is proposed to be built; and when it is a case of laying down a ship, we send for shipwrights; and so in all other matters which are considered learnable and teachable: but if anyone else, whom the people do not regard as a craftsman, attempts to advise them, no matter how handsome and wealthy and well-born he may be, not one of these things induces them to accept him; they merely laugh him to scorn and shout him down,

καὶ θορυβοῦσιν, ἕως ἂν ἢ αὐτὸς ἀποστῇ ὁ ἐπιχειρῶν λέγειν καταθορυβηθείς, ἢ οἱ τοξόται αὐτὸν
ἀφελκύσωσιν ἢ ἐξάρωνται κελευόντων τῶν πρυ-
τάνεων. περὶ μὲν οὖν ὧν οἴονται ἐν τέχνῃ εἶναι,
οὕτω διαπράττονται· ἐπειδὰν δέ τι περὶ τῆς πόλεως
D διοικήσεως δέῃ βουλεύσασθαι, συμβουλεύει αὐτοῖς ἀνιστάμενος περὶ τούτων ὁμοίως μὲν τέκτων,
ὁμοίως δὲ χαλκεύς, σκυτοτόμος, ἔμπορος, ναύ-
κληρος, πλούσιος, πένης, γενναῖος, ἀγεννής, καὶ
τούτοις οὐδεὶς τοῦτο ἐπιπλήττει ὥσπερ τοῖς
πρότερον, ὅτι οὐδαμόθεν μαθών, οὐδὲ ὄντος διδασκάλου οὐδενὸς αὐτῷ, ἔπειτα συμβουλεύειν
ἐπιχειρεῖ· δῆλον γὰρ, ὅτι οὐχ ἡγοῦνται διδακτὸν
εἶναι. μὴ τοίνυν ὅτι τὸ κοινὸν τῆς πόλεως
E οὕτως ἔχει, ἀλλὰ ἰδίᾳ ἡμῖν οἱ σοφώτατοι καὶ
ἄριστοι τῶν πολιτῶν ταύτην τὴν ἀρετὴν ἣν ἔχουσιν
οὐχ οἷοί τε ἄλλοις παραδιδόναι· ἐπεὶ Περικλῆς,
ὁ τουτωνὶ τῶν νεανίσκων πατήρ, τούτους ἃ μὲν
διδασκάλων εἴχετο καλῶς καὶ εὖ ἐπαίδευσεν, ἃ δὲ
320 αὐτὸς σοφός ἐστιν, οὔτε αὐτὸς παιδεύει οὔτε τῳ
ἄλλῳ παραδίδωσιν, ἀλλ' αὐτοὶ περιόντες νέμονται
ὥσπερ ἄφετοι, ἐάν που αὐτόματοι περιτύχωσι τῇ
ἀρετῇ. εἰ δὲ βούλει, Κλεινίαν, τὸν Ἀλκιβιάδου
τουτουὶ νεώτερον ἀδελφόν, ἐπιτροπεύων ὁ αὐτὸς
οὗτος ἀνὴρ Περικλῆς, δεδιὼς περὶ αὐτοῦ μὴ
διαφθαρῇ δὴ ὑπὸ Ἀλκιβιάδου, ἀποσπάσας ἀπὸ
τούτου, καταθέμενος ἐν Ἀρίφρονος ἐπαίδευε· καὶ
πρὶν ἓξ μῆνας γεγονέναι, ἀπέδωκε τούτῳ οὐκ
B ἔχων ὅ τι χρήσαιτο αὐτῷ. καὶ ἄλλους σοι παμ-

until either the speaker retires from his attempt,
overborne by the clamour, or the tipstaves pull him
from his place or turn him out altogether by order
of the chair. Such is their procedure in matters
which they consider professional. But when they
have to deliberate on something connected with the
administration of the State, the man who rises to
advise them on this may equally well be a smith, a
shoemaker, a merchant, a sea-captain, a rich man, a
poor man, of good family or of none, and nobody
thinks of casting in his teeth, as one would in the
former case, that his attempt to give advice is justified
by no instruction obtained in any quarter, no guidance of any master; and obviously it is because
they hold that here the thing cannot be taught.
Nay further, it is not only so with the service of the
State, but in private life our best and wisest citizens
are unable to transmit this excellence of theirs to
others; for Pericles, the father of these young fellows
here, gave them a first-rate training in the subjects for
which he found teachers, but in those of which he is
himself a master he neither trains them personally
nor commits them to another's guidance, and so they
go about grazing at will like sacred oxen, on the
chance of their picking up excellence here or there
for themselves. Or, if you like, there is Cleinias,
the younger brother of Alcibiades here, whom this
same Pericles, acting as his guardian, and fearing he
might be corrupted, I suppose, by Alcibiades, carried off from his brother and placed in Ariphron's
family to be educated: but before six months had
passed he handed him back to Alcibiades, at a
loss what to do with him. And there are a great
many others whom I could mention to you as having

πολλοὺς ἔχω λέγειν, οἳ αὐτοὶ ἀγαθοὶ ὄντες οὐδένα
πώποτε βελτίω ἐποίησαν οὔτε τῶν οἰκείων οὔτε
τῶν ἀλλοτρίων. ἐγὼ οὖν, ὦ Πρωταγόρα, εἰς
ταῦτα ἀποβλέπων οὐχ ἡγοῦμαι διδακτὸν εἶναι
ἀρετήν· ἐπειδὴ δέ σου ἀκούω ταῦτα λέγοντος,
κάμπτομαι καὶ οἶμαί τί σε λέγειν διὰ τὸ ἡγεῖσθαί
σε πολλῶν μὲν ἔμπειρον γεγονέναι, πολλὰ δὲ
μεμαθηκέναι, τὰ δὲ αὐτὸν ἐξευρηκέναι. εἰ οὖν
ἔχεις ἐναργέστερον ἡμῖν ἐπιδεῖξαι, ὡς διδακτόν
C ἐστιν ἡ ἀρετή, μὴ φθονήσῃς, ἀλλ᾽ ἐπίδειξον. Ἀλλ᾽,
ὦ Σώκρατες, ἔφη, οὐ φθονήσω· ἀλλὰ πότερον
ὑμῖν, ὡς πρεσβύτερος νεωτέροις, μῦθον λέγων
ἐπιδείξω ἢ λόγῳ διεξελθών; πολλοὶ οὖν αὐτῷ
ὑπέλαβον τῶν παρακαθημένων, ὁποτέρως βούλοιτο,
οὕτω διεξιέναι. Δοκεῖ τοίνυν μοι, ἔφη, χαριέ-
στερον εἶναι μῦθον ὑμῖν λέγειν.

Ἦν γάρ ποτε χρόνος, ὅτε θεοὶ μὲν ἦσαν, θνητὰ
D δὲ γένη οὐκ ἦν. ἐπειδὴ δὲ καὶ τούτοις χρόνος
ἦλθεν εἱμαρμένος γενέσεως, τυποῦσιν αὐτὰ θεοὶ
γῆς ἔνδον ἐκ γῆς καὶ πυρὸς μίξαντες καὶ τῶν ὅσα
πυρὶ καὶ γῇ κεράννυται. ἐπειδὴ δ᾽ ἄγειν αὐτὰ
πρὸς φῶς ἔμελλον, προσέταξαν Προμηθεῖ καὶ
Ἐπιμηθεῖ κοσμῆσαί τε καὶ νεῖμαι δυνάμεις ἑκάστοις ὡς πρέπει. Προμηθέα δὲ παραιτεῖται
Ἐπιμηθεὺς αὐτὸς νεῖμαι, νείμαντος δ᾽ ἐμοῦ, ἔφη,
E ἐπίσκεψαι· καὶ οὕτω πείσας νέμει. νέμων δὲ
τοῖς μὲν ἰσχὺν ἄνευ τάχους προσῆπτε, τοὺς δ᾽
ἀσθενεστέρους τάχει ἐκόσμει· τοὺς δὲ ὥπλιζε,

never succeeded, though virtuous themselves, in
making anyone else better, either of their own or
of other families. I therefore, Protagoras, in view
of these facts, believe that virtue is not teachable:
but when I hear you speak thus, I am swayed over,
and suppose there is something in what you say,
because I consider you to have gained experience
in many things and to have learnt many, besides
finding out some for yourself. So if you can demon-
strate to us more explicitly that virtue is teachable,
do not grudge us your demonstration.

No, Socrates, I will not grudge it you; but shall
I, as an old man speaking to his juniors, put my
demonstration in the form of a fable, or of a regular
exposition?

Many of the company sitting by him instantly
bade him treat his subject whichever way he pleased.

Well then, he said, I fancy the more agreeable
way is for me to tell you a fable.

There was once a time when there were gods, but
no mortal creatures. And when to these also came
their destined time to be created, the gods moulded
their forms within the earth, of a mixture made of
earth and fire and all substances that are compounded
with fire and earth. When they were about to bring
these creatures to light, they charged Prometheus
and Epimetheus to deal to each the equipment of
his proper faculty. Epimetheus besought Prometheus that he might do the dealing himself;
" And when I have dealt," he said, " you shall
examine." Having thus persuaded him he dealt;
and in dealing he attached strength without speed
to some, while the weaker he equipped with speed;
and some he armed, while devising for others, along

320

τοῖς δ' ἄοπλον διδοὺς φύσιν ἄλλην τιν' αὐτοῖς
ἐμηχανᾶτο δύναμιν εἰς σωτηρίαν. ἃ μὲν γὰρ
αὐτῶν σμικρότητι ἤμπισχε, πτηνὸν φυγὴν ἢ
κατάγειον οἴκησιν ἔνεμεν· ἃ δὲ ηὖξε μεγέθει,
321 τῷδε αὐτῷ αὐτὰ ἔσωζε· καὶ τἆλλα οὕτως ἐπανισῶν
ἔνεμε. ταῦτα δὲ ἐμηχανᾶτο εὐλάβειαν ἔχων μή
τι γένος ἀϊστωθείη· ἐπειδὴ δὲ αὐτοῖς ἀλληλο-
φθοριῶν διαφυγὰς ἐπήρκεσε, πρὸς τὰς ἐκ Διὸς
ὥρας εὐμάρειαν ἐμηχανᾶτο ἀμφιεννὺς αὐτὰ πυ-
κναῖς τε θριξὶ καὶ στερεοῖς δέρμασιν, ἱκανοῖς μὲν
ἀμῦναι χειμῶνα, δυνατοῖς δὲ καὶ καύματα, καὶ
εἰς εὐνὰς ἰοῦσιν ὅπως ὑπάρχοι τὰ αὐτὰ ταῦτα
στρωμνὴ οἰκεία τε καὶ αὐτοφυὴς ἑκάστῳ· καὶ
B ὑπὸ ποδῶν τὰ μὲν ὁπλαῖς, τὰ δὲ ὄνυξι[1] καὶ δέρμασι
στερεοῖς καὶ ἀναίμοις. τοὐντεῦθεν τροφὰς ἄλλοις
ἄλλας ἐξεπόριζε, τοῖς μὲν ἐκ γῆς βοτάνην, ἄλλοις
δὲ δένδρων καρπούς, τοῖς δὲ ῥίζας· ἔστι δ' οἷς
ἔδωκεν εἶναι τροφὴν ζῴων ἄλλων βοράν· καὶ τοῖς
μὲν ὀλιγογονίαν προσῆψε, τοῖς δ' ἀναλισκομένοις
ὑπὸ τούτων πολυγονίαν, σωτηρίαν τῷ γένει πο-
ρίζων. ἅτε δὴ οὖν οὐ πάνυ τι σοφὸς ὢν ὁ Ἐπιμη-
C θεὺς ἔλαθεν αὑτὸν καταναλώσας τὰς δυνάμεις εἰς
τὰ ἄλογα· λοιπὸν δὴ ἀκόσμητον ἔτι αὐτῷ ἦν τὸ
ἀνθρώπων γένος, καὶ ἠπόρει ὅ τι χρήσαιτο.
ἀποροῦντι δὲ αὐτῷ ἔρχεται Προμηθεὺς ἐπισκε-
ψόμενος τὴν νομήν, καὶ ὁρᾷ τὰ μὲν ἄλλα ζῷα
ἐμμελῶς πάντων ἔχοντα, τὸν δὲ ἄνθρωπον γυμνόν
τε καὶ ἀνυπόδητον καὶ ἄστρωτον καὶ ἄοπλον·
ἤδη δὲ καὶ ἡ εἱμαρμένη ἡμέρα παρῆν, ἐν ᾗ ἔδει καὶ
ἄνθρωπον ἐξιέναι ἐκ γῆς εἰς φῶς. ἀπορίᾳ οὖν

---

[1] ὄνυξι Baiter: θριξὶν MSS.

with an unarmed condition, some different faculty
for preservation. To those which he invested with
smallness he dealt a winged escape or an under-
ground habitation; those which he increased in
largeness he preserved by this very means; and he
dealt all the other properties on this plan of com-
pensation. In contriving all this he was taking precaution that no kind should be extinguished; and
when he had equipped them with avoidances of
mutual destruction, he devised a provision against
the seasons ordained by Heaven, in clothing them
about with thick-set hair and solid hides, sufficient to
ward off winter yet able to shield them also from
the heats, and so that on going to their lairs they
might find in these same things a bedding of their
own that was native to each; and some he shod
with hoofs, others with claws and solid, bloodless
hides. Then he proceeded to furnish each of them
with its proper food, some with pasture of the earth,
others with fruits of trees, and others again with
roots; and to a certain number for food he gave
other creatures to devour: to some he attached a
paucity in breeding, and to others, which were being
consumed by these, a plenteous brood, and so procured survival of their kind. Now Epimetheus, being
not so wise as he might be, heedlessly squandered
his stock of properties on the brutes; he still had
left unequipped the race of men, and was at a
loss what to do with it. As he was casting about,
Prometheus arrived to examine his distribution, and
saw that whereas the other creatures were fully and
suitably provided, man was naked, unshod, unbedded,
unarmed; and already the destined day was come,
whereon man like the rest should emerge from earth

ἐχόμενος ὁ Προμηθεύς, ἥντινα σωτηρίαν τῷ
ἀνθρώπῳ εὕροι, κλέπτει Ἡφαίστου καὶ Ἀθηνᾶς
D τὴν ἔντεχνον σοφίαν σὺν πυρί—ἀμήχανον γὰρ ἦν
ἄνευ πυρὸς αὐτὴν κτητήν τῳ ἢ χρησίμην γενέσθαι—καὶ οὕτω δὴ δωρεῖται ἀνθρώπῳ. τὴν μὲν
οὖν περὶ τὸν βίον σοφίαν ἄνθρωπος ταύτῃ ἔσχε,
τὴν δὲ πολιτικὴν οὐκ εἶχεν· ἦν γὰρ παρὰ τῷ Διί·
τῷ δὲ Προμηθεῖ εἰς μὲν τὴν ἀκρόπολιν τὴν τοῦ
Διὸς οἴκησιν οὐκέτι ἐνεχώρει εἰσελθεῖν· πρὸς δὲ
καὶ αἱ Διὸς φυλακαὶ φοβεραὶ ἦσαν· εἰς δὲ τὸ τῆς
E Ἀθηνᾶς καὶ Ἡφαίστου οἴκημα τὸ κοινόν, ἐν ᾧ
ἐφιλοτεχνείτην, λαθὼν εἰσέρχεται, καὶ κλέψας τήν
τε ἔμπυρον τέχνην τὴν τοῦ Ἡφαίστου καὶ τὴν
ἄλλην τὴν τῆς Ἀθηνᾶς δίδωσιν ἀνθρώπῳ, καὶ ἐκ
322 τούτου εὐπορία μὲν ἀνθρώπῳ τοῦ βίου γίγνεται,
Προμηθέα δὲ δι᾿ Ἐπιμηθέα ὕστερον, ᾗπερ λέγεται,
κλοπῆς δίκη μετῆλθεν.

Ἐπειδὴ δὲ ὁ ἄνθρωπος θείας μετέσχε μοίρας,
πρῶτον μὲν διὰ τὴν τοῦ θεοῦ συγγένειαν ζῴων
μόνον θεοὺς ἐνόμισε, καὶ ἐπεχείρει βωμούς τε
ἱδρύεσθαι καὶ ἀγάλματα θεῶν· ἔπειτα φωνὴν καὶ
ὀνόματα ταχὺ διηρθρώσατο τῇ τέχνῃ, καὶ οἰκήσεις
καὶ ἐσθῆτας καὶ ὑποδέσεις καὶ στρωμνὰς καὶ τὰς
ἐκ γῆς τροφὰς ηὕρετο. οὕτω δὴ παρεσκευασμένοι
κατ᾿ ἀρχὰς ἄνθρωποι ᾤκουν σποράδην, πόλεις δὲ
B οὐκ ἦσαν· ἀπώλλυντο οὖν ὑπὸ τῶν θηρίων διὰ τὸ
πανταχῇ αὐτῶν ἀσθενέστεροι εἶναι, καὶ ἡ δημιουρ-
γικὴ τέχνη αὐτοῖς πρὸς μὲν τροφὴν ἱκανὴ βοηθὸς
ἦν, πρὸς δὲ τὸν τῶν θηρίων πόλεμον ἐνδεής·
πολιτικὴν γὰρ τέχνην οὔπω εἶχον, ἧς μέρος πολε-
μική. ἐζήτουν δὴ ἀθροίζεσθαι καὶ σῴζεσθαι

---

[1] i.e. of arts originally apportioned to gods alone.

to light. Then Prometheus, in his perplexity as to
what preservation he could devise for man, stole
from Hephaestus and Athena wisdom in the arts
together with fire—since by no means without fire
could it be acquired or helpfully used by any—and
he handed it there and then as a gift to man. Now
although man acquired in this way the wisdom of
daily life, civic wisdom he had not, since this was in
the possession of Zeus ; Prometheus could not make
so free as to enter the citadel which is the dwelling-
place of Zeus, and moreover the guards of Zeus were
terrible : but he entered unobserved the building
shared by Athena and Hephaestus for the pursuit
of their arts, and stealing Hephaestus's fiery art and
all Athena's also he gave them to man, and hence it
is that man gets facility for his livelihood, but
Prometheus, through Epimetheus' fault, later on
(the story goes) stood his trial for theft.

And now that man was partaker of a divine
portion,[1] he, in the first place, by his nearness of
kin to deity, was the only creature that worshipped
gods, and set himself to establish altars and holy
images ; and secondly, he soon was enabled by his
skill to articulate speech and words, and to invent
dwellings, clothes, sandals, beds, and the foods that
are of the earth. Thus far provided, men dwelt
separately in the beginning, and cities there were
none ; so that they were being destroyed by the
wild beasts, since these were in all ways stronger
than they ; and although their skill in handiwork
was a sufficient aid in respect of food, in their warfare
with the beasts it was defective ; for as yet they
had no civic art, which includes the art of war. So
they sought to band themselves together and secure

κτίζοντες πόλεις· ὅτ' οὖν ἀθροισθεῖεν, ἠδίκουν
ἀλλήλους ἅτε οὐκ ἔχοντες τὴν πολιτικὴν τέχνην,
C ὥστε πάλιν σκεδαννύμενοι διεφθείροντο. Ζεὺς οὖν
δείσας περὶ τῷ γένει ἡμῶν, μὴ ἀπόλοιτο πᾶν,
Ἑρμῆν πέμπει ἄγοντα εἰς ἀνθρώπους αἰδῶ τε καὶ
δίκην, ἵν' εἶεν πόλεων κόσμοι τε καὶ δεσμοὶ φιλίας
συναγωγοί. ἐρωτᾷ οὖν Ἑρμῆς Δία, τίνα οὖν
τρόπον δοίη δίκην καὶ αἰδῶ ἀνθρώποις· πότερον
ὡς αἱ τέχναι νενέμηνται, οὕτω καὶ ταύτας νείμω;
νενέμηνται δὲ ὧδε· εἷς ἔχων ἰατρικὴν πολλοῖς
ἱκανὸς ἰδιώταις, καὶ οἱ ἄλλοι δημιουργοί· καὶ
δίκην δὴ καὶ αἰδῶ οὕτω θῶ ἐν τοῖς ἀνθρώποις, ἢ
D ἐπὶ πάντας νείμω; ἐπὶ πάντας, ἔφη ὁ Ζεύς, καὶ
πάντες μετεχόντων· οὐ γὰρ ἂν γένοιντο πόλεις, εἰ
ὀλίγοι αὐτῶν μετέχοιεν ὥσπερ ἄλλων τεχνῶν· καὶ
νόμον γε θὲς παρ' ἐμοῦ, τὸν μὴ δυνάμενον αἰδοῦς
καὶ δίκης μετέχειν κτείνειν ὡς νόσον πόλεως.
οὕτω δή, ὦ Σώκρατες, καὶ διὰ ταῦτα οἵ τε ἄλλοι
καὶ Ἀθηναῖοι, ὅταν μὲν περὶ ἀρετῆς τεκτονικῆς ᾖ
λόγος ἢ ἄλλης τινὸς δημιουργικῆς, ὀλίγοις οἴονται
E μετεῖναι συμβουλῆς, καὶ ἐάν τις ἐκτὸς ὢν τῶν
ὀλίγων συμβουλεύῃ, οὐκ ἀνέχονται, ὡς σὺ φῄς·
εἰκότως, ὡς ἐγώ φημι· ὅταν δὲ εἰς συμβουλὴν
323 πολιτικῆς ἀρετῆς ἴωσιν, ἣν δεῖ διὰ δικαιοσύνης
πᾶσαν ἰέναι καὶ σωφροσύνης, εἰκότως ἅπαντος ἀνδρὸς ἀνέχονται, ὡς παντὶ προσῆκον ταύτης γε
μετέχειν τῆς ἀρετῆς, ἢ μὴ εἶναι πόλεις. αὕτη, ὦ
Σώκρατες, τούτου αἰτία· ἵνα δὲ μὴ οἴῃ ἀπατᾶσθαι,
ὡς τῷ ὄντι ἡγοῦνται πάντες ἄνθρωποι πάντα ἄνδρα

their lives by founding cities. Now as often as they were banded together they did wrong to one another through the lack of civic art, and thus they began to be scattered again and to perish. So Zeus, fearing that our race was in danger of utter destruction, sent Hermes to bring respect and right among men, to the end that there should be regulation of cities and friendly ties to draw them together. Then Hermes asked Zeus in what manner then was he to give men right and respect: " Am I to deal them out as the arts have been dealt? That dealing was done in such wise that one man possessing medical art is able to treat many ordinary men, and so with the other craftsmen. Am I to place among men right and respect in this way also, or deal them out to all?" " To all," replied Zeus; " let all have their share; for cities cannot be formed if only a few have a share of these as of other arts. And make thereto a law of my ordaining, that he who cannot partake of respect and right shall die the death as a public pest.'' Hence it comes about, Socrates, that people in cities, and especially in Athens, consider it the concern of a few to advise on cases of artistic excellence or good craftsmanship, and if anyone outside the few gives advice they disallow it, as you say, and not without reason, as I think: but when they meet for a consultation on civic art, where they should be guided throughout by justice and good sense, they naturally allow advice from everybody, since it is held that everyone should partake of this excellence, or else that states cannot be. This, Socrates, is the explanation of it. And that you may not think you are mistaken, to show how all men verily believe that everyone

μετέχειν δικαιοσύνης τε καὶ τῆς ἄλλης πολιτικῆς
ἀρετῆς, τόδε αὖ λαβὲ τεκμήριον. ἐν γὰρ ταῖς
ἄλλαις ἀρεταῖς, ὥσπερ σὺ λέγεις, ἐάν τις φῇ
ἀγαθὸς αὐλητὴς εἶναι, ἢ ἄλλην ἡντινοῦν τέχνην,
ἣν μή ἐστιν, ἢ καταγελῶσιν ἢ χαλεπαίνουσι, καὶ
οἱ οἰκεῖοι προσιόντες νουθετοῦσιν ὡς μαινόμενον·
B ἐν δὲ δικαιοσύνῃ καὶ ἐν τῇ ἄλλῃ πολιτικῇ ἀρετῇ,
ἐάν τινα καὶ εἰδῶσιν ὅτι ἄδικός ἐστιν, ἐὰν οὗτος
αὐτὸς καθ’ αὑτοῦ τἀληθῆ λέγῃ ἐναντίον πολλῶν, ὃ
ἐκεῖ σωφροσύνην ἡγοῦντο εἶναι, τἀληθῆ λέγειν,
ἐνταῦθα μανίαν, καί φασιν πάντας δεῖν φάναι εἶναι
δικαίους, ἐάν τε ὦσιν ἐάν τε μή, ἢ μαίνεσθαι
τὸν μὴ προσποιούμενον δικαιοσύνην· ὡς ἀναγκαῖον
C οὐδένα ὄντιν’ οὐχὶ ἁμῶς γέ πως μετέχειν αὐτῆς, ἢ
μὴ εἶναι ἐν ἀνθρώποις.

Ὅτι μὲν οὖν πάντ’ ἄνδρα εἰκότως ἀποδέχονται
περὶ ταύτης τῆς ἀρετῆς σύμβουλον διὰ τὸ ἡγεῖσθαι
παντὶ μετεῖναι αὐτῆς, ταῦτα λέγω· ὅτι δὲ αὐτὴν
οὐ φύσει ἡγοῦνται εἶναι οὐδ’ ἀπὸ τοῦ αὐτομάτου,
ἀλλὰ διδακτόν τε καὶ ἐξ ἐπιμελείας παραγίγνεσθαι
ᾧ ἂν παραγίγνηται, τοῦτό σοι μετὰ τοῦτο πει-
D ράσομαι ἀποδεῖξαι. ὅσα γὰρ ἡγοῦνται ἀλλήλους
κακὰ ἔχειν ἄνθρωποι φύσει ἢ τύχῃ, οὐδεὶς θυμοῦται
οὐδὲ νουθετεῖ οὐδὲ διδάσκει οὐδὲ κολάζει τοὺς
ταῦτα ἔχοντας, ἵνα μὴ τοιοῦτοι ὦσιν, ἀλλ’ ἐλεοῦ-
σιν· οἷον τοὺς αἰσχροὺς ἢ σμικροὺς ἢ ἀσθενεῖς τίς
οὕτως ἀνόητος, ὥστε τι τούτων ἐπιχειρεῖν ποιεῖν;
ταῦτα μὲν γάρ, οἶμαι, ἴσασιν ὅτι φύσει τε καὶ
τύχῃ τοῖς ἀνθρώποις γίγνεται, τὰ καλὰ καὶ τἄναν-
136

partakes of justice and the rest of civic virtue, I can offer yet a further proof. In all other excellences, as you say, when a man professes to be good at flute-playing or any other art in which he has no such skill, they either laugh him to scorn or are annoyed with him, and his people come and reprove him for being so mad : but where justice or any other civic virtue is involved, and they happen to know that a certain person is unjust, if he confesses the truth about his conduct before the public, that truthfulness which in the former arts they would regard as good sense they here call madness. Everyone, they say, should profess to be just, whether he is so or not, and whoever does not make some pretension to justice is mad ; since it is held that all without exception must needs partake of it in some way or other, or else not be of human kind.

Take my word for it, then, that they have good reason for admitting everybody as adviser on this virtue, owing to their belief that everyone has some of it ; and next, that they do not regard it as natural or spontaneous, but as something taught and acquired after careful preparation by those who acquire it,—of this I will now endeavour to convince you. In all cases of evils which men deem to have befallen their neighbours by nature or fortune, nobody is wroth with them or reproves or lectures or punishes them, when so afflicted, with a view to their being other than they are ; one merely pities them. Who, for instance, is such a fool as to try to do anything of the sort to the ugly, the puny, or the weak ? Because, I presume, men know that it is by nature and fortune that people get these things, the graces of life and their opposites. But

323

τία τούτοις· ὅσα δὲ ἐξ ἐπιμελείας καὶ ἀσκήσεως
καὶ διδαχῆς οἴονται γίγνεσθαι ἀγαθὰ ἀνθρώποις,
E ἐάν τις ταῦτα μὴ ἔχῃ, ἀλλὰ τἀναντία τούτων κακά,
ἐπὶ τούτοις που οἵ τε θυμοὶ γίγνονται καὶ αἱ
κολάσεις καὶ αἱ νουθετήσεις. ὧν ἐστὶν ἓν καὶ ἡ
ἀδικία καὶ ἡ ἀσέβεια καὶ συλλήβδην πᾶν τὸ
324 ἐναντίον τῆς πολιτικῆς ἀρετῆς· ἔνθα δὴ πᾶς παντὶ
θυμοῦται καὶ νουθετεῖ, δῆλον ὅτι ὡς ἐξ ἐπιμελείας
καὶ μαθήσεως κτητῆς οὔσης. εἰ γὰρ ἐθέλεις
ἐννοῆσαι τὸ κολάζειν, ὦ Σώκρατες, τοὺς ἀδικοῦντας τί ποτε δύναται, αὐτό σε διδάξει, ὅτι οἵ γε
ἄνθρωποι ἡγοῦνται παρασκευαστὸν εἶναι ἀρετήν.
οὐδεὶς γὰρ κολάζει τοὺς ἀδικοῦντας πρὸς τούτῳ τὸν
B νοῦν ἔχων καὶ τούτου ἕνεκα, ὅτι ἠδίκησεν, ὅστις
μὴ ὥσπερ θηρίον ἀλογίστως τιμωρεῖται· ὁ δὲ
μετὰ λόγου ἐπιχειρῶν κολάζειν οὐ τοῦ παρ-
εληλυθότος ἕνεκα ἀδικήματος τιμωρεῖται—οὐ γὰρ
ἂν τό γε πραχθὲν ἀγένητον θείη—ἀλλὰ τοῦ μέλλοντος χάριν, ἵνα μὴ αὖθις ἀδικήσῃ μήτε αὐτὸς
οὗτος μήτε ἄλλος ὁ τοῦτον ἰδὼν κολασθέντα· καὶ
τοιαύτην διάνοιαν ἔχων διανοεῖται παιδευτὴν εἶναι
ἀρετήν· ἀποτροπῆς γοῦν ἕνεκα κολάζει. ταύτην
C οὖν τὴν δόξαν πάντες ἔχουσιν, ὅσοιπερ τιμωροῦνται
καὶ ἰδίᾳ καὶ δημοσίᾳ· τιμωροῦνται δὲ καὶ κολά-
ζονται οἵ τε ἄλλοι ἄνθρωποι οὓς ἂν οἴωνται
ἀδικεῖν, καὶ οὐχ ἥκιστα Ἀθηναῖοι, οἱ σοὶ πολῖται·
ὥστε κατὰ τοῦτον τὸν λόγον καὶ Ἀθηναῖοί εἰσι
τῶν ἡγουμένων παρασκευαστὸν εἶναι καὶ διδακτὸν
ἀρετήν. ὡς μὲν οὖν εἰκότως ἀποδέχονται οἱ σοὶ
πολῖται καὶ χαλκέως καὶ σκυτοτόμου συμβου-
λεύοντος τὰ πολιτικά, καὶ ὅτι διδακτὸν καὶ παρα-

as to all the good things that people are supposed to get by application and practice and teaching, where these are lacking in anyone and only their opposite evils are found, here surely are the occasions for wrath and punishment and reproof. One of them is injustice, and impiety, and in short all that is opposed to civic virtue ; in such case anyone will be wroth with his neighbour and reprove him, clearly because the virtue is to be acquired by application and learning. For if you will consider punishment, Socrates, and what control it has over wrong-doers, the facts will inform you that men agree in regarding virtue as procured. No one punishes a wrong-doer from the mere contemplation or on account of his wrong-doing, unless one takes unreasoning vengeance like a wild beast. But he who undertakes to punish with reason does not avenge himself for the past offence, since he cannot make what was done as though it had not come to pass ; he looks rather to the future, and aims at preventing that particular person and others who see him punished from doing wrong again. And being so minded he must have in mind that virtue comes by training : for you observe that he punishes to deter. This then is the accepted view of all who seek requital in either private or public life ; and while men in general exact requital and punishment from those whom they suppose to have wronged them, this is especially the case with the Athenians, your fellow-citizens, so that by our argument the Athenians also share the view that virtue is procured and taught. Thus I have shown that your fellow-citizens have good reason for admitting a smith's or cobbler's counsel in public affairs, and that they hold virtue to be

324

D σκευαστὸν ἡγοῦνται ἀρετήν, ἀποδέδεικταί σοι, ὦ
Σώκρατες, ἱκανῶς, ὥς γ᾽ ἐμοὶ φαίνεται.

Ἔτι δὴ λοιπὴ ἀπορία ἐστίν, ἣν ἀπορεῖς περὶ
τῶν ἀνδρῶν τῶν ἀγαθῶν, τί δήποτε οἱ ἄνδρες οἱ
ἀγαθοὶ τὰ μὲν ἄλλα τοὺς αὑτῶν υἱεῖς διδάσκουσιν, ἃ
διδασκάλων ἔχεται, καὶ σοφοὺς ποιοῦσιν, ἣν δὲ
αὐτοὶ ἀρετὴν ἀγαθοί, οὐδενὸς βελτίους ποιοῦσι.
τούτου δὴ πέρι, ὦ Σώκρατες, οὐκέτι μῦθόν σοι
ἐρῶ, ἀλλὰ λόγον. ὧδε γὰρ ἐννόησον· πότερον
E ἔστι τι ἕν, ἢ οὐκ ἔστιν, οὗ ἀναγκαῖον πάντας τοὺς
πολίτας μετέχειν, εἴπερ μέλλει πόλις εἶναι; ἐν
τούτῳ γὰρ αὕτη λύεται ἡ ἀπορία, ἣν σὺ ἀπορεῖς, ἢ
ἄλλοθι οὐδαμοῦ. εἰ μὲν γὰρ ἔστι καὶ τοῦτό ἐστι
τὸ ἓν οὐ τεκτονικὴ οὐδὲ χαλκεία οὐδὲ κεραμεία,
ἀλλὰ δικαιοσύνη καὶ σωφροσύνη καὶ τὸ ὅσιον
325 εἶναι, καὶ συλλήβδην ἓν αὐτὸ προσαγορεύω εἶναι
ἀνδρὸς ἀρετήν· εἰ τοῦτ᾽ ἐστίν, οὗ δεῖ πάντας
μετέχειν καὶ μετὰ τούτου πάντ᾽ ἄνδρα, ἐάν τι καὶ
ἄλλο βούληται μανθάνειν ἢ πράττειν, οὕτω πράττειν, ἄνευ δὲ τούτου μή, ἢ τὸν μὴ μετέχοντα καὶ
διδάσκειν καὶ κολάζειν, καὶ παῖδα καὶ ἄνδρα καὶ
γυναῖκα, ἕωσπερ ἂν κολαζόμενος βελτίων γένηται,
ὃς δ᾽ ἂν μὴ ὑπακούῃ κολαζόμενος καὶ διδασκόμενος,
B ὡς ἀνίατον ὄντα τοῦτον ἐκβάλλειν ἐκ τῶν πόλεων
ἢ ἀποκτείνειν· εἰ οὕτω μὲν ἔχει, οὕτω δ᾽ αὐτοῦ
πεφυκότος οἱ ἀγαθοὶ ἄνδρες εἰ τὰ μὲν ἄλλα διδάσκονται τοὺς υἱεῖς, τοῦτο δὲ μή, σκέψαι ὡς
θαυμάσιοι[1] γίγνονται οἱ ἀγαθοί. ὅτι μὲν γὰρ
διδακτὸν αὐτὸ ἡγοῦνται καὶ ἰδίᾳ καὶ δημοσίᾳ,
ἀπεδείξαμεν· διδακτοῦ δὲ ὄντος καὶ θεραπευτοῦ τὰ
μὲν ἄλλα ἄρα τοὺς υἱεῖς διδάσκονται, ἐφ᾽ οἷς οὐκ

---

[1] θαυμάσιοι Kroschel : θαυμασίως MSS.

taught and procured : of this I have given you satisfactory demonstration, Socrates, as it appears to me.

I have yet to deal with your remaining problem about good men, why it is that these good men have their sons taught the subjects in the regular teachers' courses, and so far make them wise, but do not make them excel in that virtue wherein consists their own goodness. On this point, Socrates, I shall give you argument instead of fable. Now consider : is there, or is there not, some one thing whereof all the citizens must needs partake, if there is to be a city ? Here, and nowhere if not here, is the solution of this problem of yours. For if there is such a thing, and that one thing, instead of being the joiner's or smith's or potter's art, is rather justice and temperance and holiness — in short, what I may put together and call a man's virtue ; and if it is this whereof all should partake and wherewith everyone should proceed to any further knowledge or action, but should not if he lacks it ; if we should instruct and punish such as do not partake of it, whether child or husband or wife, until the punishment of such persons has made them better, and should cast forth from our cities or put to death as incurable whoever fails to respond to such punishment and instruction ; —if it is like this, and yet, its nature being so, good men have their sons instructed in everything else but this, what very surprising folk the good are found to be ! For we have proved that they regard this thing as teachable both in private and in public life, and then, though it may be taught and fostered, are we to say that they have their sons taught everything

325

ἔστι θάνατος ἢ ζημία, ἐὰν μὴ ἐπίστωνται, ἐφ' ᾧ
δὲ ἦ τε ζημία θάνατος αὐτῶν τοῖς παισὶ καὶ
C φυγαὶ μὴ μαθοῦσι μηδὲ θεραπευθεῖσιν εἰς ἀρετήν,
καὶ πρὸς τῷ θανάτῳ χρημάτων τε δημεύσεις καὶ
ὡς ἔπος εἰπεῖν συλλήβδην τῶν οἴκων ἀνατροπαί,
ταῦτα δ' ἄρα οὐ διδάσκονται οὐδ' ἐπιμελοῦνται
πᾶσαν ἐπιμέλειαν; οἴεσθαί γε χρή, ὦ Σώκρατες.

Ἐκ παίδων σμικρῶν ἀρξάμενοι, μέχρι οὗπερ
ἂν ζῶσι, καὶ διδάσκουσι καὶ νουθετοῦσιν. ἐπειδὰν
θᾶττον συνιῇ τις τὰ λεγόμενα, καὶ τροφὸς καὶ
μήτηρ καὶ παιδαγωγὸς καὶ αὐτὸς ὁ πατὴρ περὶ
D τούτου διαμάχονται, ὅπως ὡς βέλτιστος ἔσται
ὁ παῖς, παρ' ἕκαστον καὶ ἔργον καὶ λόγον διδάσκοντες καὶ ἐνδεικνύμενοι, ὅτι τὸ μὲν δίκαιον, τὸ
δὲ ἄδικον, καὶ τόδε μὲν καλόν, τόδε δὲ αἰσχρόν,
καὶ τόδε μὲν ὅσιον, τόδε δὲ ἀνόσιον, καὶ τὰ μὲν
ποίει, τὰ δὲ μὴ ποίει· καὶ ἐὰν μὲν ἑκὼν πείθηται·
εἰ δὲ μή, ὥσπερ ξύλον διαστρεφόμενον καὶ καμ-
πτόμενον εὐθύνουσιν ἀπειλαῖς καὶ πληγαῖς. μετὰ
δὲ ταῦτα εἰς διδασκάλων πέμποντες πολὺ μᾶλλον
ἐντέλλονται ἐπιμελεῖσθαι εὐκοσμίας τῶν παίδων
E ἢ γραμμάτων τε καὶ κιθαρίσεως· οἱ δὲ διδάσκαλοι τούτων τε ἐπιμελοῦνται, καὶ ἐπειδὰν αὖ
γράμματα μάθωσι καὶ μέλλωσι συνήσειν τὰ
γεγραμμένα, ὥσπερ τότε τὴν φωνήν, παρα-
τιθέασιν αὐτοῖς ἐπὶ τῶν βάθρων ἀναγιγνώσκειν
ποιητῶν ἀγαθῶν ποιήματα καὶ ἐκμανθάνειν ἀναγ-
326 κάζουσιν, ἐν οἷς πολλαὶ μὲν νουθετήσεις ἔνεισι,
πολλαὶ δὲ διέξοδοι καὶ ἔπαινοι καὶ ἐγκώμια
παλαιῶν ἀνδρῶν ἀγαθῶν, ἵνα ὁ παῖς ζηλῶν μι-
μῆται καὶ ὀρέγηται τοιοῦτος γενέσθαι. οἵ τ'
αὖ κιθαρισταί, ἕτερα τοιαῦτα, σωφροσύνης τε

in which the penalty for ignorance is not death, but in a matter where the death-penalty or exile awaits their children if not instructed and cultivated in virtue—and not merely death, but confiscation of property and practically the entire subversion of their house—here they do not have them taught or take the utmost care of them? So at any rate we must conclude, Socrates.

They teach and admonish them from earliest childhood till the last day of their lives. As soon as one of them grasps what is said to him, the nurse, the mother, the tutor, and the father himself strive hard that the child may excel, and as each act and word occurs they teach and impress upon him that this is just, and that unjust, one thing noble, another base, one holy, another unholy, and that he is to do this, and not do that. If he readily obeys,—so; but if not, they treat him as a bent and twisted piece of wood and straighten him with threats and blows. After this they send them to school and charge the master to take far more pains over their children's good behaviour than over their letters and harp-playing. The masters take pains accordingly, and the children, when they have learnt their letters and are getting to understand the written word as before they did only the spoken, are furnished with works of good poets to read as they sit in class, and are made to learn them off by heart : here they meet with many admonitions, many descriptions and praises and eulogies of good men in times past, that the boy in envy may imitate them and yearn to become even as they. Then also the music-masters, in a similar

ἐπιμελοῦνται καὶ ὅπως ἂν οἱ νέοι μηδὲν κακουρ-
γῶσι· πρὸς δὲ τούτοις, ἐπειδὰν κιθαρίζειν μάθωσιν, ἄλλων αὖ ποιητῶν ἀγαθῶν ποιήματα
B διδάσκουσι μελοποιῶν, εἰς τὰ κιθαρίσματα ἐν-
τείνοντες, καὶ τοὺς ῥυθμούς τε καὶ τὰς ἁρμονίας
ἀναγκάζουσιν οἰκειοῦσθαι ταῖς ψυχαῖς τῶν παίδων,
ἵνα ἡμερώτεροί τε ὦσι, καὶ εὐρυθμότεροι καὶ
εὐαρμοστότεροι γιγνόμενοι χρήσιμοι ὦσιν εἰς τὸ
λέγειν τε καὶ πράττειν· πᾶς γὰρ ὁ βίος τοῦ ἀνθρώπου εὐρυθμίας τε καὶ εὐαρμοστίας δεῖται. ἔτι
τοίνυν πρὸς τούτοις εἰς παιδοτρίβου πέμπουσιν,
ἵνα τὰ σώματα βελτίω ἔχοντες ὑπηρετῶσι τῇ
C διανοίᾳ χρηστῇ οὔσῃ, καὶ μὴ ἀναγκάζωνται
ἀποδειλιᾶν διὰ τὴν πονηρίαν τῶν σωμάτων καὶ
ἐν τοῖς πολέμοις καὶ ἐν ταῖς ἄλλαις πράξεσι·
καὶ ταῦτα ποιοῦσιν οἱ μάλιστα δυνάμενοι· μάλιστα
δὲ δύνανται οἱ πλουσιώτατοι· καὶ οἱ τούτων υἱεῖς,
πρωιαίτατα εἰς διδασκάλων τῆς ἡλικίας ἀρξάμενοι
φοιτᾶν, ὀψιαίτατα ἀπαλλάττονται. ἐπειδὰν δὲ ἐκ
διδασκάλων ἀπαλλαγῶσιν, ἡ πόλις αὖ τούς τε
νόμους ἀναγκάζει μανθάνειν καὶ κατὰ τούτους ζῆν
D καθάπερ[1] παράδειγμα, ἵνα μὴ αὐτοὶ ἐφ᾽ αὑτῶν
εἰκῇ πράττωσιν, ἀλλ᾽ ἀτεχνῶς ὥσπερ οἱ γραμμα-
τισταὶ τοῖς μήπω δεινοῖς γράφειν τῶν παίδων
ὑπογράψαντες γραμμὰς τῇ γραφίδι οὕτω τὸ
γραμματεῖον διδόασι καὶ ἀναγκάζουσι γράφειν
κατὰ τὴν ὑφήγησιν τῶν γραμμῶν, ὣς δὲ καὶ
ἡ πόλις νόμους ὑπογράψασα, ἀγαθῶν καὶ παλαιῶν
νομοθετῶν εὑρήματα, κατὰ τούτους ἀναγκάζει
καὶ ἄρχειν καὶ ἄρχεσθαι· ὃς δ᾽ ἂν ἐκτὸς βαίνῃ
τούτων, κολάζει, καὶ ὄνομα τῇ κολάσει ταύτῃ

---

[1] καθάπερ Heindorf: κατὰ MSS.

sort, take pains for their self-restraint, and see that
their young charges do not go wrong : moreover,
when they learn to play the harp, they are taught
the works of another set of good poets, the song-
makers, while the master accompanies them on the
harp ; and they insist on familiarizing the boys' souls
with the rhythms and scales, that they may gain in
gentleness, and by advancing in rhythmic and har-
monic grace may be efficient in speech and action ;
for the whole of man's life requires the graces of
rhythm and harmony. Again, over and above
all this, people send their sons to a trainer, that
having improved their bodies they may perform
the orders of their minds, which are now in
fit condition, and that they may not be forced by
bodily faults to play the coward in wars and other
duties. This is what people do, who are most able ;
and the most able are the wealthiest. Their sons
begin school at the earliest age, and are freed from
it at the latest. And when they are released from
their schooling the city next compels them to learn
the laws and to live according to them as after a
pattern, that their conduct may not be swayed by
their own light fancies, but just as writing-masters
first draw letters in faint outline with the pen for
their less advanced pupils, and then give them the
copy-book and make them write according to the
guidance of their lines, so the city sketches out for
them the laws devised by good lawgivers of yore, and
constrains them to govern and be governed according
to these. She punishes anyone who steps outside
these borders, and this punishment among you and

E καὶ παρ᾽ ὑμῖν καὶ ἄλλοθι πολλαχοῦ, ὡς εὐθυ-
νούσης τῆς δίκης, εὐθῦναι. τοσαύτης οὖν τῆς
ἐπιμελείας οὔσης περὶ ἀρετῆς ἰδίᾳ καὶ δημοσίᾳ,
θαυμάζεις, ὦ Σώκρατες, καὶ ἀπορεῖς, εἰ διδακτόν
ἐστιν ἀρετή; ἀλλ᾽ οὐ χρὴ θαυμάζειν, ἀλλὰ πολὺ
μᾶλλον, εἰ μὴ διδακτόν.

Διὰ τί οὖν τῶν ἀγαθῶν πατέρων πολλοὶ υἱεῖς
φαῦλοι γίγνονται; τοῦτο αὖ μάθε· οὐδὲν γὰρ
θαυμαστόν, εἴπερ ἀληθῆ ἐγὼ ἐν τοῖς ἔμπροσθεν
ἔλεγον, ὅτι τούτου τοῦ πράγματος, τῆς ἀρετῆς,
327 εἰ μέλλει πόλις εἶναι, οὐδένα δεῖ ἰδιωτεύειν.
εἰ γὰρ δὴ ὃ λέγω οὕτως ἔχει—ἔχει δὲ μάλιστα
πάντων οὕτως—ἐνθυμήθητι ἄλλο τῶν ἐπιτηδευμάτων ὁτιοῦν καὶ μαθημάτων προελόμενος. εἰ μὴ
οἷόν τ᾽ ἦν πόλιν εἶναι, εἰ μὴ πάντες αὐληταὶ ἦμεν,
ὁποῖός τις ἐδύνατο ἕκαστος, καὶ τοῦτο καὶ ἰδίᾳ
καὶ δημοσίᾳ πᾶς πάντα καὶ ἐδίδασκε καὶ ἐπέ-
πληττε τὸν μὴ καλῶς αὐλοῦντα, καὶ μὴ ἐφθόνει
τούτου, ὥσπερ νῦν τῶν δικαίων καὶ τῶν νομίμων
B οὐδεὶς φθονεῖ οὐδ᾽ ἀποκρύπτεται ὥσπερ τῶν
ἄλλων τεχνημάτων· λυσιτελεῖ γάρ, οἶμαι, ἡμῖν
ἡ ἀλλήλων δικαιοσύνη καὶ ἀρετή· διὰ ταῦτα πᾶς
παντὶ προθύμως λέγει καὶ διδάσκει καὶ τὰ δίκαια
καὶ τὰ νόμιμα· εἰ οὖν οὕτω καὶ ἐν αὐλήσει
πᾶσαν προθυμίαν καὶ ἀφθονίαν εἴχομεν ἀλλήλους
διδάσκειν, οἴει ἄν τι, ἔφη, μᾶλλον, ὦ Σώκρατες,
τῶν ἀγαθῶν αὐλητῶν ἀγαθοὺς αὐλητὰς τοὺς
υἱεῖς γίγνεσθαι ἢ τῶν φαύλων; οἶμαι μὲν οὔ,
C ἀλλὰ ὅτου ἔτυχεν ὁ υἱὸς εὐφυέστατος γενόμενος
εἰς αὔλησιν, οὗτος ἂν ἐλλόγιμος ηὐξήθη, ὅτου

in many other cities, from the corrective purpose of the prosecution, is called a Correction.[1] Seeing then that so much care is taken in the matter of both private and public virtue, do you wonder, Socrates, and make it a great difficulty, that virtue may be taught? Surely there is no reason to wonder at that: you would have far greater reason, if it were not so.

Then why is it that many sons of good fathers turn out so meanly? Let me explain this also: it is no wonder, granted that I was right in stating just now that no one, if we are to have a city, must be a mere layman in this affair of virtue. For if what I say is the case—and it is supremely true—reflect on the nature of any other pursuit or study that you choose to mention. Suppose that there could be no state unless we were all flute-players, in such sort as each was able, and suppose that everyone were giving his neighbour both private and public lessons in the art, and rebuked him too, if he failed to do it well, without grudging him the trouble—even as no one now thinks of grudging or reserving his skill in what is just and lawful as he does in other expert knowledge; for our neighbours' justice and virtue, I take it, is to our advantage, and consequently we all tell and teach one another what is just and lawful—well, if we made the same zealous and ungrudging efforts to instruct each other in flute-playing, do you think, Socrates, that the good flute-players would be more likely than the bad to have sons who were good flute-players? I do not think they would: no, wherever the son had happened to be born with a nature most apt for flute-playing, he would be found to have

[1] The public inquiry to which a magistrate was liable after his term of office.

δὲ ἀφυής, ἀκλεής· καὶ πολλάκις μὲν ἀγαθοῦ
αὐλητοῦ φαῦλος ἂν ἀπέβη, πολλάκις δ᾽ ἂν φαύλου
ἀγαθός· ἀλλ᾽ οὖν αὐληταί γ᾽ ἂν[1] πάντες ἦσαν
ἱκανοὶ ὡς πρὸς τοὺς ἰδιώτας καὶ μηδὲν αὐλήσεως
ἐπαΐοντας. οὕτως οἴου καὶ νῦν, ὅστις σοι ἀδι-
κώτατος φαίνεται ἄνθρωπος τῶν ἐν νόμοις καὶ
ἀνθρώποις τεθραμμένων, δίκαιον αὐτὸν εἶναι καὶ

D δημιουργὸν τούτου τοῦ πράγματος, εἰ δέοι αὐτὸν
κρίνεσθαι πρὸς ἀνθρώπους, οἷς μήτε παιδεία
ἐστὶ μήτε δικαστήρια μήτε νόμοι μηδὲ ἀνάγκη
μηδεμία διὰ παντὸς ἀναγκάζουσα ἀρετῆς ἐπιμελεῖσθαι, ἀλλ᾽ εἶεν ἄγριοί τινες, οἷοίπερ οὓς πέρυσι
Φερεκράτης ὁ ποιητὴς ἐδίδαξεν ἐπὶ Ληναίῳ. ἦ
σφόδρα ἐν τοῖς τοιούτοις ἀνθρώποις γενόμενος,
ὥσπερ οἱ ἐν ἐκείνῳ τῷ χορῷ μισάνθρωποι, ἀγα-
πήσαις ἄν, εἰ ἐντύχοις Εὐρυβάτῳ καὶ Φρυνώνδᾳ,

E καὶ ἀνολοφύραι᾽ ἂν ποθῶν τὴν τῶν ἐνθάδε ἀνθρώπων
πονηρίαν· νῦν δὲ τρυφᾷς, ὦ Σώκρατες, διότι
πάντες διδάσκαλοί εἰσιν ἀρετῆς, καθ᾽ ὅσον δύνανται ἕκαστος, καὶ οὐδείς σοι φαίνεται· εἶθ᾽,
ὥσπερ ἂν εἰ ζητοῖς τίς διδάσκαλος τοῦ ἑλληνίζειν,

328 οὐδ᾽ ἂν εἷς φανείη, οὐδέ γ᾽ ἄν, οἶμαι, εἰ ζητοῖς
τίς ἂν ἡμῖν διδάξειε τοὺς τῶν χειροτεχνῶν υἱεῖς
αὐτὴν ταύτην τὴν τέχνην, ἣν δὴ παρὰ τοῦ πατρὸς
μεμαθήκασι, καθ᾽ ὅσον οἷός τ᾽ ἦν ὁ πατὴρ καὶ
οἱ τοῦ πατρὸς φίλοι ὄντες ὁμότεχνοι, τούτους ἔτι
τίς ἂν διδάξειεν, οὐ ῥᾴδιον οἶμαι εἶναι, ὦ Σώκρατες,
τούτων διδάσκαλον φανῆναι, τῶν δὲ ἀπείρων
παντάπασι ῥᾴδιον, οὕτω δὲ ἀρετῆς καὶ τῶν ἄλλων

---

[1] γ᾽ ἂν Shilleto : γοῦν MSS.

advanced to distinction, and where unapt, to obscurity. Often the son of a good player would turn out a bad one, and often of a bad, a good. But, at any rate, all would be capable players as compared with ordinary persons who had no inkling of the art. Likewise in the present case you must regard any man who appears to you the most unjust person ever reared among human laws and society as a just man and a craftsman of justice, if he had to stand comparison with people who lacked education and law courts and laws and any constant compulsion to the pursuit of virtue, but were a kind of wild folk such as Pherecrates the poet brought on the scene at last year's Lenaeum.[1] Sure enough, if you found yourself among such people, as did the misanthropes among his chorus, you would be very glad to meet with Eurybatus and Phrynondas,[2] and would bewail yourself with longing for the wickedness of the people here. Instead of that you give yourself dainty airs, Socrates, because everyone is a teacher of virtue to the extent of his powers, and you think there is no teacher. Why, you might as well ask who is a teacher of Greek; you would find none anywhere; and I suppose you might ask, who can teach the sons of our artisans the very crafts which of course they have learnt from their fathers, as far as the father was competent in each case, and his friends who followed the same trade,—I say if you asked who is to give these further instruction, I imagine it would be hard, Socrates, to find them a teacher, but easy enough in the case of those starting with no skill at all. And so it must be with virtue and everything else; if

[1] A dramatic festival, chiefly for comedies, held about the end of January. [2] Two notorious rogues.

πάντων· ἀλλὰ κἂν εἰ ὀλίγον ἔστι τις ὅστις δια-
B φέρει ἡμῶν προβιβάσαι εἰς ἀρετήν, ἀγαπητόν.
ὧν δὴ ἐγὼ οἶμαι εἷς εἶναι, καὶ διαφερόντως ἂν
τῶν ἄλλων ἀνθρώπων ὀνῆσαί[1] τινα πρὸς τὸ καλὸν
καὶ ἀγαθὸν γενέσθαι, καὶ ἀξίως τοῦ μισθοῦ ὃν
πράττομαι, καὶ ἔτι πλείονος, ὥστε καὶ αὐτῷ
δοκεῖν τῷ μαθόντι. διὰ ταῦτα καὶ τὸν τρόπον
τῆς πράξεως τοῦ μισθοῦ τοιοῦτον πεποίημαι·
ἐπειδὰν γάρ τις παρ' ἐμοῦ μάθῃ, ἐὰν μὲν βούληται,
ἀποδέδωκεν ὃ ἐγὼ πράττομαι ἀργύριον· ἐὰν δὲ
C μή, ἐλθὼν εἰς ἱερόν, ὀμόσας, ὅσου ἂν φῇ ἄξια
εἶναι τὰ μαθήματα, τοσοῦτον κατέθηκεν. τοιοῦτόν σοι, ἔφη, ὦ Σώκρατες, ἐγὼ καὶ μῦθον καὶ
λόγον εἴρηκα, ὡς διδακτὸν ἀρετὴ καὶ Ἀθηναῖοι
οὕτως ἡγοῦνται, καὶ ὅτι οὐδὲν θαυμαστὸν τῶν
ἀγαθῶν πατέρων φαύλους υἱεῖς γίγνεσθαι καὶ
τῶν φαύλων ἀγαθούς, ἐπεὶ καὶ οἱ Πολυκλείτου
υἱεῖς, Παράλου καὶ Ξανθίππου τοῦδε ἡλικιῶται,
οὐδὲν πρὸς τὸν πατέρα εἰσί, καὶ ἄλλοι ἄλλων
δημιουργῶν. τῶνδε δὲ οὔπω ἄξιον τοῦτο κατη-
D γορεῖν· ἔτι γὰρ ἐν αὐτοῖς εἰσιν ἐλπίδες· νέοι
γάρ.

Πρωταγόρας μὲν τοσαῦτα καὶ τοιαῦτα ἐπι-
δειξάμενος ἀπεπαύσατο τοῦ λόγου. καὶ ἐγὼ
ἐπὶ μὲν πολὺν χρόνον κεκηλημένος ἔτι πρὸς αὐτὸν
ἔβλεπον ὡς ἐροῦντά τι, ἐπιθυμῶν ἀκούειν· ἐπεὶ
δὲ δὴ ᾐσθόμην ὅτι τῷ ὄντι πεπαυμένος εἴη, μόγις
πως ἐμαυτὸν ὡσπερεὶ συναγείρας εἶπον, βλέψας
πρὸς τὸν Ἱπποκράτη· Ὦ παῖ Ἀπολλοδώρου,
ὡς χάριν σοι ἔχω ὅτι προύτρεψάς με ὧδε ἀφικέσθαι·
E πολλοῦ γὰρ ποιοῦμαι ἀκηκοέναι ἃ ἀκήκοα Πρωτ-

[1] ὀνῆσαι Dobree : νοῆσαι MSS.

there is somebody who excels us ever so little in
showing the way to virtue, we must be thankful.
Such an one I take myself to be, excelling all other
men in the gift of assisting people to become good
and true, and giving full value for the fee that I
charge—nay, so much more than full, that the learner
himself admits it. For this reason I have arranged
my charges on a particular plan : when anyone has
had lessons from me, if he likes he pays the sum that
I ask ; if not, he goes to a temple, states on oath the
value he sets on what he has learnt, and disburses
that amount. So now, Socrates, I have shown you
by both fable and argument that virtue is teachable
and is so deemed by the Athenians, and that it is no
wonder that bad sons are born of good fathers and
good of bad, since even the sons of Polycleitus, companions of Paralus and Xanthippus here, are not
to be compared with their father, and the same is
the case in other craftsmen's families. As for these
two, it is not fair to make this complaint of them yet ;
there is still hope in their case, for they are young.

After this great and fine performance Protagoras
ceased from speaking. As for me, for a good while I
was still under his spell and kept on looking at him
as though he were going to say more, such was my
eagerness to hear :[1] but when I perceived that he
had really come to a stop, I pulled myself together,
as it were, with an effort, and looking at Hippocrates
I said : Son of Apollodorus, I am very grateful to
you for inducing me to come hither ; for it is a great
treat to have heard what I have heard from Prot-

[1] Or in Milton's version, *Par. Lost*, viii. 1–3 :

in [my] eare
So charming left his voice, that [I] the while
Thought him still speaking, still stood fixt to hear.

αγόρου. ἐγὼ γὰρ ἐν μὲν τῷ ἔμπροσθεν χρόνῳ
ἡγούμην οὐκ εἶναι ἀνθρωπίνην ἐπιμέλειαν, ᾗ ἀγαθοὶ οἱ ἀγαθοὶ γίγνονται· νῦν δὲ πέπεισμαι. πλὴν
σμικρόν τί μοι ἐμποδών, ὃ δῆλον ὅτι Πρωταγόρας
ῥᾳδίως ἐπεκδιδάξει, ἐπειδὴ καὶ τὰ πολλὰ ταῦτα
ἐξεδίδαξε. καὶ γὰρ εἰ μέν τις περὶ αὐτῶν τούτων
329 συγγένοιτο ὁτῳοῦν τῶν δημηγόρων, τάχ' ἂν καὶ
τοιούτους λόγους ἀκούσειεν ἢ Περικλέους ἢ
ἄλλου τινὸς τῶν ἱκανῶν εἰπεῖν· εἰ δὲ ἐπανέροιτό
τινά τι, ὥσπερ βιβλία οὐδὲν ἔχουσιν οὔτε ἀποκρίνασθαι οὔτε αὐτοὶ ἐρέσθαι, ἀλλ' ἐάν τις καὶ σμικρὸν
ἐπερωτήσῃ τι τῶν ῥηθέντων, ὥσπερ τὰ χαλκία[1]
πληγέντα μακρὸν ἠχεῖ καὶ ἀποτείνει, ἐὰν μὴ
ἐπιλάβηταί τις, καὶ οἱ ῥήτορες οὕτω σμικρὰ
B ἐρωτηθέντες δόλιχον κατατείνουσι τοῦ λόγου.
Πρωταγόρας δὲ ὅδε ἱκανὸς μὲν μακροὺς λόγους
καὶ καλοὺς εἰπεῖν, ὡς αὐτὰ δηλοῖ, ἱκανὸς δὲ
καὶ ἐρωτηθεὶς ἀποκρίνασθαι κατὰ βραχὺ καὶ
ἐρόμενος περιμεῖναί τε καὶ ἀποδέξασθαι τὴν
ἀπόκρισιν, ἃ ὀλίγοις ἐστὶ παρεσκευασμένα. νῦν
οὖν, ὦ Πρωταγόρα, σμικροῦ τινὸς ἐνδεής εἰμι
πάντ' ἔχειν, εἴ μοι ἀποκρίναιο τόδε. τὴν ἀρετὴν
φῂς διδακτὸν εἶναι, καὶ ἐγὼ εἴπερ ἄλλῳ τῳ
ἀνθρώπων πειθοίμην ἄν, καὶ σοὶ πείθομαι· ὃ
C δ' ἐθαύμασά σου λέγοντος, τοῦτό μοι ἐν τῇ ψυχῇ
ἀποπλήρωσον. ἔλεγες γὰρ ὅτι ὁ Ζεὺς τὴν
δικαιοσύνην καὶ τὴν αἰδῶ πέμψειε τοῖς ἀνθρώποις,
καὶ αὖ πολλαχοῦ ἐν τοῖς λόγοις ἐλέγετο ὑπὸ σοῦ
ἡ δικαιοσύνη καὶ σωφροσύνη καὶ ὁσιότης καὶ

---

[1] χαλκία Cobet: χαλκεῖα mss.

agoras. I used formerly to think that there was no
human treatment by which the good were made good,
but now I am convinced that there is. Only I find
one slight difficulty, which Protagoras will of course
easily explain away, since he has explained so many
puzzles already. If one should be present when any
of the public speakers were dealing with these same
subjects, one could probably hear similar discourses
from Pericles or some other able speaker : but
suppose you put a question to one of them—they
are just like books, incapable of either answering you
or putting a question of their own ; if you question
even a small point in what has been said, just as
brazen vessels ring a long time after they have been
struck and prolong the note unless you put your hand
on them, these orators too, on being asked a little
question, extend their speech over a full-length
course.[1] But Protagoras here, while able to deliver,
as events have shown, a long and excellent speech,
is also able when questioned to reply briefly, and
after asking a question to await and accept the
answer—accomplishments that few can claim. And
now, Protagoras, there is one little thing wanting to
the completeness of what I have got, so please
answer me this. You say that virtue may be taught,
and if there is anybody in the world who could
convince me, you are the man : but there was a
point in your speech at which I wondered, and on
which my spirit would fain be satisfied. You said
that Zeus had sent justice and respect to mankind,
and furthermore it was frequently stated in your
discourse that justice, temperance, holiness and the

---

[1] The metaphor is of a long-distance race of about 2¾
miles.

πάντα ταῦτα ὡς ἕν τι εἴη συλλήβδην, ἀρετή·
ταῦτ' οὖν αὐτὰ δίελθέ μοι ἀκριβῶς τῷ λόγῳ,
πότερον ἓν μέν τί ἐστιν ἡ ἀρετή, μόρια δὲ αὐτῆς
ἐστὶν ἡ δικαιοσύνη καὶ σωφροσύνη καὶ ὁσιότης,
D ἢ ταῦτ' ἐστὶν ἃ νῦν δὴ ἐγὼ ἔλεγον πάντα ὀνόματα
τοῦ αὐτοῦ ἑνὸς ὄντος· τοῦτ' ἐστὶν ὃ ἔτι ἐπιποθῶ.

Ἀλλὰ ῥᾴδιον τοῦτό γ', ἔφη, ὦ Σώκρατες,
ἀποκρίνασθαι, ὅτι ἑνὸς ὄντος τῆς ἀρετῆς μόριά
ἐστιν ἃ ἐρωτᾷς. Πότερον, ἔφην, ὥσπερ προσώπου τὰ μόρια μόριά ἐστι, στόμα τε καὶ ῥὶς καὶ
ὀφθαλμοὶ καὶ ὦτα, ἢ ὥσπερ τὰ τοῦ χρυσοῦ μόρια
οὐδὲν διαφέρει τὰ ἕτερα τῶν ἑτέρων, ἀλλήλων
καὶ τοῦ ὅλου, ἀλλ' ἢ μεγέθει καὶ σμικρότητι;
Ἐκείνως μοι φαίνεται, ὦ Σώκρατες, ὥσπερ τὰ
E τοῦ προσώπου μόρια ἔχει πρὸς τὸ ὅλον πρόσωπον.
Πότερον οὖν, ἦν δ' ἐγώ, καὶ μεταλαμβάνουσιν
οἱ ἄνθρωποι τούτων τῶν τῆς ἀρετῆς μορίων οἱ
μὲν ἄλλο, οἱ δὲ ἄλλο, ἢ ἀνάγκη, ἐάνπερ τις ἓν
λάβῃ, ἅπαντ' ἔχειν; Οὐδαμῶς, ἔφη, ἐπεὶ πολλοὶ
ἀνδρεῖοί εἰσιν, ἄδικοι δέ, καὶ δίκαιοι αὖ, σοφοὶ
δὲ οὔ. Ἔστι γὰρ οὖν καὶ ταῦτα μόρια τῆς
330 ἀρετῆς, ἔφην ἐγώ, σοφία τε καὶ ἀνδρεία; Πάντων
μάλιστα δήπου, ἔφη· καὶ μέγιστόν γε ἡ σοφία
τῶν μορίων. Ἕκαστον δὲ αὐτῶν ἐστιν, ἦν δ' ἐγώ,
ἄλλο, τὸ δὲ ἄλλο; Ναί. Ἦ καὶ δύναμιν αὐτῶν
ἕκαστον ἰδίαν ἔχει; ὥσπερ τὰ τοῦ προσώπου,
οὐκ ἔστιν ὀφθαλμὸς οἷον τὰ ὦτα, οὐδ' ἡ δύναμις
αὐτοῦ ἡ αὐτή· οὐδὲ τῶν ἄλλων οὐδέν ἐστιν οἷον
τὸ ἕτερον οὔτε κατὰ τὴν δύναμιν οὔτε κατὰ τὰ
ἄλλα· ἆρ' οὖν οὕτω καὶ τὰ τῆς ἀρετῆς μόρια οὐκ

rest were all but one single thing, virtue : pray, now proceed to deal with these in more precise exposition, stating whether virtue is a single thing, of which justice and temperance and holiness are parts, or whether the qualities I have just mentioned are all names of the same single thing. This is what I am still hankering after.

Why, the answer to that is easy, Socrates, he replied : it is that virtue is a single thing and the qualities in question are parts of it.

Do you mean parts, I asked, in the sense of the parts of a face, as mouth, nose, eyes, and ears ; or, as in the parts of gold, is there no difference among the pieces, either between the parts or between a part and the whole, except in greatness and smallness ?

In the former sense, I think, Socrates ; as the parts of the face are to the whole face.

Well then, I continued, when men partake of these portions of virtue, do some have one, and some another, or if you get one, must you have them all ?

By no means, he replied, since many are brave but unjust, and many again are just but not wise.

Then are these also parts of virtue, I asked—wisdom and courage ?

Most certainly, I should say, he replied ; and of the parts, wisdom is the greatest.

Each of them, I proceeded, is distinct from any other ?

Yes.

Does each also have its particular function ? Just as, in the parts of the face, the eye is not like the ears, nor is its function the same ; nor is any of the other parts like another, in its function or in any other respect : in the same way, are the parts of

B ἔστι τὸ ἕτερον οἷον τὸ ἕτερον, οὔτε αὐτὸ οὔτε
ἡ δύναμις αὐτοῦ; ἢ δῆλα δὴ ὅτι οὕτως ἔχει,
εἴπερ τῷ παραδείγματί γε ἔοικεν; Ἀλλ᾿ οὕτως,
ἔφη, ἔχει, ὦ Σώκρατες. καὶ ἐγὼ εἶπον· Οὐδὲν
ἄρα ἐστὶ τῶν τῆς ἀρετῆς μορίων ἄλλο οἷον ἐπιστήμη, οὐδ᾿ οἷον δικαιοσύνη, οὐδ᾿ οἷον ἀνδρεία,
οὐδ᾿ οἷον σωφροσύνη, οὐδ᾿ οἷον ὁσιότης. Οὐκ
ἔφη. Φέρε δή, ἔφην ἐγώ, κοινῇ σκεψώμεθα
ποῖόν τι αὐτῶν ἐστὶν ἕκαστον. πρῶτον μὲν
C τὸ τοιόνδε· ἡ δικαιοσύνη πρᾶγμά τί ἐστιν ἢ
οὐδὲν πρᾶγμα; ἐμοὶ μὲν γὰρ δοκεῖ· τί δὲ σοί;
Καὶ ἐμοί, ἔφη. Τί οὖν; εἴ τις ἔροιτο ἐμέ τε
καὶ σέ· ὦ Πρωταγόρα τε καὶ Σώκρατες, εἴπετον
δή μοι, τοῦτο τὸ πρᾶγμα, ὃ ὠνομάσατε ἄρτι,
ἡ δικαιοσύνη, αὐτὸ τοῦτο δίκαιόν ἐστιν ἢ ἄδικον;
ἐγὼ μὲν ἂν αὐτῷ ἀποκριναίμην ὅτι δίκαιον· σὺ
δὲ τίν᾿ ἂν ψῆφον θεῖο; τὴν αὐτὴν ἐμοὶ ἢ ἄλλην;
Τὴν αὐτήν, ἔφη. Ἔστιν ἄρα τοιοῦτον ἡ δικαιο-
D σύνη οἷον δίκαιον εἶναι, φαίην ἂν ἔγωγε ἀποκρινόμενος τῷ ἐρωτῶντι· οὐκοῦν καὶ σύ; Ναί,
ἔφη. Εἰ οὖν μετὰ τοῦτο ἡμᾶς ἔροιτο· οὐκοῦν
καὶ ὁσιότητά τινά φατε εἶναι; φαῖμεν ἄν, ὡς
ἐγᾦμαι. Ναί, ἦ δ᾿ ὅς. Οὐκοῦν φατε καὶ
τοῦτο πρᾶγμά τι εἶναι; φαῖμεν ἄν· ἢ οὔ; Καὶ
τοῦτο συνέφη. Πότερον δὲ τοῦτο αὐτὸ τὸ πρᾶγμά φατε τοιοῦτον πεφυκέναι οἷον ἀνόσιον εἶναι
ἢ οἷον ὅσιον; ἀγανακτήσαιμ᾿ ἂν ἔγωγ᾿, ἔφην,
τῷ ἐρωτήματι, καὶ εἴποιμ᾿ ἄν· εὐφήμει, ὦ
E ἄνθρωπε· σχολῇ μέντ᾿ ἄν τι ἄλλο ὅσιον εἴη, εἰ

virtue unlike each other, both in themselves and in their functions? Are they not evidently so, if the analogy holds?

Yes, they are so, Socrates, he said.

So then, I went on, among the parts of virtue, no other part is like knowledge, or like justice, or like courage, or like temperance, or like holiness.

He agreed.

Come now, I said, let us consider together what sort of thing is each of these parts. First let us ask, is justice something, or not a thing at all? I think it is; what do you say?

So do I, he replied.

Well then, suppose someone should ask you and me: Protagoras and Socrates, pray tell me this—the thing you named just now, justice, is that itself just or unjust? I should reply, it is just: what would your verdict be? The same as mine or different?

The same, he said.

Then justice, I should say in reply to our questioner, is of a kind that is just: would you also?

Yes, he said.

Now suppose he proceeded to ask us: Do you also speak of a "holiness"? We should say we do, I fancy.

Yes, he said.

Then do you call this a thing also? We should say we do, should we not?

He assented again.

Do you say this thing itself is of such nature as to be unholy, or holy? For my part I should be annoyed at this question, I said, and should answer: Hush, my good sir! It is hard to see how anything

157

μὴ αὐτή γε ἡ ὁσιότης ὅσιον ἔσται. τί δὲ σύ; οὐχ
οὕτως ἂν ἀποκρίναιο; Πάνυ μὲν οὖν, ἔφη.

Εἰ οὖν μετὰ τοῦτ' εἴποι ἐρωτῶν ἡμᾶς· πῶς
οὖν ὀλίγον πρότερον ἐλέγετε; ἆρ' οὐκ ὀρθῶς
ὑμῶν κατήκουσα; ἐδόξατέ μοι φάναι τὰ τῆς
ἀρετῆς μόρια εἶναι οὕτως ἔχοντα πρὸς ἄλληλα,
ὡς οὐκ εἶναι τὸ ἕτερον αὐτῶν οἷον τὸ ἕτερον·
εἴποιμ' ἂν ἔγωγε ὅτι τὰ μὲν ἄλλα ὀρθῶς ἤκουσας,
ὅτι δὲ καὶ ἐμὲ οἴει εἰπεῖν τοῦτο, παρήκουσας·
331 Πρωταγόρας γὰρ ὅδε ταῦτα ἀπεκρίνατο, ἐγὼ
δὲ ἠρώτων. εἰ οὖν εἴποι· ἀληθῆ ὅδε λέγει, ὦ
Πρωταγόρα; σὺ φῂς οὐκ εἶναι τὸ ἕτερον μόριον
οἷον τὸ ἕτερον τῶν τῆς ἀρετῆς; σὸς οὗτος ὁ
λόγος ἐστί; τί ἂν αὐτῷ ἀποκρίναιο; Ἀνάγκη,
ἔφη, ὦ Σώκρατες, ὁμολογεῖν. Τί οὖν, ὦ Πρωταγόρα, ἀποκρινούμεθα αὐτῷ, ταῦτα ὁμολογή-
σαντες, ἐὰν ἡμᾶς ἐπανέρηται· οὐκ ἄρα ἐστὶν
ὁσιότης οἷον δίκαιον εἶναι πρᾶγμα, οὐδὲ δικαιοσύνη οἷον ὅσιον, ἀλλ' οἷον μὴ ὅσιον· ἡ δ' ὁσιότης
οἷον μὴ δίκαιον, ἀλλ' ἄδικον ἄρα, τὸ δὲ ἀνόσιον;
B τί αὐτῷ ἀποκρινούμεθα; ἐγὼ μὲν γὰρ αὐτὸς
ὑπέρ γε ἐμαυτοῦ φαίην ἂν καὶ τὴν δικαιοσύνην
ὅσιον εἶναι καὶ τὴν ὁσιότητα δίκαιον· καὶ ὑπὲρ
σοῦ δέ, εἴ με ἐῴης, ταὐτὰ ἂν ταῦτα ἀποκρινοίμην,
ὅτι ἤτοι ταὐτόν γ' ἐστι δικαιότης ὁσιότητι ἢ ὅτι
ὁμοιότατον, καὶ μάλιστα πάντων ἥ τε δικαιοσύνη
οἷον ὁσιότης καὶ ἡ ὁσιότης οἷον δικαιοσύνη.
ἀλλ' ὅρα, εἰ διακωλύεις ἀποκρίνεσθαι, ἢ καὶ σοὶ
συνδοκεῖ οὕτως. Οὐ πάνυ μοι δοκεῖ, ἔφη, ὦ
C Σώκρατες, οὕτως ἁπλοῦν εἶναι, ὥστε συγχω-
ρῆσαι τήν τε δικαιοσύνην ὅσιον εἶναι καὶ τὴν

could be holy, if holiness itself is not to be holy!
And you—would you not make the same reply?

Certainly I would, he said.

Now suppose he went on to ask us: Well, and
what of your statement a little while since? Perhaps
I did not hear you aright, but I understood you two
to say that the parts of virtue are in such a relation
to each other that one of them is not like another.
Here my answer would be: As to the substance of
it, you heard aright, but you made a mistake in
thinking that I had any share in that statement. It
was Protagoras here who made that answer; I was
only the questioner. Then suppose he were to ask:
Is our friend telling the truth, Protagoras? Is it
you who say that one part of virtue is not like another? Is this statement yours? What answer
would you give him?

I must needs admit it, Socrates, he said.

Well now, Protagoras, after that admission, what
answer shall we give him, if he goes on to ask this
question: Is not holiness something of such nature
as to be just, and justice such as to be holy, or can
it be unholy? Can holiness be not just, and therefore
unjust, and justice unholy? What is to be our
reply? I should say myself, on my own behalf, that
both justice is holy and holiness just, and with your
permission I would make this same reply for you
also; since justness is either the same thing as
holiness or extremely like it, and above all, justice is
of the same kind as holiness, and holiness as justice.
Are you minded to forbid this answer, or are you in
agreement with it?

I do not take quite so simple a view of it, Socrates,
as to grant that justice is holy and holiness just. I

ὁσιότητα δίκαιον, ἀλλά τί μοι δοκεῖ ἐν αὐτῷ
διάφορον εἶναι. ἀλλὰ τί τοῦτο διαφέρει; ἔφη·
εἰ γὰρ βούλει, ἔστω ἡμῖν καὶ δικαιοσύνη ὅσιον
καὶ ὁσιότης δίκαιον. Μή μοι, ἦν δ' ἐγώ· οὐδὲν
γὰρ δέομαι τὸ εἰ βούλει τοῦτο καὶ εἴ σοι δοκεῖ
ἐλέγχεσθαι, ἀλλ' ἐμέ τε καὶ σέ· τὸ δ' ἐμέ τε καὶ
σέ τοῦτο λέγω, οἰόμενος οὕτω τὸν λόγον βέλτιστ'
D ἂν ἐλέγχεσθαι, εἴ τις τὸ εἴ ἀφέλοι αὐτοῦ. Ἀλλὰ
μέντοι, ἦ δ' ὅς, προσέοικέ τι δικαιοσύνη ὁσιότητι·
καὶ γὰρ ὁτιοῦν ὁτῳοῦν ἀμῇ γέ πῃ προσέοικε.
τὸ γὰρ λευκὸν τῷ μέλανι ἔστιν ὅπῃ προσέοικε,
καὶ τὸ σκληρὸν τῷ μαλακῷ, καὶ τἆλλα ἃ δοκεῖ
ἐναντιώτατα εἶναι ἀλλήλοις· καὶ ἃ τότε ἔφαμεν
ἄλλην δύναμιν ἔχειν καὶ οὐκ εἶναι τὸ ἕτερον οἷον
τὸ ἕτερον, τὰ τοῦ προσώπου μόρια, ἀμῇ γέ πῃ
προσέοικε καὶ ἔστι τὸ ἕτερον οἷον τὸ ἕτερον·
ὥστε τούτῳ γε τῷ τρόπῳ κἂν ταῦτα ἐλέγχοις,
E εἰ βούλοιο, ὡς ἅπαντά ἐστιν ὅμοια ἀλλήλοις.
ἀλλ' οὐχὶ τὰ ὅμοιόν τι ἔχοντα ὅμοια δίκαιον
καλεῖν, οὐδὲ τὰ ἀνόμοιόν τι ἔχοντα ἀνόμοια, κἂν
πάνυ σμικρὸν ἔχῃ τὸ ὅμοιον. καὶ ἐγὼ θαυμάσας
εἶπον πρὸς αὐτόν, Ἦ γὰρ οὕτω σοι τὸ δίκαιον
καὶ τὸ ὅσιον πρὸς ἄλληλα ἔχει, ὥστε ὅμοιόν τι
σμικρὸν ἔχειν ἀλλήλοις; Οὐ πάνυ, ἔφη, οὕτως,
332 οὐ μέντοι οὐδὲ αὖ ὡς σύ μοι δοκεῖς οἴεσθαι.
Ἀλλὰ μήν, ἔφην ἐγώ, ἐπειδὴ δυσχερῶς δοκεῖς
μοι ἔχειν πρὸς τοῦτο, τοῦτο μὲν ἐάσωμεν, τόδε
δὲ ἄλλο ὧν ἔλεγες ἐπισκεψώμεθα.

Ἀφροσύνην τι καλεῖς; Ἔφη. Τούτῳ τῷ
πράγματι οὐ πᾶν τοὐναντίον ἐστὶν ἡ σοφία;

think we have to make a distinction here. Yet what difference does it make ? he said : if you like, let us assume that justice is holy and holiness just.

No, no, I said ; I do not want this " if you like " or " if you agree " sort of thing[1] to be put to the proof, but you and me together ; and when I say " you and me " I mean that our statement will be most properly tested if we take away the " if."

Well, at any rate, he said, justice has some resemblance to holiness ; for anything in the world has some sort of resemblance to any other thing. Thus there is a point in which white resembles black, and hard soft, and so with all the other things which are regarded as most opposed to each other ; and the things which we spoke of before as having different faculties and not being of the same kind as each other—the parts of the face—these in some sense resemble one another and are of like sort. In this way therefore you could prove, if you chose, that even these things are all like one another. But it is not fair to describe things as like which have some point alike, however small, or as unlike that have some point unlike.

This surprised me, and I said to him : What, do you regard just and holy as so related to each other that they have only some small point of likeness ?

Not so, he replied, at all, nor yet, on the other hand, as I believe you regard them.

Well then, I said, since I find you chafe at this suggestion, we will let it pass, and consider another instance that you gave. Is there a thing you call folly ?

Yes, he said.

Is not the direct opposite to that thing wisdom ?

[1] *Cf.* below, 333 c.

Ἔμοιγε δοκεῖ, ἔφη. Πότερον δὲ ὅταν πράττωσιν ἄνθρωποι ὀρθῶς τε καὶ ὠφελίμως, τότε
σωφρονεῖν σοι δοκοῦσιν οὕτω πράττοντες, ἢ
[εἰ] τοὐναντίον [ἔπραττον]¹; Σωφρονεῖν, ἔφη.
B Οὐκοῦν σωφροσύνῃ σωφρονοῦσιν; Ἀνάγκη. Οὐκοῦν οἱ μὴ ὀρθῶς πράττοντες ἀφρόνως πράττουσι
καὶ οὐ σωφρονοῦσιν οὕτω πράττοντες; Συνδοκεῖ
μοι, ἔφη. Τοὐναντίον ἄρα ἐστὶ τὸ ἀφρόνως
πράττειν τῷ σωφρόνως; Ἔφη. Οὐκοῦν τὰ
μὲν ἀφρόνως πραττόμενα ἀφροσύνῃ πράττεται,
τὰ δὲ σωφρόνως σωφροσύνῃ; Ὡμολόγει. Οὐκοῦν εἴ τι ἰσχύι πράττεται, ἰσχυρῶς πράττεται,
καὶ εἴ τι ἀσθενείᾳ, ἀσθενῶς; Ἐδόκει. Καὶ εἴ
τι μετὰ τάχους, ταχέως, καὶ εἴ τι μετὰ βραδυτῆτος,
C βραδέως; Ἔφη. Καὶ εἴ τι δὴ ὡσαύτως πράττεται, ὑπὸ τοῦ αὐτοῦ πράττεται, καὶ εἴ τι ἐναντίως, ὑπὸ τοῦ ἐναντίου; Συνέφη. Φέρε δή, ἦν
δ' ἐγώ, ἔστι τι καλόν; Συνεχώρει. Τούτῳ
ἔστι τι ἐναντίον πλὴν τὸ αἰσχρόν; Οὐκ ἔστιν.
Τί δέ; ἔστι τι ἀγαθόν; Ἔστιν. Τούτῳ ἔστι

¹ εἰ et ἔπραττον secl. Stallbaum.

I think so, he said.

And when men behave rightly and usefully, do you consider them temperate in so behaving, or the opposite?

Temperate, he said.

Then is it by temperance that they are temperate?

Necessarily.

Now those who do not behave rightly behave foolishly, and are not temperate in so behaving?

I agree, he said.

And behaving foolishly is the opposite to behaving temperately?

Yes, he said.

Now foolish behaviour is due to folly, and temperate behaviour to temperance?

He assented.

And whatever is done by strength is done strongly, and whatever by weakness, weakly?

He agreed.

And whatever with swiftness, swiftly, and whatever with slowness, slowly?

Yes, he said.

And so whatever is done in a certain way is done by that kind of faculty, and whatever in an opposite way, by the opposite kind?

He agreed.

Pray now, I proceeded, is there such a thing as the beautiful?

He granted it.

Has this any opposite except the ugly?

None.

Well, is there such a thing as the good?

There is.

Has it any opposite but the evil?

τι ἐναντίον πλὴν τὸ κακόν; Οὐκ ἔστιν. Τί δέ;
ἔστι τι ὀξὺ ἐν φωνῇ; Ἔφη. Τούτῳ μὴ ἔστι
τι ἐναντίον ἄλλο πλὴν τὸ βαρύ; Οὐκ ἔφη. Οὐκοῦν, ἦν δ' ἐγώ, ἑνὶ ἑκάστῳ τῶν ἐναντίων ἓν
D μόνον ἐστὶν ἐναντίον καὶ οὐ πολλά; Συνωμολόγει.
Ἴθι δή, ἦν δ' ἐγώ, ἀναλογισώμεθα τὰ ὡμολογημένα ἡμῖν. ὡμολογήκαμεν ἓν ἑνὶ μόνον ἐναντίον εἶναι, πλείω δὲ μή; Ὡμολογήκαμεν. Τὸ
δὲ ἐναντίως πραττόμενον ὑπὸ ἐναντίων πράττεσθαι;
Ἔφη. Ὡμολογήκαμεν δὲ ἐναντίως πράττεσθαι
ὃ ἂν ἀφρόνως πράττηται τῷ σωφρόνως πραττο-
μένῳ; Ἔφη. Τὸ δὲ σωφρόνως πραττόμενον
ὑπὸ σωφροσύνης πράττεσθαι, τὸ δὲ ἀφρόνως
E ὑπὸ ἀφροσύνης; Συνεχώρει. Οὐκοῦν εἴπερ ἐναντίως πράττεται, ὑπὸ ἐναντίου πράττοιτ' ἄν;
Ναί. Πράττεται δὲ τὸ μὲν ὑπὸ σωφροσύνης,
τὸ δὲ ὑπὸ ἀφροσύνης; Ναί. Ἐναντίως; Πάνυ
γε. Οὐκοῦν ὑπὸ ἐναντίων ὄντων; Ναί. Ἐναντίον ἄρ' ἐστὶν ἀφροσύνη σωφροσύνης; Φαίνεται.

None.

Tell me, is there such a thing as " shrill " in the voice ?

Yes, he said.

Has it any other opposite than " deep."

No, he said.

Now, I went on, each single opposite has but one opposite, not many ?

He admitted this.

Come now, I said, let us reckon up our points of agreement. We have agreed that one thing has but one opposite, and no more ?

We have.

And that what is done in an opposite way is done by opposites ?

Yes, he said.

And we have agreed that what is done foolishly is done in an opposite way to what is done temperately ?

Yes, he said.

And that what is done temperately is done by temperance, and what foolishly by folly ?

He assented.

Now if it is done in an opposite way, it must be done by an opposite ?

Yes ?

And one is done by temperance, and the other by folly ?

Yes.

In an opposite way ?

Certainly.

And by opposite faculties ?

Yes.

Then folly is opposite to temperance ?

Apparently.

Μέμνησαι οὖν ὅτι ἐν τοῖς ἔμπροσθεν ὡμολόγηται
ἡμῖν ἀφροσύνη σοφίᾳ ἐναντίον εἶναι; Συνωμολόγει. Ἓν δὲ ἑνὶ μόνον ἐναντίον εἶναι; Φημί.
333 Πότερον οὖν, ὦ Πρωταγόρα, λύσωμεν τῶν λόγων;
τὸ ἓν ἑνὶ μόνον ἐναντίον εἶναι, ἢ ἐκεῖνον ἐν ᾧ
ἐλέγετο ἕτερον εἶναι σωφροσύνης σοφία, μόριον
δὲ ἑκάτερον ἀρετῆς, καὶ πρὸς τῷ ἕτερον εἶναι
καὶ ἀνόμοια καὶ αὐτὰ καὶ αἱ δυνάμεις αὐτῶν,
ὥσπερ τὰ τοῦ προσώπου μόρια; πότερον οὖν
δὴ λύσωμεν; οὗτοι γὰρ οἱ λόγοι ἀμφότεροι οὐ
πάνυ μουσικῶς λέγονται· οὐ γὰρ συνᾴδουσιν
οὐδὲ συναρμόττουσιν ἀλλήλοις. πῶς γὰρ ἂν
B συνᾴδοιεν, εἴπερ γε ἀνάγκη ἑνὶ μὲν ἓν μόνον
ἐναντίον εἶναι, πλείοσιν δὲ μή, τῇ δὲ ἀφροσύνῃ
ἑνὶ ὄντι σοφία ἐναντία καὶ σωφροσύνη αὖ φαίνεται·
ἢ γάρ, ὦ Πρωταγόρα, ἔφην ἐγώ, ἢ ἄλλως πως;
Ὡμολόγησε καὶ μάλ' ἀκόντως. Οὐκοῦν ἓν ἂν
εἴη ἡ σωφροσύνη καὶ ἡ σοφία; τὸ δὲ πρότερον
αὖ ἐφάνη ἡμῖν ἡ δικαιοσύνη καὶ ἡ ὁσιότης σχεδόν
τι ταὐτὸν ὄν. ἴθι δή, ἦν δ' ἐγώ, ὦ Πρωταγόρα,
μὴ ἀποκάμωμεν, ἀλλὰ καὶ τὰ λοιπὰ διασκε-
ψώμεθα. ἆρά τίς σοι δοκεῖ ἀδικῶν ἄνθρωπος
C σωφρονεῖν, ὅτι ἀδικεῖ; Αἰσχυνοίμην ἂν ἔγωγ',
ἔφη, ὦ Σώκρατες, τοῦτο ὁμολογεῖν, ἐπεὶ πολλοί
γέ φασι τῶν ἀνθρώπων. Πότερον οὖν πρὸς
ἐκείνους τὸν λόγον ποιήσομαι, ἔφην, ἢ πρὸς σέ;
Εἰ βούλει, ἔφη, πρὸς τοῦτον πρῶτον τὸν λόγον
διαλέχθητι τὸν τῶν πολλῶν. Ἀλλ' οὐδέν μοι
διαφέρει, ἐὰν μόνον σύ γε ἀποκρίνῃ, εἴτ' οὖν

Now do you recollect that in the previous stage we have agreed that folly is opposite to wisdom ?

He admitted this.

And that one thing has but one opposite ?

Yes.

Then which, Protagoras, of our propositions are we to reject—the statement that one thing has but one opposite ; or the other, that wisdom is different from temperance, and each is a part of virtue, and moreover, a different part, and that the two are as unlike, both in themselves and in their faculties, as the parts of the face ? Which are we to upset ? The two of them together are not quite in tune ; they do not chime in harmony. How could they, if one thing must needs have but one opposite and no more, while wisdom, and temperance likewise, appear both to be opposite to folly, which is a single thing ? Such is the position, Protagoras, I said ; or is it otherwise ?

He admitted it was so, much against his will.

Then temperance and wisdom must be one thing ? And indeed we found before that justice and holiness were almost the same thing. Come, Protagoras, I said, let us not falter, but carry out our inquiry to the end. Tell me, does a man who acts unjustly seem to you to be temperate in so acting ?

I should be ashamed, Socrates, he replied, to admit that, in spite of what many people say.

Then shall I address my argument to them, I asked, or to you ?

If you please, he answered, debate first against that popular theory.

It is all the same to me, I said, so long as you make answer, whether it be your own opinion or

167

δοκεῖ σοι ταῦτα, εἴτε μή. τὸν γὰρ λόγον ἔγωγε
μάλιστα ἐξετάζω, συμβαίνει μέντοι ἴσως καὶ
ἐμὲ τὸν ἐρωτῶντα καὶ τὸν ἀποκρινόμενον ἐξε-
τάζεσθαι.

D Τὸ μὲν οὖν πρῶτον ἐκαλλωπίζετο ἡμῖν ὁ Πρωτ-
αγόρας· τὸν γὰρ λόγον ᾐτιᾶτο δυσχερῆ εἶναι·
ἔπειτα μέντοι συνεχώρησεν ἀποκρίνεσθαι. Ἴθι
δή, ἔφην ἐγώ, ἐξ ἀρχῆς μοι ἀπόκριναι. δοκοῦσί
τινές σοι σωφρονεῖν ἀδικοῦντες; Ἔστω, ἔφη.
Τὸ δὲ σωφρονεῖν λέγεις εὖ φρονεῖν; Ἔφη. Τὸ
δ᾽ εὖ φρονεῖν εὖ βουλεύεσθαι, ὅτι ἀδικοῦσιν;
Ἔστω, ἔφη. Πότερον, ἦν δ᾽ ἐγώ, εἰ εὖ πράττουσιν ἀδικοῦντες ἢ εἰ κακῶς; Εἰ εὖ. Λέγεις
οὖν ἀγαθὰ ἄττα εἶναι; Λέγω. Ἆρ᾽ οὖν, ἦν
δ᾽ ἐγώ, ταῦτ᾽ ἐστὶν ἀγαθά, ἅ ἐστιν ὠφέλιμα τοῖς
E ἀνθρώποις; Καὶ ναὶ μὰ Δί᾽, ἔφη, κἂν μὴ τοῖς
ἀνθρώποις ὠφέλιμα ᾖ, ἔγωγε καλῶ ἀγαθά. καί
μοι ἐδόκει ὁ Πρωταγόρας ἤδη τετραχύνθαι τε
καὶ ἀγωνιᾶν καὶ παρατετάχθαι πρὸς τὸ ἀπο-
κρίνεσθαι· ἐπειδὴ οὖν ἑώρων αὐτὸν οὕτως ἔχοντα,
εὐλαβούμενος ἠρέμα ἠρόμην. Πότερον, ἦν δ᾽
334 ἐγώ, λέγεις, ὦ Πρωταγόρα, ἃ μηδενὶ ἀνθρώπων
ὠφέλιμά ἐστιν, ἢ ἃ μηδὲ τὸ παράπαν ὠφέλιμα;
καὶ τὰ τοιαῦτα σὺ ἀγαθὰ καλεῖς; Οὐδαμῶς,
ἔφη· ἀλλ᾽ ἔγωγε πολλὰ οἶδ᾽ ἃ ἀνθρώποις μὲν

not. For although my first object is to test the argument, the result perhaps will be that both I, the questioner, and my respondent are brought to the test.

At first Protagoras appeared to be coy, alleging that the argument was too disconcerting : however he consented at length to make answer. Well now, I said, begin at the beginning, and tell me, do you consider people to be temperate when they are unjust ?

Let us suppose so, he said.

And by being temperate you mean being sensible ? Yes.

And being sensible is being well-advised in their injustice ?

Let us grant it, he said.

Does this mean, I asked, if they fare well by their injustice, or if they fare ill ?

If they fare well.

Now do you say there are things that are good ? I do.

Then, I asked, are those things good which are profitable to men ?

Oh yes, to be sure, he replied, and also when they are not profitable to men I call them good.

Here Protagoras seemed to me to be in a thoroughly provoked and harassed state, and to have set his face against answering : so when I saw him in this mood I grew wary and went gently with my questions. Do you mean, Protagoras, I asked, things that are profitable to no human being, or things not profitable in any way at all ? Can you call such things as these good ?

By no means, he replied ; but I know a number of

ἀνωφελῆ ἐστί, καὶ σιτία καὶ ποτὰ καὶ φάρμακα
καὶ ἄλλα μυρία, τὰ δέ γε ὠφέλιμα· τὰ δὲ ἀνθρώποις μὲν οὐδέτερα, ἵπποις δέ· τὰ δὲ βουσὶ μόνον,
τὰ δὲ κυσί· τὰ δέ γε τούτων μὲν οὐδενί, δένδροις
δέ· τὰ δὲ τοῦ δένδρου ταῖς μὲν ῥίζαις ἀγαθά,
ταῖς δὲ βλάσταις πονηρά, οἷον καὶ ἡ κόπρος,
B πάντων τῶν φυτῶν ταῖς μὲν ῥίζαις ἀγαθὸν παρα-
βαλλομένη, εἰ δ᾽ ἐθέλοις ἐπὶ τοὺς πτόρθους καὶ
τοὺς νέους κλῶνας ἐπιβάλλειν, πάντα ἀπόλλυσιν·
ἐπεὶ καὶ τὸ ἔλαιον τοῖς μὲν φυτοῖς ἅπασίν ἐστι
πάγκακον καὶ ταῖς θριξὶ πολεμιώτατον ταῖς
τῶν ἄλλων ζώων πλὴν ταῖς τοῦ ἀνθρώπου, ταῖς
δὲ τοῦ ἀνθρώπου ἀρωγὸν καὶ τῷ ἄλλῳ σώματι.
οὕτω δὲ ποικίλον τί ἐστι τὸ ἀγαθὸν καὶ παντο-
δαπόν, ὥστε καὶ ἐνταῦθα τοῖς μὲν ἔξωθεν τοῦ
C σώματος ἀγαθόν ἐστι τῷ ἀνθρώπῳ, τοῖς δ᾽ ἐντὸς
ταὐτὸ τοῦτο κάκιστον· καὶ διὰ τοῦτο οἱ ἰατροὶ
πάντες ἀπαγορεύουσι τοῖς ἀσθενοῦσι μὴ χρῆσθαι
ἐλαίῳ ἀλλ᾽ ἢ ὅτι σμικροτάτῳ ἐν τούτοις οἷς
μέλλει ἔδεσθαι, ὅσον μόνον τὴν δυσχέρειαν κατα-
σβέσαι τὴν ἐπὶ ταῖς αἰσθήσεσι ταῖς διὰ τῶν ῥινῶν
γιγνομένην ἐν τοῖς σιτίοις τε καὶ ὄψοις.

Εἰπόντος οὖν ταῦτα αὐτοῦ οἱ παρόντες ἀν-
εθορύβησαν ὡς εὖ λέγοι· καὶ ἐγὼ εἶπον· Ὦ
Πρωταγόρα, ἐγὼ τυγχάνω ἐπιλήσμων τις ὢν
D ἄνθρωπος, καὶ ἐάν τίς μοι μακρὰ λέγῃ, ἐπιλανθάνομαι περὶ οὗ ἂν ᾖ ὁ λόγος. ὥσπερ οὖν,
εἰ ἐτύγχανον ὑπόκωφος ὤν, ᾤου ἂν χρῆναι,
εἴπερ ἔμελλές μοι διαλέξεσθαι, μεῖζον φθέγγεσθαι
ἢ πρὸς τοὺς ἄλλους, οὕτω καὶ νῦν, ἐπειδὴ ἐπι-

things that are unprofitable to men, namely, foods, drinks, drugs, and countless others, and some that are profitable ; some that are neither one nor the other to men, but are one or the other to horses ; and some that are profitable only to cattle, or again to dogs ; some also that are not profitable to any of those, but are to trees ; and some that are good for the roots of a tree, but bad for its shoots—such as dung, which is a good thing when applied to the roots of all plants, whereas if you chose to cast it on the young twigs and branches, it will ruin all. And oil too is utterly bad for all plants, and most deadly for the hair of all animals save that of man, while to the hair of man it is helpful, as also to the rest of his body. The good is such an elusive and diverse thing that in this instance it is good for the outward parts of man's body, but at the same time as bad as can be for the inward ; and for this reason all doctors forbid the sick to take oil, except the smallest possible quantity, in what one is going to eat—just enough to quench the loathing that arises in the sensations of one's nostrils from food and its dressings.[1]

When he had thus spoken, the company acclaimed it as an excellent answer ; and then I remarked : Protagoras, I find I am a forgetful sort of person, and if someone addresses me at any length I forget the subject on which he is talking. So, just as you, in entering on a discussion with me, would think fit to speak louder to me than to others if I happened to be hard of hearing, please bear in mind now that you have to deal with a forgetful person, and there-

[1] Probably such oil had a specially appetizing flavour or scent.

334

λήσμονι ἐνέτυχες, σύντεμνέ μοι τὰς ἀποκρίσεις
καὶ βραχυτέρας ποίει, εἰ μέλλω σοι ἔπεσθαι.
Πῶς οὖν κελεύεις με βραχέα ἀποκρίνεσθαι; ἢ
βραχύτερά σοι, ἔφη, ἀποκρίνωμαι ἢ δεῖ; Μηδαμῶς, ἦν δ' ἐγώ. 'Αλλ' ὅσα δεῖ; ἔφη. Ναί,
E ἦν δ' ἐγώ. Πότερα οὖν ὅσα ἐμοὶ δοκεῖ δεῖν
ἀποκρίνεσθαι, τοσαῦτά σοι ἀποκρίνωμαι, ἢ ὅσα
σοί; 'Ακήκοα γοῦν, ἦν δ' ἐγώ, ὅτι σὺ οἷός τ'
εἶ καὶ αὐτὸς καὶ ἄλλον διδάξαι περὶ τῶν αὐτῶν
καὶ μακρὰ λέγειν, ἐὰν βούλῃ, οὕτως, ὥστε τὸν
λόγον μηδέποτε ἐπιλιπεῖν, καὶ αὖ βραχέα οὕτως,
335 ὥστε μηδένα σοῦ ἐν βραχυτέροις εἰπεῖν· εἰ οὖν
μέλλεις ἐμοὶ διαλέξεσθαι, τῷ ἑτέρῳ χρῶ τρόπῳ
πρός με, τῇ βραχυλογίᾳ. 'Ω Σώκρατες, ἔφη, ἐγὼ
πολλοῖς ἤδη εἰς ἀγῶνα λόγων ἀφικόμην ἀνθρώποις, καὶ εἰ τοῦτο ἐποίουν ὃ σὺ κελεύεις, ὡς ὁ
ἀντιλέγων ἐκέλευέ με διαλέγεσθαι, οὕτω διελε-
γόμην, οὐδενὸς ἂν βελτίων ἐφαινόμην οὐδ' ἂν
ἐγένετο Πρωταγόρου ὄνομα ἐν τοῖς Ἕλλησιν.
καὶ ἐγώ—ἔγνων γὰρ ὅτι οὐκ ἤρεσεν αὐτὸς αὑτῷ
ταῖς ἀποκρίσεσι ταῖς ἔμπροσθεν, καὶ ὅτι οὐκ
B ἐθελήσοι ἑκὼν εἶναι ἀποκρινόμενος διαλέγεσθαι—
ἡγησάμενος οὐκέτι ἐμὸν ἔργον εἶναι παρεῖναι ἐν
ταῖς συνουσίαις, 'Αλλά τοι, ἔφη, ὦ Πρωταγόρα,
οὐδ' ἐγὼ λιπαρῶς ἔχω παρὰ τὰ σοὶ δοκοῦντα
τὴν συνουσίαν ἡμῖν γίγνεσθαι, ἀλλ' ἐπειδὰν σὺ
βούλῃ διαλέγεσθαι ὡς ἐγὼ δύναμαι ἔπεσθαι,
τότε σοι διαλέξομαι. σὺ μὲν γάρ, ὡς λέγεται
172

fore cut up your answers into shorter pieces, that I may be able to follow you.

Well, what do you mean by short answers? he asked : do you want me to make them shorter than they should be?

Not at all, I said.

As long as they should be? he asked.

Yes, I said.

Then are my answers to be as long as I think they should be, or as you think they should be?

Well, for instance, I have heard, I said, that you yourself are able, in treating one and the same subject, not only to instruct another person in it but to speak on it at length, if you choose, without ever being at a loss for matter; or again briefly, so as to yield to no one in brevity of expression. So, if you are going to argue with me, employ with me the latter method, that of brevity.

Socrates, he said, I have undertaken in my time many contests of speech, and if I were to do what you demand, and argue just in the way that my opponent demanded, I should not be held superior to anyone nor would Protagoras have made a name among the Greeks.

Then, as I saw that he had not been quite satisfied with himself in making his former answers, and that he would not readily accept the part of answerer in debate, I considered it was not my business to attend his meetings further, and remarked : But you know, Protagoras, I too feel uncomfortable about our having this discussion against your inclination ; but when you agree to argue in such a way that I can follow, then I will argue with you. For you—as people relate of you, and you yourself

περὶ σοῦ, φῇς δὲ καὶ αὐτός, καὶ ἐν μακρολογίᾳ
καὶ ἐν βραχυλογίᾳ οἷός τ᾽ εἶ συνουσίας ποιεῖσθαι·
C σοφὸς γὰρ εἶ· ἐγὼ δὲ τὰ μακρὰ ταῦτα ἀδύνατος,
ἐπεὶ ἐβουλόμην ἂν οἷός τ᾽ εἶναι. ἀλλὰ σὲ ἐχρῆν
ἡμῖν συγχωρεῖν τὸν ἀμφότερα δυνάμενον, ἵνα
ἡ συνουσία ἐγίγνετο· νῦν δὲ ἐπειδὴ οὐκ ἐθέλεις
καὶ ἐμοί τις ἀσχολία ἐστὶ καὶ οὐκ ἂν οἷός τ᾽ εἴην
σοι παραμεῖναι ἀποτείνοντι μακροὺς λόγους—
ἐλθεῖν γάρ ποί με δεῖ—εἶμι· ἐπεὶ καὶ ταῦτ᾽ ἂν
ἴσως οὐκ ἀηδῶς σου ἤκουον. καὶ ἅμα ταῦτ᾽
εἰπὼν ἀνιστάμην ὡς ἀπιών· καί μου ἀνιστα-
D μένου ἐπιλαμβάνεται ὁ Καλλίας τῆς χειρὸς τῇ
δεξιᾷ, τῇ δ᾽ ἀριστερᾷ ἀντελάβετο τοῦ τρίβωνος
τουτουί, καὶ εἶπεν· Οὐκ ἀφήσομέν σε, ὦ Σώκρα-
τες· ἐὰν γὰρ σὺ ἐξέλθῃς, οὐχ ὁμοίως ἡμῖν ἔσονται
οἱ διάλογοι. δέομαι οὖν σου παραμεῖναι ἡμῖν·
ὡς ἐγὼ οὐδ᾽ ἂν ἑνὸς ἥδιον ἀκούσαιμι ἢ σοῦ
τε καὶ Πρωταγόρου διαλεγομένων· ἀλλὰ χάρισαι
ἡμῖν πᾶσιν. καὶ ἐγὼ εἶπον—ἤδη δὲ ἀνειστήκη
ὡς ἐξιών—Ὦ παῖ Ἱππονίκου, ἀεὶ μὲν ἔγωγέ
σου τὴν φιλοσοφίαν ἄγαμαι, ἀτὰρ καὶ νῦν ἐπαινῶ
E καὶ φιλῶ, ὥστε βουλοίμην ἂν χαρίζεσθαί σοι,
εἴ μου δυνατὰ δέοιο· νῦν δ᾽ ἐστὶν ὥσπερ ἂν εἰ
δέοιό μου Κρίσωνι τῷ Ἱμεραίῳ δρομεῖ ἀκμάζοντι
ἕπεσθαι, ἢ τῶν δολιχοδρόμων τῳ ἢ τῶν ἡμερο-
δρόμων διαθεῖν τε καὶ ἕπεσθαι, εἴποιμι ἄν σοι
336 ὅτι πολὺ σοῦ μᾶλλον ἐγὼ ἐμαυτοῦ δέομαι θέουσι
τούτοις ἀκολουθεῖν, ἀλλ᾽ οὐ γὰρ δύναμαι, ἀλλ᾽
εἴ τι δέει θεάσασθαι ἐν τῷ αὐτῷ ἐμέ τε καὶ
Κρίσωνα θέοντας, τούτου δέου συγκαθεῖναι· ἐγὼ

---

[1] See 329 B, note.
[2] Cf. Pheidippides in Herodotus, vi. 105.

assert—are able to hold a discussion in the form of
either long or short speeches ; you are a man of
knowledge : but I have no ability for these long
speeches, though I could wish that I had it. Surely
you, who are proficient in both ways, ought to have
made us this concession, that so we might have had
our debate. But now that you refuse, and I am somewhat pressed for time and could not stay to hear you
expatiate at any length—for I have an appointment—
I will be off ; though I daresay I should be happy
enough to hear your views.

With these words I rose as if to go away ; but, as
I was getting up, Callias laid hold of my arm with
his right hand, and grasped this cloak of mine with
his left, and said : We will not let you go, Socrates ;
for if you leave us our discussions will not go so well.
I beg you therefore to stay with us, for there is
nothing I would rather hear than an argument
between you and Protagoras. Come, you must
oblige us all.

Then I said (I was now standing up as though to
go out) : Son of Hipponicus, I always admire your
love of knowledge, but especially do I commend
and love it now, so that I should be very glad to
oblige you if you asked of me something that I
could do : but I am afraid it is as though you asked
me to keep pace with Criso the runner of Himera
in his prime, or to keep up in a match with one
of the long-distance[1] or day-course[2] racers, and I
could only tell you that I wish that of myself, without
your asking, I could keep pace with such runners,
but of course I cannot. If you want to have the
spectacle of Criso and me running together, you
must ask him to adapt his pace ; for whereas I

μὲν γὰρ οὐ δύναμαι ταχὺ θεῖν, οὗτος δὲ δύναται
βραδέως. εἰ οὖν ἐπιθυμεῖς ἐμοῦ καὶ Πρωταγόρου ἀκούειν, τούτου δέου, ὥσπερ τὸ πρῶτόν
μοι ἀπεκρίνατο διὰ βραχέων τε καὶ αὐτὰ τὰ
ἐρωτώμενα, οὕτω καὶ νῦν ἀποκρίνεσθαι· εἰ δὲ
B μή, τίς ὁ τρόπος ἔσται τῶν διαλόγων; χωρὶς
γὰρ ἔγωγ᾽ ᾤμην εἶναι τὸ συνεῖναί τε ἀλλήλοις
διαλεγομένους καὶ τὸ δημηγορεῖν. Ἀλλ᾽ ὁρᾷς,
ἔφη, ὦ Σώκρατες· δίκαια δοκεῖ λέγειν Πρωταγόρας ἀξιῶν αὑτῷ τε ἐξεῖναι διαλέγεσθαι ὅπως
βούλεται καὶ σὺ ὅπως ἂν αὖ σὺ βούλῃ.

Ὑπολαβὼν οὖν ὁ Ἀλκιβιάδης, Οὐ καλῶς
λέγεις, ἔφη, ὦ Καλλία· Σωκράτης μὲν γὰρ ὅδε
ὁμολογεῖ μὴ μετεῖναί οἱ μακρολογίας καὶ παρα-
C χωρεῖ Πρωταγόρᾳ, τοῦ δὲ διαλέγεσθαι οἷός τ᾽
εἶναι καὶ ἐπίστασθαι λόγον τε δοῦναι καὶ δέξασθαι
θαυμάζοιμ᾽ ἂν εἴ τῳ ἀνθρώπων παραχωρεῖ. εἰ
μὲν οὖν καὶ Πρωταγόρας ὁμολογεῖ φαυλότερος
εἶναι Σωκράτους διαλεχθῆναι, ἐξαρκεῖ Σωκράτει·
εἰ δὲ ἀντιποιεῖται, διαλεγέσθω ἐρωτῶν τε καὶ
ἀποκρινόμενος, μὴ ἐφ᾽ ἑκάστῃ ἐρωτήσει μακρὸν
λόγον ἀποτείνων, ἐκκρούων τοὺς λόγους καὶ
οὐκ ἐθέλων διδόναι λόγον, ἀλλ᾽ ἀπομηκύνων
D ἕως ἂν ἐπιλάθωνται περὶ ὅτου τὸ ἐρώτημα ἦν
οἱ πολλοὶ τῶν ἀκουόντων· ἐπεὶ Σωκράτη γε
ἐγὼ ἐγγυῶμαι μὴ ἐπιλήσεσθαι, οὐχ ὅτι παίζει
καί φησιν ἐπιλήσμων εἶναι. ἐμοὶ μὲν οὖν δοκεῖ
ἐπιεικέστερα Σωκράτης λέγειν· χρὴ γὰρ ἕκαστον
τὴν ἑαυτοῦ γνώμην ἀποφαίνεσθαι. μετὰ δὲ τὸν
Ἀλκιβιάδην, ὡς ἐγῷμαι, Κριτίας ἦν ὁ εἰπών·
Ὦ Πρόδικε καὶ Ἱππία, Καλλίας μὲν δοκεῖ μοι
μάλα πρὸς Πρωταγόρου εἶναι, Ἀλκιβιάδης δὲ

cannot run fast, he can run slowly. So if you desire
to hear Protagoras and me, ask him to resume the
method of answering which he used at first — in
short sentences and keeping to the point raised.
Otherwise what is to be our mode of discussion ?
For I thought that to hold a joint discussion and to
make a harangue were two distinct things.

Ah, but you see, Socrates, he said, Protagoras
thinks it only fair to claim that he be allowed to
discuss in his chosen style, in return for your claim
that it should be in yours.

At this Alcibiades intervened, saying : You
do not state it quite philosophically, Callias,[1] for
Socrates here confesses he is no hand at long discourses, and yields therein to Protagoras ; but I
should be surprised if he yields to any man in ability
to argue, or in understanding the interchange of
reason. Now if Protagoras confesses himself inferior
to Socrates in argumentation, Socrates has no more
to ask : but if he challenges him, let him discuss by
question and answer ; not spinning out a lecture
on each question—beating off the arguments, refusing to give a reason, and so dilating until most
of his hearers have forgotten the point at issue.
For Socrates, I warrant you, will not forget, despite
his jesting way of calling himself forgetful. Now
I think Socrates' proposal is the more equitable —
for each of us should declare his personal opinion.

After Alcibiades, the next, I believe, to speak
was Critias : Prodicus and Hippias, he said, it seems
to me that Callias is all for supporting Protagoras,
while Alcibiades is always for a contest in anything

---

[1] The translation attempts to follow the jingle of καλῶς . . .
Καλλία.

E ἀεὶ φιλόνικός ἐστι πρὸς ὃ ἂν ὁρμήσῃ· ἡμᾶς δὲ
οὐδὲν δεῖ συμφιλονικεῖν οὔτε Σωκράτει οὔτε
Πρωταγόρᾳ, ἀλλὰ κοινῇ ἀμφοτέρων δεῖσθαι μὴ
337 μεταξὺ διαλῦσαι τὴν ξυνουσίαν· εἰπόντος δὲ
αὐτοῦ ταῦτα, ὁ Πρόδικος, Καλῶς μοι, ἔφη, δοκεῖς
λέγειν, ὦ Κριτία· χρὴ γὰρ τοὺς ἐν τοιοῖσδε
λόγοις παραγιγνομένους κοινοὺς μὲν εἶναι ἀμφοῖν
τοῖν διαλεγομένοιν ἀκροατάς, ἴσους δὲ μή. ἔστι
γὰρ οὐ ταὐτόν· κοινῇ μὲν γὰρ ἀκοῦσαι δεῖ ἀμφοτέρων, μὴ ἴσον δὲ νεῖμαι ἑκατέρῳ, ἀλλὰ τῷ μὲν
σοφωτέρῳ πλέον, τῷ δὲ ἀμαθεστέρῳ ἔλαττον.
ἐγὼ μὲν καὶ αὐτός, ὦ Πρωταγόρα τε καὶ Σώκρατες, ἀξιῶ ὑμᾶς συγχωρεῖν καὶ ἀλλήλοις περὶ
B τῶν λόγων ἀμφισβητεῖν μέν, ἐρίζειν δὲ μή· ἀμφι-
σβητοῦσι μὲν γὰρ καὶ δι᾽ εὔνοιαν οἱ φίλοι τοῖς
φίλοις, ἐρίζουσι δὲ οἱ διάφοροί τε καὶ ἐχθροὶ
ἀλλήλοις. καὶ οὕτως ἂν καλλίστη ἡμῖν ἡ συνουσία γίγνοιτο· ὑμεῖς τε γὰρ οἱ λέγοντες μάλιστ᾽
ἂν οὕτως ἐν ἡμῖν τοῖς ἀκούουσιν εὐδοκιμοῖτε
καὶ οὐκ ἐπαινοῖσθε· εὐδοκιμεῖν μὲν γὰρ ἔστι
παρὰ ταῖς ψυχαῖς τῶν ἀκουόντων ἄνευ ἀπάτης,
ἐπαινεῖσθαι δὲ ἐν λόγῳ πολλάκις παρὰ δόξαν
C ψευδομένων· ἡμεῖς τ᾽ αὖ οἱ ἀκούοντες μάλιστ᾽
ἂν οὕτως εὐφραινοίμεθα, οὐχ ἡδοίμεθα· εὐφραί-
νεσθαι μὲν γὰρ ἔστι μανθάνοντά τι καὶ φρονήσεως
μεταλαμβάνοντα αὐτῇ τῇ διανοίᾳ, ἥδεσθαι δὲ
ἐσθίοντά τι ἢ ἄλλο ἡδὺ πάσχοντα αὐτῷ τῷ σώματι.

Ταῦτα οὖν εἰπόντος τοῦ Προδίκου πολλοὶ
πάνυ τῶν παρόντων ἀπεδέξαντο· μετὰ δὲ τὸν
Πρόδικον Ἱππίας ὁ σοφὸς εἶπεν, Ὦ ἄνδρες, ἔφη,

---

[1] Prodicus was specially expert in nice verbal distinctions.

he takes up. It is not for us to contend on either side for Socrates or for Protagoras, but jointly to request them both not to break off our conference unconcluded.

When he had said this, Prodicus[1] remarked: I think you are right, Critias: those who attend this sort of discussion ought to be joint, but not equal, hearers of both disputants. For there is a difference: we should listen jointly to them both, yet not give equal heed to each, but more to the wiser and less to the less intelligent. I on my part also, Protagoras and Socrates, call upon you to accede to our request, and to dispute, but not wrangle, with each other over your arguments: for friends dispute with friends, just from good feeling; whereas wrangling is between those who are at variance and enmity with one another. In this way our meeting will have highest success, since you the speakers will thus earn the greatest measure of good repute, not praise, from us who hear you. For good repute is present in the hearers' souls without deception, but praise is too often in the words of liars who hide what they really think. Again, we listeners would thus be most comforted, not pleased; for he is comforted who learns something and gets a share of good sense in his mind alone, whereas he is pleased who eats something or has some other pleasant sensation only in his body.

When Prodicus had thus spoken, quite a number of the company showed their approval: then after Prodicus the learned Hippias[2] spoke: Gentlemen,

[2] Hippias professed to teach a great variety of subjects. His frequent metaphors were evidently designed to display his wide range of knowledge.

οἱ παρόντες, ἡγοῦμαι ἐγὼ ὑμᾶς συγγενεῖς τε
καὶ οἰκείους καὶ πολίτας ἅπαντας εἶναι φύσει,
D οὐ νόμῳ· τὸ γὰρ ὅμοιον τῷ ὁμοίῳ φύσει συγ-
γενές ἐστιν, ὁ δὲ νόμος, τύραννος ὢν τῶν ἀνθρώπων, πολλὰ παρὰ τὴν φύσιν βιάζεται. ἡμᾶς
οὖν αἰσχρὸν τὴν μὲν φύσιν τῶν πραγμάτων εἰδέναι,
σοφωτάτους δὲ ὄντας τῶν Ἑλλήνων, καὶ κατ᾽
αὐτὸ τοῦτο νῦν συνεληλυθότας τῆς τε Ἑλλάδος
εἰς αὐτὸ τὸ πρυτανεῖον τῆς σοφίας καὶ αὐτῆς
τῆς πόλεως εἰς τὸν μέγιστον καὶ ὀλβιώτατον
οἶκον τόνδε, μηδὲν τούτου τοῦ ἀξιώματος ἄξιον
E ἀποφήνασθαι, ἀλλ᾽ ὥσπερ τοὺς φαυλοτάτους τῶν
ἀνθρώπων διαφέρεσθαι ἀλλήλοις. ἐγὼ μὲν οὖν
καὶ δέομαι καὶ συμβουλεύω, ὦ Πρωταγόρα τε
καὶ Σώκρατες, συμβῆναι ὑμᾶς ὥσπερ ὑπὸ διαι-
τητῶν ἡμῶν συμβιβαζόντων εἰς τὸ μέσον, καὶ
338 μήτε σὲ τὸ ἀκριβὲς τοῦτο εἶδος τῶν διαλόγων
ζητεῖν τὸ κατὰ βραχὺ λίαν, εἰ μὴ ἡδὺ Πρωταγόρᾳ,
ἀλλ᾽ ἐφεῖναι καὶ χαλάσαι τὰς ἡνίας τοῖς λόγοις,
ἵνα μεγαλοπρεπέστεροι καὶ εὐσχημονέστεροι ἡμῖν
φαίνωνται, μήτ᾽ αὖ Πρωταγόραν πάντα κάλων
ἐκτείναντα, οὐρίᾳ ἐφέντα, φεύγειν εἰς τὸ πέλαγος
τῶν λόγων, ἀποκρύψαντα γῆν, ἀλλὰ μέσον τι
ἀμφοτέρους τεμεῖν. ὡς οὖν ποιήσετε, καὶ πεί-
θεσθέ μοι ῥαβδοῦχον καὶ ἐπιστάτην καὶ πρύτανιν
B ἑλέσθαι, ὃς ὑμῖν φυλάξει τὸ μέτριον μῆκος τῶν
λόγων ἑκατέρου.

Ταῦτα ἤρεσε τοῖς παροῦσι, καὶ πάντες ἐπ-
ῄνεσαν, καὶ ἐμέ τε ὁ Καλλίας οὐκ ἔφη ἀφήσειν
καὶ ἑλέσθαι ἐδέοντο ἐπιστάτην. εἶπον οὖν ἐγὼ
ὅτι αἰσχρὸν εἴη βραβευτὴν ἑλέσθαι τῶν λόγων.
εἴτε γὰρ χείρων ἔσται ἡμῶν ὁ αἱρεθείς, οὐκ ὀρθῶς

he said, who are here present, I regard you all as kinsmen and intimates and fellow-citizens by nature, not by law : for like is akin to like by nature, whereas law, despot of mankind, often constrains us against nature. Hence it would be shameful if we, while knowing the nature of things, should yet—being the wisest of the Greeks, and having met together for the very purpose in the very sanctuary of the wisdom of Greece, and in this the greatest and most auspicious house of the city of cities—display no worthy sign of this dignity, but should quarrel with each other like low churls. Now let me beg and advise you, Protagoras and Socrates, to come to terms arranged, as it were, under our arbitration : you, Socrates, must not require that precise form of discussion with its extreme brevity, if it is disagreeable to Protagoras, but let the speeches have their head with a loose rein, that they may give us a more splendid and elegant impression ; nor must you, Protagoras, let out full sail, as you run before the breeze, and so escape into the ocean of speech leaving the land nowhere in sight ; rather, both of you must take a middle course. So you shall do as I say, and I strongly urge you to choose an umpire or supervisor or chairman who will keep watch for you over the due measure of either's speeches.

His proposal was approved by the company, and they all applauded it : Callias said he would not let me go, and they requested me to choose a supervisor. To this I replied that it would be a shame to choose an arbiter for our discussion ; for if he who is chosen, said I, is to be our inferior, it would

ἂν ἔχοι τὸν χείρω τῶν βελτιόνων ἐπιστατεῖν,
εἴτε ὅμοιος, οὐδ' οὕτως ὀρθῶς· ὁ γὰρ ὅμοιος
ἡμῖν ὅμοια καὶ ποιήσει, ὥστε ἐκ περιττοῦ ᾑρή-
C σεται. ἀλλὰ δὴ βελτίονα ἡμῶν αἱρήσεσθε. τῇ
μὲν ἀληθείᾳ, ὡς ἐγῷμαι, ἀδύνατον ὑμῖν ὥστε
Πρωταγόρου τοῦδε σοφώτερόν τινα ἑλέσθαι· εἰ
δὲ αἱρήσεσθε μὲν μηδὲν βελτίω, φήσετε δέ, αἰσχρὸν καὶ τοῦτο τῷδε γίγνεται, ὥσπερ φαύλῳ
ἀνθρώπῳ ἐπιστάτην αἱρεῖσθαι, ἐπεὶ τό γ' ἐμὸν
οὐδέν μοι διαφέρει. ἀλλ' οὑτωσὶ ἐθέλω ποιῆσαι,
ἵν' ὃ προθυμεῖσθε συνουσία τε καὶ διάλογοι ἡμῖν
γίγνωνται· εἰ μὴ βούλεται Πρωταγόρας ἀποκρί-
D νεσθαι, οὗτος μὲν ἐρωτάτω, ἐγὼ δὲ ἀποκρινοῦμαι,
καὶ ἅμα πειράσομαι αὐτῷ δεῖξαι, ὡς ἐγώ φημι
χρῆναι τὸν ἀποκρινόμενον ἀποκρίνεσθαι· ἐπειδὰν
δὲ ἐγὼ ἀποκρίνωμαι ὁπόσ' ἂν οὗτος βούληται
ἐρωτᾶν, πάλιν οὗτος ἐμοὶ λόγον ὑποσχέτω ὁμοίως.
ἐὰν οὖν μὴ δοκῇ πρόθυμος εἶναι πρὸς αὐτὸ τὸ
ἐρωτώμενον ἀποκρίνεσθαι, καὶ ἐγὼ καὶ ὑμεῖς
κοινῇ δεησόμεθα αὐτοῦ ἅπερ ὑμεῖς ἐμοῦ, μὴ
διαφθείρειν τὴν συνουσίαν· καὶ οὐδὲν δεῖ τούτου
E ἕνεκα ἕνα ἐπιστάτην γενέσθαι, ἀλλὰ πάντες κοινῇ
ἐπιστατήσετε. ἐδόκει πᾶσιν οὕτω ποιητέον εἶναι·
καὶ ὁ Πρωταγόρας πάνυ μὲν οὐκ ἤθελεν, ὅμως
δὲ ἠναγκάσθη ὁμολογῆσαι ἐρωτήσειν, καὶ ἐπειδὰν
ἱκανῶς ἐρωτήσῃ, πάλιν δώσειν λόγον κατὰ σμικρὸν ἀποκρινόμενος.

Ἤρξατο οὖν ἐρωτᾶν οὑτωσί πως· Ἡγοῦμαι,
ἔφη, ὦ Σώκρατες, ἐγὼ ἀνδρὶ παιδείας μέγιστον
339 μέρος εἶναι περὶ ἐπῶν δεινὸν εἶναι· ἔστι δὲ τοῦτο

not be right to have the inferior overseeing the superior; while if he is our equal, that will be just as wrong, for our equal will only do very much as we do, and it will be superfluous to choose him. You may say you will choose one who is our superior. This, in very truth, I hold to be impossible—to choose someone who is wiser than our friend Protagoras; and if you choose one who is not his superior, though you may say he is, that again would cast a slur on him, as if he were some paltry fellow requiring a supervisor; for, as far as I am concerned, the matter is indifferent. But let me tell you how I would have the thing done, so that your eagerness for a conference and a discussion may be satisfied. If Protagoras does not wish to answer, let him ask questions, and I will answer: at the same time I will try to show him how the answerer, in my view, ought to answer; and when I have answered all the questions that he wishes to ask, in his turn he shall render account in like manner to me. So if he does not seem very ready to answer the particular question put to him, you and I will join in beseeching him, as you have besought me, not to upset our conference. And for this plan there is no need to have one man as supervisor; you will all supervise it together.

They all resolved that it should be done in this way: Protagoras, though very unwilling, was obliged after all to agree to ask questions and then, when he had asked a sufficient number, to take his turn at making due response in short answers.

And so he began to put questions in this sort of way: I consider, Socrates, that the greatest part of a man's education is to be skilled in the matter of

τὰ ὑπὸ τῶν ποιητῶν λεγόμενα οἷόν τ᾽ εἶναι συνιέναι ἅ τε ὀρθῶς πεποίηται καὶ ἃ μή, καὶ ἐπίστασθαι διελεῖν τε καὶ ἐρωτώμενον λόγον δοῦναι. καὶ δὴ καὶ νῦν ἔσται τὸ ἐρώτημα περὶ τοῦ αὐτοῦ μέν, περὶ οὗπερ ἐγώ τε καὶ σὺ νῦν διαλεγόμεθα, περὶ ἀρετῆς, μετενηνεγμένον δὲ εἰς ποίησιν· τοσοῦτον μόνον διοίσει. λέγει γάρ που Σιμωνίδης πρὸς Σκόπαν, τὸν Κρέοντος υἱὸν τοῦ Θετταλοῦ, ὅτι

B ἄνδρ᾽ ἀγαθὸν μὲν ἀλαθέως γενέσθαι χαλεπόν,
χερσίν τε καὶ ποσὶ καὶ νόῳ τετράγωνον, ἄνευ
ψόγου τετυγμένον.

τοῦτο ἐπίστασαι τὸ ᾆσμα, ἢ πᾶν σοι διεξέλθω; καὶ ἐγὼ εἶπον ὅτι Οὐδὲν δεῖ· ἐπίσταμαί τε γάρ, καὶ πάνυ μοι τυγχάνει μεμεληκὸς τοῦ ᾄσματος. Εὖ, ἔφη, λέγεις. πότερον οὖν καλῶς σοι δοκεῖ πεποιῆσθαι καὶ ὀρθῶς, ἢ οὔ; Πάνυ, ἔφην ἐγώ, <καλῶς>[1] τε καὶ ὀρθῶς. Δοκεῖ δέ σοι καλῶς πεποιῆσθαι, εἰ ἐναντία λέγει αὐτὸς αὑτῷ ὁ ποιητής; Οὐ καλῶς, ἦν δ᾽ ἐγώ. Ὅρα δή, ἔφη,

C βέλτιον. Ἀλλ᾽, ὦ ᾽γαθέ, ἔσκεμμαι ἱκανῶς. Οἶσθα οὖν, ἔφη, ὅτι προϊόντος τοῦ ᾄσματος λέγει που·

οὐδέ μοι ἐμμελέως τὸ Πιττάκειον νέμεται,
καίτοι σοφοῦ παρὰ φωτὸς εἰρημένον· χαλεπὸν φάτ᾽
ἐσθλὸν ἔμμεναι.

ἐννοεῖς ὅτι ὁ αὐτὸς οὗτος καὶ τάδε λέγει κἀκεῖνα

---

[1] καλῶς add. Bekker.

verses; that is, to be able to apprehend, in the
utterances of the poets, what has been rightly and
what wrongly composed, and to know how to distinguish them and account for them when questioned.
Accordingly my question now will be on the same
subject that you and I are now debating, namely
virtue, but taken in connexion with poetry: that
will be the only difference. Now, Simonides, I
think, somewhere remarks to Scopas, the son of
Creon of Thessaly—

> For a man, indeed, to become good truly is hard,
> In hands and feet and mind foursquare,
> Fashioned without reproach.

Do you know the ode, or shall I recite the whole?

To this I replied: There is no need, for I know it;
it happens that I have especially studied that ode.

I am glad to hear it, he said. Now do you regard
it as finely and correctly composed or not?

Very finely and correctly, I replied.

And do you regard it as finely composed, if the
poet contradicts himself?

No, I replied.

Then observe it more closely, he said.

My good sir, I have given it ample attention.

Are you aware, then, he asked, that as the ode
proceeds he says at one point—

> Nor ringeth true to me
> That word of Pittacus [1]—
> And yet 'twas a sage who spake—
> Hard, quoth he, to be good.

Do you note that this and the former are statements
of the same person?

[1] Pittacus, ruler of Mytilene, despaired of ruling well on
the ground here stated.

τὰ ἔμπροσθεν; Οἶδα, ἦν δ᾽ ἐγώ. Δοκεῖ οὖν
σοι, ἔφη, ταῦτα ἐκείνοις ὁμολογεῖσθαι; Φαίνεται ἔμοιγε (καὶ ἅμα μέντοι ἐφοβούμην μὴ
τί λέγοι). ἀτάρ, ἔφην ἐγώ, σοὶ οὐ φαίνεται;

D Πῶς γὰρ ἂν φαίνοιτο ὁμολογεῖν αὐτὸς ἑαυτῷ ὁ
ταῦτα ἀμφότερα λέγων, ὅς γε τὸ μὲν πρῶτον
αὐτὸς ὑπέθετο χαλεπὸν εἶναι ἄνδρα ἀγαθὸν γενέσθαι ἀληθείᾳ, ὀλίγον δὲ τοῦ ποιήματος εἰς τὸ
πρόσθεν προελθὼν ἐπελάθετο, καὶ Πιττακὸν τὸν
ταῦτα λέγοντα ἑαυτῷ, ὅτι χαλεπὸν ἐσθλὸν ἔμμεναι, τοῦτον μέμφεταί τε καὶ οὔ φησιν ἀποδέχεσθαι αὐτοῦ τὰ αὐτὰ ἑαυτῷ λέγοντος. καίτοι
ὁπότε τὸν ταὐτὰ λέγοντα αὐτῷ μέμφεται, δῆλον
ὅτι καὶ ἑαυτὸν μέμφεται, ὥστε ἤτοι τὸ πρότερον
ἢ ὕστερον οὐκ ὀρθῶς λέγει.

Εἰπὼν οὖν ταῦτα πολλοῖς θόρυβον παρέσχε
E καὶ ἔπαινον τῶν ἀκουόντων· καὶ ἐγὼ τὸ μὲν
πρῶτον, ὡσπερεὶ ὑπὸ ἀγαθοῦ πύκτου πληγείς,
ἐσκοτώθην τε καὶ ἰλιγγίασα εἰπόντος αὐτοῦ
ταῦτα καὶ τῶν ἄλλων ἐπιθορυβησάντων· ἔπειτα,
ὥς γε πρὸς σὲ εἰρῆσθαι τἀληθῆ, ἵνα μοι χρόνος
ἐγγένηται τῇ σκέψει τί λέγοι ὁ ποιητής, τρέ-
πομαι πρὸς τὸν Πρόδικον, καὶ καλέσας αὐτόν,
Ὦ Πρόδικε, ἔφην ἐγώ, σὸς μέντοι Σιμωνίδης
πολίτης· δίκαιος εἶ βοηθεῖν τῷ ἀνδρί. δοκῶ
340 οὖν μοι ἐγὼ παρακαλεῖν σέ, ὥσπερ ἔφη Ὅμηρος
τὸν Σκάμανδρον πολιορκούμενον ὑπὸ τοῦ Ἀχιλ-
λέως τὸν Σιμόεντα παρακαλεῖν, εἰπόντα·

φίλε κασίγνητε, σθένος ἀνέρος ἀμφότεροί περ
σχῶμεν.

---

[1] *Iliad* xxi. 308 foll.

I know that, I said.

Then do you think the second agrees with the first?

So far as I can see, it does, I replied (at the same time, though, I was afraid there was something in what he said). Why, I asked, does it not seem so to you?

How can anyone, he replied, be thought consistent, who says both of these things? First he laid it down himself that it is hard for a man to become good in truth, and then a little further on in his poem he forgot, and he proceeds to blame Pittacus for saying the same as he did—that it is hard to be good, and refuses to accept from him the same statement that he made himself. Yet, as often as he blames the man for saying the same as himself he obviously blames himself too, so that in either the former or the latter place his statement is wrong.

This speech of his won a clamorous approval from many of his hearers; and at first I felt as though I had been struck by a skilful boxer, and was quite blind and dizzy with the effect of his words and the noise of their applause. Then—to tell you the honest truth—in order to gain time for considering the poet's meaning, I turned to Prodicus and calling him—Prodicus, I said, surely Simonides was your townsman: it behoves you to come to the man's rescue. Accordingly I allow myself to call for your assistance—just as Scamander, in Homer,[1] when besieged by Achilles, called Simois to his aid, saying—

Dear brother, let us both together stay this warrior's might.

187

ἀτὰρ καὶ ἐγώ σε παρακαλῶ, μὴ ἡμῖν ὁ Πρωταγόρας τὸν Σιμωνίδην ἐκπέρσῃ. καὶ γὰρ οὖν
καὶ δεῖται τὸ ὑπὲρ Σιμωνίδου ἐπανόρθωμα τῆς
B σῆς μουσικῆς, ᾗ τό τε βούλεσθαι καὶ ἐπιθυμεῖν
διαιρεῖς ὡς οὐ ταὐτὸν ὄν, καὶ ἃ νῦν δὴ εἶπες
πολλά τε καὶ καλά. καὶ νῦν σκόπει, εἴ σοι
συνδοκεῖ ὅπερ ἐμοί. οὐ γὰρ φαίνεται ἐναντία
λέγειν αὐτὸς αὑτῷ Σιμωνίδης. σὺ γάρ, ὦ Πρόδικε, προαπόφηναι τὴν σὴν γνώμην· ταὐτόν
σοι δοκεῖ εἶναι τὸ γενέσθαι καὶ τὸ εἶναι, ἢ ἄλλο;
"Αλλο νὴ Δί', ἔφη ὁ Πρόδικος. Οὐκοῦν, ἔφην
ἐγώ, ἐν μὲν τοῖς πρώτοις αὐτὸς ὁ Σιμωνίδης τὴν
ἑαυτοῦ γνώμην ἀπεφήνατο, ὅτι ἄνδρα ἀγαθὸν
C ἀληθείᾳ γενέσθαι χαλεπὸν εἴη; 'Αληθῆ λέγεις,
ἔφη ὁ Πρόδικος. Τὸν δέ γε Πιττακόν, ἦν δ'
ἐγώ, μέμφεται, οὐχ ὡς οἴεται Πρωταγόρας,
ταὐτὸν ἑαυτῷ λέγοντα, ἀλλ' ἄλλο. οὐ γὰρ
τοῦτο ὁ Πιττακὸς ἔλεγε τὸ χαλεπόν, γενέσθαι
ἐσθλόν, ὥσπερ ὁ Σιμωνίδης, ἀλλὰ τὸ ἔμμεναι·
ἔστι δὲ οὐ ταὐτόν, ὦ Πρωταγόρα, ὥς φησι Πρόδικος ὅδε, τὸ εἶναι καὶ τὸ γενέσθαι· εἰ δὲ μὴ
τὸ αὐτό ἐστι τὸ εἶναι τῷ γενέσθαι, οὐκ ἐναντία
λέγει ὁ Σιμωνίδης αὐτὸς αὑτῷ. καὶ ἴσως ἂν
D φαίη Πρόδικος ὅδε καὶ ἄλλοι πολλοί, καθ' Ἡσίοδον, γενέσθαι μὲν ἀγαθὸν χαλεπὸν εἶναι· τῆς
γὰρ ἀρετῆς ἔμπροσθεν τοὺς θεοὺς ἱδρῶτα θεῖναι·
ὅταν δέ τις αὐτῆς εἰς ἄκρον ἵκηται, ῥῃδίην δή-
πειτα πέλειν, χαλεπήν περ ἐοῦσαν, ἐκτῆσθαι.

Ὁ μὲν οὖν Πρόδικος ἀκούσας ταῦτα ἐπῄνεσέ
με· ὁ δὲ Πρωταγόρας, Τὸ ἐπανόρθωμά σοι,
ἔφη, ὦ Σώκρατες, μεῖζον ἁμάρτημα ἔχει ἢ ὃ

In the same way I call upon you, lest Protagoras
lay Simonides in ruins. For indeed to rehabilitate
Simonides requires your artistry, by which you can
discriminate between wishing and desiring as two
distinct things in the fine and ample manner of
your statement just now. So please consider if
you agree with my view. For it is not clear that
Simonides does contradict himself. Now you, Prodicus, shall declare your verdict first : do you consider
becoming and being to be the same or different ?

Different, to be sure, said Prodicus.

Now in the first passage, I said, Simonides gave
it as his own opinion that it is hard for a man to
become good in truth.

Quite true, said Prodicus.

And he blames Pittacus, I went on, for saying
not, as Protagoras holds, the same as himself, but
something different. For what Pittacus said was
not, as Simonides said, that it is hard "to become"
but "to be" good. Now being and becoming,
Protagoras, as our friend Prodicus says, are not the
same thing ; and if being and becoming are not
the same thing, Simonides does not contradict
himself. Perhaps Prodicus and many others might
say with Hesiod that to become good is hard, " for
Heaven hath set hard travail on the way to virtue ;
and when one reacheth the summit thereof, 'tis an
easy thing to possess, though hard before." [1]

When Prodicus heard this he gave me his approval :
but Protagoras observed : Your correction, Socrates,
contains an error greater than that which you are
correcting.

[1] A not quite exact quotation of Hesiod, *Works and Days*,
289 foll.

ἐπανορθοῖς. καὶ ἐγὼ εἶπον, Κακὸν ἄρα μοι
εἴργασται, ὡς ἔοικεν, ὦ Πρωταγόρα, καὶ εἰμί
E τις γελοῖος ἰατρός· ἰώμενος μεῖζον τὸ νόσημα
ποιῶ. Ἀλλ' οὕτως ἔχει, ἔφη. Πῶς δή; ἦν
δ' ἐγώ. Πολλὴ ἄν, ἔφη, ἀμαθία εἴη τοῦ ποιητοῦ,
εἰ οὕτω φαῦλόν τί φησιν εἶναι τὴν ἀρετὴν ἐκτῆσθαι, ὅ ἐστι πάντων χαλεπώτατον, ὡς ἅπασι
δοκεῖ ἀνθρώποις. καὶ ἐγὼ εἶπον, Νὴ τὸν Δία,
εἰς καιρόν γε παρατετύχηκεν ἡμῖν ἐν τοῖς λόγοις
Πρόδικος ὅδε. κινδυνεύει γάρ τοι, ὦ Πρωταγόρα, ἡ Προδίκου σοφία θεία τις εἶναι πάλαι,
341 ἤτοι ἀπὸ Σιμωνίδου ἀρξαμένη, ἢ καὶ ἔτι παλαιο-
τέρα. σὺ δὲ ἄλλων πολλῶν ἔμπειρος ὢν ταύτης
ἄπειρος εἶναι φαίνει, οὐχ ὥσπερ ἐγὼ ἔμπειρος
διὰ τὸ μαθητὴς εἶναι Προδίκου τουτουΐ· καὶ
νῦν μοι δοκεῖς οὐ μανθάνειν, ὅτι καὶ τὸ χαλεπὸν
τοῦτο ἴσως οὐχ οὕτω Σιμωνίδης ὑπελάμβανεν,
ὥσπερ σὺ ὑπολαμβάνεις, ἀλλ' ὥσπερ περὶ τοῦ
δεινοῦ Πρόδικός με οὑτοσὶ νουθετεῖ ἑκάστοτε,
ὅταν ἐπαινῶν ἐγὼ ἢ σὲ ἢ ἄλλον τινὰ λέγω ὅτι
B Πρωταγόρας σοφὸς καὶ δεινός ἐστιν ἀνήρ, ἐρωτᾷ
εἰ οὐκ αἰσχύνομαι τἀγαθὰ δεινὰ καλῶν. τὸ
γὰρ δεινόν, φησί, κακόν ἐστιν· οὐδεὶς γοῦν λέγει
ἑκάστοτε δεινοῦ πλούτου οὐδὲ δεινῆς εἰρήνης
οὐδὲ δεινῆς ὑγιείας, ἀλλὰ δεινῆς νόσου καὶ δεινοῦ
πολέμου καὶ δεινῆς πενίας, ὡς τοῦ δεινοῦ κακοῦ
ὄντος. ἴσως οὖν καὶ τὸ χαλεπὸν αὖ οἱ Κεῖοι
καὶ ὁ Σιμωνίδης ἢ κακὸν ὑπολαμβάνουσιν ἢ
ἄλλο τι ὃ σὺ οὐ μανθάνεις· ἐρώμεθα οὖν Πρό-
δικον· δίκαιον γὰρ τὴν Σιμωνίδου φωνὴν τοῦτον

To which I answered : then it is a bad piece of work I have done, it would seem, Protagoras, and I am an absurd sort of physician ; my treatment increases the malady.

Just so, he said.

How is that ? I asked.

Great, he replied, would be the ignorance of the poet, if he calls it such a slight matter to possess virtue, which is the hardest thing in the world, as all men agree.

Then I remarked : Upon my word, how opportunely it has happened that Prodicus is here to join in our discussion ! For it is very likely, Protagoras, that Prodicus' wisdom is a gift of long ago from heaven, beginning either in the time of Simonides or even earlier. But you, so skilled in many other things, appear to be unskilled in this, and lack the skill that I can boast because I am a disciple of the great Prodicus ; and so now I find you do not understand that perhaps Simonides did not conceive " hard " in the way that you conceive it — just as, in the case of " awful," Prodicus here corrects me each time I use the word in praising you or someone else ; when I say, for instance, that Protagoras is an awfully wise man, he asks if I am not ashamed to call good things awful. For awful, he says, is bad ; thus no one on this or that occasion speaks of " awful wealth " or " awful peace " or " awful health," but we say " awful disease," " awful war " or " awful poverty," taking " awful " to be " bad." So perhaps " hard " also was intended by the Ceans and Simonides as either " bad " or something else that you do not understand : let us therefore ask Prodicus, for it is fair to question him

C ἐρωτᾶν· τί ἔλεγεν, ὦ Πρόδικε, τὸ χαλεπὸν Σιμωνίδης; Κακόν, ἔφη. Διὰ ταῦτ᾽ ἄρα καὶ
μέμφεται, ἦν δ᾽ ἐγώ, ὦ Πρόδικε, τὸν Πιττακὸν
λέγοντα χαλεπὸν ἐσθλὸν ἔμμεναι, ὥσπερ ἂν εἰ
ἤκουεν αὐτοῦ λέγοντος ὅτι ἐστὶ κακὸν ἐσθλὸν
ἔμμεναι. Ἀλλὰ τί οἴει, ἔφη, λέγειν, ὦ Σώκρατες, Σιμωνίδην ἄλλο ἢ τοῦτο, καὶ ὀνειδίζειν
τῷ Πιττακῷ, ὅτι τὰ ὀνόματα οὐκ ἠπίστατο
ὀρθῶς διαιρεῖν ἅτε Λέσβιος ὢν καὶ ἐν φωνῇ
βαρβάρῳ τεθραμμένος; Ἀκούεις δή, ἔφην ἐγώ,
D ὦ Πρωταγόρα, Προδίκου τοῦδε. ἔχεις τι πρὸς
ταῦτα λέγειν; καὶ ὁ Πρωταγόρας, Πολλοῦ γε
δεῖ, ἔφη, οὕτως ἔχειν, ὦ Πρόδικε· ἀλλ᾽ ἐγὼ εὖ
οἶδ᾽ ὅτι καὶ Σιμωνίδης τὸ χαλεπὸν ἔλεγεν ὅπερ
ἡμεῖς οἱ ἄλλοι, οὐ τὸ κακόν, ἀλλ᾽ ὃ ἂν μὴ ῥάδιον
ᾖ, ἀλλὰ διὰ πολλῶν πραγμάτων γίγνηται. Ἀλλὰ
καὶ ἐγὼ οἶμαι, ἔφην, ὦ Πρωταγόρα, τοῦτο λέγειν
Σιμωνίδην, καὶ Πρόδικόν γε τόνδε εἰδέναι, ἀλλὰ
παίζειν καὶ σοῦ δοκεῖν ἀποπειρᾶσθαι, εἰ οἷός τ᾽
ἔσει τῷ σαυτοῦ λόγῳ βοηθεῖν· ἐπεὶ ὅτι γε Σι-
E μωνίδης οὐ λέγει τὸ χαλεπὸν κακόν, μέγα τεκμήριόν ἐστιν εὐθὺς τὸ μετὰ τοῦτο ῥῆμα· λέγει
γὰρ ὅτι

θεὸς ἂν μόνος τοῦτ᾽ ἔχοι γέρας.

οὐ δήπου τοῦτό γε λέγων, κακὸν ἐσθλὸν ἔμμεναι,
εἶτα τὸν θεόν φησι μόνον τοῦτο ἂν ἔχειν καὶ τῷ
θεῷ τοῦτο γέρας ἀπένειμε μόνῳ· ἀκόλαστον γὰρ
ἄν τινα λέγοι Σιμωνίδην ὁ Πρόδικος καὶ οὐδαμῶς
Κεῖον. ἀλλ᾽ ἅ μοι δοκεῖ διανοεῖσθαι Σιμωνίδης
ἐν τούτῳ τῷ ᾄσματι, ἐθέλω σοι εἰπεῖν, εἰ βούλει
342 λαβεῖν μου πεῖραν ὅπως ἔχω, ὃ σὺ λέγεις τοῦτο,

on the dialect of Simonides. What did Simonides mean, Prodicus, by " hard " ?

" Bad," he replied.

Then it is on this account, Prodicus, I said, that he blames Pittacus for saying it is hard to be good, just as though he heard him say it is bad to be good.

Well, Socrates, he said, what else do you think Simonides meant ? Was he not reproaching Pittacus for not knowing how to distinguish words correctly, Lesbian as he was, and nurtured in a foreign tongue ?

You hear, Protagoras, I said, what Prodicus here suggests : have you anything to say upon it ?

The case, said Protagoras, is far otherwise, Prodicus : I am quite sure that Simonides meant by " hard " the same as we generally do—not " bad," but whatever is not easy and involves a great amount of trouble.

Ah, I agree with you, Protagoras, I said, that this is Simonides' meaning, and that our friend Prodicus knows it, but is joking and chooses to experiment on you to see if you will be able to support your own statement. For that Simonides does not mean that " hard " is " bad " we have clear proof forthwith in the next phrase, where he says—

God alone can have this privilege.

Surely he cannot mean that it is bad to be good, if he proceeds here to say that God alone can have this thing, and attributes this privilege to God only : otherwise Prodicus would call Simonides a rake, and no true Cean. But I should like to tell you what I take to be Simonides' intention in this ode, if you care to test my powers, as you put it,[1] in the matter

[1] *Cf.* 339 A above.

περὶ ἐπῶν· ἐὰν δὲ βούλῃ, σοῦ ἀκούσομαι. ὁ μὲν
οὖν Πρωταγόρας ἀκούσας μου ταῦτα λέγοντος,
Εἰ σὺ βούλει, ἔφη, ὦ Σώκρατες· ὁ δὲ Πρόδικός
τε καὶ ὁ Ἱππίας ἐκελευέτην πάνυ, καὶ οἱ ἄλλοι.

Ἐγὼ τοίνυν, ἦν δ' ἐγώ, ἅ γέ μοι δοκεῖ περὶ
τοῦ ᾄσματος τούτου, πειράσομαι ὑμῖν διεξελθεῖν.
φιλοσοφία γάρ ἐστι παλαιοτάτη τε καὶ πλείστη
τῶν Ἑλλήνων ἐν Κρήτῃ τε καὶ ἐν Λακεδαίμονι,
B καὶ σοφισταὶ πλεῖστοι γῆς ἐκεῖ εἰσίν· ἀλλ' ἐξ-
αρνοῦνται καὶ σχηματίζονται ἀμαθεῖς εἶναι, ἵνα
μὴ κατάδηλοι ὦσιν ὅτι σοφίᾳ τῶν Ἑλλήνων
περίεισιν, ὥσπερ οὓς Πρωταγόρας ἔλεγε τοὺς
σοφιστάς, ἀλλὰ δοκῶσι τῷ μάχεσθαι καὶ ἀνδρείᾳ
περιεῖναι, ἡγούμενοι, εἰ γνωσθεῖεν ᾧ περίεισι,
πάντας τοῦτο ἀσκήσειν, τὴν σοφίαν. νῦν δὲ
ἀποκρυψάμενοι ἐκεῖνο ἐξηπατήκασι τοὺς ἐν ταῖς
πόλεσι λακωνίζοντας, καὶ οἱ μὲν ὦτά τε κατ-
C άγνυνται μιμούμενοι αὐτούς, καὶ ἱμάντας περι-
ειλίττονται καὶ φιλογυμναστοῦσι καὶ βραχείας ἀνα-
βολὰς φοροῦσιν, ὡς δὴ τούτοις κρατοῦντας τῶν
Ἑλλήνων τοὺς Λακεδαιμονίους· οἱ δὲ Λακεδαιμόνιοι ἐπειδὰν βούλωνται ἀνέδην τοῖς παρ'
αὑτοῖς συγγενέσθαι σοφισταῖς, καὶ ἤδη ἄχθωνται
λάθρᾳ ξυγγιγνόμενοι, ξενηλασίας ποιούμενοι τῶν
τε λακωνιζόντων τούτων καὶ ἐάν τις ἄλλος ξένος
ὢν ἐπιδημήσῃ, συγγίγνονται τοῖς σοφισταῖς λαν-
θάνοντες τοὺς ξένους, καὶ αὐτοὶ οὐδένα ἐῶσι
D τῶν νέων εἰς τὰς ἄλλας πόλεις ἐξιέναι, ὥσπερ

---

[1] *Cf.* 316 D. This whole passage is a mocking answer to
Protagoras's eulogy of sophistry.

[2] Short cloaks or capes worn in a fashion imitated from
the Spartans.

of verses ; though if you would rather, I will hear your account.

When Protagoras heard me say this—As you please, Socrates, he said ; then Prodicus and Hippias strongly urged me, and the rest of them also.

Well then, I said, I will try to explain to you my own feeling about this poem. Now philosophy is of more ancient and abundant growth in Crete and Lacedaemon than in any other part of Greece, and sophists are more numerous in those regions : but the people there deny it and make pretence of ignorance, in order to prevent the discovery that it is by wisdom that they have ascendancy over the rest of the Greeks, like those sophists of whom Protagoras was speaking [1] ; they prefer it to be thought that they owe their superiority to fighting and valour, conceiving that the revelation of its real cause would lead everyone to practise this wisdom. So well have they kept their secret that they have deceived the followers of the Spartan cult in our cities, with the result that some get broken ears by imitating them, bind their knuckles with thongs, go in for muscular exercises, and wear dashing little cloaks,[2] as though it were by these means that the Spartans were the masters of Greece. And when the Spartans wish to converse unrestrainedly with their sophists, and begin to chafe at the secrecy of their meetings, they pass alien acts against the laconizing set [3] and any other strangers within their gates, and have meetings with the sophists unknown to the foreigners ; while on their part they do not permit any of their young men to travel abroad

[3] *i.e.* people who have come to acquire the Spartan way of life, in order to spread it in other cities.

οὐδὲ Κρῆτες, ἵνα μὴ ἀπομανθάνωσιν ἃ αὐτοὶ
διδάσκουσιν. εἰσὶ δὲ ἐν ταύταις ταῖς πόλεσιν
οὐ μόνον ἄνδρες ἐπὶ παιδεύσει μέγα φρονοῦντες,
ἀλλὰ καὶ γυναῖκες. γνοῖτε δ' ἄν, ὅτι ἐγὼ ταῦτα
ἀληθῆ λέγω καὶ Λακεδαιμόνιοι πρὸς φιλοσοφίαν
καὶ λόγους ἄριστα πεπαίδευνται, ὧδε· εἰ γὰρ
ἐθέλει τις Λακεδαιμονίων τῷ φαυλοτάτῳ συγ-
E γενέσθαι, τὰ μὲν πρῶτα ἐν τοῖς λόγοις εὑρήσει
αὐτὸν φαῦλόν τινα φαινόμενον, ἔπειτα, ὅπου ἂν
τύχῃ τῶν λεγομένων, ἐνέβαλε ῥῆμα ἄξιον λόγου
βραχὺ καὶ συνεστραμμένον ὥσπερ δεινὸς ἀκοντι-
στής, ὥστε φαίνεσθαι τὸν προσδιαλεγόμενον παιδὸς μηδὲν βελτίω. τοῦτο οὖν αὐτὸ καὶ τῶν
νῦν εἰσιν οἳ κατανενοήκασι καὶ τῶν πάλαι, ὅτι
τὸ λακωνίζειν πολὺ μᾶλλόν ἐστι φιλοσοφεῖν ἢ
φιλογυμναστεῖν, εἰδότες ὅτι τοιαῦτα οἷόν τ'
343 εἶναι ῥήματα φθέγγεσθαι τελέως πεπαιδευμένου
ἐστὶν ἀνθρώπου. τούτων ἦν καὶ Θαλῆς ὁ Μι-
λήσιος καὶ Πιττακὸς ὁ Μυτιληναῖος καὶ Βίας
ὁ Πριηνεὺς καὶ Σόλων ὁ ἡμέτερος καὶ Κλεόβουλος
ὁ Λίνδιος καὶ Μύσων ὁ Χηνεύς, καὶ ἕβδομος
ἐν τούτοις ἐλέγετο Λακεδαιμόνιος Χίλων. οὗτοι
πάντες ζηλωταὶ καὶ ἐρασταὶ καὶ μαθηταὶ ἦσαν
τῆς Λακεδαιμονίων παιδείας· καὶ καταμάθοι ἄν
τις αὐτῶν τὴν σοφίαν τοιαύτην οὖσαν, ῥήματα
βραχέα ἀξιομνημόνευτα ἑκάστῳ εἰρημένα, ⟨ἃ⟩[1]
B οὗτοι καὶ κοινῇ ξυνελθόντες ἀπαρχὴν τῆς σοφίας
ἀνέθεσαν τῷ Ἀπόλλωνι εἰς τὸν νεὼν τὸν ἐν Δελφοῖς, γράψαντες ταῦτα, ἃ δὴ πάντες ὑμνοῦσι,
γνῶθι σαυτόν καὶ μηδὲν ἄγαν. τοῦ δὴ ἕνεκα
ταῦτα λέγω; ὅτι οὗτος ὁ τρόπος ἦν τῶν παλαιῶν
τῆς φιλοσοφίας, βραχυλογία τις Λακωνική· καὶ δὴ

to the other cities—in this rule they resemble the
Cretans—lest they unlearn what they are taught at
home. In those two states there are not only men
but women also who pride themselves on their
education; and you can tell that what I say is
true and that the Spartans have the best education
in philosophy and argument by this : if you choose
to consort with the meanest of Spartans, at first
you will find him making a poor show in the conversation ; but soon, at some point or other in the
discussion, he gets home with a notable remark,
short and compressed—a deadly shot that makes
his interlocutor seem like a helpless child. Hence
this very truth has been observed by certain persons
both in our day and in former times—that the
Spartan cult is much more the pursuit of wisdom
than of athletics ; for they know that a man's
ability to utter such remarks is to be ascribed to
his perfect education. Such men were Thales of
Miletus, Pittacus of Mytilene, Bias of Priene, Solon
of our city, Cleobulus of Lindus, Myson of Chen, and,
last of the traditional seven, Chilon of Sparta. All
these were enthusiasts, lovers and disciples of the
Spartan culture ; and you can recognize that character in their wisdom by the short, memorable
sayings that fell from each of them : they assembled
together and dedicated these as the first-fruits of
their lore to Apollo in his Delphic temple, inscribing
there those maxims which are on every tongue—
" Know thyself " and " Nothing overmuch." To
what intent do I say this ? To show how the ancient
philosophy had this style of laconic brevity ; and

---

[1] ἀ add. Hermann.

καὶ τοῦ Πιττακοῦ ἰδίᾳ περιεφέρετο τοῦτο τὸ
ῥῆμα ἐγκωμιαζόμενον ὑπὸ τῶν σοφῶν, τὸ χαλεπὸν
C ἐσθλὸν ἔμμεναι. ὁ οὖν Σιμωνίδης, ἅτε φιλό-
τιμος ὢν ἐπὶ σοφίᾳ, ἔγνω ὅτι, εἰ καθέλοι τοῦτο
τὸ ῥῆμα ὥσπερ εὐδοκιμοῦντα ἀθλητὴν καὶ περι-
γένοιτο αὐτοῦ, αὐτὸς εὐδοκιμήσει ἐν τοῖς τότε
ἀνθρώποις. εἰς τοῦτο οὖν τὸ ῥῆμα καὶ τούτου
ἕνεκα τούτῳ ἐπιβουλεύων κολοῦσαι αὐτὸ ἅπαν
τὸ ᾆσμα πεποίηκεν, ὥς μοι φαίνεται.

Ἐπισκεψώμεθα δὴ αὐτὸ κοινῇ ἅπαντες, εἰ
ἄρα ἐγὼ ἀληθῆ λέγω. εὐθὺς γὰρ τὸ πρῶτον
τοῦ ᾄσματος μανικὸν ἂν φανείη, εἰ βουλόμενος
D λέγειν, ὅτι ἄνδρα ἀγαθὸν γενέσθαι χαλεπόν,
ἔπειτα ἐνέβαλε τὸ μέν. τοῦτο γὰρ οὐδὲ πρὸς
ἕνα λόγον φαίνεται ἐμβεβλῆσθαι, ἐὰν μή τις
ὑπολάβῃ πρὸς τὸ τοῦ Πιττακοῦ ῥῆμα ὥσπερ
ἐρίζοντα λέγειν τὸν Σιμωνίδην· λέγοντος τοῦ
Πιττακοῦ ὅτι χαλεπὸν ἐσθλὸν ἔμμεναι, ἀμφι-
σβητοῦντα εἰπεῖν ὅτι οὔκ, ἀλλὰ γενέσθαι μὲν
χαλεπὸν ἄνδρα ἀγαθόν ἐστιν, ὦ Πιττακέ, ὡς
ἀληθῶς, οὐκ ἀληθείᾳ ἀγαθόν, οὐκ ἐπὶ τούτῳ
E λέγει τὴν ἀλήθειαν, ὡς ἄρα ὄντων τινῶν τῶν
μὲν ὡς ἀληθῶς ἀγαθῶν, τῶν δὲ ἀγαθῶν μέν,
οὐ μέντοι ἀληθῶς· εὔηθες γὰρ τοῦτό γε φανείη
ἂν καὶ οὐ Σιμωνίδου· ἀλλ' ὑπερβατὸν δεῖ θεῖναι
ἐν τῷ ᾄσματι τὸ ἀλαθέως, οὑτωσί πως ὑπ-
ειπόντα τὸ τοῦ Πιττακοῦ, ὥσπερ ἂν εἰ θεῖμεν
αὐτὸν λέγοντα τὸν Πιττακὸν καὶ Σιμωνίδην
ἀποκρινόμενον, εἰπόντα ὦ ἄνθρωποι, χαλεπὸν
ἐσθλὸν ἔμμεναι, τὸν δὲ ἀποκρινόμενον ὅτι ὦ

---

[1] In this view of the purpose of the poem (which is to
show that there is no lasting perfection in human life), and

so it was that the saying of Pittacus was privately handed about with high approbation among the sages—that it is hard to be good. Then Simonides, ambitious to get a name for wisdom, perceived that if he could overthrow this saying, as one might some famous athlete, and become its conqueror, he would win fame himself amongst men of that day. Accordingly it was against this saying, and with this aim, that he composed the whole poem as a means of covertly assailing and abasing this maxim, as it seems to me.[1]

Now let us all combine in considering whether my account is really true. The opening of the ode must at once appear crazy if, while intending to say that it is hard for a man to become good, he inserted "indeed." There is no sort of sense, I imagine, in this insertion, unless we suppose that Simonides is addressing himself to the saying of Pittacus as a disputant : Pittacus says—It is hard to be good ; and the poet controverts this by observing—No, but to become good, indeed, is hard for a man, Pittacus, truly—not truly good ; he does not mention truth in this connexion, or imply that some things are truly good, while others are good but not truly so : this would seem silly and unlike Simonides. We must rather take the " truly " as a poetical transposition, and first quote the saying of Pittacus in some such way as this : let us suppose Pittacus himself to be speaking and Simonides replying, as thus—Good people, he says, it is hard to be good ; and the poet answers—Pittacus, what you

in the detailed commentary that follows, Socrates is aping the disquisitions of the more literary sophists (*e.g.* Hippias, who warmly approves, 347 A).

344 Πιττακέ, οὐκ ἀληθῆ λέγεις· οὐ γὰρ εἶναι ἀλλὰ
γενέσθαι μέν ἐστιν ἄνδρα ἀγαθὸν χερσί τε καὶ
ποσὶ καὶ νόῳ τετράγωνον, ἄνευ ψόγου τετυγμένον,
χαλεπὸν ἀλαθέως. οὕτω φαίνεται [τὸ]¹ πρὸς
λόγον τὸ μέν ἐμβεβλημένον καὶ τὸ ἀλαθέως
ὀρθῶς ἐπ᾽ ἐσχάτῳ κείμενον· καὶ τὰ ἐπιόντα
πάντα τούτῳ μαρτυρεῖ, ὅτι οὕτως εἴρηται. πολλὰ μὲν γὰρ ἔστι καὶ περὶ ἑκάστου τῶν ἐν τῷ
B ᾄσματι εἰρημένων ἀποδεῖξαι ὡς εὖ πεποίηται·
πάνυ γὰρ χαριέντως καὶ μεμελημένως ἔχει· ἀλλὰ
μακρὸν ἂν εἴη αὐτὸ οὕτω διελθεῖν· ἀλλὰ τὸν
τύπον αὐτοῦ τὸν ὅλον διεξέλθωμεν καὶ τὴν βού-
λησιν, ὅτι παντὸς μᾶλλον ἔλεγχός ἐστι τοῦ Πιτ-
τακείου ῥήματος διὰ παντὸς τοῦ ᾄσματος.

Λέγει γὰρ μετὰ τοῦτο ὀλίγα διελθών, ὡς ἂν
εἰ λέγοι λόγον, ὅτι γενέσθαι μὲν ἄνδρα ἀγαθὸν
χαλεπὸν ἀλαθέως, οἷόν τε μέντοι ἐπί γε χρόνον
τινά· γενόμενον δὲ διαμένειν ἐν ταύτῃ τῇ ἕξει
C καὶ εἶναι ἄνδρα ἀγαθόν, ὡς σὺ λέγεις, ὦ Πιττακέ,
ἀδύνατον καὶ οὐκ ἀνθρώπειον, ἀλλὰ θεὸς ἂν μόνος
τοῦτο ἔχοι τὸ γέρας,

ἄνδρα δ᾽ οὐκ ἔστι μὴ οὐ κακὸν ἔμμεναι,
ὃν ἂν ἀμήχανος συμφορὰ καθέλῃ.

τίνα οὖν ἀμήχανος συμφορὰ καθαιρεῖ ἐν πλοίου
ἀρχῇ; δῆλον ὅτι οὐ τὸν ἰδιώτην· ὁ μὲν γὰρ
ἰδιώτης ἀεὶ καθῄρηται· ὥσπερ οὖν οὐ τὸν κεί-
μενόν τις ἂν καταβάλοι, ἀλλὰ τὸν μὲν ἑστῶτά
ποτε καταβάλοι ἄν τις, ὥστε κείμενον ποιῆσαι,
D τὸν δὲ κείμενον οὔ, οὕτω καὶ τὸν εὐμήχανον ὄντα
ποτὲ ἀμήχανος ἂν συμφορὰ καθέλοι, τὸν δὲ ἀεὶ

¹ τὸ secl. Heindorf.

200

say is not true, for it is not being but becoming good,
indeed—in hands and feet and mind foursquare,
fashioned without reproach—that is truly hard.
In this way we see a purpose in the insertion of
" indeed," and that the " truly " is correctly placed
at the end ; and all that comes after corroborates
this view of his meaning. There are many points
in the various expressions of the poem which might
be instanced to show its fine composition, for it is a
work of very elegant and elaborate art ; but it would
take too long to detail all its beauties. However,
let us go over its general outline and intention,
which is assuredly to refute Pittacus' saying, throughout the ode.

Proceeding a little way on from our passage, just
as though he were making a speech, he says to
become, indeed, a good man is truly hard (not but
what it is possible for a certain space of time) ;
" but to continue in this state of what one has
become, and to *be* a good man is, as you say, Pittacus,
impossible, superhuman : God alone can have this
privilege—

> For that man cannot help but be bad
> Whom irresistible mischance has overthrown.

Now who is it that an irresistible mischance overthrows in the command of a ship ? Clearly not the
ordinary man, for he may be overcome at any time ;
just as you cannot knock over one who is lying
down, but one who is standing ; you might knock
over a standing man so as to make him lie down,
not one who is lying down already. So it is a man
apt to resist that an irresistible mischance would
overthrow, and not one who could never resist

201

ἀμήχανον ὄντα οὔ· καὶ τὸν κυβερνήτην μέγας
χειμὼν ἐπιπεσὼν ἀμήχανον ἂν ποιήσειε, καὶ
γεωργὸν χαλεπὴ ὥρα ἐπελθοῦσα ἀμήχανον ἂν
θείη, καὶ ἰατρὸν ταὐτὰ ταῦτα. τῷ μὲν γὰρ
ἐσθλῷ ἐγχωρεῖ κακῷ γενέσθαι, ὥσπερ καὶ παρ'
ἄλλου ποιητοῦ μαρτυρεῖται τοῦ εἰπόντος

αὐτὰρ ἀνὴρ ἀγαθὸς τοτὲ μὲν κακός, ἄλλοτε
δ' ἐσθλός·

τῷ δὲ κακῷ οὐκ ἐγχωρεῖ γενέσθαι, ἀλλ' ἀεὶ
E εἶναι ἀνάγκη· ὥστε τὸν μὲν εὐμήχανον καὶ σοφὸν
καὶ ἀγαθὸν ἐπειδὰν ἀμήχανος συμφορὰ καθέλῃ,
οὐκ ἔστι μὴ οὐ κακὸν ἔμμεναι· σὺ δὲ φής, ὦ
Πιττακέ, χαλεπὸν ἐσθλὸν ἔμμεναι· τὸ δ' ἐστὶ
γενέσθαι μὲν χαλεπόν, δυνατὸν δέ, ἐσθλόν, ἔμμεναι δὲ ἀδύνατον·

πράξας μὲν γὰρ εὖ πᾶς ἀνὴρ ἀγαθός,
κακὸς δ' εἰ κακῶς.

τίς οὖν εἰς γράμματα ἀγαθὴ πρᾶξίς ἐστι, καὶ
345 τίς ἄνδρα ἀγαθὸν ποιεῖ εἰς γράμματα; δῆλον
ὅτι ἡ τούτων μάθησις. τίς δὲ εὐπραγία ἀγαθὸν
ἰατρὸν ποιεῖ; δῆλον ὅτι ἡ τῶν καμνόντων τῆς
θεραπείας μάθησις. κακὸς δὲ κακῶς· τίς οὖν
ἂν κακὸς ἰατρὸς γένοιτο; δῆλον ὅτι ᾧ πρῶτον
μὲν ὑπάρχει ἰατρῷ εἶναι, ἔπειτα ἀγαθῷ ἰατρῷ·
οὗτος γὰρ ἂν καὶ κακὸς γένοιτο· ἡμεῖς δὲ οἱ
ἰατρικῆς ἰδιῶται οὐκ ἄν ποτε γενοίμεθα κακῶς
πράξαντες οὔτε ἰατροὶ οὔτε τέκτονες οὔτε ἄλλο
B οὐδὲν τῶν τοιούτων· ὅστις δὲ μὴ ἰατρὸς ἂν γένοιτο κακῶς πράξας, δῆλον ὅτι οὐδὲ κακὸς ἰατρός.
οὕτω καὶ ὁ μὲν ἀγαθὸς ἀνὴρ γένοιτ' ἄν ποτε καὶ

anything. A great storm breaking over a steersman will render him helpless, and a severe season will leave a farmer helpless, and a doctor will be in the same case. For the good has the capacity of becoming bad, as we have witness in another poet[1] who said—

Nay more, the virtuous man is at one time bad, at another good.

whereas the bad man has no capacity for becoming, but must ever be, what he is ; so that when an irresistible mischance overthrows him who is re-sourceful, wise, and good, he cannot but be bad ; and you say, Pittacus, that it is hard to be good— that is, to become good, indeed, is hard, though possible, but to be good is impossible : for—[2]

If he hath fared well, every man is good ;
Bad, if ill.

Now what is good faring in letters—the thing that makes a man good at them ? Clearly, the study of letters. What welfare makes a good doctor ? Clearly, the study of the cure of the ailing. " Bad, if ill " : who could become a bad doctor ? Clearly, he who in the first place is a doctor, and in the second, a good doctor ; for he could become a bad one also : whereas we, who are laymen in respect of medicine, could never by faring ill become either doctors or joiners or anything else of that sort ; and if one cannot become a doctor by faring ill, clearly one cannot become a bad one either. In the same way the good man may one day become

[1] Unknown.
[2] The quotation of Simonides' poem is resumed (from 344 c).

κακὸς ἢ ὑπὸ χρόνου ἢ ὑπὸ πόνου ἢ ὑπὸ νόσου
ἢ ὑπὸ ἄλλου τινὸς περιπτώματος· αὕτη γὰρ
μόνη ἐστὶ κακὴ πρᾶξις, ἐπιστήμης στερηθῆναι·
ὁ δὲ κακὸς ἀνὴρ οὐκ ἄν ποτε γένοιτο κακός·
ἔστι γὰρ ἀεί· ἀλλ᾽ εἰ μέλλει κακὸς γενέσθαι,
δεῖ αὐτὸν πρότερον ἀγαθὸν γενέσθαι. ὥστε καὶ
C τοῦτο τοῦ ᾄσματος πρὸς τοῦτο τείνει, ὅτι εἶναι
μὲν ἄνδρα ἀγαθὸν οὐχ οἷόν τε διατελοῦντα ἀγαθόν, γενέσθαι δὲ ἀγαθὸν οἷόν τε, καὶ κακόν γε
τὸν αὐτὸν τοῦτον· ἐπὶ πλεῖστον δὲ καὶ ἄριστοί
εἰσιν οὓς ἂν οἱ θεοὶ φιλῶσιν.

Ταῦτά τε οὖν πάντα πρὸς τὸν Πιττακὸν εἴρηται, καὶ τὰ ἐπιόντα γε τοῦ ᾄσματος ἔτι μᾶλλον
δηλοῖ. φησὶ γάρ·

> τοὔνεκεν οὔ ποτ᾽ ἐγὼ τὸ μὴ γενέσθαι δυνατὸν
> διζήμενος κενεὰν ἐς ἄπρακτον ἐλπίδα μοῖραν
>   αἰῶνος βαλέω,
> πανάμωμον ἄνθρωπον, εὐρυεδοῦς ὅσοι καρπὸν
>   αἰνύμεθα χθονός·
D ἐπί θ᾽¹ ὑμῖν εὑρὼν ἀπαγγελέω,

φησίν· οὕτω σφόδρα καὶ δι᾽ ὅλου τοῦ ᾄσματος
ἐπεξέρχεται τῷ τοῦ Πιττακοῦ ῥήματι·

> πάντας δ᾽ ἐπαίνημι καὶ φιλέω
> ἑκὼν ὅστις ἔρδῃ
> μηδὲν αἰσχρόν· ἀνάγκῃ δ᾽ οὐδὲ θεοὶ μάχονται·

καὶ τοῦτ᾽ ἐστὶ πρὸς τὸ αὐτὸ τοῦτο εἰρημένον.
οὐ γὰρ οὕτως ἀπαίδευτος ἦν Σιμωνίδης, ὥστε
τούτους φάναι ἐπαινεῖν, ὃς ἂν ἑκὼν μηδὲν κακὸν
ποιῇ, ὡς ὄντων τινῶν οἳ ἑκόντες κακὰ ποιοῦσιν.
ἐγὼ γὰρ σχεδόν τι οἶμαι τοῦτο, ὅτι οὐδεὶς τῶν

bad through the effect either of time or work or
illness or some other accident; for there is only
one sort of ill fare—the deprivation of knowledge.
But the bad man can never become bad: he is that
always. If he is to become bad, he must previously
become good. Hence the upshot of this part of the
poem is that it is impossible to be a good man,
continuing to be good, but possible to become
good, and bad also, in the case of the same person.
And then—

Best also for the longest space are they whom the gods love.[1]

All this has been said with reference to Pittacus,
as is made still plainer by the ensuing verses, in
which he says—

Therefore never shall I, in quest of what cannot come to
pass, vainly cast my life's lot upon a hope impracticable—
of finding a man wholly blameless amongst us who partake
of the fruit of the broad-based earth. If I light upon him,
be sure I will report it—

says he; and in this vehement tone he pursues the
saying of Pittacus all through the poem:

But I praise and love everyone willingly committing no
baseness; for against necessity not even the gods make
war.

This also is spoken with the same intent. For
Simonides was not so ill-educated as to say that he
praised a person who willingly did no evil, as though
there were some who did evil willingly. I am
fairly sure of this—that none of the wise men con-

[1] Probably a loose quotation of a line of the poem which
was καὶ τὸ πλεῖστον ἄριστοι, τούς κε θεοὶ φιλῶσιν (Aars).

---

[1] ἐπί θ' Adam: ἐπὶ δ' ὕμμιν Bergk: ἔπειθ' MSS.

σοφῶν ἀνδρῶν ἡγεῖται οὐδένα ἀνθρώπων ἑκόντα

E ἐξαμαρτάνειν οὐδὲ αἰσχρά τε καὶ κακὰ ἑκόντα
ἐργάζεσθαι, ἀλλ᾽ εὖ ἴσασιν ὅτι πάντες οἱ τὰ
αἰσχρὰ καὶ τὰ κακὰ ποιοῦντες ἄκοντες ποιοῦσι·
καὶ δὴ καὶ ὁ Σιμωνίδης οὐχ ὃς ἂν μὴ κακὰ ποιῇ
ἑκών, τούτων φησὶν ἐπαινέτης εἶναι, ἀλλὰ περὶ
ἑαυτοῦ λέγει τοῦτο τὸ ἑκών. ἡγεῖτο γὰρ ἄνδρα καλὸν κἀγαθὸν πολλάκις αὑτὸν ἐπαναγκάζειν

346 φίλον τινὶ γίγνεσθαι καὶ ἐπαινέτην [φιλεῖν καὶ
ἐπαινεῖν],[1] οἷον ἀνδρὶ πολλάκις συμβῆναι μητέρα
ἢ πατέρα ἀλλόκοτον ἢ πατρίδα ἢ ἄλλο τι τῶν
τοιούτων. τοὺς μὲν οὖν πονηρούς, ὅταν τοιοῦτόν
τι αὐτοῖς συμβῇ, ὥσπερ ἀσμένους ὁρᾶν καὶ ψέ-
γοντας ἐπιδεικνύναι καὶ κατηγορεῖν τὴν πονηρίαν
τῶν γονέων ἢ πατρίδος, ἵνα αὐτοῖς ἀμελοῦσιν
αὐτῶν μὴ ἐγκαλῶσιν οἱ ἄνθρωποι μηδ᾽ ὀνειδί-
ζωσιν ὅτι ἀμελοῦσιν, ὥστε ἔτι μᾶλλον ψέγειν

B τε αὐτοὺς καὶ ἔχθρας ἑκουσίους πρὸς ταῖς ἀναγ-
καίαις[2] προστίθεσθαι· τοὺς δ᾽ ἀγαθοὺς ἐπικρύ-
πτεσθαί τε καὶ ἐπαινεῖν ἀναγκάζεσθαι, καὶ ἄν τι
ὀργισθῶσι τοῖς γονεῦσιν ἢ πατρίδι ἀδικηθέντες,
αὐτοὺς ἑαυτοὺς παραμυθεῖσθαι καὶ διαλλάττεσθαι
προσαναγκάζοντας ἑαυτοὺς φιλεῖν τοὺς ἑαυτῶν
καὶ ἐπαινεῖν. πολλάκις δέ, οἶμαι, καὶ Σιμωνίδης ἡγήσατο καὶ αὐτὸς ἢ τύραννον ἢ ἄλλον
τινὰ τῶν τοιούτων ἐπαινέσαι καὶ ἐγκωμιάσαι

C οὐχ ἑκών, ἀλλ᾽ ἀναγκαζόμενος. ταῦτα δὴ καὶ
τῷ Πιττακῷ λέγει ὅτι ἐγώ, ὦ Πιττακέ, οὐ διὰ
ταῦτά σε ψέγω, ὅτι εἰμὶ φιλόψογος, ἐπεὶ

ἔμοιγ᾽ ἐξαρκεῖ ὃς ἂν μὴ κακὸς ᾖ

---

[1] φιλεῖν καὶ ἐπαινεῖν secl. Grou.

siders that anybody ever willingly errs or willingly does base and evil deeds ; they are well aware that all who do base and evil things do them unwillingly ; and so Simonides does not say he gives his praise to the person who willingly does no evil, but uses the word "willingly" of himself. For he considered that a man of sense and honour often constrains himself to become a friend and approver of some person, as when a man chances to have an uncongenial mother or father or country or other such connexion. Now when this sort of thing befalls the wicked, they seem glad to see their parents' or country's faults, and complainingly point them out and inveigh against them, in order that their own neglect of them may not be denounced by their neighbours, who might otherwise reproach them for being so neglectful ; and hence they multiply their complaints and add voluntary to unavoidable feuds. But good men, he knew, conceal the trouble and constrain themselves to praise, and if they have any reason to be angered against their parents or country for some wrong done to them they pacify and conciliate their feelings, compelling themselves to love and praise their own people. And many a time, I think, Simonides was conscious that he had praised and eulogized some tyrant or other such person, not willingly, but under compulsion. So he proceeds to tell Pittacus—I, Pittacus, do not reproach you merely because I am apt to reproach, since—

For my part I am content with whosoever is not evil or

---

³ ἀναγκαίαις Heusde : ἀνάγκαις MSS.

μηδ' ἄγαν ἀπάλαμνος, εἰδώς τ' ὀνησίπολιν¹ δίκαν
  ὑγιὴς ἀνήρ·
οὔ μιν² ἐγὼ μωμήσομαι.
οὐ γὰρ εἰμι φιλόμωμος·
τῶν γὰρ ἠλιθίων ἀπείρων γενέθλα,
ὥστ' εἴ τις χαίρει ψέγων, ἐμπλησθείη ἂν ἐκείνους
μεμφόμενος.

πάντα τοι καλά, τοῖσί τ' αἰσχρὰ μὴ μέμικται.

οὐ τοῦτο λέγει, ὥσπερ ἂν εἰ ἔλεγε πάντα τοι
D λευκά, οἷς μέλανα μὴ μέμικται· γελοῖον γὰρ ἂν
εἴη πολλαχῇ· ἀλλ' ὅτι αὐτὸς καὶ τὰ μέσα ἀπο-
δέχεται ὥστε μὴ ψέγειν· καὶ οὐ ζητῶ, ἔφη,
πανάμωμον ἄνθρωπον, εὐρυεδοῦς ὅσοι καρπὸν
αἰνύμεθα χθονός, ἐπί θ' ὑμῖν εὑρὼν ἀπαγγελέω·
ὥστε τούτου γ' ἕνεκα οὐδένα ἐπαινέσομαι, ἀλλά
μοι ἐξαρκεῖ, ἂν ᾖ μέσος καὶ μηδὲν κακὸν ποιῇ,
ὡς ἐγὼ πάντας φιλέω καὶ ἐπαίνημι—καὶ τῇ φωνῇ
ἐνταῦθα κέχρηται τῇ τῶν Μυτιληναίων, ὡς πρὸς
E Πιττακὸν λέγων τὸ πάντας δὲ ἐπαίνημι καὶ
φιλέω ἑκών (ἐνταῦθα δεῖ ἐν τῷ ἑκών διαλαβεῖν
λέγοντα) ὅστις ἔρδῃ μηδὲν αἰσχρόν, ἄκων δ'
ἔστιν οὓς ἐγὼ ἐπαινῶ καὶ φιλῶ. σὲ οὖν, καὶ
εἰ μέσως ἔλεγες ἐπιεικῆ καὶ ἀληθῆ, ὦ Πιττακέ,
347 οὐκ ἄν ποτε ἔψεγον. νῦν δέ—σφόδρα γὰρ καὶ
περὶ τῶν μεγίστων ψευδόμενος δοκεῖς ἀληθῆ
λέγειν, διὰ ταῦτά σε ἐγὼ ψέγω.

Ταῦτά μοι δοκεῖ, ὦ Πρόδικε καὶ Πρωταγόρα,
ἦν δ' ἐγώ, Σιμωνίδης διανοούμενος πεποιηκέναι
τοῦτο τὸ ᾆσμα. καὶ ὁ Ἱππίας, Εὖ μέν μοι δο-

¹ τ' ὀνησίπολιν G. Hermann : γε ὀνήσει πόλιν MSS.
² μιν Schleiermacher : μὴν MSS.

too intractable. He who knows Right, the support of a
city, is a healthy man; him I shall never blame, for to
blame I am not apt. Infinite is the race of fools.

So that whoever delights in reproaching would have
his fill of blaming them:

Verily, all things are fair that have in them no admixture
of base.

By this he does not mean to say, as it were, that
all things are white that have no admixture of
black; that would be ridiculous in many ways; but
that he himself accepts the average sort without
reproaching them. "I do not seek," said he, "a
man wholly blameless amongst us who partake of
the fruit of the broad-based earth: if I light upon
him, be sure I will report it"—meaning, "If I wait
for that, I shall never find anyone to praise. No, I
am content if a man be average and do nothing
evil, since I love and praise all"—and there he has
used a Mytilenaean word,[1] for his "I praise and
love all willingly" is addressed to Pittacus (here at
"willingly" one should make a pause);—"all who
commit nothing base, but some there are whom I
praise and love unwillingly. Hence I should never
reproach you, Pittacus, if you would only speak
what is moderately reasonable and true. But as it
is, since you lie so grievously about the greatest
matters with an air of speaking the truth, on this
score I reproach you."

Such is my view, Prodicus and Protagoras, I said,
of Simonides' intention in composing this ode.

Then Hippias remarked: It certainly seems to

---

[1] The form of the word ἐπαίνημι is pedantically adduced
to emphasize the poet's censure of Pittacus.

κεῖς, ἔφη, ὦ Σώκρατες, καὶ σὺ περὶ τοῦ ᾄσματος
διεληλυθέναι· ἔστι μέντοι, ἔφη, καὶ ἐμοὶ λόγος
B περὶ αὐτοῦ εὖ ἔχων, ὃν ὑμῖν ἐπιδείξω, ἂν βούλησθε. καὶ ὁ Ἀλκιβιάδης, Ναί, ἔφη, ὦ Ἱππία,
εἰσαῦθίς γε· νῦν δὲ δίκαιόν ἐστιν, ἃ ὡμολογησάτην πρὸς ἀλλήλω Πρωταγόρας καὶ Σωκράτης,
Πρωταγόρας μὲν εἰ ἔτι βούλεται ἐρωτᾶν, ἀποκρίνεσθαι Σωκράτη, εἰ δὲ δὴ βούλεται Σωκράτει
ἀποκρίνεσθαι, ἐρωτᾶν τὸν ἕτερον. καὶ ἐγὼ εἶπον
Ἐπιτρέπω μὲν ἔγωγε Πρωταγόρᾳ ὁπότερον αὐτῷ
C ἥδιον· εἰ δὲ βούλεται, περὶ μὲν ᾀσμάτων τε καὶ
ἐπῶν ἐάσωμεν, περὶ δὲ ὧν τὸ πρῶτον ἐγώ σε
ἠρώτησα, ὦ Πρωταγόρα, ἡδέως ἂν ἐπὶ τέλος
ἔλθοιμι μετὰ σοῦ σκοπούμενος. καὶ γὰρ δοκεῖ
μοι τὸ περὶ ποιήσεως διαλέγεσθαι ὁμοιότατον
εἶναι τοῖς συμποσίοις τοῖς τῶν φαύλων καὶ ἀγο-
ραίων ἀνθρώπων. καὶ γὰρ οὗτοι, διὰ τὸ μὴ
δύνασθαι ἀλλήλοις δι᾽ ἑαυτῶν συνεῖναι ἐν τῷ
πότῳ μηδὲ διὰ τῆς ἑαυτῶν φωνῆς καὶ τῶν λόγων
D τῶν ἑαυτῶν ὑπὸ ἀπαιδευσίας, τιμίας ποιοῦσι
τὰς αὐλητρίδας, πολλοῦ μισθούμενοι ἀλλοτρίαν
φωνὴν τὴν τῶν αὐλῶν, καὶ διὰ τῆς ἐκείνων φωνῆς
ἀλλήλοις σύνεισιν· ὅπου δὲ καλοὶ κἀγαθοὶ συμ-
πόται καὶ πεπαιδευμένοι εἰσίν, οὐκ ἂν ἴδοις
οὔτ᾽ αὐλητρίδας οὔτε ὀρχηστρίδας οὔτε ψαλτρίας,
ἀλλ᾽ αὐτοὺς αὑτοῖς ἱκανοὺς ὄντας συνεῖναι ἄνευ
τῶν λήρων τε καὶ παιδιῶν τούτων διὰ τῆς αὐτῶν
φωνῆς, λέγοντάς τε καὶ ἀκούοντας ἐν μέρει ἑαυτῶν
E κοσμίως, κἂν πάνυ πολὺν οἶνον πίωσιν. οὕτω
δὲ καὶ αἱ τοιαίδε συνουσίαι, ἐὰν μὲν λάβωνται
ἀνδρῶν, οἷοίπερ ἡμῶν οἱ πολλοί φασιν εἶναι,
οὐδὲν δέονται ἀλλοτρίας φωνῆς οὐδὲ ποιητῶν,

me, Socrates, that you have given a good exposition of the poem ; but I also have an elegant discourse upon it, which I will perform for you if you wish.

Yes, Hippias, said Alcibiades, but some other time : for the moment the proper thing, according to the agreement which Protagoras and Socrates made between them, will be for Socrates to answer any questions that Protagoras may still wish to put to him, but if he prefers to answer Socrates, then it will be for Socrates to ask.

On this I remarked : For my part I place it in Protagoras's hands to do whichever he likes best. But if he does not mind, let us talk no more of poems and verses, but consider the points on which I questioned you at first, Protagoras, and on which I should be glad to reach, with your help, a conclusion. For it seems to me that arguing about poetry is comparable to the wine-parties of common market-folk. These people, owing to their inability to carry on a familiar conversation over their wine by means of their own voices and discussions—such is their lack of education—put a premium on flute-girls by hiring the extraneous voice of the flute at a high price, and carry on their intercourse by means of its utterance. But where the party consists of thorough gentlemen who have had a proper education, you will see neither flute-girls nor dancing-girls nor harp-girls, but only the company contenting themselves with their own conversation, and none of these fooleries and frolics—each speaking and listening decently in his turn, even though they may drink a great deal of wine. And so a gathering like this of ours, when it includes such men as most of us claim to be, requires no extraneous voices,

οὓς οὔτε ἀνερέσθαι οἷόν τ' ἐστὶ περὶ ὧν λέγουσιν,
ἐπαγόμενοί τε αὐτοὺς οἱ πολλοὶ ἐν τοῖς λόγοις
οἱ μὲν ταῦτά φασι τὸν ποιητὴν νοεῖν, οἱ δ' ἕτερα,
περὶ πράγματος διαλεγόμενοι ὃ ἀδυνατοῦσιν ἐξ-
ελέγξαι· ἀλλὰ τὰς μὲν τοιαύτας συνουσίας ἐῶσι
348 χαίρειν, αὐτοὶ δ' ἑαυτοῖς σύνεισι δι' ἑαυτῶν, ἐν
τοῖς ἑαυτῶν λόγοις πεῖραν ἀλλήλων λαμβάνοντες
καὶ διδόντες. τοὺς τοιούτους μοι δοκεῖ χρῆναι
μᾶλλον μιμεῖσθαι ἐμέ τε καὶ σέ, καταθεμένους
τοὺς ποιητὰς αὐτοὺς δι' ἡμῶν αὐτῶν πρὸς ἀλλήλους
τοὺς λόγους ποιεῖσθαι, τῆς ἀληθείας καὶ ἡμῶν
αὐτῶν πεῖραν λαμβάνοντας· κἂν μὲν βούλῃ ἔτι
ἐρωτᾶν, ἕτοιμός εἰμί σοι παρέχειν ἀποκρινόμε-
νος· ἐὰν δὲ βούλῃ, σὺ ἐμοὶ παράσχες, περὶ ὧν
μεταξὺ ἐπαυσάμεθα διεξιόντες, τούτοις τέλος ἐπι-
B θεῖναι. λέγοντος οὖν ἐμοῦ ταῦτα καὶ τοιαῦτα
ἄλλα οὐδὲν ἀπεσάφει ὁ Πρωταγόρας ὁπότερα
ποιήσοι. εἶπεν οὖν ὁ Ἀλκιβιάδης πρὸς τὸν
Καλλίαν βλέψας, Ὦ Καλλία, δοκεῖ σοι, ἔφη, καὶ
νῦν καλῶς Πρωταγόρας ποιεῖν, οὐκ ἐθέλων εἴτε
δώσει λόγον εἴτε μὴ διασαφεῖν; ἐμοὶ γὰρ οὐ
δοκεῖ· ἀλλ' ἤτοι διαλεγέσθω ἢ εἰπέτω ὅτι οὐκ
ἐθέλει διαλέγεσθαι, ἵνα τούτῳ μὲν ταῦτα συνει-
δῶμεν, Σωκράτης δὲ ἄλλῳ τῳ διαλέγηται ἢ ἄλλος
C ὅστις ἂν βούληται ἄλλῳ. καὶ ὁ Πρωταγόρας
αἰσχυνθείς, ὥς γέ μοι ἔδοξε, τοῦ τε Ἀλκιβιάδου
ταῦτα λέγοντος καὶ τοῦ Καλλίου δεομένου καὶ
τῶν ἄλλων σχεδόν τι τῶν παρόντων, μόγις πρου-

not even of the poets, whom one cannot question on the sense of what they say ; when they are adduced in discussion we are generally told by some that the poet thought so and so, and by others, something different, and they go on arguing about a matter which they are powerless to determine. No, this sort of meeting is avoided by men of culture, who prefer to converse directly with each other, and to use their own way of speech in putting one another by turns to the test. It is this sort of person that I think you and I ought rather to imitate ; putting the poets aside, let us hold our discussion together in our own persons, making trial of the truth and of ourselves. So if you wish to question me further, I am at your service as answerer ; but if you like, put yourself at my service, so that we may clear up the several points of the inquiry in which we stopped half-way.

On my saying this and something more of the sort, Protagoras gave no indication as to which course he would take. So Alcibiades, looking at Callias, said : Do you consider, Callias, that Protagoras is behaving properly now in refusing to signify whether he will or will not answer ? I do not think he is. Let him either debate or say that he does not want to debate, so that we may have this understanding with him ; then Socrates can debate with someone else, or another of us with some other, as may be agreed.

Then Protagoras was ashamed, as it seemed to me, at these words of Alcibiades, and the more so when Callias requested him, together with almost the whole of the company ; and so he reluctantly prevailed on himself to take up the debate, and

τράπετο εἰς τὸ διαλέγεσθαι καὶ ἐκέλευεν ἐρωτᾶν αὐτὸν ὡς ἀποκρινούμενος.

Εἶπον δὴ ἐγώ, ᾿Ω Πρωταγόρα, μὴ οἴου δια-λέγεσθαί μέ σοι ἄλλο τι βουλόμενον ἢ ἃ αὐτὸς ἀπορῶ ἑκάστοτε, ταῦτα διασκέψασθαι. ἡγοῦμαι γὰρ πάνυ λέγειν τι τὸν ῞Ομηρον τὸ

D σύν τε δύ' ἐρχομένω, καί τε πρὸ ὃ τοῦ ἐνόησεν.

εὐπορώτεροι γάρ πως ἅπαντές ἐσμεν οἱ ἄνθρωποι πρὸς ἅπαν ἔργον καὶ λόγον καὶ διανόημα· μοῦνος δ' εἴπερ τε νοήσῃ, αὐτίκα περιιὼν ζητεῖ ὅτῳ ἐπιδείξηται καὶ μεθ' ὅτου βεβαιώσηται, ἕως ἂν ἐντύχῃ. ὥσπερ καὶ ἐγὼ ἕνεκα τούτου σοὶ ἡδέως διαλέγομαι μᾶλλον ἢ ἄλλῳ τινί, ἡγού-μενός σε βέλτιστ' ἂν ἐπισκέψασθαι καὶ περὶ
E τῶν ἄλλων περὶ ὧν εἰκὸς σκοπεῖσθαι τὸν ἐπιεικῆ, καὶ δὴ καὶ περὶ ἀρετῆς. τίνα γὰρ ἄλλον ἢ σέ; ὅς γε οὐ μόνον αὐτὸς οἴει καλὸς κἀγαθὸς εἶναι, ὥσπερ τινὲς ἄλλοι αὐτοὶ μὲν ἐπιεικεῖς εἰσίν, ἄλλους δὲ οὐ δύνανται ποιεῖν· σὺ δὲ καὶ αὐτὸς ἀγαθὸς εἶ καὶ ἄλλους οἷός τ' εἶ ποιεῖν ἀγαθούς. καὶ οὕτω πεπίστευκας σαυτῷ, ὥστε καὶ ἄλλων ταύτην τὴν τέχνην ἀποκρυπτομένων σύ γ' ἀνα-
349 φανδὸν σεαυτὸν ὑποκηρυξάμενος εἰς πάντας τοὺς ῞Ελληνας, σοφιστὴν ἐπονομάσας, σεαυτὸν ἀπέ-φηνας παιδεύσεως καὶ ἀρετῆς διδάσκαλον, πρῶτος τούτου μισθὸν ἀξιώσας ἄρνυσθαι. πῶς οὖν οὐ σε χρῆν παρακαλεῖν ἐπὶ τὴν τούτων σκέψιν καὶ ἐρωτᾶν καὶ ἀνακοινοῦσθαι; οὐκ ἔσθ' ὅπως οὔ. καὶ νῦν δὴ ἐγὼ ἐκεῖνα, ἅπερ τὸ πρῶτον ἠρώτων

---

asked to have questions put to him, since he was ready to answer.

So I proceeded to say—Protagoras, do not suppose that I have any other desire in debating with you than to examine the difficulties which occur to myself at each point. For I hold that there is a good deal in what Homer [1] says—

When two go together, one observes before the other;

for somehow it makes all of us human beings more resourceful in every deed or word or thought; but if one observes something alone, forthwith one has to go about searching until one discovers somebody to whom one can show it off and who can corroborate it. And I also have my reason for being glad to debate with you rather than with anyone else; it is that I regard you as the best person to investigate in general any matters that a sensible man may be expected to examine, and virtue in particular. Whom else should I choose but you? Not only do you consider yourself a worthy gentleman, like sundry other people, who are sensible enough themselves, but cannot make others so; but you are both good yourself and have the gift of making others good. And you are so confident of yourself that, while others make a secret of this art, you have had yourself publicly proclaimed to all the Greeks with the title of sophist, and have appointed yourself preceptor of culture and virtue, and are the first who has ever demanded a regular fee for such work. What then could I do but call upon you to deal with our problem both by question and communication? I had no other course. So now with regard to those points which I have raised

περὶ τούτων, πάλιν ἐπιθυμῶ ἐξ ἀρχῆς τὰ μὲν
B ἀναμνησθῆναι παρὰ σοῦ, τὰ δὲ συνδιασκέψασθαι.
ἦν δέ, ὡς ἐγῷμαι, τὸ ἐρώτημα τόδε· σοφία καὶ
σωφροσύνη καὶ ἀνδρεία καὶ δικαιοσύνη καὶ ὁσιότης
πότερον ταῦτα, πέντε ὄντα ὀνόματα, ἐπὶ ἑνὶ πράγ-
ματί ἐστιν, ἢ ἑκάστῳ τῶν ὀνομάτων τούτων
ὑπόκειταί τις ἴδιος οὐσία καὶ πρᾶγμα ἔχον ἑαυτοῦ
δύναμιν ἕκαστον, οὐκ ὂν οἷον τὸ ἕτερον αὐτῶν τὸ
ἕτερον; ἔφησθα οὖν σὺ οὐκ ὀνόματα ἐπὶ ἑνὶ εἶναι,
C ἀλλὰ ἕκαστον ἰδίῳ πράγματι τῶν ὀνομάτων τούτων
ἐπικεῖσθαι, πάντα δὲ ταῦτα μόρια εἶναι ἀρετῆς,
οὐχ ὡς τὰ τοῦ χρυσοῦ μόρια ὅμοιά ἐστιν ἀλλήλοις
καὶ τῷ ὅλῳ οὗ μόριά ἐστιν, ἀλλ' ὡς τὰ τοῦ προσώπου μόρια καὶ τῷ ὅλῳ οὗ μόριά ἐστιν καὶ ἀλλήλοις ἀνόμοια, ἰδίαν ἕκαστα δύναμιν ἔχοντα. ταῦτα
εἰ μέν σοι δοκεῖ ἔτι ὥσπερ τότε, φάθι· εἰ δὲ ἄλλως
πως, τοῦτο διόρισαι, ὡς ἔγωγε οὐδέν σοι ὑπόλογον
τίθεμαι, ἐάν πῃ ἄλλῃ νῦν φῇς· οὐ γὰρ ἂν θαυμά-
D ζοιμι, εἰ τότε ἀποπειρώμενός μου ταῦτα ἔλεγες.

Ἀλλ' ἐγώ σοι, ἔφη, λέγω, ὦ Σώκρατες, ὅτι
ταῦτα πάντα μόρια μέν ἐστιν ἀρετῆς, καὶ τὰ μὲν
τέτταρα αὐτῶν ἐπιεικῶς παραπλήσια ἀλλήλοις
ἐστίν, ἡ δὲ ἀνδρεία πάνυ πολὺ διαφέρον πάντων
τούτων. ὧδε δὲ γνώσει ὅτι ἐγὼ ἀληθῆ λέγω·
εὑρήσεις γὰρ πολλοὺς τῶν ἀνθρώπων ἀδικωτάτους
μὲν ὄντας καὶ ἀνοσιωτάτους καὶ ἀκολαστοτάτους
καὶ ἀμαθεστάτους, ἀνδρειοτάτους δὲ διαφερόντως.
E Ἔχε δή, ἔφην ἐγώ· ἄξιον γάρ τοι ἐπισκέψασθαι
ὃ λέγεις. πότερον τοὺς ἀνδρείους θαρραλέους
λέγεις ἢ ἄλλο τι; Καὶ ἴτας γε, ἔφη, ἐφ' ἃ οἱ πολλοὶ

---

[1] Cf. 329 c foll.

on the subject in my opening questions, I desire to be reminded of some by you and to have your help in investigating others. The question, I believe, was this :[1] Are the five names of wisdom, temperance, courage, justice, and holiness attached to one thing, or underlying each of these names is there a distinct existence or thing that has its own particular function, each thing being different from the others ? And your answer was that they are not names attached to one thing, but that each of these names applies to a distinct thing, and that all these are parts of virtue ; not like the parts of gold, which are similar to each other and to the whole of which they are parts, but like the parts of the face, dissimilar to the whole of which they are parts and to each other, and each having a distinct function. If you still hold the same opinion of them, say so ; if you have a new one, define what it is, for I make no objection to your replying now on other lines. Indeed I should not be surprised if you were merely experimenting upon me when you spoke before.

Well, Socrates, he replied, I say that all these are parts of virtue, and that while four of them are fairly on a par with each other, courage is something vastly different from all the rest. You may perceive the truth of what I say from this : you will find many people extremely unjust, unholy, dissolute, and ignorant, and yet pre-eminently courageous.

Stop now, I said : we must duly examine what you say. Do you call courageous men bold, or something else ?

Yes, and impetuous also, he replied, where most men fear to tread.

φοβοῦνται ἰέναι. Φέρε δή, τὴν ἀρετὴν καλόν τι
φὴς εἶναι, καὶ ὡς καλοῦ ὄντος αὐτοῦ σὺ διδάσκαλον
σαυτὸν παρέχεις; Κάλλιστον μὲν οὖν, ἔφη, εἰ
μὴ μαίνομαί γε. Πότερον οὖν, ἦν δ᾽ ἐγώ, τὸ μέν
τι αὐτοῦ αἰσχρόν, τὸ δέ τι καλόν, ἢ ὅλον καλόν;
Ὅλον που καλὸν ὡς οἷόν τε μάλιστα. Οἶσθα οὖν
350 τίνες εἰς τὰ φρέατα κολυμβῶσι θαρραλέως;
Ἔγωγε, ὅτι οἱ κολυμβηταί. Πότερον διότι ἐπίστανται ἢ δι᾽ ἄλλο τι; Ὅτι ἐπίστανται. Τίνες δὲ
ἀπὸ τῶν ἵππων πολεμεῖν θαρραλέοι εἰσί; πότερον
οἱ ἱππικοὶ ἢ οἱ ἄφιπποι; Οἱ ἱππικοί. Τίνες δὲ
πέλτας ἔχοντες; οἱ πελταστικοὶ ἢ οἱ μή; Οἱ
πελταστικοί. καὶ τὰ ἄλλα γε πάντα, εἰ τοῦτο
ζητεῖς, ἔφη, οἱ ἐπιστήμονες τῶν μὴ ἐπισταμένων
θαρραλεώτεροί εἰσι, καὶ αὐτοὶ ἑαυτῶν, ἐπειδὰν
B μάθωσιν, ἢ πρὶν μαθεῖν. Ἤδη δέ τινας ἑώρακας,
ἔφην, πάντων τούτων ἀνεπιστήμονας ὄντας, θαρροῦντας δὲ πρὸς ἕκαστα τούτων; Ἔγωγε, ἦ δ᾽ ὅς,
καὶ λίαν γε θαρροῦντας. Οὐκοῦν οἱ θαρραλέοι
οὗτοι καὶ ἀνδρεῖοί εἰσιν; Αἰσχρὸν μέντ᾽ ἄν, ἔφη,
εἴη ἡ ἀνδρεία· ἐπεὶ οὗτοί γε μαινόμενοί εἰσιν. Πῶς
οὖν, ἔφην ἐγώ, λέγεις τοὺς ἀνδρείους; οὐχὶ τοὺς
C θαρραλέους εἶναι; Καὶ νῦν γ᾽, ἔφη. Οὐκοῦν

Well now, do you say that virtue is a good thing, and of this good thing offer yourself as teacher?

Nay, it is the best of things, he said, unless I am out of my senses.

Then is one part of it base and another good, or is the whole good?

Surely the whole is good in the highest possible degree.

Now do you know who dive boldly into wells?

I do; divers.

Is this because they have knowledge, or for some other reason?

Because they have knowledge.

And who are bold in going to war on horseback— those who are practised horsemen, or those who are not?

Practised horsemen.

And who with bucklers—buckler-men, or those who are not?

Buckler-men: and so with all other cases, he went on, if that is your point; those who have knowledge are bolder than those who lack it, and individually they are bolder when they have learnt than before learning.

But you must have seen at times, I said, persons who are without knowledge of any of these affairs, yet behaving boldly in each of them.

I have, he said, and very boldly too.

Then are these bold ones courageous also?

Nay, that would make courage a base thing, he replied; for those you speak of are out of their senses.

What then, I asked, do you mean by courageous men? Surely the same as bold men?

Yes, I do still, he said.

οὗτοι, ἦν δ' ἐγώ, οἱ οὕτω θαρραλέοι ὄντες οὐκ
ἀνδρεῖοι ἀλλὰ μαινόμενοι φαίνονται; καὶ ἐκεῖ αὖ
οἱ σοφώτατοι οὗτοι καὶ θαρραλεώτατοί εἰσι, θαρρα-
λεώτατοι δὲ ὄντες ἀνδρειότατοι; καὶ κατὰ τοῦτον
τὸν λόγον ἡ σοφία ἂν ἀνδρεία εἴη; Οὐ καλῶς, ἔφη,
μνημονεύεις, ὦ Σώκρατες, ἃ ἔλεγόν τε καὶ ἀπεκρι-
νόμην σοι. ἔγωγε ἐρωτηθεὶς ὑπὸ σοῦ, εἰ οἱ ἀνδρεῖοι
θαρραλέοι εἰσίν, ὡμολόγησα· εἰ δὲ καὶ οἱ θαρραλέοι
ἀνδρεῖοι, οὐκ ἠρωτήθην· εἰ γάρ με τότε ἤρου,
D εἶπον ἂν ὅτι οὐ πάντες· τοὺς δὲ ἀνδρείους ὡς οὐ
θαρραλέοι εἰσί, τὸ ἐμὸν ὁμολόγημα οὐδαμοῦ
ἐπέδειξας ὡς οὐκ ὀρθῶς ὡμολόγησα. ἔπειτα τοὺς
ἐπισταμένους αὐτοὺς ἑαυτῶν θαρραλεωτέρους
ὄντας ἀποφαίνεις καὶ μὴ ἐπισταμένων ἄλλων, καὶ
ἐν τούτῳ οἴει τὴν ἀνδρείαν καὶ τὴν σοφίαν ταὐτὸν
εἶναι· τούτῳ δὲ τῷ τρόπῳ μετιὼν καὶ τὴν ἰσχὺν
οἰηθείης ἂν εἶναι σοφίαν. πρῶτον μὲν γὰρ εἰ οὕτω
μετιὼν ἔροιό με εἰ οἱ ἰσχυροὶ δυνατοί εἰσι, φαίην ἄν·
E ἔπειτα, εἰ οἱ ἐπιστάμενοι παλαίειν δυνατώτεροί εἰσι
τῶν μὴ ἐπισταμένων παλαίειν καὶ αὐτοὶ αὑτῶν,
ἐπειδὰν μάθωσιν, ἢ πρὶν μαθεῖν, φαίην ἄν· ταῦτα
δὲ ἐμοῦ ὁμολογήσαντος ἐξείη ἄν σοι, χρωμένῳ τοῖς
αὐτοῖς τεκμηρίοις τούτοις, λέγειν ὡς κατὰ τὴν ἐμὴν
ὁμολογίαν ἡ σοφία ἐστὶν ἰσχύς. ἐγὼ δὲ οὐδαμοῦ
οὐδ' ἐνταῦθα ὁμολογῶ τοὺς δυνατοὺς ἰσχυροὺς
εἶναι, τοὺς μέντοι ἰσχυροὺς δυνατούς· οὐ γὰρ
351 ταὐτὸν εἶναι δύναμίν τε καὶ ἰσχύν, ἀλλὰ τὸ μὲν
καὶ ἀπὸ ἐπιστήμης γίγνεσθαι, τὴν δύναμιν, καὶ
ἀπὸ μανίας γε καὶ θυμοῦ, ἰσχὺν δὲ ἀπὸ φύσεως
καὶ εὐτροφίας τῶν σωμάτων. οὕτω δὲ κἀκεῖ οὐ

Then these men, I went on, who are so brave, are found to be not courageous but mad? And in those former cases our wisest men are boldest too, and being boldest are most courageous? And on this reasoning, wisdom will be courage?

You do not rightly recall, Socrates, what I stated in replying to you. When you asked me whether courageous men are bold, I admitted it: I was not asked whether bold men are courageous. Had you asked me this before, I should have said—" Not all." And as to proving that courageous men are not bold, you have nowhere pointed out that I was wrong in my admission that they are. Next you show that such persons individually are bolder when they have knowledge, and bolder than others who lack it, and therewith you take courage and wisdom to be the same: proceeding in this manner you might even take strength to be wisdom. On this method you might begin by asking me whether the strong are powerful, and I should say " Yes "; and then, whether those who know how to wrestle are more powerful than those who do not know how to wrestle, and whether individually they are more powerful when they have learnt than before learning, and I should say " Yes." And on my admitting these points it would be open to you to say, by the same token, that according to my admission wisdom is strength. But neither there nor elsewhere do I admit that the powerful are strong, only that the strong are powerful; for I hold that power and strength are not the same, but that one of them, power, comes from knowledge, or from madness or rage, whereas strength comes from constitution and fit nurture of the body. So, in the other instance,

ταὐτὸν εἶναι θάρσος τε καὶ ἀνδρείαν· ὥστε συμβαίνει τοὺς μὲν ἀνδρείους θαρραλέους εἶναι, μὴ
μέντοι τούς γε θαρραλέους ἀνδρείους πάντας· θάρσος
μὲν γὰρ καὶ ἀπὸ τέχνης γίγνεται ἀνθρώποις καὶ
B ἀπὸ θυμοῦ γε καὶ ἀπὸ μανίας, ὥσπερ ἡ δύναμις,
ἀνδρεία δὲ ἀπὸ φύσεως καὶ εὐτροφίας τῶν ψυχῶν
γίγνεται.

Λέγεις δέ τινας, ἔφην, ὦ Πρωταγόρα, τῶν
ἀνθρώπων εὖ ζῆν, τοὺς δὲ κακῶς; Ἔφη. Ἆρ'
οὖν δοκεῖ σοι ἄνθρωπος ἂν εὖ ζῆν, εἰ ἀνιώμενός τε
καὶ ὀδυνώμενος ζῴη; Οὐκ ἔφη. Τί δ', εἰ ἡδέως
βιοὺς τὸν βίον τελευτήσειεν, οὐκ εὖ ἄν σοι δοκεῖ
οὕτως βεβιωκέναι; Ἔμοιγ', ἔφη. Τὸ μὲν ἄρα
C ἡδέως ζῆν ἀγαθόν, τὸ δ' ἀηδῶς κακόν; Εἴπερ τοῖς
καλοῖς γ', ἔφη, ζῴη ἡδόμενος. Τί δή, ὦ Πρωταγόρα; μὴ καὶ σύ, ὥσπερ οἱ πολλοί, ἡδέα ἄττα
καλεῖς κακὰ καὶ ἀνιαρὰ ἀγαθά; ἐγὼ γὰρ λέγω,
καθ' ὃ ἡδέα ἐστίν, ἆρα κατὰ τοῦτο οὐκ ἀγαθά, μὴ
εἴ τι ἀπ' αὐτῶν ἀποβήσεται ἄλλο; καὶ αὖθις αὖ
τὰ ἀνιαρὰ ὡσαύτως οὕτως οὐ καθ' ὅσον ἀνιαρά,
κακά; Οὐκ οἶδα, ὦ Σώκρατες, ἔφη, ἁπλῶς οὕτως,
D ὡς σὺ ἐρωτᾷς, εἰ ἐμοὶ ἀποκριτέον ἐστίν, ὡς τὰ ἡδέα
τε ἀγαθά ἐστιν ἅπαντα καὶ τὰ ἀνιαρὰ κακά· ἀλλά
μοι δοκεῖ οὐ μόνον πρὸς τὴν νῦν ἀπόκρισιν ἐμοὶ
ἀσφαλέστερον εἶναι ἀποκρίνασθαι, ἀλλὰ καὶ πρὸς
πάντα τὸν ἄλλον βίον τὸν ἐμόν, ὅτι ἔστι μὲν ἃ τῶν
ἡδέων οὐκ ἔστιν ἀγαθά, ἔστι δ' αὖ καὶ ἃ τῶν

boldness and courage are not the same, and therefore it results that the courageous are bold, but not that the bold are courageous; for boldness comes to a man from art, or from rage or madness, like power, whereas courage comes from constitution and fit nurture of the soul.

Do you speak of some men, Protagoras, I asked, as living well, and others ill?

Yes.

Then do you consider that a man would live well if he lived in distress and anguish?

No, he said.

Well now, if he lived pleasantly and so ended his life, would you not consider he had thus contrived to live well?

I would, he said.

And, I suppose, to live pleasantly is good, and unpleasantly, bad?

Yes, he said, if one lived in the enjoyment of honourable things.

But, Protagoras, will you tell me you agree with the majority in calling some pleasant things bad and some painful ones good? I mean to say—Are not things good in so far as they are pleasant, putting aside any other result they may have; and again, are not painful things in just the same sense bad— in so far as they are painful?

I cannot tell, Socrates, he replied, whether I am to answer, in such absolute fashion as that of your question, that all pleasant things are good and painful things bad: I rather think it safer for me to reply, with a view not merely to my present answer but to all the rest of my life, that some pleasant things are not good, and also that some

ἀνιαρῶν οὐκ ἔστι κακά, ἔστι δ' ἃ ἔστι, καὶ τρίτον
ἃ οὐδέτερα, οὔτε κακὰ οὔτ' ἀγαθά. Ἡδέα δὲ
καλεῖς, ἦν δ' ἐγώ, οὐ τὰ ἡδονῆς μετέχοντα ἢ
E ποιοῦντα ἡδονήν; Πάνυ γ', ἔφη. Τοῦτο τοίνυν
λέγω, καθ' ὅσον ἡδέα ἐστίν, εἰ οὐκ ἀγαθά, τὴν
ἡδονὴν αὐτὴν ἐρωτῶν εἰ οὐκ ἀγαθόν ἐστιν. Ὥσπερ
σὺ λέγεις, ἔφη, ἑκάστοτε, ὦ Σώκρατες, σκοπώμεθα
αὐτό, καὶ ἐὰν μὲν πρὸς λόγον δοκῇ εἶναι τὸ σκέμμα
καὶ τὸ αὐτὸ φαίνηται ἡδύ τε καὶ ἀγαθόν, συγχωρη-
σόμεθα· εἰ δὲ μή, τότε ἤδη ἀμφισβητήσομεν.
Πότερον οὖν, ἦν δ' ἐγώ, σὺ βούλει ἡγεμονεύειν τῆς
σκέψεως, ἢ ἐγὼ ἡγῶμαι; Δίκαιος, ἔφη, σὺ
ἡγεῖσθαι· σὺ γὰρ καὶ κατάρχεις τοῦ λόγου. Ἆρ'
352 οὖν, ἦν δ' ἐγώ, τῇδέ πη καταφανὲς ἂν ἡμῖν γένοιτο;
ὥσπερ εἴ τις ἄνθρωπον σκοπῶν ἐκ τοῦ εἴδους ἢ
πρὸς ὑγίειαν ἢ πρὸς ἄλλο τι τῶν τοῦ σώματος
ἔργων, ἰδὼν τὸ πρόσωπον καὶ τὰς χεῖρας ἄκρας
εἴποι· ἴθι δή μοι ἀποκαλύψας καὶ τὰ στήθη καὶ τὸ
μετάφρενον ἐπίδειξον, ἵνα ἐπισκέψωμαι σαφέστερον·
καὶ ἐγὼ τοιοῦτόν τι ποθῶ πρὸς τὴν σκέψιν· θεασά-
μενος ὅτι οὕτως ἔχεις πρὸς τὸ ἀγαθὸν καὶ τὸ ἡδύ,
ὡς φῄς, δέομαι τοιοῦτόν τι εἰπεῖν· ἴθι δή μοι, ὦ
Πρωταγόρα, καὶ τόδε τῆς διανοίας ἀποκάλυψον·
B πῶς ἔχεις πρὸς ἐπιστήμην; πότερον καὶ τοῦτό σοι
δοκεῖ ὥσπερ τοῖς πολλοῖς ἀνθρώποις, ἢ ἄλλως;
δοκεῖ δὲ τοῖς πολλοῖς περὶ ἐπιστήμης τοιοῦτόν τι,
οὐκ ἰσχυρὸν οὐδ' ἡγεμονικὸν οὐδ' ἀρχικὸν εἶναι·

painful things are not bad, and some are, while a third class of them are indifferent—neither bad nor good.

You call pleasant, do you not, I asked, things that partake of pleasure or cause pleasure?

Certainly, he said.

So when I put it to you, whether things are not good in so far as they are pleasant, I am asking whether pleasure itself is not a good thing.

Let us examine the matter, Socrates, he said, in the form in which you put it at each point, and if the proposition seems to be reasonable, and pleasant and good are found to be the same, we shall agree upon it; if not, we shall dispute it there and then.

And would you like, I asked, to be leader in the inquiry, or am I to lead?

You ought to lead, he replied, since you are the inaugurator of this discussion.

Well then, I proceeded, will the following example give us the light we need? Just as, in estimating a man's health or bodily efficiency by his appearance, one might look at his face and the lower part of his arms and say: Come now, uncover your chest too and your back and show them, that I may examine you thoroughly—so the same sort of desire comes over me in regard to our inquiry. Observing your condition to be as you describe in respect of the good and the pleasant, I am fain to say something like this: Come, my good Protagoras, uncover some more of your thoughts: how are you in regard to knowledge? Do you share the view that most people take of this, or have you some other? The opinion generally held of knowledge is something of this sort—that it is no strong or guiding or govern-

οὐδὲ ὡς περὶ τοιούτου αὐτοῦ ὄντος διανοοῦνται, ἀλλ'
ἐνούσης πολλάκις ἀνθρώπῳ ἐπιστήμης οὐ τὴν ἐπιστήμην αὐτοῦ ἄρχειν, ἀλλ' ἄλλο τι, τοτὲ μὲν θυμόν,
τοτὲ δὲ ἡδονήν, τοτὲ δὲ λύπην, ἐνίοτε δὲ ἔρωτα,
πολλάκις δὲ φόβον, ἀτεχνῶς διανοούμενοι περὶ τῆς
C ἐπιστήμης, ὥσπερ περὶ ἀνδραπόδου, περιελκομένης
ὑπὸ τῶν ἄλλων ἁπάντων. ἆρ' οὖν καὶ σοὶ τοιοῦτόν
τι περὶ αὐτῆς δοκεῖ, ἢ καλόν τε εἶναι ἡ ἐπιστήμη καὶ
οἷον ἄρχειν τοῦ ἀνθρώπου, καὶ ἐάνπερ γιγνώσκῃ
τις τἀγαθὰ καὶ τὰ κακά, μὴ ἂν κρατηθῆναι ὑπὸ
μηδενός, ὥστε ἄλλ' ἄττα πράττειν ἢ ἂν ἡ ἐπιστήμη
κελεύῃ, ἀλλ' ἱκανὴν εἶναι τὴν φρόνησιν βοηθεῖν τῷ
ἀνθρώπῳ; Καὶ δοκεῖ, ἔφη, ὥσπερ σὺ λέγεις, ὦ
D Σώκρατες, καὶ ἅμα, εἴπερ τῳ ἄλλῳ, αἰσχρόν ἐστι
καὶ ἐμοὶ σοφίαν καὶ ἐπιστήμην μὴ οὐχὶ πάντων
κράτιστον φάναι εἶναι τῶν ἀνθρωπείων πραγμάτων.
Καλῶς γε, ἔφην ἐγώ, σὺ λέγων καὶ ἀληθῆ. οἶσθα
οὖν ὅτι οἱ πολλοὶ τῶν ἀνθρώπων ἐμοί τε καὶ σοὶ οὐ
πείθονται, ἀλλὰ πολλούς φασι γιγνώσκοντας τὰ
βέλτιστα οὐκ ἐθέλειν πράττειν, ἐξὸν αὐτοῖς, ἀλλὰ
ἄλλα πράττειν· καὶ ὅσους δὴ ἐγὼ ἠρόμην ὅ τί
ποτε αἴτιόν ἐστι τούτου, ὑπὸ ἡδονῆς φασιν ἡττω-
E μένους ἢ λύπης ἢ ὧν νῦν δὴ ἐγὼ ἔλεγον ὑπό τινος
τούτων κρατουμένους ταῦτα ποιεῖν τοὺς ποιοῦντας.
Πολλὰ γὰρ οἶμαι, ἔφη, ὦ Σώκρατες, καὶ ἄλλα οὐκ
ὀρθῶς λέγουσιν οἱ ἄνθρωποι. Ἴθι δὴ μετ' ἐμοῦ
ἐπιχείρησον πείθειν τοὺς ἀνθρώπους καὶ διδάσκειν
ὅ ἐστιν αὐτοῖς τοῦτο τὸ πάθος, ὅ φασιν ὑπὸ τῶν
353 ἡδονῶν ἡττᾶσθαι καὶ οὐ πράττειν διὰ ταῦτα τὰ

ing thing; it is not regarded as anything of that kind, but people think that, while a man often has knowledge in him, he is not governed by it, but by something else—now by passion, now by pleasure, now by pain, at times by love, and often by fear; their feeling about knowledge is just what they have about a slave, that it may be dragged about by any other force. Now do you agree with this view of it, or do you consider that knowledge is something noble and able to govern man, and that whoever learns what is good and what is bad will never be swayed by anything to act otherwise than as knowledge bids, and that intelligence is a sufficient succour for mankind?

My view, Socrates, he replied, is precisely that which you express, and what is more, it would be a disgrace for me above all men to assert that wisdom and knowledge were aught but the highest of all human things.

Well and truly spoken, I said. Now you know that most people will not listen to you and me, but say that many, while knowing what is best, refuse to perform it, though they have the power, and do other things instead. And whenever I have asked them to tell me what can be the reason of this, they say that those who act so are acting under the influence of pleasure or pain, or under the control of one of the things I have just mentioned.

Yes, Socrates, he replied, I regard this as but one of the many erroneous sayings of mankind.

Come then, and join me in the endeavour to persuade the world and explain what is this experience of theirs, which they call " being overcome by pleasure," and which they give as the

βέλτιστα, ἐπεὶ γιγνώσκειν γε αὐτά. ἴσως γὰρ ἂν
λεγόντων ἡμῶν ὅτι οὐκ ὀρθῶς λέγετε, ὦ ἄνθρωποι,
ἀλλὰ ψεύδεσθε, ἔροιντ' ἂν ἡμᾶς· ὦ Πρωταγόρα τε
καὶ Σώκρατες, εἰ μὴ ἔστι τοῦτο τὸ πάθημα ἡδονῆς ἡττᾶσθαι, ἀλλὰ τί ποτ' ἐστί, καὶ τί ὑμεῖς αὐτό
φατε εἶναι; εἴπατον ἡμῖν. Τί δέ, ὦ Σώκρατες,
δεῖ ἡμᾶς σκοπεῖσθαι τὴν τῶν πολλῶν δόξαν
B ἀνθρώπων, οἳ ὅ τι ἂν τύχωσι τοῦτο λέγουσιν; Οἴ-
μαι, ἦν δ' ἐγώ, εἶναί τι ἡμῖν τοῦτο πρὸς τὸ ἐξευρεῖν
περὶ ἀνδρείας, πρὸς τἆλλα μόρια τὰ τῆς ἀρετῆς πῶς
ποτ' ἔχει. εἰ οὖν σοι δοκεῖ ἐμμένειν οἷς ἄρτι
ἔδοξεν ἡμῖν, ἐμὲ ἡγήσασθαι, ᾗ οἶμαι ἂν ἔγωγε
κάλλιστα φανερὸν γενέσθαι, ἕπου· εἰ δὲ μὴ βούλει,
εἴ σοι φίλον, ἐῶ χαίρειν. 'Αλλ', ἔφη, ὀρθῶς
λέγεις· καὶ πέραινε ὥσπερ ἤρξω.

C   Πάλιν τοίνυν, ἔφην ἐγώ, εἰ ἔροιντο ἡμᾶς· τί οὖν
φατὲ τοῦτο εἶναι, ὃ ἡμεῖς ἥττω εἶναι τῶν ἡδονῶν
ἐλέγομεν; εἴποιμ' ἂν ἔγωγε πρὸς αὐτοὺς ὡδί·
ἀκούετε δή· πειρασόμεθα γὰρ ὑμῖν ἐγώ τε καὶ
Πρωταγόρας φράσαι. ἄλλο τι γάρ, ὦ ἄνθρωποι,
φατὲ ὑμῖν τοῦτο γίγνεσθαι ἐν τοῖσδε, οἷον πολλάκις ὑπὸ σίτων καὶ ποτῶν καὶ ἀφροδισίων κρατού-
μενοι ἡδέων ὄντων, γιγνώσκοντες ὅτι πονηρά ἐστιν,
ὅμως αὐτὰ πράττειν; Φαῖεν ἄν. Οὐκοῦν ἐροίμεθ'
ἂν αὐτοὺς ἐγώ τε καὶ σὺ πάλιν· πονηρὰ δὲ αὐτὰ
D πῇ φατὲ εἶναι; πότερον ὅτι τὴν ἡδονὴν ταύτην ἐν
τῷ παραχρῆμα παρέχει καὶ ἡδύ ἐστιν ἕκαστον
αὐτῶν, ἢ ὅτι εἰς τὸν ὕστερον χρόνον νόσους τε
ποιεῖ καὶ πενίας καὶ ἄλλα τοιαῦτα πολλὰ παρα-

reason why they fail to do what is best though they have knowledge of it. For perhaps if we said to them: What you assert, good people, is not correct, but quite untrue — they might ask us: Protagoras and Socrates, if this experience is not "being overcome by pleasure" what on earth is it, and what do you call it? Tell us that.

Why, Socrates, must we consider the opinion of the mass of mankind, who say just what occurs to them?

I fancy, I replied, that this will be a step towards discovering how courage is related to the other parts of virtue. So if you think fit to abide by the arrangement we made a while ago—that I should lead in the direction which seems best for elucidating the matter—you must now follow; but if you would rather not, to suit your wishes I will let it pass.

No, he said, your plan is quite right: go on to the end as you began.

Once more then, I proceeded, suppose they should ask us: Then what do you call this thing which we described as "being overcome by pleasures"? The answer I should give them would be this: Please attend; Protagoras and I will try to explain it to you. Do you not say that this thing occurs, good people, in the common case of a man being overpowered by the pleasantness of food or drink or sexual acts, and doing what he does though he knows it to be wicked? They would admit it. Then you and I would ask them again: In what sense do you call such deeds wicked? Is it that they produce those pleasures and are themselves pleasant at the moment, or that later on they cause diseases and poverty, and have many more such ills

353

σκευάζει; ἢ κἂν εἴ τι τούτων εἰς τὸ ὕστερον μηδὲν
παρασκευάζει, χαίρειν δὲ μόνον ποιεῖ, ὅμως δ' ἂν
κακὰ ἦν, ὅτι μαθόντα χαίρειν ποιεῖ καὶ ὁπηοῦν;
ἆρ' οἰόμεθ' ἂν αὐτούς, ὦ Πρωταγόρα, ἄλλο τι
ἀποκρίνασθαι, ἢ ὅτι οὐ κατὰ τὴν αὐτῆς τῆς ἡδονῆς
Ε τῆς παραχρῆμα ἐργασίαν κακά ἐστιν, ἀλλὰ διὰ τὰ
ὕστερον γιγνόμενα, νόσους τε καὶ τἆλλα. Ἐγὼ
μὲν οἶμαι, ἔφη ὁ Πρωταγόρας, τοὺς πολλοὺς ἂν
ταῦτα ἀποκρίνασθαι. Οὐκοῦν νόσους ποιοῦντα
ἀνίας ποιεῖ, καὶ πενίας ποιοῦντα ἀνίας ποιεῖ;
354 ὁμολογοῖεν ἄν, ὡς ἐγᾦμαι. Συνέφη ὁ Πρωταγόρας. Οὐκοῦν φαίνεται, ὦ ἄνθρωποι, ὑμῖν, ὥς
φαμεν ἐγώ τε καὶ Πρωταγόρας, δι' οὐδὲν ἄλλο
ταῦτα κακὰ ὄντα, ἢ διότι εἰς ἀνίας τε ἀποτελευτᾷ
καὶ ἄλλων ἡδονῶν ἀποστερεῖ; ὁμολογοῖεν ἄν;
Συνεδόκει ἡμῖν ἀμφοῖν. Οὐκοῦν πάλιν ἂν αὐτοὺς
τὸ ἐναντίον εἰ ἐροίμεθα· ὦ ἄνθρωποι οἱ λέγοντες
αὖ ἀγαθὰ ἀνιαρὰ εἶναι, ἆρα οὐ τὰ τοιάδε λέγετε,
οἷον τά τε γυμνάσια καὶ τὰς στρατείας καὶ τὰς
ὑπὸ τῶν ἰατρῶν θεραπείας τὰς διὰ καύσεών τε καὶ
τομῶν καὶ φαρμακειῶν καὶ λιμοκτονιῶν γιγνο-
μένας, ὅτι ταῦτα ἀγαθὰ μέν ἐστιν, ἀνιαρὰ δέ;
Β φαῖεν ἄν; Συνεδόκει. Πότερον οὖν κατὰ τόδε
ἀγαθὰ αὐτὰ καλεῖτε, ὅτι ἐν τῷ παραχρῆμα ὀδύνας
τὰς ἐσχάτας παρέχει καὶ ἀλγηδόνας, ἢ ὅτι εἰς τὸν
ὕστερον χρόνον ὑγίειαί τε ἀπ' αὐτῶν γίγνονται καὶ
εὐεξίαι τῶν σωμάτων καὶ τῶν πόλεων σωτηρίαι
καὶ ἄλλων ἀρχαὶ καὶ πλοῦτοι; φαῖεν ἄν, ὡς ἐγᾦμαι.

in store for us? Or, even though they have none
of these things in store for a later day, and cause
us only enjoyment, would they still be evil just
because, forsooth, they cause enjoyment in some way
or other? Can we suppose, Protagoras, that they
will make any other answer than that these things
are evil, not according to the operation of the actual
pleasure of the moment, but owing to the later
results in disease and those other ills?

I think, said Protagoras, that most people would
answer thus.

Then in causing diseases they cause pains? And
in causing poverty they cause pains? They would
admit this, I imagine.

Protagoras agreed.

Then does it seem to you, my friends, as Protagoras
and I assert, that the only reason why these things
are evil is that they end at last in pains, and deprive
us of other pleasures? Would they admit this?

We both agreed that they would.

Then again, suppose we should ask them the
opposite: You, sirs, who tell us on the other
hand that good things are painful—do you not give
such instances as physical training, military service,
and medical treatment conducted by cautery,
incision, drugs, or starvation, and say that these are
good, but painful? Would they not grant it?

He agreed that they would.

Then do you call them good because they produce
extreme pangs and anguish for the moment, or
because later on they result in health and good
bodily condition, the deliverance of cities, dominion
over others, and wealth? They would assent to
this, I suppose.

Συνεδόκει. Ταῦτα δὲ ἀγαθά ἐστι δι' ἄλλο τι, ἢ
ὅτι εἰς ἡδονὰς ἀποτελευτᾷ καὶ λυπῶν ἀπαλλαγάς
τε καὶ ἀποτροπάς; ἢ ἔχετέ τι ἄλλο τέλος λέγειν,
C εἰς ὃ ἀποβλέψαντες αὐτὰ ἀγαθὰ καλεῖτε, ἀλλ' ⟨ἢ⟩[1]
ἡδονάς τε καὶ λύπας; οὐκ ἂν φαῖεν, ὡς ἐγῷμαι.
Οὐδ' ἐμοὶ δοκεῖ, ἔφη ὁ Πρωταγόρας. Οὐκοῦν
τὴν μὲν ἡδονὴν διώκετε ὡς ἀγαθὸν ὄν, τὴν δὲ
λύπην φεύγετε ὡς κακόν; Συνεδόκει. Τοῦτ' ἄρα
ἡγεῖσθ' εἶναι κακόν, τὴν λύπην, καὶ ἀγαθὸν τὴν
ἡδονήν, ἐπεὶ καὶ αὐτὸ τὸ χαίρειν τότε λέγετε
κακὸν εἶναι, ὅταν μειζόνων ἡδονῶν ἀποστερῇ ἢ
ὅσας αὐτὸ ἔχει, ἢ λύπας μείζους παρασκευάζῃ τῶν
D ἐν αὐτῷ ἡδονῶν· ἐπεὶ εἰ κατ' ἄλλο τι αὐτὸ τὸ
χαίρειν κακὸν καλεῖτε καὶ εἰς ἄλλο τι τέλος ἀποβλέψαντες, ἔχοιτε ἂν καὶ ἡμῖν εἰπεῖν· ἀλλ' οὐχ
ἕξετε. Οὐδ' ἐμοὶ δοκοῦσιν, ἔφη ὁ Πρωταγόρας.
Ἄλλο τι οὖν πάλιν καὶ περὶ αὐτοῦ τοῦ λυπεῖσθαι ὁ
αὐτὸς τρόπος; τότε καλεῖτε αὐτὸ τὸ λυπεῖσθαι
ἀγαθόν, ὅταν ἢ μείζους λύπας τῶν ἐν αὐτῷ οὐσῶν
ἀπαλλάττῃ ἢ μείζους ἡδονὰς τῶν λυπῶν παρασκευάζῃ; ἐπεὶ εἰ πρὸς ἄλλο τι τέλος ἀποβλέπετε,
E ὅταν καλῆτε αὐτὸ τὸ λυπεῖσθαι ἀγαθόν, ἢ πρὸς ὃ
ἐγὼ λέγω, ἔχετε ἡμῖν εἰπεῖν· ἀλλ' οὐχ ἕξετε.
Ἀληθῆ, ἔφη, λέγεις, ὁ Πρωταγόρας. Πάλιν
τοίνυν, ἔφην ἐγώ, εἴ με ἀνέροισθε, ὦ ἄνθρωποι,
τίνος οὖν δήποτε ἕνεκα πολλὰ περὶ τούτου λέγεις
καὶ πολλαχῇ; συγγιγνώσκετέ μοι, φαίην ἂν ἔγωγε.

[1] ἢ add. Stephanus.

He agreed.

And are these things good for any other reason than that they end at last in pleasures and relief and riddance of pains? Or have you some other end to mention, with respect to which you call them good, apart from pleasures and pains? They could not find one, I fancy.

I too think they could not, said Protagoras.

Then do you pursue pleasure as being a good thing, and shun pain as being a bad one?

He agreed that we do.

So one thing you hold to be bad—pain; and pleasure you hold to be good, since the very act of enjoying you call bad as soon as it deprives us of greater pleasures than it has in itself, or leads to greater pains than the pleasures it contains. For if it is with reference to something else that you call the act of enjoyment bad, and with a view to some other end, you might be able to tell it us; but this you will be unable to do.

I too think that they cannot, said Protagoras.

Then is not the same thing repeated in regard to the state of being pained? You call being pained a good thing as soon as it either rids us of greater pains than those it comprises, or leads to greater pleasures than its pains. Now if you have in view some other end than those which I mention when you call being pained good, you can tell it us; but you never can.

Truly spoken, said Protagoras.

Once more then, I proceeded; if you were to ask me, my friends, Now why on earth do you speak at such length on this point, and in so many ways? I should reply, Forgive me: in the first

πρῶτον μὲν γὰρ οὐ ῥᾴδιον ἀποδεῖξαι, τί ἐστί ποτε
τοῦτο, ὃ ὑμεῖς καλεῖτε τῶν ἡδονῶν ἥττω εἶναι·
ἔπειτα ἐν τούτῳ εἰσὶ πᾶσαι αἱ ἀποδείξεις. ἀλλ'
ἔτι καὶ νῦν ἀναθέσθαι ἔξεστιν, εἴ πῃ ἔχετε ἄλλο τι
355 φάναι εἶναι τὸ ἀγαθὸν ἢ τὴν ἡδονήν, ἢ τὸ κακὸν
ἄλλο τι ἢ τὴν ἀνίαν, ἢ ἀρκεῖ ὑμῖν τὸ ἡδέως κατα-
βιῶναι τὸν βίον ἄνευ λυπῶν; εἰ δὲ ἀρκεῖ καὶ
μὴ ἔχετε μηδὲν ἄλλο φάναι εἶναι ἀγαθὸν ἢ κακόν,
ὃ μὴ εἰς ταῦτα τελευτᾷ, τὸ μετὰ τοῦτο ἀκούετε.
φημὶ γὰρ ὑμῖν τούτου οὕτως ἔχοντος γελοῖον τὸν
λόγον γίγνεσθαι, ὅταν λέγητε, ὅτι πολλάκις γιγνώσκων τὰ κακὰ ἄνθρωπος, ὅτι κακά ἐστιν, ὅμως
πράττει αὐτά, ἐξὸν μὴ πράττειν, ὑπὸ τῶν ἡδονῶν
B ἀγόμενος καὶ ἐκπληττόμενος. καὶ αὖθις αὖ λέγετε,
ὅτι γιγνώσκων ὁ ἄνθρωπος τἀγαθὰ πράττειν οὐκ
ἐθέλει διὰ τὰς παραχρῆμα ἡδονάς, ὑπὸ τούτων
ἡττώμενος.

Ὡς δὲ ταῦτα γελοῖά ἐστι, κατάδηλον ἔσται, ἐὰν
μὴ πολλοῖς ὀνόμασι χρώμεθα ἅμα, ἡδεῖ τε καὶ
ἀνιαρῷ καὶ ἀγαθῷ καὶ κακῷ, ἀλλ' ἐπειδὴ δύο
ἐφάνη ταῦτα, δυοῖν καὶ ὀνόμασι προσαγορεύωμεν
αὐτά, πρῶτον μὲν ἀγαθῷ καὶ κακῷ, ἔπειτα αὖθις
ἡδεῖ τε καὶ ἀνιαρῷ. θέμενοι δὴ οὕτω λέγωμεν,
C ὅτι γιγνώσκων ὁ ἄνθρωπος τὰ κακὰ ὅτι κακά
ἐστιν, ὅμως αὐτὰ ποιεῖ. ἐὰν οὖν τις ἡμᾶς ἔρηται,
διὰ τί, ἡττώμενος, φήσομεν· ὑπὸ τοῦ; ἐκεῖνος
ἐρήσεται ἡμᾶς· ἡμῖν δὲ ὑπὸ μὲν ἡδονῆς οὐκέτι
ἔξεστιν εἰπεῖν· ἄλλο γὰρ ὄνομα μετείληφεν ἀντὶ
τῆς ἡδονῆς τὸ ἀγαθόν· ἐκείνῳ δὴ ἀποκρινώμεθα καὶ
λέγωμεν, ὅτι ἡττώμενος. ὑπὸ τίνος; φήσει· τοῦ
ἀγαθοῦ, φήσομεν νὴ Δία. ἂν οὖν τύχῃ ὁ ἐρόμενος
ἡμᾶς ὑβριστὴς ὤν, γελάσεται καὶ ἐρεῖ· ἢ γελοῖον

place, it is not easy to conclude what it is that you
mean when you say "overcome by pleasures";
and secondly, on this point hang all our conclusions
But it is still quite possible to retract, if you can
somehow contrive to say that the good is different
from pleasure, or the bad from pain. Is it enough
for you to live out your life pleasantly, without
pain? If it is, and you are unable to tell us of any
other good or evil that does not end in pleasure or
pain, listen to what I have to say next. I tell you
that if this is so, the argument becomes absurd,
when you say that it is often the case that a man,
knowing the evil to be evil, nevertheless commits
it, when he might avoid it, because he is driven
and dazed by his pleasures; while on the other
hand you say that a man, knowing the good, refuses
to do good because of the momentary pleasures by
which he is overcome.

The absurdity of all this will be manifest if we
refrain from using a number of terms at once, such
as pleasant, painful, good, and bad; and as there
appeared to be two things, let us call them by
two names—first, good and evil, and then later on,
pleasant and painful. Let us then lay it down as
our statement, that a man does evil in spite of
knowing the evil of it. Now if someone asks us:
Why? we shall answer: Because he is overcome.
By what? the questioner will ask us; and this time
we shall be unable to reply: By pleasure—for this
has exchanged its name for "the good." So we
must answer only with the words: Because he is
overcome. By what? says the questioner. The
good—must surely be our reply. Now if our questioner chance to be an arrogant person he will laugh

I

235

D λέγετε πρᾶγμα, εἰ πράττει τις κακά, γιγνώσκων
ὅτι κακά ἐστιν, οὐ δέον αὐτὸν πράττειν, ἡττώμενος
ὑπὸ τῶν ἀγαθῶν. ἆρα, φήσει, οὐκ ἀξίων ὄντων
νικᾶν ἐν ὑμῖν τῶν ἀγαθῶν τὰ κακά, ἢ ἀξίων;
φήσομεν δῆλον ὅτι ἀποκρινόμενοι, ὅτι οὐκ ἀξίων
ὄντων. οὐ γὰρ ἂν ἐξημάρτανεν ὃν φαμεν ἥττω
εἶναι τῶν ἡδονῶν. κατὰ τί δέ, φήσει ἴσως,
ἀνάξιά ἐστι τἀγαθὰ τῶν κακῶν ἢ τὰ κακὰ τῶν
ἀγαθῶν; ἢ κατ᾽ ἄλλο τι ἢ ὅταν τὰ μὲν μείζω, τὰ
δὲ σμικρότερα ᾖ; ἢ πλείω, τὰ δὲ ἐλάττω ᾖ; οὐχ
E ἕξομεν εἰπεῖν ἄλλο ἢ τοῦτο. δῆλον ἄρα, φήσει, ὅτι
τὸ ἡττᾶσθαι τοῦτο λέγετε, ἀντὶ ἐλαττόνων ἀγαθῶν
μείζω κακὰ λαμβάνειν. ταῦτα μὲν οὖν οὕτω.
μεταλάβωμεν δὴ τὰ ὀνόματα πάλιν τὸ ἡδύ τε καὶ
ἀνιαρὸν ἐπὶ τοῖς αὐτοῖς τούτοις, καὶ λέγωμεν ὅτι
ἄνθρωπος πράττει, τότε μὲν ἐλέγομεν τὰ κακά,
νῦν δὲ λέγωμεν τὰ ἀνιαρά, γιγνώσκων ὅτι ἀνιαρά
ἐστιν, ἡττώμενος ὑπὸ τῶν ἡδέων, δῆλον ὅτι
356 ἀναξίων ὄντων νικᾶν. καὶ τίς ἄλλη ἀναξία ἡδονῇ
πρὸς λύπην ἐστίν, ἀλλ᾽ ἢ ὑπερβολὴ ἀλλήλων καὶ
ἔλλειψις; ταῦτα δ᾽ ἐστὶ μείζω τε καὶ σμικρότερα γιγνόμενα ἀλλήλων καὶ πλείω καὶ ἐλάττω
καὶ μᾶλλον καὶ ἧττον. εἰ γάρ τις λέγοι ὅτι ἀλλὰ
πολὺ διαφέρει, ὦ Σώκρατες, τὸ παραχρῆμα ἡδὺ
τοῦ εἰς τὸν ὕστερον χρόνον καὶ ἡδέος καὶ λυπηροῦ,
μῶν ἄλλῳ τῳ, φαίην ἂν ἔγωγε, ἢ ἡδονῇ καὶ λύπῃ;
B οὐ γὰρ ἔσθ᾽ ὅτῳ ἄλλῳ. ἀλλ᾽ ὥσπερ ἀγαθὸς
ἱστάναι ἄνθρωπος, συνθεὶς τὰ ἡδέα καὶ συνθεὶς
τὰ λυπηρά, καὶ τὸ ἐγγὺς καὶ τὸ πόρρω στήσας ἐν

and exclaim: What a ridiculous statement, that a
man does evil, knowing it to be evil, and not having
to do it, because he is overcome by the good! Is
this, he will ask, because the good is not worthy
of conquering the evil in you, or because it is worthy?
Clearly we must reply: Because it is not worthy;
otherwise he whom we speak of as overcome by
pleasures would not have offended. But in what
sense, he might ask us, is the good unworthy of the
bad, or the bad of the good? This can only be when
the one is greater and the other smaller, or when
there are more on the one side and fewer on the
other. We shall not find any other reason to give.
So it is clear, he will say, that by " being overcome "
you mean getting the greater evil in exchange for
the lesser good. That must be agreed. Then let
us apply the terms " pleasant " and " painful "
to these things instead, and say that a man does
what we previously called evil, but now call painful,
knowing it to be painful, because he is overcome
by the pleasant, which is obviously unworthy to
conquer. What unworthiness can there be in
pleasure as against pain, save an excess or defect
of one compared with the other? That is, when
one becomes greater and the other smaller, or when
there are more on one side and fewer on the other,
or here a greater degree and there a less. For if
you should say: But, Socrates, the immediately
pleasant differs widely from the subsequently
pleasant or painful, I should reply: Do they differ
in anything but pleasure and pain? That is the
only distinction. Like a practised weigher, put
pleasant things and painful in the scales, and with
them the nearness and the remoteness, and tell me

τῷ ζυγῷ, εἰπὲ πότερα πλείω ἐστίν. ἐὰν μὲν γὰρ
ἡδέα πρὸς ἡδέα ἱστῇς, τὰ μείζω ἀεὶ καὶ πλείω
ληπτέα· ἐὰν δὲ λυπηρὰ πρὸς λυπηρά, τὰ ἐλάττω
καὶ σμικρότερα· ἐὰν δὲ ἡδέα πρὸς λυπηρά, ἐὰν
μὲν τὰ ἀνιαρὰ ὑπερβάλληται ὑπὸ τῶν ἡδέων, ἐάν
τε τὰ ἐγγὺς ὑπὸ τῶν πόρρω ἐάν τε τὰ πόρρω ὑπὸ
τῶν ἐγγύς, ταύτην τὴν πρᾶξιν πρακτέον ἐν ᾗ ἂν
C ταῦτ᾽ ἐνῇ· ἐὰν δὲ τὰ ἡδέα ὑπὸ τῶν ἀνιαρῶν, οὐ
πρακτέα· μή πῃ ἄλλῃ ἔχει, φαίην ἄν, ταῦτα, ὦ
ἄνθρωποι; οἶδ᾽ ὅτι οὐκ ἂν ἔχοιεν ἄλλως λέγειν.
Συνεδόκει καὶ ἐκείνῳ. Ὅτε δὴ τοῦτο οὕτως
ἔχει, τόδε μοι ἀποκρίνασθε, φήσω. φαίνεται
ὑμῖν τῇ ὄψει τὰ αὐτὰ μεγέθη ἐγγύθεν μὲν μείζω,
πόρρωθεν δὲ ἐλάττω· ἢ οὔ; Φήσουσιν. Καὶ τὰ
παχέα καὶ τὰ πολλὰ ὡσαύτως; καὶ αἱ φωναὶ
⟨αἱ⟩[1] ἴσαι ἐγγύθεν μὲν μείζους, πόρρωθεν δὲ
D σμικρότεραι; Φαῖεν ἄν. Εἰ οὖν ἐν τούτῳ ἡμῖν
ἦν τὸ εὖ πράττειν, ἐν τῷ τὰ μὲν μεγάλα μήκη
καὶ πράττειν καὶ λαμβάνειν, τὰ δὲ σμικρὰ καὶ
φεύγειν καὶ μὴ πράττειν, τίς ἂν ἡμῖν σωτηρία
ἐφάνη τοῦ βίου; ἆρα ἡ μετρητικὴ τέχνη ἢ ἡ τοῦ
φαινομένου δύναμις; ἢ αὕτη μὲν ἡμᾶς ἐπλάνα
καὶ ἐποίει ἄνω τε καὶ κάτω πολλάκις μεταλαμ-
βάνειν ταὐτὰ καὶ μεταμέλειν καὶ ἐν ταῖς πράξεσι
καὶ ἐν ταῖς αἱρέσεσι τῶν μεγάλων τε καὶ σμικρῶν,
ἡ δὲ μετρητικὴ ἄκυρον μὲν ἂν ἐποίησε τοῦτο τὸ
E φάντασμα, δηλώσασα δὲ τὸ ἀληθὲς ἡσυχίαν ἂν
ἐποίησεν ἔχειν τὴν ψυχὴν μένουσαν ἐπὶ τῷ ἀληθεῖ
καὶ ἔσωσεν ἂν τὸν βίον; ἆρ᾽ ἂν ὁμολογοῖεν οἱ

[1] αἱ add. Heindorf.

which count for more. For if you weigh pleasant things against pleasant, the greater and the more are always to be preferred: if painful against painful, then always the fewer and smaller. If you weigh pleasant against painful, and find that the painful are outbalanced by the pleasant—whether the near by the remote or the remote by the near—you must take that course of action to which the pleasant are attached ; but not that course if the pleasant are outweighed by the painful. Can the case be otherwise, I should ask, than thus, my friends ? I am certain they could state no alternative.

To this he too assented.

Since that is the case, then, I shall say, please answer me this : Does not the same size appear larger to your sight when near, and smaller when distant ? They will admit this. And it is the same with thickness and number ? And sounds of equal strength are greater when near, and smaller when distant ? They would agree to this. Now if our welfare consisted in doing and choosing things of large dimensions, and avoiding and not doing those of small, what would be our salvation in life ? Would it be the art of measurement, or the power of appearance ? Is it not the latter that leads us astray, as we saw, and many a time causes us to take things topsy-turvy and to have to change our minds both in our conduct and in our choice of great or small ? Whereas the art of measurement would have made this appearance ineffective, and by showing us the truth would have brought our soul into the repose of abiding by the truth, and so would have saved our life. Would men acknowledge, in view of all this,

ἄνθρωποι πρὸς ταῦτα ἡμᾶς τὴν μετρητικὴν σώζειν
ἂν τέχνην, ἢ ἄλλην; Τὴν μετρητικήν, ὡμολόγει.
Τί δ᾽, εἰ ἐν τῇ τοῦ περιττοῦ καὶ ἀρτίου αἱρέσει
ἡμῖν ἦν ἡ σωτηρία τοῦ βίου, ὁπότε τὸ πλέον
ὀρθῶς ἔδει ἑλέσθαι καὶ ὁπότε τὸ ἔλαττον, ἢ αὐτὸ
πρὸς ἑαυτὸ ἢ τὸ ἕτερον πρὸς τὸ ἕτερον, εἴτ᾽ ἐγγὺς
357 εἴτε πόρρω εἴη, τί ἂν ἔσωζεν ἡμῖν τὸν βίον; ἆρ᾽
ἂν οὐκ ἐπιστήμη; καὶ ἆρ᾽ ἂν οὐ μετρητική τις,
ἐπειδήπερ ὑπερβολῆς τε καὶ ἐνδείας ἐστὶν ἡ τέχνη;
ἐπειδὴ δὲ περιττοῦ τε καὶ ἀρτίου, ἆρα ἄλλη τις
ἢ ἀριθμητική; ὁμολογοῖεν ἂν ἡμῖν οἱ ἄνθρωποι,
ἢ οὔ; Ἐδόκουν ἂν καὶ τῷ Πρωταγόρᾳ ὁμολογεῖν.
Εἶεν, ὦ ἄνθρωποι· ἐπεὶ δὲ δὴ[1] ἡδονῆς τε καὶ
λύπης ἐν ὀρθῇ τῇ αἱρέσει ἐφάνη ἡμῖν ἡ σωτηρία
τοῦ βίου οὖσα, τοῦ τε πλέονος καὶ ἐλάττονος καὶ
B μείζονος καὶ σμικροτέρου καὶ πορρωτέρου καὶ ἐγ-
γυτέρω, ἆρα πρῶτον μὲν οὐ μετρητικὴ φαίνεται,
ὑπερβολῆς τε καὶ ἐνδείας οὖσα καὶ ἰσότητος πρὸς
ἀλλήλας σκέψις; Ἀλλ᾽ ἀνάγκη. Ἐπεὶ δὲ μετρητική, ἀνάγκη δήπου τέχνη καὶ ἐπιστήμη. Συμ-
φήσουσιν. Ἥτις μὲν τοίνυν τέχνη καὶ ἐπιστήμη
ἐστὶν αὕτη, εἰσαῦθις σκεψόμεθα· ὅτι δὲ ἐπιστήμη
ἐστί, τοσοῦτον ἐξαρκεῖ πρὸς τὴν ἀπόδειξιν, ἣν
C ἐμὲ δεῖ καὶ Πρωταγόραν ἀποδεῖξαι περὶ ὧν
ἤρεσθ᾽ ἡμᾶς. ἤρεσθε δέ, εἰ μέμνησθε, ἡνίκα
ἡμεῖς ἀλλήλοις ὡμολογοῦμεν ἐπιστήμης μηδὲν

---

[1] ἐπεὶ δὲ δὴ Adam : ἐπὶ δὲ δὴ . . . ἐπειδὴ δὲ mss.

---

[1] The intellectual control of our sense-perceptions, which
differ as to the size or number of the same things when near
and when distant, etc., has an important part in the educa-

that the art which saves our life is measurement,
or some other ?

It is measurement, he agreed.

Well now, if the saving of our life depended on
the choice of odd or even, and on knowing when
to make a right choice of the greater and when of
the less—taking each by itself or comparing it with
the other, and whether near or distant—what would
save our life ? Would it not be knowledge ; a
knowledge of measurement, since the art here is
concerned with excess and defect, and of numeration,
as it has to do with odd and even ? People would
admit this, would they not ?

Protagoras agreed that they would.

Well then, my friends, since we have found that
the salvation of our life depends on making a right
choice of pleasure and pain—of the more and the
fewer, the greater and the smaller, and the nearer
and the remoter—is it not evident, in the first place,
that measurement is a study of their excess and
defect and equality in relation to each other ?

This must needs be so.

And being measurement, I presume it must be an
art or science ?

They will assent to this.

Well, the nature of this art or science we shall
consider some other time [1] ; but the mere fact of its
being a science will suffice for the proof which
Protagoras and I are required to give in answer to
the question you have put to us. You asked it,
if you remember, when we were agreeing [2] that
there is nothing stronger than knowledge, and

tional scheme of the *Republic.* The measuring art is further
considered in the *Politicus* (283 foll.).   [2] *Cf.* 352 B foll.

εἶναι κρεῖττον, ἀλλὰ τοῦτο ἀεὶ κρατεῖν, ὅπου ἂν
ἐνῇ, καὶ ἡδονῆς καὶ τῶν ἄλλων ἁπάντων· ὑμεῖς
δὲ δὴ ἔφατε τὴν ἡδονὴν πολλάκις κρατεῖν καὶ
τοῦ εἰδότος ἀνθρώπου, ἐπειδὴ δὲ ὑμῖν οὐχ ὡμολογοῦμεν, μετὰ τοῦτο ἤρεσθε ἡμᾶς· ὦ Πρωταγόρα
τε καὶ Σώκρατες, εἰ μὴ ἔστι τοῦτο τὸ πάθημα
D ἡδονῆς ἡττᾶσθαι, ἀλλὰ τί ποτ' ἐστὶ καὶ τί ὑμεῖς
αὐτό φατε εἶναι; εἴπατε ἡμῖν. εἰ μὲν οὖν τότε
εὐθὺς ὑμῖν εἴπομεν ὅτι ἀμαθία, κατεγελᾶτε ἂν
ἡμῶν· νῦν δὲ ἂν ἡμῶν καταγελᾶτε, καὶ ὑμῶν
αὐτῶν καταγελάσεσθε. καὶ γὰρ ὑμεῖς ὡμολογήκατε ἐπιστήμης ἐνδείᾳ ἐξαμαρτάνειν περὶ
τὴν τῶν ἡδονῶν αἵρεσιν καὶ λυπῶν τοὺς ἐξαμαρ-
τάνοντας· ταῦτα δέ ἐστιν ἀγαθά τε καὶ κακά·
καὶ οὐ μόνον ἐπιστήμης, ἀλλὰ καὶ ἧς τὸ πρόσθεν
ἔτι ὡμολογήκατε ὅτι μετρητικῆς· ἡ δὲ ἐξαμαρ-
E τανομένη πρᾶξις ἄνευ ἐπιστήμης ἴστε που καὶ
αὐτοὶ ὅτι ἀμαθίᾳ πράττεται. ὥστε τοῦτ' ἐστὶ
τὸ ἡδονῆς ἥττω εἶναι, ἀμαθία ἡ μεγίστη· ἧς
Πρωταγόρας ὅδε φησὶν ἰατρὸς εἶναι καὶ Πρόδικος
καὶ Ἱππίας· ὑμεῖς δὲ διὰ τὸ οἴεσθαι ἄλλο τι ἢ
ἀμαθίαν εἶναι οὔτε αὐτοὶ ⟨ἴτε⟩[1] οὔτε τοὺς ὑμε-
τέρους παῖδας παρὰ τοὺς τούτων διδασκάλους
τούσδε τοὺς σοφιστὰς πέμπετε, ὡς οὐ διδακτοῦ
ὄντος, ἀλλὰ κηδόμενοι τοῦ ἀργυρίου καὶ οὐ διδόν-
358 τες τούτοις κακῶς πράττετε καὶ ἰδίᾳ καὶ δημοσίᾳ.

Ταῦτα μὲν τοῖς πολλοῖς ἀποκεκριμένοι ἂν ἦμεν·
ὑμᾶς δὲ δὴ μετὰ Πρωταγόρου ἐρωτῶ, ⟨ὦ⟩[2]
Ἱππία τε καὶ Πρόδικε—κοινὸς γὰρ δὴ ἔστω ὑμῖν
ὁ λόγος—πότερον δοκῶ ὑμῖν ἀληθῆ λέγειν ἢ

---

[1] ἴτε add. Madvig.   [2] ὦ add. Rückert.

that knowledge, wherever it may be found, has always the upper hand of pleasure or anything else ; and then you said that pleasure often masters even the man of knowledge, and on our refusing to agree with you, you went on to ask us: Protagoras and Socrates, if this experience is not " being overcome by pleasure," whatever can it be, and what do you call it ? Tell us. If on the spur of the moment we had replied, " Ignorance," you would have laughed us to scorn : but now if you laugh at us you will be laughing at yourselves as well. For you have admitted that it is from defect of knowledge that men err, when they do err, in their choice of pleasures and pains—that is, in the choice of good and evil ; and from defect not merely of knowledge but of the knowledge which you have now admitted also to be that of measurement. And surely you know well enough for yourselves that the erring act committed without knowledge is done through ignorance. Accordingly " to be overcome by pleasure " means just this—ignorance in the highest degree, which Protagoras here and Prodicus and Hippias profess to cure. But you, through supposing it to be something else than ignorance, will neither go yourselves nor send your children to these sophists, who are the teachers of those things—you say it cannot be taught ; you are chary of your money and will give them none, and so you fare badly both in private and in public life.

Such would have been our answer to the world at large. And I ask you now, Hippias and Prodicus, as well as Protagoras—for I would have you make a joint reply—whether you think what I say is true or false.

ψεύδεσθαι. Ὑπερφυῶς ἐδόκει ἅπασιν ἀληθῆ εἶναι
τὰ εἰρημένα. Ὁμολογεῖτε ἄρα, ἦν δ᾽ ἐγώ, τὸ
μὲν ἡδὺ ἀγαθὸν εἶναι, τὸ δὲ ἀνιαρὸν κακόν. τὴν
δὲ Προδίκου τοῦδε διαίρεσιν τῶν ὀνομάτων παρ-
B αιτοῦμαι· εἴτε γὰρ ἡδὺ εἴτε τερπνὸν λέγεις εἴτε
χαρτόν, εἴτε ὁπόθεν καὶ ὅπως χαίρεις τὰ τοιαῦτα
ὀνομάζων, ὦ βέλτιστε Πρόδικε, τοῦτό μοι πρὸς
ὃ βούλομαι ἀπόκριναι. Γελάσας οὖν ὁ Πρόδικος
συνωμολόγησε, καὶ οἱ ἄλλοι. Τί δὲ δή, ὦ ἄνδρες,
ἔφην ἐγώ, τὸ τοιόνδε; αἱ ἐπὶ τούτου πράξεις
ἅπασαι, ἐπὶ τοῦ ἀλύπως ζῆν καὶ ἡδέως, ἆρ᾽ οὐ
καλαί [καὶ ὠφέλιμοι[1]]; καὶ τὸ καλὸν ἔργον
ἀγαθόν τε καὶ ὠφέλιμον; Συνεδόκει. Εἰ ἄρα,
ἔφην ἐγώ, τὸ ἡδὺ ἀγαθόν ἐστιν, οὐδεὶς οὔτε εἰδὼς
C οὔτε οἰόμενος ἄλλα βελτίω εἶναι, ἢ ἃ ποιεῖ,[2] καὶ
δυνατά,[3] ἔπειτα ποιεῖ ταῦτα, ἐξὸν τὰ βελτίω· οὐδὲ
τὸ ἥττω εἶναι αὐτοῦ ἄλλο τι τοῦτ᾽ ἐστὶν ἢ ἀμαθία,
οὐδὲ κρείττω ἑαυτοῦ ἄλλο τι ἢ σοφία. Συνεδόκει πᾶσιν. Τί δὲ δή; ἀμαθίαν ἄρα τὸ τοιόνδε
λέγετε, τὸ ψευδῆ ἔχειν δόξαν καὶ ἐψεῦσθαι περὶ
τῶν πραγμάτων τῶν πολλοῦ ἀξίων; Καὶ τοῦτο
πᾶσι συνεδόκει. Ἄλλο τι οὖν, ἔφην ἐγώ, ἐπί
γε τὰ κακὰ οὐδεὶς ἑκὼν ἔρχεται οὐδὲ ἐπὶ ἃ οἴεται
D κακὰ εἶναι, οὐδ᾽ ἔστι τοῦτο, ὡς ἔοικεν, ἐν ἀνθρώπου
φύσει, ἐπὶ ἃ οἴεται κακὰ εἶναι ἐθέλειν ἰέναι ἀντὶ
τῶν ἀγαθῶν· ὅταν τε ἀναγκασθῇ δυοῖν κακοῖν τὸ

---

[1] καὶ ὠφέλιμοι secl. Schleiermacher.
[2] ποιεῖ Heindorf: ἐποίει MSS.
[3] δυνατά Schleiermacher: δύναται MSS.

---

[1] "Yielding to oneself" and "mastery of oneself" are
here put instead of "being overcome by pleasure" and

They all thought what I had said was absolutely true.

Then you agree, I continued, that the pleasant is good and the painful bad. And let me entreat my friend Prodicus to spare me his distinction of terms: for whether you say pleasant or delightful or enjoyable, my excellent Prodicus, or in whatever style or manner you may be pleased to name these things, pray reply to the sense of my question.

At this Prodicus laughed and consented, as did the rest.

Well now, my friends, I said, what of this? All actions aimed at living painlessly and pleasantly are honourable, are they not? And the honourable work is both good and useful?

They agreed.

Then if, I proceeded, the pleasant is good, no one who has knowledge or thought of other actions as better than those he is doing, and as possible, will do as he proposes if he is free to do the better ones; and this yielding to oneself is nothing but ignorance, and mastery of[1] oneself is as certainly wisdom.

They all agreed.

Well then, by ignorance do you mean having a false opinion and being deceived about matters of importance?

They all agreed to this also.

Then surely, I went on, no one willingly goes after evil or what he thinks to be evil; it is not in human nature, apparently, to do so—to wish to go after what one thinks to be evil in preference to the good; and when compelled to choose one of

the opposite state. The conflict between the better and worse self is discussed in *Rep.* iv. 430 e foll.

ἕτερον αἱρεῖσθαι, οὐδεὶς τὸ μεῖζον αἱρήσεται ἐξὸν
τὸ ἔλαττον. Ἅπαντα ταῦτα συνεδόκει ἅπασιν
ἡμῖν. Τί οὖν; ἔφην ἐγώ, καλεῖτέ ⟨τι⟩¹ δέος
καὶ φόβον; καὶ ἆρα ὅπερ ἐγώ; πρὸς σὲ λέγω,
Πρόδικε. προσδοκίαν τινὰ λέγω κακοῦ τοῦτο,
εἴτε φόβον εἴτε δέος καλεῖτε. Ἐδόκει Πρωτ-
E αγόρᾳ μὲν καὶ Ἱππίᾳ δέος τε καὶ φόβος εἶναι
τοῦτο, Προδίκῳ δὲ δέος, φόβος δ' οὔ. Ἀλλ'
οὐδέν, ἔφην ἐγώ, Πρόδικε, διαφέρει· ἀλλὰ τόδε.
εἰ ἀληθῆ τὰ ἔμπροσθέν ἐστιν, ἆρά τις ἀνθρώπων
ἐθελήσει ἐπὶ ταῦτα ἰέναι ἃ δέδοικεν, ἐξὸν ἐπὶ ἃ
μή; ἢ ἀδύνατον ἐκ τῶν ὡμολογημένων; ἃ γὰρ
δέδοικεν, ὡμολόγηται ἡγεῖσθαι κακὰ εἶναι· ἃ δὲ
ἡγεῖται κακά, οὐδένα οὔτε ἰέναι ἐπὶ ταῦτα οὔτε
359 λαμβάνειν ἑκόντα. Ἐδόκει καὶ ταῦτα πᾶσιν.

Οὕτω δὴ τούτων ὑποκειμένων, ἦν δ' ἐγώ,
Πρόδικέ τε καὶ Ἱππία, ἀπολογείσθω ἡμῖν Πρωταγόρας ὅδε, ἃ τὸ πρῶτον ἀπεκρίνατο, πῶς ὀρθῶς
ἔχει, μὴ ἃ τὸ πρῶτον παντάπασι· τότε μὲν γὰρ
δὴ πέντε ὄντων μορίων τῆς ἀρετῆς οὐδὲν ἔφη
εἶναι τὸ ἕτερον οἷον τὸ ἕτερον, ἰδίαν δὲ αὐτοῦ
ἕκαστον ἔχειν δύναμιν· ἀλλ' οὐ ταῦτα λέγω, ἀλλ'
ἃ τὸ ὕστερον εἶπε. τὸ γὰρ ὕστερον ἔφη τὰ μὲν
τέτταρα ἐπιεικῶς παραπλήσια ἀλλήλοις εἶναι,
B τὸ δὲ ἓν πάνυ πολὺ διαφέρειν τῶν ἄλλων, τὴν
ἀνδρείαν, γνώσεσθαι δέ μ' ἔφη τεκμηρίῳ τῷδε·
εὑρήσεις γάρ, ὦ Σώκρατες, ἀνθρώπους ἀνοσιωτά-

¹ τι add. Heindorf.

two evils, nobody will choose the greater when he may the lesser.

All this met with the assent of everyone.

Well, I said, is there something you call dread, or fear ? And is it—I address myself to you, Prodicus —the same as I have in mind—something I describe as an expectation of evil, whether you call it fear or dread ?

Protagoras and Hippias agreed to this description of dread or fear ; but Prodicus thought this was dread, not fear.

No matter, Prodicus, I said, but my point is this : if our former statements are true, will any man wish to go after what he dreads, when he may pursue what he does not ? Surely this is impossible after what we have admitted—that he regards as evil that which he dreads ? And what is regarded as evil is neither pursued nor accepted willingly, we saw, by anyone.

Here also they were all in agreement.

So much, then, being granted, Prodicus and Hippias, I said, let our friend Protagoras vindicate the correctness of the answer he made at first— not that which he made at the very beginning,[1] when he said that, while there were five parts of virtue, none of them was like any other, but each had its particular function : I do not refer to that, but the statement he made afterwards,[2] when he proceeded to say that four of them had a considerable resemblance to each other, but one was quite different from the rest—courage ; and he told me I should perceive this by the following token : You will find, Socrates, said he, that men may be most

[1] Cf. 330 A foll.

Cf. 349 D foll.

τοὺς μὲν ὄντας καὶ ἀδικωτάτους καὶ ἀκολαστοτάτους καὶ ἀμαθεστάτους, ἀνδρειοτάτους δέ· ᾧ
γνώσει ὅτι πολὺ διαφέρει ἡ ἀνδρεία τῶν ἄλλων μορίων τῆς ἀρετῆς. καὶ ἐγὼ εὐθὺς τότε πάνυ
ἐθαύμασα τὴν ἀπόκρισιν, καὶ ἔτι μᾶλλον ἐπειδὴ
ταῦτα μεθ᾽ ὑμῶν διεξῆλθον. ἠρόμην δ᾽ οὖν
τοῦτον, εἰ τοὺς ἀνδρείους λέγοι θαρραλέους· ὁ δέ,
C καὶ ἴτας γ᾽, ἔφη. μέμνησαι, ἦν δ᾽ ἐγώ, ὦ Πρωταγόρα, ταῦτα ἀποκρινόμενος; Ὡμολόγει. Ἴθι δή,
ἔφην ἐγώ, εἰπὲ ἡμῖν, ἐπὶ τί λέγεις ἴτας εἶναι τοὺς
ἀνδρείους; ἦ ἐφ᾽ ἅπερ οἱ δειλοί; Οὐκ ἔφη. Οὐκοῦν ἐφ᾽ ἕτερα. Ναί, ἦ δ᾽ ὅς. Πότερον οἱ μὲν
δειλοὶ ἐπὶ τὰ θαρραλέα ἔρχονται, οἱ δὲ ἀνδρεῖοι ἐπὶ
τὰ δεινά; Λέγεται δή, ὦ Σώκρατες, οὕτως ὑπὸ
τῶν ἀνθρώπων. Ἀληθῆ, ἔφην ἐγώ, λέγεις· ἀλλ᾽ οὐ
D τοῦτο ἐρωτῶ, ἀλλὰ σὺ ἐπὶ τί φὴς ἴτας εἶναι τοὺς
ἀνδρείους; ἆρ᾽ ἐπὶ τὰ δεινά, ἡγουμένους δεινὰ
εἶναι, ἦ ἐπὶ τὰ μή; Ἀλλὰ τοῦτό γ᾽, ἔφη, ἐν οἷς σὺ
ἔλεγες τοῖς λόγοις ἀπεδείχθη ἄρτι ὅτι ἀδύνατον.
Καὶ τοῦτο, ἔφην ἐγώ, ἀληθὲς λέγεις· ὥστ᾽ εἰ τοῦτο
ὀρθῶς ἀπεδείχθη, ἐπὶ μὲν ἃ δεινὰ ἡγεῖται εἶναι
οὐδεὶς ἔρχεται, ἐπειδὴ τὸ ἥττω εἶναι ἑαυτοῦ ηὑρέθη
ἀμαθία οὖσα. Ὡμολόγει. Ἀλλὰ μὴν ἐπὶ ἅ γε
θαρροῦσι πάντες αὖ ἔρχονται, καὶ δειλοὶ καὶ
ἀνδρεῖοι, καὶ ταύτῃ γε ἐπὶ τὰ αὐτὰ ἔρχονται οἱ
E δειλοί τε καὶ οἱ ἀνδρεῖοι. Ἀλλὰ μέντοι, ἔφη, ὦ
Σώκρατες, πᾶν γε τοὐναντίον ἐστὶν ἐπὶ ἃ οἵ τε

unholy, most unjust, most dissolute, and most ignorant, yet most courageous; whence you may judge that courage is very different from the other parts of virtue. His answer caused me great surprise at the moment, and still more when I went into the matter with your help. But anyhow, I asked him whether by the brave he meant " bold." Yes, he replied, and impetuous. Protagoras, I said, do you remember making this answer?

He admitted he did.

Well now, I said, tell us, towards what do you mean they are impetuous when they are courageous? Towards the same things as cowards?

No, he said.

Then towards other things?

Yes, he said.

Do cowards go after things that allow boldness, and the courageous after dreadful things?

So people say, Socrates.

Quite true, I said. But my point is rather, towards what, according to you, are the brave impetuous? Dreadful things, in the belief that they are dreadful, or towards what is not dreadful?

No, he said; the former has just been shown, by the arguments you put forward, to be impossible.

Quite true again, I said; so that if this proof was correct, no one goes to meet what he regards as dreadful, since to be overcome by oneself was found to be ignorance.

He admitted this.

And yet all men go also to meet what they can face boldly, whether cowardly or brave, and in this respect cowardly and brave go to meet the same things.

But still, Socrates, he said, what cowards go to

249

δειλοὶ ἔρχονται καὶ οἱ ἀνδρεῖοι. αὐτίκα εἰς τὸν
πόλεμον οἱ μὲν ἐθέλουσιν ἰέναι, οἱ δὲ οὐκ ἐθέλουσιν.
Πότερον, ἔφην ἐγώ, καλὸν ὂν ἰέναι ἢ αἰσχρόν;
Καλόν, ἔφη. Οὐκοῦν εἴπερ καλόν, καὶ ἀγαθὸν
ὡμολογήσαμεν ἐν τοῖς ἔμπροσθεν. τὰς γὰρ καλὰς
πράξεις ἁπάσας ἀγαθὰς ὡμολογήσαμεν. Ἀληθῆ
λέγεις, καὶ ἀεὶ ἔμοιγε δοκεῖ οὕτως. Ὀρθῶς γε,
360 ἔφην ἐγώ. ἀλλὰ ποτέρους φὴς εἰς τὸν πόλεμον
οὐκ ἐθέλειν ἰέναι, καλὸν ὂν καὶ ἀγαθόν; Τοὺς
δειλούς, ἦ δ' ὅς. Οὐκοῦν, ἦν δ' ἐγώ, εἴπερ καλὸν
καὶ ἀγαθόν, καὶ ἡδύ; Ὡμολόγηται γοῦν, ἔφη.
Ἆρ' οὖν γιγνώσκοντες οἱ δειλοὶ οὐκ ἐθέλουσιν
ἰέναι ἐπὶ τὸ κάλλιόν¹ τε καὶ ἄμεινον καὶ ἥδιον;
Ἀλλὰ καὶ τοῦτο ἐὰν ὁμολογῶμεν, ἔφη, δια-
φθεροῦμεν τὰς ἔμπροσθεν ὁμολογίας. Τί δ' ὁ
ἀνδρεῖος; οὐκ ἐπὶ τὸ κάλλιόν τε καὶ ἄμεινον καὶ
B ἥδιον ἔρχεται; Ἀνάγκη, ἔφη, ὁμολογεῖν. Οὐκοῦν
ὅλως οἱ ἀνδρεῖοι οὐκ αἰσχροὺς φόβους φοβοῦνται,
ὅταν φοβῶνται, οὐδὲ αἰσχρὰ θάρρη θαρροῦσιν;
Ἀληθῆ, ἔφη. Εἰ δὲ μὴ αἰσχρά, ἆρ' οὐ καλά;
Ὡμολόγει. Εἰ δὲ καλά, καὶ ἀγαθά; Ναί. Οὐκοῦν καὶ οἱ δειλοὶ καὶ οἱ θρασεῖς καὶ οἱ μαινόμενοι
τοὐναντίον αἰσχρούς τε φόβους φοβοῦνται καὶ

¹ κάλλιόν Stephanus: καλόν MSS.

meet is the very opposite of what the courageous go to meet. For instance, the latter are willing to go to war, but the former are not.

Is going to war an honourable thing, I asked, or a base thing?

Honourable, he replied.

Then if it is honourable, we have admitted, by our former argument, that it is also good; for we agreed that all honourable actions were good.

True, and I abide by that decision.

You are right to do so, I said. But which sort of men do you say are not willing to go to war, that being an honourable and good thing to do?

The cowardly, he replied.

Then, I went on, if it is honourable and good, is it also pleasant?

That certainly has been admitted, he said.

Now do the cowards wittingly refuse to go to what is more honourable, better, and pleasanter?

Well, if we admit that too, he replied, we shall undo our previous admissions.

But what of the courageous man? Does he not go to the more honourable and better and pleasanter?

I am forced to admit that, he said.

Now, in general, courageous men do not feel base fears, when they fear, nor is there anything base in their boldness?

True, he said.

And if not base, then it must be honourable?

He admitted this.

And if honourable, then good?

Yes.

And the cowardly and the bold and the mad, on the contrary, feel base fears and base boldness?

αἰσχρὰ θάρρη θαρροῦσιν; Ὡμολόγει. Θαρροῦσι

δὲ τὰ αἰσχρὰ καὶ κακὰ δι᾽ ἄλλο τι ἢ δι᾽ ἄγνοιαν

C καὶ ἀμαθίαν; Οὕτως ἔχει, ἔφη. Τί οὖν; τοῦτο δι᾽

ὃ δειλοί εἰσιν οἱ δειλοί, δειλίαν ἢ ἀνδρείαν καλεῖς;

Δειλίαν ἔγωγ᾽, ἔφη. Δειλοὶ δὲ οὐ διὰ τὴν τῶν

δεινῶν ἀμαθίαν ἐφάνησαν ὄντες; Πάνυ γ᾽, ἔφη.

Διὰ ταύτην ἄρα τὴν ἀμαθίαν δειλοί εἰσιν; Ὡμολόγει.

Δι᾽ ὃ δὲ δειλοί εἰσι, δειλία ὁμολογεῖται παρὰ σοῦ;

Συνέφη. Οὐκοῦν ἡ τῶν δεινῶν καὶ μὴ δεινῶν

ἀμαθία δειλία ἂν εἴη; Ἐπένευσεν. Ἀλλὰ μήν,

D ἦν δ᾽ ἐγώ, ἐναντίον ἀνδρεία δειλίᾳ. Ἔφη.

Οὐκοῦν ἡ τῶν δεινῶν καὶ μὴ δεινῶν σοφία ἐναντία

τῇ τούτων ἀμαθίᾳ ἐστίν; Καὶ ἐνταῦθα ἔτι ἐπένευ-

σεν. Ἡ δὲ τούτων ἀμαθία δειλία; Πάνυ μόγις ἐν-

ταῦθα ἐπένευσεν. Ἡ σοφία ἄρα τῶν δεινῶν καὶ

μὴ δεινῶν ἀνδρεία ἐστίν, ἐναντία οὖσα τῇ τούτων

ἀμαθίᾳ; Οὐκέτι ἐνταῦθα οὔτ᾽ ἐπινεῦσαι ἠθέλησεν

ἐσίγα τε· καὶ ἐγὼ εἶπον· Τί δή, ὦ Πρωταγόρα,

He agreed.

Do they feel base and evil boldness solely through stupidity and ignorance ?

Just so, he said.

Well now, the cause of cowards being cowardly, do you call this cowardice or courage ?

Cowardice, I call it, he replied.

And were they not found to be cowards through ignorance of what is dreadful ?

Certainly, he said.

And so they are cowards because of that ignorance ?

He agreed.

And the cause of their being cowards is admitted by you to be cowardice ?

He assented.

Then ignorance of what is dreadful and not dreadful will be cowardice ?

He nodded assent.

But surely courage, I went on, is the opposite of cowardice.

Yes.

Then the wisdom that knows what is and what is not dreadful is opposed to the ignorance of these things ?

To this he could still nod assent.

And the ignorance of them is cowardice ?

To this he nodded very reluctantly.

So the wisdom that knows what is and what is not dreadful is courage, being opposed to the ignorance of these things ?

Here he could no longer bring himself to nod agreement, and remained silent.   Then I proceeded : Why is it, Protagoras, that you neither affirm nor deny what I ask you ?

360

οὔτε σὺ φῇς ἃ ἐρωτῶ οὔτε ἀπόφῃς; Αὐτός, ἔφη,
E πέρανον. Ἕν γ᾽, ἔφην ἐγώ, μόνον ἐρόμενος
ἔτι σέ, εἴ σοι ὥσπερ τὸ πρῶτον ἔτι δοκοῦσιν εἶναί
τινες ἄνθρωποι ἀμαθέστατοι μέν, ἀνδρειότατοι δέ.
Φιλονικεῖν μοι, ἔφη, δοκεῖς, ὦ Σώκρατες, τὸ
ἐμὲ εἶναι τὸν ἀποκρινόμενον· χαριοῦμαι οὖν σοι,
καὶ λέγω ὅτι ἐκ τῶν ὡμολογημένων ἀδύνατόν μοι
δοκεῖ εἶναι.

Οὗτοι, ἦν δ᾽ ἐγώ, ἄλλου ἕνεκα ἐρωτῶ πάντα
ταῦτα, ἢ σκέψασθαι βουλόμενος, πῶς ποτ᾽ ἔχει τὰ
περὶ τῆς ἀρετῆς καὶ τί ποτ᾽ ἐστὶν αὐτό, ἡ ἀρετή.
361 οἶδα γὰρ ὅτι τούτου φανεροῦ γενομένου μάλιστ᾽
ἂν κατάδηλον γένοιτο ἐκεῖνο, περὶ οὗ ἐγώ τε καὶ
σὺ μακρὸν λόγον ἑκάτερος ἀπετείναμεν, ἐγὼ μὲν
λέγων ὡς οὐ διδακτὸν ἀρετή, σὺ δ᾽ ὡς διδακτόν.
καί μοι δοκεῖ ἡμῶν ἡ ἄρτι ἔξοδος τῶν λόγων
ὥσπερ ἄνθρωπος κατηγορεῖν τε καὶ καταγελᾶν,
καὶ εἰ φωνὴν λάβοι, εἰπεῖν ἂν ὅτι ἄτοποί γ᾽ ἐστέ,
ὦ Σώκρατές τε καὶ Πρωταγόρα· σὺ μὲν λέγων
ὅτι οὐ διδακτόν ἐστιν ἀρετὴ ἐν τοῖς ἔμπροσθεν,
B νῦν σεαυτῷ τἀναντία σπεύδεις, ἐπιχειρῶν ἀποδεῖξαι
ὡς πάντα χρήματα ἐστὶν ἐπιστήμη, καὶ ἡ δικαιοσύνη
καὶ ἡ σωφροσύνη καὶ ἡ ἀνδρεία, ᾧ τρόπῳ μάλιστ᾽
ἂν διδακτὸν φανείη ἡ ἀρετή· εἰ μὲν γὰρ ἄλλο τι
ἦν ἢ ἐπιστήμη ἡ ἀρετή, ὥσπερ Πρωταγόρας
ἐπεχείρει λέγειν, σαφῶς οὐκ ἂν ἦν διδακτόν· νῦν
δὲ εἰ φανήσεται ἐπιστήμη ὅλον, ὡς σὺ σπεύδεις, ὦ
Σώκρατες, θαυμάσιον ἔσται μὴ διδακτὸν ὄν. Πρωταγόρας δ᾽ αὖ διδακτὸν τότε ὑποθέμενος νῦν
C τοὐναντίον ἔοικε σπεύδοντι, ὀλίγου πάντα μᾶλλον
φανῆναι αὐτὸ ἢ ἐπιστήμην. καὶ οὕτως ἂν ἥκιστα

Finish it, he said, by yourself.

I must first ask you, I said, just one more question: Do you still think, as at the beginning, that there are any people who are most ignorant and yet most courageous?

I see, Socrates, you have set your heart on making me your answerer; so, to oblige you, I will say that by what we have admitted I consider it impossible.

My only motive, I then said, in asking all these questions has been a desire to examine the various relations of virtue and its own special nature. For I know that, were it once made plain, that other question on which you and I have argued at such length on either side—you maintaining and I denying that virtue can be taught—would be cleared up satisfactorily. Our discussion, in its present result, seems to me as though it accused and mocked us like some human person; if it were given a voice it would say : "What strange creatures you are, Socrates and Protagoras! You on the one hand, after having said at first that virtue cannot be taught, are now hot in opposition to yourself, endeavouring to prove that all things are knowledge—justice, temperance, and courage—which is the best way to make virtue appear teachable : for if virtue were anything else than knowledge, as Protagoras tried to make out, obviously it would not be teachable ; but if as a matter of fact it turns out to be entirely knowledge, as you urge, Socrates, I shall be surprised if it is not teachable. Protagoras, on the other hand, though at first he claimed that it was teachable, now seems as eager for the opposite, declaring that it has been found to be almost anything but knowledge, which would make it quite unteachable ! "

εἴη διδακτόν· ἐγὼ οὖν, ὦ Πρωταγόρα, πάντα
ταῦτα καθορῶν ἄνω κάτω ταραττόμενα δεινῶς,
πᾶσαν προθυμίαν ἔχω καταφανῆ αὐτὰ γενέσθαι,
καὶ βουλοίμην ἂν ταῦτα διεξελθόντας ἡμᾶς ἐξελ-
θεῖν καὶ ἐπὶ τὴν ἀρετὴν ὅ τι ἔστι, καὶ πάλιν ἐπισκέψασθαι περὶ αὐτοῦ, εἴτε διδακτὸν εἴτε μὴ διδακτόν,
μὴ πολλάκις ἡμᾶς ὁ Ἐπιμηθεὺς ἐκεῖνος καὶ ἐν τῇ
D σκέψει σφήλῃ ἐξαπατήσας, ὥσπερ καὶ ἐν τῇ δια-
νομῇ ἠμέλησεν ἡμῶν, ὡς φῂς σύ. ἤρεσεν οὖν μοι
καὶ ἐν τῷ μύθῳ ὁ Προμηθεὺς μᾶλλον τοῦ Ἐπι-
μηθέως· ᾧ χρώμενος ἐγὼ καὶ προμηθούμενος ὑπὲρ
τοῦ βίου τοῦ ἐμαυτοῦ παντὸς πάντα ταῦτα πραγ-
ματεύομαι, καὶ εἰ σὺ ἐθέλοις, ὅπερ καὶ κατ᾽ ἀρχὰς
ἔλεγον, μετὰ σοῦ ἂν ἥδιστα ταῦτα συνδιασκοποίην.
καὶ ὁ Πρωταγόρας, Ἐγὼ μέν, ἔφη, ὦ Σώκρατες,
ἐπαινῶ σου τὴν προθυμίαν καὶ τὴν διέξοδον τῶν
E λόγων. καὶ γὰρ οὔτε τἆλλα οἶμαι κακὸς εἶναι
ἄνθρωπος, φθονερός τε ἥκιστ᾽ ἀνθρώπων, ἐπεὶ καὶ
περὶ σοῦ πρὸς πολλοὺς δὴ εἴρηκα, ὅτι ὧν ἐντυγχάνω
πολὺ μάλιστα ἄγαμαι σέ, τῶν μὲν τηλικούτων καὶ
πάνυ· καὶ λέγω γε ὅτι οὐκ ἂν θαυμάζοιμι, εἰ τῶν
ἐλλογίμων γένοιο ἀνδρῶν ἐπὶ σοφίᾳ. καὶ περὶ
τούτων δὲ εἰσαῦθις, ὅταν βούλῃ, διέξιμεν· νῦν δ᾽
362 ὥρα ἤδη καὶ ἐπ᾽ ἄλλο τι τρέπεσθαι. Ἀλλ᾽, ἦν δ᾽
ἐγώ, οὕτω χρὴ ποιεῖν, εἴ σοι δοκεῖ. καὶ γὰρ ἐμοὶ
οἵπερ ἔφην ἰέναι πάλαι ὥρα, ἀλλὰ Καλλίᾳ τῷ καλῷ
χαριζόμενος παρέμεινα. ταῦτ᾽ εἰπόντες καὶ ἀκούσαντες ἀπῇμεν.

Now I, Protagoras, observing the extraordinary tangle into which we have managed to get the whole matter, am most anxious to have it thoroughly cleared up. And I should like to work our way through it until at last we reach what virtue is, and then go back and consider whether it is teachable or not, lest perchance your Epimetheus beguile and trip us up in our investigation as he overlooked us in your account of his distribution.[1] I like the Prometheus of your fable better than the Epimetheus ; for he is of use to me, and I take Promethean thought continually for my own life when I am occupied with all these questions ; so, with your consent, as I said at the beginning, I should be delighted to have your aid in the inquiry.

I approve your zeal, Socrates, said Protagoras, and the way you develop your arguments ; for I think I am not ill-natured, and I am the last person on earth to be envious. Indeed I have told many people how I regard you—as the man I admire far above any that I meet, and as quite an exception to men of your age ; and I say I should not be surprised if you won high repute for wisdom. We shall pursue the subject on some other occasion, at your pleasure : for the present, it is time to turn to another affair.

I quite agree, said I, if you think so : for I was long ago due to be where I told you I was going ; I stayed merely to oblige our excellent Callias.

Here our colloquy ended, and each went his way.

[1] *Cf.* 321 o.

MENO

INTRODUCTION TO THE *MENO*

THE *Meno* takes up the question which the *Protagoras* left waiting for an answer—Can virtue be taught? This dialogue proceeds in the direct dramatic form, without descriptive introduction or connecting narrative, and in a series of five scenes we are shown the various resources of Socratic method in a determined attempt to solve that important problem. Thus (1) (70 A–80 D) we find that the first requisite for progress in the search is a definition of virtue; (2) (80 D–86 C) the inquiry is shifted to the origin of knowledge, which is demonstrated, by an experiment on one of Meno's young attendants, to be latent in us, and recoverable by the proper stimulation of our memory; (3) (86 C–90 B) we return to the question of what virtue is, and while it appears to be teachable we are faced with the awkward fact that it has no real teachers—it is not taught; (4) (90 B–95 A) Anytus, the typical man of affairs, is convicted of error in his reliance on convention and common sense; and lastly (5) (95 A–100 B) Socrates discusses with Meno the relation of knowledge, in which virtue must somehow consist, to the true opinion which guides practical men along the right path in everyday life.

The first two of these scenes are preparatory: they point out that by some means or other we must obtain a definition of the thing itself—virtue—on which our inquiry is bent, and then we are given a specimen of the method by which we are most likely to acquire such a piece of real knowledge. With these two lessons in mind, we return to the question as it stood at the end of the *Protagoras*, and come to grips once more with that great defaulter—the received system of education. The only hope of finding our way to the truth for which we are groping seems to lie in a study of the instinctive opinion which occasionally guides men of superior character to the right course of action, and in a comparison of this " inspired " thought—which has helped us already (81) towards the educational principle of " recollection " — with the reasoned knowledge which we may look to as an abiding and unfailing support to ourselves and as a power that we can transmit to others.

The sane and profound wisdom which moves beneath the whole discussion is as remarkable as the clearness and acuteness of its argumentation. The detection of insufficiency in existing modes of instruction, and the recognition of rightness in certain high examples of conduct, are marked by a gentle humour and a breadth of vision and sympathy which doubtless distinguished the actual Socrates : the purpose to which those points are applied—of turning our gaze to a higher level of education and a surer basis of all thought and action—is derived indeed from the Master, but brought into full flower, with promise of later fruit, by the personal ardour and art of Plato. We feel the splendid determination of a new master-mind ; and although his attempt at a deeper probing of the question has to be given up for the present without an answer, we are subtly prepared for the ambitious elaboration and demonstration of the *Republic* and the *Phaedo*.

Besides this main impression, the *Meno* has many subsidiary interests. The sophists Protagoras and Gorgias are referred to with respect, though their teaching is proved to be seriously defective. We find here (81) perhaps the first, because so tentative and diffident, statement in Plato of the soul's experience of previous existence, and its present possession of a sort of latent or suppressed knowledge of general notions, which has to be elicited and revived by methodical inquiry. We have also (79) an account of the effect of Socrates' conversations upon his disciples, which is a useful counterpart and complement to the excited rhapsody of Alcibiades in the *Symposium* (215) ; while the humorous, mystifying modesty of Socrates in ascribing his highest beliefs to converse with poets, priests, and priestesses (81) is of a piece with his manner in the *Symposium* and elsewhere. Finally we should notice the suddenness of Anytus' appearance on the scene, and his abrupt exit : remembering that he was afterwards the accuser of Socrates, and observing the language and tone of his warning to that reckless critic of the democracy, we must conclude that Plato contrived the episode with the deliberate purpose of showing that he did not blame any single person for his beloved Master's death, but cherished a nobler grudge against a world that was politically and intellectually out of joint. He thus brings us almost unawares to the edge of the rift which was opening in his mind between philosophy and the ordinary life of affairs : we see it gaping

INTRODUCTION TO THE *MENO*

wide and grim in the *Gorgias* ; when we come to the *Republic*, it is a well-known gulf, to be carefully measured and mapped.

Meno was a young Thessalian of noble and wealthy family. He is supposed here to be on a visit to Athens about 402 B.C., three years before the death of Socrates. He has acquired some literary and scientific knowledge by association with Gorgias, who spent his last few years in Thessaly. He took part as a general in the great march of the Ten Thousand with Cyrus in 401 B.C. Xenophon depicts him in the *Anabasis* as greedy, self-seeking and treacherous. Plato shows us his pleasanter side, though we find here that he is rather conceited and lacking in self-control (76 A, 80 B, C, 86 D).

The *Meno* has been edited, with ample introduction and notes, by E. S. Thompson (Macmillan, 1901).

ΜΕΝΩΝ

[Η ΠΕΡΙ ΑΡΕΤΗΣ · ΠΕΙΡΑΣΤΙΚΟΣ]

ΤΑ ΤΟΥ ΔΙΑΛΟΓΟΥ ΠΡΟΣΩΠΑ

ΜΕΝΩΝ, ΣΩΚΡΑΤΗΣ, ΠΑΙΣ ΜΕΝΩΝΟΣ, ΑΝΥΤΟΣ

ΜΕΝ. Ἔχεις μοι εἰπεῖν, ὦ Σώκρατες, ἆρα διδακτὸν ἡ ἀρετή; ἢ οὐ διδακτὸν ἀλλ' ἀσκητόν; ἢ οὔτε ἀσκητὸν οὔτε μαθητόν, ἀλλὰ φύσει παραγίγνεται τοῖς ἀνθρώποις ἢ ἄλλῳ τινὶ τρόπῳ;

ΣΩ. Ὦ Μένων, πρὸ τοῦ μὲν Θετταλοὶ εὐδόκιμοι ἦσαν ἐν τοῖς Ἕλλησι καὶ ἐθαυμάζοντο ἐφ' ἱππικῇ
B τε καὶ πλούτῳ, νῦν δέ, ὡς ἐμοὶ δοκεῖ, καὶ ἐπὶ σοφίᾳ, καὶ οὐχ ἥκιστα οἱ τοῦ σοῦ ἑταίρου Ἀριστίππου πολῖται Λαρισαῖοι. τούτου δὲ ὑμῖν αἴτιός ἐστι Γοργίας· ἀφικόμενος γὰρ εἰς τὴν πόλιν ἐραστὰς ἐπὶ σοφίᾳ εἴληφεν Ἀλευαδῶν τε τοὺς πρώτους, ὧν ὁ σὸς ἐραστής ἐστιν Ἀρίστιππος, καὶ τῶν ἄλλων Θετταλῶν· καὶ δὴ καὶ τοῦτο τὸ ἔθος ὑμᾶς εἴθικεν, ἀφόβως τε καὶ μεγαλοπρεπῶς ἀποκρίνεσθαι, ἐάν τίς τι ἔρηται, ὥσπερ
C εἰκὸς τοὺς εἰδότας, ἅτε καὶ αὐτὸς παρέχων αὑτὸν ἐρωτᾶν τῶν Ἑλλήνων τῷ βουλομένῳ ὅ τι ἄν τις βούληται, καὶ οὐδενὶ ὅτῳ οὐκ ἀποκρινόμενος. ἐν-

264

MENO

[OR ON VIRTUE: TESTING]

CHARACTERS

MENO, SOCRATES, MENO'S BOY, ANYTUS

MEN. Can you tell me, Socrates, whether virtue can be taught, or is acquired by practice, not teaching? Or if neither by practice nor by learning, whether it comes to mankind by nature or in some other way?

SOC. Meno, of old the Thessalians were famous and admired among the Greeks for their riding and their riches; but now they have a name, I believe, for wisdom also, especially your friend Aristippus's people, the Larisaeans. For this you have to thank Gorgias; for when he came to that city he made the leading men of the Aleuadae—among them your lover Aristippus—and the Thessalians generally enamoured of wisdom. Nay more, he has given you the regular habit of answering any chance question in a fearless, magnificent manner, as befits those who know: for he sets the example of offering himself to be questioned by any Greek who chooses, and on any point one likes, and he has an answer for everybody. Now in this place, my dear Meno,

θάδε δέ, ὦ φίλε Μένων, τὸ ἐναντίον περιέστηκεν·
71 ὥσπερ αὐχμός τις τῆς σοφίας γέγονεν, καὶ κινδυνεύει ἐκ τῶνδε τῶν τόπων παρ᾽ ὑμᾶς οἴχεσθαι
ἡ σοφία· εἰ γοῦν τινὰ ἐθέλεις οὕτως ἐρέσθαι τῶν
ἐνθάδε, οὐδεὶς ὅστις οὐ γελάσεται καὶ ἐρεῖ· ὦ
ξένε, κινδυνεύω σοι δοκεῖν μακάριός τις εἶναι,
ἀρετὴν γοῦν εἴτε διδακτὸν εἴθ᾽ ὅτῳ τρόπῳ παραγίγνεται εἰδέναι· ἐγὼ δὲ τοσοῦτον δέω εἴτε
διδακτὸν εἴτε μὴ διδακτὸν εἰδέναι, ὥστ᾽ οὐδὲ αὐτό,
ὅ τι ποτ᾽ ἐστὶ τὸ παράπαν ἀρετή, τυγχάνω εἰδώς.
B   Ἐγὼ οὖν καὶ αὐτός, ὦ Μένων, οὕτως ἔχω· συμ-
πένομαι τοῖς πολίταις τούτου τοῦ πράγματος, καὶ
ἐμαυτὸν καταμέμφομαι ὡς οὐκ εἰδὼς περὶ ἀρετῆς
τὸ παράπαν· ὃ δὲ μὴ οἶδα τί ἐστι, πῶς ἂν ὁποῖόν
γέ τι εἰδείην; ἢ δοκεῖ σοι οἷόν τε εἶναι, ὅστις
Μένωνα μὴ γιγνώσκει τὸ παράπαν ὅστις ἐστί,
τοῦτον εἰδέναι εἴτε καλὸς εἴτε πλούσιος εἴτε καὶ
γενναῖός ἐστιν, εἴτε καὶ τἀναντία τούτων; δοκεῖ
σοι οἷόν τ᾽ εἶναι;
    ΜΕΝ. Οὐκ ἔμοιγε. ἀλλὰ σύ, ὦ Σώκρατες,
C ἀληθῶς οὐδ᾽ ὅ τι ἀρετή ἐστιν οἶσθα, ἀλλὰ ταῦτα
περὶ σοῦ καὶ οἴκαδε ἀπαγγέλλωμεν;
    ΣΩ. Μὴ μόνον γε, ὦ ἑταῖρε, ἀλλὰ καὶ ὅτι οὐδ᾽
ἄλλῳ πω ἐνέτυχον εἰδότι, ὡς ἐμοὶ δοκῶ.
    ΜΕΝ. Τί δέ; Γοργίᾳ οὐκ ἐνέτυχες ὅτε ἐνθάδε
ἦν;
    ΣΩ. Ἔγωγε.
    ΜΕΝ. Εἶτα οὐκ ἐδόκει σοι εἰδέναι;
    ΣΩ. Οὐ πάνυ εἰμὶ μνήμων, ὦ Μένων, ὥστε
οὐκ ἔχω εἰπεῖν ἐν τῷ παρόντι, πῶς μοι τότε
ἔδοξεν. ἀλλ᾽ ἴσως ἐκεῖνός τε οἶδε, καὶ σὺ ἃ
D ἐκεῖνος ἔλεγεν· ἀνάμνησον οὖν με, πῶς ἔλεγεν.

we have a contrary state of things : a drought of wisdom, as it were, has come on ; and it seems as though wisdom had deserted our borders in favour of yours. You have only to ask one of our people a question such as that, and he will be sure to laugh and say : Stranger, you must think me a specially favoured mortal, to be able to tell whether virtue can be taught, or in what way it comes to one : so far am I from knowing whether it can be taught or not, that I actually do not even know what the thing itself, virtue, is at all.

And I myself, Meno, am in the same case ; I share my townsmen's poverty in this matter : I have to reproach myself with an utter ignorance about virtue ; and if I do not know what a thing is, how can I know what its nature may be ? Or do you imagine it possible, if one has no cognisance at all of Meno, that one could know whether he is handsome or rich or noble, or the reverse of these ? Do you suppose that one could ?

MEN. Not I. But is it true, Socrates, that you do not even know what virtue is ? Are we to return home with this report of you ?

SOC. Not only this, my friend, but also that I never yet came across anybody who did know, in my opinion.

MEN. What ? You did not meet Gorgias when he was here ?

SOC. I did.

MEN. And you didn't consider that he knew ?

SOC. I have not a very good memory, Meno, so I cannot tell at the moment how he struck me then. It may be that he did know, and that you know what he said : remind me therefore how he expressed

εἰ δὲ βούλει, αὐτὸς εἰπέ· δοκεῖ γὰρ δήπου σοὶ
ἅπερ ἐκείνῳ.

ΜΕΝ. Ἔμοιγε.

ΣΩ. Ἐκεῖνον μὲν τοίνυν ἐῶμεν, ἐπειδὴ καὶ
ἄπεστιν· σὺ δὲ αὐτός, ὦ πρὸς θεῶν, Μένων, τί
φὴς ἀρετὴν εἶναι; εἶπον καὶ μὴ φθονήσῃς, ἵνα
εὐτυχέστατον ψεῦσμα ἐψευσμένος ὦ, ἂν φανῇς
σὺ μὲν εἰδὼς καὶ Γοργίας, ἐγὼ δὲ εἰρηκὼς μηδενὶ
πώποτε εἰδότι ἐντετυχηκέναι.

E   ΜΕΝ. Ἀλλ' οὐ χαλεπόν, ὦ Σώκρατες, εἰπεῖν.
πρῶτον μέν, εἰ βούλει ἀνδρὸς ἀρετήν, ῥᾴδιον, ὅτι
αὕτη ἐστὶν ἀνδρὸς ἀρετή, ἱκανὸν εἶναι τὰ τῆς
πόλεως πράττειν, καὶ πράττοντα τοὺς μὲν φίλους
εὖ ποιεῖν, τοὺς δ' ἐχθροὺς κακῶς, καὶ αὐτὸν
εὐλαβεῖσθαι μηδὲν τοιοῦτον παθεῖν. εἰ δὲ βούλει
γυναικὸς ἀρετήν, οὐ χαλεπὸν διελθεῖν, ὅτι δεῖ
αὐτὴν τὴν οἰκίαν εὖ οἰκεῖν, σῴζουσάν τε τὰ ἔνδον
καὶ κατήκοον οὖσαν τοῦ ἀνδρός. καὶ ἄλλη ἐστὶ
παιδὸς ἀρετή, καὶ θηλείας καὶ ἄρρενος, καὶ πρεσβυτέρου ἀνδρός, εἰ μὲν βούλει, ἐλευθέρου, εἰ δὲ
72 βούλει, δούλου. καὶ ἄλλαι πάμπολλαι ἀρεταί
εἰσιν, ὥστε οὐκ ἀπορία εἰπεῖν ἀρετῆς πέρι ὅ τι
ἔστιν· καθ' ἑκάστην γὰρ τῶν πράξεων καὶ τῶν
ἡλικιῶν πρὸς ἕκαστον ἔργον ἑκάστῳ ἡμῶν ἡ ἀρετή
ἐστιν· ὡσαύτως δέ, οἶμαι, ὦ Σώκρατες, καὶ ἡ
κακία.

ΣΩ. Πολλῇ γέ τινι εὐτυχίᾳ ἔοικα κεχρῆσθαι,
ὦ Μένων, εἰ μίαν ζητῶν ἀρετὴν σμῆνός τι ἀν-
ηύρηκα ἀρετῶν παρὰ σοὶ κειμένων. ἀτάρ, ὦ
Μένων, κατὰ ταύτην τὴν εἰκόνα τὴν περὶ τὰ
B   σμήνη, εἴ μου ἐρομένου μελίττης περὶ οὐσίας

it ; or if you like, make your own statement, for I expect you share his views.

MEN. I do.

SOC. Then let us pass him over, since in fact he is not present, and do you tell me, in heaven's name, what is your own account of virtue. Speak out frankly, that I may find myself the victim of a most fortunate falsehood, if you and Gorgias prove to have knowledge of it, while I have said that I never yet came across anyone who had.

MEN. Why, there is no difficulty, Socrates, in telling. First of all, if you take the virtue of a man, it is easily stated that a man's virtue is this—that he be competent to manage the affairs of his city, and to manage them so as to benefit his friends and harm his enemies, and to take care to avoid suffering harm himself. Or take a woman's virtue : there is no difficulty in describing it as the duty of ordering the house well, looking after the property indoors, and obeying her husband. And the child has another virtue—one for the female, and one for the male ; and there is another for elderly men—one, if you like, for freemen, and yet another for slaves. And there are very many other virtues besides, so that one cannot be at a loss to explain what virtue is ; for it is according to each activity and age that every one of us, in whatever we do, has his virtue ; and the same, I take it, Socrates, will hold also of vice.

SOC. I seem to be in a most lucky way, Meno ; for in seeking one virtue I have discovered a whole swarm of virtues there in your keeping. Now, Meno, to follow this figure of a swarm, suppose I should ask you what is the real nature of the bee,

ὅ τί ποτ᾿ ἔστι, πολλὰς καὶ παντοδαπὰς ἔλεγες
αὐτὰς εἶναι, τί ἂν ἀπεκρίνω μοι, εἴ σε ἠρόμην·
ἆρα τούτῳ φῂς πολλὰς καὶ παντοδαπὰς εἶναι
καὶ διαφερούσας ἀλλήλων, τῷ μελίττας εἶναι;
ἢ τούτῳ μὲν οὐδὲν διαφέρουσιν, ἄλλῳ δέ τῳ,
οἷον ἢ κάλλει ἢ μεγέθει ἢ ἄλλῳ τῳ τῶν τοιούτων·
εἰπέ, τί ἂν ἀπεκρίνω οὕτως ἐρωτηθείς;

MEN. Τοῦτ᾿ ἔγωγε, ὅτι οὐδὲν διαφέρουσιν,
ᾗ μέλιτται εἰσίν, ἡ ἑτέρα τῆς ἑτέρας.

C   ΣΩ. Εἰ οὖν εἶπον μετὰ ταῦτα· τοῦτο τοίνυν
μοι αὐτὸ εἰπέ, ὦ Μένων· ᾧ οὐδὲν διαφέρουσιν
ἀλλὰ ταὐτόν εἰσιν ἅπασαι, τί τοῦτο φῂς εἶναι;
εἶχες δήπου ἄν τί μοι εἰπεῖν;

MEN. Ἔγωγε.

ΣΩ. Οὕτω δὴ καὶ περὶ τῶν ἀρετῶν· κἂν εἰ
πολλαὶ καὶ παντοδαπαί εἰσιν, ἕν γέ τι εἶδος ταὐτὸν
ἅπασαι ἔχουσι, δι᾿ ὃ εἰσὶν ἀρεταί, εἰς ὃ καλῶς
που ἔχει ἀποβλέψαντα τὸν ἀποκρινόμενον τῷ
ἐρωτήσαντι ἐκεῖνο δηλῶσαι, ὃ τυγχάνει οὖσα
D ἀρετή· ἢ οὐ μανθάνεις ὅ τι λέγω;

MEN. Δοκῶ γέ μοι μανθάνειν· οὐ μέντοι ὡς
βούλομαί γέ πω κατέχω τὸ ἐρωτώμενον.

ΣΩ. Πότερον δὲ περὶ ἀρετῆς μόνον σοι οὕτω
δοκεῖ, ὦ Μένων, ἄλλη μὲν ἀνδρὸς εἶναι, ἄλλη δὲ
γυναικὸς καὶ τῶν ἄλλων, ἢ καὶ περὶ ὑγιείας καὶ
περὶ μεγέθους καὶ περὶ ἰσχύος ὡσαύτως; ἄλλη
μὲν ἀνδρὸς δοκεῖ σοι εἶναι ὑγίεια, ἄλλη δὲ γυναικός; ἢ ταὐτὸν πανταχοῦ εἶδός ἐστιν, ἐάνπερ
E ὑγίεια ᾖ, ἐάντε ἐν ἀνδρὶ ἐάντε ἐν ἄλλῳ ὁτῳοῦν ᾖ;

and you replied that there are many different kinds of bees, and I rejoined : Do you say it is by being bees that they are of many and various kinds and differ from each other, or does their difference lie not in that, but in something else—for example, in their beauty or size or some other quality ? Tell me, what would be your answer to this question ?

MEN. Why, this—that they do not differ, as bees, the one from the other.

soc. And if I went on to say : Well now, there is this that I want you to tell me, Meno : what do you call the quality by which they do not differ, but are all alike ? You could find me an answer, I presume ?

MEN. I could.

soc. And likewise also with the virtues, however many and various they may be, they all have one common character whereby they are virtues, and on which one would of course be wise to keep an eye when one is giving a definitive answer to the question of what virtue really is. You take my meaning, do you not ?

MEN. My impression is that I do; but still I do not yet grasp the meaning of the question as I could wish.

soc. Is it only in the case of virtue, do you think, Meno, that one can say there is one kind belonging to a man, another to a woman, and so on with the rest, or is it just the same, too, in the case of health and size and strength ? Do you consider that there is one health for a man, and another for a woman ? Or, wherever we find health, is it of the same character universally, in a man or in anyone else ?

ΜΕΝ. Ἡ αὐτή μοι δοκεῖ ὑγίειά γε εἶναι καὶ
ἀνδρὸς καὶ γυναικός.

ΣΩ. Οὐκοῦν καὶ μέγεθος καὶ ἰσχύς; ἐάνπερ
ἰσχυρὰ γυνὴ ᾖ, τῷ αὐτῷ εἴδει καὶ τῇ αὐτῇ ἰσχύι
ἰσχυρὰ ἔσται; τὸ γὰρ τῇ αὐτῇ τοῦτο λέγω· οὐδὲν
διαφέρει πρὸς τὸ ἰσχὺς εἶναι ἡ ἰσχύς, ἐάντε ἐν
ἀνδρὶ ᾖ ἐάντε ἐν γυναικί· ἢ δοκεῖ τί σοι διαφέρειν;

ΜΕΝ. Οὐκ ἔμοιγε.

73 ΣΩ. Ἡ δὲ ἀρετὴ πρὸς τὸ ἀρετὴ εἶναι διοίσει τι,
ἐάντε ἐν παιδὶ ᾖ ἐάντε ἐν πρεσβύτῃ, ἐάντε ἐν
γυναικὶ ἐάντε ἐν ἀνδρί;

ΜΕΝ. Ἔμοιγέ πως δοκεῖ, ὦ Σώκρατες, τοῦτο
οὐκέτι ὅμοιον εἶναι τοῖς ἄλλοις τούτοις.

ΣΩ. Τί δέ; οὐκ ἀνδρὸς μὲν ἀρετὴν ἔλεγες
πόλιν εὖ διοικεῖν, γυναικὸς δὲ οἰκίαν;

ΜΕΝ. Ἔγωγε.

ΣΩ. Ἆρ᾿ οὖν οἷόν τε εὖ διοικεῖν ἢ πόλιν ἢ
οἰκίαν ἢ ἄλλο ὁτιοῦν, μὴ σωφρόνως καὶ δικαίως
διοικοῦντα;

Β ΜΕΝ. Οὐ δῆτα.

ΣΩ. Οὐκοῦν ἄνπερ δικαίως καὶ σωφρόνως
διοικῶσι, δικαιοσύνῃ καὶ σωφροσύνῃ διοικήσουσιν;

ΜΕΝ. Ἀνάγκη.

ΣΩ. Τῶν αὐτῶν ἄρα ἀμφότεροι δέονται, εἴπερ
μέλλουσιν ἀγαθοὶ εἶναι, καὶ ἡ γυνὴ καὶ ὁ ἀνήρ,
δικαιοσύνης καὶ σωφροσύνης.

ΜΕΝ. Φαίνονται.

ΣΩ. Τί δὲ παῖς καὶ πρεσβύτης; μῶν ἀκό-
λαστοι ὄντες καὶ ἄδικοι ἀγαθοὶ ἄν ποτε γένοιντο;

ΜΕΝ. Οὐ δῆτα.

ΣΩ. Ἀλλὰ σώφρονες καὶ δίκαιοι;

MENO

MEN. I think that health is the same, both in man and in woman.

SOC. Then is it not so with size and strength also ? If a woman is strong, she will be strong by reason of the same form and the same strength ; by " the same " I mean that strength does not differ as strength, whether it be in a man or in a woman. Or do you think there is any difference ?

MEN. I do not.

SOC. And will virtue, as virtue, differ at all whether it be in a child or in an elderly person, in a woman or in a man ?

MEN. I feel somehow, Socrates, that here we cease to be on the same ground as in those other cases.

SOC. Why ? Were you not saying that a man's virtue is to manage a state well, and a woman's a house ?

MEN. I was.

SOC. And is it possible to manage a state well, or a house, or anything at all, if you do not manage it temperately and justly ?

MEN. Surely not.

SOC. Then whoever manages temperately and justly will manage with temperance and justice ?

MEN. That must be.

SOC. Then both the woman and the man require the same qualities of justice and temperance, if they are to be good.

MEN. Evidently.

SOC. And what of a child or an old man ? Can they ever hope to be good if they are intemperate and unjust ?

MEN. Surely not.

SOC. Only if they are temperate and just ?

ΜΕΝ. Ναί.

Σω. Πάντες ἄρ' ἄνθρωποι τῷ αὐτῷ τρόπῳ ἀγαθοί εἰσι· τῶν αὐτῶν γὰρ τυχόντες ἀγαθοὶ γίγνονται.

ΜΕΝ. Ἔοικεν.

Σω. Οὐκ ἂν δήπου, εἴ γε μὴ ἡ αὐτὴ ἀρετὴ ἦν αὐτῶν, τῷ αὐτῷ ἂν τρόπῳ ἀγαθοὶ ἦσαν.

ΜΕΝ. Οὐ δῆτα.

Σω. Ἐπειδὴ τοίνυν ἡ αὐτὴ ἀρετὴ πάντων ἐστί, πειρῶ εἰπεῖν καὶ ἀναμνησθῆναι, τί αὐτό φησι Γοργίας εἶναι καὶ σὺ μετ' ἐκείνου.

ΜΕΝ. Τί ἄλλο γ' ἢ ἄρχειν οἷόν τ' εἶναι τῶν ἀνθρώπων; εἴπερ ἕν γέ τι ζητεῖς κατὰ πάντων.

Σω. Ἀλλὰ μὴν ζητῶ γε. ἀλλ' ἆρα καὶ παιδὸς ἡ αὐτὴ ἀρετή, ὦ Μένων, καὶ δούλου, ἄρχειν οἵῳ τε εἶναι τοῦ δεσπότου, καὶ δοκεῖ σοι ἔτι ἂν δοῦλος εἶναι ὁ ἄρχων;

ΜΕΝ. Οὐ πάνυ μοι δοκεῖ, ὦ Σώκρατες.

Σω. Οὐ γὰρ εἰκός, ὦ ἄριστε. ἔτι γὰρ καὶ τόδε σκόπει· ἄρχειν φῂς οἷόν τ' εἶναι· οὐ προσθήσομεν αὐτόσε τὸ δικαίως, ἀδίκως δὲ μή;

ΜΕΝ. Οἶμαι ἔγωγε· ἡ γὰρ δικαιοσύνη, ὦ Σώκρατες, ἀρετή ἐστιν.

Σω. Πότερον ἀρετή, ὦ Μένων, ἢ ἀρετή τις;

ΜΕΝ. Πῶς τοῦτο λέγεις;

Σω. Ὡς περὶ ἄλλου ὁτουοῦν. οἷον, εἰ βούλει, στρογγυλότητος πέρι εἴποιμ' ἂν ἔγωγε, ὅτι σχῆμά τί ἐστιν, οὐχ οὕτως ἁπλῶς ὅτι σχῆμα. διὰ ταῦτα δὲ οὕτως ἂν εἴποιμι, ὅτι καὶ ἄλλα ἔστι σχήματα.

ΜΕΝ. Ὀρθῶς γε λέγων σύ, ἐπεὶ καὶ ἐγὼ λέγω οὐ μόνον δικαιοσύνην ἀλλὰ καὶ ἄλλας εἶναι ἀρετάς.

MEN. Yes.

soc. So all mankind are good in the same way; for they become good when they acquire the same qualities.

MEN. So it seems.

soc. And I presume, if they had not the same virtue, they would not be good in the same way.

MEN. No, indeed.

soc. Seeing then that it is the same virtue in all cases, try and tell me, if you can recollect, what Gorgias—and you in agreement with him—say it is.

MEN. Simply that it is the power of governing mankind—if you want some single description to cover all cases.

soc. That is just what I am after. But is virtue the same in a child, Meno, and in a slave—an ability to govern each his master? And do you think he who governed would still be a slave?

MEN. I should say certainly not, Socrates.

soc. No, indeed, it would be unlikely, my excellent friend. And again, consider this further point: you say it is "to be able to govern"; shall we not add to that—"justly, not unjustly"?

MEN. Yes, I think so; for justice, Socrates, is virtue.

soc. Virtue, Meno, or a virtue?

MEN. What do you mean by that?

soc. What I would in any other case. To take roundness, for instance; I should call it a figure, and not figure pure and simple. And I should name it so because there are other figures as well.

MEN. You would be quite right—just as I say there are other virtues besides justice.

74 ΣΩ. Τίνας ταύτας; εἰπέ· οἷον καὶ ἐγώ σοι εἴποιμι ἂν καὶ ἄλλα σχήματα, εἴ με κελεύοις· καὶ σὺ οὖν ἐμοὶ εἰπὲ ἄλλας ἀρετάς.

ΜΕΝ. Ἡ ἀνδρεία τοίνυν ἔμοιγε δοκεῖ ἀρετὴ εἶναι καὶ σωφροσύνη καὶ σοφία καὶ μεγαλοπρέπεια καὶ ἄλλαι πάμπολλαι.

ΣΩ. Πάλιν, ὦ Μένων, ταὐτὸν πεπόνθαμεν· πολλὰς αὖ ηὑρήκαμεν ἀρετὰς μίαν ζητοῦντες, ἄλλον τρόπον ἢ νυνδή· τὴν δὲ μίαν, ἣ διὰ πάντων τούτων ἐστίν, οὐ δυνάμεθα ἀνευρεῖν.

B ΜΕΝ. Οὐ γὰρ δύναμαί πω, ὦ Σώκρατες, ὡς σὺ ζητεῖς, μίαν ἀρετὴν λαβεῖν κατὰ πάντων, ὥσπερ ἐν τοῖς ἄλλοις.

ΣΩ. Εἰκότως γε· ἀλλ᾽ ἐγὼ προθυμήσομαι, ἐὰν οἷός τ᾽ ὦ, ἡμᾶς προβιβάσαι. μανθάνεις γάρ που, ὅτι οὑτωσὶ ἔχει περὶ παντός· εἴ τίς σε ἀνέροιτο τοῦτο, ὃ νυνδὴ ἐγὼ ἔλεγον, τί ἐστι σχῆμα, ὦ Μένων; εἰ αὐτῷ εἶπες ὅτι στρογγυλότης, εἴ σοι εἶπεν ἅπερ ἐγώ, πότερον σχῆμα ἡ στρογγυλότης ἐστὶν ἢ σχῆμά τι; εἶπες δήπου ἂν ὅτι σχῆμά τι.

ΜΕΝ. Πάνυ γε.

C ΣΩ. Οὐκοῦν διὰ ταῦτα, ὅτι καὶ ἄλλα ἔστι σχήματα;

ΜΕΝ. Ναί.

ΣΩ. Καὶ εἴ γε προσανηρώτα σε ὁποῖα, ἔλεγες ἄν;

ΜΕΝ. Ἔγωγε.

ΣΩ. Καὶ αὖ εἰ περὶ χρώματος ὡσαύτως ἀνήρετο ὅ τι ἔστι, καὶ εἰπόντος σου, ὅτι τὸ λευκόν, μετὰ ταῦτα ὑπέλαβεν ὁ ἐρωτῶν, πότερον τὸ λευκὸν χρῶμά ἐστιν ἢ χρῶμά τι; εἶπες ἂν ὅτι χρῶμά τι, διότι καὶ ἄλλα τυγχάνει ὄντα;

soc. What are they ? Tell me. In the same way as I can tell you of other figures, if you request me, so do you tell me of other virtues.

men. Well then, courage, I consider, is a virtue, and temperance, and wisdom, and loftiness of mind ; and there are a great many others.

soc. Once more, Meno, we are in the same plight : again we have found a number of virtues when we were looking for one, though not in the same way as we did just now ; but the one that runs through them all, this we are not able to find.

men. No, for I am not yet able, Socrates, to follow your line of search, and find a single virtue common to all, as one can in other cases.

soc. And no wonder ; but I will make an effort, so far as I can, to help us onward. You understand, of course, that this principle of mine applies to everything : if someone asked you the question I put to you just now: What is figure, Meno ? and you replied : Roundness ; and then he said, as I did : Is roundness figure or a figure ? I suppose you would answer: A figure.

men. Certainly.

soc. And for this reason—that there are other figures as well ?

men. Yes.

soc. And if he went on to ask you of what sort they were, you would tell him ?

men. I would.

soc. And if he asked likewise what colour is, and on your answering " white " your questioner then rejoined: Is " white " colour or a colour ? your reply would be : A colour ; because there are other colours besides.

ΜΕΝ. Ἔγωγε.

ΣΩ. Καὶ εἴ γέ σε ἐκέλευε λέγειν ἄλλα χρώματα,
D ἔλεγες ἂν ἄλλα, ἃ οὐδὲν ἧττον τυγχάνει ὄντα χρώματα τοῦ λευκοῦ;

ΜΕΝ. Ναί.

ΣΩ. Εἰ οὖν ὥσπερ ἐγὼ μετῄει τὸν λόγον,
καὶ ἔλεγεν ὅτι ἀεὶ εἰς πολλὰ ἀφικνούμεθα, ἀλλὰ
μή μοι οὕτως, ἀλλ᾽ ἐπειδὴ τὰ πολλὰ ταῦτα ἑνί
τινι προσαγορεύεις ὀνόματι, καὶ φῂς οὐδὲν αὐτῶν
ὅ τι οὐ σχῆμα εἶναι, καὶ ταῦτα καὶ ἐναντία ὄντα
ἀλλήλοις, ὅ τι ἔστι τοῦτο, ὃ οὐδὲν ἧττον κατέχει
τὸ στρογγύλον ἢ τὸ εὐθύ, ὃ δὴ ὀνομάζεις σχῆμα
E καὶ οὐδὲν μᾶλλον φῂς τὸ στρογγύλον σχῆμα εἶναι
ἢ τὸ εὐθύ; ἢ οὐχ οὕτω λέγεις;

ΜΕΝ. Ἔγωγε.

ΣΩ. Ἆρ᾽ οὖν, ὅταν οὕτω λέγῃς, τότε οὐδὲν
μᾶλλον φῂς τὸ στρογγύλον εἶναι στρογγύλον ἢ
εὐθύ, οὐδὲ τὸ εὐθὺ εὐθὺ ἢ στρογγύλον;

ΜΕΝ. Οὐ δήπου, ὦ Σώκρατες.

ΣΩ. Ἀλλὰ μὴν σχῆμά γε οὐδὲν μᾶλλον φῂς
εἶναι τὸ στρογγύλον τοῦ εὐθέος, οὐδὲ τὸ ἕτερον
τοῦ ἑτέρου.

ΜΕΝ. Ἀληθῆ λέγεις.

ΣΩ. Τί ποτε οὖν τοῦτο, οὗ τοῦτο ὄνομά ἐστι,
τὸ σχῆμα; πειρῶ λέγειν. εἰ οὖν τῷ ἐρωτῶντι
75 οὕτως ἢ περὶ σχήματος ἢ χρώματος εἶπες ὅτι
ἀλλ᾽ οὐδὲ μανθάνω ἔγωγε ὅ τι βούλει, ὦ ἄνθρωπε,
οὐδὲ οἶδα ὅ τι λέγεις· ἴσως ἂν ἐθαύμασε καὶ
εἶπεν· οὐ μανθάνεις, ὅτι ζητῶ τὸ ἐπὶ πᾶσι τούτοις
ταὐτόν; ἢ οὐδὲ ἐπὶ τούτοις, ὦ Μένων, ἔχοις ἂν

MEN. It would.

SOC. And if he bade you mention other colours, you would tell him of others that are colours just as much as white?

MEN. Yes.

SOC. Now suppose that, like me, he pursued the argument and said: We are always arriving at a variety of things, but let me have no more of that: since you call these many things by one single name, and say they are figures, every one of them, even when they are opposed to one another, tell me what is that which comprises round and straight alike, and which you call figure—including straight equally with round under that term. For that is your statement, is it not?

MEN. It is.

SOC. And in making it, do you mean to say that round is no more round than straight, or straight no more straight than round?

MEN. No, to be sure, Socrates.

SOC. What you mean is that the round shape is no more a figure than the straight, or the straight than the round.

MEN. Quite right.

SOC. Then what can this thing be, which bears the name of figure? Try and tell me. Suppose that, on being asked this question by someone, either about figure or about colour, you had replied: Why, I don't so much as understand what you want, sir, or even know what you are saying: he might well have shown surprise, and said: Do you not understand that I am looking for that which is the same common element in all these things? Or would you still be unable to reply, Meno, if you were

εἰπεῖν, εἴ τις ἐρωτῴη· τί ἐστιν ἐπὶ τῷ στρογ-
γύλῳ καὶ εὐθεῖ καὶ ἐπὶ τοῖς ἄλλοις, ἃ δὴ σχήματα
καλεῖς, ταὐτὸν ἐπὶ πᾶσι; πειρῶ εἰπεῖν, ἵνα καὶ
γένηταί σοι μελέτη πρὸς τὴν περὶ τῆς ἀρετῆς
ἀπόκρισιν.

B ΜΕΝ. Μή, ἀλλὰ σύ, ὦ Σώκρατες, εἰπέ.

ΣΩ. Βούλει σοι χαρίσωμαι;

ΜΕΝ. Πάνυ γε.

ΣΩ. Ἐθελήσεις οὖν καὶ σὺ ἐμοὶ εἰπεῖν περὶ
τῆς ἀρετῆς;

ΜΕΝ. Ἔγωγε.

ΣΩ. Προθυμητέον τοίνυν· ἄξιον γάρ.

ΜΕΝ. Πάνυ μὲν οὖν.

ΣΩ. Φέρε δή, πειρώμεθά σοι εἰπεῖν, τί ἐστι
σχῆμα. σκόπει οὖν εἰ τόδε ἀποδέχῃ αὐτὸ εἶναι·
ἔστω γὰρ δὴ ἡμῖν τοῦτο σχῆμα, ὃ μόνον τῶν
ὄντων τυγχάνει χρώματι ἀεὶ ἑπόμενον. ἱκανῶς
σοι, ἢ ἄλλως πως ζητεῖς; ἐγὼ γὰρ κἂν οὕτως
ἀγαπῴην εἴ μοι ἀρετὴν εἴποις.

C ΜΕΝ. Ἀλλὰ τοῦτό γε εὔηθες, ὦ Σώκρατες.

ΣΩ. Πῶς λέγεις;

ΜΕΝ. Ὅτι σχῆμά πού ἐστι κατὰ τὸν σὸν
λόγον, ὃ ἀεὶ χρόᾳ ἕπεται. εἶεν· εἰ δὲ δὴ τὴν
χρόαν τις μὴ φαίη εἰδέναι, ἀλλὰ ὡσαύτως ἀποροῖ
ὥσπερ περὶ τοῦ σχήματος, τί ἂν οἴει σοι ἀπο-
κεκρίσθαι;

ΣΩ. Τἀληθῆ ἔγωγε· καὶ εἰ μέν γε τῶν σοφῶν
τις εἴη καὶ ἐριστικῶν τε καὶ ἀγωνιστικῶν ὁ
D ἐρόμενος, εἴποιμ᾽ ἂν αὐτῷ ὅτι ἐμοὶ μὲν εἴρηται·
εἰ δὲ μὴ ὀρθῶς λέγω, σὸν ἔργον λαμβάνειν λόγον
καὶ ἐλέγχειν. εἰ δὲ ὥσπερ ἐγώ τε καὶ σὺ νυνὶ
φίλοι ὄντες βούλοιντο ἀλλήλοις διαλέγεσθαι, δεῖ

approached on other terms, and were asked: What
is it that is common to the round and the straight
and everything else that you call figures—the same
in all? Try and tell me; it will be good practice
for your answer about virtue.

MEN. No, it is you who must answer, Socrates.

SOC. You wish me to do you the favour?

MEN. By all means.

SOC. And then you will agree to take your turn
and answer me on virtue?

MEN. I will.

SOC. Well then, I must make the effort, for it is
worth our while.

MEN. Certainly.

SOC. Come now, let me try and tell you what
figure is. Just consider if you accept this description
of it: figure, let us say, is the only existing thing that
is found always following colour. Are you satisfied,
or are you looking for something different? I am
sure I should be content with a similar account of
virtue from you.

MEN. But it is such a silly one, Socrates.

SOC. How do you mean?

MEN. Well, figure, as I understand by your account,
is what always follows colour. Very good; but if
some one said he did not know colour, and was in the
same difficulty about it as about figure, what answer
do you suppose would have come from you?

SOC. The truth, from me; and if my questioner
were a professor of the eristic and contentious sort,
I should say to him: I have made my statement;
if it is wrong, your business is to examine and refute
it. But if, like you and me on this occasion, we were
friends and chose to have a discussion together, I

δὴ πραότερόν πως καὶ διαλεκτικώτερον ἀποκρίνεσθαι. ἔστι δὲ ἴσως τὸ διαλεκτικώτερον μὴ
μόνον τἀληθῆ ἀποκρίνεσθαι, ἀλλὰ καὶ δι' ἐκείνων
ὧν ἂν προσομολογῇ εἰδέναι ὁ ἐρωτώμενος. πειράσομαι δὴ καὶ ἐγώ σοι οὕτως εἰπεῖν. λέγε
γάρ μοι· τελευτὴν καλεῖς τι; τοιόνδε λέγω οἷον
Ε πέρας καὶ ἔσχατον· πάντα ταῦτα ταὐτόν τι λέγω·
ἴσως δ' ἂν ἡμῖν Πρόδικος διαφέροιτο· ἀλλὰ σύ
γέ που καλεῖς πεπεράνθαι τι καὶ τετελευτηκέναι·
τὸ τοιοῦτον βούλομαι λέγειν, οὐδὲν ποικίλον.

ΜΕΝ. Ἀλλὰ καλῶ, καὶ οἶμαι μανθάνειν ὃ
λέγεις.

76 ΣΩ. Τί δ'; ἐπίπεδον καλεῖς τι, καὶ ἕτερον
αὖ στερεόν, οἷον ταῦτα τὰ ἐν γεωμετρίαις;

ΜΕΝ. Ἔγωγε καλῶ.

ΣΩ. Ἤδη τοίνυν ἂν μάθοις μου ἐκ τούτων,
σχῆμα ὃ λέγω. κατὰ γὰρ παντὸς σχήματος
τοῦτο λέγω, εἰς ὃ τὸ στερεὸν περαίνει, τοῦτ'
εἶναι σχῆμα· ὅπερ ἂν συλλαβὼν εἴποιμι στερεοῦ
πέρας σχῆμα εἶναι.

ΜΕΝ. Τὸ δὲ χρῶμα τί λέγεις, ὦ Σώκρατες;

ΣΩ. Ὑβριστής γ' εἶ, ὦ Μένων· ἀνδρὶ πρεσβύτῃ
πράγματα προστάττεις ἀποκρίνεσθαι, αὐτὸς δὲ
Β οὐκ ἐθέλεις ἀναμνησθεὶς εἰπεῖν, ὅ τί ποτε λέγει
Γοργίας ἀρετὴν εἶναι.

ΜΕΝ. Ἀλλ' ἐπειδάν μοι σὺ τοῦτ' εἴπῃς, ὦ
Σώκρατες, ἐρῶ σοι.

ΣΩ. Κἂν κατακεκαλυμμένος τις γνοίη, ὦ
Μένων, διαλεγομένου σου, ὅτι καλὸς εἶ καὶ ἐρασταί
σοι ἔτι εἰσίν.

MENO

should have to reply in some milder tone more suited to dialectic. The more dialectical way, I suppose, is not merely to answer what is true, but also to make use of those points which the questioned person acknowledges he knows. And this is the way in which I shall now try to argue with you. Tell me, is there something you call an end ? Such a thing, I mean, as a limit, or extremity—I use all these terms in the same sense, though I daresay Prodicus[1] might quarrel with us. But you, I am sure, refer to a thing as terminated or ended : something of that sort is what I mean—nothing complicated.

MEN. Yes, I do, and I think I grasp your meaning.

SOC. Well then, you speak of a surface, and also of a solid—the terms employed in geometrical problems ?

MEN. I do.

SOC. So now you are able to comprehend from all this what I mean by figure. In every instance of figure I call that figure in which the solid ends ; and I may put that more succinctly by saying that figure is " limit of solid."

MEN. And what do you say of colour, Socrates ?

SOC. How overbearing of you, Meno, to press an old man with demands for answers, when you will not trouble yourself to recollect and tell me what account Gorgias gives of virtue !

MEN. When you have answered my question, Socrates, I will answer yours.

SOC. One might tell even blindfolded, Meno, by the way you discuss, that you are handsome and still have lovers.

---

[1] *Cf. Protag.* 337 A.

ΜΕΝ. Τί δή;

ΣΩ. Ὅτι οὐδὲν ἀλλ’ ἢ ἐπιτάττεις ἐν τοῖς λόγοις· ὅπερ ποιοῦσιν οἱ τρυφῶντες, ἅτε τυραννεύοντες, ἕως ἂν ἐν ὥρᾳ ὦσι. καὶ ἅμα ἐμοῦ C ἴσως κατέγνωκας, ὅτι εἰμὶ ἥττων τῶν καλῶν. χαριοῦμαι οὖν σοι καὶ ἀποκρινοῦμαι.

ΜΕΝ. Πάνυ μὲν οὖν χάρισαι.

ΣΩ. Βούλει οὖν σοι κατὰ Γοργίαν ἀποκρίνωμαι, ᾗ ἂν σὺ μάλιστα ἀκολουθήσαις;

ΜΕΝ. Βούλομαι· πῶς γὰρ οὔ;

ΣΩ. Οὐκοῦν λέγετε ἀπορροάς τινας τῶν ὄντων κατὰ Ἐμπεδοκλέα;

ΜΕΝ. Σφόδρα γε.

ΣΩ. Καὶ πόρους, εἰς οὓς καὶ δι’ ὧν αἱ ἀπορροαὶ πορεύονται;

ΜΕΝ. Πάνυ γε.

ΣΩ. Καὶ τῶν ἀπορροῶν τὰς μὲν ἁρμόττειν D ἐνίοις τῶν πόρων, τὰς δὲ ἐλάττους ἢ μείζους εἶναι;

ΜΕΝ. Ἔστι ταῦτα.

ΣΩ. Οὐκοῦν καὶ ὄψιν καλεῖς τι;

ΜΕΝ. Ἔγωγε.

ΣΩ. Ἐκ τούτων δὴ ξύνες ὅ τοι λέγω, ἔφη Πίνδαρος. ἔστι γὰρ χρόα ἀπορροὴ σχημάτων ὄψει σύμμετρος καὶ αἰσθητός.

ΜΕΝ. Ἄριστά μοι δοκεῖς, ὦ Σώκρατες, ταύτην τὴν ἀπόκρισιν εἰρηκέναι.

ΣΩ. Ἴσως γάρ σοι κατὰ συνήθειαν εἴρηται·

---

[1] There is something of Gorgias's stately style in the definition that follows; but the implication seems mainly to be that the substance of it will be familiar to Meno because

MEN. Why so?

SOC. Because you invariably speak in a peremptory tone, after the fashion of spoilt beauties, holding as they do a despotic power so long as their bloom is on them. You have also, I daresay, made a note of my weakness for handsome people. So I will indulge you, and answer.

MEN. You must certainly indulge me.

SOC. Then would you like me to answer you in the manner of Gorgias,[1] which you would find easiest to follow?

MEN. I should like that, of course.

SOC. Do not both of you say there are certain effluences [2] of existent things, as Empedocles held?

MEN. Certainly.

SOC. And passages into which and through which the effluences pass?

MEN. To be sure.

SOC. And some of the effluences fit into various passages, while some are too small or too large?

MEN. That is so.

SOC. And further, there is what you call sight?

MEN. Yes.

SOC. So now " conceive my meaning," as Pindar [3] says : colour is an effluence of figures, commensurate with sight and sensible.

MEN. Your answer, Socrates, seems to me excellently put.

SOC. Yes, for I expect you find its terms familiar ;

he was a pupil of Gorgias, who had learnt his science from Empedocles.

[2] Empedocles taught that material objects are known to us by means of effluences or films given off by them and suited in various ways to our sense-organs.

[3] Fr. 82 (Bergk); *cf.* Aristoph. *Birds*, 939.

καὶ ἅμα, οἶμαι, ἐννοεῖς, ὅτι ἔχοις ἂν ἐξ αὐτῆς
εἰπεῖν καὶ φωνήν, ὃ ἔστι, καὶ ὀσμὴν καὶ ἄλλα
Ε πολλὰ τῶν τοιούτων.

ΜΕΝ. Πάνυ μὲν οὖν.

ΣΩ. Τραγικὴ γάρ ἐστιν, ὦ Μένων, ἡ ἀπόκρισις,
ὥστε ἀρέσκει σοι μᾶλλον ἢ ἡ περὶ τοῦ σχήματος.

ΜΕΝ. Ἔμοιγε.

ΣΩ. Ἀλλ' οὐκ ἔστιν, ὦ παῖ Ἀλεξιδήμου, ὡς
ἐγὼ ἐμαυτὸν πείθω, ἀλλ' ἐκείνη βελτίων· οἶμαι
δὲ οὐδ' ἂν σοὶ δόξαι, εἰ μή, ὥσπερ χθὲς ἔλεγες,
ἀναγκαῖόν σοι ἀπιέναι πρὸ τῶν μυστηρίων, ἀλλ'
εἰ περιμείναις τε καὶ μυηθείης.

77 ΜΕΝ. Ἀλλὰ περιμένοιμ' ἄν, ὦ Σώκρατες, εἴ
μοι πολλὰ τοιαῦτα λέγοις.

ΣΩ. Ἀλλὰ μὴν προθυμίας γε οὐδὲν ἀπολείψω,
καὶ σοῦ ἕνεκα καὶ ἐμαυτοῦ, λέγων τοιαῦτα· ἀλλ'
ὅπως μὴ οὐχ οἷός τ' ἔσομαι πολλὰ τοιαῦτα λέγειν.
ἀλλ' ἴθι δὴ πειρῶ καὶ σὺ ἐμοὶ τὴν ὑπόσχεσιν
ἀποδοῦναι, κατὰ ὅλου εἰπὼν ἀρετῆς πέρι, ὅ τι ἔστι,
καὶ παῦσαι πολλὰ ποιῶν ἐκ τοῦ ἑνός, ὅπερ φασὶ
τοὺς συντρίβοντάς τι ἑκάστοτε οἱ σκώπτοντες, ἀλλ'
Β ἐάσας ὅλην καὶ ὑγιῆ εἰπὲ τί ἐστιν ἀρετή. τὰ δέ
γε παραδείγματα παρ' ἐμοῦ εἴληφας.

ΜΕΝ. Δοκεῖ τοίνυν μοι, ὦ Σώκρατες, ἀρετὴ
εἶναι, καθάπερ ὁ ποιητὴς λέγει, χαίρειν τε καλοῖσι
καὶ δύνασθαι· καὶ ἐγὼ τοῦτο λέγω ἀρετήν, ἐπιθυμοῦντα τῶν καλῶν δυνατὸν εἶναι πορίζεσθαι.

ΣΩ. Ἆρα λέγεις τὸν τῶν καλῶν ἐπιθυμοῦντα
ἀγαθῶν ἐπιθυμητὴν εἶναι;

ΜΕΝ. Μάλιστά γε.

ΣΩ. Ἆρα ὡς ὄντων τινῶν οἳ τῶν κακῶν ἐπι-

---

[1] Perhaps from Simonides.

and at the same time I fancy you observe that it enables you to tell what sound and smell are, and numerous other things of the kind.

MEN. Certainly.

SOC. It is an answer in the high poetic style, Meno, and so more agreeable to you than that about figure.

MEN. Yes, it is.

SOC. But yet, son of Alexidemus, I am inclined to think the other was the better of the two ; and I believe you also would prefer it, if you were not compelled, as you were saying yesterday, to go away before the mysteries, and could stay awhile and be initiated.

MEN. But I should stay, Socrates, if you would give me many such answers.

SOC. Well then, I will spare no endeavour, both for your sake and for my own, to continue in that style ; but I fear I may not succeed in keeping for long on that level. But come now, you in your turn must try and fulfil your promise by telling me what virtue is in a general way ; and you must stop producing a plural from the singular, as the wags say whenever one breaks something, but leave virtue whole and sound, and tell me what it is. The pattern you have now got from me.

MEN. Well, in my view, Socrates, virtue is, in the poet's words, " to rejoice in things honourable and be able for them "[1]; and that, I say, is virtue—to desire what is honourable and be able to procure it.

SOC. Do you say that he who desires the honourable is desirous of the good ?

MEN. Certainly.

SOC. Implying that there are some who desire

θυμοῦσιν, ἑτέρων δὲ οἱ τῶν ἀγαθῶν; οὐ πάντες,
C ὥριστε, δοκοῦσί σοι τῶν ἀγαθῶν ἐπιθυμεῖν;

ΜΕΝ. Οὐκ ἔμοιγε.

ΣΩ. Ἀλλά τινες τῶν κακῶν;

ΜΕΝ. Ναί.

ΣΩ. Οἰόμενοι τὰ κακὰ ἀγαθὰ εἶναι, λέγεις, ἢ
καὶ γιγνώσκοντες, ὅτι κακά ἐστιν, ὅμως ἐπιθυμοῦσιν αὐτῶν;

ΜΕΝ. Ἀμφότερα ἔμοιγε δοκεῖ.

ΣΩ. Ἦ γὰρ δοκεῖ τίς σοι, ὦ Μένων, γιγνώσκων
τὰ κακὰ ὅτι κακά ἐστιν ὅμως ἐπιθυμεῖν αὐτῶν;

ΜΕΝ. Μάλιστα.

ΣΩ. Τί ἐπιθυμεῖν λέγεις; ἢ γενέσθαι αὐτῷ;
D ΜΕΝ. Γενέσθαι· τί γὰρ ἄλλο;

ΣΩ. Πότερον ἡγούμενος τὰ κακὰ ὠφελεῖν
ἐκεῖνον ᾧ ἂν γένηται, ἢ γιγνώσκων τὰ κακὰ ὅτι
βλάπτει ᾧ ἂν παρῇ;

ΜΕΝ. Εἰσὶ μὲν οἱ ἡγούμενοι τὰ κακὰ ὠφελεῖν,
εἰσὶ δὲ καὶ οἱ γιγνώσκοντες ὅτι βλάπτει.

ΣΩ. Ἦ καὶ δοκοῦσί σοι γιγνώσκειν τὰ κακά,
ὅτι κακά ἐστιν, οἱ ἡγούμενοι τὰ κακὰ ὠφελεῖν;

ΜΕΝ. Οὐ πάνυ μοι δοκεῖ τοῦτό γε.

ΣΩ. Οὐκοῦν δῆλον ὅτι οὗτοι μὲν οὐ τῶν κακῶν
ἐπιθυμοῦσιν, οἱ ἀγνοοῦντες αὐτά, ἀλλὰ ἐκείνων, ἃ
E ᾤοντο ἀγαθὰ εἶναι, ἔστι δὲ ταῦτά γε κακά· ὥστε
οἱ ἀγνοοῦντες αὐτὰ καὶ οἰόμενοι ἀγαθὰ εἶναι δῆλον
ὅτι τῶν ἀγαθῶν ἐπιθυμοῦσιν· ἢ οὔ;

ΜΕΝ. Κινδυνεύουσιν οὗτοί γε.

ΣΩ. Τί δέ; οἱ τῶν κακῶν μὲν ἐπιθυμοῦντες,
ὡς φῂς σύ, ἡγούμενοι δὲ τὰ κακὰ βλάπτειν ἐκεῖνον,
ᾧ ἂν γίγνηται, γιγνώσκουσι δήπου ὅτι βλαβήσονται
ὑπ᾽ αὐτῶν;

the evil, and others the good? Do not all men, in your opinion, my dear sir, desire the good?

MEN. I think not.

SOC. There are some who desire the evil?

MEN. Yes.

SOC. Thinking the evil to be good, do you mean, or actually recognizing it to be evil, and desiring it nevertheless?

MEN. Both, I believe.

SOC. Do you really believe, Meno, that a man knows the evil to be evil, and still desires it?

MEN. Certainly.

SOC. What do you mean by " desires "? Desires the possession of it?

MEN. Yes; what else could it be?

SOC. And does he think the evil benefits him who gets it, or does he know that it harms him who has it?

MEN. There are some who think the evil is a benefit, and others who know that it does harm.

SOC. And, in your opinion, do those who think the evil a benefit know that it is evil?

MEN. I do not think that at all.

SOC. Obviously those who are ignorant of the evil do not desire it, but only what they supposed to be good, though it is really evil; so that those who are ignorant of it and think it good are really desiring the good. Is not that so?

MEN. It would seem to be so in their case.

SOC. Well now, I presume those who, as you say, desire the evil, and consider that the evil harms him who gets it, know that they will be harmed by it?

ΜΕΝ. Ἀνάγκη.

78 ΣΩ. Ἀλλὰ τοὺς βλαπτομένους οὗτοι οὐκ οἴονται ἀθλίους εἶναι καθ᾽ ὅσον βλάπτονται;

ΜΕΝ. Καὶ τοῦτο ἀνάγκη.

ΣΩ. Τοὺς δὲ ἀθλίους οὐ κακοδαίμονας;

ΜΕΝ. Οἶμαι ἔγωγε.

ΣΩ. Ἔστιν οὖν ὅστις βούλεται ἄθλιος καὶ κακοδαίμων εἶναι;

ΜΕΝ. Οὔ μοι δοκεῖ, ὦ Σώκρατες.

ΣΩ. Οὐκ ἄρα βούλεται, ὦ Μένων, τὰ κακὰ οὐδείς, εἴπερ μὴ βούλεται τοιοῦτος εἶναι. τί γὰρ ἄλλο ἐστὶν ἄθλιον εἶναι, ἢ ἐπιθυμεῖν τε τῶν κακῶν καὶ κτᾶσθαι;

Β ΜΕΝ. Κινδυνεύεις ἀληθῆ λέγειν, ὦ Σώκρατες· καὶ οὐδεὶς βούλεσθαι τὰ κακά.

ΣΩ. Οὐκοῦν νῦν δὴ ἔλεγες, ὅτι ἔστιν ἡ ἀρετὴ βούλεσθαί τε τἀγαθὰ καὶ δύνασθαι;

ΜΕΝ. Εἶπον γάρ.

ΣΩ. Οὐκοῦν τοῦ[1] λεχθέντος τὸ μὲν βούλεσθαι πᾶσιν ὑπάρχει, καὶ ταύτῃ γε οὐδὲν ὁ ἕτερος τοῦ ἑτέρου βελτίων;

ΜΕΝ. Φαίνεται.

ΣΩ. Ἀλλὰ δῆλον ὅτι, εἴπερ ἐστὶ βελτίων ἄλλος ἄλλου, κατὰ τὸ δύνασθαι ἂν εἴη ἀμείνων.

ΜΕΝ. Πάνυ γε.

ΣΩ. Τοῦτ᾽ ἔστιν ἄρα, ὡς ἔοικε, κατὰ τὸν σὸν
C λόγον ἀρετή, δύναμις τοῦ πορίζεσθαι τἀγαθά.

ΜΕΝ. Παντάπασί μοι δοκεῖ, ὦ Σώκρατες, οὕτως ἔχειν, ὡς σὺ νῦν ὑπολαμβάνεις.

ΣΩ. Ἴδωμεν δὴ καὶ τοῦτο εἰ ἀληθὲς λέγεις· ἴσως γὰρ ἂν εὖ λέγοις. τἀγαθὰ φῂς οἷόν τ᾽ εἶναι πορίζεσθαι ἀρετὴν εἶναι;

MENO

MEN. They needs must.

soc. But do they not hold that those who are harmed are miserable in proportion to the harm they suffer ?

MEN. That too must be.

soc. And are not the miserable ill-starred ?

MEN. I think so.

soc. Then is there anyone who wishes to be miserable and ill-starred ?

MEN. I do not suppose there is, Socrates.

soc. No one, then, Meno, desires evil, if no one desires to be such an one : for what is being miserable but desiring evil and obtaining it ?

MEN. It seems that what you say is true, Socrates, and that nobody desires evil.

soc. Well now, you were saying a moment ago that virtue is the desire and ability for good ?

MEN. Yes, I was.

soc. One part of the statement—the desire—belongs to our common nature, and in this respect one man is no better than another ?

MEN. Apparently.

soc. But it is plain that if one man is not better than another in this, he must be superior in the ability.

MEN. Certainly.

soc. Then virtue, it seems by your account, is ability to procure goods.

MEN. I entirely agree, Socrates, with the view which you now take of the matter.

soc. Then let us see whether your statement is true in another respect ; for very likely you may be right. You say virtue is the ability to procure goods ?

---

¹ τοῦ Ast : τούτου MSS.

ΜΕΝ. Ἔγωγε.

ΣΩ. Ἀγαθὰ δὲ καλεῖς οὐχὶ οἷον ὑγίειάν τε καὶ πλοῦτον;

ΜΕΝ. Καὶ χρυσίον λέγω καὶ ἀργύριον κτᾶσθαι καὶ τιμὰς ἐν πόλει καὶ ἀρχάς.

ΣΩ. Μὴ ἄλλ' ἄττα λέγεις τἀγαθὰ ἢ τὰ τοιαῦτα;

ΜΕΝ. Οὔκ, ἀλλὰ πάντα λέγω τὰ τοιαῦτα.

D ΣΩ. Εἶεν· χρυσίον δὲ δὴ καὶ ἀργύριον πορίζεσθαι ἀρετή ἐστιν, ὥς φησι Μένων ὁ τοῦ μεγάλου βασιλέως πατρικὸς ξένος. πότερον προστιθεῖς τούτῳ τῷ πόρῳ, ὦ Μένων, τὸ δικαίως καὶ ὁσίως, ἢ οὐδέν σοι διαφέρει, ἀλλὰ κἂν ἀδίκως τις αὐτὰ πορίζηται, ὁμοίως σὺ αὐτὰ ἀρετὴν καλεῖς;

ΜΕΝ. Οὐ δήπου, ὦ Σώκρατες.

ΣΩ. Ἀλλὰ κακίαν.

ΜΕΝ. Πάντως δήπου.

ΣΩ. Δεῖ ἄρα, ὡς ἔοικε, τούτῳ τῷ πόρῳ δικαιοσύνην ἢ σωφροσύνην ἢ ὁσιότητα προσεῖναι, ἢ ἄλλο
E τι μόριον ἀρετῆς· εἰ δὲ μή, οὐκ ἔσται ἀρετή, καίπερ ἐκπορίζουσα τἀγαθά.

ΜΕΝ. Πῶς γὰρ ἄνευ τούτων ἀρετὴ γένοιτ' ἄν;

ΣΩ. Τὸ δὲ μὴ ἐκπορίζειν χρυσίον καὶ ἀργύριον, ὅταν μὴ δίκαιον ᾖ, μήτε αὐτῷ μήτε ἄλλῳ, οὐκ ἀρετὴ καὶ αὕτη ἐστὶν ἡ ἀπορία;

ΜΕΝ. Φαίνεται.

ΣΩ. Οὐδὲν ἄρα μᾶλλον ὁ πόρος τῶν τοιούτων ἀγαθῶν ἢ ἡ ἀπορία ἀρετὴ ἂν εἴη, ἀλλά, ὡς ἔοικεν, ὃ μὲν ἂν μετὰ δικαιοσύνης γίγνηται, ἀρετὴ ἔσται,
79 ὃ δ' ἂν ἄνευ πάντων τῶν τοιούτων, κακία.

MEN. I do.

SOC. And do you not mean by goods such things as health and wealth?

MEN. Yes, and I include the acquisition of gold and silver, and of state honours and offices.

SOC. Are there any things besides this sort, that you class as goods?

MEN. No, I refer only to everything of that sort.

SOC. Very well: procuring gold and silver is virtue, according to Meno, the ancestral friend of the Great King. Tell me, do you add to such procuring, Meno, that it is to be done justly and piously, or is this indifferent to you, but even though a man procures these things unjustly, do you call them virtue all the same?

MEN. Surely not, Socrates.

SOC. Rather, vice.

MEN. Yes, of course.

SOC. Then it seems that justice or temperance or holiness or some other part of virtue must accompany the procuring of these things; otherwise it will not be virtue, though it provides one with goods.

MEN. Yes, for how, without these, could it be virtue?

SOC. And not to procure gold and silver, when it would be unjust—what we call the want of such things—is virtue, is it not?

MEN. Apparently.

SOC. So the procuring of this sort of goods will be no more virtue than the want of them; but it seems that whatever comes accompanied by justice will be virtue, and whatever comes without any such quality, vice.

ΜΕΝ. Δοκεῖ μοι ἀναγκαῖον εἶναι ὡς λέγεις.

ΣΩ. Οὐκοῦν τούτων ἕκαστον ὀλίγον πρότερον μόριον ἀρετῆς ἔφαμεν εἶναι, τὴν δικαιοσύνην καὶ σωφροσύνην καὶ πάντα τὰ τοιαῦτα;

ΜΕΝ. Ναί.

ΣΩ. Εἶτα, ὦ Μένων, παίζεις πρός με;

ΜΕΝ. Τί δή, ὦ Σώκρατες;

ΣΩ. Ὅτι ἄρτι ἐμοῦ δεηθέντος σου μὴ κατ- αγνύναι μηδὲ κερματίζειν τὴν ἀρετήν, καὶ δόντος παραδείγματα καθ' ἃ δέοι ἀποκρίνεσθαι, τούτου μὲν ἠμέλησας, λέγεις δέ μοι, ὅτι ἀρετή ἐστιν οἷόν B τ' εἶναι τἀγαθὰ πορίζεσθαι μετὰ δικαιοσύνης· τοῦτο δὲ φῂς μόριον ἀρετῆς εἶναι;

ΜΕΝ. Ἔγωγε.

ΣΩ. Οὐκοῦν συμβαίνει ἐξ ὧν σὺ ὁμολογεῖς, τὸ μετὰ μορίου ἀρετῆς πράττειν, ὅ τι ἂν πράττῃ, τοῦτο ἀρετὴν εἶναι· τὴν γὰρ δικαιοσύνην μόριον φῂς ἀρετῆς εἶναι, καὶ ἕκαστα τούτων. τί οὖν δὴ τοῦτο λέγω; ὅτι ἐμοῦ δεηθέντος ὅλον εἰπεῖν τὴν ἀρετήν, αὐτὴν μὲν πολλοῦ δεῖς εἰπεῖν ὅ τι ἔστι, πᾶσαν δὲ φῂς πρᾶξιν ἀρετὴν εἶναι, ἐάνπερ μετὰ C μορίου ἀρετῆς πράττηται, ὥσπερ εἰρηκὼς ὅ τι ἀρετή ἐστι τὸ ὅλον καὶ ἤδη γνωσομένου ἐμοῦ, καὶ ἐὰν σὺ κατακερματίζῃς αὐτὴν κατὰ μόρια. δεῖται οὖν σοι πάλιν ἐξ ἀρχῆς, ὡς ἐμοὶ δοκεῖ, τῆς αὐτῆς ἐρωτήσεως, ὦ φίλε Μένων, τί ἐστιν ἀρετή, εἰ μετὰ μορίου ἀρετῆς πᾶσα πρᾶξις ἀρετὴ ἂν εἴη; τοῦτο γάρ ἐστι λέγειν, ὅταν λέγῃ τις, ὅτι πᾶσα ἡ μετὰ δικαιοσύνης πρᾶξις ἀρετή ἐστιν. ἢ οὐ δοκεῖ σοι πάλιν δεῖσθαι τῆς αὐτῆς ἐρωτήσεως, ἀλλ' οἴει τινὰ εἰδέναι μόριον ἀρετῆς ὅ τι ἔστιν, αὐτὴν μὴ εἰδότα;

MEN. I agree that it must be as you say.

soc. And were we saying a little while ago that each of these things was a part of virtue—justice and temperance and the rest of them?

MEN. Yes.

soc. And here you are, Meno, making fun of me?

MEN. How so, Socrates?

soc. Because after my begging you not to break up virtue into small change, and giving you a pattern on which you should answer, you have ignored all this, and now tell me that virtue is the ability to procure good things with justice; and this, you tell me, is a part of virtue?

MEN. I do.

soc. Then it follows from your own admission that doing whatever one does with a part of virtue is itself virtue; for you say that justice is a part of virtue, and so is each of such qualities. You ask the meaning of my remark. It is that after my requesting you to speak of virtue as a whole, you say not a word as to what it is in itself, but tell me that every action is virtue provided that it is done with a part of virtue; as though you had told me what virtue is in the whole, and I must understand it forthwith —when you are really splitting it up into fragments! I think therefore that you must face the same question all over again, my dear Meno—What is virtue?—if we are to be told that every action accompanied by a part of virtue is virtue; for that is the meaning of the statement that every action accompanied by justice is virtue. Or do you not agree that you have to meet the same question afresh? Do you suppose that anyone can know a part of virtue when he does not know virtue itself?

ΜΕΝ. Οὐκ ἔμοιγε δοκεῖ.

D ΣΩ. Εἰ γὰρ καὶ μέμνησαι, ὅτ᾽ ἐγώ σοι ἄρτι
ἀπεκρινάμην περὶ τοῦ σχήματος, ἀπεβάλλομέν
που τὴν τοιαύτην ἀπόκρισιν τὴν διὰ τῶν ἔτι ζη-
τουμένων καὶ μήπω ὡμολογημένων ἐπιχειροῦσαν
ἀποκρίνεσθαι.

ΜΕΝ. Καὶ ὀρθῶς γε ἀπεβάλλομεν, ὦ Σώκρατες.

ΣΩ. Μὴ τοίνυν, ὦ ἄριστε, μηδὲ σὺ ἔτι ζητου-
μένης ἀρετῆς ὅλης ὅ τι ἔστιν οἴου διὰ τῶν ταύτης
μορίων ἀποκρινόμενος δηλώσειν αὐτὴν ὁτῳοῦν, ἢ
E ἄλλο ὁτιοῦν τούτῳ τῷ αὐτῷ τρόπῳ λέγων, ἀλλὰ
πάλιν τῆς αὐτῆς δεήσεσθαι ἐρωτήσεως, τίνος
ὄντος ἀρετῆς λέγεις ἃ λέγεις· ἢ οὐδέν σοι δοκῶ
λέγειν;

ΜΕΝ. Ἔμοιγε δοκεῖς ὀρθῶς λέγειν.

ΣΩ. Ἀπόκριναι τοίνυν πάλιν ἐξ ἀρχῆς· τί φῂς
ἀρετὴν εἶναι καὶ σὺ καὶ ὁ ἑταῖρός σου;

ΜΕΝ. Ὦ Σώκρατες, ἤκουον μὲν ἔγωγε πρὶν
80 καὶ συγγενέσθαι σοι, ὅτι σὺ οὐδὲν ἄλλο ἢ αὐτός
τε ἀπορεῖς καὶ τοὺς ἄλλους ποιεῖς ἀπορεῖν· καὶ
νῦν, ὥς γέ μοι δοκεῖς, γοητεύεις με καὶ φαρμάττεις
καὶ ἀτεχνῶς κατεπᾴδεις, ὥστε μεστὸν ἀπορίας γε-
γονέναι· καὶ δοκεῖς μοι παντελῶς, εἰ δεῖ τι καὶ
σκῶψαι, ὁμοιότατος εἶναι τό τε εἶδος καὶ τἆλλα
ταύτῃ τῇ πλατείᾳ νάρκῃ τῇ θαλαττίᾳ. καὶ γὰρ
αὕτη τὸν ἀεὶ πλησιάζοντα καὶ ἁπτόμενον ναρκᾶν
ποιεῖ· καὶ σὺ δοκεῖς μοι νῦν ἐμὲ τοιοῦτόν τι
πεποιηκέναι [ναρκᾶν].[1] ἀληθῶς γὰρ ἔγωγε καὶ
B τὴν ψυχὴν καὶ τὸ στόμα ναρκῶ, καὶ οὐκ ἔχω ὅ τι
ἀποκρίνωμαί σοι. καίτοι μυριάκις γε περὶ ἀρετῆς

---

[1] ναρκᾶν secl. Dobree.

MEN. No, I do not.

soc. And I daresay you remember, when I answered you a while ago about figure, how we rejected the sort of answer that attempts to proceed in terms which are still under inquiry and has not yet been admitted.

MEN. Yes, and we were right in rejecting it, Socrates.

soc. Well then, my good sir, you must not in your turn suppose that while the nature of virtue as a whole is still under inquiry you will explain it to anyone by replying in terms of its parts, or by any other statement on the same lines : you will only have to face the same question over again— What *is* this virtue, of which you are speaking all the time ? Or do you see no force in what I say ?

MEN. I think what you say is right.

soc. Then answer me again from the beginning : what do both you and your associate say that virtue is ?

MEN. Socrates, I used to be told, before I began to meet you, that yours was just a case of being in doubt yourself and making others doubt also ; and so now I find you are merely bewitching me with your spells and incantations, which have reduced me to utter perplexity. And if I am indeed to have my jest, I consider that both in your appearance and in other respects you are extremely like the flat torpedo sea-fish ; for it benumbs anyone who approaches and touches it, and something of the sort is what I find you have done to me now. For in truth I feel my soul and my tongue quite benumbed, and I am at a loss what answer to give you. And yet on countless occasions I have made abundant

παμπόλλους λόγους εἴρηκα καὶ πρὸς πολλούς, καὶ
πάνυ εὖ, ὥς γε ἐμαυτῷ ἐδόκουν· νῦν δὲ οὐδ᾽ ὅ τι
ἔστι τὸ παράπαν ἔχω εἰπεῖν. καί μοι δοκεῖς εὖ
βουλεύεσθαι οὐκ ἐκπλέων ἐνθένδε οὐδ᾽ ἀποδημῶν·
εἰ γὰρ ξένος ἐν ἄλλῃ πόλει τοιαῦτα ποιοῖς, τάχ᾽
ἂν ὡς γόης ἀπαχθείης.

ΣΩ. Πανοῦργος εἶ, ὦ Μένων, καὶ ὀλίγου ἐξ-
ηπάτησάς με.

ΜΕΝ. Τί μάλιστα, ὦ Σώκρατες;

C ΣΩ. Γιγνώσκω οὗ ἕνεκά με εἴκασας.

ΜΕΝ. Τίνος δὴ οἴει;

ΣΩ. Ἵνα σε ἀντεικάσω. ἐγὼ δὲ τοῦτο οἶδα
περὶ πάντων τῶν καλῶν, ὅτι χαίρουσιν εἰκαζόμενοι.
λυσιτελεῖ γὰρ αὐτοῖς· καλαὶ γάρ, οἶμαι, τῶν
καλῶν καὶ αἱ εἰκόνες. ἀλλ᾽ οὐκ ἀντεικάσομαί σε.
ἐγὼ δέ, εἰ μὲν ἡ νάρκη αὐτὴ ναρκῶσα οὕτω καὶ
τοὺς ἄλλους ποιεῖ ναρκᾶν, ἔοικα αὐτῇ· εἰ δὲ μή,
οὔ. οὐ γὰρ εὐπορῶν αὐτὸς τοὺς ἄλλους ποιῶ ἀπορεῖν, ἀλλὰ παντὸς μᾶλλον αὐτὸς ἀπορῶν οὕτως καὶ
D τοὺς ἄλλους ποιῶ ἀπορεῖν. καὶ νῦν περὶ ἀρετῆς,
ὃ ἔστιν, ἐγὼ μὲν οὐκ οἶδα, σὺ μέντοι ἴσως πρότερον
μὲν ᾔδησθα πρὶν ἐμοῦ ἅψασθαι, νῦν μέντοι ὅμοιος
εἶ οὐκ εἰδότι. ὅμως δὲ ἐθέλω μετὰ σοῦ σκέψασθαι
καὶ συζητῆσαι ὅ τί ποτέ ἐστιν.

ΜΕΝ. Καὶ τίνα τρόπον ζητήσεις, ὦ Σώκρατες,
τοῦτο, ὃ μὴ οἶσθα τὸ παράπαν ὅ τι ἔστι; ποῖον γὰρ
ὧν οὐκ οἶσθα προθέμενος ζητήσεις; ἢ εἰ καὶ ὅτι
μάλιστα ἐντύχοις αὐτῷ, πῶς εἴσῃ ὅτι τοῦτό ἐστιν,
ὃ σὺ οὐκ ᾔδησθα;

MENO

speeches on virtue to various people—and very good
speeches they were, so I thought—but now I cannot
say one word as to what it is. You are well advised,
I consider, in not voyaging or taking a trip away
from home ; for if you went on like this as a stranger
in any other city you would very likely be taken up
for a wizard.

soc. You are a rogue, Meno, and had almost
deceived me.

men. How is that, Socrates ?

soc. I perceive your aim in thus comparing me.

men. What was it ?

soc. That I might compare you in return. One
thing I know about all handsome people is this—
they delight in being compared to something.
They do well over it, since fine features, I suppose,
must have fine similes. But I am not for playing
your game. As for me, if the torpedo is torpid
itself while causing others to be torpid, I am like
it, but not otherwise. For it is not from any sure-
ness in myself that I cause others to doubt : it is
from being in more doubt than anyone else that I
cause doubt in others. So now, for my part, I
have no idea what virtue is, whilst you, though
perhaps you may have known before you came in
touch with me, are now as good as ignorant of it
also. But none the less I am willing to join you in
examining it and inquiring into its nature.

men. Why, on what lines will you look, Socrates,
for a thing of whose nature you know nothing at all ?
Pray, what sort of thing, amongst those that you know
not, will you treat us to as the object of your search ?
Or even supposing, at the best, that you hit upon it,
how will you know it is the thing you did not know ?

ΣΩ. Μανθάνω οἷον βούλει λέγειν, ὦ Μένων.
Ε ὁρᾷς τοῦτον ὡς ἐριστικὸν λόγον κατάγεις, ὡς οὐκ
ἄρα ἔστι ζητεῖν ἀνθρώπῳ οὔτε ὃ οἶδεν οὔτε ὃ μὴ
οἶδεν; οὔτε γὰρ ἂν ὅ γε οἶδε ζητοῖ· οἶδε γάρ, καὶ
οὐδὲν δεῖ τῷ γε τοιούτῳ ζητήσεως· οὔτε ὃ μὴ
οἶδεν· οὐδὲ γὰρ οἶδεν ὅ τι ζητήσει.

81 ΜΕΝ. Οὐκοῦν καλῶς σοι δοκεῖ λέγεσθαι ὁ
λόγος οὗτος, ὦ Σώκρατες;

ΣΩ. Οὐκ ἔμοιγε.

ΜΕΝ. Ἔχεις λέγειν ὅπη;

ΣΩ. Ἔγωγε· ἀκήκοα γὰρ ἀνδρῶν τε καὶ γυναικῶν σοφῶν περὶ τὰ θεῖα πράγματα—

ΜΕΝ. Τίνα λόγον λεγόντων;

ΣΩ. Ἀληθῆ, ἔμοιγε δοκεῖν, καὶ καλόν.

ΜΕΝ. Τίνα τοῦτον, καὶ τίνες οἱ λέγοντες;

ΣΩ. Οἱ μὲν λέγοντές εἰσι τῶν ἱερέων τε καὶ
ἱερειῶν ὅσοις μεμέληκε περὶ ὧν μεταχειρίζονται
λόγον οἵοις τ' εἶναι διδόναι· λέγει δὲ καὶ Πίνδαρος
Β καὶ ἄλλοι πολλοὶ τῶν ποιητῶν, ὅσοι θεῖοί εἰσιν.
ἃ δὲ λέγουσι, ταυτί ἐστιν· ἀλλὰ σκόπει, εἴ σοι
δοκοῦσιν ἀληθῆ λέγειν. φασὶ γὰρ τὴν ψυχὴν
τοῦ ἀνθρώπου εἶναι ἀθάνατον, καὶ τοτὲ μὲν
τελευτᾶν, ὃ δὴ ἀποθνήσκειν καλοῦσι, τοτὲ δὲ
πάλιν γίγνεσθαι, ἀπόλλυσθαι δ' οὐδέποτε· δεῖν
δὴ διὰ ταῦτα ὡς ὁσιώτατα διαβιῶναι τὸν βίον·
οἷσι γὰρ ἂν—

Φερσεφόνα ποινὰν παλαιοῦ πένθεος
δέξεται, εἰς τὸν ὕπερθεν ἅλιον κείνων ἐνάτῳ ἔτεϊ
ἀνδιδοῖ ψυχὰς πάλιν,

MENO

soc. I understand the point you would make, Meno. Do you see what a captious argument you are introducing—that, forsooth, a man cannot inquire either about what he knows or about what he does not know? For he cannot inquire about what he knows, because he knows it, and in that case is in no need of inquiry; nor again can he inquire about what he does not know, since he does not know about what he is to inquire.

MEN. Now does it seem to you to be a good argument, Socrates?

soc. It does not.

MEN. Can you explain how not?

soc. I can; for I have heard from wise men and women who told of things divine that—

MEN. What was it they said?

soc. Something true, as I thought, and admirable.

MEN. What was it? And who were the speakers?

soc. They were certain priests and priestesses who have studied so as to be able to give a reasoned account of their ministry; and Pindar also and many another poet of heavenly gifts. As to their words, they are these: mark now, if you judge them to be true. They say that the soul of man is immortal, and at one time comes to an end, which is called dying, and at another is born again, but never perishes. Consequently one ought to live all one's life in the utmost holiness.

For from whomsoever Persephone shall accept requital for ancient wrong,[1] the souls of these she restores in the ninth year to the upper sun again; from them arise glorious

---

[1] πένθος (" affliction ") in mystic language means something like " fall " or " sin." These lines are probably from one of Pindar's *Dirges* (Bergk, fr. 133).

81

C ἐκ τᾶν βασιλῆες ἀγαυοὶ
καὶ σθένει κραιπνοὶ σοφίᾳ τε μέγιστοι
ἄνδρες αὔξοντ'.[1] ἐς δὲ τὸν λοιπὸν χρόνον ἥρωες
ἁγνοὶ πρὸς ἀνθρώπων καλεῦνται.

"Ατε οὖν ἡ ψυχὴ ἀθάνατός τε οὖσα καὶ πολλάκις
γεγονυῖα, καὶ ἑωρακυῖα καὶ τὰ ἐνθάδε καὶ τὰ
ἐν "Αιδου καὶ πάντα χρήματα, οὐκ ἔστιν ὅ τι
οὐ μεμάθηκεν· ὥστε οὐδὲν θαυμαστὸν καὶ περὶ
ἀρετῆς καὶ περὶ ἄλλων οἷόν τε εἶναι αὐτὴν ἀναμνησθῆναι, ἅ γε καὶ πρότερον ἠπίστατο. ἅτε γὰρ
D τῆς φύσεως ἁπάσης συγγενοῦς οὔσης, καὶ μεμα-
θηκυίας τῆς ψυχῆς ἅπαντα, οὐδὲν κωλύει ἓν μόνον
ἀναμνησθέντα, ὃ δὴ μάθησιν καλοῦσιν ἄνθρωποι,
τἄλλα πάντα αὐτὸν ἀνευρεῖν, ἐάν τις ἀνδρεῖος ᾖ καὶ
μὴ ἀποκάμνῃ ζητῶν· τὸ γὰρ ζητεῖν ἄρα καὶ τὸ
μανθάνειν ἀνάμνησις ὅλον ἐστίν. οὔκουν δεῖ
πείθεσθαι τούτῳ τῷ ἐριστικῷ λόγῳ· οὗτος μὲν
γὰρ ἂν ἡμᾶς ἀργοὺς ποιήσειε καὶ ἔστι τοῖς μαλα-
κοῖς τῶν ἀνθρώπων ἡδὺς ἀκοῦσαι, ὅδε δὲ ἐργα-
E στικούς τε καὶ ζητητικοὺς ποιεῖ· ᾧ ἐγὼ πιστεύων
ἀληθεῖ εἶναι ἐθέλω μετὰ σοῦ ζητεῖν ἀρετὴ ὅ τι ἔστιν.

ΜΕΝ. Ναί, ὦ Σώκρατες· ἀλλὰ πῶς λέγεις
τοῦτο, ὅτι οὐ μανθάνομεν, ἀλλὰ ἣν καλοῦμεν
μάθησιν ἀνάμνησίς ἐστιν; ἔχεις με τοῦτο διδάξαι
ὡς οὕτως ἔχει;

ΣΩ. Καὶ ἄρτι εἶπον, ὦ Μένων, ὅτι πανοῦργος
εἶ, καὶ νῦν ἐρωτᾷς εἰ ἔχω σε διδάξαι, ὃς οὔ φημι
82 διδαχὴν εἶναι ἀλλ' ἀνάμνησιν, ἵνα δὴ εὐθὺς φαίνωμαι αὐτὸς ἐμαυτῷ τἀναντία λέγων.

ΜΕΝ. Οὐ μὰ τὸν Δία, ὦ Σώκρατες, οὐ πρὸς
τοῦτο βλέψας εἶπον, ἀλλ' ὑπὸ τοῦ ἔθους· ἀλλ' εἴ

---

[1] αὔξοντ' Boeckh: αὔξονται mss.

kings and men of splendid might and surpassing wisdom, and for all remaining time are they called holy heroes amongst mankind.

Seeing then that the soul is immortal and has been born many times, and has beheld all things both in this world and in the nether realms, she has acquired knowledge of all and everything ; so that it is no wonder that she should be able to recollect all that she knew before about virtue and other things. For as all nature is akin, and the soul has learned all things, there is no reason why we should not, by remembering but one single thing—an act which men call learning—discover everything else, if we have courage and faint not in the search ; since, it would seem, research and learning are wholly recollection. So we must not hearken to that captious argument : it would make us idle, and is pleasing only to the indolent ear, whereas the other makes us energetic and inquiring. Putting my trust in its truth, I am ready to inquire with you into the nature of virtue.

MEN. Yes, Socrates, but what do you mean by saying that we do not learn, and that what we call learning is recollection ? Can you instruct me that this is so ?

SOC. I remarked just now, Meno, that you are a rogue ; and so here you are asking if I can instruct you, when I say there is no teaching but only recollection : you hope that I may be caught contradicting myself forthwith.

MEN. I assure you, Socrates, that was not my intention ; I only spoke from habit. But if you can

πώς μοι ἔχεις ἐνδείξασθαι, ὅτι ἔχει ὥσπερ λέγεις, ἔνδειξαι.

ΣΩ. Ἀλλ' ἔστι μὲν οὐ ῥᾴδιον, ὅμως δὲ ἐθέλω προθυμηθῆναι σοῦ ἕνεκα. ἀλλά μοι προσκάλεσον τῶν πολλῶν ἀκολούθων τουτωνὶ τῶν σαυτοῦ ἕνα, B ὅντινα βούλει, ἵνα ἐν τούτῳ σοι ἐπιδείξωμαι.

ΜΕΝ. Πάνυ γε. δεῦρο πρόσελθε.

ΣΩ. Ἕλλην μέν ἐστι καὶ ἑλληνίζει;

ΜΕΝ. Πάνυ γε σφόδρα, οἰκογενής γε.

ΣΩ. Πρόσεχε δὴ τὸν νοῦν, ὁπότερ' ἄν σοι φαίνηται, ἢ ἀναμιμνησκόμενος ἢ μανθάνων παρ' ἐμοῦ.

ΜΕΝ. Ἀλλὰ προσέξω.

ΣΩ. Εἰπὲ δή μοι, ὦ παῖ, γιγνώσκεις τετράγωνον χωρίον ὅτι τοιοῦτόν ἐστιν;

ΠΑΙΣ. Ἔγωγε.

C ΣΩ. Ἔστιν οὖν τετράγωνον χωρίον ἴσας ἔχον τὰς γραμμὰς ταύτας πάσας, τέτταρας οὔσας;

ΠΑΙΣ. Πάνυ γε.

ΣΩ. Οὐ καὶ ταυτασὶ τὰς διὰ μέσου ἐστὶν ἴσας ἔχον;

ΠΑΙΣ. Ναί.

ΣΩ. Οὐκοῦν εἴη ἂν τοιοῦτον χωρίον καὶ μεῖζον καὶ ἔλαττον;

ΠΑΙΣ. Πάνυ γε.

ΣΩ. Εἰ οὖν εἴη αὕτη ἡ πλευρὰ δυοῖν ποδοῖν καὶ αὕτη δυοῖν, πόσων ἂν εἴη ποδῶν τὸ ὅλον; ὧδε δὲ σκόπει· εἰ ἦν ταύτῃ δυοῖν ποδοῖν, ταύτῃ δὲ ἑνὸς ποδὸς μόνον, ἄλλο τι ἅπαξ ἂν ἦν δυοῖν ποδοῖν τὸ χωρίον;

ΠΑΙΣ. Ναί.

D ΣΩ. Ἐπειδὴ δὲ δυοῖν ποδοῖν καὶ ταύτῃ, ἄλλο τι ἢ δὶς δυοῖν γίγνεται;

somehow prove to me that it is as you say, pray do so.

soc. It is no easy matter, but still I am willing to try my best for your sake. Just call one of your own troop of attendants there, whichever one you please, that he may serve for my demonstration.

men. Certainly. You, I say, come here.

soc. He is a Greek, I suppose, and speaks Greek?

men. Oh yes, to be sure—born in the house.

soc. Now observe closely whether he strikes you as recollecting or as learning from me.

men. I will.

soc. Tell me, boy, do you know that a square figure is like this? [1]

boy. I do.

soc. Now, a square figure has these lines, four in number, all equal?

boy. Certainly.

soc. And these, drawn through the middle,[2] are equal too, are they not?

boy. Yes.

soc. And a figure of this sort may be larger or smaller?

boy. To be sure.

soc. Now if this side were two feet and that also two, how many feet would the whole be? Or let me put it thus: if one way it were two feet, and only one foot the other, of course the space would be two feet taken once?

boy. Yes.

soc. But as it is two feet also on that side, it must be twice two feet?

---

[1] Socrates draws in the sand.
[2] *i.e.* the middle of each side of the square.

ΠΑΙΣ. Γίγνεται.

ΣΩ. Δυοῖν ἄρα δὶς γίγνεται ποδῶν;

ΠΑΙΣ. Ναί.

ΣΩ. Πόσοι οὖν εἰσὶν οἱ δύο δὶς πόδες; λογισάμενος εἰπέ.

ΠΑΙΣ. Τέτταρες, ὦ Σώκρατες.

ΣΩ. Οὐκοῦν γένοιτ᾽ ἂν τούτου τοῦ χωρίου ἕτερον διπλάσιον, τοιοῦτον δέ, ἴσας ἔχον πάσας τὰς γραμμὰς ὥσπερ τοῦτο;

ΠΑΙΣ. Ναί.

ΣΩ. Πόσων οὖν ἔσται ποδῶν;

ΠΑΙΣ. Ὀκτώ.

ΣΩ. Φέρε δή, πειρῶ μοι εἰπεῖν πηλίκη τις ἔσται
Ε ἐκείνου ἡ γραμμὴ ἑκάστη. ἡ μὲν γὰρ τοῦδε δυοῖν ποδοῖν· τί δὲ ἡ ἐκείνου τοῦ διπλασίου;

ΠΑΙΣ. Δῆλον δή, ὦ Σώκρατες, ὅτι διπλασία.

ΣΩ. Ὁρᾷς, ὦ Μένων, ὡς ἐγὼ τοῦτον οὐδὲν διδάσκω, ἀλλ᾽ ἐρωτῶ πάντα; καὶ νῦν οὗτος οἴεται εἰδέναι, ὁποία ἐστὶν ἀφ᾽ ἧς τὸ ὀκτώπουν χωρίον γενήσεται· ἢ οὐ δοκεῖ σοι;

ΜΕΝ. Ἔμοιγε.

ΣΩ. Οἶδεν οὖν;

ΜΕΝ. Οὐ δῆτα.

ΣΩ. Οἴεται δέ γε ἀπὸ τῆς διπλασίας;

ΜΕΝ. Ναί.

ΣΩ. Θεῶ δὴ αὐτὸν ἀναμιμνησκόμενον ἐφεξῆς, ὡς δεῖ ἀναμιμνήσκεσθαι. σὺ δέ μοι λέγε· ἀπὸ
83 τῆς διπλασίας γραμμῆς φὴς τὸ διπλάσιον χωρίον γίγνεσθαι; τοιόνδε λέγω, μὴ ταύτῃ μὲν μακρόν, τῇ δὲ βραχύ, ἀλλὰ ἴσον πανταχῇ ἔστω ὥσπερ τουτί,

BOY. It is.

SOC. Then the space is twice two feet?

BOY. Yes.

SOC. Well, how many are twice two feet? Count and tell me.

BOY. Four, Socrates.

SOC. And might there not be another figure twice the size of this, but of the same sort, with all its sides equal like this one?

BOY. Yes.

SOC. Then how many feet will it be?

BOY. Eight.

SOC. Come now, try and tell me how long will each side of that figure be. This one is two feet long : what will be the side of the other, which is double in size?

BOY. Clearly, Socrates, double.

SOC. Do you observe, Meno, that I am not teaching the boy anything, but merely asking him each time? And now he supposes that he knows about the line required to make a figure of eight square feet ; or do you not think he does?

MEN. I do.

SOC. Well, does he know?

MEN. Certainly not.

SOC. He just supposes it, from the double size required?

MEN. Yes.

SOC. Now watch his progress in recollecting, by the proper use of memory. Tell me, boy, do you say we get the double space from the double line? The space I speak of is not long one way and short the other, but must be equal each way like this one,

διπλάσιον δὲ τούτου, ὀκτώπουν· ἀλλ᾽ ὅρα, εἰ ἔτι σοι ἀπὸ τῆς διπλασίας δοκεῖ ἔσεσθαι.

ΠΑΙΣ. Ἔμοιγε.

ΣΩ. Οὐκοῦν διπλασία αὕτη ταύτης γίγνεται, ἂν ἑτέραν τοσαύτην προσθῶμεν ἐνθένδε;

ΠΑΙΣ. Πάνυ γε.

ΣΩ. Ἀπὸ ταύτης δή, φῄς, ἔσται τὸ ὀκτώπουν χωρίον, ἂν τέτταρες τοσαῦται γένωνται;

ΠΑΙΣ. Ναί.

B ΣΩ. Ἀναγραψώμεθα δὴ ἀπ᾽ αὐτῆς ἴσας τέτταρας. ἄλλο τι ἢ τουτὶ ἂν εἴη ὃ φῂς τὸ ὀκτώπουν εἶναι;

ΠΑΙΣ. Πάνυ γε.

ΣΩ. Οὐκοῦν ἐν αὐτῷ ἐστι ταυτὶ τέτταρα, ὧν ἕκαστον ἴσον τούτῳ ἐστὶ τῷ τετράποδι;

ΠΑΙΣ. Ναί.

ΣΩ. Πόσον οὖν γίγνεται; οὐ τετράκις τοσοῦτον;

ΠΑΙΣ. Πῶς δ᾽ οὔ;

ΣΩ. Διπλάσιον οὖν ἐστὶ τὸ τετράκις τοσοῦτον;

ΠΑΙΣ. Οὐ μὰ Δία.

ΣΩ. Ἀλλὰ ποσαπλάσιον;

ΠΑΙΣ. Τετραπλάσιον.

C ΣΩ. Ἀπὸ τῆς διπλασίας ἄρα, ὦ παῖ, οὐ διπλάσιον ἀλλὰ τετραπλάσιον γίγνεται χωρίον.

ΠΑΙΣ. Ἀληθῆ λέγεις.

ΣΩ. Τεττάρων γὰρ τετράκις ἐστὶν ἑκκαίδεκα. οὐχί;

ΠΑΙΣ. Ναί.

ΣΩ. Ὀκτώπουν δ᾽ ἀπὸ ποίας γραμμῆς; οὐχὶ ἀπὸ μὲν ταύτης τετραπλάσιον;

ΠΑΙΣ. Φημί.

while being double its size—eight square feet. Now
see if you still think we get this from a double length
of line.

BOY. I do.

SOC. Well, this line is doubled, if we add here
another of the same length ?

BOY. Certainly.

SOC. And you say we shall get our eight-foot space
from four lines of this length ?

BOY. Yes.

SOC. Then let us describe the square, drawing
four equal lines of that length. This will be what
you say is the eight-foot figure, will it not ?

BOY. Certainly.

SOC. And here, contained in it, have we not four
squares, each of which is equal to this space of four
feet ?

BOY. Yes.

SOC. Then how large is the whole ? Four times
that space, is it not ?

BOY. It must be.

SOC. And is four times equal to double ?

BOY. No, to be sure.

SOC. But how much is it ?

BOY. Fourfold.

SOC. Thus, from the double-sized line, boy, we get
a space, not of double, but of fourfold size.

BOY. That is true.

SOC. And if it is four times four it is sixteen, is it
not ?

BOY. Yes.

SOC. What line will give us a space of eight feet ?
This one gives us a fourfold space, does it not ?

BOY. It does.

ΣΩ. Τετράπουν δὲ ἀπὸ τῆς ἡμισέας ταυτησὶ
τουτί;

ΠΑΙΣ. Ναί.

ΣΩ. Εἶεν· τὸ δὲ ὀκτώπουν οὐ τοῦδε μὲν δι-
πλάσιόν ἐστι, τούτου δὲ ἥμισυ;

ΠΑΙΣ. ⟨Ναί⟩[1].

ΣΩ. Οὐκ ἀπὸ μὲν μείζονος ἔσται ἢ τοσαύτης
D γραμμῆς, ἀπὸ ἐλάττονος δὲ ἢ τοσησδί; ἢ οὔ;

ΠΑΙΣ. Ἔμοιγε δοκεῖ οὕτως.

ΣΩ. Καλῶς· τὸ γάρ σοι δοκοῦν τοῦτο ἀποκρίνου.
καί μοι λέγε· οὐχ ἥδε μὲν δυοῖν ποδοῖν ἦν, ἡ δὲ
τεττάρων;

ΠΑΙΣ. Ναί.

ΣΩ. Δεῖ ἄρα τὴν τοῦ ὀκτώποδος χωρίου
γραμμὴν μείζω μὲν εἶναι τῆσδε τῆς δίποδος,
ἐλάττω δὲ τῆς τετράποδος.

ΠΑΙΣ. Δεῖ.

E   ΣΩ. Πειρῶ δὴ λέγειν πηλίκην τινὰ φῂς αὐτὴν
εἶναι.

ΠΑΙΣ. Τρίποδα.

ΣΩ. Οὐκοῦν ἄνπερ τρίπους ᾖ, τὸ ἥμισυ ταύτης
προσληψόμεθα καὶ ἔσται τρίπους; δύο μὲν γὰρ
οἶδε, ὁ δὲ εἷς· καὶ ἐνθένδε ὡσαύτως δύο μὲν οἶδε,
ὁ δὲ εἷς· καὶ γίγνεται τοῦτο τὸ χωρίον ὃ φῄς.

ΠΑΙΣ. Ναί.

ΣΩ. Οὐκοῦν ἂν ᾖ τῇδε τριῶν καὶ τῇδε τριῶν, τὸ
ὅλον χωρίον τριῶν τρὶς ποδῶν γίγνεται;

ΠΑΙΣ. Φαίνεται.

ΣΩ. Τρεῖς δὲ τρὶς πόσοι εἰσὶ πόδες;

ΠΑΙΣ. Ἐννέα.

ΣΩ. Ἔδει δὲ τὸ διπλάσιον πόσων εἶναι ποδῶν;

---

[1] Ναί om. mss.

soc. And a space of four feet is made from this line of half the length?

boy. Yes.

soc. Very well; and is not a space of eight feet double the size of this one, and half the size of this other?

boy. Yes.

soc. Will it not be made from a line longer than the one of these, and shorter than the other?

boy. I think so.

soc. Excellent: always answer just what you think. Now tell me, did we not draw this line two feet, and that four?

boy. Yes.

soc. Then the line on the side of the eight-foot figure should be more than this of two feet, and less than the other of four?

boy. It should.

soc. Try and tell me how much you would say it is.

boy. Three feet.

soc. Then if it is to be three feet, we shall add on a half to this one, and so make it three feet? For here we have two, and here one more, and so again on that side there are two, and another one; and that makes the figure of which you speak.

boy. Yes.

soc. Now if it be three this way and three that way, the whole space will be thrice three feet, will it not?

boy. So it seems.

soc. And thrice three feet are how many?

boy. Nine.

soc. And how many feet was that double one to be?

ΠΑΙΣ. Ὀκτώ.

ΣΩ. Οὐδ' ἄρα ἀπὸ τῆς τρίποδός πω τὸ ὀκτώπουν χωρίον γίγνεται.

ΠΑΙΣ. Οὐ δῆτα.

ΣΩ. Ἀλλ' ἀπὸ ποίας; πειρῶ ἡμῖν εἰπεῖν ἀκρι-
84 βῶς· καὶ εἰ μὴ βούλει ἀριθμεῖν, ἀλλὰ δεῖξον ἀπὸ ποίας.

ΠΑΙΣ. Ἀλλὰ μὰ τὸν Δία, ὦ Σώκρατες, ἔγωγε οὐκ οἶδα.

ΣΩ. Ἐννοεῖς αὖ, ὦ Μένων, οὗ ἐστὶν ἤδη βαδίζων ὅδε τοῦ ἀναμιμνήσκεσθαι; ὅτι τὸ μὲν πρῶτον ᾔδει μὲν οὔ, ἥ τις ἔστιν ἡ τοῦ ὀκτώποδος χωρίου γραμμή, ὥσπερ οὐδὲ νῦν πω οἶδεν, ἀλλ' οὖν ᾤετό γ' αὐτὴν τότε εἰδέναι, καὶ θαρραλέως ἀπεκρίνετο ὡς εἰδώς, καὶ οὐχ ἡγεῖτο ἀπορεῖν· νῦν δὲ ἡγεῖται ἀπορεῖν ἤδη, καὶ ὥσπερ οὐκ οἶδεν, οὐδ' οἴεται
B εἰδέναι.

ΜΕΝ. Ἀληθῆ λέγεις.

ΣΩ. Οὐκοῦν νῦν βέλτιον ἔχει περὶ τὸ πρᾶγμα ὃ οὐκ ᾔδει;

ΜΕΝ. Καὶ τοῦτό μοι δοκεῖ.

ΣΩ. Ἀπορεῖν οὖν αὐτὸν ποιήσαντες καὶ ναρκᾶν ὥσπερ ἡ νάρκη, μῶν τι ἐβλάψαμεν;

ΜΕΝ. Οὐκ ἔμοιγε δοκεῖ.

ΣΩ. Προὔργου γοῦν τι πεποιήκαμεν, ὡς ἔοικε, πρὸς τὸ ἐξευρεῖν ὅπη ἔχει· νῦν μὲν γὰρ καὶ ζητή-σειεν ἂν ἡδέως οὐκ εἰδώς, τότε δὲ ῥᾳδίως ἂν καὶ πρὸς πολλοὺς καὶ πολλάκις ᾤετ' ἂν εὖ λέγειν περὶ
C τοῦ διπλασίου χωρίου, ὡς δεῖ διπλασίαν τὴν γραμ-μὴν ἔχειν μήκει.

BOY. Eight.

SOC. So we fail to get our eight-foot figure from this three-foot line.

BOY. Yes, indeed.

SOC. But from what line shall we get it? Try and tell us exactly; and if you would rather not reckon it out, just show what line it is.

BOY. Well, on my word, Socrates, I for one do not know.

SOC. There now, Meno, do you observe what progress he has already made in his recollection? At first he did not know what is the line that forms the figure of eight feet, and he does not know even now: but at any rate he thought he knew then, and confidently answered as though he knew, and was aware of no difficulty; whereas now he feels the difficulty he is in, and besides not knowing does not think he knows.

MEN. That is true.

SOC. And is he not better off in respect of the matter which he did not know?

MEN. I think that too is so.

SOC. Now, by causing him to doubt and giving him the torpedo's shock, have we done him any harm?

MEN. I think not.

SOC. And we have certainly given him some assistance, it would seem, towards finding out the truth of the matter: for now he will push on in the search gladly, as lacking knowledge; whereas then he would have been only too ready to suppose he was right in saying, before any number of people any number of times, that the double space must have a line of double the length for its side.

PLATO

ΜΕΝ. Ἔοικεν.

ΣΩ. Οἴει οὖν ἂν αὐτὸν πρότερον ἐπιχειρῆσαι ζητεῖν ἢ μανθάνειν τοῦτο, ὃ ᾤετο εἰδέναι οὐκ εἰδώς, πρὶν εἰς ἀπορίαν κατέπεσεν ἡγησάμενος μὴ εἰδέναι, καὶ ἐπόθησε τὸ εἰδέναι;

ΜΕΝ. Οὔ μοι δοκεῖ, ὦ Σώκρατες.

ΣΩ. Ὤνητο ἄρα ναρκήσας;

ΜΕΝ. Δοκεῖ μοι.

ΣΩ. Σκέψαι δὴ ἐκ ταύτης τῆς ἀπορίας ὅ τι καὶ ἀνευρήσει ζητῶν μετ᾽ ἐμοῦ, οὐδὲν ἀλλ᾽ ἢ ἐρωτῶντος D ἐμοῦ καὶ οὐ διδάσκοντος· φύλαττε δὲ ἂν πού εὕρῃς με διδάσκοντα καὶ διεξιόντα αὐτῷ, ἀλλὰ μὴ τὰς τούτου δόξας ἀνερωτῶντα.

Λέγε γάρ μοι σύ· οὐ τὸ μὲν τετράπουν τοῦτο ἡμῖν ἐστὶ χωρίον; μανθάνεις;

ΠΑΙΣ. Ἔγωγε.

ΣΩ. Ἕτερον δὲ αὐτῷ προσθεῖμεν ἂν τουτὶ ἴσον;

ΠΑΙΣ. Ναί.

ΣΩ. Καὶ τρίτον τόδε ἴσον ἑκατέρῳ τούτων;

ΠΑΙΣ. Ναί.

ΣΩ. Οὐκοῦν προσαναπληρωσαίμεθ᾽ ἂν τὸ ἐν τῇ γωνίᾳ τόδε;

ΠΑΙΣ. Πάνυ γε.

ΣΩ. Ἄλλο τι οὖν γένοιτ᾽ ἂν τέτταρα ἴσα χωρία τάδε;

E ΠΑΙΣ. Ναί.

MENO

MEN. It seems so.

SOC. Now do you imagine he would have attempted to inquire or learn what he thought he knew, when he did not know it, until he had been reduced to the perplexity of realizing that he did not know, and had felt a craving to know ?

MEN. I think not, Socrates.

SOC. Then the torpedo's shock was of advantage to him ?

MEN. I think so.

SOC. Now you should note how, as a result of this perplexity, he will go on and discover something by joint inquiry with me, while I merely ask questions and do not teach him ; and be on the watch to see if at any point you find me teaching him or expounding to him, instead of questioning him on his opinions.

Tell me, boy : here we have a square of four feet,[1] have we not ? You understand ?

BOY. Yes.

SOC. And here we add another square[2] equal to it ?

BOY. Yes.

SOC. And here a third,[3] equal to either of them ?

BOY. Yes.

SOC. Now shall we fill up this vacant space[4] in the corner ?

BOY. By all means.

SOC. So here we must have four equal spaces ?

BOY. Yes.

1 ABCD. 2 DCFE.
3 CHGF. 4 BIHC.

ΣΩ. Τί οὖν; τὸ ὅλον τόδε ποσαπλάσιον τοῦδε γίγνεται;

ΠΑΙΣ. Τετραπλάσιον.

ΣΩ. Ἔδει δὲ διπλάσιον ἡμῖν γενέσθαι· ἢ οὐ μέμνησαι;

ΠΑΙΣ. Πάνυ γε.

ΣΩ. Οὐκοῦν ἐστιν αὕτη γραμμὴ ἐκ γωνίας εἰς
85 γωνίαν τείνουσα, τέμνουσα δίχα ἕκαστον τούτων τῶν χωρίων;

ΠΑΙΣ. Ναί.

ΣΩ. Οὐκοῦν τέτταρες αὗται γίγνονται γραμμαὶ ἴσαι, περιέχουσαι τουτὶ τὸ χωρίον;

ΠΑΙΣ. Γίγνονται γάρ.

ΣΩ. Σκόπει δή· πηλίκον τί ἐστι τοῦτο τὸ χωρίον;

ΠΑΙΣ. Οὐ μανθάνω.

ΣΩ. Οὐχὶ τεττάρων ὄντων τούτων ἥμισυ ἑκά-στου ἑκάστη ἡ γραμμὴ ἀποτέτμηκεν ἐντός; ἢ οὔ;

ΠΑΙΣ. Ναί.

ΣΩ. Πόσα οὖν τηλικαῦτα ἐν τούτῳ ἔνεστιν;

ΠΑΙΣ. Τέτταρα.

ΣΩ. Πόσα δὲ ἐν τῷδε;

ΠΑΙΣ. Δύο.

ΣΩ. Τὰ δὲ τέτταρα τοῖν δυοῖν τί ἐστιν;

ΠΑΙΣ. Διπλάσια.

B ΣΩ. Τόδε οὖν ποσάπουν γίγνεται;

ΠΑΙΣ. Ὀκτώπουν.

ΣΩ. Ἀπὸ ποίας γραμμῆς;

ΠΑΙΣ. Ἀπὸ ταύτης.

ΣΩ. Ἀπὸ τῆς ἐκ γωνίας εἰς γωνίαν τεινούσης τοῦ τετράποδος;

ΠΑΙΣ. Ναί.

soc. Well now, how many times larger is this whole space than this other?

boy. Four times.

soc. But it was to have been only twice, you remember?

boy. To be sure.

soc. And does this line,[1] drawn from corner to corner, cut in two each of these spaces?

boy. Yes.

soc. And have we here four equal lines[2] containing this space[3]?

boy. We have.

soc. Now consider how large this space[3] is.

boy. I do not understand.

soc. Has not each of the inside lines cut off half of each of these four spaces?

boy. Yes.

soc. And how many spaces of that size are there in this part?

boy. Four.

soc. And how many in this[4]?

boy. Two.

soc. And four is how many times two?

boy. Twice.

soc. And how many feet is this space[5]?

boy. Eight feet.

soc. From what line do we get this figure?

boy. From this.

soc. From the line drawn corner-wise across the four-foot figure?

boy. Yes.

---

[1] BD.   [2] BD, DF, FH, HB.   [3] BDFH.
[4] ABCD.   [5] BDFH.

ΣΩ. Καλοῦσι δέ γε ταύτην διάμετρον οἱ σοφισταί· ὥστ' εἰ ταύτῃ διάμετρος ὄνομα, ἀπὸ τῆς διαμέτρου ἄν, ὡς σὺ φῄς, ὦ παῖ Μένωνος, γίγνοιτ' ἂν τὸ διπλάσιον χωρίον.

ΠΑΙΣ. Πάνυ μὲν οὖν, ὦ Σώκρατες.

ΣΩ. Τί σοι δοκεῖ, ὦ Μένων; ἔστιν ἥντινα δόξαν οὐχ αὑτοῦ οὗτος ἀπεκρίνατο;

C   ΜΕΝ. Οὔκ, ἀλλ' ἑαυτοῦ.

ΣΩ. Καὶ μὴν οὐκ ᾔδει γε, ὡς ἔφαμεν ὀλίγον πρότερον.

ΜΕΝ. Ἀληθῆ λέγεις.

ΣΩ. Ἐνῆσαν δέ γε αὐτῷ αὗται αἱ δόξαι· ἢ οὔ;

ΜΕΝ. Ναί.

ΣΩ. Τῷ οὐκ εἰδότι ἄρα περὶ ὧν ἂν μὴ εἰδῇ ἔνεισιν ἀληθεῖς δόξαι περὶ τούτων ὧν οὐκ οἶδεν;

ΜΕΝ. Φαίνεται.

ΣΩ. Καὶ νῦν μέν γε αὐτῷ ὥσπερ ὄναρ ἄρτι ἀνακεκίνηνται αἱ δόξαι αὗται· εἰ δὲ αὐτόν τις ἀνερήσεται πολλάκις τὰ αὐτὰ ταῦτα καὶ πολλαχῇ, οἶσθ' ὅτι τελευτῶν οὐδενὸς ἧττον ἀκριβῶς ἐπι-
D στήσεται περὶ τούτων.

ΜΕΝ. Ἔοικεν.

ΣΩ. Οὐκοῦν οὐδενὸς διδάξαντος ἀλλ' ἐρωτήσαντος ἐπιστήσεται, ἀναλαβὼν αὐτὸς ἐξ αὑτοῦ τὴν ἐπιστήμην;

ΜΕΝ. Ναί.

ΣΩ. Τὸ δὲ ἀναλαμβάνειν αὐτὸν ἐν αὑτῷ ἐπιστήμην οὐκ ἀναμιμνήσκεσθαί ἐστιν;

ΜΕΝ. Πάνυ γε.

ΣΩ. Ἆρ' οὖν οὐ τὴν ἐπιστήμην, ἣν νῦν οὗτος ἔχει, ἤτοι ἔλαβέ ποτε ἢ ἀεὶ εἶχεν

ΜΕΝ. Ναί.

soc. The professors call it the diagonal : so if the diagonal is its name, then according to you, Meno's boy, the double space is the square of the diagonal.

boy. Yes, certainly it is, Socrates.

soc. What do you think, Meno ? Was there any opinion that he did not give as an answer of his own thought ?

men. No, they were all his own.

soc. But you see, he did not know, as we were saying a while since.

men. That is true.

soc. Yet he had in him these opinions, had he not ?

men. Yes.

soc. So that he who does not know about any matters, whatever they be, may have true opinions on such matters, about which he knows nothing ?

men. Apparently.

soc. And at this moment those opinions have just been stirred up in him, like a dream ; but if he were repeatedly asked these same questions in a variety of forms, you know he will have in the end as exact an understanding of them as anyone.

men. So it seems.

soc. Without anyone having taught him, and only through questions put to him, he will understand, recovering the knowledge out of himself ?

men. Yes.

soc. And is not this recovery of knowledge, in himself and by himself, recollection ?

men. Certainly.

soc. And must he not have either once acquired or always had the knowledge he now has ?

men. Yes.

ΣΩ. Οὐκοῦν εἰ μὲν ἀεὶ εἶχεν, ἀεὶ καὶ ἦν ἐπιστήμων· εἰ δὲ ἔλαβέ ποτε, οὐκ ἂν ἔν γε τῷ νῦν βίῳ
E εἰληφὼς εἴη. ἢ δεδίδαχέ τις τοῦτον γεωμετρεῖν; οὗτος γὰρ ποιήσει περὶ πάσης γεωμετρίας ταὐτὰ ταῦτα, καὶ τῶν ἄλλων μαθημάτων ἁπάντων. ἔστιν οὖν ὅστις τοῦτον πάντα δεδίδαχε; δίκαιος γάρ που εἶ εἰδέναι, ἄλλως τε ἐπειδὴ ἐν τῇ σῇ οἰκίᾳ γέγονε καὶ τέθραπται.

ΜΕΝ. Ἀλλ᾽ οἶδα ἔγωγε ὅτι οὐδεὶς πώποτε ἐδίδαξεν.

ΣΩ. Ἔχει δὲ ταύτας τὰς δόξας, ἢ οὐχί;

ΜΕΝ. Ἀνάγκη, ὦ Σώκρατες, φαίνεται.

ΣΩ. Εἰ δὲ μὴ ἐν τῷ νῦν βίῳ λαβών, οὐκ ἤδη
86 τοῦτο δῆλον, ὅτι ἐν ἄλλῳ τινὶ χρόνῳ εἶχε καὶ ἐμεμαθήκει;

ΜΕΝ. Φαίνεται.

ΣΩ. Οὐκοῦν οὗτός γέ ἐστιν ὁ χρόνος, ὅτ᾽ οὐκ ἦν ἄνθρωπος;

ΜΕΝ. Ναί.

ΣΩ. Εἰ οὖν ὅν τ᾽ ἂν¹ ᾖ χρόνον καὶ ὃν ἂν μὴ ᾖ ἄνθρωπος, ἐνέσονται αὐτῷ ἀληθεῖς δόξαι, αἳ ἐρωτήσει ἐπεγερθεῖσαι ἐπιστῆμαι γίγνονται, ἆρ᾽ οὖν τὸν ἀεὶ χρόνον μεμαθηκυῖα ἔσται ἡ ψυχὴ αὐτοῦ; δῆλον γὰρ ὅτι τὸν πάντα χρόνον ἔστιν ἢ οὐκ ἔστιν ἄνθρωπος.

ΜΕΝ. Φαίνεται.

ΣΩ. Οὐκοῦν εἰ ἀεὶ ἡ ἀλήθεια ἡμῖν τῶν ὄντων
B ἐστὶν ἐν τῇ ψυχῇ, ἀθάνατος ἂν ἡ ψυχὴ εἴη, ὥστε θαρροῦντα χρή, ὃ μὴ τυγχάνεις ἐπιστάμενος νῦν, τοῦτο δ᾽ ἐστὶν ὃ μὴ μεμνημένος, ἐπιχειρεῖν ζητεῖν καὶ ἀναμιμνήσκεσθαι;

¹ ὅν τ᾽ ἂν Baiter: ὅταν, ὅτ᾽ ἂν MSS.

soc. Now if he always had it, he was always in a state of knowing; and if he acquired it at some time, he could not have acquired it in this life. Or has someone taught him geometry? You see, he can do the same as this with all geometry and every branch of knowledge. Now, can anyone have taught him all this? You ought surely to know, especially as he was born and bred in your house.

MEN. Well, I know that no one has ever taught him.

soc. And has he these opinions, or has he not?

MEN. He must have them, Socrates, evidently.

soc. And if he did not acquire them in this present life, is it not obvious at once that he had them and learnt them during some other time?

MEN. Apparently.

soc. And this must have been the time when he was not a human being?

MEN. Yes.

soc. So if in both of these periods—when he was and was not a human being—he has had true opinions in him which have only to be awakened by questioning to become knowledge, his soul must have had this cognisance throughout all time? For clearly he has always either been or not been a human being.

MEN. Evidently.

soc. And if the truth of all things that are is always in our soul, then the soul must be immortal; so that you should take heart and, whatever you do not happen to know at present—that is, what you do not remember—you must endeavour to search out and recollect?

ΜΕΝ. Εὖ μοι δοκεῖς λέγειν, ὦ Σώκρατες, οὐκ οἶδ' ὅπως.

ΣΩ. Καὶ γὰρ ἐγὼ ἐμοί, ὦ Μένων. καὶ τὰ μέν γε ἄλλα οὐκ ἂν πάνυ ὑπὲρ τοῦ λόγου διισχυρισαίμην· ὅτι δ' οἰόμενοι δεῖν ζητεῖν, ἃ μή τις οἶδε, βελτίους ἂν εἶμεν καὶ ἀνδρικώτεροι καὶ ἧττον ἀργοὶ ἢ εἰ οἰοίμεθα, ἃ μὴ ἐπιστάμεθα, μηδὲ δυνατὸν εἶναι C εὑρεῖν μηδὲ δεῖν ζητεῖν, περὶ τούτου πάνυ ἂν δια- μαχοίμην, εἰ οἷός τε εἴην, καὶ λόγῳ καὶ ἔργῳ.

ΜΕΝ. Καὶ τοῦτο μέν γε δοκεῖς μοι εὖ λέγειν, ὦ Σώκρατες.

ΣΩ. Βούλει οὖν, ἐπειδὴ ὁμονοοῦμεν, ὅτι ζη- τητέον περὶ οὗ μή τις οἶδεν, ἐπιχειρήσωμεν κοινῇ ζητεῖν τί ποτ' ἔστιν ἀρετή;

ΜΕΝ. Πάνυ μὲν οὖν. οὐ μέντοι, ὦ Σώκρατες, ἀλλ' ἔγωγε ἐκεῖνο ἂν ἥδιστα, ὅπερ ἠρόμην τὸ πρῶτον, καὶ σκεψαίμην καὶ ἀκούσαιμι, πότερον ὡς διδακτῷ ὄντι αὐτῷ δεῖ ἐπιχειρεῖν, ἢ ὡς φύσει D ἢ ὡς τίνι ποτὲ τρόπῳ παραγιγνομένης τοῖς ἀνθρώ- ποις τῆς ἀρετῆς.

ΣΩ. Ἀλλ' εἰ μὲν ἐγὼ ἦρχον, ὦ Μένων, μὴ μόνον ἐμαυτοῦ ἀλλὰ καὶ σοῦ, οὐκ ἂν ἐσκεψάμεθα πρότερον εἴτε διδακτὸν εἴτε οὐ διδακτὸν ἡ ἀρετή, πρὶν ὅ τι ἔστι πρῶτον ἐζητήσαμεν αὐτό· ἐπειδὴ δὲ σὺ σαυτοῦ μὲν οὐδ' ἐπιχειρεῖς ἄρχειν, ἵνα δὴ ἐλεύθερος ᾖς, ἐμοῦ δὲ ἐπιχειρεῖς τε ἄρχειν καὶ ἄρχεις, συγχωρήσομαί σοι· τί γὰρ χρὴ ποιεῖν; E ἔοικεν οὖν σκεπτέον εἶναι, ποῖόν τί ἐστιν ὃ μήπω

---

[1] Socrates characteristically pretends to be at the mercy of the wayward young man.

MENO

MEN. What you say commends itself to me, Socrates, I know not how.

soc. And so it does to me, Meno. Most of the points I have made in support of my argument are not such as I can confidently assert; but that the belief in the duty of inquiring after what we do not know will make us better and braver and less helpless than the notion that there is not even a possibility of discovering what we do not know, nor any duty of inquiring after it—this is a point for which I am determined to do battle, so far as I am able, both in word and deed.

MEN. There also I consider that you speak aright, Socrates.

soc. Then since we are of one mind as to the duty of inquiring into what one does not know, do you agree to our attempting a joint inquiry into the nature of virtue?

MEN. By all means. But still, Socrates, for my part I would like best of all to examine that question I asked at first, and hear your view as to whether in pursuing it we are to regard it as a thing to be taught, or as a gift of nature to mankind, or as arriving to them in some other way which I should be glad to know.

soc. Had I control over you, Meno, as over myself, we should not have begun considering whether virtue can or cannot be taught until we had first inquired into the main question of what it is. But as you do not so much as attempt to control yourself—you are so fond of your liberty— and both attempt and hold control over me,[1] I will yield to your request—what else am I to do? So it seems we are to consider what sort of thing it is of

323

ἴσμεν ὅ τι ἔστιν. εἰ μή τι οὖν ἀλλὰ σμικρόν γέ
μοι τῆς ἀρχῆς χάλασον, καὶ συγχώρησον ἐξ ὑποθέσεως αὐτὸ σκοπεῖσθαι, εἴτε διδακτόν ἐστιν εἴτε
ὁπωσοῦν. λέγω δὲ τὸ ἐξ ὑποθέσεως ὧδε, ὥσπερ
οἱ γεωμέτραι πολλάκις σκοποῦνται, ἐπειδάν τις
ἔρηται αὐτούς, οἷον περὶ χωρίου, εἰ οἷόν τε ἐς
87 τόνδε τὸν κύκλον τόδε τὸ χωρίον τρίγωνον ἐν-
ταθῆναι, εἴποι ἄν τις ὅτι οὔπω οἶδα εἰ ἔστι τοῦτο
τοιοῦτον, ἀλλ' ὥσπερ μέν τινα ὑπόθεσιν προὔργου
οἶμαι ἔχειν πρὸς τὸ πρᾶγμα τοιάνδε. εἰ μέν
ἐστι τοῦτο τὸ χωρίον τοιοῦτον, οἷον παρὰ τὴν
δοθεῖσαν αὐτοῦ γραμμὴν παρατείναντα ἐλλείπειν
τοιούτῳ χωρίῳ, οἷον ἂν αὐτὸ τὸ παρατεταμένον
ᾖ, ἄλλο τι συμβαίνειν μοι δοκεῖ, καὶ ἄλλο αὖ, εἰ
ἀδύνατόν ἐστι ταῦτα παθεῖν· ὑποθέμενος οὖν
ἐθέλω εἰπεῖν σοι τὸ συμβαῖνον περὶ τῆς ἐντάσεως
B αὐτοῦ εἰς τὸν κύκλον, εἴτε ἀδύνατον εἴτε μή.
οὕτω δὴ καὶ περὶ ἀρετῆς ἡμεῖς, ἐπειδὴ οὐκ ἴσμεν
οὔθ' ὅ τί ἐστιν οὔθ' ὁποῖόν τι, ὑποθέμενοι αὐτὸ
σκοπῶμεν εἴτε διδακτὸν εἴτε οὐ διδακτόν ἐστιν,
ὧδε λέγοντες· εἰ ποῖόν τί ἐστι τῶν περὶ τὴν
ψυχὴν ὄντων ἀρετή, διδακτὸν ἂν εἴη ἢ οὐ διδακτόν;
πρῶτον μὲν εἰ ἔστιν ἀλλοῖον ἢ οἷον ἐπιστήμη,

which we do not yet know what it is ! Well, the least you can do is to relax just a little of your authority, and allow the question — whether virtue comes by teaching or some other way—to be examined by means of hypothesis. I mean by hypothesis what the geometricians often do in dealing with a question put to them ; for example, whether a certain area is capable of being inscribed as a triangular space in a given circle : they reply— " I cannot yet tell whether it has that capability ; but I think, if I may put it so, that I have a certain helpful hypothesis for the problem, and it is as follows : If this area[1] is such that when you apply it to the given line [2] of the circle you find it falls short [3] by a space similar to that which you have just applied, then I take it you have one conse- quence, and if it is impossible for it to fall so, then some other. Accordingly I wish to put a hypothesis, before I state our conclusion as regards inscribing this figure in the circle by saying whether it is im- possible or not." In the same way with regard to our question about virtue, since we do not know either what it is or what kind of thing it may be, we had best make use of a hypothesis in considering whether it can be taught or not, as thus : what kind of thing must virtue be in the class of mental properties, so as to be teachable or not ? In the first place, if it is something

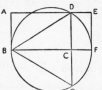

[1] The problem seems to be that of inscribing in a circle a triangle (BDG) equal in area to a given rectangle (ABCD).

[2] *i.e.* the diameter (BF).

[3] *i.e.* falls short of the rectangle on the diameter (ABFE).

ἆρα διδακτὸν ἢ οὔ, ἢ ὃ νῦν δὴ ἐλέγομεν, ἀναμνηστόν·
διαφερέτω δὲ μηδὲν ἡμῖν ὁποτέρῳ ἂν τῷ ὀνόματι
C χρώμεθα· ἀλλ᾽ ἆρα διδακτόν; ἢ τοῦτό γε παντὶ
δῆλον, ὅτι οὐδὲν ἄλλο διδάσκεται ἄνθρωπος ἢ
ἐπιστήμην;

ΜΕΝ. Ἔμοιγε δοκεῖ.

ΣΩ. Εἰ δέ γ᾽ ἐστὶν ἐπιστήμη τις ἡ ἀρετή, δῆλον
ὅτι διδακτὸν ἂν εἴη.

ΜΕΝ. Πῶς γὰρ οὔ;

ΣΩ. Τούτου μὲν ἄρα ταχὺ ἀπηλλάγμεθα, ὅτι
τοιοῦδε μὲν ὄντος διδακτόν, τοιοῦδε δ᾽ οὔ.

ΜΕΝ. Πάνυ γε.

ΣΩ. Τὸ δὴ μετὰ τοῦτο, ὡς ἔοικε, δεῖ σκέψασθαι,
πότερόν ἐστιν ἐπιστήμη ἡ ἀρετὴ ἢ ἀλλοῖον ἐπιστήμης.

D ΜΕΝ. Ἔμοιγε δοκεῖ τοῦτο μετὰ τοῦτο σκεπτέον
εἶναι.

ΣΩ. Τί δὲ δή; ἄλλο τι ἢ ἀγαθὸν αὐτό φαμεν
εἶναι τὴν ἀρετήν, καὶ αὕτη ἡ ὑπόθεσις μένει ἡμῖν,
ἀγαθὸν αὐτὸ εἶναι;

ΜΕΝ. Πάνυ μὲν οὖν.

ΣΩ. Οὐκοῦν εἰ μέν τί ἐστιν ἀγαθὸν καὶ ἄλλο
χωριζόμενον ἐπιστήμης, τάχ᾽ ἂν εἴη ἡ ἀρετὴ οὐκ
ἐπιστήμη τις· εἰ δὲ μηδέν ἐστιν ἀγαθόν, ὃ οὐκ
ἐπιστήμη περιέχει, ἐπιστήμην ἄν τιν᾽ αὐτὸ ὑπ-
οπτεύοντες εἶναι ὀρθῶς ὑποπτεύοιμεν.

ΜΕΝ. Ἔστι ταῦτα.

ΣΩ. Καὶ μὴν ἀρετῇ γ᾽ ἐσμὲν ἀγαθοί;

ΜΕΝ. Ναί.

E ΣΩ. Εἰ δὲ ἀγαθοί, ὠφέλιμοι· πάντα γὰρ ἀγαθὰ
ὠφέλιμα. οὐχί;

ΜΕΝ. Ναί.

dissimilar or similar to knowledge, is it taught or not—or, as we were saying just now, remembered? Let us have no disputing about the choice of a name: is it taught? Or is not this fact plain to everyone —that the one and only thing taught to men is knowledge?

MEN. I agree to that.

SOC. Then if virtue is a kind of knowledge, clearly it must be taught?

MEN. Certainly.

SOC. So you see we have made short work of this question—if virtue belongs to one class of things it is teachable, and if to another, it is not.

MEN. To be sure.

SOC. The next question, it would seem, that we have to consider is whether virtue is knowledge, or of another kind than knowledge.

MEN. I should say that is the next thing we have to consider.

SOC. Well now, surely we call virtue a good thing, do we not, and our hypothesis stands, that it is good?

MEN. Certainly we do.

SOC. Then if there is some good apart and separable from knowledge, it may be that virtue is not a kind of knowledge; but if there is nothing good that is not embraced by knowledge, our suspicion that virtue is a kind of knowledge would be well founded.

MEN. Quite so.

SOC. Now it is by virtue that we are good?

MEN. Yes.

SOC. And if good, profitable; for all good things are profitable, are they not?

MEN. Yes.

ΣΩ. Καὶ ἡ ἀρετὴ δὴ ὠφέλιμόν ἐστιν;

ΜΕΝ. Ἀνάγκη ἐκ τῶν ὡμολογημένων.

ΣΩ. Σκεψώμεθα δὴ καθ᾽ ἕκαστον ἀναλαμ-
βάνοντες, ποῖά ἐστιν ἃ ἡμᾶς ὠφελεῖ. ὑγίεια,
φαμέν, καὶ ἰσχὺς καὶ κάλλος καὶ πλοῦτος δή·
ταῦτα λέγομεν καὶ τὰ τοιαῦτα ὠφέλιμα. οὐχί;

ΜΕΝ. Ναί.

88   ΣΩ. Ταὐτὰ δὲ ταῦτά φαμεν ἐνίοτε καὶ βλάπτειν·
ἢ σὺ ἄλλως φῂς ἢ οὕτως;

ΜΕΝ. Οὔκ, ἀλλ᾽ οὕτως.

ΣΩ. Σκόπει δή, ὅταν τί ἑκάστου τούτων
ἡγῆται, ὠφελεῖ ἡμᾶς, καὶ ὅταν τί, βλάπτει; ἆρ᾽ οὐχ
ὅταν μὲν ὀρθὴ χρῆσις, ὠφελεῖ, ὅταν δὲ μή, βλάπτει;

ΜΕΝ. Πάνυ γε.

ΣΩ. Ἔτι τοίνυν καὶ τὰ κατὰ τὴν ψυχὴν σκεψώμεθα. σωφροσύνην τι καλεῖς καὶ δικαιοσύνην
καὶ ἀνδρείαν καὶ εὐμαθίαν καὶ μνήμην καὶ μεγαλο-
πρέπειαν καὶ πάντα τὰ τοιαῦτα;

B   ΜΕΝ. Ἔγωγε.

ΣΩ. Σκόπει δή, τούτων ἄττα σοι δοκεῖ μὴ
ἐπιστήμη εἶναι ἀλλ᾽ ἄλλο ἐπιστήμης, εἰ οὐχὶ τοτὲ
μὲν βλάπτει, τοτὲ δὲ ὠφελεῖ· οἷον ἀνδρεία, εἰ μὴ
ἔστι φρόνησις ἡ ἀνδρεία ἀλλ᾽ οἷον θάρρος τι· οὐχ
ὅταν μὲν ἄνευ νοῦ θαρρῇ ἄνθρωπος, βλάπτεται,
ὅταν δὲ σὺν νῷ, ὠφελεῖται;

ΜΕΝ. Ναί.

ΣΩ. Οὐκοῦν καὶ σωφροσύνη ὡσαύτως καὶ εὐ-
μαθία· μετὰ μὲν νοῦ καὶ μανθανόμενα καὶ κατ-
αρτυόμενα ὠφέλιμα, ἄνευ δὲ νοῦ βλαβερά;

soc. So virtue is profitable ?

MEN. That must follow from what has been admitted.

soc. Then let us see, in particular instances, what sort of things they are that profit us. Health, let us say, and strength, and beauty, and wealth— these and their like we call profitable, do we not ?

MEN. Yes.

soc. But these same things, we admit, actually harm us at times ; or do you dispute that statement ?

MEN. No, I agree.

soc. Consider now, what is the guiding condition in each case that makes them at one time profitable, and at another harmful. Are they not profitable when the use of them is right, and harmful when it is not ?

MEN. To be sure.

soc. Then let us consider next the goods of the soul : by these you understand temperance, justice, courage, intelligence, memory, magnanimity, and so forth ?

MEN. Yes.

soc. Now tell me ; such of these as you think are not knowledge, but different from knowledge—do they not sometimes harm us, and sometimes profit us ? For example, courage, if it is courage apart from prudence, and only a sort of boldness : when a man is bold without sense, he is harmed ; but when he has sense at the same time, he is profited, is he not ?

MEN. Yes.

soc. And the same holds of temperance and intelligence : things learnt and co-ordinated with the aid of sense are profitable, but without sense they are harmful ?

88

C   ΜΕΝ. Πάνυ σφόδρα.

ΣΩ. Οὐκοῦν συλλήβδην πάντα τὰ τῆς ψυχῆς ἐπιχειρήματα καὶ καρτερήματα ἡγουμένης μὲν φρονήσεως εἰς εὐδαιμονίαν τελευτᾷ, ἀφροσύνης δ᾽ εἰς τοὐναντίον;

ΜΕΝ. Ἔοικεν.

ΣΩ. Εἰ ἄρα ἀρετὴ τῶν ἐν τῇ ψυχῇ τί ἐστι καὶ ἀναγκαῖον αὐτῷ ὠφελίμῳ εἶναι, φρόνησιν αὐτὸ δεῖ εἶναι, ἐπειδήπερ πάντα τὰ κατὰ τὴν ψυχὴν αὐτὰ μὲν καθ᾽ αὑτὰ οὔτε ὠφέλιμα οὔτε βλαβερά ἐστι, προσγενομένης δὲ φρονήσεως ἢ ἀφροσύνης

D βλαβερά τε καὶ ὠφέλιμα γίγνεται. κατὰ δὴ τοῦτον τὸν λόγον ὠφέλιμόν γε οὖσαν τὴν ἀρετὴν φρόνησιν δεῖ τιν᾽ εἶναι.

ΜΕΝ. Ἔμοιγε δοκεῖ.

ΣΩ. Καὶ μὲν δὴ καὶ τἆλλα, ἃ νῦν δὴ ἐλέγομεν, πλοῦτόν τε καὶ τὰ τοιαῦτα, τοτὲ μὲν ἀγαθὰ τοτὲ δὲ βλαβερὰ εἶναι, ἆρ᾽ οὐχ ὥσπερ τῇ ἄλλῃ ψυχῇ ἡ φρόνησις ἡγουμένη ὠφέλιμα τὰ τῆς ψυχῆς ἐποίει,

E ἡ δὲ ἀφροσύνη βλαβερά, οὕτως αὖ καὶ τούτοις ἡ ψυχὴ ὀρθῶς μὲν χρωμένη καὶ ἡγουμένη ὠφέλιμα αὐτὰ ποιεῖ, μὴ ὀρθῶς δὲ βλαβερά;

ΜΕΝ. Πάνυ γε.

ΣΩ. Ὀρθῶς δέ γε ἡ ἔμφρων ἡγεῖται, ἡμαρτημένως δ᾽ ἡ ἄφρων;

ΜΕΝ. Ἔστι ταῦτα.

ΣΩ. Οὐκοῦν οὕτω δὴ κατὰ πάντων εἰπεῖν ἔστι, τῷ ἀνθρώπῳ τὰ μὲν ἄλλα πάντα εἰς τὴν ψυχὴν ἀνηρτῆσθαι, τὰ δὲ τῆς ψυχῆς αὐτῆς εἰς

89 φρόνησιν, εἰ μέλλει ἀγαθὰ εἶναι· καὶ τούτῳ τῷ λόγῳ φρόνησις ἂν εἴη τὸ ὠφέλιμον· φαμὲν δὲ τὴν ἀρετὴν ὠφέλιμον εἶναι;

MENO

MEN. Most certainly.

SOC. And in brief, all the undertakings and endurances of the soul, when guided by wisdom, end in happiness, but when folly guides, in the opposite ?

MEN. So it seems.

SOC. Then if virtue is something that is in the soul, and must needs be profitable, it ought to be wisdom, seeing that all the properties of the soul are in themselves neither profitable nor harmful, but are made either one or the other by the addition of wisdom or folly ; and hence, by this argument, virtue being profitable must be a sort of wisdom.

MEN. I agree.

SOC. Then as to the other things, wealth and the like, that we mentioned just now as being sometimes good and sometimes harmful—are not these also made profitable or harmful by the soul according as she uses and guides them rightly or wrongly : just as, in the case of the soul generally, we found that the guidance of wisdom makes profitable the properties of the soul, while that of folly makes them harmful ?

MEN. Certainly.

SOC. And the wise soul guides rightly, and the foolish erroneously ?

MEN. That is so.

SOC. Then may we assert this as a universal rule, that in man all other things depend upon the soul, while the things of the soul herself depend upon wisdom, if they are to be good ; and so by this account the profitable will be wisdom, and virtue, we say, is profitable ?

ΜΕΝ. Πάνυ γε.

ΣΩ. Φρόνησιν ἄρα φαμὲν ἀρετὴν εἶναι, ἤτοι σύμπασαν ἢ μέρος τι;

ΜΕΝ. Δοκεῖ μοι καλῶς λέγεσθαι, ὦ Σώκρατες, τὰ λεγόμενα.

ΣΩ. Οὐκοῦν εἰ ταῦτα οὕτως ἔχει, οὐκ ἂν εἶεν φύσει οἱ ἀγαθοί.

ΜΕΝ. Οὔ μοι δοκεῖ.

B ΣΩ. Καὶ γὰρ ἄν που καὶ τόδ' ἦν· εἰ φύσει οἱ ἀγαθοὶ ἐγίγνοντο, ἦσάν που ἂν ἡμῖν οἳ ἐγίγνωσκον τῶν νέων τοὺς ἀγαθοὺς τὰς φύσεις, οὓς ἡμεῖς ἂν παραλαβόντες ἐκείνων ἀποφηνάντων ἐφυλάττομεν ἐν ἀκροπόλει, κατασημηνάμενοι πολὺ μᾶλλον ἢ τὸ χρυσίον, ἵνα μηδεὶς αὐτοὺς διέφθειρεν, ἀλλ' ἐπειδὴ ἀφίκοιντο εἰς τὴν ἡλικίαν, χρήσιμοι γίγνοιντο ταῖς πόλεσιν.

ΜΕΝ. Εἰκός γέ τοι, ὦ Σώκρατες.

ΣΩ. Ἆρ' οὖν ἐπειδὴ οὐ φύσει οἱ ἀγαθοὶ ἀγαθοὶ C γίγνονται, ἆρα μαθήσει;

ΜΕΝ. Δοκεῖ μοι ἤδη ἀναγκαῖον εἶναι· καὶ δῆλον, ὦ Σώκρατες, κατὰ τὴν ὑπόθεσιν, εἴπερ ἐπιστήμη ἐστὶν ἀρετή, ὅτι διδακτόν ἐστιν.

ΣΩ. Ἴσως νὴ Δία· ἀλλὰ μὴ τοῦτο οὐ καλῶς ὡμολογήσαμεν;

ΜΕΝ. Καὶ μὴν ἐδόκει γε ἄρτι καλῶς λέγεσθαι.

ΣΩ. Ἀλλὰ μὴ οὐκ ἐν τῷ ἄρτι μόνον δέῃ αὐτὸ δοκεῖν καλῶς λέγεσθαι, ἀλλὰ καὶ ἐν τῷ νῦν καὶ ἐν τῷ ἔπειτα, εἰ μέλλει τι αὐτοῦ ὑγιὲς εἶναι.

D ΜΕΝ. Τί οὖν δή; πρὸς τί βλέπων δυσχεραίνεις αὐτὸ καὶ ἀπιστεῖς μὴ οὐκ ἐπιστήμη ᾖ ἡ ἀρετή;

MEN. Certainly.

soc. Hence we conclude that virtue is either wholly or partly wisdom ?

MEN. It seems to me that your statement, Socrates, is excellent.

soc. Then if this is so, good men cannot be good by nature.

MEN. I think not.

soc. No, for then, I presume, we should have had this result : if good men were so by nature, we surely should have had men able to discern who of the young were good by nature, and on their pointing them out we should have taken them over and kept them safe in the citadel, having set our mark on them far rather than on our gold treasure, in order that none might have tampered with them, and that when they came to be of age, they might be useful to their country.

MEN. Yes, most likely, Socrates.

soc. So since it is not by nature that the good become good, is it by education ?

MEN. We must now conclude, I think, that it is ; and plainly, Socrates, on our hypothesis that virtue is knowledge, it must be taught.

soc. Yes, I daresay ; but what if we were not right in agreeing to that ?

MEN. Well, it seemed to be a correct statement a moment ago.

soc. Yes, but not only a moment ago must it seem correct, but now also and hereafter, if it is to be at all sound.

MEN. Why, what reason have you to make a difficulty about it, and feel a doubt as to virtue being knowledge ?

ΣΩ. Ἐγώ σοι ἐρῶ, ὦ Μένων. τὸ μὲν γὰρ διδακτὸν αὐτὸ εἶναι, εἴπερ ἐπιστήμη ἐστίν, οὐκ ἀνατίθεμαι μὴ οὐ καλῶς λέγεσθαι· ὅτι δ' οὐκ ἔστιν ἐπιστήμη, σκέψαι ἐάν σοι δοκῶ εἰκότως ἀπιστεῖν. τόδε γάρ μοι εἰπέ· εἰ ἔστι διδακτὸν ὁτιοῦν πρᾶγμα, μὴ μόνον ἀρετή, οὐκ ἀναγκαῖον αὐτοῦ καὶ διδασκάλους καὶ μαθητὰς εἶναι;

Ε   ΜΕΝ. Ἔμοιγε δοκεῖ.

ΣΩ. Οὐκοῦν τοὐναντίον αὖ, οὗ μήτε διδάσκαλοι μήτε μαθηταὶ εἶεν, καλῶς ἂν αὐτὸ εἰκάζοντες εἰκάζοιμεν μὴ διδακτὸν εἶναι;

ΜΕΝ. Ἔστι ταῦτα· ἀλλ' ἀρετῆς διδάσκαλοι οὐ δοκοῦσί σοι εἶναι;

ΣΩ. Πολλάκις γοῦν ζητῶν, εἴ τινες εἶεν αὐτῆς διδάσκαλοι, πάντα ποιῶν οὐ δύναμαι εὑρεῖν. καίτοι μετὰ πολλῶν γε ζητῶ, καὶ τούτων μάλιστα, οὓς ἂν οἴωμαι ἐμπειροτάτους εἶναι τοῦ πράγματος. καὶ δὴ καὶ νῦν, ὦ Μένων, εἰς καλὸν ἡμῖν Ἄνυτος

90 ὅδε παρεκαθέζετο, ᾧ μεταδῶμεν τῆς ζητήσεως. εἰκότως δ' ἂν μεταδοῖμεν· Ἄνυτος γὰρ ὅδε πρῶτον μέν ἐστι πατρὸς πλουσίου τε καὶ σοφοῦ Ἀνθεμίωνος, ὃς ἐγένετο πλούσιος οὐκ ἀπὸ τοῦ αὐτομάτου οὐδὲ δόντος τινός, ὥσπερ ὁ νῦν νεωστὶ εἰληφὼς τὰ Πολυκράτους χρήματα Ἰσμηνίας ὁ Θηβαῖος, ἀλλὰ τῇ αὑτοῦ σοφίᾳ κτησάμενος καὶ ἐπιμελείᾳ, ἔπειτα καὶ τὰ ἄλλα οὐχ ὑπερήφανος δοκῶν εἶναι

Β πολίτης οὐδὲ ὀγκώδης τε καὶ ἐπαχθής, ἀλλὰ κόσμιος καὶ εὐσταλὴς ἀνήρ· ἔπειτα τοῦτον εὖ ἔθρεψε καὶ ἐπαίδευσεν, ὡς δοκεῖ Ἀθηναίων τῷ

---

[1] A democratic leader at Thebes who assisted Anytus and the other exiled Athenian democrats in 403 B.C., shortly

MENO

soc. I will tell you, Meno. I do not withdraw as incorrect the statement that it is taught, if it is knowledge; but as to its being knowledge, consider if you think I have grounds for misgiving. For tell me now: if anything at all, not merely virtue, is teachable, must there not be teachers and learners of it?

men. I think so.

soc. Then also conversely, if a thing had neither teachers nor learners, we should be right in surmising that it could not be taught?

men. That is so: but do you think there are no teachers of virtue?

soc. I must say I have often inquired whether there were any, but for all my pains I cannot find one. And yet many have shared the search with me, and particularly those persons whom I regard as best qualified for the task. But look, Meno: here, at the very moment when he was wanted, we have Anytus sitting down beside us, to take his share in our quest. And we may well ask his assistance; for our friend Anytus, in the first place, is the son of a wise and wealthy father, Anthemion, who became rich not by a fluke or a gift—like that man the other day, Ismenias [1] the Theban, who has come into the fortune of a Polycrates [2]—but as the product of his own skill and industry [3]; and secondly, he has the name of being in general a well-conducted, mannerly person, not insolent towards his fellow-citizens or arrogant and annoying; and further, he gave his son a good upbringing and education, as the Athenian people think, for they choose him

before their return to Athens and the supposed time of this dialogue (about 402 B.C.). *Cf. Rep.* i. 336 A.

[2] Tyrant of Samos about 530 B.C. *Cf.* Herodot. iii. 39 foll.   [3] As a tanner.

πλήθει· αἱροῦνται γοῦν αὐτὸν ἐπὶ τὰς μεγίστας
ἀρχάς. δίκαιον δὴ μετὰ τοιούτων ζητεῖν ἀρετῆς
πέρι διδασκάλους, εἴτ᾽ εἰσὶν εἴτε μή, καὶ οἵτινες.
σὺ οὖν ἡμῖν, ὦ Ἄνυτε, συζήτησον, ἐμοί τε καὶ τῷ
σαυτοῦ ξένῳ Μένωνι τῷδε, περὶ τούτου τοῦ πράγματος, τίνες ἂν εἶεν διδάσκαλοι. ὧδε δὲ σκέψαι·
εἰ βουλοίμεθα Μένωνα τόνδε ἀγαθὸν ἰατρὸν γενέσθαι,
C παρὰ τίνας ἂν αὐτὸν πέμποιμεν διδασκάλους;
ἆρ᾽ οὐ παρὰ τοὺς ἰατρούς;

ΑΝ. Πάνυ γε.

ΣΩ. Τί δ᾽ εἰ σκυτοτόμον ἀγαθὸν βουλοίμεθα
γενέσθαι, ἆρ᾽ οὐ παρὰ τοὺς σκυτοτόμους;

ΑΝ. Ναί.

ΣΩ. Καὶ τἆλλα οὕτως;

ΑΝ. Πάνυ γε.

ΣΩ. Ὧδε δή μοι πάλιν περὶ τῶν αὐτῶν εἰπέ.
παρὰ τοὺς ἰατρούς, φαμέν, πέμποντες τόνδε
καλῶς ἂν ἐπέμπομεν, βουλόμενοι ἰατρὸν γενέσθαι·
D ἆρ᾽ ὅταν τοῦτο λέγωμεν, τόδε λέγομεν, ὅτι παρὰ
τούτους πέμποντες αὐτὸν σωφρονοῖμεν ἄν, τοὺς
ἀντιποιουμένους τε τῆς τέχνης μᾶλλον ἢ τοὺς
μή, καὶ τοὺς μισθὸν πραττομένους ἐπ᾽ αὐτῷ
τούτῳ, ἀποφήναντας αὑτοὺς διδασκάλους τοῦ
βουλομένου ἰέναι τε καὶ μανθάνειν; ἆρ᾽ οὐ πρὸς
ταῦτα βλέψαντες καλῶς ἂν πέμποιμεν;

ΑΝ. Ναί.

ΣΩ. Οὐκοῦν καὶ περὶ αὐλήσεως καὶ τῶν ἄλλων
τὰ αὐτὰ ταῦτα; πολλὴ ἄνοιά ἐστι βουλομένους
E αὐλητήν τινα ποιῆσαι παρὰ μὲν τοὺς ὑπισχνουμένους διδάξειν τὴν τέχνην καὶ μισθὸν πραττομένους
μὴ ἐθέλειν πέμπειν, ἄλλοις δέ τισι πράγματα
παρέχειν, ζητοῦντα μανθάνειν παρὰ τούτων, οἳ

for the highest offices. This is the sort of man to whom one may look for help in the inquiry as to whether there are teachers of virtue or not, and who they may be. So please, Anytus, join with me and your family-friend Meno in our inquiry about this matter—who can be the teachers. Consider it thus: if we wanted Meno here to be a good doctor, to whom should we send him for instruction? Would it not be to the doctors?

AN. Certainly.

SOC. And if we wanted him to become a good cobbler, should we not send him to the cobblers?

AN. Yes.

SOC. And in the same way with every other trade?

AN. Certainly.

SOC. Now let me ask you something more about these same instances. We should be right, we say, in sending him to the doctors if we wanted him to be a doctor. When we say this, do we mean that we should be wise in sending him to those who profess the art rather than those who do not, and to those who charge a fee for the particular thing they do, as avowed teachers of anyone who wishes to come and learn of them? If these were our reasons, should we not be right in sending him?

AN. Yes.

SOC. And the same would hold in the case of flute-playing, and so on with the rest? What folly, when we wanted to make someone a flute-player, to refuse to send him to the professed teachers of the art, who charge a regular fee, and to bother with requests for instruction other people who neither set up to

PLATO

μήτε προσποιοῦνται διδάσκαλοι εἶναι μήτ' ἔστιν
αὐτῶν μαθητὴς μηδεὶς τούτου τοῦ μαθήματος,
ὃ ἡμεῖς ἀξιοῦμεν μανθάνειν παρ' αὐτῶν ὃν ἂν
πέμπωμεν. οὐ πολλή σοι δοκεῖ ἀλογία εἶναι;

ΑΝ. Ναὶ μὰ Δία ἔμοιγε, καὶ ἀμαθία γε πρός.

ΣΩ. Καλῶς λέγεις. νῦν τοίνυν ἔξεστί σε
91 μετ' ἐμοῦ κοινῇ βουλεύεσθαι περὶ τοῦ ξένου
τουτουὶ Μένωνος. οὗτος γάρ, ὦ Ἄνυτε, πάλαι
λέγει πρός με, ὅτι ἐπιθυμεῖ ταύτης τῆς σοφίας
καὶ ἀρετῆς, ᾗ οἱ ἄνθρωποι τάς τε οἰκίας καὶ
τὰς πόλεις καλῶς διοικοῦσι, καὶ τοὺς γονέας
τοὺς αὑτῶν θεραπεύουσι, καὶ πολίτας καὶ ξένους
ὑποδέξασθαί τε καὶ ἀποπέμψαι ἐπίστανται ἀξίως
B ἀνδρὸς ἀγαθοῦ. ταύτην οὖν τὴν ἀρετὴν ⟨μαθησό-
μενον⟩[1] σκόπει παρὰ τίνας ἂν πέμποντες αὐτὸν
ὀρθῶς πέμποιμεν. ἢ δῆλον δὴ κατὰ τὸν ἄρτι
λόγον, ὅτι παρὰ τούτους τοὺς ὑπισχνουμένους
ἀρετῆς διδασκάλους εἶναι καὶ ἀποφήναντας αὑτοὺς
κοινοὺς τῶν Ἑλλήνων τῷ βουλομένῳ μανθάνειν,
μισθὸν τούτου ταξαμένους τε καὶ πραττομένους;

ΑΝ. Καὶ τίνας λέγεις τούτους, ὦ Σώκρατες;

ΣΩ. Οἶσθα δήπου καὶ σύ, ὅτι οὗτοί εἰσιν
οὓς οἱ ἄνθρωποι καλοῦσι σοφιστάς.

C ΑΝ. Ἡράκλεις, εὐφήμει, ὦ Σώκρατες. μηδένα
τῶν γ' ἐμῶν[2] μήτε οἰκείων μήτε φίλων, μήτε
ἀστὸν μήτε ξένον, τοιαύτη μανία λάβοι, ὥστε
παρὰ τούτους ἐλθόντα λωβηθῆναι, ἐπεὶ οὗτοί γε
φανερά ἐστι λώβη τε καὶ διαφθορὰ τῶν συγ-
γιγνομένων.

ΣΩ. Πῶς λέγεις, ὦ Ἄνυτε; οὗτοι ἄρα μόνοι

---

[1] μαθησόμενον intercidisse coni. Cobet.
[2] γ' ἐμῶν Burnet: γεμῶν, συγγενῶν MSS.

be teachers nor have a single pupil in that sort of
study which we expect him, when sent, to pursue !
Do you not consider this would be grossly
unreasonable ?

AN. Yes, on my word, I do, and stupid to boot.

soc. Quite right. And now there is an oppor-
tunity of your joining me in a consultation on my
friend Meno here. He has been declaring to me
ever so long, Anytus, that he desires to have that
wisdom and virtue whereby men keep their house
or their city in good order, and honour their parents,
and know when to welcome and when to speed
citizens and strangers as befits a good man. Now
tell me, to whom ought we properly to send him
for lessons in this virtue ? Or is it clear enough,
from our argument just now, that he should go to
these men who profess to be teachers of virtue and
advertise themselves as the common teachers of
the Greeks, and are ready to instruct anyone
who chooses in return for fees charged on a fixed
scale ?

AN. To whom are you referring, Socrates ?

soc. Surely you know as well as anyone ; they
are the men whom people call sophists.

AN. For heaven's sake hold your tongue, Socrates !
May no kinsman or friend of mine, whether of this
city or another, be seized with such madness as to
let himself be infected with the company of those
men ; for they are a manifest plague and corruption to those who frequent them.[1]

soc. What is this, Anytus ? Of all the people

---

[1] Anytus' vehemence expresses the hostility of the
ordinary practical democrat, after the restoration of 403 B.C.,
towards any novel movement in the state.

τῶν ἀντιποιουμένων τι ἐπίστασθαι εὐεργετεῖν
τοσοῦτον τῶν ἄλλων διαφέρουσιν, ὅσον οὐ μόνον
οὐκ ὠφελοῦσιν, ὥσπερ οἱ ἄλλοι, ὅ τι ἄν τις αὐτοῖς
D παραδῷ, ἀλλὰ καὶ τὸ ἐναντίον διαφθείρουσι;
καὶ τούτων φανερῶς χρήματα ἀξιοῦσι πράττεσθαι;
ἐγὼ μὲν οὖν οὐκ ἔχω ὅπως σοι πιστεύσω· οἶδα
γὰρ ἄνδρα ἕνα Πρωταγόραν πλείω χρήματα
κτησάμενον ἀπὸ ταύτης τῆς σοφίας ἢ Φειδίαν τε,
ὃς οὕτω περιφανῶς καλὰ ἔργα εἰργάζετο, καὶ
ἄλλους δέκα τῶν ἀνδριαντοποιῶν· καίτοι τέρας
λέγεις, εἰ οἱ μὲν τὰ ὑποδήματα ἐργαζόμενοι τὰ
παλαιὰ καὶ τὰ ἱμάτια ἐξακούμενοι οὐκ ἂν δύναιντο
E λαθεῖν τριάκονθ' ἡμέρας μοχθηρότερα ἀποδιδόντες
ἢ παρέλαβον τὰ ἱμάτιά τε καὶ ὑποδήματα, ἀλλ' εἰ
τοιαῦτα ποιοῖεν, ταχὺ ἂν τῷ λιμῷ ἀποθάνοιεν,
Πρωταγόρας δὲ ἄρα ὅλην τὴν Ἑλλάδα ἐλάνθανε
διαφθείρων τοὺς συγγιγνομένους καὶ μοχθηροτέ-
ρους ἀποπέμπων ἢ παρελάμβανε πλέον ἢ τετταράκοντα ἔτη· οἶμαι γὰρ αὐτὸν ἀποθανεῖν ἐγγὺς
καὶ ἑβδομήκοντα ἔτη γεγονότα, τετταράκοντα
δὲ ἐν τῇ τέχνῃ ὄντα· καὶ ἐν ἅπαντι τῷ χρόνῳ
τούτῳ ἔτι εἰς τὴν ἡμέραν ταυτηνὶ εὐδοκιμῶν
οὐδὲν πέπαυται· καὶ οὐ μόνον Πρωταγόρας,
92 ἀλλὰ καὶ ἄλλοι πάμπολλοι, οἱ μὲν πρότερον γεγονότες ἐκείνου, οἱ δὲ καὶ νῦν ἔτι ὄντες. πότερον
δὴ οὖν φῶμεν κατὰ τὸν σὸν λόγον εἰδότας αὐτοὺς
ἐξαπατᾶν καὶ λωβᾶσθαι τοὺς νέους, ἢ λεληθέναι
καὶ ἑαυτούς; καὶ οὕτω μαίνεσθαι ἀξιώσομεν
τούτους, οὓς ἔνιοί φασι σοφωτάτους ἀνθρώπων
εἶναι;

ΑΝ. Πολλοῦ γε δέουσι μαίνεσθαι, ὦ Σώκρατες,
ἀλλὰ πολὺ μᾶλλον οἱ τούτοις διδόντες ἀργύριον

who set up to understand how to do us good, do you mean to single out these as conveying not merely no benefit, such as the rest can give, but actually corruption to anyone placed in their hands? And is it for doing this that they openly claim the payment of fees? For my part I cannot bring myself to believe you; for I know of one man, Protagoras, who amassed more money by his craft than Pheidias —so famous for the noble works he produced—or any ten other sculptors. And yet how surprising that menders of old shoes and furbishers of clothes should not be able to go undetected thirty days if they should return the clothes or shoes in worse condition than they received them, and that such doings on their part would quickly starve them to death, while for more than forty years all Greece failed to notice that Protagoras was corrupting his classes and sending his pupils away in a worse state than when he took charge of them! For I believe he died about seventy years old, forty of which he spent in the practice of his art; and he retains undiminished to this day the high reputation he has enjoyed all that time—and not only Protagoras, but a multitude of others too: some who lived before him, and others still living. Now are we to take it, according to you, that they wittingly deceived and corrupted the youth, or that they were themselves unconscious of it? Are we to conclude those who are frequently termed the wisest of mankind to have been so demented as that?

AN. Demented! Not they, Socrates: far rather the young men who pay them money, and still

τῶν νέων· τούτων δ' ἔτι μᾶλλον οἱ τούτοις ἐπι-
B τρέποντες, οἱ προσήκοντες· πολὺ δὲ μάλιστα πάντων
αἱ πόλεις, ἐῶσαι αὐτοὺς εἰσαφικνεῖσθαι καὶ οὐκ
ἐξελαύνουσαι, εἴτε τις ξένος ἐπιχειρεῖ τοιοῦτόν
τι ποιεῖν εἴτε ἀστός.

ΣΩ. Πότερον δέ, ὦ Ἄνυτε, ἠδίκηκέ τίς σε
τῶν σοφιστῶν, ἢ τί οὕτως αὐτοῖς χαλεπὸς εἶ;

ΑΝ. Οὐδὲ μὰ Δία ἔγωγε συγγέγονα πώποτε
αὐτῶν οὐδενί, οὐδ' ἂν ἄλλον ἐάσαιμι τῶν ἐμῶν
οὐδένα.

ΣΩ. Ἄπειρος ἄρ' εἶ παντάπασι τῶν ἀνδρῶν;
C ΑΝ. Καὶ εἴην γε.

ΣΩ. Πῶς οὖν ἄν, ὦ δαιμόνιε, εἰδείης περὶ
τούτου τοῦ πράγματος, εἴτε τι ἀγαθὸν ἔχει ἐν
ἑαυτῷ εἴτε φλαῦρον, οὗ παντάπασιν ἄπειρος
εἴης;

ΑΝ. Ῥᾳδίως· τούτους γοῦν οἶδα οἵ εἰσιν,
εἴτ' οὖν ἄπειρος αὐτῶν εἰμι εἴτε μή.

ΣΩ. Μάντις εἶ ἴσως, ὦ Ἄνυτε· ἐπεὶ ὅπως γε
ἄλλως οἶσθα τούτων πέρι, ἐξ ὧν αὐτὸς λέγεις
θαυμάζοιμ' ἄν. ἀλλὰ γὰρ οὐ τούτους ἐπιζητοῦμεν
D τίνες εἰσί, παρ' οὓς ἂν Μένων ἀφικόμενος μοχθηρὸς
γένοιτο· οὗτοι μὲν γάρ, εἰ σὺ βούλει, ἔστων οἱ
σοφισταί· ἀλλὰ δὴ ἐκείνους εἰπὲ ἡμῖν, καὶ τὸν
πατρικὸν τόνδε ἑταῖρον εὐεργέτησον, φράσας αὐτῷ,
παρὰ τίνας ἀφικόμενος ἐν τοσαύτῃ πόλει τὴν
ἀρετὴν ἣν νυνδὴ ἐγὼ διῆλθον γένοιτ' ἂν ἄξιος
λόγου.

ΑΝ. Τί δὲ αὐτῷ οὐ σὺ ἔφρασας;

ΣΩ. Ἀλλ' οὓς μὲν ἐγὼ ᾤμην διδασκάλους
τούτων εἶναι, εἶπον, ἀλλὰ τυγχάνω οὐδὲν λέγων,
E ὡς σὺ φῄς· καὶ ἴσως τὶ λέγεις. ἀλλὰ σὺ δὴ ἐν

more the relations who let the young men have their way ; and most of all the cities that allow them to enter, and do not expel them, whether such attempt be made by stranger or citizen.

soc. Tell me, Anytus, has any of the sophists wronged you ? What makes you so hard on them ?

an. No, heaven knows I have never in my life had dealings with any of them, nor would I let any of my people have to do with them either.

soc. Then you have absolutely no experience of those persons ?

an. And trust I never may.

soc. How then, my good sir, can you tell whether a thing has any good or evil in it, if you are quite without experience of it ?

an. Easily : the fact is, I know what these people are, whether I have experience of them or not.

soc. You are a wizard, perhaps, Anytus ; for I really cannot see, from what you say yourself, how else you can know anything about them. But we are not inquiring now who the teachers are whose lessons would make Meno wicked ; let us grant, if you will, that they are the sophists : I only ask you to tell us, and do Meno a service as a friend of your family by letting him know, to whom in all this great city he should apply in order to become eminent in the virtue which I described just now.

an. Why not tell him yourself ?

soc. I did mention to him the men whom I supposed to be teachers of these things ; but I find, from what you say, that I am quite off the track, and I daresay you are on it. Now you take

τῷ μέρει αὐτῷ εἰπὲ παρὰ τίνας ἔλθῃ Ἀθηναίων·
εἰπὲ ὄνομα ὅτου βούλει.

ΑΝ. Τί δὲ ἑνὸς ἀνθρώπου ὄνομα δεῖ ἀκοῦσαι;
ὅτῳ γὰρ ἂν ἐντύχῃ Ἀθηναίων τῶν καλῶν κἀγα-
θῶν, οὐδείς ἐστιν ὃς οὐ βελτίω αὐτὸν ποιήσει ἢ
οἱ σοφισταί, ἐάνπερ ἐθέλῃ πείθεσθαι.

ΣΩ. Πότερον δὲ οὗτοι οἱ καλοὶ κἀγαθοὶ ἀπὸ
τοῦ αὐτομάτου ἐγένοντο τοιοῦτοι, παρ' οὐδενὸς
μαθόντες ὅμως μέντοι ἄλλους διδάσκειν οἷοί τε
93 ὄντες ταῦτα, ἃ αὐτοὶ οὐκ ἔμαθον;

ΑΝ. Καὶ τούτους ἔγωγε ἀξιῶ παρὰ τῶν προτέρων μαθεῖν, ὄντων καλῶν κἀγαθῶν· ἢ οὐ δοκοῦσί
σοι πολλοὶ καὶ ἀγαθοὶ γεγονέναι ἐν τῇδε τῇ πόλει
ἄνδρες;

ΣΩ. Ἔμοιγε, ὦ Ἄνυτε, καὶ εἶναι δοκοῦσιν
ἐνθάδε ἀγαθοὶ τὰ πολιτικά, καὶ γεγονέναι ἔτι
οὐχ ἧττον ἢ εἶναι· ἀλλὰ μῶν καὶ διδάσκαλοι
ἀγαθοὶ γεγόνασι τῆς αὑτῶν ἀρετῆς; τοῦτο γάρ
ἐστι περὶ οὗ ὁ λόγος ἡμῖν τυγχάνει ὤν· οὐκ εἰ
Β εἰσὶν ἀγαθοὶ ἢ μὴ ἄνδρες ἐνθάδε, οὐδ' εἰ γεγόνασιν
ἐν τῷ πρόσθεν, ἀλλ' εἰ διδακτόν ἐστιν ἀρετὴ πάλαι
σκοπούμεν. τοῦτο δὲ σκοποῦντες τόδε σκοποῦμεν, ἆρα οἱ ἀγαθοὶ ἄνδρες καὶ τῶν νῦν καὶ τῶν
προτέρων ταύτην τὴν ἀρετήν, ἣν αὐτοὶ ἀγαθοὶ
ἦσαν, ἠπίσταντο καὶ ἄλλῳ παραδοῦναι, ἢ οὐ
παραδοτὸν τοῦτο ἀνθρώπῳ οὐδὲ παραληπτὸν ἄλλῳ
παρ' ἄλλου. τοῦτ' ἔστιν ὃ πάλαι ζητοῦμεν ἐγώ τε
καὶ Μένων. ὧδε οὖν σκόπει ἐκ τοῦ σαυτοῦ λόγου·
C Θεμιστοκλέα οὐκ ἀγαθὸν ἂν φαίης ἄνδρα γεγονέναι;

ΑΝ. Ἔγωγε, πάντων γε μάλιστα.

your turn, and tell him to whom of the Athenians he is to go. Give us a name—anyone you please.

AN. Why mention a particular one? Any Athenian gentleman he comes across, without exception, will do him more good, if he will do as he is bid, than the sophists.

SOC. And did those gentlemen grow spontaneously into what they are, and without learning from anybody are they able, nevertheless, to teach others what they did not learn themselves?

AN. I expect they must have learnt in their turn from the older generation, who were gentlemen: or does it not seem to you that we have had many good men in this city?

SOC. Yes, I agree, Anytus; we have also many who are good at politics, and have had them in the past as well as now. But I want to know whether they have proved good teachers besides of their own virtue: that is the question with which our discussion is actually concerned; not whether there are, or formerly have been, good men here amongst us or not, but whether virtue is teachable; this has been our problem all the time. And our inquiry into this problem resolves itself into the question: Did the good men of our own and of former times know how to transmit to another man the virtue in respect of which they were good, or is it something not to be transmitted or taken over from one human being to another? That is the question I and Meno have been discussing all this time. Well, just consider it in your own way of speaking: would you not say that Themistocles was a good man?

AN. I would, particularly so.

ΣΩ. Οὐκοῦν καὶ διδάσκαλον ἀγαθόν, εἴπερ τις ἄλλος τῆς αὐτοῦ ἀρετῆς διδάσκαλος ἦν, κἀκεῖνον εἶναι;

ΑΝ. Οἶμαι ἔγωγε, εἴπερ ἐβούλετό γε.

ΣΩ. 'Αλλ', οἴει, οὐκ ἂν ἐβουλήθη ἄλλους τέ τινας καλοὺς κἀγαθοὺς γενέσθαι, μάλιστα δέ που τὸν υἱὸν τὸν αὑτοῦ; ἢ οἴει αὐτὸν φθονεῖν αὐτῷ καὶ ἐξεπίτηδες οὐ παραδιδόναι τὴν ἀρετήν, D ἣν αὐτὸς ἀγαθὸς ἦν; ἢ οὐκ ἀκήκοας, ὅτι Θεμιστοκλῆς Κλεόφαντον τὸν υἱὸν ἱππέα μὲν ἐδιδάξατο ἀγαθόν; ἐπέμενε γοῦν ἐπὶ τῶν ἵππων ὀρθὸς ἑστηκώς, καὶ ἠκόντιζεν ἀπὸ τῶν ἵππων ὀρθός, καὶ ἄλλα πολλὰ καὶ θαυμαστὰ εἰργάζετο, ἃ ἐκεῖνος αὐτὸν ἐπαιδεύσατο καὶ ἐποίησε σοφόν, ὅσα διδασκάλων ἀγαθῶν εἴχετο· ἢ ταῦτα οὐκ ἀκήκοας τῶν πρεσβυτέρων;

ΑΝ. 'Ακήκοα.

ΣΩ. Οὐκ ἂν ἄρα τήν γε φύσιν τοῦ υἱέος αὐτοῦ ᾐτιάσατ' ἄν τις εἶναι κακήν.

E ΑΝ. "Ισως οὐκ ἄν.

ΣΩ. Τί δὲ τόδε; ὡς Κλεόφαντος ὁ Θεμιστοκλέους ἀνὴρ ἀγαθὸς καὶ σοφὸς ἐγένετο ἅπερ ὁ πατὴρ αὐτοῦ, ἤδη του ἀκήκοας ἢ νεωτέρου ἢ πρεσβυτέρου;

ΑΝ. Οὐ δῆτα.

ΣΩ. 'Αρ' οὖν ταῦτα μὲν οἰόμεθα βούλεσθαι αὐτὸν τὸν αὑτοῦ υἱὸν παιδεῦσαι, ἣν δὲ αὐτὸς σοφίαν ἦν σοφός, οὐδὲν τῶν γειτόνων βελτίω ποιῆσαι, εἴπερ ἦν γε διδακτὸν ἡ ἀρετή;

ΑΝ. "Ισως μὰ Δί' οὔ.

ΣΩ. Οὗτος μὲν δή σοι τοιοῦτος διδάσκαλος

soc. And if any man ever was a teacher of his own virtue, he especially was a good teacher of his?

AN. In my opinion, yes, assuming that he wished to be so.

soc. But can you suppose he would not have wished that other people should become good, honourable men—above all, I presume, his own son? Or do you think he was jealous of him, and deliberately refused to impart the virtue of his own goodness to him? Have you never heard how Themistocles had his son Cleophantus taught to be a good horseman? Why, he could keep his balance standing upright on horseback, and hurl the javelin while so standing, and perform many other wonderful feats in which his father had had him trained, so as to make him skilled in all that could be learnt from good masters. Surely you must have heard all this from your elders?

AN. I have.

soc. Then there could be no complaints of badness in his son's nature?

AN. I daresay not.

soc. But I ask you—did you ever hear anybody, old or young, say that Cleophantus, son of Themistocles, had the same goodness and accomplishments as his father?

AN. Certainly not.

soc. And can we believe that his father chose to train his own son in those feats, and yet made him no better than his neighbours in his own particular accomplishments—if virtue, as alleged, was to be taught?

AN. On my word, I think not.

soc. Well, there you have a fine teacher of virtue

347

93

94 ἀρετῆς, ὃν καὶ σὺ ὁμολογεῖς ἐν τοῖς ἄριστον τῶν
προτέρων εἶναι· ἄλλον δὲ δὴ σκεψώμεθα, Ἀριστείδην τὸν Λυσιμάχου· ἢ τοῦτον οὐχ ὁμολογεῖς
ἀγαθὸν γεγονέναι;

ΑΝ. Ἔγωγε, πάντως δήπου.

ΣΩ. Οὐκοῦν καὶ οὗτος τὸν υἱὸν τὸν αὑτοῦ
Λυσίμαχον, ὅσα μὲν διδασκάλων εἴχετο, κάλλιστα
Ἀθηναίων ἐπαίδευσεν, ἄνδρα δὲ βελτίω δοκεῖ
σοι ὁτουοῦν πεποιηκέναι; τούτῳ γάρ που καὶ
συγγέγονας καὶ ὁρᾷς οἷός ἐστιν. εἰ δὲ βούλει,
B Περικλέα, οὕτω μεγαλοπρεπῶς σοφὸν ἄνδρα,
οἶσθ᾽ ὅτι δύο υἱεῖς ἔθρεψε, Πάραλον καὶ Ξάνθ-
ιππον;

ΑΝ. Ἔγωγε.

ΣΩ. Τούτους μέντοι, ὡς οἶσθα καὶ σύ, ἱππέας
μὲν ἐδίδαξεν οὐδενὸς χείρους Ἀθηναίων, καὶ
μουσικὴν καὶ ἀγωνίαν καὶ τἆλλα ἐπαίδευσεν, ὅσα
τέχνης ἔχεται, οὐδενὸς χείρους· ἀγαθοὺς δὲ ἄρα
ἄνδρας οὐκ ἐβούλετο ποιῆσαι; δοκῶ μέν, ἐβούλετο,
ἀλλὰ μὴ οὐκ ᾖ διδακτόν. ἵνα δὲ μὴ ὀλίγους
οἴῃ καὶ τοὺς φαυλοτάτους Ἀθηναίων ἀδυνάτους
C γεγονέναι τοῦτο τὸ πρᾶγμα, ἐνθυμήθητι ὅτι Θουκυδίδης αὖ δύο υἱεῖς ἔθρεψε, Μελησίαν καὶ Στέφανον,
καὶ τούτους ἐπαίδευσε τά τε ἄλλα εὖ καὶ ἐπάλαισαν
κάλλιστα Ἀθηναίων· τὸν μὲν γὰρ Ξανθίᾳ ἔδωκε,
τὸν δὲ Εὐδώρῳ· οὗτοι δέ που ἐδόκουν τῶν τότε
κάλλιστα παλαίειν· ἢ οὐ μέμνησαι;

ΑΝ. Ἔγωγε, ἀκοῇ.

[1] Thucydides (son of Melesias, and no relation of the
historian) was an aristocrat of high principle and con-
348

who, you admit, was one of the best men of past times. Let us take another, Aristeides, son of Lysimachus : do you not admit that he was a good man ?

AN. I do, absolutely, of course.

SOC. Well, did he not train his son Lysimachus better than any other Athenian in all that masters could teach him ? And in the result, do you consider he has turned out better than anyone else ? You have been in his company, I know, and you see what he is like. Or take another example—the splendidly accomplished Pericles : he, as you are aware, brought up two sons, Paralus and Xanthippus.

AN. Yes.

SOC. And, you know as well as I, he taught them to be the foremost horsemen of Athens, and trained them to excel in music and gymnastics and all else that comes under the head of the arts ; and with all that, had he no desire to make them good men ? He wished to, I imagine, but presumably it is not a thing one can be taught. And that you may not suppose it was only a few of the meanest sort of Athenians who failed in this matter, let me remind you that Thucydides[1] also brought up two sons, Melesias and Stephanus, and that besides giving them a good general education he made them the best wrestlers in Athens : one he placed with Xanthias, and the other with Eudorus—masters who, I should think, had the name of being the best exponents of the art. You remember them, do you not ?

AN. Yes, by hearsay.

servative views who opposed the plans of Pericles for enriching and adorning Athens.

ΣΩ. Οὐκοῦν δῆλον ὅτι οὗτος οὐκ ἄν ποτε, οὗ μὲν ἔδει δαπανώμενον διδάσκειν, ταῦτα μὲν D ἐδίδαξε τοὺς παῖδας τοὺς αὑτοῦ, οὗ δὲ οὐδὲν ἔδει ἀναλώσαντα ἀγαθοὺς ἄνδρας ποιῆσαι, ταῦτα δὲ οὐκ ἐδίδαξεν, εἰ διδακτὸν ἦν; ἀλλὰ γὰρ ἴσως ὁ Θουκυδίδης φαῦλος ἦν, καὶ οὐκ ἦσαν αὐτῷ πλεῖστοι φίλοι 'Αθηναίων καὶ τῶν συμμάχων; καὶ οἰκίας μεγάλης ἦν καὶ ἐδύνατο μέγα ἐν τῇ πόλει καὶ ἐν τοῖς ἄλλοις Ἕλλησιν, ὥστε εἴπερ ἦν τοῦτο διδακτόν, ἐξευρεῖν ἂν ὅστις ἔμελλεν αὐτοῦ τοὺς υἱεῖς ἀγαθοὺς ποιήσειν, ἢ τῶν ἐπιχωρίων E τις ἢ τῶν ξένων, εἰ αὐτὸς μὴ ἐσχόλαζε διὰ τὴν τῆς πόλεως ἐπιμέλειαν. ἀλλὰ γάρ, ὦ ἑταῖρε Ἄνυτε, μὴ οὐκ ᾖ διδακτὸν ἀρετή.

ΑΝ. Ὦ Σώκρατες, ῥᾳδίως μοι δοκεῖς κακῶς λέγειν ἀνθρώπους. ἐγὼ μὲν οὖν ἄν σοι συμβουλεύσαιμι, εἰ ἐθέλεις ἐμοὶ πείθεσθαι, εὐλαβεῖσθαι· ὡς ἴσως μὲν καὶ ἐν ἄλλῃ πόλει ῥᾷον[1] ἐστι κακῶς ποιεῖν ἀνθρώπους ἢ εὖ, ἐν τῇδε δὲ 95 καὶ πάνυ· οἶμαι δὲ σὲ καὶ αὐτὸν εἰδέναι.

ΣΩ. Ὦ Μένων, Ἄνυτος μέν μοι δοκεῖ χαλεπαίνειν· καὶ οὐδὲν θαυμάζω· οἴεται γάρ με πρῶτον μὲν κακηγορεῖν τούτους τοὺς ἄνδρας, ἔπειτα ἡγεῖται καὶ αὐτὸς εἶναι εἷς τούτων. ἀλλ' οὗτος μὲν ἐάν ποτε γνῷ, οἷόν ἐστι τὸ κακῶς λέγειν, παύσεται χαλεπαίνων, νῦν δὲ ἀγνοεῖ· σὺ δέ μοι εἰπέ, οὐ καὶ παρ' ὑμῖν εἰσὶ καλοὶ κἀγαθοὶ ἄνδρες;

---

¹ ῥᾷον Buttmann: ῥᾴδιον mss.

---

¹ Anytus goes away. His parting words show that (in Plato's view) he regarded Socrates as an enemy of the restored democracy which, he hints, has popular juries only too ready to condemn such an awkward critic.

soc. Well, is it not obvious that this father would never have spent his money on having his children taught all those things, and then have omitted to teach them at no expense the others that would have made them good men, if virtue was to be taught? Will you say that perhaps Thucydides was one of the meaner sort, and had no great number of friends among the Athenians and allies? He, who was of a great house and had much influence in our city and all over Greece, so that if virtue were to be taught he would have found out the man who was likely to make his sons good, whether one of our own people or a foreigner, were he himself too busy owing to the cares of state! Ah no, my dear Anytus, it looks as though virtue were not a teachable thing.

an. Socrates, I consider you are too apt to speak ill of people. I, for one, if you will take my advice, would warn you to be careful: in most cities it is probably easier to do people harm than good, and particularly in this one; I think you know that yourself.[1]

soc. Meno, I think Anytus is angry, and I am not at all surprised: for he conceives, in the first place, that I am speaking ill of these gentlemen; and in the second place, he considers he is one of them himself. Yet, should the day come when he knows what "speaking ill" means, his anger will cease; at present he does not know.[2] Now you must answer me: are there not good and honourable men among your people also?

[2] This is probably not a reference to a prosecution of Anytus himself, but a suggestion that what he needs is a Socratic discussion on "speaking ill," for "ill" may mean "maliciously," "untruthfully," "ignorantly," etc.

ΜΕΝ. Πάνυ γε.

Β ΣΩ. Τί οὖν; ἐθέλουσιν οὗτοι παρέχειν αὑτοὺς διδασκάλους τοῖς νέοις, καὶ ὁμολογεῖν διδάσκαλοί τε εἶναι καὶ διδακτὸν ἀρετήν;

ΜΕΝ. Οὐ μὰ τὸν Δία, ὦ Σώκρατες, ἀλλὰ τοτὲ μὲν ἂν αὐτῶν ἀκούσαις ὡς διδακτόν, τοτὲ δὲ ὡς οὔ.

ΣΩ. Φῶμεν οὖν τούτους διδασκάλους εἶναι τούτου τοῦ πράγματος, οἷς μηδὲ αὐτὸ τοῦτο ὁμολογεῖται;

ΜΕΝ. Οὔ μοι δοκεῖ, ὦ Σώκρατες.

ΣΩ. Τί δὲ δή; οἱ σοφισταί σοι οὗτοι, οἵπερ
C μόνοι ἐπαγγέλλονται, δοκοῦσι διδάσκαλοι εἶναι ἀρετῆς;

ΜΕΝ. Καὶ Γοργίου μάλιστα, ὦ Σώκρατες, ταῦτα ἄγαμαι, ὅτι οὐκ ἄν ποτε αὐτοῦ τοῦτο ἀκούσαις ὑπισχνουμένου, ἀλλὰ καὶ τῶν ἄλλων καταγελᾷ, ὅταν ἀκούσῃ ὑπισχνουμένων· ἀλλὰ λέγειν οἴεται δεῖν ποιεῖν δεινούς.

ΣΩ. Οὐδ᾽ ἄρα σοὶ δοκοῦσιν οἱ σοφισταὶ διδάσκαλοι εἶναι;

ΜΕΝ. Οὐκ ἔχω λέγειν, ὦ Σώκρατες. καὶ γὰρ αὐτὸς ὅπερ οἱ πολλοὶ πέπονθα· τοτὲ μέν μοι δοκοῦσι, τοτὲ δὲ οὔ.

ΣΩ. Οἶσθα δὲ ὅτι οὐ μόνον σοί τε καὶ τοῖς
D ἄλλοις τοῖς πολιτικοῖς τοῦτο δοκεῖ τοτὲ μὲν εἶναι διδακτόν, τοτὲ δ᾽ οὔ, ἀλλὰ καὶ Θέογνιν τὸν ποιητὴν οἶσθ᾽ ὅτι ταὐτὰ ταῦτα λέγει;

ΜΕΝ. Ἐν ποίοις ἔπεσιν;

ΣΩ. Ἐν τοῖς ἐλεγείοις, οὗ λέγει—

κ αὶ παρὰ τοῖσιν πῖνε καὶ ἔσθιε, καὶ μετὰ τοῖσιν
ἷζε, καὶ ἄνδανε τοῖς, ὧν μεγάλη δύναμις.

MEN. Certainly.

SOC. Well then, are they willing to put themselves forward as teachers of the young, and avow that they are teachers and that virtue is to be taught?

MEN. No, no, Socrates, I assure you: sometimes you may hear them refer to it as teachable, but sometimes as not.

SOC. Then are we to call those persons teachers of this thing, when they do not even agree on that great question?

MEN. I should say not, Socrates.

SOC. Well, and what of the sophists? Do you consider these, its only professors, to be teachers of virtue?

MEN. That is a point, Socrates, for which I admire Gorgias: you will never hear him promising this, and he ridicules the others when he hears them promise it. Skill in speaking is what he takes it to be their business to produce.

SOC. Then you do not think the sophists are teachers of virtue?

MEN. I cannot say, Socrates. I am in the same plight as the rest of the world: sometimes I think that they are, sometimes that they are not.

SOC. And are you aware that not only you and other political folk are in two minds as to whether virtue is to be taught, but Theognis the poet also says, you remember, the very same thing?

MEN. In which part of his poems?

SOC. In those elegiac lines where he says—

"Eat and drink with these men; sit with them, and be pleasing unto them, who wield great power; for from the

353

95

ἐσθλῶν μὲν γὰρ ἄπ᾽ ἐσθλὰ διδάξεαι· ἢν δὲ

E κακοῖσιν

συμμίσγῃς, ἀπολεῖς καὶ τὸν ἐόντα νόον.

οἶσθ᾽ ὅτι ἐν τούτοις μὲν ὡς διδακτοῦ οὔσης τῆς ἀρετῆς λέγει;

MEN. Φαίνεταί γε.

ΣΩ. Ἐν ἄλλοις δέ γε ὀλίγον μεταβάς,

εἰ δ᾽ ἦν ποιητόν, φησί, καὶ ἔνθετον ἀνδρὶ νόημα, λέγει πως ὅτι

πολλοὺς ἂν μισθοὺς καὶ μεγάλους ἔφερον
οἱ δυνάμενοι τοῦτο ποιεῖν, καὶ
οὔ ποτ᾽ ἂν ἐξ ἀγαθοῦ πατρὸς ἔγεντο κακός,

96 πειθόμενος μύθοισι σαόφροσιν. ἀλλὰ διδάσκων
οὔ ποτε ποιήσεις τὸν κακὸν ἄνδρ᾽ ἀγαθόν.

ἐννοεῖς ὅτι αὐτὸς αὑτῷ πάλιν περὶ τῶν αὐτῶν τἀναντία λέγει;

MEN. Φαίνεται.

ΣΩ. Ἔχεις οὖν εἰπεῖν ἄλλου ὁτουοῦν πράγματος, οὗ οἱ μὲν φάσκοντες διδάσκαλοι εἶναι οὐχ ὅπως ἄλλων διδάσκαλοι ὁμολογοῦνται, ἀλλ᾽ οὐδὲ αὐτοὶ

B ἐπίστασθαι, ἀλλὰ πονηροὶ εἶναι περὶ αὐτὸ τοῦτο τὸ πρᾶγμα οὗ φασὶ διδάσκαλοι εἶναι, οἱ δὲ ὁμολογούμενοι αὐτοὶ καλοὶ κἀγαθοὶ τοτὲ μέν φασιν αὐτὸ διδακτὸν εἶναι, τοτὲ δὲ οὔ; τοὺς οὖν οὕτω τεταραγμένους περὶ ὁτουοῦν φαίης ἂν σὺ κυρίως διδασκάλους εἶναι;

MEN. Μὰ Δί᾽ οὐκ ἔγωγε.

ΣΩ. Οὐκοῦν εἰ μήτε οἱ σοφισταὶ μήτε οἱ αὐτοὶ

---

[1] Bergk, 33–36.   [2] Bergk, 434–438.

good wilt thou win thee lessons in the good; but mingle with the bad, and thou wilt lose even the sense that thou hast."[1]

Do you observe how in these words he implies that virtue is to be taught?

MEN. He does, evidently.

soc. But in some other lines he shifts his ground a little, saying—

"Could understanding be created and put into a man" (I think it runs thus) "many high rewards would they obtain" (that is, the men who were able to do such a thing): and again—
"Never would a bad son have sprung from a good father, for he would have followed the precepts of wisdom: but not by teaching wilt thou ever make the bad man good."[2]

You notice how in the second passage he contradicts himself on the same point?

MEN. Apparently.

soc. Well, can you name any other subject in which the professing teachers are not only refused recognition as teachers of others, but regarded as not even understanding it themselves, and indeed as inferior in the very quality of which they claim to be teachers; while those who are themselves recognized as men of worth and honour say at one time that it is teachable, and at another that it is not? When people are so confused about this or that matter, can you say they are teachers in any proper sense of the word?

MEN. No, indeed, I cannot.

soc. Well, if neither the sophists nor the men

καλοὶ κἀγαθοὶ ὄντες διδάσκαλοί εἰσι τοῦ πράγματος,
δῆλον ὅτι οὐκ ἂν ἄλλοι γε;

ΜΕΝ. Οὔ μοι δοκεῖ.

C   ΣΩ. Εἰ δέ γε μὴ διδάσκαλοι, οὐδὲ μαθηταί;

ΜΕΝ. Δοκεῖ μοι ἔχειν ὡς λέγεις.

ΣΩ. Ὡμολογήκαμεν δέ γε, πράγματος οὗ μήτε
διδάσκαλοι μήτε μαθηταὶ εἶεν, τοῦτο μηδὲ διδακτὸν εἶναι;

ΜΕΝ. Ὡμολογήκαμεν.

ΣΩ. Οὐκοῦν ἀρετῆς οὐδαμοῦ φαίνονται διδάσκαλοι;

ΜΕΝ. Ἔστι ταῦτα.

ΣΩ. Εἰ δέ γε μὴ διδάσκαλοι, οὐδὲ μαθηταί;

ΜΕΝ. Φαίνεται οὕτως.

ΣΩ. Ἀρετὴ ἄρα οὐκ ἂν εἴη διδακτόν;

D   ΜΕΝ. Οὐκ ἔοικεν, εἴπερ ὀρθῶς ἡμεῖς ἐσκέμ-
μεθα. ὥστε καὶ θαυμάζω δή, ὦ Σώκρατες,
πότερόν ποτε οὐδ᾽ εἰσὶν ἀγαθοὶ ἄνδρες, ἢ τίς ἂν
εἴη τρόπος τῆς γενέσεως τῶν ἀγαθῶν γιγνομένων.

ΣΩ. Κινδυνεύομεν, ὦ Μένων, ἐγώ τε καὶ σὺ
φαῦλοί τινες εἶναι ἄνδρες, καὶ σέ τε Γοργίας οὐχ
ἱκανῶς πεπαιδευκέναι καὶ ἐμὲ Πρόδικος. παντὸς
μᾶλλον οὖν προσεκτέον τὸν νοῦν ἡμῖν αὐτοῖς, καὶ
ζητητέον ὅστις ἡμᾶς ἑνί γέ τῳ τρόπῳ βελτίους
E ποιήσει· λέγω δὲ ταῦτα ἀποβλέψας πρὸς τὴν
ἄρτι ζήτησιν, ὡς ἡμᾶς ἔλαθε καταγελάστως,
ὅτι οὐ μόνον ἐπιστήμης ἡγουμένης ὀρθῶς τε καὶ
εὖ τοῖς ἀνθρώποις πράττεται τὰ πράγματα, ᾗ[1]
ἴσως καὶ διαφεύγει ἡμᾶς τὸ γνῶναι, τίνα ποτὲ
τρόπον γίγνονται οἱ ἀγαθοὶ ἄνδρες.

ΜΕΝ. Πῶς τοῦτο λέγεις, ὦ Σώκρατες;

---

[1] ᾗ Madvig: ἢ MSS.

who are themselves good and honourable are teachers of the subject, clearly no others can be ?

MEN. I agree.

soc. And if there are no teachers, there can be no disciples either ?

MEN. I think that statement is true.

soc. And we have admitted that a thing of which there are neither teachers nor disciples cannot be taught ?

MEN. We have.

soc. So nowhere are any teachers of virtue to be found ?

MEN. That is so.

soc. And if no teachers, then no disciples ?

MEN. So it appears.

soc. Hence virtue cannot be taught ?

MEN. It seems likely, if our investigation is correct. And that makes me wonder, I must say, Socrates, whether perhaps there are no good men at all, or by what possible sort of process good people can come to exist ?

soc. I fear, Meno, you and I are but poor creatures, and Gorgias has been as faulty an educator of you as Prodicus of me. So our first duty is to look to ourselves, and try to find somebody who will have some means or other of making us better. I say this with special reference to our recent inquiry, in which I see that we absurdly failed to note that it is not only through the guidance of knowledge that human conduct is right and good ; and it is probably owing to this that we fail to perceive by what means good men can be produced.

MEN. To what are you alluding, Socrates ?

ΣΩ. Ὧδε· ὅτι μὲν τοὺς ἀγαθοὺς ἄνδρας δεῖ ὠφελίμους εἶναι, ὀρθῶς ὡμολογήκαμεν τοῦτό 97 γε, ὅτι οὐκ ἂν ἄλλως ἔχοι· ἢ γάρ;

ΜΕΝ. Ναί.

ΣΩ. Καὶ ὅτι γε ὠφέλιμοι ἔσονται, ἂν ὀρθῶς ἡμῖν ἡγῶνται τῶν πραγμάτων, καὶ τοῦτό που καλῶς ὡμολογοῦμεν;

ΜΕΝ. Ναί.

ΣΩ. Ὅτι δ' οὐκ ἔστιν ὀρθῶς ἡγεῖσθαι, ἐὰν μὴ φρόνιμος ᾖ, τοῦτο ὅμοιοί ἐσμεν οὐκ ὀρθῶς ὡμολογηκόσιν.

ΜΕΝ. Πῶς δὴ [ὀρθῶς] λέγεις;

ΣΩ. Ἐγὼ ἐρῶ. εἴ τις εἰδὼς τὴν ὁδὸν τὴν εἰς Λάρισαν ἢ ὅποι βούλει ἄλλοσε βαδίζοι καὶ ἄλλοις ἡγοῖτο, ἄλλο τι ὀρθῶς ἂν καὶ εὖ ἡγοῖτο;

ΜΕΝ. Πάνυ γε.

B ΣΩ. Τί δ' εἴ τις ὀρθῶς μὲν δοξάζων, ἥτις ἐστὶν ἡ ὁδός, ἐληλυθὼς δὲ μὴ μηδ' ἐπιστάμενος, οὐ καὶ οὗτος ἂν ὀρθῶς ἡγοῖτο;

ΜΕΝ. Πάνυ γε.

ΣΩ. Καὶ ἕως γ' ἄν που ὀρθὴν δόξαν ἔχῃ περὶ ὧν ὁ ἕτερος ἐπιστήμην, οὐδὲν χείρων ἡγεμὼν ἔσται, οἰόμενος μὲν ἀληθῆ, φρονῶν δὲ μή, τοῦ τοῦτο φρονοῦντος.

ΜΕΝ. Οὐδὲν γάρ.

ΣΩ. Δόξα ἄρα ἀληθὴς πρὸς ὀρθότητα πράξεως οὐδὲν χείρων ἡγεμὼν φρονήσεως· καὶ τοῦτό ἐστιν ὃ νυνδὴ παρελείπομεν ἐν τῇ περὶ τῆς ἀρετῆς C σκέψει, ὁποῖόν τι εἴη, λέγοντες ὅτι φρόνησις μόνον ἡγεῖται τοῦ ὀρθῶς πράττειν· τὸ δὲ ἄρα καὶ δόξα ἦν ἀληθής.

soc. I mean that good men must be useful: we were right, were we not, in admitting that this must needs be so?

MEN. Yes.

soc. And in thinking that they will be useful if they give us right guidance in conduct: here also, I suppose, our admission was correct?

MEN. Yes.

soc. But our assertion that it is impossible to give right guidance unless one has knowledge looks very like a mistake.

MEN. What do you mean by that?

soc. I will tell you. If a man knew the way to Larisa, or any other place you please, and walked there and led others, would he not give right and good guidance?

MEN. Certainly.

soc. Well, and a person who had a right opinion as to which was the way, but had never been there and did not really know, might give right guidance, might he not?

MEN. Certainly.

soc. And so long, I presume, as he has right opinion about that which the other man really knows, he will be just as good a guide—if he thinks the truth instead of knowing it—as the man who has the knowledge.

MEN. Just as good.

soc. Hence true opinion is as good a guide to rightness of action as knowledge; and this is a point we omitted just now in our consideration of the nature of virtue, when we stated that knowledge is the only guide of right action; whereas we find there is also true opinion.

ΜΕΝ. Ἔοικέ γε.

ΣΩ. Οὐδὲν ἄρα ἧττον ὠφέλιμόν ἐστιν ὀρθὴ δόξα ἐπιστήμης.

ΜΕΝ. Τοσούτῳ γε, ὦ Σώκρατες, ὅτι ὁ μὲν τὴν ἐπιστήμην ἔχων ἀεὶ ἂν ἐπιτυγχάνοι, ὁ δὲ τὴν ὀρθὴν δόξαν τοτὲ μὲν ἂν τυγχάνοι, τοτὲ δ' οὔ.

ΣΩ. Πῶς λέγεις; ὁ ἀεὶ ἔχων ὀρθὴν δόξαν οὐκ ἀεὶ τυγχάνοι, ἕωσπερ ὀρθὰ δοξάζοι;

ΜΕΝ. Ἀνάγκη μοι φαίνεται· ὥστε θαυμάζω, D ὦ Σώκρατες, τούτου οὕτως ἔχοντος, ὅτι δή ποτε πολὺ τιμιωτέρα ἡ ἐπιστήμη τῆς ὀρθῆς δόξης, καὶ δι' ὅ τι τὸ μὲν ἕτερον, τὸ δὲ ἕτερόν ἐστιν αὐτῶν.

ΣΩ. Οἶσθα οὖν δι' ὅ τι θαυμάζεις, ἢ ἐγώ σοι εἴπω;

ΜΕΝ. Πάνυ γ' εἰπέ.

ΣΩ. Ὅτι τοῖς Δαιδάλου ἀγάλμασιν οὐ προσέσχηκας τὸν νοῦν· ἴσως δὲ οὐδ' ἔστι παρ' ὑμῖν.

ΜΕΝ. Πρὸς τί δὲ δὴ τοῦτο λέγεις;

ΣΩ. Ὅτι καὶ ταῦτα, ἐὰν μὲν μὴ δεδεμένα ᾖ, ἀποδιδράσκει καὶ δραπετεύει, ἐὰν δὲ δεδεμένα, παραμένει.

E ΜΕΝ. Τί οὖν δή;

ΣΩ. Τῶν ἐκείνου ποιημάτων λελυμένον μὲν ἐκτῆσθαι οὐ πολλῆς τινὸς ἄξιόν ἐστι τιμῆς, ὥσπερ δραπέτην ἄνθρωπον· οὐ γὰρ παραμένει· δεδεμένον δὲ πολλοῦ ἄξιον· πάνυ γὰρ καλὰ τὰ ἔργα ἐστί. πρὸς τί οὖν δὴ λέγω ταῦτα; πρὸς τὰς δόξας τὰς ἀληθεῖς. καὶ γὰρ αἱ δόξαι αἱ ἀληθεῖς,

---

[1] Cf. Euthyphro 11. Socrates pretends to believe the old legend according to which Daedalus, the first sculptor, con-

MEN. So it seems.

soc. Then right opinion is just as useful as knowledge.

MEN. With this difference, Socrates, that he who has knowledge will always hit on the right way, whereas he who has right opinion will sometimes do so, but sometimes not.

soc. How do you mean ? Will not he who always has right opinion be always right, so long as he opines rightly ?

MEN. It appears to me that he must ; and therefore I wonder, Socrates, this being the case, that knowledge should ever be more prized than right opinion, and why they should be two distinct and separate things.

soc. Well, do you know why it is that you wonder, or shall I tell you ?

MEN. Please tell me.

soc. It is because you have not observed with attention the images of Daedalus.[1] But perhaps there are none in your country.

MEN. What is the point of your remark ?

soc. That if they are not fastened up they play truant and run away ; but, if fastened, they stay where they are.

MEN. Well, what of that ?

soc. To possess one of his works which is let loose does not count for much in value ; it will not stay with you any more than a runaway slave : but when fastened up it is worth a great deal, for his productions are very fine things And to what am I referring in all this ? To true opinions.

trived a wonderful mechanism in his statues by which they could move.

ὅσον μὲν ἂν χρόνον παραμένωσι, καλὸν τὸ χρῆμα
98 καὶ πάντα τἀγαθὰ ἐργάζονται· πολὺν δὲ χρόνον
οὐκ ἐθέλουσι παραμένειν, ἀλλὰ δραπετεύουσιν ἐκ
τῆς ψυχῆς τοῦ ἀνθρώπου, ὥστε οὐ πολλοῦ ἄξιαί
εἰσιν, ἕως ἄν τις αὐτὰς δήσῃ αἰτίας λογισμῷ.
τοῦτο δ᾽ ἐστίν, Μένων ἑταῖρε, ἀνάμνησις, ὡς ἐν
τοῖς πρόσθεν ἡμῖν ὡμολόγηται. ἐπειδὰν δὲ δε-
θῶσι, πρῶτον μὲν ἐπιστῆμαι γίγνονται, ἔπειτα
μόνιμοι· καὶ διὰ ταῦτα δὴ τιμιώτερον ἐπιστήμη
ὀρθῆς δόξης ἐστί, καὶ διαφέρει δεσμῷ ἐπιστήμη
ὀρθῆς δόξης.

ΜΕΝ. Νὴ τὸν Δία, ὦ Σώκρατες, ἔοικε τοιούτῳ
τινί.

Β ΣΩ. Καὶ μὴν καὶ ἐγὼ ὡς οὐκ εἰδὼς λέγω,
ἀλλ᾽ εἰκάζων· ὅτι δέ ἐστί τι ἀλλοῖον ὀρθὴ δόξα
καὶ ἐπιστήμη, οὐ πάνυ μοι δοκῶ τοῦτο εἰκάζειν,
ἀλλ᾽ εἴπερ τι ἄλλο φαίην ἂν εἰδέναι, ὀλίγα δ᾽ ἂν
φαίην, ἓν δ᾽ οὖν καὶ τοῦτο ἐκείνων θείην ἂν ὧν
οἶδα.

ΜΕΝ. Καὶ ὀρθῶς γε, ὦ Σώκρατες, λέγεις.

ΣΩ. Τί δέ; τόδε οὐκ ὀρθῶς, ὅτι ἀληθὴς δόξα
ἡγουμένη τὸ ἔργον ἑκάστης τῆς πράξεως οὐδὲν
χεῖρον ἀπεργάζεται ἢ ἐπιστήμη;

ΜΕΝ. Καὶ τοῦτο δοκεῖς μοι ἀληθῆ λέγειν.

C ΣΩ. Οὐδὲν ἄρα ὀρθὴ δόξα ἐπιστήμης χεῖρον
οὐδὲ ἧττον ὠφελίμη ἔσται εἰς τὰς πράξεις, οὐδὲ
ἀνὴρ ὁ ἔχων ὀρθὴν δόξαν ἢ ὁ ἐπιστήμην.

ΜΕΝ. Ἔστι ταῦτα.

ΣΩ. Καὶ μὴν ὅ γε ἀγαθὸς ἀνὴρ ὠφέλιμος
ἡμῖν ὡμολόγηται εἶναι.

For these, so long as they stay with us, are a fine possession, and effect all that is good; but they do not care to stay for long, and run away out of the human soul, and thus are of no great value until one makes them fast with causal reasoning. And this process, friend Meno, is recollection, as in our previous talk we have agreed. But when once they are fastened, in the first place they turn into knowledge, and in the second, are abiding. And this is why knowledge is more prized than right opinion: the one transcends the other by its trammels.

MEN. Upon my word, Socrates, it seems to be very much as you say.

soc. And indeed I too speak as one who does not know but only conjectures: yet that there is a difference between right opinion and knowledge is not at all a conjecture with me but something I would particularly assert that I knew: there are not many things of which I would say that, but this one, at any rate, I will include among those that I know.

MEN. Yes, and you are right, Socrates, in so saying.

soc. Well, then, am I not right also in saying that true opinion leading the way renders the effect of each action as good as knowledge does?

MEN. There again, Socrates, I think you speak the truth.

soc. So that right opinion will be no whit inferior to knowledge in worth or usefulness as regards our actions, nor will the man who has right opinion be inferior to him who has knowledge.

MEN. That is so.

soc. And you know that the good man has been admitted by us to be useful.

PLATO

98

ΜΕΝ. Ναί.

ΣΩ. Ἐπειδὴ τοίνυν οὐ μόνον δι' ἐπιστήμην ἀγαθοὶ ἄνδρες ἂν εἶεν καὶ ὠφέλιμοι ταῖς πόλεσιν, εἴπερ εἶεν, ἀλλὰ καὶ δι' ὀρθὴν δόξαν, τούτοιν δὲ οὐδέτερον φύσει ἐστὶ τοῖς ἀνθρώποις, οὔτε ἐπι-
D στήμη οὔτε δόξα ἀληθής, ὄντ'[1] ἐπίκτητα—ἢ δοκεῖ σοι φύσει ὁποτερονοῦν αὐτοῖν ἐνῖαι;

ΜΕΝ. Οὐκ ἔμοιγε.

ΣΩ. Οὐκοῦν ἐπειδὴ οὐ φύσει, οὐδὲ οἱ ἀγαθοὶ φύσει εἶεν ἄν.

ΜΕΝ. Οὐ δῆτα.

ΣΩ. Ἐπειδὴ δέ γε οὐ φύσει, ἐσκοποῦμεν τὸ μετὰ τοῦτο, εἰ διδακτόν ἐστιν.

ΜΕΝ. Ναί.

ΣΩ. Οὐκοῦν διδακτὸν ἔδοξεν εἶναι, εἰ φρόνησις ἡ ἀρετή;

ΜΕΝ. Ναί.

ΣΩ. Κἂν εἴ γε διδακτὸν εἴη, φρόνησις ἂν εἶναι;

ΜΕΝ. Πάνυ γε.

ΣΩ. Καὶ εἰ μέν γε διδάσκαλοι εἶεν, διδακτὸν
E ἂν εἶναι, μὴ ὄντων δὲ οὐ διδακτόν;

ΜΕΝ. Οὕτως.

ΣΩ. Ἀλλὰ μὴν ὡμολογήκαμεν μὴ εἶναι αὐτοῦ διδασκάλους;

ΜΕΝ. Ἔστι ταῦτα.

ΣΩ. Ὡμολογήκαμεν ἄρα μήτε διδακτὸν αὐτὸ μήτε φρόνησιν εἶναι;

ΜΕΝ. Πάνυ γε.

ΣΩ. Ἀλλὰ μὴν ἀγαθόν γε αὐτὸ ὁμολογοῦμεν εἶναι;

ΜΕΝ. Ναί.

[1] ὄντ' Apelt: οὔτ' mss.

364

MEN. Yes.

soc. Since then it is not only because of knowledge that men will be good and useful to their country, where such men are to be found, but also on account of right opinion; and since neither of these two things—knowledge and true opinion—is a natural property of mankind, being acquired—or do you think that either of them is natural?

MEN. Not I.

soc. Then if they are not natural, good people cannot be good by nature either.

MEN. Of course not.

soc. And since they are not an effect of nature, we next considered whether virtue can be taught.

MEN. Yes.

soc. And we thought it teachable if virtue is wisdom?

MEN. Yes.

soc. And if teachable, it must be wisdom?

MEN. Certainly.

soc. And if there were teachers, it could be taught, but if there were none, it could not?

MEN. Quite so.

soc. But surely we acknowledged that it had no teachers?

MEN. That is true.

soc. Then we acknowledged it neither was taught nor was wisdom?

MEN. Certainly.

soc. But yet we admitted it was a good?

MEN. Yes.

98

ΣΩ. Ὠφέλιμον δὲ καὶ ἀγαθὸν εἶναι τὸ ὀρθῶς ἡγούμενον;

ΜΕΝ. Πάνυ γε.

ΣΩ. Ὀρθῶς δέ γε ἡγεῖσθαι δύο ὄντα ταῦτα
99 μόνα, δόξαν τε ἀληθῆ καὶ ἐπιστήμην, ἃ ἔχων
ἄνθρωπος ὀρθῶς ἡγεῖται. τὰ γὰρ ἀπὸ τύχης
γιγνόμενα οὐκ ἀνθρωπίνῃ ἡγεμονίᾳ γίγνεται· ὧν δὲ
ἄνθρωπος ἡγεμών ἐστιν ἐπὶ τὸ ὀρθόν, δύο ταῦτα,
δόξα ἀληθὴς καὶ ἐπιστήμη.

ΜΕΝ. Δοκεῖ μοι οὕτως.

ΣΩ. Οὐκοῦν ἐπειδὴ οὐ διδακτόν ἐστιν, οὐδ'
ἐπιστήμη δὴ ἔτι γίγνεται ἡ ἀρετή;

ΜΕΝ. Οὐ φαίνεται.

B ΣΩ. Δυοῖν ἄρα ὄντοιν ἀγαθοῖν καὶ ὠφελίμοιν τὸ
μὲν ἕτερον ἀπολέλυται, καὶ οὐκ ἂν εἴη ἐν πολιτικῇ πράξει ἐπιστήμη ἡγεμών.

ΜΕΝ. Οὔ μοι δοκεῖ.

ΣΩ. Οὐκ ἄρα σοφίᾳ τινὶ οὐδὲ σοφοὶ ὄντες οἱ
τοιοῦτοι ἄνδρες ἡγοῦντο ταῖς πόλεσιν, οἱ ἀμφὶ
Θεμιστοκλέα τε καὶ οὓς ἄρτι Ἄνυτος ὅδε ἔλεγε·
διὸ καὶ οὐχ οἷοί τε ἄλλους ποιεῖν τοιούτους οἷοί
αὐτοί εἰσιν, ἅτε οὐ δι' ἐπιστήμην ὄντες τοιοῦτοι.

ΜΕΝ. Ἔοικεν οὕτως ἔχειν, ὦ Σώκρατες, ὡς
λέγεις.

ΣΩ. Οὐκοῦν εἰ μὴ ἐπιστήμη, εὐδοξίᾳ δὴ τὸ
C λοιπὸν γίγνεται· ᾗ οἱ πολιτικοὶ ἄνδρες χρώμενοι
τὰς πόλεις ὀρθοῦσιν, οὐδὲν διαφερόντως ἔχοντες
πρὸς τὸ φρονεῖν ἢ οἱ χρησμῳδοί τε καὶ οἱ θεο-
μάντεις· καὶ γὰρ οὗτοι λέγουσι μὲν ἀληθῆ καὶ
πολλά, ἴσασι δὲ οὐδὲν ὧν λέγουσιν.

MENO

soc. And that which guides rightly is useful and good ?

men. Certainly.

soc. And that there are only two things—true opinion and knowledge—that guide rightly and a man guides rightly if he have these ; for things that come about by chance do not occur through human guidance ; but where a man is a guide to what is right we find these two things—true opinion and knowledge.

men. I agree.

soc. Well now, since virtue is not taught, we no longer take it to be knowledge ?

men. Apparently not.

soc. So of two good and useful things one has been rejected : knowledge cannot be our guide in political conduct.

men. I think not.

soc. Therefore it was not by any wisdom, nor because they were wise, that the sort of men we spoke of controlled their states—Themistocles and the rest of them, to whom our friend Anytus was referring a moment ago. For this reason it was that they were unable to make others like unto themselves—because their qualities were not an effect of knowledge.

men. The case is probably as you say, Socrates.

soc. And if not by knowledge, as the only alternative it must have been by good opinion. This is the means which statesmen employ for their direction of states, and they have nothing more to do with wisdom than soothsayers and diviners ; for these people utter many a true thing when inspired, but have no knowledge of anything they say.

ΜΕΝ. Κινδυνεύει οὕτως ἔχειν.

ΣΩ. Οὐκοῦν, ὦ Μένων, ἄξιον τούτους θείους καλεῖν τοὺς ἄνδρας, οἵτινες νοῦν μὴ ἔχοντες πολλὰ καὶ
μεγάλα κατορθοῦσιν ὧν πράττουσι καὶ λέγουσιν;

ΜΕΝ. Πάνυ γε.

ΣΩ. Ὀρθῶς ἄρ' ἂν καλοῖμεν θείους τε, οὓς
D νυνδὴ ἐλέγομεν χρησμῳδοὺς καὶ μάντεις καὶ τοὺς
ποιητικοὺς ἅπαντας· καὶ τοὺς πολιτικοὺς οὐχ
ἥκιστα τούτων φαῖμεν ἂν θείους τε εἶναι καὶ
ἐνθουσιάζειν, ἐπίπνους ὄντας καὶ κατεχομένους
ἐκ τοῦ θεοῦ, ὅταν κατορθῶσι λέγοντες πολλὰ
καὶ μεγάλα πράγματα, μηδὲν εἰδότες ὧν λέγουσιν.

ΜΕΝ. Πάνυ γε.

ΣΩ. Καὶ αἵ γε γυναῖκες δήπου, ὦ Μένων, τοὺς
ἀγαθοὺς ἄνδρας θείους καλοῦσι· καὶ οἱ Λάκωνες
ὅταν τινὰ ἐγκωμιάζωσιν ἀγαθὸν ἄνδρα, θεῖος
ἀνήρ, φασίν, οὗτος.

E ΜΕΝ. Καὶ φαίνονταί γε, ὦ Σώκρατες, ὀρθῶς
λέγειν. καίτοι ἴσως Ἄνυτος ὅδε σοι ἄχθεται
λέγοντι.

ΣΩ. Οὐδὲν μέλει ἔμοιγε. τούτῳ μέν, ὦ Μένων, καὶ αὖθις διαλεξόμεθα· εἰ δὲ νῦν ἡμεῖς ἐν
παντὶ τῷ λόγῳ τούτῳ καλῶς ἐζητήσαμέν τε καὶ
ἐλέγομεν, ἀρετὴ ἂν εἴη οὔτε φύσει οὔτε διδακτόν,
ἀλλὰ θείᾳ μοίρᾳ παραγιγνομένη ἄνευ νοῦ, οἷς
100 ἂν παραγίγνηται, εἰ μή τις εἴη τοιοῦτος τῶν
πολιτικῶν ἀνδρῶν, οἷος καὶ ἄλλον ποιῆσαι πολι-
τικόν. εἰ δὲ εἴη, σχεδὸν ἄν τι οὗτος λέγοιτο
τοιοῦτος ἐν τοῖς ζῶσιν, οἷον ἔφη Ὅμηρος ἐν
τοῖς τεθνεῶσι τὸν Τειρεσίαν εἶναι, λέγων περὶ
αὑτοῦ, ὅτι οἷος πέπνυται τῶν ἐν Ἅιδου, αἱ δὲ
σκιαὶ ἀΐσσουσι. ταὐτὸν ἂν καὶ ἐνθάδε ὁ τοιοῦτος

MEN. I daresay that is so.

SOC. And may we, Meno, rightly call those men divine who, having no understanding, yet succeed in many a great deed and word?

MEN. Certainly.

SOC. Then we shall be right in calling those divine of whom we spoke just now as soothsayers and prophets and all of the poetic turn; and especially we can say of the statesmen that they are divine and enraptured, as being inspired and possessed of God when they succeed in speaking many great things, while knowing nought of what they say.

MEN. Certainly.

SOC. And the women too, I presume, Meno, call good men divine; and the Spartans, when they eulogize a good man, say—"He is a divine person."

MEN. And to all appearance, Socrates, they are right; though perhaps our friend Anytus may be annoyed at your statement.

SOC. For my part, I care not. As for him, Meno, we will converse with him some other time. At the moment, if through all this discussion our queries and statements have been correct, virtue is found to be neither natural nor taught, but is imparted to us by a divine dispensation without understanding in those who receive it, unless there should be somebody among the statesmen capable of making a statesman of another. And if there should be any such, he might fairly be said to be among the living what Homer says Teiresias was among the dead—"He alone has comprehension; the rest are flitting shades."[1] In the same way he on earth, in

---

[1] *Od.* x. 494.

ὥσπερ παρὰ σκιὰς ἀληθὲς ἂν πρᾶγμα εἴη πρὸς
ἀρετήν.

B   ΜΕΝ. Κάλλιστα δοκεῖς μοι λέγειν, ὦ Σώκρατες.

ΣΩ. Ἐκ μὲν τοίνυν τούτου τοῦ λογισμοῦ, ὦ
Μένων, θείᾳ μοίρᾳ ἡμῖν φαίνεται παραγιγνομένη
ἡ ἀρετὴ οἷς παραγίγνεται· τὸ δὲ σαφὲς περὶ
αὐτοῦ εἰσόμεθα τότε, ὅταν πρὶν ᾧτινι τρόπῳ τοῖς
ἀνθρώποις παραγίγνεται ἀρετή, πρότερον ἐπιχειρήσωμεν αὐτὸ καθ’ αὑτὸ ζητεῖν τί ποτ’ ἔστιν
ἀρετή. νῦν δ’ ἐμοὶ μὲν ὥρα ποι ἰέναι, σὺ δὲ
ταῦτα ἅπερ αὐτὸς πέπεισαι πεῖθε καὶ τὸν ξένον
τόνδε Ἄνυτον, ἵνα πρᾳότερος ᾖ· ὡς ἐὰν πείσῃς
τοῦτον, ἔστιν ὅ τι καὶ Ἀθηναίους ὀνήσεις.

respect of virtue, will be a real substance among shadows.

MEN. I think you put it excellently, Socrates.

soc. Then the result of our reasoning, Meno, is found to be that virtue comes to us by a divine dispensation, when it does come. But the certainty of this we shall only know when, before asking in what way virtue comes to mankind, we set about inquiring what virtue is, in and by itself. It is time now for me to go my way, but do you persuade our friend Anytus of that whereof you are now yourself persuaded, so as to put him in a gentler mood ; for if you can persuade him, you will do a good turn to the people of Athens also.

EUTHYDEMUS

INTRODUCTION TO THE *EUTHYDEMUS*

THIS dialogue is remarkable amongst Plato's writings for the keenness and brilliance of its comic satire. In the main it is a relentless exposure of the " eristic " or disputatious side of the higher education which was fashionable at Athens towards the end of Socrates' life : the plot of the little drama is designed to ridicule the mischievous quibbles of two professors who are trying to captivate the mind of a handsome and promising youth. But at the same time it is plainly the work of an ardent teacher of philosophy, who is clearing the ground for the construction of what we now call a system of logic. The spurious argumentation of certain popular sophists had to be demolished before the Socratic method of " dialectic " could be exhibited in its full dignity and value.

There are good reasons for believing that the *Euthydemus* was written and published after the *Protagoras* and *Meno*, about 390 B.C.—some ten years after the death of Socrates, and not long before Plato founded the Academy in 387. Beneath all its mockery and laughter runs an eager tone of protest, which is only half muffled by the genial banter of Socrates. His manner towards the professors is throughout deferential and diffident, but the famous " irony " only serves to bring out

in sharper relief the unscrupulous audacity of these
sham philosophers. After allowing for some artistic
selection and intensification, we may probably take
it as a truthful picture of the actual Socrates in
contrast with two attractive and successful educators
of the day : but we cannot help perceiving also the
zeal for true education which is steadily impelling
Plato himself towards his high and responsible
position in the intellectual world.

The form of the dialogue is notable in itself,
for it is the only instance in Plato of a narrated
conversation which is broken by remarks of the
hearer (Crito) upon the story as told by Socrates,
who discusses it with him. The account of the
contest with the two sophists is moreover followed
by some serious talk between Socrates and his
friend about a person who stands half-way between
philosophy and politics, and who has hastily spurned
the former of these pursuits after listening to Euthydemus and Dionysodorus. Whether (as seems probable) the reference is to Isocrates, or to someone
else, this epilogue serves to point the important moral
that, despite the unworthiness of her ministers,
Philosophy abides, ever undefiled, august and
supreme. In relation to her, the half-way men are
as worthless as her showy professors. It seems likely
that Plato felt some apprehension lest the dramatic
and literary skill with which he had represented,
through the mouth of Socrates, the verbal antics
of the two sophists had endangered the impression
which he wished to leave of his master's and his own
great interest in life—the right education of able
and aspiring youth. Thus the whole piece is to
be regarded as a comedy annotated, as it were,

with a view to serious instruction, or an educational manifesto half concealed by lively scenes of satirical drama. Its art is entertaining in itself, and significant also for an understanding of the Aristophanic side of Plato's nature. Its real meaning, however, shows him treading in the steps of Socrates, and especially developing for his own ends his departed master's views on rhetoric and politics.

A useful modern edition of the *Euthydemus* by E. H. Gifford was published by the Clarendon Press, Oxford, in 1905.

ΕΥΘΥΔΗΜΟΣ

[Η ΕΡΙΣΤΙΚΟΣ· ΑΝΑΤΡΕΠΤΙΚΟΣ]

ΤΑ ΤΟΥ ΔΙΑΛΟΓΟΥ ΠΡΟΣΩΠΑ

ΚΡΙΤΩΝ, ΣΩΚΡΑΤΗΣ, ΕΥΘΥΔΗΜΟΣ, ΔΙΟΝΥΣΟΔΩΡΟΣ, ΚΛΕΙΝΙΑΣ, ΚΤΗΣΙΠΠΟΣ

St. I.
p. 271

ΚΡΙ. Τίς ἦν, ὦ Σώκρατες, ᾧ χθὲς ἐν Λυκείῳ διελέγου; ἦ πολὺς ὑμᾶς ὄχλος περιειστήκει, ὥστ' ἔγωγε βουλόμενος ἀκούειν προσελθὼν οὐδὲν οἷός τ' ἦ ἀκοῦσαι σαφές· ὑπερκύψας μέντοι κατεῖδον, καί μοι ἔδοξεν εἶναι ξένος τις, ᾧ διελέγου. τίς ἦν;

ΣΩ. Πότερον καὶ ἐρωτᾷς, ὦ Κρίτων; οὐ γὰρ εἷς, ἀλλὰ δύ' ἤστην.

ΚΡΙ. Ὃν μὲν ἐγὼ λέγω, ἐκ δεξιᾶς τρίτος ἀπὸ
B σοῦ καθῆστο· ἐν μέσῳ δ' ὑμῶν τὸ Ἀξιόχου μειρά- κιον ἦν. καὶ μάλα πολύ, ὦ Σώκρατες, ἐπιδεδωκέναι μοι ἔδοξεν, καὶ τοῦ ἡμετέρου οὐ πολύ τι τὴν ἡλικίαν διαφέρειν Κριτοβούλου. ἀλλ' ἐκεῖνος μὲν σκλη- φρός, οὗτος δὲ προφερὴς καὶ καλὸς καὶ ἀγαθὸς τὴν ὄψιν.

ΣΩ. Εὐθύδημος οὗτός ἐστιν, ὦ Κρίτων, ὃν ἐρωτᾷς· ὁ δὲ παρ' ἐμὲ καθήμενος ἐξ ἀριστερᾶς ἀδελφὸς τούτου, Διονυσόδωρος· μετέχει δὲ καὶ οὗτος τῶν λόγων.

378

EUTHYDEMUS

[OR ON DISPUTATION: REFUTATIVE]

CHARACTERS

CRITO, SOCRATES, EUTHYDEMUS, DIONYSODORUS, CLEINIAS, CTESIPPUS

CRI. Who was it, Socrates, that you were talking with yesterday at the Lyceum? Why, there was such a crowd standing about you that when I came up in the hope of listening I could hear nothing distinctly: still, by craning over I got a glimpse, and it appeared to me that it was a stranger with whom you were talking. Who was he?

SOC. About which are you asking, Crito? There were two of them, not one.

CRI. The man whom I mean was sitting next but one to you, on your right: between you was Axiochus' boy; and he, Socrates, seemed to me to have grown a great deal, so as to look almost the same age as my Critobulus, who is rather puny; whereas this boy has come on finely, and has a noble air about him.

SOC. Euthydemus is the person to whom you refer, Crito, and the one sitting on my left was his brother, Dionysodorus. He too takes part in our discussions.

ΚΡΙ. Οὐδέτερον γιγνώσκω, ὦ Σώκρατες. καινοὶ
C τινες αὖ οὗτοι, ὡς ἔοικε, σοφισταί· ποδαποί; καὶ
τίς ἡ σοφία;

ΣΩ. Οὗτοι τὸ μὲν γένος, ὡς ἐγῷμαι, ἐντεῦθέν
ποθέν εἰσιν ἐκ Χίου, ἀπῴκησαν δὲ ἐς Θουρίους,
φεύγοντες δὲ ἐκεῖθεν πόλλ᾽ ἤδη ἔτη περὶ τούσδε τοὺς
τόπους διατρίβουσιν· ὃ δὲ σὺ ἐρωτᾷς τὴν σοφίαν
αὐτοῖν, θαυμασία, ὦ Κρίτων· πασσοφοι ἀτεχνῶς τώ
γε, οὐδ᾽ ἤδη πρὸ τοῦ, ὅ τι εἶεν οἱ παγκρατιασταί.
τούτω γάρ ἐστον κομιδῇ παμμάχω οὐ κατὰ τὼ
Ἀκαρνᾶνε ἐγενέσθην τὼ παγκρατιαστὰ ἀδελφώ·
D ἐκείνω μὲν γὰρ τῷ σώματι μόνον οἵω τε μάχεσθαι·
τούτω δὲ πρῶτον μὲν τῷ σώματι δεινοτάτω
ἐστὸν καὶ μάχῃ, ᾗ πάντων ἔστι κρατεῖν· ἐν
ὅπλοις γὰρ αὐτώ τε σοφὼ πάνυ μάχεσθαι καὶ
272 ἄλλον, ὃς ἂν διδῷ μισθόν, οἵω τε ποιῆσαι· ἔπειτα
τὴν ἐν τοῖς δικαστηρίοις μάχην κρατίστω καὶ
ἀγωνίσασθαι καὶ ἄλλον διδάξαι λέγειν τε καὶ
συγγράφεσθαι λόγους οἵους εἰς τὰ δικαστήρια.
πρὸ τοῦ μὲν οὖν ταῦτα δεινὼ ἤστην μόνον, νῦν δὲ
τέλος ἐπιτεθήκατον παγκρατιαστικῇ τέχνῃ. ἢ γὰρ
ἦν λοιπὴ αὐτοῖν μάχη ἀργός, ταύτην νῦν ἐξείργασθον, ὥστε μηδ᾽ ἂν ἕνα αὐτοῖς οἱόν τ᾽ εἶναι μηδ᾽
ἀντᾶραι· οὕτω δεινὼ γεγόνατον ἐν τοῖς λόγοις
μάχεσθαί τε καὶ ἐξελέγχειν τὸ ἀεὶ λεγόμενον, ὁμοίως
B ἐάν τε ψεῦδος ἐάν τε ἀληθὲς ᾖ. ἐγὼ μὲν οὖν, ὦ
Κρίτων, ἐν νῷ ἔχω τοῖν ἀνδροῖν παραδοῦναι ἐμαυτόν·
καὶ γάρ φατον ἐν ὀλίγῳ χρόνῳ ποιῆσαι ἂν καὶ
ἄλλον ὁντινοῦν τὰ αὐτὰ ταῦτα δεινόν.

---

[1] The phrase refers especially to a very vigorous sport
which combined wrestling and boxing.

CRI. Neither of them is known to me, Socrates. A pair of fresh additions, I suppose, to our sophists. Where do they hail from, and what science do they profess?

SOC. By birth I believe they belong to these parts, that is to say, Chios; they went out as colonists to Thurii, but have been exiled thence and have spent a good many years now in various parts of this country. As to what you ask of their profession, it is a wonderful one, Crito. These two men are absolutely omniscient: I never knew before what "all-round sportsmen"[1] were. They are a pair of regular all-round fighters—not in the style of the famous all-round athletes, the two brothers of Acarnania; they could fight with their bodies only. But these two, in the first place, are most formidable in body and in fight against all comers—for they are not only well skilled themselves in fighting under arms, but are able to impart that skill, for a fee, to another; and further, they are most competent also to fight the battle of the law-courts and teach others how to speak, or to have composed for them, such speeches as may win their suits. Formerly they had merely some ability for this; but now they have put the finishing touch to their skill as all-round sportsmen. The one feat of fighting yet unperformed by them they have now accomplished, so that nobody dares stand up to them for a moment; such a faculty they have acquired for wielding words as their weapons and confuting any argument as readily if it be true as if it be false. And so I, Crito, am minded to place myself in these two gentlemen's hands; for they say it would take them but a little while to make anyone else clever in just the same way.

ΚΡΙ. Τί δέ, ὦ Σώκρατες; οὐ φοβῇ τὴν ἡλικίαν,
μὴ ἤδη πρεσβύτερος ᾖς;

ΣΩ. Ἥκιστά γε, ὦ Κρίτων· ἱκανὸν τεκμήριον
ἔχω καὶ παραμύθιον τοῦ μὴ φοβεῖσθαι. αὐτὼ
γὰρ τούτω, ὡς ἔπος εἰπεῖν, γέροντε ὄντε ἠρξά-
σθην ταύτης τῆς σοφίας, ἧς ἔγωγε ἐπιθυμῶ, τῆς
C ἐριστικῆς· πέρυσιν ἢ προπέρυσιν οὐδέπω ἤστην
σοφώ. ἀλλ᾽ ἐγὼ ἓν μόνον φοβοῦμαι, μὴ αὖ
ὄνειδος τοῖν ξένοιν περιάψω, ὥσπερ Κόννῳ τῷ
Μητροβίου, τῷ κιθαριστῇ, ὃς ἐμὲ διδάσκει ἔτι καὶ
νῦν κιθαρίζειν· ὁρῶντες οὖν οἱ παῖδες οἱ συμφοι-
τηταί μου ἐμοῦ τε καταγελῶσι καὶ τὸν Κόννον
καλοῦσι γεροντοδιδάσκαλον. μὴ οὖν καὶ τοῖν
ξένοιν τις ταὐτὸ τοῦτο ὀνειδίσῃ· οἱ δ᾽ αὐτὸ τοῦτο
ἴσως φοβούμενοι τάχα με οὐκ ἂν ἐθέλοιεν προσ-
δέξασθαι. ἐγὼ δ᾽, ὦ Κρίτων, ἐκεῖσε μὲν ἄλλους πέπεικα συμμαθητάς μοι φοιτᾶν πρεσβύτας,
D ἐνταῦθα δέ γε ἑτέρους πειράσομαι πείθειν. καὶ
σὺ τί οὐ συμφοιτᾷς; ὡς[1] δὲ δέλεαρ αὐτοῖς ἄξομεν
τοὺς σοὺς υἱεῖς· ἐφιέμενοι γὰρ ἐκείνων οἶδ᾽ ὅτι
καὶ ἡμᾶς παιδεύσουσιν.

ΚΡΙ. Ἀλλ᾽ οὐδὲν κωλύει, ὦ Σώκρατες, ἐάν γε
σοὶ δοκῇ. πρῶτον δέ μοι διήγησαι τὴν σοφίαν
τοῖν ἀνδροῖν τίς ἐστιν, ἵνα εἰδῶ ὅ τι καὶ μαθη-
σόμεθα.

ΣΩ. Οὐκ ἂν φθάνοις ἀκούων· ὡς οὐκ ἂν ἔχοιμί
γε εἰπεῖν, ὅτι οὐ προσεῖχον τὸν νοῦν αὐτοῖν, ἀλλὰ
πάνυ καὶ προσεῖχον καὶ μέμνημαι, καί σοι πειρά-
E σομαι ἐξ ἀρχῆς ἅπαντα διηγήσασθαι. κατὰ θεὸν

---

[1] So Winckelmann: σὺ τί που συμφοιτᾷ ἴσως mss.

CRI. What, Socrates! Are you not afraid, at your time of life, that you may be too old for that now?

SOC. Not at all, Crito: I have enough proof and reassurance to the contrary. These same two persons were little less than old men at the time of their taking up this science, which I desire to have, of disputation. Last year, or the year before, they were as yet without their science. The only thing I am afraid of is that I may bring the same disgrace upon our two visitors as upon Connus, son of Metrobius, the harper, who is still trying to teach me the harp; so that the boys who go to his lessons with me make fun of me and call Connus "the gaffers' master." This makes me fear that someone may make the same reproach to the two strangers; and, for aught I know, their dread of this very thing may make them unwilling to accept me. So, Crito, just as in the other case I have persuaded some elderly men to come and have lessons with me, in this affair I am going to try and persuade another set. Now you, I am sure, will come with me to school; and we will take your sons as a bait to entice them, for I have no doubt that the attraction of these young fellows will make them include us also in the class.

CRI. I have no objection, Socrates, if you think fit to do so. But first you must explain to me what is the science these men profess, that I may know what it is we are going to learn.

SOC. You shall be told at once; for I cannot plead that I did not give them my attention, since I not only attended closely but remember and will try to expound the whole thing from the beginning.

γάρ τινα ἔτυχον καθήμενος ἐνταῦθα, οὗπερ σύ με
εἶδες, ἐν τῷ ἀποδυτηρίῳ μόνος, καὶ ἤδη ἐν νῷ
εἶχον ἀναστῆναι· ἀνισταμένου δέ μου ἐγένετο τὸ
εἰωθὸς σημεῖον τὸ δαιμόνιον. πάλιν οὖν ἐκα-
273 θεζόμην, καὶ ὀλίγῳ ὕστερον εἰσέρχεσθον τούτω,
ὅ τ᾽ Εὐθύδημος καὶ ὁ Διονυσόδωρος, καὶ ἄλλοι
μαθηταὶ ἅμα αὖ πολλοὶ ἐμοὶ δοκεῖν· εἰσελθόντε
δὲ περιεπατείτην ἐν τῷ καταστέγῳ δρόμῳ. καὶ
οὔπω τούτω δύ᾽ ἢ τρεῖς δρόμους περιεληλυθότε
ἤστην, καὶ εἰσέρχεται Κλεινίας, ὃν σὺ φῂς πολὺ
ἐπιδεδωκέναι, ἀληθῆ λέγων· ὄπισθεν δὲ αὐτοῦ
ἐρασταὶ πάνυ πολλοί τε ἄλλοι καὶ Κτήσιππος,
νεανίσκος τις Παιανιεύς, μάλα καλός τε κἀγαθὸς
τὴν φύσιν, ὅσον μὴ ὑβριστὴς διὰ τὸ νέος εἶναι.
B ἰδὼν οὖν με ὁ Κλεινίας ἀπὸ τῆς εἰσόδου μόνον
καθήμενον, ἄντικρυς ἰὼν παρεκαθέζετο ἐκ δεξιᾶς,
ὥσπερ καὶ σὺ φῄς· ἰδόντε δὲ αὐτὸν ὅ τε Διονυσόδωρος καὶ ὁ Εὐθύδημος πρῶτον μὲν ἐπιστάντε
διελεγέσθην ἀλλήλοιν, ἄλλην καὶ ἄλλην ἀπο-
βλέποντε εἰς ἡμᾶς· καὶ γὰρ πάνυ αὐτοῖν προσεῖχον τὸν νοῦν· ἔπειτα ἰόντε ὁ μὲν παρὰ τὸ
μειράκιον ἐκαθέζετο, ὁ Εὐθύδημος, ὁ δὲ παρ᾽
αὐτὸν ἐμὲ ἐν ἀριστερᾷ· οἱ δ᾽ ἄλλοι ὡς ἕκαστος
ἐτύγχανεν.
C   Ἠσπαζόμην οὖν αὐτὼ ἅτε διὰ χρόνου ἑωρακώς·
μετὰ δὲ τοῦτο εἶπον πρὸς τὸν Κλεινίαν, Ὦ Κλεινία,
τώδε μέντοι τὼ ἄνδρε σοφώ, Εὐθύδημός τε καὶ
Διονυσόδωρος, οὐ τὰ σμικρά, ἀλλὰ τὰ μεγάλα· τὰ

---

[1] This gymnasium (the Lyceum) was a public one, open
to persons of all ages, and was a common resort of Socrates
and the sophists.
[2] Socrates believed that his conduct was occasionally

By some providence I chanced to be sitting in the place where you saw me, in the undressing-room,[1] alone, and was just intending to get up and go; but the moment I did so, there came my wonted spiritual sign.[2] So I sat down again, and after a little while these two persons entered—Euthydemus and Dionysodorus—and accompanying them, quite a number, as it seemed to me, of their pupils: the two men came in and began walking round inside the cloister.[3] Hardly had they taken two or three turns, when in stepped Cleinias, who you say has come on so much, and you are right: behind him was a whole troop of lovers, and among them Ctesippus, a young fellow from Paeania, of gentle birth and breeding, except for a certain insolence of youth. So when Cleinias as he entered caught sight of me sitting there alone, he came straight across and sat beside me on my right, just as you say. Dionysodorus and Euthydemus, when they saw him, stood at first talking with each other, and casting an occasional glance at us— for my attention was fixed on them—but then one of them, Euthydemus, took a seat by the youth, and the other next to me on my left; the rest, where each happened to find one.

So I greeted the two brothers, as not having seen them for some time; after that I said to Cleinias: My dear Cleinias, these two men, you know, are skilled not in little things, but in great. For they

---

guided by a spiritual voice or sign peculiar to himself. By Plato's account it was always negative, but the present instance shows how Xenophon might have some reason for saying that it was sometimes positive.

[3] The cloister ran round the central open court, and was reached by passing through the undressing-room.

γὰρ περὶ τὸν πόλεμον πάντα ἐπίστασθον, ὅσα δεῖ
τὸν μέλλοντα στρατηγὸν ἔσεσθαι, τάς τε τάξεις
καὶ τὰς ἡγεμονίας τῶν στρατοπέδων καὶ ὅσα ἐν
ὅπλοις μάχεσθαι διδακτέον· οἵω τε δὲ καὶ ποιῆσαι
δυνατὸν εἶναι αὐτὸν αὑτῷ βοηθεῖν ἐν τοῖς δικαστηρίοις, ἄν τις αὐτὸν ἀδικῇ. εἰπὼν οὖν ταῦτα
D κατεφρονήθην ὑπ' αὐτοῖν· ἐγελασάτην οὖν ἄμφω
βλέψαντε εἰς ἀλλήλω, καὶ ὁ Εὐθύδημος εἶπεν·
Οὗτοι ἔτι ταῦτα, ὦ Σώκρατες, σπουδάζομεν, ἀλλὰ
παρέργοις αὐτοῖς χρώμεθα. κἀγὼ θαυμάσας
εἶπον· Καλὸν ἄν τι τὸ ἔργον ὑμῶν εἴη, εἰ τηλικαῦτα πράγματα πάρεργα ὑμῖν τυγχάνει ὄντα, καὶ
πρὸς θεῶν εἴπετόν μοι, τί ἐστι τοῦτο τὸ καλόν.
Ἀρετήν, ἔφη, ὦ Σώκρατες, οἰόμεθα οἵω τ' εἶναι
παραδοῦναι κάλλιστ' ἀνθρώπων καὶ τάχιστα.
E Ὦ Ζεῦ, οἷον, ἦν δ' ἐγώ, λέγετον πρᾶγμα· πόθεν
τοῦτο τὸ ἕρμαιον εὑρέτην; ἐγὼ δὲ περὶ ὑμῶν
διενοούμην ἔτι, ὥσπερ νῦν δὴ ἔλεγον, ὡς τὸ πολὺ
τοῦτο δεινοῖν ὄντοιν, ἐν ὅπλοις μάχεσθαι, καὶ ταῦτ'
ἔλεγον περὶ σφῶν· ὅτε γὰρ τὸ πρότερον ἐπεδη-
μησάτην, τοῦτο μέμνημαι σφὼ ἐπαγγελλομένω.
εἰ δὲ νῦν ἀληθῶς ταύτην τὴν ἐπιστήμην ἔχετον,
ἵλεω εἴητον· ἀτεχνῶς γὰρ ἔγωγε σφὼ ὥσπερ θεὼ
προσαγορεύω, συγγνώμην δεόμενος ἔχειν μοι τῶν
274 ἔμπροσθεν εἰρημένων. ἀλλ' ὁρᾶτον, ὦ Εὐθύδημέ
τε καὶ Διονυσόδωρε, εἰ ἀληθῆ ἐλέγετον· ὑπὸ γὰρ
τοῦ μεγέθους τοῦ ἐπαγγέλματος οὐδὲν θαυμαστὸν
ἀπιστεῖν.

Ἀλλ' εὖ ἴσθι, ὦ Σώκρατες, ἔφατον, τοῦτο
οὕτως ἔχον.

Μακαρίζω ἄρ' ὑμᾶς ἔγωγε τοῦ κτήματος πολὺ

understand all about war, that is, as much as is
needful for him who is to be a good general; both
the tactics and the strategy of armies, and all the
teaching of troops under arms; and they can also
enable one to get redress in the law courts for a
wrong that one may have suffered.

When I had said this, I saw they despised me for
it, and they both laughed, looking at each other;
then Euthydemus said: No, no, Socrates, we do
not make those matters our business now; we deal
with them as diversions.

At this I wondered and said: Your business must
be a fine one, if such great matters are indeed
diversions to you; so I beseech you, tell me what
this fine business is.

Virtue, Socrates, he replied, is what we deem
ourselves able to purvey in a pre-eminently excellent
and speedy manner.

Good heavens, I exclaimed, a mighty affair
indeed! Where did you have the luck to pick it
up? I was still considering you, as I remarked
just now, to be chiefly skilled in fighting under arms,
and so spoke of you in those terms: for when you
visited our city before, this, I recollect, was the
profession you made. But if you now in truth
possess this other knowledge, have mercy—you see
I address you just as though you were a couple of
gods, beseeching you to forgive my former remarks.
But make sure, Euthydemus and Dionysodorus,
that you spoke the truth: for the vastness of your
promise gives me some excuse for disbelieving.

You may be sure, Socrates, they replied, it is as
we say.

Then I congratulate you on your acquisition far

μᾶλλον ἢ μέγαν βασιλέα τῆς ἀρχῆς· τοσόνδε δέ
μοι εἴπετον, εἰ ἐν νῷ ἔχετον ἐπιδεικνύναι ταύτην
τὴν σοφίαν, ἢ πῶς σφῷν βεβούλευται.

Ἐπ' αὐτό γε τοῦτο πάρεσμεν, ὦ Σώκρατες, ὡς
B ἐπιδείξοντε καὶ διδάξοντε, ἐάν τις ἐθέλῃ μανθάνειν.

Ἀλλ' ὅτι μὲν ἐθελήσουσιν ἅπαντες οἱ μὴ ἔχοντες,
ἐγὼ ὑμῖν ἐγγυῶμαι, πρῶτος μὲν ἐγώ, ἔπειτα δὲ
Κλεινίας οὑτοσί, πρὸς δ' ἡμῖν Κτήσιππός τε ὅδε
καὶ οἱ ἄλλοι οὗτοι, ἦν δ' ἐγὼ δεικνὺς αὐτῷ τοὺς
ἐραστὰς τοὺς Κλεινίου· οἱ δὲ ἐτύγχανον ἡμᾶς ἤδη
περιστάμενοι. ὁ γὰρ Κτήσιππος ἔτυχε πόρρω
καθεζόμενος τοῦ Κλεινίου, ἐμοὶ δοκεῖν· ὡς δ'
ἐτύγχανεν ὁ Εὐθύδημος ἐμοὶ διαλεγόμενος προ-
C νενευκὼς εἰς τὸ πρόσθεν, ἐν μέσῳ ὄντος ἡμῶν τοῦ
Κλεινίου ἐπεσκότει τῷ Κτησίππῳ τῆς θέας· βουλόμενός τε οὖν θεάσασθαι ὁ Κτήσιππος τὰ παιδικὰ
καὶ ἅμα φιλήκοος ὢν ἀναπηδήσας πρῶτος προσ-
έστη ἡμῖν ἐν τῷ καταντικρύ· οὕτως οὖν καὶ οἱ
ἄλλοι ἐκεῖνον ἰδόντες περιέστησαν ἡμᾶς, οἵ τε τοῦ
Κλεινίου ἐρασταὶ καὶ οἱ τοῦ Εὐθυδήμου τε καὶ
Διονυσοδώρου ἑταῖροι. τούτους δὴ ἐγὼ δεικνὺς
ἔλεγον τῷ Εὐθυδήμῳ, ὅτι πάντες ἕτοιμοι εἶεν
μανθάνειν· ὅ τε οὖν Κτήσιππος συνέφη μάλα
D προθύμως καὶ οἱ ἄλλοι, καὶ ἐκέλευον αὐτὼ κοινῇ
πάντες ἐπιδείξασθαι τὴν δύναμιν τῆς σοφίας.

Εἶπον οὖν ἐγώ, Ὦ Εὐθύδημε καὶ Διονυσόδωρε,
πάνυ μὲν οὖν παντὶ τρόπῳ καὶ τούτοις χαρίσασθον
καὶ ἐμοῦ ἕνεκα ἐπιδείξατον. τὰ μὲν οὖν πλεῖστα
δῆλον ὅτι οὐκ ὀλίγον ἔργον ἐπιδεῖξαι· τόδε δέ μοι
εἴπετον, πότερον πεπεισμένον ἤδη, ὡς χρὴ παρ'
ὑμῶν μανθάνειν, δύναισθ' ἂν ἀγαθὸν ποιῆσαι ἄνδρα
E μόνον, ἢ καὶ ἐκεῖνον τὸν μήπω πεπεισμένον διὰ τὸ

more than I do the great king on his empire: only tell me whether you intend to exhibit this science of yours, or what you have determined to do.

We are here for the very purpose, Socrates, of exhibiting and expounding it to anyone who wishes to learn.

Well, I guarantee that all who do not possess it will wish to—myself to begin with, then Cleinias here and, besides us, Ctesippus and all these others, I said, showing him the lovers of Cleinias, who were by this time standing about us. For Ctesippus, as it happened, was sitting some way from Cleinias, I noticed; and by chance, as Euthydemus leant forward in talking to me he obscured Ctesippus's view of Cleinias, who was between us. Then Ctesippus, desiring to gaze on his favourite and being also an eager listener, led the way by jumping up and placing himself opposite us; and this made the others, on seeing what he did, stand around us, both Cleinias's lovers and the followers of Euthydemus and Dionysodorus. Pointing to these, I told Euthydemus that they were all ready to learn; to which Ctesippus assented with great eagerness, and so did the rest; and they all joined in urging the two men to exhibit the power of their wisdom.

On this I remarked: My good Euthydemus and Dionysodorus, you must do your very best to gratify my friends and, for my sake also, to give us an exhibition. To do it in full, of course, would obviously be a lengthy performance: but tell me one thing— will you be able to make a good man of him only who is already convinced that he should learn of you, or of him also who is not yet so convinced, owing to

μὴ οἴεσθαι ὅλως τὸ πρᾶγμα τὴν ἀρετὴν μαθητὸν
εἶναι ἢ μὴ σφὼ εἶναι αὐτῆς διδασκάλω; φέρε, καὶ
τὸν οὕτως ἔχοντα τῆς αὐτῆς τέχνης ἔργον πεῖσαι,
ὡς καὶ διδακτὸν ἡ ἀρετὴ καὶ οὗτοι ὑμεῖς ἐστέ,
παρ᾽ ὧν ἂν κάλλιστά τις αὐτὸ μάθοι, ἢ ἄλλης;

Ταύτης μὲν οὖν, ἔφη, τῆς αὐτῆς, ὦ Σώκρατες, ὁ
Διονυσόδωρος.

Ὑμεῖς ἄρα, ἦν δ᾽ ἐγώ, ὦ Διονυσόδωρε, τῶν
νῦν ἀνθρώπων κάλλιστ᾽ ἂν προτρέψαιτε εἰς φιλο-
275 σοφίαν καὶ ἀρετῆς ἐπιμέλειαν;

Οἰόμεθά γε δή, ὦ Σώκρατες.

Τῶν μὲν τοίνυν ἄλλων τὴν ἐπίδειξιν ἡμῖν, ἔφην,
εἰσαῦθις ἀπόθεσθον, τοῦτο δ᾽ αὐτὸ ἐπιδείξασθον·
τουτονὶ τὸν νεανίσκον πείσατον, ὡς χρὴ φιλοσοφεῖν καὶ ἀρετῆς ἐπιμελεῖσθαι, καὶ χαριεῖσθον ἐμοί
τε καὶ τουτοισὶ πᾶσι. συμβέβηκε γάρ τι τοιοῦτον
τῷ μειρακίῳ τούτῳ· ἐγώ τε καὶ οἵδε πάντες
τυγχάνομεν ἐπιθυμοῦντες ὡς βέλτιστον αὐτὸν
γενέσθαι. ἔστι δὲ οὗτος ᾽Αξιόχου μὲν υἱὸς τοῦ
B ᾽Αλκιβιάδου τοῦ παλαιοῦ, αὐτανεψιὸς δὲ τοῦ
νῦν ὄντος ᾽Αλκιβιάδου· ὄνομα δ᾽ αὐτῷ Κλεινίας.
ἔστι δὲ νέος· φοβούμεθα δὴ περὶ αὐτῷ, οἷον εἰκὸς
περὶ νέῳ, μή τις φθῇ ἡμᾶς ἐπ᾽ ἄλλο τι ἐπιτήδευμα
τρέψας τὴν διάνοιαν καὶ διαφθείρῃ. σφὼ οὖν ἥκε-
τον εἰς κάλλιστον· ἀλλ᾽ εἰ μή τι διαφέρει ὑμῖν,
λάβετον πεῖραν τοῦ μειρακίου καὶ διαλέχθητον
ἐναντίον ἡμῶν.

Εἰπόντος οὖν ἐμοῦ σχεδόν τι αὐτὰ ταῦτα ὁ
Εὐθύδημος ἅμα ἀνδρείως τε καὶ θαρραλέως, ᾽Αλλ᾽

an absolute disbelief that virtue is a thing that can be learnt or that you are teachers of it? Come now, is it the business of this same art to persuade such a man that virtue is teachable and that you are the men of whom one may best learn it, or does this need some other art?

No, this same one can do it, Socrates, said Dionysodorus.

Then you two, Dionysodorus, I said, would be the best persons now on earth to incite one to the pursuit of knowledge and the practice of virtue?

We think so, at least, Socrates.

Well then, please defer the display of all the rest to some other occasion, I said, and exhibit this one thing. You are to persuade this young fellow here that he ought to ensue wisdom and practise virtue, and so you will oblige both me and all these present. This youth happens to be in just the sort of condition I speak of; and I and all of us here are at this moment anxious for him to become as good as possible. He is the son of Axiochus, son of the former Alcibiades,[1] and is own cousin to the Alcibiades that now is: his name is Cleinias. He is young; and so we have fears for him, as well one may for a young man, lest someone forestall us and turn his inclination to some other course of life, and so corrupt him. Hence your arrival now is most happy. Come now, if it is all the same to you, make trial of the lad and talk with him in our presence.

When I had thus spoken, in almost these very words, Euthydemus answered in a tone both manly

---

[1] *i.e.* the famous Alcibiades, who died in 404 B.C. at the age of 44. The supposed time of this discussion must be a year or two before Socrates' death (399 B.C.).

C οὐδὲν διαφέρει, ὦ Σώκρατες, ἔφη, ἐὰν μόνον
ἐθέλῃ ἀποκρίνεσθαι ὁ νεανίσκος.

Ἀλλὰ μὲν δή, ἔφην ἐγώ, τοῦτό γε καὶ εἴθισται·
θαμὰ γὰρ αὐτῷ οἵδε προσιόντες πολλὰ ἐρωτῶσί
τε καὶ διαλέγονται, ὥστε ἐπιεικῶς θαρρεῖ τὸ
ἀποκρίνασθαι.

Τὰ δὴ μετὰ ταῦτα, ὦ Κρίτων, πῶς ἂν καλῶς
σοι διηγησαίμην; οὐ γὰρ σμικρὸν τὸ ἔργον, δύνασθαι ἀναλαβεῖν διεξιόντα σοφίαν ἀμήχανον ὅσην·
D ὥστ᾿ ἔγωγε, καθάπερ οἱ ποιηταί, δέομαι ἀρχόμενος τῆς διηγήσεως Μούσας τε καὶ Μνήμην
ἐπικαλεῖσθαι· ἤρξατο δ᾿ οὖν ἐνθένδε ποθὲν ὁ
Εὐθύδημος, ὡς ἐγᾦμαι· Ὦ Κλεινία, πότεροί εἰσι
τῶν ἀνθρώπων οἱ μανθάνοντες, οἱ σοφοὶ ἢ οἱ
ἀμαθεῖς;

Καὶ τὸ μειράκιον, ἅτε μεγάλου ὄντος τοῦ ἐρω-
τήματος, ἠρυθρίασέ τε καὶ ἀπορήσας ἔβλεπεν εἰς
ἐμέ· καὶ ἐγὼ γνοὺς αὐτὸν τεθορυβημένον, Θάρρει,
ἦν δ᾿ ἐγώ, ὦ Κλεινία, καὶ ἀπόκριναι ἀνδρείως,
E ὁπότερά σοι φαίνεται· ἴσως γάρ τοι ὠφελεῖ τὴν
μεγίστην ὠφέλειαν.

Καὶ ἐν τούτῳ ὁ Διονυσόδωρος προσκύψας μοι
σμικρὸν πρὸς τὸ οὖς, πάνυ μειδιάσας τῷ προσώπῳ,
Καὶ μήν, ἔφη, σοί, ὦ Σώκρατες, προλέγω, ὅτι
ὁπότερ᾿ ἂν ἀποκρίνηται τὸ μειράκιον, ἐξελεγχθή-
σεται.

Καὶ αὐτοῦ μεταξὺ ταῦτα λέγοντος ὁ Κλεινίας
ἔτυχεν ἀποκρινάμενος, ὥστε οὐδὲ παρακελεύσασθαί
276 μοι ἐξεγένετο εὐλαβηθῆναι τῷ μειρακίῳ, ἀλλ᾿
ἀπεκρίνατο, ὅτι οἱ σοφοὶ εἶεν οἱ μανθάνοντες.

Καὶ ὁ Εὐθύδημος, Καλεῖς δέ τινας, ἔφη, διδασκάλους, ἢ οὔ; Ὡμολόγει. Οὐκοῦν τῶν μαν-

and dashing : Oh, it is all the same to us, Socrates, provided the youth is willing to answer us.

Why, in fact, I said, that is just what he is used to : these people here are constantly coming to him and asking him a number of questions and debating with him, so he is a fairly fearless answerer.

What ensued, Crito, how am I to relate in proper style ? For no slight matter it is to be able to recall in description such enormous knowledge as theirs. Consequently, like the poets, I must needs begin my narrative with an invocation of the Muses and Memory. Well, Euthydemus set to work, so far as I remember, in terms very much the same as these : Cleinias, which sort of men are the learners, the wise or the foolish ?

At this the young man, feeling the embarrassment of the question, blushed and glanced at me in his helplessness. So I, perceiving his confusion, said : Have no fear, Cleinias ; answer bravely, whichever you think it is : for perchance he is doing you the greatest service in the world.

Meanwhile Dionysodorus leant over a little to me, with a broad smile on his face, and whispered in my ear : Let me tell you, Socrates, beforehand that, whichever way the lad answers, he will be confuted.

While he was saying this, Cleinias made his reply, so that I was unable even to advise the boy to be wary : he replied that it was the wise who were the learners.

Then Euthydemus asked : And are there persons whom you call teachers, or not ?

He agreed that there were.

θανόντων οἱ διδάσκαλοι διδάσκαλοί εἰσιν, ὥσπερ
ὁ κιθαριστὴς καὶ ὁ γραμματιστὴς διδάσκαλοι
δήπου ἦσαν σοῦ καὶ τῶν ἄλλων παίδων, ὑμεῖς δὲ
μαθηταί; Συνέφη. Ἄλλο τι οὖν, ἡνίκα ἐμανθάνετε, οὔπω ἠπίστασθε ταῦτα, ἃ ἐμανθάνετε;
B Οὐκ ἔφη. Ἆρ᾽ οὖν σοφοὶ ἦτε, ὅτε ταῦτα οὐκ
ἠπίστασθε; Οὐ δῆτα, ἦ δ᾽ ὅς. Οὐκοῦν εἰ μὴ
σοφοί, ἀμαθεῖς; Πάνυ γε. Ὑμεῖς ἄρα μανθάνοντες ἃ οὐκ ἠπίστασθε, ἀμαθεῖς ὄντες ἐμανθάνετε. Ἐπένευσε τὸ μειράκιον. Οἱ ἀμαθεῖς
ἄρα μανθάνουσιν, ὦ Κλεινία, ἀλλ᾽ οὐχ οἱ σοφοί,
ὡς σὺ οἴει.

Ταῦτ᾽ οὖν εἰπόντος αὐτοῦ, ὥσπερ ὑπὸ διδασκάλου
χορὸς ἀποσημήναντος, ἅμα ἀνεθορύβησάν τε καὶ
ἐγέλασαν οἱ ἑπόμενοι ἐκεῖνοι μετὰ τοῦ Διονυσο-
C δώρου τε καὶ Εὐθυδήμου· καὶ πρὶν ἀναπνεῦσαι
καλῶς τε καὶ εὖ τὸ μειράκιον, ἐκδεξάμενος ὁ
Διονυσόδωρος, Τί δέ, ὦ Κλεινία, ἔφη, ὁπότε
ἀποστοματίζοι ὑμῖν ὁ γραμματιστής, πότεροι
ἐμάνθανον τῶν παίδων τὰ ἀποστοματιζόμενα, οἱ
σοφοὶ ἢ οἱ ἀμαθεῖς; Οἱ σοφοί, ἔφη ὁ Κλεινίας.
Οἱ σοφοὶ ἄρα μανθάνουσιν, ἀλλ᾽ οὐχ οἱ ἀμαθεῖς,
καὶ οὐκ εὖ σὺ[1] ἄρτι Εὐθυδήμῳ ἀπεκρίνω.

D Ἐνταῦθα δὴ καὶ πάνυ ἐγέλασάν τε καὶ ἐθορύ-
βησαν οἱ ἐρασταὶ τοῖν ἀνδροῖν, ἀγασθέντες τῆς
σοφίας αὐτοῖν· οἱ δ᾽ ἄλλοι ἡμεῖς ἐκπεπληγμένοι
ἐσιωπῶμεν. γνοὺς δὲ ἡμᾶς ὁ Εὐθύδημος ἐκ-

[1] εὖ σὺ Burnet: εὐθὺς mss.

And the teachers of the learners are teachers in the same way as your lute-master and your writing-master, I suppose, were teachers of you and the other boys, while you were pupils?

He assented.

Now, of course, when you were learning, you did not yet know the things you were learning?

No, he said.

So were you wise, when you did not know those things?

No, to be sure, he said.

Then if not wise, foolish?

Certainly.

So when you learnt what you did not know, you learnt while being foolish.

To this the lad nodded assent.

Hence it is the foolish who learn, Cleinias, and not the wise, as you suppose.

When he had thus spoken, all those followers of Dionysodorus and Euthydemus raised a cheer and a laugh, like a chorus at the signal of their director; and before the boy could fairly and fully recover his breath Dionysodorus took up the cudgels and said: Well now, Cleinias, whenever your writing-master dictated from memory, which of the boys learnt the piece recited, the wise or the foolish?

The wise, said Cleinias.

So it is the wise who learn, and not the foolish: hence the answer you gave just now to Euthydemus was a bad one.

Thereupon arose a great deal of laughter and loud applause from the pair's adorers, in admiration of their cleverness; while we on our side were dismayed and held our peace. Then Euthydemus, observing

πεπληγμένους, ἵν᾽ ἔτι μᾶλλον θαυμάζοιμεν αὐτόν,
οὐκ ἀνίει τὸ μειράκιον, ἀλλ᾽ ἠρώτα, καὶ ὥσπερ οἱ
ἀγαθοὶ ὀρχησταί, διπλᾶ ἔστρεφε τὰ ἐρωτήματα
περὶ τοῦ αὐτοῦ, καὶ ἔφη· Πότερον γὰρ οἱ μανθάνοντες μανθάνουσιν ἃ ἐπίστανται ἢ ἃ μὴ ἐπίστανται;

Καὶ ὁ Διονυσόδωρος πάλιν μικρὸν πρός με ψι-
E θυρίσας, Καὶ τοῦτ᾽, ἔφη, ὦ Σώκρατες, ἕτερον
τοιοῦτον, οἷον τὸ πρότερον.

Ὦ Ζεῦ, ἔφην ἐγώ, ἦ μὴν καὶ τὸ πρότερόν γε
καλὸν ὑμῖν ἐφάνη τὸ ἐρώτημα.

Πάντ᾽, ἔφη, ὦ Σώκρατες, τοιαῦτα ἡμεῖς ἐρωτῶ-
μεν ἄφυκτα.

Τοιγάρτοι, ἦν δ᾽ ἐγώ, δοκεῖτέ μοι εὐδοκιμεῖν
παρὰ τοῖς μαθηταῖς.

Ἐν δὲ τούτῳ ὁ μὲν Κλεινίας τῷ Εὐθυδήμῳ
ἀπεκρίνατο, ὅτι μανθάνοιεν οἱ μανθάνοντες ἃ οὐκ
ἐπίσταιντο· ὁ δὲ ἤρετο αὐτὸν διὰ τῶν αὐτῶν
277 ὧνπερ τὸ πρότερον· Τί δέ; ἦ δ᾽ ὅς, οὐκ ἐπίστασαι
σὺ γράμματα; Ναί, ἔφη. Οὐκοῦν ἅπαντα;
Ὡμολόγει. Ὅταν οὖν τις ἀποστοματίζῃ ὁτιοῦν,
οὐ γράμματα ἀποστοματίζει; Ὡμολόγει. Οὐκοῦν ὧν τι σὺ ἐπίστασαι, ἔφη, ἀποστοματίζει,
εἴπερ πάντα ἐπίστασαι; Καὶ τοῦτο ὡμολόγει.
Τί οὖν; ἦ δ᾽ ὅς, ἆρα σὺ μανθάνεις ἅττ᾽ ἂν ἀποστοματίζῃ τις, ὁ δὲ μὴ ἐπιστάμενος γράμματα
μανθάνει; Οὔκ, ἀλλ᾽, ἦ δ᾽ ὅς, μανθάνω. Οὐκοῦν ἃ ἐπίστασαι, ἔφη, μανθάνεις, εἴ πέρ γε ἅπαντα

our dismay, and seeking to astonish us still further, would not let the boy go, but went on questioning him and, like a skilful dancer, gave a twofold twist to his questions on the same point : Now, do the learners learn what they know, he asked, or what they do not ?

Then Dionysodorus whispered to me again softly : Here comes a second one, Socrates, just like the first.

Heavens ! I replied : surely the first question served you well enough.

All our questions, Socrates, he said, are like that ; they leave no escape.

And consequently, as it seems to me, I remarked, you have this high repute among your disciples.

Meanwhile Cleinias answered Euthydemus, that learners learnt what they did not know ; so he had to meet the same course of questions as before : Well then, asked the other, do you not know your letters ?

Yes, he said.

All of them ?

He admitted it.

Now when anyone dictates some piece or other, does he not dictate letters ?

He admitted it.

And he dictates things of which you know something, since you know all of them ?

He admitted this too.

Well now, said the other, surely you do not learn whatever such a person dictates ; it is rather he who does not know his letters that learns ?

No, he replied ; I learn.

Then you learn what you know, since you know all your letters.

B τὰ γράμματα ἐπίστασαι. Ὡμολόγησεν. Οὐκ
ἄρα ὀρθῶς ἀπεκρίνω, ἔφη.

Καὶ οὔπω σφόδρα τι ταῦτα εἴρητο τῷ Εὐθυδήμῳ, καὶ ὁ Διονυσόδωρος ὥσπερ σφαῖραν ἐκδεξάμενος τὸν λόγον πάλιν ἐστοχάζετο τοῦ μειρακίου,
καὶ εἶπεν· Ἐξαπατᾷ σε Εὐθύδημος, ὦ Κλεινία.
εἰπὲ γάρ μοι, τὸ μανθάνειν οὐκ ἐπιστήμην ἐστὶ
λαμβάνειν τούτου, οὗ ἄν τις μανθάνῃ; Ὡμολόγει
ὁ Κλεινίας. Τὸ δ' ἐπίστασθαι, ἦ δ' ὅς, ἄλλο τι
ἢ ἔχειν ἐπιστήμην ἤδη ἐστίν; Συνέφη. Τὸ ἄρα
C μὴ ἐπίστασθαι μήπω ἔχειν ἐπιστήμην ἐστίν;
Ὡμολόγει αὐτῷ. Πότερον οὖν εἰσὶν οἱ λαμβάνοντες ὁτιοῦν οἱ ἔχοντες ἤδη ἢ οἳ ἂν μή; Οἳ ἂν
μὴ ἔχωσιν. Οὐκοῦν ὡμολόγηκας εἶναι τούτων
καὶ τοὺς μὴ ἐπισταμένους, τῶν μὴ ἐχόντων;
Κατένευσε. Τῶν λαμβανόντων ἄρ' εἰσὶν οἱ μανθάνοντες, ἀλλ' οὐ τῶν ἐχόντων; Συνέφη. Οἱ μὴ
ἐπιστάμενοι ἄρα, ἔφη, μανθάνουσιν, ὦ Κλεινία,
ἀλλ' οὐχ οἱ ἐπιστάμενοι.

Ἔτι δὴ ἐπὶ τὸ τρίτον καταβαλὼν ὥσπερ πά-
λαισμα ὥρμα ὁ Εὐθύδημος τὸν νεανίσκον· καὶ
D ἐγὼ γνοὺς βαπτιζόμενον τὸ μειράκιον, βουλόμενος ἀναπαῦσαι αὐτό, μὴ ἡμῖν ἀποδειλιάσειε,
παραμυθούμενος εἶπον· Ὦ Κλεινία, μὴ θαύμαζε,
εἴ σοι φαίνονται ἀήθεις οἱ λόγοι. ἴσως γὰρ οὐκ
αἰσθάνει, οἷον ποιεῖτον τὼ ξένω περὶ σέ· ποιεῖτον

He agreed.

So your answer was not correct, he said.

The last word was hardly out of Euthydemus' mouth when Dionysodorus caught, as it were, the ball of the argument and, aiming at the boy again, said : Euthydemus is deceiving you, Cleinias. Tell me, is not learning the reception of knowledge of that which one learns ?

Cleinias agreed.

And is not knowing, he went on, just having knowledge at the time ?

He assented.

So that not knowing is not yet having knowledge ?

He agreed with him.

Then are those who receive anything those who have it already, or those who have it not ?

Those who have it not.

And you have admitted that those who do not know belong also to this class of those who have it not ?

He nodded assent.

And the learners belong to the class of the receiving and not to that of the having ?

He agreed.

Hence it is those who do not know that learn, Cleinias, and not those who know.

Euthydemus was proceeding to press the youth for the third fall, when I, perceiving the lad was going under, and wishing to give him some breathing-space lest he should shame us by losing heart, encouraged him with these words : Cleinias, do not be surprised that these arguments seem strange to you ; for perhaps you do not discern what our two visitors are doing to you. They are acting just like

277

δὲ ταὐτόν, ὅπερ οἱ ἐν τῇ τελετῇ τῶν Κορυβάντων,
ὅταν τὴν θρόνωσιν ποιῶσι περὶ τοῦτον, ὃν ἂν
μέλλωσι τελεῖν. καὶ γὰρ ἐκεῖ χορεία τίς ἐστι
καὶ παιδιά, εἰ ἄρα καὶ τετέλεσαι· καὶ νῦν τούτω
Ε οὐδὲν ἄλλο ἢ χορεύετον περὶ σὲ καὶ οἷον ὀρχεῖσθον
παίζοντε, ὡς μετὰ τοῦτο τελοῦντε. νῦν οὖν νό-
μισον τὰ πρῶτα τῶν ἱερῶν ἀκούειν τῶν σοφι-
στικῶν. πρῶτον γάρ, ὥς φησι Πρόδικος, περὶ
ὀνομάτων ὀρθότητος μαθεῖν δεῖ· ὃ δὴ καὶ ἐνδεί-
κνυσθόν σοι τὼ ξένω, ὅτι οὐκ ᾔδεισθα τὸ μανθάνειν
ὅτι οἱ ἄνθρωποι καλοῦσι μὲν ἐπὶ τῷ τοιῷδε, ὅταν
τις ἐξ ἀρχῆς μηδεμίαν ἔχων ἐπιστήμην περὶ πράγ-
ματός τινος ἔπειτα ὕστερον αὐτοῦ λαμβάνῃ τὴν
278 ἐπιστήμην, καλοῦσι δὲ ταὐτὸ τοῦτο καὶ ἐπειδὰν
ἔχων ἤδη τὴν ἐπιστήμην ταύτῃ τῇ ἐπιστήμῃ ταὐτὸν τοῦτο πρᾶγμα ἐπισκοπῇ ἢ πραττόμενον ἢ
λεγόμενον. μᾶλλον μὲν αὐτὸ ξυνιέναι καλοῦσιν
ἢ μανθάνειν, ἔστι δ᾽ ὅτε καὶ μανθάνειν· σὲ δὲ
τοῦτο, ὡς οὗτοι ἐνδείκνυνται, διαλέληθε, ταὐτὸ
ὄνομα ἐπ᾽ ἀνθρώποις ἐναντίως ἔχουσι κείμενον, ἐπὶ
τῷ τε εἰδότι καὶ ἐπὶ τῷ μή· παραπλήσιον δὲ
τούτῳ καὶ τὸ ἐν τῷ δευτέρῳ ἐρωτήματι, ἐν ᾧ
Β ἠρώτων σε, πότερα μανθάνουσιν οἱ ἄνθρωποι ἃ
ἐπίστανται, ἢ ἃ μή. ταῦτα δὴ τῶν μαθημάτων
παιδιά ἐστι· διὸ καί φημι ἐγώ σοι τούτους προσ-
παίζειν· παιδιὰν δὲ λέγω διὰ ταῦτα, ὅτι, εἰ καὶ
πολλά τις ἢ καὶ πάντα τὰ τοιαῦτα μάθοι, τὰ μὲν
πράγματα οὐδὲν ἂν μᾶλλον εἰδείη πῇ ἔχει, προσ-

the celebrants of the Corybantic rites, when they perform the enthronement of the person whom they
are about to initiate. There, as you know, if you
have been through it, they have dancing and merry-
making : so here these two are merely dancing
about you and performing their sportive gambols
with a view to your subsequent initiation. You
must now, accordingly, suppose you are listening
to the first part of the professorial mysteries. First
of all, as Prodicus says, you have to learn about the
correct use of words—the very point that our two
visitors are making plain to you, namely, that you
were unaware that *learning* is the name which
people apply on the one hand to the case of a man
who, having originally no knowledge about some
matter, in course of time receives such knowledge ;
and on the other hand the same word is applied
when, having the knowledge already, he uses that
knowledge for the investigation of the same matter
whether occurring in action or in speech. It is
true that they tend rather to call it *understanding* than
learning, but occasionally they call it learning too ;
and this point, as our friends are demonstrating,
has escaped your notice—how the same word is
used for people who are in the opposite conditions
of knowing and not knowing. A similar point
underlay the second question, where they asked you
whether people learn what they know, or what they
do not. Such things are the sport of the sciences—
and that is why I tell you these men are making
game of you ; I call it sport because, although one
were to learn many or even all of such tricks, one
would be not a whit the wiser as to the true state
of the matters in hand, but only able to make game

401

PLATO

παίζειν δὲ οἶός τ' ἂν εἴη τοῖς ἀνθρώποις διὰ τὴν
τῶν ὀνομάτων διαφορὰν ὑποσκελίζων καὶ ἀνατρέπων, ὥσπερ οἱ τὰ σκολύθρια τῶν μελλόντων
C καθιζήσεσθαι ὑποσπῶντες χαίρουσι καὶ γελῶσιν,
ἐπειδὰν ἴδωσιν ὕπτιον ἀνατετραμμένον. ταῦτα
μὲν οὖν σοι παρὰ τούτων νόμιζε παιδιὰν γεγονέναι·
τὸ δὲ μετὰ ταῦτα δῆλον ὅτι τούτω γέ σοι αὐτὼ τὰ
σπουδαῖα ἐνδείξεσθον, καὶ ἐγὼ ὑφηγήσομαι αὐτοῖν
ἅ μοι ὑπέσχοντο ἀποδώσειν. ἐφάτην γὰρ ἐπιδείξεσθαι[1] τὴν προτρεπτικὴν σοφίαν· νῦν δέ, μοι
δοκεῖ, ᾠηθήτην πρότερον δεῖν παῖσαι πρὸς σέ.
ταῦτα μὲν οὖν, ὦ Εὐθύδημέ τε καὶ Διονυσόδωρε,
D πεπαίσθω τε ὑμῖν, καὶ ἴσως ἱκανῶς ἔχει· τὸ δὲ δὴ
μετὰ ταῦτα ἐπιδείξατον προτρέποντε τὸ μειράκιον,
ὅπως χρὴ σοφίας τε καὶ ἀρετῆς ἐπιμεληθῆναι.
πρότερον δ' ἐγὼ σφῷν ἐνδείξομαι, οἷον αὐτὸ ὑπο-
λαμβάνω καὶ οἵου αὐτοῦ ἐπιθυμῶ ἀκοῦσαι· ἐὰν
οὖν δόξω ὑμῖν ἰδιωτικῶς τε καὶ γελοίως αὐτὸ
ποιεῖν, μή μου καταγελᾶτε· ὑπὸ προθυμίας γὰρ
E τοῦ ἀκοῦσαι τῆς ὑμετέρας σοφίας τολμήσω ἀπ-
αυτοσχεδιάσαι ἐναντίον ὑμῶν. ἀνάσχεσθον οὖν
ἀγελαστὶ ἀκούοντες αὐτοί τε καὶ οἱ μαθηταὶ ὑμῶν·
σὺ δέ μοι, ὦ παῖ Ἀξιόχου, ἀπόκριναι.

Ἆρά γε πάντες ἄνθρωποι βουλόμεθα εὖ πράττειν; ἢ τοῦτο μὲν ἐρώτημα ὧν νῦν δὴ ἐφοβούμην
ἓν τῶν καταγελάστων; ἀνόητον γὰρ δήπου καὶ τὸ
ἐρωτᾶν τὰ τοιαῦτα· τίς γὰρ οὐ βούλεται εὖ πράτ-
279 τειν; Οὐδεὶς ὅστις οὔκ, ἔφη ὁ Κλεινίας. Εἶεν,
ἦν δ' ἐγώ· τὸ δὴ μετὰ τοῦτο, ἐπειδὴ βουλόμεθα
εὖ πράττειν, πῶς ἂν εὖ πράττοιμεν; ἆρ ἂν εἰ

---

[1] ἐπιδείξασθαι mss. : ἐπιδείξεσθαι Stephanus.

of people, thanks to the difference in the sense of the words, by tripping them up and overturning them; just as those who slyly pull stools away from persons who are about to sit down make merry and laugh when they see one sprawling on one's back. So far, then, you are to regard these gentlemen's treatment of you as mere play: but after this they will doubtless display to you their own serious object, while I shall keep them on the track and see that they fulfil the promise they gave me. They said they would exhibit their skill in exhortation; but instead, I conceive, they thought fit to make sport with you first. So now, Euthydemus and Dionysodorus, let us have done with your sport: I daresay you have had as much as you want. What you have next to do is to give us a display of exhorting this youth as to how he should devote himself to wisdom and virtue. But first I shall explain to you how I regard this matter and how I desire to hear it dealt with. If I strike you as treating it in a crude and ridiculous manner, do not laugh me to scorn; for in my eagerness to listen to your wisdom I shall venture to improvise in your presence. So both you and your disciples must restrain yourselves and listen without laughing; and you, son of Axiochus, answer me this:

Do all we human beings wish to prosper? Or is this question one of the absurdities I was afraid of just now? For I suppose it is stupid merely to ask such things, since every man must wish to prosper.

Everyone in the world, said Cleinias.

Well then, I asked, as to the next step, since we wish to prosper, how can we prosper? Will it be if

ἡμῖν πολλὰ κἀγαθὰ εἴη; ἢ τοῦτο ἐκείνου ἔτι
εὐηθέστερον; δῆλον γάρ που καὶ τοῦτο ὅτι οὕτως
ἔχει. Συνέφη. Φέρε δή, ἀγαθὰ δὲ ποῖα ἄρα
τῶν ὄντων τυγχάνει ἡμῖν ὄντα; ἢ οὐ χαλεπὸν
οὐδὲ σεμνοῦ ἀνδρὸς πάνυ τι οὐδὲ τοῦτο ἔοικεν εἶναι
εὐπορεῖν; πᾶς γὰρ ἂν ἡμῖν εἴποι, ὅτι τὸ πλουτεῖν
ἀγαθόν· ἢ γάρ; Πάνυ γ’, ἔφη. Οὐκοῦν καὶ τὸ
ὑγιαίνειν καὶ τὸ καλὸν εἶναι καὶ τἆλλα κατὰ τὸ
B σῶμα ἱκανῶς παρεσκευάσθαι; Συνεδόκει. Ἀλλὰ
μὴν εὐγένειαί τε καὶ δυνάμεις καὶ τιμαὶ ἐν τῇ
ἑαυτοῦ δῆλά ἐστιν ἀγαθὰ ὄντα. Ὡμολόγει. Τί
οὖν, ἔφην, ἔτι ἡμῖν λείπεται τῶν ἀγαθῶν; τί
ἄρα ἐστὶ τὸ σώφρονά τε εἶναι καὶ δίκαιον καὶ
ἀνδρεῖον; πότερον πρὸς Διός, ὦ Κλεινία, ἡγεῖ σύ,
ἐὰν ταῦτα τιθῶμεν ὡς ἀγαθά, ὀρθῶς ἡμᾶς θήσειν,
ἢ ἐὰν μή; ἴσως γὰρ ἄν τις ἡμῖν ἀμφισβητήσειε·
σοὶ δὲ πῶς δοκεῖ; Ἀγαθά, ἔφη ὁ Κλεινίας. Εἶεν,
C ἦν δ’ ἐγώ· τὴν δὲ σοφίαν ποῦ χοροῦ τάξομεν; ἐν
τοῖς ἀγαθοῖς, ἢ πῶς λέγεις; Ἐν τοῖς ἀγαθοῖς.
Ἐνθυμοῦ δή, μή τι παραλείπωμεν τῶν ἀγαθῶν, ὅ
τι καὶ ἄξιον λόγου. Ἀλλά μοι δοκοῦμεν, ἔφη,
οὐδέν, ὁ Κλεινίας. καὶ ἐγὼ ἀναμνησθεὶς εἶπον

we have many good things? Or is this an even sillier question than the other? For surely this too must obviously be so.

He agreed.

Come now, of things that are, what sort do we hold to be really good? Or does it appear to be no difficult matter, and no problem for an important person, to find here too a ready answer? Anyone will tell us that to be rich is good, surely?

Quite true, he said.

Then it is the same with being healthy and handsome, and having the other bodily endowments in plenty?

He agreed.

Again, it is surely clear that good birth and talents and distinctions in one's own country are good things.

He admitted it.

Then what have we still remaining, I asked, in the class of goods? What of being temperate, and just, and brave? I pray you tell me, Cleinias, do you think we shall be right in ranking these as goods, or in rejecting them? For it may be that someone will dispute it. How does it strike you?

They are goods, said Cleinias.

Very well, I went on, and where in the troupe shall we station wisdom? Among the goods, or how?

Among the goods.

Then take heed that we do not pass over any of the goods that may deserve mention.

I do not think we are leaving any out, said Cleinias.

Hereupon I recollected one and said: Yes, by

ὅτι Ναὶ μὰ Δία κινδυνεύομέν γε τὸ μέγιστον τῶν
ἀγαθῶν παραλιπεῖν. Τί τοῦτο; ἦ δ' ὅς. Τὴν
εὐτυχίαν, ὦ Κλεινία· ὃ πάντες φασί, καὶ οἱ πάνυ
φαῦλοι, μέγιστον τῶν ἀγαθῶν εἶναι. Ἀληθῆ
λέγεις, ἔφη. καὶ ἐγὼ αὖ πάλιν μετανοήσας εἶπον
D ὅτι Ὀλίγου καταγέλαστοι ἐγενόμεθα ὑπὸ τῶν
ξένων ἐγώ τε καὶ σύ, ὦ παῖ Ἀξιόχου. Τί δή,
ἔφη, τοῦτο; Ὅτι εὐτυχίαν ἐν τοῖς ἔμπροσθεν
θέμενοι νῦν δὴ αὖθις περὶ τοῦ αὐτοῦ ἐλέγομεν.
Τί οὖν δὴ τοῦτο; Καταγέλαστον δήπου, ὃ πάλαι
πρόκειται, τοῦτο πάλιν προτιθέναι καὶ δὶς ταὐτὰ λέγειν. Πῶς, ἔφη, τοῦτο λέγεις; Ἡ σοφία δήπου,
ἦν δ' ἐγώ, εὐτυχία ἐστί· τοῦτο δὲ κἂν παῖς γνοίη.
καὶ ὃς ἐθαύμασεν· οὕτως ἔτι νέος τε καὶ εὐήθης
ἐστί· κἀγὼ γνοὺς αὐτὸν θαυμάζοντα, Ἆρ' οὐκ
E οἶσθα, ἔφην, ὦ Κλεινία, ὅτι περὶ αὐλημάτων
εὐπραγίαν οἱ αὐληταὶ εὐτυχέστατοί εἰσιν; Συνέφη. Οὐκοῦν, ἦν δ' ἐγώ, καὶ περὶ γραμμάτων
γραφῆς τε καὶ ἀναγνώσεως οἱ γραμματισταί;
Πάνυ γε. Τί δέ; πρὸς τοὺς τῆς θαλάττης κιν-
δύνους μῶν οἴει εὐτυχεστέρους τινὰς εἶναι τῶν
σοφῶν κυβερνητῶν, ὡς ἐπὶ πᾶν εἰπεῖν; Οὐ δῆτα.
Τί δέ; στρατευόμενος μετὰ ποτέρου ἂν ἥδιον τοῦ

---

[1] γραμματισταί were the schoolmasters who taught reading
and writing and explained the difficulties of Homer in
primary education.

Heaven, we are on the verge of omitting the greatest of the goods.

What is that? he asked.

Good fortune, Cleinias: a thing which all men, even the worst fools, refer to as the greatest of goods.

You are right, he said.

Once again I reconsidered and said: We have almost made ourselves laughing-stocks, you and I, son of Axiochus, for our visitors.

What is wrong now? he asked.

Why, after putting good fortune in our former list, we have just been discussing the same thing again.

What is the point?

Surely it is ridiculous, when a thing has been before us all the time, to set it forth again and go over the same ground twice.

To what are you referring? he asked.

Wisdom, I replied, is presumably good fortune: even a child could see that.

He wondered at this—he is still so young and simple-minded: then I, perceiving his surprise, went on: Can you be unaware, Cleinias, that for success in flute-music it is the flute-players that have the best fortune?

He agreed to this.

Then in writing and reading letters it will be the schoolmasters.[1]

Certainly.

Well now, for the dangers of a sea-voyage, do you consider any pilots to be more fortunate, as a general rule, than the wise ones?

No, to be sure.

Well, then, suppose you were on a campaign, with which kind of general would you prefer to

κινδύνου τε καὶ τῆς τύχης μετέχοις, μετὰ σοφοῦ
στρατηγοῦ ἢ μετ' ἀμαθοῦς; Μετὰ σοφοῦ. Τί
δέ; ἀσθενῶν μετὰ ποτέρου ἂν ἡδέως κινδυνεύοις,
μετὰ σοφοῦ ἰατροῦ ἢ μετ' ἀμαθοῦς; Μετὰ σοφοῦ.
280 Ἆρ' οὖν, ἦν δ' ἐγώ, ὅτι εὐτυχέστερον ἂν οἴει
πράττειν μετὰ σοφοῦ πράττων ἢ μετ' ἀμαθοῦς;
Ξυνεχώρει. Ἡ σοφία ἄρα πανταχοῦ εὐτυχεῖν
ποιεῖ τοὺς ἀνθρώπους. οὐ γὰρ δήπου ἁμαρτάνοι
γ' ἄν ποτέ τις σοφίᾳ ἀλλ' ἀνάγκη ὀρθῶς πράττειν
καὶ τυγχάνειν· ἢ γὰρ ἂν οὐκέτι σοφία εἴη.

Συνωμολογησάμεθα τελευτῶντες οὐκ οἶδ' ὅπως
B ἐν κεφαλαίῳ οὕτω τοῦτο ἔχειν, σοφίας παρούσης,
ᾧ ἂν παρῇ, μηδὲν προσδεῖσθαι εὐτυχίας· ἐπειδὴ δὲ
τοῦτο συνομολογησάμεθα, πάλιν ἐπυνθανόμην αὐτοῦ τὰ πρότερον ὡμολογημένα πῶς ἂν ἡμῖν ἔχοι.
Ὡμολογήσαμεν γάρ, ἔφην, εἰ ἡμῖν ἀγαθὰ πολλὰ
παρείη, εὐδαιμονεῖν ἂν καὶ εὖ πράττειν. Συνέφη.
Ἆρ' οὖν εὐδαιμονοῖμεν ἂν διὰ τὰ παρόντα ἀγαθά,
εἰ μηδὲν ἡμᾶς ὠφελοῖ ἢ εἰ ὠφελοῖ; Εἰ ὠφελοῖ,
ἔφη. Ἆρ' οὖν ἄν τι ὠφελοῖ, εἰ εἴη μόνον ἡμῖν,
C χρώμεθα δ' αὐτοῖς μή; οἷον σιτία εἰ ἡμῖν εἴη
πολλά, ἐσθίοιμεν δὲ μή, ἢ ποτόν, πίνοιμεν δὲ μή,
ἔσθ' ὅ τι ὠφελοίμεθ' ἄν; Οὐ δῆτα, ἔφη. Τί δέ;
οἱ δημιουργοὶ πάντες, εἰ αὐτοῖς εἴη πάντα τὰ

share both the peril and the luck—a wise one, or an ignorant?

With a wise one.

Well then, supposing you were sick, with which kind of doctor would you like to venture yourself— a wise one, or an ignorant?

With a wise one.

And your reason, I said, is this, that you would fare with better fortune in the hands of a wise one than of an ignorant one?

He assented.

So that wisdom everywhere causes men to be fortunate: since I presume she could never err, but must needs be right in act and result; otherwise she could be no longer wisdom.

We came to an agreement somehow or other in the end that the truth in general was this: when wisdom is present, he with whom it is present has no need of good fortune as well; and as we had agreed on this I began to inquire of him over again what we should think, in this case, of our previous agreements. For we agreed, said I, that if many goods were present to us we should be happy and prosper.

Yes, he said.

Then would we be happy because of our present goods, if they gave us no benefit, or if they gave us some?

If they gave us benefit, he said.

And would a thing benefit us if we merely had it and did not use it? For instance, if we had a lot of provisions, but did not eat them, or liquor, and did not drink it, could we be said to be benefited?

Of course not, he answered.

Well then, if every craftsman found the requisites

409

ἐπιτήδεια παρεσκευασμένα ἑκάστῳ εἰς τὸ ἑαυτοῦ
ἔργον, χρῷντο δ' αὐτοῖς μή, ἆρ' ἂν οὗτοι εὖ πράτ-
τοιεν διὰ τὴν κτῆσιν, ὅτι κεκτημένοι εἶεν πάντα ἃ
δεῖ κεκτῆσθαι τὸν δημιουργόν; οἷον τέκτων, εἰ
παρεσκευασμένος εἴη τά τε ὄργανα ἅπαντα καὶ
ξύλα ἱκανά, τεκταίνοιτο δὲ μή, ἔσθ' ὅ τι ὠφελοῖτ'
D ἂν ἀπὸ τῆς κτήσεως; Οὐδαμῶς, ἔφη. Τί δέ,
εἴ τις κεκτημένος εἴη πλοῦτόν τε καὶ ἃ νῦν δὴ
ἐλέγομεν πάντα τὰ ἀγαθά, χρῷτο δὲ αὐτοῖς μή,
ἆρ' ἂν εὐδαιμονοῖ διὰ τὴν τούτων κτῆσιν τῶν
ἀγαθῶν; Οὐ δῆτα, ὦ Σώκρατες. Δεῖν ἄρα,
ἔφην, ὡς ἔοικε, μὴ μόνον κεκτῆσθαι τὰ τοιαῦτα
ἀγαθὰ τὸν μέλλοντα εὐδαίμονα ἔσεσθαι, ἀλλὰ καὶ
χρῆσθαι αὐτοῖς· ὡς οὐδὲν ὄφελος τῆς κτήσεως
γίγνεται. Ἀληθῆ λέγεις. Ἆρ' οὖν, ὦ Κλεινία,
E ἤδη τούτω ἱκανὼ[1] πρὸς τὸ εὐδαίμονα ποιῆσαί τινα,
τό τε κεκτῆσθαι τἀγαθὰ καὶ τὸ χρῆσθαι αὐτοῖς;
Ἔμοιγε δοκεῖ. Πότερον, ἦν δ' ἐγώ, ἐὰν ὀρθῶς
χρῆταί τις ἢ καὶ ἐὰν μή; Ἐὰν ὀρθῶς. Καλῶς
δέ, ἦν δ' ἐγώ, λέγεις. πλεῖον γάρ που, οἶμαι,
θάτερόν ἐστιν, ἐάν τις χρῆται ὁτῳοῦν μὴ ὀρθῶς
πράγματι ἢ ἐὰν ἐᾷ· τὸ μὲν γὰρ κακόν, τὸ δὲ οὔτε
281 κακὸν οὔτε ἀγαθόν· ἢ οὐχ οὕτω φαμέν; Ξυνεχώρει. Τί οὖν; ἐν τῇ ἐργασίᾳ τε καὶ χρήσει τῇ
περὶ τὰ ξύλα μῶν ἄλλο τί ἐστι τὸ ἀπεργαζόμενον
ὀρθῶς χρῆσθαι ἢ ἐπιστήμη ἡ τεκτονική; Οὐ

---

[1] τούτω ἱκανὼ R. G. Bury : τοῦτο ἱκανὸν, τούτῳ καλλίῳ, τούτῳ
καλλίω MSS.

for his particular work all ready prepared for him, and then made no use of them, would he prosper because of these acquisitions, as having acquired all the things necessary for a craftsman to have at hand? For example, if a carpenter were furnished with all his tools and a good supply of wood, but did no carpentry, is it possible he could be benefited by what he had got?

By no means, he said.

Well now, suppose a man had got wealth and all the goods that we mentioned just now, but made no use of them; would he be happy because of his possessing these goods?

Surely not, Socrates.

So it seems one must not merely have acquired such goods if one is to be happy, but use them too; else there is no benefit gained from their possession.

True.

Then have we here enough means, Cleinias, for making a man happy—in the possession of these goods and using them?

I think so.

Shall we say, I asked, if he uses them rightly, or just as much if he does not?

If rightly.

Well answered, I said; for I suppose there is more mischief when a man uses anything wrongly than when he lets it alone. In the one case there is evil; in the other there is neither evil nor good. May we not state it so?

He agreed.

To proceed then: in the working and use connected with wood, is there anything else that effects the right use than the knowledge of carpentry?

δῆτα, ἔφη. Ἀλλὰ μήν που καὶ ἐν τῇ περὶ τὰ
σκεύη ἐργασίᾳ τὸ ὀρθῶς ἐπιστήμη ἐστὶν ἡ ἀπεργαζομένη. Συνέφη. Ἆρ' οὖν, ἦν δ' ἐγώ, καὶ
περὶ τὴν χρείαν ὧν ἐλέγομεν τὸ πρῶτον τῶν ἀγαθῶν, πλούτου τε καὶ ὑγιείας καὶ κάλλους, τὸ ὀρθῶς
πᾶσι τοῖς τοιούτοις χρῆσθαι ἐπιστήμη ἦν ἡ[1] ἡγου-
B μένη καὶ κατορθοῦσα τὴν πρᾶξιν, ἢ ἄλλο τι; Ἐπιστήμη, ἦ δ' ὅς. Οὐ μόνον ἄρα εὐτυχίαν, ἀλλὰ
καὶ εὐπραγίαν, ὡς ἔοικεν, ἡ ἐπιστήμη παρέχει ἐν
πάσῃ κτήσει τε καὶ πράξει. Ὡμολόγει. Ἆρ'
οὖν ὦ πρὸς Διός, ἦν δ' ἐγώ, ὄφελός τι τῶν ἄλλων
κτημάτων ἄνευ φρονήσεως καὶ σοφίας; ἆρά γε ἂν
ὄναιτο ἄνθρωπος πολλὰ κεκτημένος καὶ πολλὰ
πράττων νοῦν μὴ ἔχων, μᾶλλον ἢ ὀλίγα[2]; ὧδε
δὲ σκόπει· οὐκ ἐλάττω πράττων ἐλάττω ἂν ἐξ-
C αμαρτάνοι, ἐλάττω δὲ ἁμαρτάνων ἧττον ἂν κακῶς
πράττοι, ἧττον δὲ κακῶς πράττων ἄθλιος ἧττον
ἂν εἴη; Πάνυ γ', ἔφη. Πότερον οὖν ἂν μᾶλλον
ἐλάττω τις πράττοι πένης ὢν ἢ πλούσιος; Πένης,
ἔφη. Πότερον δὲ ἀσθενὴς ἢ ἰσχυρός; Ἀσθενής.
Πότερον δὲ ἔντιμος ἢ ἄτιμος; Ἄτιμος. Πότερον
δὲ ἀνδρεῖος ὢν καὶ σώφρων ἐλάττω ἂν πράττοι ἢ

---

[1] ἡ Badham.
[2] μᾶλλον ἢ ὀλίγα Iambl.: ἢ μᾶλλον ὀλίγα νοῦν ἔχων MSS.

Surely not, he said.

Further, I presume that in the working connected with furniture it is knowledge that effects the right work.

Yes, he said.

Then similarly, I went on, in the use of the goods we mentioned at first—wealth and health and beauty—was it knowledge that showed the way to the right use of all those advantages and rectified their conduct, or was it something else?

Knowledge, he replied.

So that knowledge, it would seem, supplies mankind not only with good luck, but with welfare, in all that he either possesses or conducts.

He agreed.

Then can we, in Heaven's name, get any benefit from all the other possessions without understanding and wisdom? Shall we say that a man will profit more by possessing much and doing much when he has no sense, than he will if he does and possesses little? Consider it this way: would he not err less if he did less; and so, erring less, do less ill; and hence, doing less ill, be less miserable?

Certainly, he said.

In which of the two cases, when one is poor or when one is rich, will one be more likely to do less?

When one is poor, he said.

And when one is weak, or when one is strong? Weak.

And when one has high position, or has none? None.

When one is brave and self-controlled, will one do less, or when one is a coward?

δειλός; Δειλός. Οὐκοῦν καὶ ἀργὸς μᾶλλον ἢ
ἐργάτης; Συνεχώρει. Καὶ βραδὺς μᾶλλον ἢ
D ταχύς, καὶ ἀμβλὺ ὁρῶν καὶ ἀκούων μᾶλλον ἢ ὀξύ;
Πάντα τὰ τοιαῦτα ξυνεχωροῦμεν ἀλλήλοις.

Ἐν κεφαλαίῳ δ᾽, ἔφην, ὦ Κλεινία, κινδυνεύει
σύμπαντα, ἃ τὸ πρῶτον ἔφαμεν ἀγαθὰ εἶναι, οὐ περὶ
τούτου ὁ λόγος αὐτοῖς εἶναι, ὅπως αὐτά γε καθ᾽
αὑτὰ πέφυκεν ἀγαθά, ἀλλ᾽ ὡς ἔοικεν ὧδ᾽ ἔχει· ἐὰν
μὲν αὐτῶν ἡγῆται ἀμαθία, μείζω κακὰ εἶναι τῶν
ἐναντίων, ὅσῳ δυνατώτερα ὑπηρετεῖν τῷ ἡγου-
μένῳ κακῷ ὄντι· ἐὰν δὲ φρόνησίς τε καὶ σοφία,
E μείζω ἀγαθά· αὐτὰ δὲ καθ᾽ αὑτὰ οὐδέτερα αὐτῶν
οὐδενὸς ἄξια εἶναι. Φαίνεται, ἔφη, ὡς ἔοικεν,
οὕτως, ὡς σὺ λέγεις. Τί οὖν ἡμῖν συμβαίνει ἐκ
τῶν εἰρημένων; ἄλλο τι ἢ τῶν μὲν ἄλλων οὐδὲν
ὂν οὔτε ἀγαθὸν οὔτε κακόν, τούτοιν δὲ δυοῖν ὄντοιν
ἡ μὲν σοφία ἀγαθόν, ἡ δὲ ἀμαθία κακόν; Ὡμο-
282 λόγει.

Ἔτι τοίνυν, ἔφην, τὸ λοιπὸν ἐπισκεψώμεθα.
ἐπειδὴ εὐδαίμονες μὲν εἶναι προθυμούμεθα πάντες,
ἐφάνημεν δὲ τοιοῦτοι γιγνόμενοι ἐκ τοῦ χρῆσθαί τε
τοῖς πράγμασι καὶ ὀρθῶς χρῆσθαι, τὴν δὲ ὀρθότητα καὶ εὐτυχίαν ἐπιστήμη ἡ παρέχουσα, δεῖ δή,
ὡς ἔοικεν, ἐκ παντὸς τρόπου ἅπαντα ἄνδρα τοῦτο
παρασκευάζεσθαι, ὅπως ὡς σοφώτατος ἔσται· ἢ

A coward.

So too, when idle rather than busy ?

He agreed.

And slow rather than quick, and dim of sight and hearing rather than sharp ?

We agreed with each other as to these and all such cases.

To sum up then, Cleinias, I proceeded, it seems that, as regards the whole lot of things which at first we termed goods, the discussion they demand is not on the question of how they are in themselves and by nature goods, but rather, I conceive, as follows : if they are guided by ignorance, they are greater evils than their opposites, according as they are more capable of ministering to their evil guide ; whereas if understanding and wisdom guide them, they are greater goods ; but in themselves neither sort is of any worth.

I think the case appears, he replied, to be as you suggest.

Now what result do we get from our statements ? Is it not precisely that, of all the other things, not one is either good or bad, but of these two, wisdom is good and ignorance bad ?

He agreed.

Let us consider then, I said, the further conclusion that lies before us. Since we are all eager to be happy, and since we were found to become so by not only using things but using them aright, while knowledge, we saw, was that which provided the rightness and good fortune, it seems that every man must prepare himself by all available means so that he may be as wise as possible. Is it not so ?

οὖ; Ναί, ἔφη. Καὶ παρὰ πατρός γε δήπου τοῦτο
B οἰόμενον δεῖν παραλαμβάνειν πολὺ μᾶλλον ἢ χρήματα, καὶ παρ' ἐπιτρόπων καὶ φίλων τῶν τε ἄλλων
καὶ τῶν φασκόντων ἐραστῶν εἶναι, καὶ ξένων καὶ
πολιτῶν, δεόμενον καὶ ἱκετεύοντα σοφίας μεταδιδόναι, οὐδὲν αἰσχρόν, ὦ Κλεινία, οὐδὲ νεμεσητὸν
ἕνεκα τούτου ὑπηρετεῖν καὶ δουλεύειν καὶ ἐραστῇ
καὶ παντὶ ἀνθρώπῳ, ὁτιοῦν ἐθέλοντα ὑπηρετεῖν τῶν
καλῶν ὑπηρετημάτων, προθυμούμενον σοφὸν γενέ-
σθαι· ἢ οὐ δοκεῖ σοι, ἔφην ἐγώ, οὕτως; Πάνυ μὲν
C οὖν εὖ μοι δοκεῖς λέγειν, ἦ δ' ὅς. Εἰ ἔστι γε, ὦ
Κλεινία, ἦν δ' ἐγώ, ἡ σοφία διδακτόν, ἀλλὰ μὴ
ἀπὸ ταὐτομάτου παραγίγνεται τοῖς ἀνθρώποις.
τοῦτο γὰρ ἡμῖν ἔτι ἄσκεπτον καὶ οὔπω διωμολο-
γημένον ἐμοί τε καὶ σοί. 'Αλλ' ἔμοιγε, ἔφη, ὦ
Σώκρατες, διδακτὸν εἶναι δοκεῖ. καὶ ἐγὼ ἡσθεὶς
εἶπον· Ἦ καλῶς λέγεις, ὦ ἄριστε ἀνδρῶν, καὶ εὖ
ἐποίησας ἀπαλλάξας με σκέψεως πολλῆς περὶ
τούτου αὐτοῦ, πότερον διδακτὸν ἢ οὐ διδακτὸν
ἡ σοφία. νῦν οὖν ἐπειδή σοι καὶ διδακτὸν δοκεῖ
D καὶ μόνον τῶν ὄντων εὐδαίμονα καὶ εὐτυχῆ ποιεῖν
τὸν ἄνθρωπον, ἄλλο τι ἢ φαίης ἂν ἀναγκαῖον εἶναι
φιλοσοφεῖν καὶ αὐτὸς ἐν νῷ ἔχεις αὐτὸ ποιεῖν;
Πάνυ μὲν οὖν, ἔφη, ὦ Σώκρατες, ὡς οἷόν τε
μάλιστα.

Κἀγὼ ταῦτα ἄσμενος ἀκούσας, Τὸ μὲν ἐμόν,
ἔφην, παράδειγμα, ὦ Διονυσόδωρέ τε καὶ Εὐθύδημε, οἵων ἐπιθυμῶ τῶν προτρεπτικῶν λόγων
εἶναι, τοιοῦτον, ἰδιωτικὸν ἴσως καὶ μόλις διὰ

Yes, he said.

And if a man thinks, as well he may, that he ought to get this endowment from his father much more than money, and also from his guardians and his ordinary friends, and from those who profess to be his lovers, whether strangers or fellow-citizens —praying and beseeching them to give him his share of wisdom; there is no disgrace, Cleinias, or reprobation in making this a reason for serving and being a slave to either one's lover or any man, and being ready to perform any service that is honourable in one's eagerness to become wise. Is not this your view? I asked.

I think you are perfectly right, he replied.

Yes, Cleinias, I went on, if wisdom is teachable, and does not present itself to mankind of its own accord—for this is a question that we have still to consider as not yet agreed on by you and me.

For my part, Socrates, he said, I think it is teachable.

At this I was glad, and said : Well spoken indeed, my excellent friend! How good of you to relieve me of a long inquiry into this very point, whether wisdom is teachable or not teachable! So now, since you think it is both teachable and the only thing in the world that makes man happy and fortunate, can you help saying that it is necessary to pursue wisdom or intending to pursue it yourself?

Why, said he, I do say so, Socrates, with all my might.

So I, delighted to hear this, said : There, Dionysodorus and Euthydemus, is my illustration of what I desire a hortatory argument to be—rough and ready, perhaps, and expressed at laborious length :

μακρῶν λεγόμενον· σφῶν δὲ ὁπότερος βούλεται,
ταὐτὸν τοῦτο τέχνῃ πράττων ἐπιδειξάτω ἡμῖν. εἰ
E δὲ μὴ τοῦτο βούλεσθον, ὅθεν ἐγὼ ἀπέλιπον, τὸ
ἑξῆς ἐπιδείξατον τῷ μειρακίῳ, πότερον πᾶσαν
ἐπιστήμην δεῖ αὐτὸν κτᾶσθαι, ἢ ἔστι τις μία, ἣν
δεῖ λαβόντα εὐδαιμονεῖν τε καὶ ἀγαθὸν ἄνδρα
εἶναι, καὶ τίς αὕτη. ὡς γὰρ ἔλεγον ἀρχόμενος,
περὶ πολλοῦ ἡμῖν τυγχάνει ὂν τόνδε τὸν νεανίσκον
283 σοφόν τε καὶ ἀγαθὸν γενέσθαι.

Ἐγὼ μὲν οὖν ταῦτα εἶπον, ὦ Κρίτων· τῷ δὲ
μετὰ τοῦτο ἐσομένῳ πάνυ σφόδρα προσεῖχον τὸν
νοῦν, καὶ ἐπεσκόπουν, τίνα ποτὲ τρόπον ἅψοιντο
τοῦ λόγου καὶ ὁπόθεν ἄρξοιντο παρακελευόμενοι τῷ
νεανίσκῳ σοφίαν τε καὶ ἀρετὴν ἀσκεῖν. ὁ οὖν
πρεσβύτερος αὐτῶν, ὁ Διονυσόδωρος, πρότερος
ἤρχετο τοῦ λόγου, καὶ ἡμεῖς πάντες ἐβλέπομεν
πρὸς αὐτὸν ὡς αὐτίκα μάλα ἀκουσόμενοι θαυ-
μασίους τινὰς λόγους· ὅπερ οὖν καὶ συνέβη ἡμῖν·
B θαυμαστὸν γάρ τινα, ὦ Κρίτων, ἀνὴρ κατῆρχε
λόγον, οὗ σοὶ ἄξιον ἀκοῦσαι, ὡς παρακελευστικὸς ὁ
λόγος ἦν ἐπ’ ἀρετήν.

Εἰπέ μοι, ἔφη, ὦ Σώκρατές τε καὶ ὑμεῖς οἱ
ἄλλοι, ὅσοι φατὲ ἐπιθυμεῖν τόνδε τὸν νεανίσκον
σοφὸν γενέσθαι, πότερον παίζετε ταῦτα λέγοντες
ἢ ὡς ἀληθῶς ἐπιθυμεῖτε καὶ σπουδάζετε;

Κἀγὼ διενοήθην, ὅτι ᾠηθήτην ἄρα ἡμᾶς τὸ
πρότερον παίζειν, ἡνίκα ἐκελεύομεν διαλεχθῆναι
τῷ νεανίσκῳ αὐτώ, καὶ διὰ ταῦτα προσεπαισάτην
C τε καὶ οὐκ ἐσπουδασάτην· ταῦτα οὖν διανοηθεὶς ἔτι
μᾶλλον εἶπον, ὅτι θαυμαστῶς σπουδάζοιμεν.

Καὶ ὁ Διονυσόδωρος, Σκόπει μήν, ἔφη, ὦ
Σώκρατες, ὅπως μὴ ἔξαρνος ἔσει ἃ νῦν λέγεις.

now let either of you who wishes to do so give us
an example of an artist's handling of this same matter.
If you do not wish to do that, let your display begin
where I left off, and show the lad whether he ought
to acquire every kind of knowledge, or whether
there is a single sort of it which one must obtain
if one is to be both happy and a good man, and what
it is. For as I was saying at the outset, it really
is a matter of great moment to us that this youth
should become wise and good.

These were my words, Crito; and I set about
giving the closest attention to what should follow,
and observing in what fashion they would deal with
the question, and how they would start exhorting
the youth to practise wisdom and virtue. So then
the elder of them, Dionysodorus, entered first upon
the discussion, and we all turned our eyes on him
expecting to hear, there and then, some wonderful
arguments. And this result we certainly got ; for
wondrous, in a way, Crito, was the argument that the
man then ushered forth, which is worth your hearing
as a notable incitement to virtue.

Tell me, Socrates, he said, and all you others who
say you desire this youth to become wise, whether
you say this in jest or truly and earnestly desire it.

At this I reflected that previously, as it seemed,
they took us to be jesting, when we urged them to
converse with the youth, and hence they made a
jest of it and did not take it seriously. This reflec-
tion therefore made me insist all the more that we
were in deadly earnest.

Then Dionysodorus said : Yet be careful, Socrates,
that you do not have to deny what you say now.

Ἔσκεμμαι, ἦν δ' ἐγώ· οὐ γὰρ μή ποτ' ἔξαρνος γένωμαι. Τί οὖν; ἔφη· φατὲ βούλεσθαι αὐτὸν σοφὸν γενέσθαι; Πάνυ μὲν οὖν. Νῦν δέ, ἦ δ' ὅς, Κλεινίας πότερον σοφός ἐστιν ἢ οὔ; Οὔκουν φησί γέ πω· ἔστι δὲ οὐκ ἀλαζών. Ὑμεῖς δέ, ἔφη,

D βούλεσθε γενέσθαι αὐτὸν σοφόν, ἀμαθῆ δὲ μὴ εἶναι; Ὁμολογοῦμεν. Οὐκοῦν ὃς μὲν οὐκ ἔστι, βούλεσθε αὐτὸν γενέσθαι, ὃς δ' ἔστι νῦν, μηκέτι εἶναι. καὶ ἐγὼ ἀκούσας ἐθορυβήθην· ὁ δέ μου θορυβουμένου ὑπολαβών, Ἄλλο τι οὖν, ἔφη, ἐπεὶ βούλεσθε αὐτόν, ὃς νῦν ἐστί, μηκέτι εἶναι, βούλεσθε αὐτόν, ὡς ἔοικεν, ἀπολωλέναι; καίτοι πολλοῦ ἂν ἄξιοι οἱ τοιοῦτοι εἶεν φίλοι τε καὶ ἐρασταί, οἵτινες τὰ παιδικὰ περὶ παντὸς ἂν ποιήσαιντο ἐξολωλέναι.

E Καὶ ὁ Κτήσιππος ἀκούσας ἠγανάκτησέ τε ὑπὲρ τῶν παιδικῶν καὶ εἶπεν· Ὦ ξένε Θούριε, εἰ μὴ ἀγροικότερον, ἔφη, ἦν εἰπεῖν, εἶπον ἄν, σοὶ εἰς κεφαλήν, ὅ τι μαθών μου καὶ τῶν ἄλλων καταψεύδει τοιοῦτο πρᾶγμα, ὃ ἐγὼ οἶμαι οὐδ' ὅσιον εἶναι λέγειν, ὡς ἐγὼ τόνδε βουλοίμην ἂν ἐξολωλέναι.

Τί δέ, ἔφη, ὦ Κτήσιππε, ὁ Εὐθύδημος, ἦ δοκεῖ σοι οἷόν τ' εἶναι ψεύδεσθαι; Νὴ Δία, ἔφη, εἰ μὴ μαίνομαί γε. Πότερον λέγοντα τὸ πρᾶγμα, περὶ

284 οὗ ἂν ὁ λόγος ᾖ, ἢ μὴ λέγοντα; Λέγοντα, ἔφη. Οὐκοῦν εἴπερ λέγει αὐτό, οὐκ ἄλλο λέγει τῶν

I know what I am about, I said : I know I shall never deny it.

Well now, he proceeded ; you tell me you wish him to become wise ?

Certainly.

And at present, he asked, is Cleinias wise or not ?

He says he is not yet so—he is no vain pretender.

And you, he went on, wish him to become wise, and not to be ignorant ?

We agreed.

So you wish him to become what he is not, and to be no longer what he now is.

When I heard this I was confused ; and he, striking in on my confusion, said : Of course then, since you wish him to be no longer what he now is, you wish him, apparently, to be dead. And yet what valuable friends and lovers they must be, who would give anything to know their darling was dead and gone !

Ctesippus, on hearing this, was annoyed on his favourite's account, and said : Stranger of Thurii, were it not rather a rude thing to say, I should tell you, ill betide your design of speaking so falsely of me and my friends as to make out—what to me is almost too profane even to repeat—that I could wish this boy to be dead and gone !

Why, Ctesippus, said Euthydemus, do you think it possible to lie ?

To be sure, I do, he replied : I should be mad otherwise.

Do you mean, when one tells the thing about which one is telling, or when one does not ?

When one tells it, he said.

Then if you tell it, you tell just that thing

421

ὄντων ἢ ἐκεῖνο ὅπερ λέγει; Πῶς γὰρ ἄν; ἔφη ὁ
Κτήσιππος. Ἓν μὴν κἀκεῖνό γ᾽ ἐστὶ τῶν ὄντων,
ὃ λέγει, χωρὶς τῶν ἄλλων. Πάνυ γε. Οὐκοῦν
ὁ ἐκεῖνο λέγων τὸ ὄν, ἔφη, λέγει; Ναί. Ἀλλὰ
μὴν ὅ γε τὸ ὂν λέγων καὶ τὰ ὄντα τἀληθῆ λέγει·
ὥστε ὁ Διονυσόδωρος, εἴπερ λέγει τὰ ὄντα, λέγει
τἀληθῆ καὶ οὐδὲν κατὰ σοῦ ψεύδεται. Ναί, ἔφη·
B ἀλλ᾽ ὁ ταῦτα λέγων, ἔφη ὁ Κτήσιππος, ὦ Εὐθύδημε, οὐ τὰ ὄντα λέγει. καὶ ὁ Εὐθύδημος, Τὰ δὲ
μὴ ὄντα, ἔφη, ἄλλο τι ἢ οὐκ ἔστιν; Οὐκ ἔστιν.
Ἄλλο τι οὖν οὐδαμοῦ τά γε μὴ ὄντα ὄντα ἐστίν;
Οὐδαμοῦ. Ἔστιν οὖν ὅπως περὶ ταῦτα τὰ μὴ
ὄντα πράξειεν ἄν τίς τι, ὥστε καὶ εἶναι[1] ποιήσειεν
ἂν καὶ ὁστισοῦν τὰ μηδαμοῦ ὄντα; Οὐκ ἔμοιγε
δοκεῖ, ἔφη ὁ Κτήσιππος. Τί οὖν; οἱ ῥήτορες
ὅταν λέγωσιν ἐν τῷ δήμῳ, οὐδὲν πράττουσιν;
Πράττουσι μὲν οὖν, ἦ δ᾽ ὅς. Οὐκοῦν εἴπερ
C πράττουσι, καὶ ποιοῦσιν; Ναί. Τὸ λέγειν ἄρα
πράττειν τε καὶ ποιεῖν ἐστίν; Ὡμολόγησεν. Οὐκ
ἄρα τά γε μὴ ὄντ᾽, ἔφη, λέγει οὐδείς· ποιοῖ γὰρ
ἂν ἤδη τί· σὺ δὲ ὡμολόγηκας τὸ μὴ ὂν μὴ οἷόν τ᾽

_____

[1] ὥστε καὶ εἶναι Hermann : ὥστ᾽ ἐκεῖνα, ὥς γε κλεινίᾳ κτλ. MSS.

which you tell, of all that are, and nothing else whatever?

Of course, said Ctesippus.

Now the thing that you tell is a single one, distinct from all the others there are.

Certainly.

Then the person who tells that thing tells that which is?

Yes.

But yet, surely he who tells what is, and things that are, tells the truth: so that Dionysodorus, if he tells things that are, tells the truth and speaks no lie about you.

Yes, said Ctesippus; but he who speaks as he did, Euthydemus, does not say things that are.

Then Euthydemus asked him: And the things which are not, surely are not?

They are not.

Then nowhere can the things that are not be?

Nowhere.

Then is it possible for anyone whatever so to deal with these things that are not as to make them be when they are nowhere?

I think not, said Ctesippus.

Well now, when orators speak before the people, do they do nothing?

No, they do something, he replied.

Then if they do, they also make?

Yes.

Now, is speaking doing and making?

He agreed that it is.

No one, I suppose, speaks what is not—for thereby he would be making something; and you have agreed that one cannot so much as make what is not—so

εἶναι μηδὲ ποιεῖν· ὥστε κατὰ τὸν σὸν λόγον οὐδεὶς
ψευδῆ λέγει, ἀλλ᾽ εἴπερ λέγει Διονυσόδωρος,
τἀληθῆ τε καὶ τὰ ὄντα λέγει. Νὴ Δία, ἔφη ὁ
Κτήσιππος, ὦ Εὐθύδημε· ἀλλὰ τὰ ὄντα μὲν
τρόπον τινὰ λέγει, οὐ μέντοι ὥς γε ἔχει.

Πῶς λέγεις, ἔφη ὁ Διονυσόδωρος, ὦ Κτήσιππε;
D εἰσὶ γάρ τινες, οἳ λέγουσι τὰ πράγματα ὡς ἔχει;
Εἰσὶ μέντοι, ἔφη, οἱ καλοί τε κἀγαθοὶ καὶ οἱ τἀληθῆ λέγοντες. Τί οὖν; ἦ δ᾽ ὅς· τἀγαθὰ οὐκ εὖ,
ἔφη, ἔχει, τὰ δὲ κακὰ κακῶς; Συνεχώρει. Τοὺς
δὲ καλούς τε κἀγαθοὺς ὁμολογεῖς λέγειν ὡς ἔχει
τὰ πράγματα; Ὁμολογῶ. Κακῶς ἄρα, ἔφη,
λέγουσιν, ὦ Κτήσιππε, οἱ ἀγαθοὶ τὰ κακά, εἴπερ
ὡς ἔχει λέγουσι. Ναὶ μὰ Δία, ἦ δ᾽ ὅς, σφόδρα γε,
τοὺς γοῦν κακοὺς ἀνθρώπους· ὧν σύ, ἐάν μοι
E πείθῃ, εὐλαβήσει εἶναι, ἵνα μή σε οἱ ἀγαθοὶ κακῶς
λέγωσιν. ὡς εὖ ἴσθ᾽ ὅτι κακῶς λέγουσιν οἱ
ἀγαθοὶ τοὺς κακούς. Ἦ καὶ τοὺς μεγάλους,
ἔφη ὁ Εὐθύδημος, μεγάλως λέγουσι καὶ τοὺς
θερμοὺς θερμῶς; Μάλιστα δήπου, ἔφη ὁ Κτήσ-
ιππος· τοὺς γοῦν ψυχροὺς ψυχρῶς λέγουσί τε καὶ
φασὶ διαλέγεσθαι. Σὺ μέν, ἔφη ὁ Διονυσόδωρος,
λοιδορεῖ, ὦ Κτήσιππε, λοιδορεῖ. Μὰ Δί᾽ οὐκ
ἔγωγε, ἦ δ᾽ ὅς, ὦ Διονυσόδωρε, ἐπεὶ φιλῶ σε,
ἀλλὰ νουθετῶ σ᾽ ὡς ἑταῖρον, καὶ πειρῶμαι πείθειν
μηδέποτε ἐναντίον ἐμοῦ οὕτως ἀγροίκως λέγειν,

---

[1] The quibbling throughout this passage is a wilful confusion of the two very different uses of the verb "to be"
(εἶναι), (a) in predication, where it has nothing to do with
existence, and (b) by itself, as stating existence.

[2] Euthydemus seizes on the ambiguous use of κακῶς,
which may mean either "badly" or "injuriously."

that, by your account, no one speaks what is false, while if Dionysodorus speaks, he speaks what is true and is.

Yes, in faith, Euthydemus, said Ctesippus; but somehow or other he speaks what is, only not as it is.[1]

How do you mean, Ctesippus? said Dionysodorus. Are there persons who tell things as they are?

Why surely, he replied, there are gentlemen—people who speak the truth?

Well, he went on, good things are in good case, bad in bad, are they not?

He assented.

And you admit that gentlemen tell things as they are.

I do.

Then, Ctesippus, good people speak evil of evil things, if they speak of them as they are.

Yes, I can tell you, very much so, when for instance they speak of evil men; among whom, if you take my advice, you will beware of being included, that the good may not speak ill of you. For, I assure you, the good speak ill[2] of the evil.

And they speak greatly of the great, asked Euthydemus, and hotly of the hot?

Certainly, I presume, said Ctesippus: I know they speak frigidly of the frigid, and call their way of arguing frigid.

You are turning abusive, Ctesippus, said Dionysodorus, quite abusive!

Not I, on my soul, Dionysodorus, for I like you: I am only giving you a friendly hint, and endeavouring to persuade you never to say anything so tactless

285 ὅτι ἐγὼ τούτους βούλομαι ἐξολωλέναι, οὓς περὶ
πλείστου ποιοῦμαι.

Ἐγὼ οὖν, ἐπειδή μοι ἐδόκουν ἀγριωτέρως πρὸς
ἀλλήλους ἔχειν, προσέπαιζόν τε τὸν Κτήσιππον καὶ
εἶπον ὅτι Ὦ Κτήσιππε, ἐμοὶ μὲν δοκεῖ χρῆναι
ἡμᾶς παρὰ τῶν ξένων δέχεσθαι ἃ λέγουσιν, ἐὰν
ἐθέλωσι διδόναι, καὶ μὴ ὀνόματι διαφέρεσθαι. εἰ
γὰρ ἐπίστανται οὕτως ἐξολλύναι ἀνθρώπους, ὥστ'
ἐκ πονηρῶν τε καὶ ἀφρόνων χρηστούς τε καὶ
ἔμφρονας ποιεῖν, καὶ τοῦτο εἴτε αὐτὼ εὑρήκατον
B εἴτε καὶ παρ' ἄλλου του ἐμαθέτην φθόρον τινὰ καὶ
ὄλεθρον τοιοῦτον, ὥστε ἀπολέσαντες πονηρὸν ὄντα
χρηστὸν πάλιν ἀποφῆναι· εἰ τοῦτο ἐπίστασθον—
δῆλον δέ, ὅτι ἐπίστασθον· ἐφάτην γοῦν τὴν τέχνην
σφῶν εἶναι τὴν νεωστὶ εὑρημένην ἀγαθοὺς ποιεῖν
τοὺς ἀνθρώπους ἐκ πονηρῶν—συγχωρήσωμεν οὖν
αὐτοῖν αὐτό· ἀπολεσάντων ἡμῖν τὸ μειράκιον καὶ
φρόνιμον ποιησάντων, καὶ ἅπαντάς γε ἡμᾶς τοὺς
ἄλλους. εἰ δὲ ὑμεῖς οἱ νέοι φοβεῖσθε, ὥσπερ ἐν
C Καρὶ ἐν ἐμοὶ ἔστω ὁ κίνδυνος· ὡς ἐγώ, ἐπειδὴ
καὶ πρεσβύτης εἰμί, παρακινδυνεύειν ἕτοιμος καὶ
παραδίδωμι ἐμαυτὸν Διονυσοδώρῳ τούτῳ ὥσπερ
τῇ Μηδείᾳ τῇ Κόλχῳ· ἀπολλύτω με, καὶ εἰ μὲν
βούλεται, ἑψέτω, εἰ δ', ὅ τι βούλεται, τοῦτο ποιείτω·
μόνον χρηστὸν ἀποφηνάτω. καὶ ὁ Κτήσιππος,
Ἐγὼ μέν, ἔφη, καὶ αὐτός, ὦ Σώκρατες, ἕτοιμός
εἰμι παρέχειν ἐμαυτὸν τοῖς ξένοις, καὶ ἐὰν βούλωνται δέρειν ἔτι μᾶλλον ἢ νῦν δέρουσιν, εἴ μοι ἡ
D δορὰ μὴ εἰς ἀσκὸν τελευτήσει ὥσπερ ἡ τοῦ Μαρ-

---

[1] Lit. " a Carian slave."
[2] This satyr was fabled to have challenged Apollo to a
musical contest, and on his fluting being judged inferior to

in my presence as that I wish these my most highly valued friends to be dead and gone.

So then I, observing that they were getting rather savage with each other, began to poke fun at Ctesippus, saying : Ctesippus, my feeling is that we ought to accept from our visitors what they tell us, if they are so good as to give it, and should not quarrel over a word. For if they understand how to do away with people in such sort as to change them from wicked and witless to honest and intelligent, and that too whether they have discovered for themselves or learnt from somebody else this peculiar kind of destruction or undoing, which enables them to destroy a man in his wickedness and set him up again in honesty ; if they understand this —and obviously they do ; you know they said that their newly discovered art was to turn wicked men into good — let us then accord them this power ; let them destroy the lad for us, and make him sensible, and all the rest of us likewise. If you young fellows are afraid, let the experiment be made on me as a *corpus vile* [1] ; for I, being an elderly person, am ready to take the risk and put myself in the hands of Dionysodorus here, as if he were the famous Medea of Colchis. Let him destroy me, and if he likes let him boil me down, or do to me whatever he pleases : only he must make me good.

Then Ctesippus said : I too, Socrates, am ready to offer myself to be skinned by the strangers even more, if they choose, than they are doing now, if my hide is not to end by being made into a wine-skin, like that of Marsyas,[2] but into the shape of virtue.

Apollo's harping he was flayed alive by the god for his presumption, and his skin was hung up like a bag or bottle in a cave ; *cf.* Herod. vii. 26.

σύου, ἀλλ᾽ εἰς ἀρετήν. καίτοι με οἴεται Διονυσόδωρος οὑτοσὶ χαλεπαίνειν αὐτῷ· ἐγὼ δὲ οὐ χαλεπαίνω, ἀλλ᾽ ἀντιλέγω πρὸς ταῦτα, ἅ μοι δοκεῖ πρός με μὴ καλῶς λέγειν· ἀλλὰ σὺ τὸ ἀντιλέγειν, ἔφη, ὦ γενναῖε Διονυσόδωρε, μὴ κάλει λοιδορεῖσθαι· ἕτερον γάρ τί ἐστι τὸ λοιδορεῖσθαι.

Καὶ ὁ Διονυσόδωρος, Ὡς ὄντος, ἔφη, τοῦ ἀντιλέγειν, ὦ Κτήσιππε, ποιεῖ τοὺς λόγους; Πάντως δήπου, ἔφη, καὶ σφόδρα γε· ἢ σύ, ὦ Διονυσόδωρε,
E οὐκ οἴει εἶναι ἀντιλέγειν; Οὔκουν σύ ταν, ἔφη, ἀποδείξαις πώποτε ἀκούσας οὐδενὸς ἀντιλέγοντος ἑτέρου ἑτέρῳ. Ἀληθῆ λέγεις; ἔφη· ἀλλὰ ἀκούωμεν νῦν, εἴ σοι ἀποδείκνυμι, ἀντιλέγοντος Κτησίππου Διονυσοδώρῳ. Ἦ καὶ ὑπόσχοις ἂν τούτου λόγον; Πάνυ, ἔφη. Τί οὖν; ἦ δ᾽ ὅς· εἰσὶν ἑκάστῳ τῶν ὄντων λόγοι; Πάνυ γε. Οὐκοῦν ὡς
286 ἔστιν ἕκαστον ἢ ὡς οὐκ ἔστιν; Ὡς ἔστιν. Εἰ γὰρ μέμνησαι, ἔφη, ὦ Κτήσιππε, καὶ ἄρτι ἐπεδείξαμεν μηδένα λέγοντα ὡς οὐκ ἔστι· τὸ γὰρ μὴ ὂν οὐδεὶς ἐφάνη λέγων. Τί οὖν δὴ τοῦτο; ἦ δ᾽ ὃς ὁ Κτήσιππος· ἧττόν τι ἀντιλέγομεν ἐγώ τε καὶ σύ; Πότερον οὖν, ἦ δ᾽ ὅς, ἀντιλέγοιμεν ἂν τὸν[1] τοῦ αὐτοῦ πράγματος λόγον ἀμφότεροι λέγοντες, ἢ οὕτω μὲν ἂν δήπου ταὐτὰ λέγοιμεν; Συνεχώρει. Ἀλλ᾽

---

[1] τὸν add. Heindorf.

And yet Dionysodorus here believes I am vexed with him. I am not vexed at all; I only contradict the remarks which I think he has improperly aimed at me. Come now, my generous Dionysodorus, do not call contradiction abuse : abuse is quite another thing.

On this Dionysodorus said : As though there were such a thing as contradiction ! Is that the way you argue, Ctesippus ?

Yes, to be sure, he replied, indeed I do ; and do you, Dionysodorus, hold that there is not ?

Well, you at any rate, he said, could not prove that you had ever heard a single person contradicting another.

Is that so ? he replied : well, let us hear now whether I can prove a case of it—Ctesippus contradicting Dionysodorus.

Now, will you make that good ?

Certainly, he said.

Well then, proceeded the other, each thing that is has its own description ?

Certainly.

Then do you mean, as each is, or as it is not ?

As it is.

Yes, he said, for if you recollect, Ctesippus, we showed just now that no one speaks of a thing as it is not ; since we saw that no one speaks what is not.

Well, what of that ? asked Ctesippus : are you and I contradicting any the less ?

Now tell me, he said, could we contradict if we both spoke the description of the same thing ? In this case should we not surely speak the same words ?

He agreed.

ὅταν μηδέτερος, ἔφη, τὸν τοῦ πράγματος λόγον
B λέγῃ, τότε ἀντιλέγοιμεν ἄν; ἢ οὕτω γε τὸ παράπαν
οὐδ᾽ ἂν μεμνημένος εἴη τοῦ πράγματος οὐδέτερος
ἡμῶν; Καὶ τοῦτο συνωμολόγει. Ἀλλ᾽ ἄρα, ὅταν
ἐγὼ μὲν τὸν τοῦ πράγματος λόγον λέγω, σὺ δὲ
ἄλλου τινὸς ἄλλον, τότε ἀντιλέγομεν; ἢ ἐγὼ λέγω
μὲν τὸ πρᾶγμα, σὺ δὲ οὐδὲ λέγεις τὸ παράπαν· ὁ
δὲ μὴ λέγων τῷ λέγοντι πῶς ἂν ἀντιλέγοι;

Καὶ ὁ μὲν Κτήσιππος ἐσίγησεν· ἐγὼ δὲ θαυμάσας τὸν λόγον, Πῶς, ἔφην, ὦ Διονυσόδωρε,
C λέγεις; οὐ γάρ τοι ἀλλὰ τοῦτόν γε τὸν λόγον
πολλῶν δὴ καὶ πολλάκις ἀκηκοὼς ἀεὶ θαυμάζω·
καὶ γὰρ οἱ ἀμφὶ Πρωταγόραν σφόδρα ἐχρῶντο
αὐτῷ καὶ οἱ ἔτι παλαιότεροι· ἐμοὶ δὲ ἀεὶ θαυμαστός
τις δοκεῖ εἶναι καὶ τούς τε ἄλλους ἀνατρέπων καὶ
αὐτὸς αὐτόν—οἶμαι δὲ αὐτοῦ τὴν ἀλήθειαν παρὰ
σοῦ κάλλιστα πεύσεσθαι. ἄλλο τι ψευδῆ λέγειν
οὐκ ἔστι; τοῦτο γὰρ δύναται ὁ λόγος· ἢ γάρ;
ἀλλ᾽ ἢ λέγοντ᾽ ἀληθῆ λέγειν ἢ μὴ λέγειν; Συν-
D εχώρει. Πότερον οὖν ψευδῆ μὲν λέγειν οὐκ ἔστι,
δοξάζειν μέντοι ἔστιν; Οὐδὲ δοξάζειν, ἔφη. Οὐδ᾽
ἄρα ψευδής, ἦν δ᾽ ἐγώ, δόξα ἔστι τὸ παράπαν.
Οὐκ ἔφη. Οὐδ᾽ ἄρα ἀμαθία οὐδ᾽ ἀμαθεῖς ἄνθρω-
ποι· ἢ οὐ τοῦτ᾽ ἂν εἴη ἀμαθία, εἴπερ εἴη, τὸ ψεύδεσθαι τῶν πραγμάτων; Πάνυ γε, ἔφη. Ἀλλὰ

---

[1] The argument is that, if we cannot speak *what is not*, or
falsely, of a thing (this assumption being based on the old
confusion of *being* with *existence*), there can be only one
description of a thing in any given relation, and so there is
no room for contradiction. This argument is commonly
ascribed to Antisthenes, the founder of the Cynic sect and
opponent of Plato. It is not clear who exactly are meant
by "the followers of Protagoras" or the "others before his
time."

But when neither of us speaks the description of the thing, he asked, then we should contradict? Or in this case shall we say that neither of us touched on the matter at all?

This also he admitted.

Well now, when I for my part speak the description of the thing, while you give another of another thing, do we contradict then? Or do I describe the thing, while you do not describe it at all? How can he who does not describe contradict him who does?[1]

At this Ctesippus was silent; but I, wondering at the argument, said: How do you mean, Dionysodorus? For, to be plain with you, this argument, though I have heard it from many people on various occasions, never fails to set me wondering—you know the followers of Protagoras made great use of it, as did others even before his time, but to me it always seems to have a wonderful way of upsetting not merely other views but itself also— and I believe I shall learn the truth of it from you far better than from anyone else. There is no such thing as speaking false—that is the substance of your statement, is it not? Either one must speak and speak the truth, or else not speak?

He agreed.

Then shall we say that speaking false "is not," but thinking false "is"?

No, it is the same with thinking, he said.

So neither is there any false opinion, I said, at all.

No, he said.

Nor ignorance, nor ignorant men; or must not ignorance occur, if it ever can, when we put things falsely?

Certainly, he said.

τοῦτο οὐκ ἔστιν, ἦν δ' ἐγώ. Οὐκ ἔφη. Λόγου
ἕνεκα, ὦ Διονυσόδωρε, λέγεις τὸν λόγον, ἵνα δὴ
ἄτοπον λέγῃς, ἢ ὡς ἀληθῶς δοκεῖ σοι οὐδεὶς εἶναι
E ἀμαθὴς ἀνθρώπων; Ἀλλὰ σύ, ἔφη, ἔλεγξον. Ἦ
καὶ ἔστι τοῦτο κατὰ τὸν σὸν λόγον, ἐξελέγξαι,
μηδενὸς ψευδομένου; Οὐκ ἔστιν, ἔφη ὁ Εὐθύδημος.
Οὐδ' ἄρα ἐκέλευεν, ἔφην ἐγώ, νῦν δὴ Διονυσόδωρος
ἐξελέγξαι; Τὸ γὰρ μὴ ὂν πῶς ἄν τις κελεύσαι; σὺ
δὲ κελεύεις; Ὅτι, ἦν δ' ἐγώ, ὦ Εὐθύδημε, τὰ
σοφὰ ταῦτα καὶ τὰ εὖ ἔχοντα οὐ πάνυ τι μανθάνω,
ἀλλὰ παχέως πως ἐννοῶ. ἴσως μὲν οὖν φορτι-
κώτερόν τι ἐρήσομαι. ἀλλὰ συγγίγνωσκε, ὅρα
287 δέ· εἰ γὰρ μήτε ψεύδεσθαι ἔστι μήτε ψευδῆ δοξάζειν μήτε ἀμαθῆ εἶναι, ἄλλο τι οὐδ' ἐξαμαρτάνειν
ἔστιν, ὅταν τίς τι πράττῃ; πράττοντα γὰρ οὐκ
ἔστιν ἁμαρτάνειν τούτου ὃ πράττει· οὐχ οὕτω
λέγετε; Πάνυ γ', ἔφη. Τοῦτό ἐστιν ἤδη, ἦν δ'
ἐγώ, τὸ φορτικὸν ἐρώτημα. εἰ γὰρ μὴ ἁμαρτάνομεν
μήτε πράττοντες μήτε λέγοντες μήτε διανοούμενοι, ὑμεῖς, ὦ πρὸς Διός, εἰ ταῦτα οὕτως ἔχει,
τίνος διδάσκαλοι ἥκετε; ἢ οὐκ ἄρτι ἔφατε ἀρετὴν
B κάλλιστ' ἂν παραδοῦναι ἀνθρώπων τῷ ἐθέλοντι
μανθάνειν;

Εἶτ', ἔφη, ὦ Σώκρατες, ὁ Διονυσόδωρος ὑπο-

But there is no such thing as this, I said.

No, he said.

Is it merely to save your statement, Dionysodorus, that you state it so—just to say something startling— or is it really and truly your view that there is no such thing as an ignorant man?

But you, he replied, are to refute me.

Well, does your argument allow of such a thing as refutation, if there is nobody to speak false?

There is no such thing, said Euthydemus.

So neither did Dionysodorus just now bid me refute him? I asked.

No, for how can one bid something that is not? Do you bid such a thing?

Well, Euthydemus, I said, it is because I do not at all understand these clever devices and palpable hits: I am only a dull sort of thinker. And so I may perhaps be going to say something rather clownish; but you must forgive me. Here it is: if there is no such thing as speaking false or think- ing false or being stupid, surely there can be no making a mistake either, when one does some- thing. For in doing it there is no mistaking the thing that is done. You will state it so, will you not?

Certainly, he said.

My clownish question, I went on, is now already before you. If we make no mistake either in doing or saying or intending, I ask you what in Heaven's name, on that assumption, is the subject you two set up to teach. Or did you not say just now that your speciality was to put any man who wished in the way of learning virtue?

Now really, Socrates, interposed Dionysodorus,

λαβών, οὕτως εἶ Κρόνος, ὥστε ἃ τὸ πρῶτον
εἴπομεν νῦν ἀναμιμνήσκει, καὶ εἴ τι πέρυσιν εἶπον,
νῦν ἀναμνησθήσει, τοῖς δ' ἐν τῷ παρόντι λεγομένοις
οὐχ ἕξεις ὅ τι χρῇ; Καὶ γάρ, ἔφην ἐγώ, χαλεποί
εἰσι πάνυ, εἰκότως· παρὰ σοφῶν γὰρ λέγονται·
ἐπεὶ καὶ τούτῳ τῷ τελευταίῳ παγχάλεπον χρήσα-
σθαί ἐστιν, ᾧ λέγεις. τὸ γὰρ οὐκ ἔχω ὅ τι
χρῶμαι τί ποτε λέγεις, ὦ Διονυσόδωρε; ἢ δῆλον
C ὅτι ὡς οὐκ ἔχω ἐξελέγξαι αὐτόν; ἐπεὶ εἰπέ, τί
σοι ἄλλο νοεῖ τοῦτο τὸ ῥῆμα, τὸ οὐκ ἔχω ὅ τι
χρήσωμαι τοῖς λόγοις; Ἀλλ' ὃ σὺ λέγεις, ἔφη,
τούτῳ γ' οὐ[1] πάνυ χαλεπὸν χρῆσθαι· ἐπεὶ ἀπόκριναι.
Πρὶν σὲ ἀποκρίνασθαι, ἦν δ' ἐγώ, ὦ Διονυσόδωρε;
Οὐκ ἀποκρίνει; ἔφη. Ἦ καὶ δίκαιον; Δίκαιον μέντοι, ἔφη. Κατὰ τίνα λόγον; ἦν δ'
ἐγώ· ἢ δῆλον ὅτι κατὰ τόνδε, ὅτι σὺ νῦν πάνσοφός
τις ἡμῖν ἀφῖξαι περὶ λόγους, καὶ οἶσθ' ὅτε δεῖ
ἀποκρίνασθαι καὶ ὅτε μή; καὶ νῦν οὐδ' ἂν ὁτιοῦν
D ἀποκρίνει, ἅτε γιγνώσκων ὅτι οὐ δεῖ; Λαλεῖς,
ἔφη, ἀμελήσας ἀποκρίνασθαι· ἀλλ', ὦ 'γαθέ,
πείθου καὶ ἀπόκρινου, ἐπειδὴ καὶ ὁμολογεῖς με
σοφὸν εἶναι. Πειστέον τοίνυν, ἦν δ' ἐγώ, καὶ
ἀνάγκη, ὡς ἔοικε· σὺ γὰρ ἄρχεις· ἀλλ' ἐρώτα.
Πότερον οὖν ψυχὴν ἔχοντα νοεῖ τὰ νοοῦντα,
ἢ καὶ τὰ ἄψυχα; Τὰ ψυχὴν ἔχοντα. Οἶσθα οὖν

---

[1] γ' οὐ Badham : τῷ mss.

---

[1] *i.e.* νοεῖ, " intend."

are you such an old dotard as to recollect now what we said at first, and will you now recollect what I may have said last year, and yet be at a loss how to deal with the arguments urged at the moment?

Well, you see, I replied, they are so very hard, and naturally so; for they fall from the lips of wise men; and this is further shown by the extreme difficulty of dealing with this last one you put forward. For what on earth do you mean, Dionysodorus, by saying I am at a loss how to deal with it? Or is it clear that you mean I am at a loss how to refute it? You must tell me what else your phrase can intend, " at a loss how to deal with the arguments."

But it is not so very hard to deal with that phrase [1] of yours, he said. Just answer me.

Before you answer me, Dionysodorus? I protested.

You refuse to answer? he said.

Is it fair?

Oh yes, it is fair enough, he replied.

On what principle? I asked: or is it plainly on this one—that you present yourself to us at this moment as universally skilled in discussion, and thus can tell when an answer is to be given, and when not? So now you will not answer a word, because you discern that you ought not to

What nonsense you talk, he said, instead of answering as you should. Come, good sir, do as I bid you and answer, since you confess to my wisdom.

Well then, I must obey, I said, and of necessity, it seems; for you are the master here. Now for your question.

Then tell me, do things that " intend " have life when they intend, or do lifeless things do it too?

Only those that have life.

τι, ἔφη, ῥῆμα ψυχὴν ἔχον; Μὰ Δί' οὐκ ἔγωγε.
Ε Τί οὖν ἄρτι ἤρου, ὅ τί μοι νοοῖ τὸ ῥῆμα; Τί ἄλλο
γε, ἦν δ' ἐγώ, ἢ ἐξήμαρτον διὰ τὴν βλακείαν; ἢ
οὐκ ἐξήμαρτον, ἀλλὰ καὶ τοῦτο ὀρθῶς εἶπον,
εἰπὼν ὅτι νοεῖ τὰ ῥήματα; πότερα φῂς ἐξαμαρτάνειν με ἢ οὔ; εἰ γὰρ μὴ ἐξήμαρτον, οὐδὲ σὺ
ἐξελέγξεις, καίπερ σοφὸς ὤν, οὐδ' ἔχεις ὅ τι
χρῇ τῷ λόγῳ· εἰ δ' ἐξήμαρτον, οὐδ' οὕτως ὀρθῶς
288 λέγεις, φάσκων οὐκ εἶναι ἐξαμαρτάνειν· καὶ
ταῦτα οὐ πρὸς ἃ πέρυσιν ἔλεγες λέγω. ἀλλὰ
ἔοικεν, ἔφην ἐγώ, ὦ Διονυσόδωρέ τε καὶ Εὐθύδημε,
οὗτος μὲν ὁ λόγος ἐν ταὐτῷ μένειν, καὶ ἔτι ὥσπερ
τὸ παλαιὸν καταβαλὼν πίπτειν, καὶ ὥστε τοῦτο
μὴ πάσχειν, οὐδ' ὑπὸ τῆς ὑμετέρας πω τέχνης
ἐξευρῆσθαι, καὶ ταῦτα οὑτωσὶ θαυμαστῆς οὔσης
εἰς ἀκρίβειαν λόγων.

Καὶ ὁ Κτήσιππος, Θαυμάσιά γε λέγετ', ἔφη,
Β ὦ ἄνδρες Θούριοι εἴτε Χῖοι εἴθ' ὁπόθεν καὶ ὅπῃ
χαίρετον ὀνομαζόμενοι· ὡς οὐδὲν ὑμῖν μέλει τοῦ
παραληρεῖν.

Καὶ ἐγὼ φοβηθείς, μὴ λοιδορία γένηται, πάλιν
κατεπράϋνον τὸν Κτήσιππον καὶ εἶπον· Ὦ Κτήσιππε, καὶ νῦν δὴ ἃ πρὸς Κλεινίαν ἔλεγον, καὶ
πρὸς σὲ ταὐτὰ ταῦτα λέγω, ὅτι οὐ γιγνώσκεις
τῶν ξένων τὴν σοφίαν, ὅτι θαυμασία ἐστίν· ἀλλ'
οὐκ ἐθέλετον ἡμῖν ἐπιδείξασθαι σπουδάζοντε,
ἀλλὰ τὸν Πρωτέα μιμεῖσθον τὸν Αἰγύπτιον σοφι-

---

[1] Cf. above, 271 c.
[2] Cf. Homer, Od. iv. 385 foll. Proteus was an ancient
seer of the sea who, if one could catch him as he slept on
the shore and hold him fast while he transformed himself
into a variety of creatures, would tell one the intentions of
the gods, the fate of absent friends, etc.

Now do you know any phrase that has life?

Upon my soul, I do not.

Why then did you ask just now what my phrase intended?

Of course I made a great mistake, I said; I am such a dullard. Or perhaps it was not a mistake, and I was right in saying what I did, that phrases intend. Do you say I was mistaken or not? If I was not, then you will not refute me, with all your skill, and you are at a loss how to deal with the argument; while if I was mistaken, you are in the wrong there, too, for you assert that there is no such thing as making a mistake; and what I say is not aimed at what you said last year. But it seems, I went on, Dionysodorus and Euthydemus, that our argument remains just where it was, and still suffers from the old trouble of knocking others down and then falling itself, and even your art has not yet discovered a way of avoiding this failure—in spite, too, of the wonderful show it makes of accurate reasoning.

Here Ctesippus exclaimed: Yes, your way of discussion is marvellous, you men of Thurii or Chios [1] or wherever or however it is you are pleased to get your names; for you have no scruple about babbling like fools.

At this I was afraid we might hear some abuse, so I soothed Ctesippus down once more, saying: Ctesippus, I repeat to you what I said to Cleinias just now, that you do not perceive the wonderful nature of our visitors' skill. Only they are unwilling to give us a display of it in real earnest, but treat us to jugglers' tricks in the style of Proteus [2] the

C στὴν γοητεύοντε ἡμᾶς. ἡμεῖς οὖν τὸν Μενέλαον
μιμώμεθα, καὶ μὴ ἀφιώμεθα τοῖν ἀνδροῖν, ἕως
ἂν ἡμῖν ἐκφανῆτον, ἐφ᾽ ᾧ αὐτὼ σπουδάζετον·
οἶμαι γάρ τι αὐτοῖν πάγκαλον φανεῖσθαι, ἐπειδὰν
ἄρξωνται σπουδάζειν· ἀλλὰ δεώμεθα καὶ παρα-
μυθώμεθα καὶ προσευχώμεθα αὐτοῖν ἐκφανῆναι.
ἐγὼ οὖν μοι δοκῶ καὶ αὐτὸς πάλιν ὑφηγήσασθαι,
οἵω προσεύχομαι αὐτὼ φανῆναί μοι· ὅθεν γὰρ
D τὸ πρότερον ἀπέλιπον, τὸ ἑξῆς τούτοις πειράσομαι,
ὅπως ἂν δύνωμαι, διελθεῖν, ἐάν πως ἐκκαλέ-
σωμαι καὶ ἐλεήσαντέ με καὶ οἰκτείραντε συν-
τεταμένον καὶ σπουδάζοντα καὶ αὐτὼ σπουδάσητον.

Σὺ δέ, ὦ Κλεινία, ἔφην, ἀνάμνησόν με, πόθεν
τότ᾽ ἀπελίπομεν. ὡς μὲν οὖν ἐγῷμαι, ἐνθένδε
ποθέν. φιλοσοφητέον ὡμολογήσαμεν τελευτῶντες·
ἦ γάρ; Ναί, ἦ δ᾽ ὅς. Ἡ δέ γε φιλοσοφία κτῆσις
ἐπιστήμης· οὐχ οὕτως; ἔφην. Ναί, ἔφη. Τίνα
ποτ᾽ οὖν ἂν κτησάμενοι ἐπιστήμην ὀρθῶς κτη-
E σαίμεθα; ἆρ᾽ οὐ τοῦτο μὲν ἁπλοῦν, ἥτις ἡμᾶς
ὀνήσει; Πάνυ γ᾽, ἔφη. Ἆρ᾽ οὖν ἄν τι ἡμᾶς
ὀνήσειεν, εἰ ἐπισταίμεθα γιγνώσκειν περιιόντες,
ὅπου τῆς γῆς χρυσίον πλεῖστον κατορώρυκται;
Ἴσως, ἔφη. Ἀλλὰ τὸ πρότερον, ἦν δ᾽ ἐγώ,
τοῦτό γε ἐξηλέγξαμεν, ὅτι οὐδὲν πλέον, οὐδ᾽ εἰ
ἄνευ πραγμάτων καὶ τοῦ ὀρύττειν τὴν γῆν τὸ
πᾶν ἡμῖν χρυσίον γένοιτο· ὥστε οὐδ᾽ εἰ τὰς
289 πέτρας χρυσᾶς ἐπισταίμεθα ποιεῖν, οὐδενὸς ἂν

---

[1] Cf. Hom. Od. iv. 456.   [2] Cf. 282 D.

Egyptian adept. So let us take our cue from
Menelaus,[1] and not leave hold of these gentlemen
till they give us a sight of their own serious business.
I believe something very fine will be found in them
as soon as they begin to be serious. Come, let us
beg and exhort and beseech them to let their light
shine. For my part, then, I am minded to take the
lead once more in showing what sort of persons I
pray may be revealed in them : starting from where
I left off before, I shall try, as best I can, to describe
what follows on from that, to see if I can rouse them
to action and make them, in merciful commiseration
of my earnest endeavour, be earnest themselves.

Will you, Cleinias, I asked, please remind me of the
point at which we left off ? Now, as far as I can tell,
it was something like this : we ended by agreeing
that one ought to pursue wisdom, did we not ?[2]

Yes, he said.

And this pursuit—called philosophy—is an acquiring of knowledge. Is it not so ? I asked.

Yes, he said.

Then what knowledge should we acquire if we
acquired it rightly ? Is it not absolutely clear that
it must be that knowledge which will profit us ?

Certainly, he said.

Now will it profit us at all, if we know how to tell,
as we go about, where the earth has most gold buried
in it ?

Perhaps, he said.

But yet, I went on, we refuted that former proposition, agreeing that even if without any trouble
or digging the earth we got all the gold in the world,
we should gain nothing, so that not if we knew how
to turn the rocks into gold would our knowledge

ἀξία ἡ ἐπιστήμη εἴη· εἰ γὰρ μὴ καὶ χρῆσθαι
ἐπιστησόμεθα τῷ χρυσίῳ, οὐδὲν ὄφελος αὐτὸ
ἐφάνη ὄν· ἢ οὐ μέμνησαι; ἔφην ἐγώ. Πάνυ γ᾽,
ἔφη, μέμνημαι. Οὐδέ γε, ὡς ἔοικε, τῆς ἄλλης
ἐπιστήμης ὄφελος γίγνεται οὐδέν, οὔτε χρημα-
τιστικῆς οὔτε ἰατρικῆς οὔτε ἄλλης οὐδεμιᾶς,
ἥτις ποιεῖν τι ἐπίσταται, χρῆσθαι δὲ μὴ ᾧ ἂν
ποιήσῃ· οὐχ οὕτως; Συνέφη. Οὐδέ γε εἴ τις
B ἔστιν ἐπιστήμη, ὥστε ἀθανάτους ποιεῖν, ἄνευ
τοῦ ἐπίστασθαι τῇ ἀθανασίᾳ χρῆσθαι, οὐδὲ ταύτης
ἔοικεν ὄφελος οὐδὲν εἶναι, εἰ τοῖς πρόσθεν ὡμολο-
γημένοις τεκμαίρεσθαι δεῖ. Συνεδόκει ἡμῖν
πάντα ταῦτα. Τοιαύτης τινὸς ἄρα ἡμῖν ἐπιστήμης δεῖ, ὦ καλὲ παῖ, ἦν δ᾽ ἐγώ, ἐν ᾗ συμπέ-
πτωκεν ἅμα τό τε ποιεῖν καὶ τὸ ἐπίστασθαι χρῆσθαι
τούτῳ, ὃ ἂν ποιῇ. Φαίνεται, ἔφη. Πολλοῦ
ἄρα δεῖ, ὡς ἔοικεν, ἡμᾶς λυροποιοὺς δεῖν εἶναι
C καὶ τοιαύτης τινὸς ἐπιστήμης ἐπηβόλους. ἐνταῦθα γὰρ δὴ χωρὶς μὲν ἡ ποιοῦσα τέχνη, χωρὶς
δὲ ἡ χρωμένη, διῄρηται δὲ τοῦ αὐτοῦ πέρι· ἡ
γὰρ λυροποιικὴ καὶ ἡ κιθαριστικὴ πολὺ δια-
φέρετον ἀλλήλοιν· οὐχ οὕτως; Συνέφη. Οὐδὲ
μὴν αὐλοποιικῆς γε δῆλον ὅτι δεόμεθα· καὶ γὰρ
αὕτη ἑτέρα τοιαύτη. Συνεδόκει. Ἀλλὰ πρὸς
θεῶν, ἔφην ἐγώ, εἰ τὴν λογοποιικὴν τέχνην μάθοιμεν,
440

be of any worth. For unless we know how to use the gold, we found no advantage in it. Do you not remember? I asked.

Certainly I do, he said.

Nor, it seems, do we get any advantage from all other knowledge, whether of money-making or medicine or any other that knows how to make things, without knowing how to use the thing made. Is it not so?

He agreed.

Nor again, if there is a knowledge enabling one to make men immortal, does this, if we lack the knowledge how to use immortality, seem to bring any advantage either, if we are to infer anything from our previous admissions.

On all these points we agreed.

Then the sort of knowledge we require, fair youth, I said, is that in which there happens to be a union of making and knowing how to use the thing made.

Apparently, he said.

So we ought, it seems, to aim at something far other than being lyre-makers or possessing that kind of knowledge. For in this case the art that makes and the art that uses are quite distinct, dealing in separation with the same thing; since there is a wide difference between the art of making lyres and that of harp - playing. Is it not so?

He agreed.

Nor again, obviously, do we require an art of flute-making; for this is another of the same kind.

He assented.

Now in good earnest, I asked, if we were to learn

ἆρά ἐστιν αὕτη, ἣν ἔδει κεκτημένους ἡμᾶς εὐδαίμονας εἶναι; Οὐκ οἶμαι, ἔφη, ἐγώ, ὁ Κλεινίας
D ὑπολαβών. Τίνι τεκμηρίῳ, ἦν δ' ἐγώ, χρῇ;

Ὁρῶ, ἔφη, τινὰς λογοποιούς, οἳ τοῖς ἰδίοις
λόγοις, οἷς αὐτοὶ ποιοῦσιν, οὐκ ἐπίστανται χρῆσθαι,
ὥσπερ οἱ λυροποιοὶ ταῖς λύραις, ἀλλὰ καὶ ἐνταῦθα
ἄλλοι δυνατοὶ χρῆσθαι οἷς ἐκεῖνοι εἰργάσαντο, οἱ
λογοποιεῖν αὐτοὶ ἀδύνατοι· δῆλον οὖν ὅτι καὶ
περὶ λόγους χωρὶς ἡ τοῦ ποιεῖν τέχνη καὶ ἡ τοῦ
χρῆσθαι.

Ἱκανόν μοι δοκεῖς, ἔφην ἐγώ, τεκμήριον λέγειν,
ὅτι οὐχ αὕτη ἐστὶν ἡ τῶν λογοποιῶν τέχνη, ἣν ἂν
κτησάμενός τις εὐδαίμων εἴη. καίτοι ἐγὼ ᾤμην
ἐνταῦθά που φανήσεσθαι τὴν ἐπιστήμην, ἣν δὴ
E πάλαι ζητοῦμεν. καὶ γάρ μοι οἵ τε ἄνδρες αὐτοὶ
οἱ λογοποιοί, ὅταν συγγένωμαι αὐτοῖς, ὑπέρσοφοι,
ὦ Κλεινία, δοκοῦσιν εἶναι, καὶ αὐτὴ ἡ τέχνη αὐτῶν
θεσπεσία τις καὶ ὑψηλή. καὶ μέντοι οὐδὲν
θαυμαστόν· ἔστι γὰρ τῆς τῶν ἐπῳδῶν τέχνης
290 μόριον σμικρῷ τε ἐκείνης ὑποδεεστέρα. ἡ μὲν
γὰρ τῶν ἐπῳδῶν ἔχεών τε καὶ φαλαγγίων καὶ
σκορπίων καὶ τῶν ἄλλων θηρίων τε καὶ νόσων
κήλησίς ἐστιν, ἡ δὲ δικαστῶν τε καὶ ἐκκλησιαστῶν
καὶ τῶν ἄλλων ὄχλων κήλησίς τε καὶ παραμυθία
τυγχάνει οὖσα· ἤ σοι, ἔφην ἐγώ, ἄλλως πως δοκεῖ;
Οὔκ, ἀλλ' οὕτω μοι φαίνεται, ἔφη, ὡς σὺ λέγεις.
Ποῖ οὖν, ἔφην ἐγώ, τραποίμεθ' ἂν ἔτι; ἐπὶ ποίαν
τέχνην; Ἐγὼ μὲν οὐκ εὐπορῶ, ἔφη. Ἀλλ',
ἦν δ' ἐγώ, ἐμὲ οἶμαι εὑρηκέναι. Τίνα; ἔφη ὁ

the art of speech-making, can that be the art we should acquire if we would be happy ?

I for one think not, said Cleinias, interposing.

On what proof do you rely ? I asked.

I see, he said, certain speech-writers who do not know how to use the special arguments composed by themselves, just as lyre-makers in regard to their lyres : in the former case also there are other persons able to use what the makers produced, while being themselves unable to make the written speech. Hence it is clear that in speech likewise there are two distinct arts, one of making and one of using.

I think you give sufficient proof, I said, that this art of the speech-writers cannot be that whose acquisition would make one happy. And yet I fancied that somewhere about this point would appear the knowledge which we have been seeking all this while. For not only do these speech-writers themselves, when I am in their company, impress me as prodigiously clever, Cleinias, but their art itself seems so exalted as to be almost inspired. However, this is not surprising ; for it is a part of the sorcerer's art, and only slightly inferior to that. The sorcerer's art is the charming of snakes and tarantulas and scorpions and other beasts and diseases, while the other is just the charming and soothing of juries, assemblies, crowds, and so forth. Or does it strike you differently ? I asked.

No, it appears to me, he replied, to be as you say.

Which way then, said I, shall we turn now ? What kind of art shall we try ?

For my part, he said, I have no suggestion.

Why, I think I have found it myself, I said.

What is it ? said Cleinias.

B Κλεινίας. Ἡ στρατηγική μοι δοκεῖ, ἔφην ἐγώ
τέχνη παντὸς μᾶλλον εἶναι, ἣν ἄν τις κτησάμενος
εὐδαίμων εἴη. Οὐκ ἔμοιγε δοκεῖ. Πῶς; ἦν
δ' ἐγώ. Θηρευτική τις ἥδε γέ ἐστι τέχνη ἀνθρώπων. Τί δὴ οὖν; ἔφην ἐγώ. Οὐδεμία, ἔφη,
τῆς θηρευτικῆς αὐτῆς ἐπὶ πλέον ἐστὶν ἢ ὅσον
θηρεῦσαι καὶ χειρώσασθαι· ἐπειδὰν δὲ χειρώ-
σωνται τοῦτο, ὃ ἂν θηρεύωνται, οὐ δύνανται
τούτῳ χρῆσθαι, ἀλλ' οἱ μὲν κυνηγέται καὶ οἱ
ἁλιεῖς τοῖς ὀψοποιοῖς παραδιδόασιν, οἱ δ' αὖ
γεωμέτραι καὶ οἱ ἀστρονόμοι καὶ οἱ λογιστικοί—
C θηρευτικοὶ γάρ εἰσι καὶ οὗτοι· οὐ γὰρ ποιοῦσι
τὰ διαγράμματα ἕκαστοι τούτων, ἀλλὰ τὰ ὄντα
ἀνευρίσκουσιν—ἅτε οὖν χρῆσθαι αὐτοῖς οὐκ ἐπιστάμενοι, ἀλλὰ θηρεῦσαι μόνον, παραδιδόασι δήπου
τοῖς διαλεκτικοῖς καταχρῆσθαι αὐτῶν τοῖς εὑρή-
μασιν, ὅσοι γε αὐτῶν μὴ παντάπασιν ἀνόητοί εἰσιν.

Εἶεν, ἦν δ' ἐγώ, ὦ κάλλιστε καὶ σοφώτατε
Κλεινία· τοῦτο οὕτως ἔχει;

Πάνυ μὲν οὖν· καὶ οἵ γε στρατηγοί, ἔφη, οὕτω
τὸν αὐτὸν τρόπον, ἐπειδὰν ἢ πόλιν τινὰ θηρεύσων-
D ται ἢ στρατόπεδον, παραδιδόασι τοῖς πολιτικοῖς
ἀνδράσιν· αὐτοὶ γὰρ οὐκ ἐπίστανται χρῆσθαι
τούτοις, ἃ ἐθήρευσαν ὥσπερ, οἶμαι, οἱ ὀρτυγο-
θῆραι τοῖς ὀρτυγοτρόφοις παραδιδόασιν. εἰ οὖν,
ἦ δ' ὅς, δεόμεθα ἐκείνης τῆς τέχνης, ἥτις ᾧ ἂν
κτήσηται ἢ ποιήσασα ἢ θηρευσαμένη αὐτὴ καὶ
ἐπιστήσεται χρῆσθαι, καὶ ἡ τοιαύτη ποιήσει
ἡμᾶς μακαρίους, ἄλλην δή τινα, ἔφη, ζητητέον
ἀντὶ τῆς στρατηγικῆς.

---

[1] *i.e.* geometers etc. are not to be regarded as mere
makers of diagrams, these being only the necessary and

Generalship, I replied, strikes me as the art whose acquisition above all others would make one happy.

I do not think so.

Why not ? I asked.

In a sense, this is an art of hunting men.

What then ? I said.

No part of actual hunting, he replied, covers more than the province of chasing and overcoming ; and when they have overcome the creature they are chasing, they are unable to use it : the huntsmen or the fishermen hand it over to the caterers, and so it is too with the geometers, astronomers, and calculators—for these also are hunters in their way, since they are not in each case diagram-makers, but discover the realities of things [1]—and so, not knowing how to use their prey, but only how to hunt, I take it they hand over their discoveries to the dialecticians to use properly, those of them, at least, who are not utter blockheads.

Very good, I said, most handsome and ingenious Cleinias ; and is this really so ?

To be sure it is ; and so, in the same way, with the generals. When they have hunted either a city or an army, they hand it over to the politicians—since they themselves do not know how to use what they have hunted—just as quail-hunters, I suppose, hand over their birds to the quail-keepers. If, therefore, he went on, we are looking for that art which itself shall know how to use what it has acquired either in making or chasing, and if this is the sort that will make us blest, we must reject generalship, he said, and seek out some other.

common machinery for their real business, the discovery of mathematical and other abstract truths.

290

Ε   ΚΡΙ. Τί λέγεις σύ, ὦ Σώκρατες, ἐκεῖνο τὸ μειράκιον τοιαῦτ᾿ ἐφθέγξατο;

ΣΩ. Οὐκ οἴει, ὦ Κρίτων;

ΚΡΙ. Μὰ Δί᾿ οὐ μέντοι. οἶμαι γὰρ αὐτὸν ἐγώ, εἰ ταῦτ᾿ εἶπεν, οὔτ᾿ Εὐθυδήμου οὔτε ἄλλου οὐδενὸς ἔτ᾿ ἀνθρώπου δεῖσθαι εἰς παιδείαν.

ΣΩ. Ἀλλ᾿ ἄρα, ὦ πρὸς Διός, μὴ ὁ Κτήσιππος ἦν ὁ ταῦτ᾿ εἰπών, ἐγὼ δὲ οὐ μέμνημαι;

291   ΚΡΙ. Ποῖος Κτήσιππος;

ΣΩ. Ἀλλὰ μὴν τό γε εὖ οἶδα, ὅτι οὔτε Εὐθύδημος οὔτε Διονυσόδωρος ἦν ὁ εἰπὼν ταῦτα· ἀλλ᾿, ὦ δαιμόνιε Κρίτων, μή τις τῶν κρειττόνων παρὼν αὐτὰ ἐφθέγξατο; ὅτι γὰρ ἤκουσά γε ταῦτα, εὖ οἶδα.

ΚΡΙ. Ναὶ μὰ Δία, ὦ Σώκρατες· τῶν κρειττόνων μέντοι τις ἐμοὶ δοκεῖ, καὶ πολύ γε. ἀλλὰ μετὰ τοῦτο ἔτι τινὰ ἐζητήσατε τέχνην; καὶ ηὕρετε ἐκείνην ἢ οὐχ ηὕρετε, ἧς ἕνεκα ἐζητεῖτε;

Β   ΣΩ. Πόθεν, ὦ μακάριε, εὕρομεν; ἀλλ᾿ ἦμεν πάνυ γελοῖοι, ὥσπερ τὰ παιδία τὰ τοὺς κορύδους διώκοντα· ἀεὶ ᾠόμεθα ἑκάστην τῶν ἐπιστημῶν αὐτίκα λήψεσθαι, αἱ δ᾿ ἀεὶ ὑπεξέφυγον. τὰ μὲν οὖν πολλὰ τί ἄν σοι λέγοιμι; ἐπὶ δὲ δὴ τὴν βασιλικὴν ἐλθόντες τέχνην καὶ διασκοπούμενοι αὐτήν, εἰ αὕτη εἴη ἡ τὴν εὐδαιμονίαν παρέχουσά τε καὶ ἀπεργαζομένη, ἐνταῦθα ὥσπερ εἰς λαβύρινθον ἐμπεσόντες, οἰόμενοι ἤδη ἐπὶ τέλει εἶναι, περι-

C   κάμψαντες πάλιν ὥσπερ ἐν ἀρχῇ τῆς ζητήσεως ἀνεφάνημεν ὄντες καὶ τοῦ ἴσου δεόμενοι, ὅσουπερ ὅτε τὸ πρῶτον ἐζητοῦμεν.

ΚΡΙ. Πῶς δὴ τοῦτο ὑμῖν συνέβη, ὦ Σώκρατες;

CRI. What is this, Socrates? Such a pronouncement from that stripling!

SOC. You do not believe it is his, Crito?

CRI. I should rather think not. For I am sure, if he spoke thus, he has no need of education from Euthydemus or anyone else.

SOC. But then, Heaven help me! I wonder if it was Ctesippus who said it, and my memory fails me.

CRI. Very like Ctesippus!

SOC. Well, of this at any rate I am certain, that it was neither Euthydemus nor Dionysodorus who said it. Tell me, mysterious Crito, was it some superior power that was there to speak it? For that speech I heard, I am sure.

CRI. Yes, I promise you, Socrates : I fancy it was indeed some superior power—very much so. But after that, did you go on looking for a suitable art? Did you find the one which you had as the object of your search, or not?

SOC. Find it, my good fellow! No, we were in a most ridiculous state ; like children who run after crested larks, we kept on believing each moment we were just going to catch this or that one of the knowledges, while they as often slipped from our grasp. What need to tell you the story at length? When we reached the kingly art, and were examining it to see if we had here what provides and produces happiness, at this point we were involved in a labyrinth : when we supposed we had arrived at the end, we twisted about again and found ourselves practically at the beginning of our search, and just as sorely in want as when we first started on it.

CRI. How did this happen to you, Socrates?

ΣΩ. Ἐγὼ φράσω. ἔδοξε γὰρ δὴ ἡμῖν ἡ πολιτικὴ καὶ ἡ βασιλικὴ τέχνη ἡ αὐτὴ εἶναι.

ΚΡΙ. Τί οὖν δή;

ΣΩ. Ταύτῃ τῇ τέχνῃ ἥ τε στρατηγικὴ καὶ αἱ ἄλλαι παραδιδόναι ἄρχειν τῶν ἔργων, ὧν αὐταὶ δημιουργοί εἰσιν, ὡς μόνῃ ἐπισταμένῃ χρῆσθαι. σαφῶς οὖν ἐδόκει ἡμῖν αὕτη εἶναι, ἣν ἐζητοῦμεν, D καὶ ἡ αἰτία τοῦ ὀρθῶς πράττειν ἐν τῇ πόλει, καὶ ἀτεχνῶς κατὰ τὸ Αἰσχύλου ἰαμβεῖον μόνη ἐν τῇ πρύμνῃ καθῆσθαι τῆς πόλεως, πάντα κυβερνῶσα καὶ πάντων ἄρχουσα πάντα χρήσιμα ποιεῖν.

ΚΡΙ. Οὐκοῦν καλῶς ὑμῖν ἐδόκει, ὦ Σώκρατες;

ΣΩ. Σὺ κρινεῖς, ὦ Κρίτων, ἐὰν βούλῃ ἀκούειν καὶ τὰ μετὰ ταῦτα συμβάντα ἡμῖν. αὖθις γὰρ δὴ πάλιν ἐσκοποῦμεν ὡδέ πως· Φέρε, πάντων ἄρχουσα ἡ βασιλικὴ τέχνη τὶ ἡμῖν ἀπεργάζεται E ἔργον, ἢ οὐδέν; Πάντως δήπου, ἡμεῖς ἔφαμεν πρὸς ἀλλήλους. Οὐ καὶ σὺ ἂν ταῦτα φαίης, ὦ Κρίτων;

ΚΡΙ. Ἔγωγε.

ΣΩ. Τί οὖν ἂν φαίης αὐτῆς ἔργον εἶναι; ὥσπερ εἰ σὲ ἐγὼ ἐρωτῴην, πάντων ἄρχουσα ἡ ἰατρική, ὧν ἄρχει, τί ἔργον παρέχεται; οὐ τὴν ὑγίειαν φαίης;

ΚΡΙ. Ἔγωγε.

ΣΩ. Τί δέ; ἡ ὑμετέρα τέχνη ἡ γεωργία, πάντων 292 ἄρχουσα, ὧν ἄρχει, τί ἔργον ἀπεργάζεται; οὐ τὴν τροφὴν ἂν φαίης τὴν ἐκ τῆς γῆς παρέχειν ἡμῖν;

ΚΡΙ. Ἔγωγε.

---

[1] *Cf.* Aesch. *Septem*, 2 "Whoso at helm of the state keeps watch upon affairs, guiding the tiller without resting his eyelids in sleep."

soc. I will tell you. We took the view that the statesman's and the monarch's arts were one and the same.

cri. Well, what then?

soc. To this art, we thought, generalship and the other arts handed over the management of the productions of their own trades, as this one alone knew how to use them. So it seemed clear to us that this was the one we were seeking, and was the cause of right conduct in the state, and precisely as Aeschylus' line [1] expresses it, is seated alone at the helm of the city, steering the whole, commanding the whole, and making the whole useful.

cri. And surely your notion was a good one, Socrates?

soc. You shall judge of that, Crito, if you care to hear what befell us thereafter. For later on we reconsidered it somewhat in this manner: Look now, does the monarch's art, that rules over all, produce any effect or not? Certainly it does, of course, we said to one another. Would you not say so too, Crito?

cri. I would.

soc. Then what would you say is its effect? For instance, if I were to ask you whether medicine, in ruling over all that comes under its rule, has any effect to show; would you not say: Yes, health?

cri. I would.

soc. And what about your art of agriculture? In ruling over all that comes under its rule, what effect does it produce? Would you not say that it supplies us with food from the earth?

cri. I would.

ΣΩ. Τί δέ; ἡ βασιλικὴ πάντων ἄρχουσα, ὧν ἄρχει, τί ἀπεργάζεται; ἴσως οὐ πάνυ γ᾽ εὐπορεῖς.

ΚΡΙ. Μὰ τὸν Δία, ὦ Σώκρατες.

ΣΩ. Οὐδὲ γὰρ ἡμεῖς, ὦ Κρίτων· ἀλλὰ τοσόνδε γε οἶσθα, ὅτι εἴπερ ἐστὶν αὕτη ἣν ἡμεῖς ζητοῦμεν, ὠφέλιμον αὐτὴν δεῖ εἶναι.

ΚΡΙ. Πάνυ γε.

ΣΩ. Οὐκοῦν ἀγαθόν γέ τι δεῖ ἡμῖν αὐτὴν παραδιδόναι;

ΚΡΙ. Ἀνάγκη, ὦ Σώκρατες.

B ΣΩ. Ἀγαθὸν δέ γέ που ὡμολογήσαμεν ἀλλήλοις ἐγώ τε καὶ Κλεινίας οὐδὲν εἶναι ἄλλο ἢ ἐπιστήμην τινά.

ΚΡΙ. Ναί, οὕτως ἔλεγες.

ΣΩ. Οὐκοῦν τὰ μὲν ἄλλα ἔργα, ἃ φαίη ἄν τις πολιτικῆς εἶναι—πολλὰ δέ που ταῦτ᾽ ἂν εἴη, οἷον πλουσίους τοὺς πολίτας παρέχειν καὶ ἐλευθέρους καὶ ἀστασιάστους—πάντα ταῦτα οὔτε κακὰ οὔτε ἀγαθὰ ἐφάνη, ἔδει δὲ σοφοὺς ποιεῖν καὶ ἐπιστήμης μεταδιδόναι, εἴπερ ἔμελλεν αὕτη εἶναι ἡ ὠφελοῦσά C τε καὶ εὐδαίμονας ποιοῦσα.

ΚΡΙ. Ἔστι ταῦτα· τότε γοῦν οὕτως ὑμῖν ὡμολογήθη, ὡς σὺ τοὺς λόγους ἀπήγγειλας.

ΣΩ. Ἆρ᾽ οὖν ἡ βασιλικὴ σοφοὺς ποιεῖ τοὺς ἀνθρώπους καὶ ἀγαθούς;

ΚΡΙ. Τί γὰρ κωλύει, ὦ Σώκρατες;

ΣΩ. Ἀλλ᾽ ἆρα πάντας καὶ πάντα ἀγαθούς; καὶ πᾶσαν ἐπιστήμην, σκυτοτομικήν τε καὶ τεκτονικὴν καὶ τὰς ἄλλας ἁπάσας, αὕτη ἡ παραδιδοῦσά ἐστιν;

ΚΡΙ. Οὐκ οἶμαι ἔγωγε, ὦ Σώκρατες.

D ΣΩ. Ἀλλὰ τίνα δὴ ἐπιστήμην; ἢ τί χρησόμεθα,

450

soc. And what of the monarch's art ? In ruling over all that comes under its rule, what does it produce ? Perhaps you are not quite ready with the answer.

cri. I am not indeed, Socrates.

soc. Nor were we, Crito ; yet so much you know, that if this is really the one we are seeking, it must be beneficial.

cri. Certainly.

soc. Then surely it must purvey something good ?

cri. Necessarily, Socrates.

soc. And you know we agreed with each other, Cleinias and I, that nothing can be good but some sort of knowledge.

cri. Yes, so you told me.

soc. And it was found that all effects in general that you may ascribe to statesmanship—and a great many of them there must be, presumably, if the citizens are to be made wealthy and free and immune from faction—all these things were neither bad nor good, while this art must make us wise and impart knowledge, if it really was to be the one which benefited us and made us happy.

cri. True : so at all events you agreed then, by your account of the discussion.

soc. Then do you think that kingship makes men wise and good ?

cri. Why not, Socrates ?

soc. But does it make all men good, and in all things ? And is this the art that confers every sort of knowledge—shoe-making and carpentry and so forth ?

cri. No, I think not, Socrates.

soc. Well, what knowledge does it give ? What

τῶν μὲν γὰρ ἔργων οὐδενὸς δεῖ αὐτὴν δημιουργὸν
εἶναι τῶν μήτε κακῶν μήτε ἀγαθῶν, ἐπιστήμην
δὲ παραδιδόναι μηδεμίαν ἄλλην ἢ αὐτὴν ἑαυτήν.
λέγωμεν δὴ οὖν, τίς ποτε ἔστιν αὕτη, ᾗ τί χρησόμεθα; βούλει φῶμεν, ὦ Κρίτων, ᾗ ἄλλους ἀγαθοὺς
ποιήσομεν;

ΚΡΙ. Πάνυ γε.

ΣΩ. Οἳ τί ἔσονται ἡμῖν ἀγαθοὶ καὶ τί χρήσιμοι;
ἢ ἔτι λέγωμεν, ὅτι ἄλλους ποιήσουσιν, οἱ δὲ ἄλλοι
ἐκεῖνοι ἄλλους; ὅ τι δέ ποτε ἀγαθοί εἰσιν, οὐδαμοῦ
E ἡμῖν φαίνονται, ἐπειδήπερ τὰ ἔργα τὰ λεγόμενα
εἶναι τῆς πολιτικῆς ἠτιμάσαμεν, ἀλλ' ἀτεχνῶς
τὸ λεγόμενον ὁ Διὸς Κόρινθος γίγνεται, καὶ ὅπερ
ἔλεγον, τοῦ ἴσου ἡμῖν ἐνδεῖ ἢ ἔτι πλέονος πρὸς
τὸ εἰδέναι, τίς ποτ' ἐστὶν ἡ ἐπιστήμη ἐκείνη, ᾗ
ἡμᾶς εὐδαίμονας ποιήσει;

ΚΡΙ. Νὴ τὸν Δία, ὦ Σώκρατες, εἰς πολλήν γε
ἀπορίαν, ὡς ἔοικεν, ἀφίκεσθε.

ΣΩ. Ἔγωγε οὖν καὶ αὐτός, ὦ Κρίτων, ἐπειδὴ
293 ἐν ταύτῃ τῇ ἀπορίᾳ ἐνεπεπτώκη, πᾶσαν ἤδη
φωνὴν ἠφίειν, δεόμενος τοῖν ξένοιν ὥσπερ Διοσ-
κούρων ἐπικαλούμενος σῶσαι ἡμᾶς, ἐμέ τε καὶ
τὸ μειράκιον, ἐκ τῆς τρικυμίας τοῦ λόγου, καὶ
παντὶ τρόπῳ σπουδάσαι, καὶ σπουδάσαντας ἐπιδεῖξαι, τίς ποτ' ἔστιν ἡ ἐπιστήμη, ἧς τυχόντες
ἂν καλῶς τὸν ἐπίλοιπον βίον διέλθοιμεν.

ΚΡΙ. Τί οὖν; ἠθέλησέ τι ὑμῖν ἐπιδεῖξαι ὁ
Εὐθύδημος;

---

[1] *Cf.* Pindar, *Nem.* vii. *fin.* Megara, a colony of Corinth,
revolted, and when the Corinthians appealed to the sentiment
attaching to Corinthus, the mythical founder of Megara,

use can we make of it? It is not to be a producer
of any of the effects which are neither bad nor good,
while it is to confer no other knowledge but itself.
Shall we try and say what it is, and what use we shall
make of it? Do you mind if we describe it, Crito, as
that whereby we shall make other men good?

CRI. I quite agree.

SOC. And in what respect are we going to have these
men good, and in what useful? Or shall we venture
to say they are to make others so, and these again
others? In what respect they can possibly be good
is nowhere evident to us, since we have discredited
all the business commonly called politics, and it is
merely a case of the proverbial "Corinthus Divine"[1];
and, as I was saying, we are equally or even worse at
fault as to what that knowledge can be which is to
make us happy.

CRI. Upon my word, Socrates, you got yourselves
there, it seems, into a pretty fix.

SOC. So then I myself, Crito, finding I had fallen
into this perplexity, began to exclaim at the top of
my voice, beseeching the two strangers as though
I were calling upon the Heavenly Twins to save
us, the lad and myself, from the mighty wave[2] of the
argument, and to give us the best of their efforts,
and this done, to make plain to us what that knowledge can be of which we must get hold if we
are to spend the remainder of our lives in a proper
way.

CRI. Well, did Euthydemus consent to propound
anything for you?

the Megarians drove them off, taunting them with using a
"vain repetition."

[2] Lit. "the big wave that comes in every three."

ΣΩ. Πῶς γὰρ οὔ; καὶ ἤρξατό γε, ὦ ἑταῖρε,
πάνυ μεγαλοφρόνως τοῦ λόγου ὧδε·

B Πότερον δή σε, ἔφη, ὦ Σώκρατες, ταύτην τὴν
ἐπιστήμην, περὶ ἣν πάλαι ἀπορεῖτε, διδάξω, ἢ
ἐπιδείξω ἔχοντα; Ὦ μακάριε, ἦν δ᾽ ἐγώ, ἔστι δὲ
ἐπὶ σοὶ τοῦτο; Πάνυ μὲν οὖν, ἔφη. Ἐπίδειξον
τοίνυν με νὴ Δί᾽, ἔφην ἐγώ, ἔχοντα· πολὺ γὰρ
ῥᾷον ἢ μανθάνειν τηλικόνδε ἄνδρα. Φέρε δή
μοι ἀπόκριναι, ἔφη· ἔστιν ὅ τι ἐπίστασαι; Πάνυ
γε, ἦν δ᾽ ἐγώ, καὶ πολλά, σμικρά γε. Ἀρκεῖ,
ἔφη. ἆρ᾽ οὖν δοκεῖς οἷόν τέ τι τῶν ὄντων τοῦτο,
ὃ τυγχάνει ὄν, αὐτὸ τοῦτο μὴ εἶναι; Ἀλλὰ μὰ
C Δί᾽ οὐκ ἔγωγε. Οὐκοῦν σύ, ἔφης, ἐπίστασαί
τι; Ἔγωγε. Οὐκοῦν ἐπιστήμων εἶ, εἴπερ ἐπίστασαι; Πάνυ γε, τούτου γε αὐτοῦ. Οὐδὲν
διαφέρει· ἀλλ᾽ οὐκ ἀνάγκη σε ἔχει πάντα ἐπίστασθαι ἐπιστήμονά γε ὄντα; Μὰ Δί᾽, ἔφην ἐγώ·
ἐπεὶ πολλὰ ἄλλ᾽ οὐκ ἐπίσταμαι. Οὐκοῦν εἴ τι
μὴ ἐπίστασαι, οὐκ ἐπιστήμων εἶ. Ἐκείνου γε,
ὦ φίλε, ἦν δ᾽ ἐγώ. Ἧττον οὖν τι, ἔφη, οὐκ
ἐπιστήμων εἶ; ἄρτι δὲ ἐπιστήμων ἔφησθα εἶναι·
D καὶ οὕτω τυγχάνεις ὢν αὐτὸς οὗτος, ὃς εἶ, καὶ

soc. Why, certainly ; and he began his discourse, my good friend, in this very lofty-minded fashion :

Would you rather, Socrates, that I instructed you as to this knowledge which has baffled you all this while, or propound that you have it ?

O gifted sir, I exclaimed, and have you the power to do this ?

Certainly I have, he replied.

Then for Heaven's sake, I cried, propound that I have it ! This will be much easier than learning for a man of my age.

Come then, answer me this, he said : Do you know anything ?

Yes, indeed, I replied, and many things, though trifles.

That is enough, he said ; now do you think it possible that anything that is should not be just that which it actually is ?

On my soul, not I.

Now you, he said, know something ?

I do.

Then you are knowing, if you really know ?

Certainly, in just that something.

That makes no difference ; you are not under a necessity of knowing everything, if you are knowing ?

No, to be sure, I replied ; for there are many other things which I do not know.

Then if you do not know something, you are not knowing ?

Not in that thing, my dear sir, I replied.

Are you therefore any the less unknowing ? Just now you said you were knowing ; so here you are, actually the very man that you are, and again,

αὖ πάλιν οὐκ εἶ, κατὰ ταὐτὰ ἅμα. Εἶεν, ἦν δ'
ἐγώ, Εὐθύδημε· τὸ γὰρ λεγόμενον, καλὰ δὴ
πάντα λέγεις· πῶς οὖν ἐπίσταμαι ἐκείνην τὴν
ἐπιστήμην, ἣν ἐζητοῦμεν; ὡς δὴ τοῦτο ἀδύνατόν
ἐστι τὸ αὐτὸ εἶναί τε καὶ μή· εἴπερ ἓν ἐπίσταμαι,
ἅπαντα ἐπίσταμαι· οὐ γὰρ ἂν εἴην ἐπιστήμων
τε καὶ ἀνεπιστήμων ἅμα· ἐπεὶ δὲ πάντα ἐπίσταμαι,
κἀκείνην δὴ τὴν ἐπιστήμην ἔχω· ἆρα οὕτως
λέγεις, καὶ τοῦτό ἐστι τὸ σοφόν;

E   Αὐτὸς σαυτόν γε δὴ ἐξελέγχεις, ἔφη, ὦ Σώκρατες.
   Τί δέ, ἦν δ' ἐγώ, ὦ Εὐθύδημε, σὺ οὐ πέπονθας
τοῦτο τὸ αὐτὸ πάθος; ἐγὼ γάρ τοι μετὰ σοῦ
ὁτιοῦν ἂν πάσχων καὶ μετὰ Διονυσοδώρου τοῦδε,
φίλης κεφαλῆς, οὐκ ἂν πάνυ ἀγανακτοίην. εἰπέ μοι,
σφὼ οὐχὶ τὰ μὲν ἐπίστασθον τῶν ὄντων, τὰ δὲ
οὐκ ἐπίστασθον; Ἥκιστά γε, ἔφη, ὦ Σώκρατες,
ὁ Διονυσόδωρος. Πῶς λέγετον; ἔφην ἐγώ·
ἀλλ' οὐδὲν ἄρα ἐπίστασθον; Καὶ μάλα, ἦ δ' ὅς.
294 Πάντ' ἄρα, ἔφην ἐγώ, ἐπίστασθον, ἐπειδήπερ καὶ
ὁτιοῦν; Πάντ', ἔφη· καὶ σύ γε προς, εἴπερ καὶ
ἓν ἐπίστασαι, πάντα ἐπίστασαι. Ὦ Ζεῦ, ἔφην
ἐγώ, ὡς θαυμαστὸν λέγεις καὶ ἀγαθὸν μέγα
πεφάνθαι. μῶν καὶ οἱ ἄλλοι πάντες ἄνθρωποι
πάντ' ἐπίστανται, ἢ οὐδέν; Οὐ γὰρ δήπου, ἔφη,
τὰ μὲν ἐπίστανται, τὰ δ' οὐκ ἐπίστανται, καὶ
εἰσὶν ἅμα ἐπιστήμονές τε καὶ ἀνεπιστήμονες.

not that man, in regard to the same matter and at the same time!

Admitted, Euthydemus, I said: as the saying goes, " well said whate'er you say." How therefore do I know that knowledge which we were seeking? Since forsooth it is impossible for the same thing to be so and not be so; by knowing one thing I know all;—for I could not be at once both knowing and unknowing;—and as I know everything I have that knowledge to boot: is that your line of argument? Is this your wisdom?

Yes, you see, Socrates, he said, your own words refute you.

Well, but, Euthydemus, I continued, are you not in the same plight? I assure you, so long as I had you and this dear fellow Dionysodorus to share my lot, however hard, I should have nothing to complain of. Tell me, you both know some existent things, of course, and others you do not?

By no means, Socrates, said Dionysodorus.

How do you mean? I asked: do you then not know anything?

Oh yes, we do, he said.

So you know everything, I asked, since you know anything?

Everything, he replied; yes, and you too, if you know one thing, know all.

Good Heavens, I cried, what a wonderful statement! What a great blessing to boast of! And the rest of mankind, do they know everything or nothing?

Surely, he said, they cannot know some things and not others, and so be at once knowing and unknowing.

457

Ἀλλὰ τί; ἦν δ' ἐγώ. Πάντες, ἦ δ' ὅς, πάντα
ἐπίστανται, εἴπερ καὶ ἕν. Ὦ πρὸς τῶν θεῶν,
B ἦν δ' ἐγώ, ὦ Διονυσόδωρε· δῆλοι γάρ μοί ἐστον
ἤδη ὅτι σπουδάζετον, καὶ μόλις ὑμᾶς προὐκαλε-
σάμην σπουδάζειν· αὐτὼ τῷ ὄντι πάντα ἐπίστασθον; οἷον τεκτονικὴν καὶ σκυτικήν; Πάνυ γ',
ἔφη. Ἦ καὶ νευρορραφεῖν δυνατώ ἐστον; Καὶ
ναὶ μὰ Δία καττύειν, ἔφη. Ἦ καὶ τὰ τοιαῦτα,
τοὺς ἀστέρας, ὁπόσοι εἰσί, καὶ τὴν ἄμμον; Πάνυ
γε, ἦ δ' ὅς· εἶτ' οὐκ ἂν οἴει ὁμολογῆσαι ἡμᾶς;

Καὶ ὁ Κτήσιππος ὑπολαβών· Πρὸς Διός,
C ἔφη, Διονυσόδωρε, τεκμήριόν τί μοι τούτων
ἐπιδείξατον τοιόνδε, ᾧ εἴσομαι, ὅτι ἀληθῆ λέγετον.
Τί ἐπιδείξω; ἔφη. Οἶσθα Εὐθύδημον, ὁπόσους
ὀδόντας ἔχει, καὶ ὁ Εὐθύδημος, ὁπόσους σύ;

Οὐκ ἐξαρκεῖ σοι, ἔφη, ἀκοῦσαι, ὅτι πάντα
ἐπιστάμεθα;

Μηδαμῶς, ἦ δ' ὅς, ἀλλὰ τοῦτο ἔτι ἡμῖν μόνον
εἴπατον καὶ ἐπιδείξατον, ὅτι ἀληθῆ λέγετον· καὶ
ἐὰν εἴπητον, ὁπόσους ἑκάτερος ἔχει ὑμῶν, καὶ
φαίνησθε γνόντες ἡμῶν ἀριθμησάντων, ἤδη πεισό-
μεθα ὑμῖν καὶ τἆλλα.

D Ἡγουμένω οὖν σκώπτεσθαι οὐκ ἠθελέτην, ἀλλ'
ὡμολογησάτην πάντα χρήματα ἐπίστασθαι, καθ'
ἓν ἕκαστον ἐρωτώμενοι ὑπὸ Κτησίππου. ὁ γὰρ
458

But what then? I asked.

All men, he replied, know all things, if they know one.

In the name of goodness, Dionysodorus, I said—for now I can see both of you are serious; before, I could hardly prevail on you to be so—do you yourselves really know everything? Carpentry, for instance, and shoe-making?

Certainly, he said.

And you are good hands at leather-stitching?

Why yes, in faith, and cobbling, he said.

And are you good also at such things as counting the stars, and the sand?

Certainly, he said: can you think we would not admit that also?

Here Ctesippus broke in: Be so good, Dionysodorus, he said, as to place some such evidence before me as will convince me that what you say is true.

What shall I put forward? he asked.

Do you know how many teeth Euthydemus has, and does Euthydemus know how many you have?

Are you not content, he rejoined, to be told that we know everything?

No, do not say that, he replied: only tell us this one thing more, and propound to us that you speak the truth. Then, if you tell us how many teeth each of you has, and you are found by our counting to have known it, we shall believe you thenceforth in everything else likewise.

Well, as they supposed we were making fun of them, they would not do it: only they agreed that they knew all subjects, when questioned on them, one after the other, by Ctesippus; who, before he

Κτήσιππος πάνυ ἀπαρακαλύπτως οὐδὲν ὅ τι
οὐκ ἠρώτα τελευτῶν, καὶ τὰ αἴσχιστα, εἰ ἐπισταί-
σθην· τὼ δὲ ἀνδρειότατα ὁμόσε ἤτην τοῖς ἐρωτή-
μασιν, ὁμολογοῦντες εἰδέναι, ὥσπερ οἱ κάπροι
οἱ πρὸς τὴν πληγὴν ὁμόσε ὠθούμενοι, ὥστ' ἔγωγε
καὶ αὐτός, ὦ Κρίτων, ὑπ' ἀπιστίας ἠναγκάσθην
τελευτῶν ἐρέσθαι [τὸν Εὐθύδημον],[1] εἰ καὶ ὀρχεῖ-
E σθαι ἐπίσταιτο ὁ Διονυσόδωρος· ὁ δέ, Πάνυ,
ἔφη. Οὐ δήπου, ἦν δ' ἐγώ, καὶ ἐς μαχαίρας
γε κυβιστᾶν καὶ ἐπὶ τροχοῦ δινεῖσθαι τηλικοῦτος
ὤν, οὕτω πόρρω σοφίας ἥκεις; Οὐδέν, ἔφη, ὅ
τι οὔ. Πότερον δέ, ἦν δ' ἐγώ, πάντα νῦν μόνον
ἐπίστασθον ἢ καὶ ἀεί; Καὶ ἀεί, ἔφη. Καὶ ὅτε
παιδία ἤστην καὶ εὐθὺς γενόμενοι ἠπίστασθε;
Πάντα, ἐφάτην ἅμα ἀμφοτέρω.

295 Καὶ ἡμῖν μὲν ἄπιστον ἐδόκει τὸ πρᾶγμα εἶναι·
ὁ δ' Εὐθύδημος, Ἀπιστεῖς, ἔφη, ὦ Σώκρατες;
Πλήν γ' ὅτι, ⟨ἦν δ'⟩[2] ἐγώ, εἰκὸς ὑμᾶς ἐστι σοφοὺς
εἶναι. Ἀλλ' ἤν, ἔφη, ἐθελήσῃς μοι ἀποκρίνεσθαι,
ἐγὼ ἐπιδείξω καὶ σὲ ταῦτα τὰ θαυμαστὰ ὁμολο-
γοῦντα. Ἀλλὰ μήν, ἦν δ' ἐγώ, ἥδιστα ταῦτα
ἐξελέγχομαι. εἰ γάρ τοι λέληθα ἐμαυτὸν σοφὸς
ὤν, σὺ δὲ τοῦτο ἐπιδείξεις ὡς πάντα ἐπίσταμαι
καὶ ἀεί, τί μεῖζον ἕρμαιον αὐτοῦ ἂν εὕροιμι ἐν
παντὶ τῷ βίῳ;

Ἀποκρίνου δή, ἔφη. Ὡς ἀποκρινουμένου

---

[1] τὸν Εὐθύδημον secl. Hermann.
[2] ἦν δ' add. Cornarius.

had done with them, asked them if they knew
every kind of thing, even the most unseemly, without the least reserve; while they most valiantly
encountered his questions, agreeing that they had
the knowledge in each case, like boars when driven
up to face the spears : so that I for my part, Crito,
became quite incredulous,and had to ask in the end
if Dionysodorus knew also how to dance. To which
he replied: Certainly.

I do not suppose, I said, that you have attained
such a degree of skill as to do sword-dancing, or be
whirled about on a wheel, at your time of life ?

There is nothing, he said, that I cannot do.

Then tell me, I went on, do you know everything
at present only, or for ever ?

For ever too, he said.

And when you were children, and were just born,
you knew ?

Everything, they both replied together.

Now, to us the thing seemed incredible : then
Euthydemus said : You do not believe it, Socrates ?

I will only say, I replied, that you must indeed
be clever.

Why, he said, if you will consent to answer me, I
will propound that you too admit these surprising
facts.

Oh, I am only too glad, I replied, to be refuted
in the matter. For if I am not aware of my own
cleverness, and you are going to show me that I
know everything always, what greater stroke of
luck than this could befall me in all my living
days ?

Then answer me, he said.

Ask : I am ready to answer.

B ἐρώτα. Ἆρ᾽ οὖν, ἔφη, ὦ Σώκρατες, ἐπιστήμων
του εἶ ἢ οὔ; Ἔγωγε. Πότερον οὖν ᾧ ἐπιστήμων
εἶ, τούτῳ καὶ ἐπίστασαι, ἢ ἄλλῳ τῳ; Ὧι ἐπιστήμων. οἶμαι γάρ σε τὴν ψυχὴν λέγειν· ἢ οὐ
τοῦτο λέγεις; Οὐκ αἰσχύνῃ, ἔφη, ὦ Σώκρατες;
ἐρωτώμενος ἀντερωτᾷς; Εἶεν, ἦν δ᾽ ἐγώ· ἀλλὰ
πῶς ποιῶ; οὕτω γὰρ ποιήσω, ὅπως ἂν σὺ κελεύῃς.
ὅταν μὴ εἰδῶ ὅ τι ἐρωτᾷς, κελεύεις με ὅμως
ἀποκρίνεσθαι, ἀλλὰ μὴ ἐπανερέσθαι; Ὑπολαμ-
C βάνεις γὰρ δήπου τι, ἔφη, ὃ λέγω; Ἔγωγε, ἦν
δ᾽ ἐγώ. Πρὸς τοῦτο τοίνυν ἀποκρίνου, ὃ ὑπολαμβάνεις. Τί οὖν, ἔφην, ἂν σὺ μὲν ἄλλῃ ἐρωτᾷς
διανοούμενος, ἐγὼ δὲ ἄλλῃ ὑπολάβω, ἔπειτα πρὸς
τοῦτο ἀποκρίνωμαι, ἐξαρκεῖ σοι, ἐὰν μηδὲν πρὸς
ἔπος ἀποκρίνωμαι; Ἔμοιγε, ἦ δ᾽ ὅς· οὐ μέντοι
σοί γε, ὡς ἐγῷμαι. Οὐ τοίνυν μὰ Δία ἀποκρινοῦμαι, ἦν δ᾽ ἐγώ, πρότερον, πρὶν ἂν πύθωμαι.
Οὐκ ἀποκρινῇ, ἔφη, πρὸς ἃ ἂν ἀεὶ ὑπολαμβάνῃς,
D ὅτι ἔχων φλυαρεῖς καὶ ἀρχαιότερος εἶ τοῦ δέοντος.

Κἀγὼ ἔγνων αὐτὸν ὅτι μοι χαλεπαίνοι δια-
στέλλοντι τὰ λεγόμενα, βουλόμενός με θηρεῦσαι
τὰ ὀνόματα περιστήσας. ἀνεμνήσθην οὖν τοῦ
Κόννου, ὅτι μοι κἀκεῖνος χαλεπαίνει ἑκάστοτε,
ὅταν αὐτῷ μὴ ὑπείκω, ἔπειτά μου ἧττον ἐπι-
462

Well then, Socrates, he asked, have you knowledge of something, or not ?

I have.

And tell me, do you know with that whereby you
have knowledge, or with something else ?

With that whereby I have knowledge : I think
you mean the soul, or is not that your meaning ?

Are you not ashamed, Socrates, he said, to ask a
question on your side when you are being questioned ?

Very well, I said : but how am I to proceed ? I
will do just as you bid me. When I cannot tell
what you are asking, is it your order that I answer
all the same, without asking a question upon it ?

Why, he replied, you surely conceive some meaning
in what I say ?

I do, I replied.

Answer then to the meaning you conceive to be
in my words.

Well, I said, if you ask a question with a different
meaning in your mind from that which I conceive,
and I answer to the latter, are you content I should
answer nothing to the point ?

For my part, he replied, I shall be content : you,
however, will not, so far as I can see.

Then I declare I shall not answer, I said, before
I get it right.

You refuse to answer, he said, to the meaning you
conceive in each case, because you will go on drivel-
ling, you hopeless old dotard !

Here I perceived he was annoyed with me for
distinguishing between the phrases used, when he
wanted to entrap me in his verbal snares. So I
remembered Connus, how he too is annoyed with
me whenever I do not give in to him, with the

μελεῖται ὡς ἀμαθοῦς ὄντος· ἐπεὶ δὲ οὖν διενενοήμην
καὶ παρὰ τοῦτον φοιτᾶν, ᾠήθην δεῖν ὑπείκειν,
μή με σκαιὸν ἡγησάμενος φοιτητὴν μὴ προσ-
δέχοιτο. εἶπον οὖν· Ἀλλ᾽ εἰ δοκεῖ σοι, Εὐθύδημε,
Ε οὕτω ποιεῖν, ποιητέον· σὺ γὰρ πάντως που κάλλιον ἐπίστασαι διαλέγεσθαι ἢ ἐγώ, τέχνην ἔχων
ἰδιώτου ἀνθρώπου· ἐρώτα οὖν πάλιν ἐξ ἀρχῆς.

Ἀποκρίνου δή, ἔφη, πάλιν, πότερον ἐπίστασαί
τῳ ἃ ἐπίστασαι, ἢ οὔ; Ἔγωγε, ἔφην, τῇ γε ψυχῇ.
296 Οὗτος αὖ, ἔφη, προσαποκρίνεται τοῖς ἐρωτω-
μένοις. οὐ γὰρ ἔγωγε ἐρωτῶ ὅτῳ, ἀλλ᾽ εἰ
ἐπίστασαί τῳ. Πλέον αὖ, ἔφην ἐγώ, τοῦ δέοντος
ἀπεκρινάμην ὑπὸ ἀπαιδευσίας· ἀλλὰ συγ-
γίγνωσκέ μοι· ἀποκρινοῦμαι γὰρ ἤδη ἁπλῶς ὅτι
ἐπίσταμαί τῳ ἃ ἐπίσταμαι. Πότερον, ἦ δ᾽ ὅς,
τῷ αὐτῷ τούτῳ γ᾽ ἀεί, ἢ ἔστι μὲν ὅτε τούτῳ, ἔστι
δὲ ὅτε ἑτέρῳ; Ἀεί, ὅταν ἐπίστωμαι, ἦν δ᾽ ἐγώ,
τούτῳ. Οὐκ αὖ, ἔφη, παύσει παραφθεγγόμενος;
Β Ἀλλ᾽ ὅπως μή τι ἡμᾶς σφαλεῖ τὸ ἀεὶ τοῦτο.
Οὔκουν ἡμᾶς γε, ἔφη, ἀλλ᾽ εἴπερ, σέ. ἀλλ᾽
ἀποκρίνου· ἦ ἀεὶ τούτῳ ἐπίστασαι; Ἀεί, ἦν δ᾽
ἐγώ, ἐπειδὴ δεῖ ἀφελεῖν τὸ ὅταν. Οὐκοῦν ἀεὶ
μὲν τούτῳ ἐπίστασαι· ἀεὶ δ᾽ ἐπιστάμενος πότερον

result that he now takes less trouble over me as being a stupid person. So being minded to take lessons from this new teacher, I decided that I had better give in, lest he should take me for a blockhead and not admit me to his classes. So I said : Well, if you think fit, Euthydemus, to proceed thus, we must do so ; in any case I suppose you understand debating better than I do—you are versed in the method, and I am but a layman. Begin your questions, then, over again.

Now, answer me once more, he said : do you know what you know by means of something, or not ?

I do, I replied ; by means of my soul.

There he is again, he said, answering more than he is asked. For I am not asking what the means is, but only whether you know by some means.

Yes, I did again answer more than I ought, I said, through lack of education. But forgive me, and I will now simply reply that I know what I know by some means.

By one and the same means always, he asked, or sometimes by one and sometimes by another ?

Always, whenever I know, I replied, it is by this means.

There again, he cried, you really must stop adding these qualifications.

But I am so afraid this word " always " may bring us to grief.

Not us, he rejoined, but, if anyone, you. Now answer : do you know by this means always ?

Always, I replied, since I must withdraw the " whenever."

Then you always know by this means : that being

τὰ μὲν τούτῳ ἐπίστασαι ᾧ ἐπίστασαι, τὰ δ' ἄλλῳ,
ἢ τούτῳ πάντα; Τούτῳ, ἔφην ἐγώ, ἅπαντα, ἅ γ'
ἐπίσταμαι. Τοῦτ' ἐκεῖνο, ἔφη· ἧκει τὸ αὐτὸ
παράφθεγμα. 'Αλλ' ἀφαιρῶ, ἔφην ἐγώ, τὸ ἅ γ'
ἐπίσταμαι. 'Αλλὰ μηδὲ ἕν, ἔφη, ἀφέλῃς· οὐ-
C δὲν γάρ σου δέομαι. ἀλλά μοι ἀπόκριναι· δύναιο
ἂν ἅπαντα ἐπίστασθαι, εἰ μὴ πάντα ἐπίσταιο;
Τέρας γὰρ ἂν εἴη, ἦν δ' ἐγώ. καὶ ὃς εἶπε·
Προστίθει τοίνυν ἤδη ὅ τι βούλει· ἅπαντα
γὰρ ὁμολογεῖς ἐπίστασθαι. "Εοικα, ἔφην ἐγώ,
ἐπειδήπερ γε οὐδεμίαν ἔχει δύναμιν τὸ ἃ
ἐπίσταμαι, πάντα δὲ ἐπίσταμαι. Οὐκοῦν καὶ ἀεὶ
ὡμολόγηκας ἐπίστασθαι τούτῳ, ᾧ ἐπίστασαι,
εἴτε ὅταν ἐπίστῃ εἴτε ὅπως βούλει· ἀεὶ γὰρ
ὡμολόγηκας ἐπίστασθαι καὶ ἅμα πάντα δῆλον
D οὖν, ὅτι καὶ παῖς ὢν ἠπίστω, καὶ ὅτ' ἐγίγνου,
καὶ ὅτ' ἐφύου· καὶ πρὶν αὐτὸς γενέσθαι, καὶ
πρὶν οὐρανὸν καὶ γῆν γενέσθαι, ἠπίστω ἅπαντα,
εἴπερ ἀεὶ ἐπίστασαι. καὶ ναὶ μὰ Δία, ἔφη,
αὐτὸς ἀεὶ ἐπιστήσει καὶ ἅπαντα, ἂν ἐγὼ βούλωμαι.

'Αλλὰ βουληθείης, ἦν δ' ἐγώ, ὦ πολυτίμητε
Εὐθύδημε, εἰ δὴ τῷ ὄντι ἀληθῆ λέγεις. ἀλλ'
οὔ σοι πάνυ πιστεύω ἱκανῷ εἶναι, εἰ μή σοι συμ-
βουληθείη ὁ ἀδελφός σου οὑτοσὶ Διονυσόδωρος·
οὕτω τάχα ἄν. εἴπετον δέ μοι, ἦν δ' ἐγώ·

the case, do you know some things by this means of knowing, and some things by another means, or everything by this?

Everything by this, I replied; everything, that is, that I know.

There it comes again, he cried; the same qualification!

Well, I withdraw my " that is, that I know."

No, do not withdraw a single word, he said: I ask you for no concession. Only answer me: could you know all things if you did not know everything?

It would be most surprising, I said.

Then he went on: You may therefore add on now whatever you please: for you admit that you know all things.

It seems I do, I replied, seeing that my " that I know " has no force, and I know everything.

Now you have also admitted that you know always by the means whereby you know, whenever you know—or however you like to put it. For you have admitted that you always know and, at the same time, everything. Hence it is clear that even as a child you knew, both when you were being born and when you were being conceived: and before you yourself came into being or heaven and earth existed, you knew all things, since you always know. Yes, and I declare, he said, you yourself will always know all things, if it be my pleasure.

Oh, pray let it be your pleasure, I replied, most worshipful Euthydemus, if what you say is really true. Only I do not quite trust in your efficacy, if your pleasure is not to be also that of your brother here, Dionysodorus: if it is, you will probably prevail. And tell me, I went on, since I cannot

296

E τὰ μὲν γὰρ ἄλλα οὐκ ἔχω ὑμῖν πῶς ἀμφισβητοίην,
οὕτως εἰς σοφίαν τερατώδεσιν ἀνθρώποις, ὅπως
οὐ πάντα ἐπίσταμαι, ἐπειδὴ ὑμεῖς φατέ· τὰ δὲ
τοιάδε πῶς φῶ ἐπίστασθαι, Εὐθύδημε, ὡς οἱ
ἀγαθοὶ ἄνδρες ἄδικοί εἰσι; φέρε εἰπέ, τοῦτο
ἐπίσταμαι ἢ οὐκ ἐπίσταμαι; Ἐπίστασαι μέντοι,
ἔφη. Τί; ἦν δ' ἐγώ. Ὅτι οὐκ ἄδικοί εἰσιν
οἱ ἀγαθοί. Πάνυ γε, ἦν δ' ἐγώ, πάλαι· ἀλλ'
297 οὐ τοῦτο ἐρωτῶ· ἀλλ' ὡς ἄδικοί εἰσιν οἱ ἀγαθοί,
ποῦ ἐγὼ τοῦτο ἔμαθον; Οὐδαμοῦ, ἔφη ὁ Διονυσόδωρος. Οὐκ ἄρα ἐπίσταμαι, ἔφην, τοῦτο ἐγώ.
Διαφθείρεις, ἔφη, τὸν λόγον, ὁ Εὐθύδημος πρὸς
τὸν Διονυσόδωρον, καὶ φανήσεται οὑτοσὶ οὐκ
ἐπιστάμενος, καὶ ἐπιστήμων ἅμα ὢν καὶ ἀνεπιστήμων. καὶ ὁ Διονυσόδωρος ἠρυθρίασεν.
Ἀλλὰ σύ, ἦν δ' ἐγώ, πῶς λέγεις, ὦ Εὐθύδημε;
B οὐ δοκεῖ σοι ὀρθῶς ἀδελφὸς λέγειν ὁ πάντα εἰδώς;
Ἀδελφὸς γάρ, ἔφη, ἐγώ εἰμι Εὐθυδήμου, ταχὺ
ὑπολαβὼν ὁ Διονυσόδωρος; κἀγὼ εἶπον, Ἔασον,
ὦ 'γαθέ, ἕως ἂν Εὐθύδημός με διδάξῃ, ὡς ἐπίσταμαι τοὺς ἀγαθοὺς ἄνδρας ὅτι ἄδικοί εἰσι, καὶ
μή μοι φθονήσῃς τοῦ μαθήματος. Φεύγεις, ἔφη,
ὦ Σώκρατες, ὁ Διονυσόδωρος, καὶ οὐκ ἐθέλεις
ἀποκρίνεσθαι. Εἰκότως γ', εἶπον ἐγώ· ἥττων γάρ
C εἰμι καὶ τοῦ ἑτέρου ὑμῶν, ὥστε πολλοῦ δέω μὴ
οὐ δύο γε φεύγειν. πολὺ γὰρ πού εἰμι φαυλότερος τοῦ Ἡρακλέους, ὃς οὐχ οἷός τε ἦν τῇ τε
ὕδρᾳ διαμάχεσθαι, σοφιστρίᾳ οὔσῃ καὶ διὰ τὴν
468

hope in a general way to dispute the statement that
I know everything with persons so prodigiously
clever—since it is *your* statement—how am I to say
I know certain things, Euthydemus; for instance,
that good men are unjust? Come, tell me, do I
know this or not?

You know it certainly, he said.

What? I said.

That the good are not unjust.

Quite so, I said: I knew that all the time; but
that is not what I ask: tell me, where did I learn
that the good are unjust?

Nowhere, said Dionysodorus.

Then I do not know this, I said.

You are spoiling the argument, said Euthydemus
to Dionysodorus, and we shall find that this fellow
does not know, and is at once both knowing and unknowing.

At this Dionysodorus reddened. But you, I said,
what do *you* mean, Euthydemus. Do you find that
your brother, who knows everything, has not spoken
aright?

I a brother of Euthydemus? quickly interposed
Dionysodorus.

Whereupon I said: Let me alone, good sir, till
Euthydemus has taught me that I know that good
men are unjust, and do not grudge me this lesson.

You are running away, Socrates, said Dionysodorus; you refuse to answer.

Yes, and with good reason, I said: for I am
weaker than either one of you, so I have no scruple
about running away from the two together. You
see, I am sadly inferior to Hercules, who was no
match for the hydra—that she-professor who was

σοφίαν ἀνιείσῃ, εἰ μίαν κεφαλὴν τοῦ λόγου τις
ἀποτέμοι, πολλὰς ἀντὶ τῆς μιᾶς, καὶ καρκίνῳ
τινὶ ἑτέρῳ σοφιστῇ, ἐκ θαλάττης ἀφιγμένῳ, νεωστί,
μοι δοκεῖν, καταπεπλευκότι· ὃς ἐπειδὴ αὐτὸν
ἐλύπει οὕτως ἐκ τοῦ ἐπ' ἀριστερὰ λέγων καὶ
δάκνων, τὸν Ἰόλεων τὸν ἀδελφιδοῦν βοηθὸν
D ἐπεκαλέσατο, ὁ δὲ αὐτῷ ἱκανῶς ἐβοήθησεν. ὁ
δ' ἐμὸς Ἰόλεως [Πατροκλῆς]¹ εἰ ἔλθοι, πλέον ἂν
θάτερον ποιήσειεν.

Ἀπόκριναι δή, ἔφη ὁ Διονυσόδωρος, ὁπότε
σοι ταῦτα ὕμνηται· πότερον ὁ Ἰόλεως τοῦ Ἡρακλέους μᾶλλον ἦν ἀδελφιδοῦς ἢ σός; Κράτιστον
τοίνυν μοι, ὦ Διονυσόδωρε, ἦν δ' ἐγώ, ἀποκρίνα-
σθαί σοι. οὐ γὰρ μὴ ἀνῇς ἐρωτῶν, σχεδόν τι
ἐγὼ τοῦτ' εὖ οἶδα, φθονῶν καὶ διακωλύων, ἵνα
μὴ διδάξῃ με Εὐθύδημος ἐκεῖνο τὸ σοφόν. Ἀποκρίνου δή, ἔφη. Ἀποκρίνομαι δή, εἶπον, ὅτι
τοῦ Ἡρακλέους ἦν ὁ Ἰόλεως ἀδελφιδοῦς, ἐμὸς
E δ', ὡς ἐμοὶ δοκεῖ, οὐδ' ὁπωστιοῦν. οὐ γὰρ
Πατροκλῆς ἦν αὐτῷ πατήρ, ὁ ἐμὸς ἀδελφός,
ἀλλὰ παραπλήσιον μὲν τοὔνομα Ἰφικλῆς, ὁ Ἡρακλέους ἀδελφός. Πατροκλῆς δέ, ἦ δ' ὅς, σός;
Πάνυ γ', ἔφην ἐγώ, ὁμομήτριός γε, οὐ μέντοι
ὁμοπάτριος. Ἀδελφὸς ἄρα ἐστί σοι καὶ οὐκ
ἀδελφός. Οὐχ ὁμοπάτριός γε, ὦ βέλτιστε, ἔφην·
ἐκείνου μὲν γὰρ Χαιρέδημος ἦν πατήρ, ἐμὸς δὲ
Σωφρονίσκος. Πατὴρ δὲ ἦν, ἔφη, Σωφρονίσκος
καὶ Χαιρέδημος; Πάνυ γ', ἔφην· ὁ μέν γε ἐμός,
298 ὁ δὲ ἐκείνου. Οὐκοῦν, ἦ δ' ὅς, ἕτερος ἦν Χαιρέ-

---

¹ Πατροκλῆς secl. Heindorf.

¹ *i.e.* any kinsman or helper I might summon would only
add to the number of your victims.

so clever that she sent forth many heads of debate in place of each one that was cut off; nor for another sort of crab-professor from the sea—freshly, I fancy, arrived on shore; and, when the hero was so bothered with its leftward barks and bites, he summoned his nephew Iolaus to the rescue, and he brought him effective relief. But if my Iolaus were to come, he would do more harm than good.[1]

Well, answer this, said Dionysodorus, now you have done your descanting: Was Iolaus more Hercules' nephew than yours?

I see I had best answer you, Dionysodorus, I said. For you will never cease putting questions—I think I may say I am sure of this—in a grudging, obstructing spirit, so that Euthydemus may not teach me that bit of cleverness.

Then answer, he said.

Well, I answer, I said, that Iolaus was Hercules' nephew, but not mine, so far as I can see, in any way whatever. For Patrocles, my brother, was not his father; only Hercules' brother Iphicles had a name somewhat similar to his.

And Patrocles, he said, is your brother?

Certainly, I said: that is, by the same mother, but not by the same father.

Then he is your brother and not your brother.

Not by the same father, worthy sir, I replied. His father was Chaeredemus, mine Sophroniscus.

So Sophroniscus and Chaeredemus, he said, were " father "?

Certainly, I said: the former mine, the latter his.

Then surely, he went on, Chaeredemus was other than " father "?

δημος τοῦ πατρός; Τοὐμοῦ γ', ἔφην ἐγώ. Ἆρ'
οὖν πατὴρ ἦν ἕτερος ὢν πατρός; ἢ σὺ εἶ ὁ αὐτὸς
τῷ λίθῳ; Δέδοικα μὲν ἔγωγ', ἔφην, μὴ φανῶ
ὑπὸ σοῦ ὁ αὐτός· οὐ μέντοι μοι δοκῶ. Οὐκοῦν
ἕτερος εἶ, ἔφη, τοῦ λίθου; Ἕτερος μέντοι. Ἄλλο
τι οὖν ἕτερος, ἦ δ' ὅς, ὢν λίθου οὐ λίθος εἶ; καὶ
ἕτερος ὢν χρυσοῦ οὐ χρυσὸς εἶ; Ἔστι ταῦτα.
Οὐκοῦν καὶ ὁ Χαιρέδημος, ἔφη, ἕτερος ὢν πατρὸς
B οὐκ ἂν πατὴρ εἴη. Ἔοικεν, ἦν δ' ἐγώ, οὐ πατὴρ
εἶναι. Εἰ γὰρ δήπου, ἔφη, πατήρ ἐστιν ὁ Χαιρέδημος, ὑπολαβὼν ὁ Εὐθύδημος, πάλιν αὖ ὁ
Σωφρονίσκος ἕτερος ὢν πατρὸς οὐ πατήρ ἐστιν,
ὥστε σύ, ὦ Σώκρατες, ἀπάτωρ εἶ.

Καὶ ὁ Κτήσιππος ἐκδεξάμενος, Ὁ δὲ ὑμέτερος,
ἔφη, αὖ πατὴρ οὐ ταὐτὰ ταῦτα πέπονθεν; ἕτερός
ἐστι τοὐμοῦ πατρός; Πολλοῦ γ', ἔφη, δεῖ, ὁ
Εὐθύδημος. Ἀλλά, ἦ δ' ὅς, ὁ αὐτός; Ὁ αὐτὸς
μέντοι. Οὐκ ἂν συμβουλοίμην. ἀλλὰ πότερον,
C ὦ Εὐθύδημε, ἐμὸς μόνος ἐστὶ πατὴρ ἢ καὶ τῶν
ἄλλων ἀνθρώπων; Καὶ τῶν ἄλλων, ἔφη· ἢ οἴει
τὸν αὐτὸν πατέρα ὄντα οὐ πατέρα εἶναι; Ὤιμην
δῆτα, ἔφη ὁ Κτήσιππος. Τί δέ; ἦ δ' ὅς· χρυσὸν
ὄντα μὴ χρυσὸν εἶναι; ἢ ἄνθρωπον ὄντα μὴ
ἄνθρωπον; Μὴ γάρ, ἔφη ὁ Κτήσιππος, ὦ Εὐθύ-

---

[1] Cf. Gorgias, 494 A, where "the life of a stone" is given
as a proverbial example of a life without pleasure or pain.

Than mine, at any rate, I said.

Why then, he was father while being other than father. Or are you the same as "the stone"?[1]

I fear you may prove that of me, I said, though I do not feel like it.

Then are you other than the stone?

Other, I must say.

Then of course, he went on, if you are other than stone, you are not stone? And if you are other than gold, you are not gold?

Quite so.

Hence Chaeredemus, he said, being other than father, cannot be "father."

It seems, I said, that he is not a father.

No, for I presume, interposed Euthydemus, that if Chaeredemus is a father Sophroniscus in his turn, being other than a father, is not a father; so that you, Socrates, are fatherless.

Here Ctesippus took it up, observing: And your father too, is he not in just the same plight? Is he other than my father?

Not in the slightest, said Euthydemus.

What, asked the other, is he the same?

The same, to be sure.

I should not like to think he was: but tell me, Euthydemus, is he my father only, or everybody else's too?

Everybody else's too, he replied; or do you suppose that the same man, being a father, can be no father?

I did suppose so, said Ctesippus.

Well, said the other, and that a thing being gold could be not gold? Or being a man, not man?

Perhaps, Euthydemus, said Ctesippus, you are

473

δημε, τὸ λεγόμενον, οὐ λίνον λίνῳ συνάπτεις·
δεινὸν γὰρ λέγεις πρᾶγμα, εἰ ὁ σὸς πατὴρ πάντων
ἐστὶ πατήρ. Ἀλλ' ἔστιν, ἔφη. Πότερον ἀνθρώπων; ἦ δ' ὃς ὁ Κτήσιππος, ἦ καὶ ἵππων;
D ἦ καὶ τῶν ἄλλων πάντων ζώων; Πάντων, ἔφη.
Ἦ καὶ μήτηρ ἡ μήτηρ; Καὶ ἡ μήτηρ γε. Καὶ
τῶν ἐχίνων ἄρα, ἔφη, ἡ σὴ μήτηρ μήτηρ ἐστὶ τῶν
θαλαττίων. Καὶ ἡ σή γ', ἔφη. Καὶ σὺ ἄρα
ἀδελφὸς εἶ τῶν κωβιῶν καὶ κυναρίων καὶ χοιρι-
δίων. Καὶ γὰρ σύ, ἔφη. κάπρος¹ ἄρα σοι
πατήρ ἐστι καὶ κύων. Καὶ γὰρ σοί, ἔφη.

Αὐτίκα δέ γε, ἦ δ' ὃς ὁ Διονυσόδωρος, ἄν μοι
ἀποκρίνῃ, ὦ Κτήσιππε, ὁμολογήσεις ταῦτα. εἰπὲ
γάρ μοι, ἔστι σοι κύων; Καὶ μάλα πονηρός, ἔφη
E ὁ Κτήσιππος. Ἔστιν οὖν αὐτῷ κυνίδια; Καὶ
μάλ', ἔφη, ἕτερα τοιαῦτα. Οὐκοῦν πατήρ ἐστιν
αὐτῶν ὁ κύων; Ἔγωγέ τοι εἶδον, ἔφη, αὐτὸν
ὀχεύοντα τὴν κύνα. Τί οὖν; οὐ σός ἐστιν ὁ
κύων; Πάνυ γ', ἔφη. Οὐκοῦν πατὴρ ὢν σός
ἐστι, ὥστε σὸς πατὴρ γίγνεται ὁ κύων καὶ σὺ
κυναρίων ἀδελφός;

Καὶ αὖθις ταχὺ ὑπολαβὼν ὁ Διονυσόδωρος,
ἵνα μὴ πρότερόν τι εἴποι ὁ Κτήσιππος, Καὶ ἔτι
γέ μοι μικρόν, ἔφη, ἀπόκριναι· τύπτεις τὸν κύνα

---

¹ κάπρος Badham : καὶ πρὸς MSS.

---

¹ *i.e.* treating two different things as the same.

knotting flax with cotton,[1] as they say : for it is a strange result that you state, if your father is father of all.

He is, though, was the reply.

Of all men, do you mean? asked Ctesippus, or of horses too, and all other animals?

Of all, he said.

And is your mother a mother in the same way?

My mother too.

And is your mother a mother of sea-urchins?

Yes, and yours is also, he replied.

So then you are a brother of the gudgeons and whelps and porkers.

Yes, and so are you, he said.

Then your father is a boar and a dog.

And so is yours, he said.

Yes, said Dionysodorus, and it will take you but a moment, if you will answer me, Ctesippus, to acknowledge all this. Just tell me, have you a dog?

Yes, a real rogue, said Ctesippus.

Has he got puppies?

Yes, a set of rogues like him.

Then is the dog their father?

Yes, indeed ; I saw him with my own eyes covering the bitch.

Well now, is not the dog yours?

Certainly, he said.

Thus he is a father, and yours, and accordingly the dog turns out to be your father, and you a brother of whelps.

Hereupon Dionysodorus struck in again quickly, lest Ctesippus should get a word in before him : Answer me just one more little point : do you beat this dog?

475

τοῦτον; καὶ ὁ Κτήσιππος γελάσας, Νὴ τοὺς
θεούς, ἔφη· οὐ γὰρ δύναμαι σέ. Οὐκοῦν τὸν
299 σαυτοῦ πατέρα, ἔφη, τύπτεις. Πολὺ μέντοι, ἔφη,
δικαιότερον τὸν ὑμέτερον πατέρα τύπτοιμι, ὅ τι
μαθὼν σοφοὺς υἱεῖς οὕτως ἔφυσεν. ἀλλ᾽ ἦ που,
ὦ Εὐθύδημε, ἔφη ὁ Κτήσιππος, πόλλ᾽ ἀγαθὰ ἀπὸ
τῆς ὑμετέρας σοφίας ταύτης ἀπολέλαυκεν ὁ πατὴρ
ὁ ὑμέτερός τε καὶ ὁ τῶν κυνιδίων. Ἀλλ᾽ οὐδὲν
δεῖται πολλῶν ἀγαθῶν, ὦ Κτήσιππε, οὔτ᾽ ἐκεῖνος
οὔτε σύ. Οὐδὲ σύ, ἦ δ᾽ ὅς, ὦ Εὐθύδημε, αὐτός;
Οὐδὲ ἄλλος γε οὐδεὶς ἀνθρώπων. εἰπὲ γάρ μοι,
B ὦ Κτήσιππε, εἰ ἀγαθὸν νομίζεις εἶναι ἀσθενοῦντι
φάρμακον πιεῖν ἢ οὐκ ἀγαθὸν εἶναι δοκεῖ σοι,
ὅταν δέηται· ἢ εἰς πόλεμον ὅταν ἴῃ, ὅπλα ἔχοντα
μᾶλλον ἰέναι ἢ ἄνοπλον. Ἔμοιγε, ἔφη. καίτοι
οἶμαί τί σε τῶν καλῶν ἐρεῖν. Σὺ ἄριστα εἴσει,
ἔφη· ἀλλ᾽ ἀποκρίνου. ἐπειδὴ γὰρ ὡμολόγεις
ἀγαθὸν εἶναι φάρμακον, ὅταν δέῃ, πίνειν ἀνθρώπῳ,
ἄλλο τι τοῦτο τὸ ἀγαθὸν ὡς πλεῖστον δεῖ τίνειν,
καὶ καλῶς ἐκεῖ ἕξει, ἐάν τις αὐτῷ τρίψας ἐγκεράσῃ
ἐλλεβόρου ἅμαξαν; καὶ ὁ Κτήσιππος εἶπε, Πάνυ
C γε σφόδρα, ὦ Εὐθύδημε, ἐὰν ᾖ γε ὁ πίνων ὅσος
ὁ ἀνδριὰς ὁ ἐν Δελφοῖς. Οὐκοῦν, ἔφη, καὶ ἐν
τῷ πολέμῳ ἐπειδὴ ἀγαθόν ἐστιν ὅπλα ἔχειν, ὡς
πλεῖστα δεῖ ἔχειν δόρατά τε καὶ ἀσπίδας, ἐπειδήπερ
ἀγαθόν ἐστιν; Μάλα δήπου, ἔφη ὁ Κτήσιππος·

Ctesippus laughed and said: My word, yes; since I cannot beat you!

So you beat your own father? he said.

There would be much more justice, though, he replied, in my beating yours, for being so ill-advised as to beget clever sons like you. Yet I doubt, Ctesippus went on, if your father, Euthydemus— the puppies' father—has derived much good from this wisdom of yours.

Why, he has no need of much good, Ctesippus, neither he nor you.

And have you no need either, yourself, Euthydemus? he asked.

No, nor has any other man. Just tell me, Ctesippus, whether you think it good for a sick man to drink physic when he wants it, or whether you consider it not good; or for a man to go to the wars with arms rather than without them.

With them, I think, he replied: and yet I believe you are about to utter one of your pleasantries.

You will gather that well enough, he said: only answer me. Since you admit that physic is good for a man to drink when necessary, surely one ought to drink this good thing as much as possible; and in such a case it will be well to pound and infuse in it a cart-load of hellebore?

To this Ctesippus replied: Quite so, to be sure, Euthydemus, at any rate if the drinker is as big as the Delphian statue.

Then, further, since in war, he proceeded, it is good to have arms, one ought to have as many spears and shields as possible, if we agree that it is a good thing?

Yes, I suppose, said Ctesippus; and you, Euthy-

σὺ δ' οὐκ οἴει, ὦ Εὐθύδημε, ἀλλὰ μίαν καὶ ἓν
δόρυ; Ἔγωγε. Ἦ καὶ τὸν Γηρυόνην ἄν, ἔφη,
καὶ τὸν Βριάρεων οὕτω σὺ ὁπλίσαις; ἐγὼ δὲ
ᾤμην σε δεινότερον εἶναι, ἅτε ὁπλομάχην ὄντα, καὶ
τόνδε τὸν ἑταῖρον.

Καὶ ὁ μὲν Εὐθύδημος ἐσίγησεν· ὁ δὲ Διονυσό-
D δωρος πρὸς τὰ πρότερον ἀποκεκριμένα τῷ Κτησίππῳ ἤρετο, Οὐκοῦν καὶ χρυσίον, ἦ δ' ὅς, ἀγαθὸν
δοκεῖ σοι εἶναι ἔχειν; Πάνυ, καὶ ταῦτά γε πολύ,
ἔφη ὁ Κτήσιππος. Τί οὖν; ἀγαθὰ οὐ δοκεῖ
σοι χρῆναι[1] ἀεί τ' ἔχειν καὶ πανταχοῦ; Σφόδρα
γ', ἔφη. Οὐκοῦν καὶ τὸ χρυσίον ἀγαθὸν ὁμολογεῖς εἶναι; Ὡμολόγηκα μὲν οὖν, ἦ δ' ὅς. Οὐκοῦν
ἀεὶ δεῖ αὐτὸ ἔχειν καὶ πανταχοῦ καὶ ὡς μάλιστα ἐν
E ἑαυτῷ; καὶ εἴη ἂν εὐδαιμονέστατος, εἰ ἔχοι
χρυσίου μὲν τρία τάλαντα ἐν τῇ γαστρί, τάλαντον
δ' ἐν τῷ κρανίῳ, στατῆρα δὲ χρυσοῦ ἐν ἑκατέρῳ
τὠφθαλμῷ; Φασί γε οὖν, ὦ Εὐθύδημε, ἔφη ὁ
Κτήσιππος, τούτους εὐδαιμονεστάτους εἶναι Σκυθῶν καὶ ἀρίστους ἄνδρας, οἳ χρυσίον τε ἐν τοῖς
κρανίοις ἔχουσι πολὺ τοῖς ἑαυτῶν, ὥσπερ σὺ
νῦν δὴ ἔλεγες τὸν κύνα τὸν πατέρα, καὶ ὃ θαυ-
μασιώτερόν γε ἔτι, ὅτι καὶ πίνουσιν ἐκ τῶν ἑαυτῶν
κρανίων κεχρυσωμένων, καὶ ταῦτα ἐντὸς καθορῶσι,
τὴν ἑαυτῶν κορυφὴν ἐν ταῖς χερσὶν ἔχοντες.
300 Πότερον δὲ ὁρῶσιν, ἔφη ὁ Εὐθύδημος, καὶ Σκύθαι
τε καὶ οἱ ἄλλοι ἄνθρωποι τὰ δυνατὰ ὁρᾶν ἢ τὰ

---

[1] χρῆναι Badham : χρήματα mss.

[a] Two fabulous giants (Geryon had three, Briareus fifty,
pairs of arms).

demus, do you take the other view, that it should be one shield and one spear ?

Yes, I do.

What, he said, and would you arm Geryon also and Briareus[1] in this way ? I thought you more of an expert than that, considering you are a man-at-arms, and your comrade here too !

At this Euthydemus was silent; then Dionyso-dorus asked some questions on Ctesippus' previous answers, saying : Well now, gold is in your opinion a good thing to have ?

Certainly, and—here I agree—plenty of it too, said Ctesippus.

Well then, do you not think it right to have good things always and everywhere ?

Assuredly, he said.

Then do you admit that gold is also a good ?

Why, I have admitted it, he replied.

Then we ought always to have it, and everywhere, and above all, in oneself ? And one will be happiest if one has three talents of gold in one's belly, a talent in one's skull, and a stater of gold in each eye ?

Well, Euthydemus, replied Ctesippus, they say that among the Scythians those are the happiest and best men who have a lot of gold in their own skulls—somewhat as you were saying a moment ago that " dog " is " father " ; and a still more marvellous thing is told, how they drink out of their skulls when gilded, and gaze inside them, holding their own headpiece in their hands.

Tell me, said Euthydemus, do the Scythians and men in general see things possible of sight, or things impossible ?

ἀδύνατα; Τὰ δυνατὰ δήπου. Οὐκοῦν καὶ σύ, ἔφη; Κἀγώ. Ὁρᾷς οὖν τὰ ἡμέτερα ἱμάτια; Ναί. Δυνατὰ οὖν ὁρᾶν ἐστι ταῦτα. Ὑπερφυῶς, ἔφη ὁ Κτήσιππος. Τί δέ; ἦ δ' ὅς. Μηδέν. σὺ δ' ἴσως οὐκ οἴει αὐτὰ ὁρᾶν· οὕτως ἡδὺς εἶ. ἀλλά μοι δοκεῖς, Εὐθύδημε, οὐ καθεύδων ἐπικεκοιμῆσθαι, καὶ εἰ οἷόν τε λέγοντα μηδὲν λέγειν,
B καὶ σὺ τοῦτο ποιεῖν.

Ἦ γὰρ οὐκ οἷόν τε, ἔφη ὁ Διονυσόδωρος, σιγῶντα λέγειν; Οὐδ' ὁπωστιοῦν, ἦ δ' ὃς ὁ Κτήσιππος. Ἆρ' οὐδὲ λέγοντα σιγᾶν; Ἔτι ἧττον, ἔφη. Ὅταν οὖν λίθους λέγῃς καὶ ξύλα καὶ σιδήρια, οὐ σιγῶντα λέγεις; Οὔκουν, εἴ γε ἐγώ, ἔφη, παρέρχομαι ἐν τοῖς χαλκείοις, ἀλλὰ φθεγγόμενα καὶ βοῶντα μέγιστον τὰ σιδήρια λέγεται, ἐάν τις ἅψηται· ὥστε τοῦτο μὲν ὑπὸ σοφίας ἔλαθες οὐδὲν εἰπών. ἀλλ' ἔτι μοι τὸ ἕτερον ἐπιδείξατον,
C ὅπως αὖ ἔστι λέγοντα σιγᾶν. καί μοι ἐδόκει ὑπεραγωνιᾶν ὁ Κτήσιππος διὰ τὰ παιδικά. Ὅταν σιγᾷς, ἔφη ὁ Εὐθύδημος, οὐ πάντα σιγᾷς; Ἔγωγε, ἦ δ' ὅς. Οὐκοῦν καὶ τὰ λέγοντα σιγᾷς, εἴπερ τῶν ἁπάντων ἐστὶ τὰ λέγοντα.[1] Τί δέ; ἔφη ὁ Κτήσιππος, οὐ σιγᾷ πάντα; Οὐ δήπου, ἔφη ὁ Εὐθύ-

---

[1] τὰ λέγοντα Stephanus : τὰ λεγόμενα MSS.

---

[1] The quibble is on the double meaning of δυνατὰ ὁρᾶν —(a) "possible," and (b) "able to see." So in what follows, σιγῶντα λέγειν may mean both "the speaking of a silent person," or "speaking of silent things."

Possible, I presume.

And you do so too ?

I too.

Then you see our cloaks ?

Yes.

And have they power of sight ?[1]

Quite extraordinarily, said Ctesippus.

What do they see ? he asked.

Nothing. Perhaps you do not think they see —you are such a sweet innocent. I should say, Euthydemus, that you have fallen asleep with your eyes open and, if it be possible to speak and at the same time say nothing, that this is what you are doing.

Why, asked Dionysodorus, may there not be a speaking of the silent ?

By no means whatever, replied Ctesippus.

Nor a silence of speaking ?

Still less, he said.

Now, when you speak of stones and timbers and irons, are you not speaking of the silent ?

Not if I walk by a smithy, for there, as they say, the irons speak and cry aloud, when they are touched ; so here your wisdom has seduced you into nonsense. But come, you have still to propound me your second point, how on the other hand there may be a silence of speaking. (It struck me that Ctesippus was specially excited on account of his young friend's presence.)

When you are silent, said Euthydemus, are you not making a silence of all things ?

Yes, he replied.

Then it is a silence of speaking things also, if the speaking are among all things.

What, said Ctesippus, are not all things silent ?

I presume not, said Euthydemus.

δημος. 'Αλλ' ἄρα, ὦ βέλτιστε, λέγει τὰ πάντα;
Τά γε δήπου λέγοντα. 'Αλλά, ἦ δ' ὅς, οὐ τοῦτο
ἐρωτῶ, ἀλλὰ τὰ πάντα σιγᾷ ἢ λέγει; Οὐδέτερα
D καὶ ἀμφότερα, ἔφη ὑφαρπάσας ὁ Διονυσόδωρος·
εὖ γὰρ οἶδα ὅτι τῇ ἀποκρίσει οὐχ ἕξεις ὅ τι χρῇ.
καὶ ὁ Κτήσιππος, ὥσπερ εἰώθει, μέγα πάνυ ἀνα-
καγχάσας, Ὦ Εὐθύδημε, ἔφη, ὁ ἀδελφός σου
ἐξημφοτέρικε τὸν λόγον, καὶ ἀπόλωλέ τε καὶ
ἥττηται. καὶ ὁ Κλεινίας πάνυ ἥσθη καὶ ἐγέλασεν,
ὥστε ὁ Κτήσιππος ἐγένετο πλεῖον ἢ δεκαπλάσιος·
ὁ δ' οἶμαι,[1] πανοῦργος ὤν, ὁ Κτήσιππος, παρ'
αὐτῶν τούτων αὐτὰ ταῦτα παρηκηκόει· οὐ γάρ
ἐστιν ἄλλων τοιαύτη σοφία τῶν νῦν ἀνθρώπων.

E Κἀγὼ εἶπον, Τί γελᾷς, ὦ Κλεινία, ἐπὶ σπου-
δαίοις οὕτω πράγμασι καὶ καλοῖς; Σὺ γὰρ ἤδη τι
πώποτε εἶδες, ὦ Σώκρατες, καλὸν πρᾶγμα; ἔφη ὁ
Διονυσόδωρος. Ἔγωγε, ἔφην, καὶ πολλά γε, ὦ
Διονυσόδωρε. Ἆρα ἕτερα ὄντα τοῦ καλοῦ, ἔφη,
301 ἢ ταὐτὰ τῷ καλῷ; κἀγὼ ἐν παντὶ ἐγενόμην ὑπὸ
ἀπορίας, καὶ ἡγούμην δίκαια πεπονθέναι, ὅτι
ἔγρυξα, ὅμως δὲ ἕτερα ἔφην αὐτοῦ γε τοῦ καλοῦ·
πάρεστι μέντοι ἑκάστῳ αὐτῶν κάλλος τι. Ἐὰν
οὖν, ἔφη, παραγένηταί σοι βοῦς, βοῦς εἶ, καὶ ὅτι
νῦν ἐγώ σοι πάρειμι, Διονυσόδωρος εἶ; Εὐφήμει

---

[1] δ' οἶμαι Badham : δέ μοι MSS.

But then, my good sir, do all things speak?

Yes, I suppose, at least those that speak.

But that is not what I ask, he said: are all things silent or do they speak?

Neither and both, said Dionysodorus, snatching the word from him: I am quite sure that is an answer that will baffle you!

At this Ctesippus, as his manner was, gave a mighty guffaw, and said: Ah, Euthydemus, your brother has made the argument ambiguous with his " both," and is worsted and done for.

Then Cleinias was greatly delighted and laughed, so that Ctesippus felt his strength was as the strength of ten: but I fancy Ctesippus—he is such a rogue— had picked up these very words by overhearing the men themselves, since in nobody else of the present age is such wisdom to be found.

So I remarked: Why are you laughing, Cleinias, at such serious and beautiful things?

What, have you, Socrates, ever yet seen a beautiful thing? asked Dionysodorus.

Yes, I have, I replied, and many of them, Dionysodorus.

Did you find them different from the beautiful, he said, or the same as the beautiful?

Here I was desperately perplexed, and felt that I had my deserts for the grunt I had made: however, I replied that they were different from the beautiful itself, though each of them had some beauty present with it.

So if an ox is present with you, he said, you are an ox, and since I am now present with you, you are Dionysodorus.

Heavens, do not say that! I cried.

τοῦτό γε, ἦν δ᾽ ἐγώ. Ἀλλὰ τίνα τρόπον, ἔφη,
ἑτέρου ἑτέρῳ παραγενομένου τὸ ἕτερον ἕτερον ἂν
B εἴη; Ἆρα τοῦτο, ἔφην ἐγώ, ἀπορεῖς; ἤδη δὲ
τοῖν ἀνδροῖν τὴν σοφίαν ἐπεχείρουν μιμεῖσθαι,
ἅτε ἐπιθυμῶν αὐτῆς. Πῶς γὰρ οὐκ ἀπορῶ, ἔφη,
καὶ ἐγὼ καὶ οἱ ἄλλοι ἅπαντες ἄνθρωποι, ὃ μὴ
ἔστιν; Τί λέγεις, ἦν δ᾽ ἐγώ, ὦ Διονυσόδωρε; οὐ
τὸ καλὸν καλόν ἐστι καὶ τὸ αἰσχρὸν αἰσχρόν; Ἐὰν
ἔμοιγε, ἔφη, δοκῇ. Οὐκοῦν δοκεῖ; Πάνυ γε,
ἔφη. Οὐκοῦν καὶ τὸ ταὐτὸν ταὐτὸν καὶ τὸ ἕτερον
ἕτερον; οὐ γὰρ δήπου τό γε ἕτερον ταὐτόν, ἀλλ᾽
C ἔγωγε οὐδ᾽ ἂν παῖδα ᾤμην τοῦτο ἀπορῆσαι, ὡς οὐ
τὸ ἕτερον ἕτερόν ἐστιν. ἀλλ᾽, ὦ Διονυσόδωρε,
τοῦτο μὲν ἑκὼν παρῆκας, ἐπεὶ τὰ ἄλλα μοι δοκεῖτε
ὥσπερ οἱ δημιουργοί, οἷς ἕκαστα προσήκει ἀπεργάζεσθαι, καὶ ὑμεῖς τὸ διαλέγεσθαι παγκάλως
ἀπεργάζεσθαι. Οἶσθα οὖν, ἔφη, ὅ τι προσήκει
ἑκάστοις τῶν δημιουγῶν; πρῶτον τίνα χαλκεύειν
προσήκει, οἶσθα; Ἔγωγε· ὅτι χαλκέα. Τί δὲ
κεραμεύειν; Κεραμέα. Τί δὲ σφάττειν τε καὶ
D ἐκδέρειν καὶ τὰ σμικρὰ κρέα κατακόψαντα ἕψειν
καὶ ὀπτᾶν; Μάγειρον, ἦν δ᾽ ἐγώ. Οὐκοῦν ἐάν
τις, ἔφη, τὰ προσήκοντα πράττῃ, ὀρθῶς πράξει;

But in what way can one thing, by having a different thing present with it, be itself different?

Are you at a loss there? I asked: already I was attempting to imitate the cleverness of these men, I was so eager to get it.

Can I help being at a loss, he said, I and likewise everybody else in the world, in face of what cannot be?

What is that you say, Dionysodorus? I asked: is not the beautiful beautiful, and the ugly ugly?

Yes, if it seems so to me, he replied.

Then does it seem so?

Certainly, he said.

Then the same also is the same, and the different different? For I presume the different cannot be the same; nay, I thought not even a child would doubt that the different is different. But, Dionysodorus, you have deliberately passed over this one point; though, on the whole, I feel that, like craftsmen finishing off each his special piece of work, you two are carrying out your disputation in excellent style.

Well, he asked, do you know what is each craftsman's special piece of work? First of all, whose proper task is it to forge brass? Can you tell?

I can: a brazier's.

Well, again, whose to make pots?

A potter's.

Once more, whose to slaughter and skin, and after cutting up the joints to stew and roast?

A caterer's, I said.

Now, if one does one's proper work, he said, one will do rightly?

301

Μάλιστα. Προσήκει δέ γε, ὡς φής, τὸν μάγειρον
κατακόπτειν καὶ ἐκδέρειν; ὡμολόγησας ταῦτα ἢ
οὔ; Ὡμολόγησα, ἔφην, ἀλλὰ συγγνώμην μοι
ἔχε. Δῆλον τοίνυν, ἦ δ᾽ ὅς, ὅτι ἄν τις σφάξας
τὸν μάγειρον καὶ κατακόψας ἑψήσῃ καὶ ὀπτήσῃ,
τὰ προσήκοντα ποιήσει· καὶ ἐὰν τὸν χαλκέα τις
αὐτὸν χαλκεύῃ καὶ τὸν κεραμέα κεραμεύῃ, καὶ
οὗτος τὰ προσήκοντα πράξει.

E   Ὦ Πόσειδον, ἦν δ᾽ ἐγώ, ἤδη κολοφῶνα ἐπιτίθης
τῇ σοφίᾳ. ἆρά μοί ποτε αὕτη παραγενήσεται,
ὥστε μοι οἰκεία γενέσθαι; Ἐπιγνοίης ἂν αὐτήν,
ὦ Σώκρατες, ἔφη, οἰκείαν γενομένην; Ἐὰν σύ γε
βούλῃ, ἔφην ἐγώ, δῆλον ὅτι. Τί δέ, ἦ δ᾽ ὅς, τὰ
σαυτοῦ οἴει γιγνώσκειν; Εἰ μή τι σὺ ἄλλο λέγεις·
ἀπὸ σοῦ γὰρ δεῖ ἄρχεσθαι, τελευτᾶν δ᾽ εἰς Εὐθύδημον τόνδε. Ἆρ᾽ οὖν, ἔφη, ταῦτα ἡγεῖ σὰ
εἶναι, ὧν ἂν ἄρξῃς καὶ ἐξῇ σοι αὐτοῖς χρῆσθαι ὃ
302 τι ἂν βούλῃ; οἷον βοῦς καὶ πρόβατον, ἆρ᾽ ἂν
ἡγοῖο ταῦτα σὰ εἶναι, ἅ σοι ἐξείη καὶ ἀποδόσθαι
καὶ δοῦναι καὶ θῦσαι ὅτῳ βούλοιο θεῶν; ἃ δ᾽ ἂν
μὴ οὕτως ἔχῃ, οὐ σά; κἀγώ, ἤδη γὰρ ὅτι ἐξ
αὐτῶν καλόν τι ἀνακύψοιτο τῶν ἐρωτημάτων,
καὶ ἅμα βουλόμενος ὅ τι τάχιστ᾽ ἀκοῦσαι, Πάνυ
μὲν οὖν, ἔφην, οὕτως ἔχει· τὰ τοιαῦτα ἐστὶ μόνα

---

[1] The Greek words follow a usual form of prayer or hymn
to the gods.

486

Yes, to be sure.

And is it, as you say, the caterer's proper work to cut up and skin? Did you admit this or not?

I did so, I replied, but pray forgive me.

It is clear then, he proceeded, that if someone slaughters the caterer and cuts him up, and then stews or roasts him, he will be doing his proper work; and if he hammers the brazier himself, and moulds the potter, he will be doing his business likewise.

Poseidon! I exclaimed, there you give the finishing-touch to your wisdom. I wonder if this skill could ever come to me in such manner as to be my very own.

Would you recognize it, Socrates, he asked, if it came to be your own?

Yes, if only you are agreeable, I replied, without a doubt.

Why, he went on, do you imagine you perceive what is yours?

Yes, if I take your meaning aright: for all my hopes arise from you, and end in Euthydemus here.[1]

Then tell me, he asked, do you count those things yours which you control and are free to use as you please? For instance, an ox or a sheep,—would you count these as yours, if you were free to sell or bestow them, or sacrifice them to any god you chose? And things which you could not treat thus are not yours?

Hereupon, since I knew that some brilliant result was sure to bob up from the mere turn of the questions, and as I also wanted to hear it as quickly as possible, I said: It is precisely as you say; only such things are mine.

ἐμά. Τί δέ; ζῷα, ἔφη, οὐ ταῦτα καλεῖς, ἃ ἂν
B ψυχὴν ἔχῃ; Ναί, ἔφην. Ὁμολογεῖς οὖν τῶν
ζῴων ταῦτα μόνα εἶναι σά, περὶ ἃ ἄν σοι ἐξουσία
ᾖ πάντα ταῦτα ποιεῖν, ἃ νῦν δὴ ἐγὼ ἔλεγον; Ὁμολογῶ. καὶ ὅς, εἰρωνικῶς πάνυ ἐπισχὼν ὥς τι
μέγα σκοπούμενος, Εἰπέ μοι, ἔφη, ὦ Σώκρατες,
ἔστι σοι Ζεὺς πατρῷος; καὶ ἐγὼ ὑποπτεύσας
ἥξειν τὸν λόγον ᾗπερ ἐτελεύτησεν, ἄπορόν τινα
στροφὴν ἔφευγόν τε καὶ ἐστρεφόμην ἤδη ὥσπερ
ἐν δικτύῳ εἰλημμένος· Οὐκ ἔστιν, ἦν δ᾽ ἐγώ, ὦ
Διονυσόδωρε. Ταλαίπωρος ἄρα τις σύ γε ἄνθρω-
C πος εἶ καὶ οὐδὲ Ἀθηναῖος, ᾧ μήτε θεοὶ πατρῷοί
εἰσι μήτε ἱερὰ μήτε ἄλλο μηδὲν καλὸν καὶ ἀγαθόν.
Ἔα, ἦν δ᾽ ἐγώ, ὦ Διονυσόδωρε, εὐφήμει τε καὶ μὴ
χαλεπῶς με προδίδασκε. ἔστι γὰρ ἔμοιγε καὶ
βωμοὶ καὶ ἱερὰ οἰκεῖα καὶ πατρῷα καὶ τὰ ἄλλα
ὅσαπερ τοῖς ἄλλοις Ἀθηναίοις τῶν τοιούτων.
Εἶτα τοῖς ἄλλοις, ἔφη, Ἀθηναίοις οὐκ ἔστι Ζεὺς ὁ
πατρῷος; Οὐκ ἔστιν, ἦν δ᾽ ἐγώ, αὕτη ἡ ἐπωνυμία
Ἰώνων οὐδενί, οὔθ᾽ ὅσοι ἐκ τῆσδε τῆς πόλεως
ἀπῳκισμένοι εἰσὶν οὔθ᾽ ἡμῖν, ἀλλὰ Ἀπόλλων
D πατρῷος διὰ τὴν τοῦ Ἴωνος γένεσιν· Ζεὺς δ᾽
ἡμῖν πατρῷος μὲν οὐ καλεῖται, ἕρκειος δὲ καὶ
φράτριος, καὶ Ἀθηναία[1] φρατρία. Ἀλλ᾽ ἀρκεῖ
γε, ἔφη ὁ Διονυσόδωρος. ἔστι γάρ σοι, ὡς ἔοικεν,
Ἀπόλλων τε καὶ Ζεὺς καὶ Ἀθηνᾶ. Πάνυ, ἦν δ᾽

---

[1] Ἀθηναία Cobet : Ἀθηνᾶ mss.

---

[1] Zeus was the ancestral or tutelary god of the Dorians.
[2] Cf. Eurip. Ion, 64-75. Apollo begot Ion upon Creusa,
daughter of Erechtheus.

Well now, he went on; you call those things animals which have life?

Yes, I said.

And you admit that only those animals are yours which you are at liberty to deal with in those various ways that I mentioned just now?

I admit that.

Then—after a very ironical pause, as though he were pondering some great matter—he proceeded: Tell me, Socrates, have you an ancestral Zeus[1]?

Here I suspected the discussion was approaching the point at which it eventually ended, and so I tried what desperate wriggle I could to escape from the net in which I now felt myself entangled. My answer was: I have not, Dionysodorus.

What a miserable fellow you must be, he said, and no Athenian at all, if you have neither ancestral gods, nor shrines, nor anything else that denotes a gentleman!

Enough, Dionysodorus; speak fair words, and don't browbeat your pupil! For I have altars and shrines, domestic and ancestral, and everything else of the sort that other Athenians have.

Then have not other Athenians, he asked, their ancestral Zeus?

None of the Ionians, I replied, give him this title, neither we nor those who have left this city to settle abroad: they have an ancestral Apollo, because of Ion's parentage.[2] Among us the name "ancestral" is not given to Zeus, but that of "house-ward" and "tribal," and we have a tribal Athena.

That will do, said Dionysodorus; you have, it seems, Apollo and Zeus and Athena.

Certainly, I said.

302

ἐγώ. Οὐκοῦν καὶ οὗτοι σοὶ θεοὶ ἂν εἶεν; ἔφη.
Πρόγονοι, ἦν δ' ἐγώ, καὶ δεσπόται. Ἀλλ' οὖν σοί
γε, ἔφη· ἢ οὐ σοὺς ὡμολόγηκας αὐτοὺς εἶναι;
Ὡμολόγηκα, ἔφην· τί γὰρ πάθω; Οὐκοῦν, ἔφη,
καὶ ζῷά εἰσιν οὗτοι οἱ θεοί; ὡμολόγηκας γάρ,
E ὅσα ψυχὴν ἔχει, ζῷα εἶναι. ἢ οὗτοι οἱ θεοὶ οὐκ
ἔχουσι ψυχήν; Ἔχουσιν, ἦν δ' ἐγώ. Οὐκοῦν
καὶ ζῷά εἰσιν; Ζῷα, ἔφην. Τῶν δέ γε ζῴων, ἔφη,
ὡμολόγηκας ταῦτ' εἶναι σά, ὅσα ἄν σοι ἐξῇ καὶ
δοῦναι καὶ ἀποδόσθαι καὶ θῦσαι ἂν θεῷ ὅτῳ ἂν βούλῃ.
Ὡμολόγηκα, ἔφην. οὐκ ἔστι γάρ μοι ἀνάδυσις, ὦ
Εὐθύδημε. Ἴθι δή μοι εὐθύς, ἦ δ' ὅς, εἰπέ
ἐπειδὴ σὸν ὁμολογεῖς εἶναι τὸν Δία καὶ τοὺς
ἄλλους θεούς, ἆρα ἔξεστί σοι αὐτοὺς ἀποδόσθαι
303 ἢ δοῦναι ἢ ἄλλ' ὅ τι ἂν βούλῃ χρῆσθαι ὥσπερ τοῖς
ἄλλοις ζῴοις; ἐγὼ μὲν οὖν, ὦ Κρίτων, ὥσπερ
πληγεὶς ὑπὸ τοῦ λόγου, ἐκείμην ἄφωνος· ὁ δὲ
Κτήσιππός μοι ἰὼν ὡς βοηθήσων, Πυππὰξ ὦ
Ἡράκλεις, ἔφη, καλοῦ λόγου. καὶ ὁ Διονυσόδωρος,
Πότερον οὖν, ἔφη, ὁ Ἡρακλῆς πυππάξ ἐστιν ἢ
ὁ πυππὰξ Ἡρακλῆς; καὶ ὁ Κτήσιππος, Ὦ Πόσειδον, ἔφη, δεινῶν λόγων· ἀφίσταμαι· ἀμάχω
τὼ ἄνδρε.

B Ἐνταῦθα μέντοι, ὦ φίλε Κρίτων, οὐδεὶς ὅστις
οὐ τῶν παρόντων ὑπερεπήνεσε τὸν λόγον καὶ τὼ
ἄνδρε, καὶ γελῶντες καὶ κροτοῦντες καὶ χαίροντες[1]
ὀλίγου παρετάθησαν. ἐπὶ μὲν γὰρ τοῖς ἔμπρο-

[1] γελῶντες ... κροτοῦντες ... χαίροντες Badham : γελῶντε
... κροτοῦντε ... χαίροντε MSS.

490

Then these must be your gods? he said.

My ancestors, I said, and lords.

Well, at least, you have them, he said: or have you not admitted they are yours?

I have admitted it, I replied: what else could I do?

And are not these gods animals? he asked: you know you have admitted that whatever has life is an animal. Or have these gods no life?

They have, I replied.

Then are they not animals?

Yes, animals, I said.

And those animals, he went on, you have admitted to be yours, which you are free to bestow and sell and sacrifice to any god you please.

I have admitted it, I replied; there is no escape for me, Euthydemus.

Come then, tell me straight off, he said; since you admit that Zeus and the other gods are yours, are you free to sell or bestow them or treat them just as you please, like the other animals?

Well, Crito, here I must say I was knocked out, as it were, by the argument, and lay speechless; then Ctesippus rushed to the rescue and—Bravo, Hercules! he cried, a fine argument!

Whereat Dionysodorus asked: Now, do you mean that Hercules is a bravo, or that bravo is Hercules?

Ctesippus replied: Poseidon, what a frightful use of words! I give up the fight: these two are invincible.

Hereupon I confess, my dear Crito, that everyone present without exception wildly applauded the argument and the two men, till they all nearly died of laughing and clapping and rejoicing. For their

σθεν ἐφ' ἑκάστοις πᾶσι παγκάλως ἐθορύβουν μόνοι
οἱ τοῦ Εὐθυδήμου ἐρασταί, ἐνταῦθα δὲ ὀλίγου καὶ
οἱ κίονες οἱ ἐν τῷ Λυκείῳ ἐθορύβησάν τ' ἐπὶ τοῖν
ἀνδροῖν καὶ ἥσθησαν. ἐγὼ μὲν οὖν καὶ αὐτὸς
οὕτω διετέθην, ὥστε ὁμολογεῖν μηδένας πώποτε
C ἀνθρώπους ἰδεῖν οὕτω σοφούς, καὶ παντάπασι
καταδουλωθεὶς ὑπὸ τῆς σοφίας αὐτοῖν ἐπὶ τὸ
ἐπαινεῖν τε καὶ ἐγκωμιάζειν αὐτὼ ἐτραπόμην, καὶ
εἶπον· ῏Ω μακάριοι σφὼ τῆς θαυμαστῆς φύσεως,
οἳ τοσοῦτον πρᾶγμα οὕτω ταχὺ καὶ ἐν ὀλίγῳ χρόνῳ
ἐξείργασθον. πολλὰ μὲν οὖν καὶ ἄλλα οἱ λόγοι
ὑμῶν καλὰ ἔχουσιν, ὦ Εὐθύδημέ τε καὶ Διονυσό-
δωρε· ἐν δὲ τοῖς καὶ τοῦτο μεγαλοπρεπέστερον,
ὅτι τῶν πολλῶν ἀνθρώπων καὶ τῶν σεμνῶν δὴ καὶ
δοκούντων τὶ εἶναι οὐδὲν ὑμῖν μέλει, ἀλλὰ τῶν
ὁμοίων ὑμῖν μόνον. ἐγὼ γὰρ εὖ οἶδα, ὅτι τούτους
D τοὺς λόγους πάνυ μὲν ἂν ὀλίγοι ἀγαπῷεν ἄνθρωποι
ὅμοιοι ὑμῖν, οἱ δ' ἄλλοι οὕτω νοοῦσιν αὐτούς, ὥστ'
εὖ οἶδ' ὅτι αἰσχυνθεῖεν ἂν μᾶλλον ἐξελέγχοντες
τοιούτοις λόγοις τοὺς ἄλλους ἢ αὐτοὶ ἐξελεγχόμενοι.
καὶ τόδε αὖ ἕτερον δημοτικόν τι καὶ πρᾷον ἐν
τοῖς λόγοις· ὁπόταν φῆτε μήτε καλὸν εἶναι μηδὲν
μήτε ἀγαθὸν πρᾶγμα μήτε λευκὸν μηδ' ἄλλο τῶν
τοιούτων μηδέν, μηδὲ τὸ παράπαν ἑτέρων ἕτερον,
ἀτεχνῶς μὲν τῷ ὄντι ξυρράπτετε τὰ στόματα τῶν
E ἀνθρώπων, ὥσπερ καὶ φατέ· ὅτι δ' οὐ μόνον τὰ
τῶν ἄλλων, ἀλλὰ δόξαιτε ἂν καὶ τὰ ὑμέτερα αὐτώ,
τοῦτο πάνυ χαρίεν τέ ἐστι καὶ τὸ ἐπαχθὲς τῶν λόγων ἀφαιρεῖται. τὸ δὲ δὴ μέγιστον, ὅτι ταῦτα
οὕτως ἔχει ὑμῖν καὶ τεχνικῶς ἐξεύρηται, ὥστε πάνυ
ὀλίγῳ χρόνῳ ὁντινοῦν ἂν μαθεῖν ἀνθρώπων, ἔγνων

previous successes had been highly acclaimed one
by one, but only by the devotees of Euthydemus ;
whereas now almost the very pillars of the Lyceum
took part in the joyful acclamations in honour of
the pair. For myself, I was quite disposed to
admit that never had I set eyes on such clever
people, and I was so utterly enthralled by their
skill that I betook myself to praising and congratulat-
ing them, and said : Ah, happy pair ! What amazing
genius, to acquire such a great accomplishment so
quickly and in so short a time ! Among the many
fine points in your arguments, Euthydemus and
Dionysodorus, there is one that stands out in
particular magnificence—that you care not a jot
for the multitude, or for any would-be important or
famous people, but only for those of your own sort.
And I am perfectly sure that there are but a few
persons like yourselves who would be satisfied with
these arguments : the rest of the world regard them
only as arguments with which, I assure you, they
would feel it a greater disgrace to refute others
than to be refuted themselves. And further, there
is at the same time a popular and kindly feature in
your talk : when you say there is nothing either
beautiful, or good, or white, and so on, and no
difference of things at all, in truth you simply
stitch up men's mouths, as you expressly say you
do ; while as to your apparent power of stitching
up your own mouths as well, this is a piece of agreeable manners that takes off any offence from your
talk. But the greatest thing of all is, that this
faculty of yours is such, and is so skilfully contrived,
that anyone in the world may learn it of you in a
very short time ; this fact I perceived myself by

ἔγωγε καὶ τῷ Κτησίππῳ τὸν νοῦν προσέχων, ὡς
ταχὺ ὑμᾶς ἐκ τοῦ παραχρῆμα μιμεῖσθαι οἷός τ'
ἦν. τοῦτο μὲν οὖν τοῦ πράγματος σφῶν πρὸς μὲν
304 τὸ ταχὺ παραδιδόναι καλόν, ἐναντίον δ' ἀνθρώπων
διαλέγεσθαι οὐκ ἐπιτήδειον, ἀλλ' ἄν γ' ἐμοὶ πεί-
θησθε, εὐλαβήσεσθε μὴ πολλῶν ἐναντίον λέγειν, ἵνα
μὴ ταχὺ ἐκμαθόντες ὑμῖν μὴ εἰδῶσι χάριν· ἀλλὰ
μάλιστα μὲν αὐτὼ πρὸς ἀλλήλω μόνω διαλέγεσθον,
εἰ δὲ μή, εἴπερ ἄλλου του ἐναντίον, ἐκείνου μόνου,
ὃς ἂν ὑμῖν διδῷ ἀργύριον. τὰ αὐτὰ δὲ ταῦτα,
B ἐὰν σωφρονῆτε, καὶ τοῖς μαθηταῖς συμβουλεύσετε,
μηδέποτε μηδενὶ ἀνθρώπων διαλέγεσθαι, ἀλλ' ἢ
ὑμῖν τε καὶ αὑτοῖς. τὸ γὰρ σπάνιον, ὦ Εὐθύδημε,
τίμιον· τὸ δὲ ὕδωρ εὐωνότατον, ἄριστον ὄν, ὡς
ἔφη Πίνδαρος. ἀλλ' ἄγετε, ἦν δ' ἐγώ, ὅπως κἀμὲ
καὶ Κλεινίαν τόνδε παραδέξεσθον.

Ταῦτα, ὦ Κρίτων, καὶ ἄλλα βραχέα διαλε-
χθέντες ἀπῇμεν. σκόπει οὖν, ὅπως συμφοιτήσεις
C παρὰ τὼ ἄνδρε, ὡς ἐκείνω φατὸν οἵω τ' εἶναι διδάξαι
τὸν ἐθέλοντ' ἀργύριον διδόναι, καὶ οὔτε φύσιν οὔθ'
ἡλικίαν ἐξείργειν οὐδεμίαν—ὃ δὲ καὶ σοὶ μάλιστα
προσήκει ἀκοῦσαι, ὅτι οὐδὲ τοῦ χρηματίζεσθαί
φατον διακωλύειν οὐδέν—μὴ οὐ παραλαβεῖν ὁντινοῦν
εὐπετῶς τὴν σφετέραν σοφίαν.

ΚΡΙ. Καὶ μήν, ὦ Σώκρατες, φιλήκοος μὲν
ἔγωγε καὶ ἡδέως ἄν τι μανθάνοιμι, κινδυνεύω
μέντοι κἀγὼ εἷς εἶναι τῶν οὐχ ὁμοίων Εὐθυδήμῳ,
ἀλλ' ἐκείνων, ὧν δὴ καὶ σὺ ἔλεγες, τῶν ἥδιον ἂν
D ἐξελεγχομένων ὑπὸ τῶν τοιούτων λόγων ἢ ἐξ-
ελεγχόντων. ἀτὰρ γελοῖον μέν μοι δοκεῖ εἶναι

watching Ctesippus and observing how quickly he was able to imitate you on the spot. Now, in so far as your accomplishment can be quickly imparted, it is excellent; but for public discussions it is not suitable : if I may advise you, beware of talking before a number of people, lest they learn the whole thing in a trice and give you no credit for it. The best thing for you is to talk to each other by yourselves, in private; failing that, if a third person is present, it must be someone who will pay you a good fee. And if you are prudent you will give this same counsel to your pupils also—that they are never to converse with anybody except you and each other. For it is the rare, Euthydemus, that is precious, while water is cheapest, though best, as Pindar[1] said. But come, I said, see if you can admit both me and Cleinias here to your class.

This, Crito, was our conversation, and after exchanging a few more words we went off. Now you must arrange to join us in taking lessons from the pair; for they say they are able to teach anyone who is willing to pay good money, and that no sort of character or age—and it is well that you especially should be told that they promise that their art is no hindrance to money-making—need deter anyone from an easy acquisition of their wisdom.

CRI. Indeed, Socrates, I love listening, and would be glad to learn from them; but I am afraid I am one of the sort who are not like Euthydemus, but who, as you described them just now, would prefer being refuted to refuting with such arguments. Now, although I feel it is absurd to admonish you,

---

[1] *Cf.* Pindar, *Ol.* i., which begins—Ἄριστον μὲν ὕδωρ.

τὸ νουθετεῖν σε, ὅμως δέ, ἅ γ᾽ ἤκουον, ἐθέλω σοι
ἀπαγγεῖλαι. τῶν ἀφ᾽ ὑμῶν ἀπιόντων ἴσθ᾽ ὅτι
προσελθών τίς μοι περιπατοῦντι, ἀνὴρ οἰόμενος
πάνυ εἶναι σοφός, τούτων τις τῶν περὶ τοὺς λόγους
τοὺς εἰς τὰ δικαστήρια δεινῶν, Ὦ Κρίτων, ἔφη,
οὐδὲν ἀκροᾷ τῶνδε τῶν σοφῶν; Οὐ μὰ τὸν Δία, ἦν
δ᾽ ἐγώ· οὐ γὰρ οἷός τ᾽ ἦ προσστὰς κατακούειν ὑπὸ
τοῦ ὄχλου. Καὶ μήν, ἔφη, ἄξιόν γ᾽ ἦν ἀκοῦσαι.
E Τί δέ; ἦν δ᾽ ἐγώ. Ἵνα ἤκουσας ἀνδρῶν διαλεγομένων, οἳ νῦν σοφώτατοί εἰσι τῶν περὶ τοὺς
τοιούτους λόγους. κἀγὼ εἶπον, Τί οὖν ἐφαί-
νοντό σοι; Τί δὲ ἄλλο, ἦ δ᾽ ὅς, ἢ οἷάπερ ἀεὶ ἄν
τις τῶν τοιούτων ἀκοῦσαι ληρούντων καὶ περὶ
οὐδενὸς ἀξίων ἀναξίαν σπουδὴν ποιουμένων; οὑτωσὶ γάρ πως καὶ εἶπε τοῖς ὀνόμασι. καὶ ἐγώ,
Ἀλλὰ μέντοι, ἔφην, χαρίεν γέ τι πρᾶγμά ἐστιν
ἡ φιλοσοφία. Ποῖον, ἔφη, χαρίεν, ὦ μακάριε;
305 οὐδενὸς μὲν οὖν ἄξιον, ἀλλὰ καὶ εἰ νῦν παρεγένου,
πάνυ ἄν σε οἶμαι αἰσχυνθῆναι ὑπὲρ τοῦ σεαυτοῦ
ἑταίρου· οὕτως ἦν ἄτοπος, ἐθέλων ἑαυτὸν παρέχειν ἀνθρώποις, οἷς οὐδὲν μέλει ὅ τι ἂν λέγωσι,
παντὸς δὲ ῥήματος ἀντέχονται. καὶ οὗτοι, ὅπερ
ἄρτι ἔλεγον, ἐν τοῖς κρατίστοις εἰσὶ τῶν νῦν.
ἀλλὰ γάρ, ὦ Κρίτων, ἔφη, τὸ πρᾶγμα αὐτὸ καὶ
οἱ ἄνθρωποι οἱ ἐπὶ τῷ πράγματι διατρίβοντες
φαῦλοί εἰσι καὶ καταγέλαστοι. ἐμοὶ δέ, ὦ
Σώκρατες, τὸ πρᾶγμα ἐδόκει οὐκ ὀρθῶς ψέγειν
B οὔθ᾽ οὗτος οὔτ᾽ εἴ τις ἄλλος ψέγει· τὸ μέντοι

I wish nevertheless to report to you what was told me just now. Do you know, one of the people who had left your discussion came up to me as I was taking a stroll—a man who thinks himself very wise, one of those who are so clever at turning out speeches for the law-courts [1]—and said: Crito, do you take no lessons from these wise men? No, in truth, I replied: there was such a crowd that, though I stood quite close, I was unable to catch what was said. Well, let me tell you, he said, it was something worth hearing. What was it? I asked. You would have heard the disputation of men who are the most accomplished of our day in that kind of speaking. To this I replied: Well, what did they show forth to you? Merely the sort of stuff, he said, that you may hear such people babbling about at any time—making an inconsequent ado about matters of no consequence (in some such parlance he expressed himself). Whereupon—Well, all the same, I said, philosophy is a charming thing. Charming is it, my dear innocent? he exclaimed: nay, a thing of no consequence. Why, had you been in that company just now, you would have been filled with shame, I fancy, for your particular friend: he was so strangely willing to lend himself to persons who care not a straw what they say, but merely fasten on any phrase that turns up. And these, as I said just now, are the heads of their profession to-day. But the fact is, Crito, he went on, the business itself and the people who follow it are worthless and ridiculous. Now, in my opinion, Socrates, he was not right in decrying the pursuit; he is wrong, and so is anyone else who decries it:

---

[1] The allusion is probably to Isocrates.

ἐθέλειν διαλέγεσθαι τοιούτοις ἐναντίον πολλῶν
ἀνθρώπων ὀρθῶς μοι ἐδόκει μέμφεσθαι.

ΣΩ. Ὦ Κρίτων, θαυμάσιοί εἰσιν οἱ τοιοῦτοι
ἄνδρες. ἀτὰρ οὔπω οἶδα ὅ τι μέλλω ἐρεῖν.
ποτέρων ἦν ὁ προσελθών σοι καὶ μεμφόμενος τὴν
φιλοσοφίαν; πότερον τῶν ἀγωνίσασθαι δεινῶν
ἐν τοῖς δικαστηρίοις, ῥήτωρ τις, ἢ τῶν τοὺς τοιούτους εἰσπεμπόντων, ποιητὴς τῶν λόγων, οἷς οἱ
ῥήτορες ἀγωνίζονται;

C   ΚΡΙ. Ἥκιστα νὴ τὸν Δία ῥήτωρ, οὐδὲ οἶμαι
πώποτ᾽ αὐτὸν ἐπὶ δικαστήριον ἀναβεβηκέναι· ἀλλ᾽
ἐπαΐειν αὐτόν φασι περὶ τοῦ πράγματος νὴ τὸν
Δία καὶ δεινὸν εἶναι καὶ δεινοὺς λόγους συντιθέναι.

ΣΩ. Ἤδη μανθάνω· περὶ τούτων καὶ αὐτὸς
νῦν δὴ ἔμελλον λέγειν. οὗτοι γάρ εἰσι μέν, ὦ
Κρίτων, οὓς ἔφη Πρόδικος μεθόρια φιλοσόφου
τε ἀνδρὸς καὶ πολιτικοῦ, οἴονται δ᾽ εἶναι πάντων
σοφώτατοι ἀνθρώπων, πρὸς δὲ τῷ εἶναι καὶ
δοκεῖν πάνυ παρὰ πολλοῖς, ὥστε παρὰ πᾶσιν
D   εὐδοκιμεῖν ἐμποδὼν σφίσιν εἶναι οὐδένας ἄλλους
ἢ τοὺς περὶ φιλοσοφίαν ἀνθρώπους. ἡγοῦνται
οὖν, ἐὰν τούτους εἰς δόξαν καταστήσωσι μηδενὸς
δοκεῖν ἀξίους εἶναι, ἀναμφισβητήτως ἤδη παρὰ
πᾶσι τὰ νικητήρια εἰς δόξαν οἴσεσθαι σοφίας πέρι.
εἶναι μὲν γὰρ τῇ ἀληθείᾳ σφᾶς σοφωτάτους, ἐν
δὲ τοῖς ἰδίοις λόγοις ὅταν ἀπολειφθῶσιν, ὑπὸ τῶν
ἀμφὶ Εὐθύδημον κολούεσθαι. σοφοὶ δὲ ἡγοῦνται
εἶναι πάνυ εἰκότως· μετρίως μὲν γὰρ φιλοσοφίας
ἔχειν, μετρίως δὲ πολιτικῶν, πάνυ ἐξ εἰκότος

though I must say I felt he was right in blaming the readiness to engage in discussion with such people before a large company.

soc. Crito, these people are very odd. But I do not yet know what answer I shall give you. Of which party was he who came up to you and blamed philosophy? Was he one of those who excel in the contests of the courts, an orator; or of those who equip the orators for the fray, a composer of the speeches they deliver in their contests?

cri. Nothing of an orator, I dare swear, nor do I think he has ever appeared in court: only he is reputed to know about the business, so they declare, and to be a clever person, and compose clever speeches.

soc. Now I understand: it was of these people that I was just now going to speak myself. They are the persons, Crito, whom Prodicus described as the border-ground between philosopher and politician, yet they fancy that they are the wisest of all mankind, and that they not merely are but are thought so by a great many people; and accordingly they feel that none but the followers of philosophy stand in the way of their universal renown. Hence they believe that, if they can reduce the latter to a status of no esteem, the prize of victory will by common consent be awarded to them, without dispute or delay, and their claim to wisdom will be won. For they consider themselves to be in very truth the wisest, but find that, when caught in private conversation, they are cut off short by Euthydemus and his set. This conceit of their wisdom is very natural, since they regard themselves as moderately versed in philosophy, and moderately too in politics, on

305

Ε λόγου· μετέχειν γὰρ ἀμφοτέρων ὅσον ἔδει, ἐκτὸς
δὲ ὄντες κινδύνων καὶ ἀγώνων καρποῦσθαι τὴν
σοφίαν.

ΚΡΙ. Τί οὖν; δοκοῦσί σοι τὶ, ὦ Σώκρατες,
λέγειν; οὐ γάρ τοι ἀλλ' ὅ γε λόγος ἔχει τινὰ εὐπρέπειαν τῶν ἀνδρῶν.

ΣΩ. Καὶ γὰρ ἔχει οὕτως, ὦ Κρίτων, εὐπρέπειαν
306 μᾶλλον ἢ ἀλήθειαν. οὐ γὰρ ῥᾴδιον αὐτοὺς
πεῖσαι, ὅτι καὶ ἄνθρωποι καὶ τἆλλα πάντα, ὅσα
μεταξύ τινοῖν δυοῖν ἐστὶ καὶ ἀμφοτέροιν τυγχάνει
μετέχοντα, ὅσα μὲν ἐκ κακοῦ καὶ ἀγαθοῦ, τοῦ
μὲν βελτίω, τοῦ δὲ χείρω γίγνεται· ὅσα δὲ ἐκ
δυοῖν ἀγαθοῖν μὴ πρὸς ταὐτόν, ἀμφοῖν χείρω,
πρὸς ὃ ἂν ἑκάτερον ᾖ χρηστὸν ἐκείνων, ἐξ ὧν
συνετέθη· ὅσα δὲ ἐκ δυοῖν κακοῖν συντεθέντα
μὴ πρὸς τὸ αὐτὸ ὄντοιν ἐν τῷ μέσῳ ἐστί, ταῦτα
Β μόνα βελτίω ἑκατέρου ἐκείνων ἐστίν, ὧν ἀμφοτέρων
μέρος μετέχουσιν. εἰ μὲν οὖν ἡ φιλοσοφία
ἀγαθόν ἐστι καὶ ἡ πολιτικὴ πρᾶξις, πρὸς ἄλλο
δὲ ἑκάτερα, οὗτοι δ' ἀμφοτέρων μετέχοντες
τούτων ἐν μέσῳ εἰσίν, οὐδὲν λέγουσιν· ἀμφοτέρων
γάρ εἰσι φαυλότεροι· εἰ δὲ ἀγαθὸν καὶ κακόν,
τῶν μὲν βελτίους, τῶν δὲ χείρους· εἰ δὲ κακὰ
ἀμφότερα, οὕτως ἄν τι λέγοιεν ἀληθές, ἄλλως
δ' οὐδαμῶς. οὐκ ἂν οὖν οἶμαι αὐτοὺς ὁμολο-
C γῆσαι οὔτε κακὼ αὐτὼ ἀμφοτέρω εἶναι οὔτε τὸ
μὲν κακόν, τὸ δὲ ἀγαθόν· ἀλλὰ τῷ ὄντι οὗτοι
ἀμφοτέρων μετέχοντες ἀμφοτέρων ἥττους εἰσὶ

quite reasonable grounds : for they have dipped into both as far as they needed, and, evading all risk and struggle, are content to gather the fruits of wisdom.

CRI. Well, now, do you consider, Socrates, that there is anything in what they say ? It is not to be denied that these men have some colour for their statements.

SOC. Yes, that is so, Crito ; colour rather than truth. It is no easy matter to persuade them that either people or things, which are between two other things and have a certain share of both, if compounded of bad and good are found to be better than the one and worse than the other ; but if compounded of two good things which have not the same object, they are worse than either of their components in relation to the object to which each of them is adapted ; while if they are compounded of two bad things which have not the same object, and stand between them, this is the only case where they are better than either of the two things of which they have a share. Now if philosophy and the statesman's business are both good things, and each of them has a different object, and if these persons, partaking of both, are between them, their claims are nought ; for they are inferior to both : if one is good and the other bad, they are better than the one and worse than the other : while if both are bad, in this case there would be some truth in their statement, but in any other case there is none. Now I do not think they will admit either that both these things are bad, or that one is bad and the other good : the truth is that these people, partaking of both, are inferior to both in respect of

πρὸς ἑκάτερον, πρὸς ὃ ἥ τε πολιτικὴ καὶ ἡ φιλοσοφία ἀξίω λόγου ἐστόν, καὶ τρίτοι ὄντες τῇ
ἀληθείᾳ ζητοῦσι πρῶτοι δοκεῖν εἶναι. συγγι-
γνώσκειν μὲν οὖν αὐτοῖς χρὴ τῆς ἐπιθυμίας καὶ
μὴ χαλεπαίνειν, ἡγεῖσθαι μέντοι τοιούτους εἶναι
οἷοί εἰσι· πάντα γὰρ ἄνδρα χρὴ ἀγαπᾶν, ὅστις
καὶ ὁτιοῦν λέγει ἐχόμενον φρονήσεως πρᾶγμα
D καὶ ἀνδρείως ἐπεξιὼν διαπονεῖται.

ΚΡΙ. Καὶ μήν, ὦ Σώκρατες, καὶ αὐτὸς περὶ
τῶν υἱέων, ὥσπερ ἀεὶ πρός σε λέγω, ἐν ἀπορίᾳ
εἰμί, τί δεῖ αὐτοῖς χρήσασθαι. ὁ μὲν οὖν νεώτερος ἔτι καὶ σμικρός ἐστι, Κριτόβουλος δ' ἤδη
ἡλικίαν ἔχει καὶ δεῖταί τινος, ὅστις αὐτὸν ὀνήσει.
ἐγὼ μὲν οὖν ὅταν σοὶ ξυγγένωμαι, οὕτω δια-
τίθεμαι, ὥστε μοι δοκεῖν μανίαν εἶναι τὸ ἕνεκα
τῶν παίδων ἄλλων μὲν πολλῶν σπουδὴν τοιαύτην
E ἐσχηκέναι, καὶ περὶ τοῦ γάμου, ὅπως ἐκ γεν-
ναιοτάτης ἔσονται μητρός, καὶ περὶ τῶν χρημάτων,
ὅπως ὡς πλουσιώτατοι, αὐτῶν δὲ περὶ παιδείας
ἀμελῆσαι· ὅταν δὲ εἴς τινα ἀποβλέψω τῶν φασκόντων ἂν παιδεῦσαι ἀνθρώπους, ἐκπέπληγμαι,
καί μοι δοκεῖ εἰς ἕκαστος αὐτῶν σκοποῦντι πάνυ
307 ἀλλόκοτος εἶναι, ὥς γε πρὸς σὲ τἀληθῆ εἰρῆσθαι·
ὥστε οὐκ ἔχω ὅπως προτρέπω τὸ μειράκιον
ἐπὶ φιλοσοφίαν.

ΣΩ. Ὦ φίλε Κρίτων, οὐκ οἶσθα, ὅτι ἐν παντὶ
ἐπιτηδεύματι οἱ μὲν φαῦλοι πολλοὶ καὶ οὐδενὸς
ἄξιοι, οἱ δὲ σπουδαῖοι ὀλίγοι καὶ παντὸς ἄξιοι;
ἐπεὶ γυμναστικὴ οὐ καλὸν δοκεῖ σοι εἶναι, καὶ
χρηματιστικὴ καὶ ῥητορικὴ καὶ στρατηγία;

the objects for which statesmanship and philosophy are important; and while they are really in the third place they seek to be accorded the first. However, we ought to be indulgent towards their ambition and not feel annoyed, while still judging them to be what they actually are. For we should be glad of anyone, whoever he may be, who says anything that verges on good sense, and labours steadily and manfully in its pursuit.

CRI. Now I myself, Socrates, as I so often tell you, am in doubt about my sons, as to what I am to do with them. The younger is as yet quite small; but Critobulus is already grown up, and needs someone who will be of service to him. When I am in your company, the effect on me is such as to make me feel it is mere madness to have taken ever so much pains in various directions for the good of my children—first in so marrying that they should be of very good blood on their mother's side; then in making money so that they might be as well off as possible; while I have neglected the training of the boys themselves. But when I glance at one of the persons who profess to educate people, I am dismayed, and feel that each one of them, when I consider them, is wholly unsuitable—to tell you the truth between ourselves. So that I cannot see how I am to incline the lad towards philosophy.

SOC. My dear Crito are you not aware that in every trade the duffers are many and worthless, whereas the good workers are few and worth any price? Why, do you not hold athletics, and money-making, and rhetoric, and generalship, to be fine things?

ΚΡΙ. Ἔμοιγε πάντως δήπου.

Β   ΣΩ. Τί οὖν· ἐν ἑκάστῃ τούτων τοὺς πολλοὺς πρὸς ἕκαστον τὸ ἔργον οὐ καταγελάστους ὁρᾷς;

ΚΡΙ. Ναὶ μὰ τὸν Δία, καὶ μάλα ἀληθῆ λέγεις.

ΣΩ. Ἦ οὖν τούτου ἕνεκα αὐτός τε φεύξει πάντα τὰ ἐπιτηδεύματα καὶ τῷ υἱεῖ οὐκ ἐπιτρέψεις;

ΚΡΙ. Οὔκουν δίκαιόν γε, ὦ Σώκρατες.

ΣΩ. Μὴ τοίνυν ὅ γε οὐ χρὴ ποίει, ὦ Κρίτων, ἀλλ' ἐάσας χαίρειν τοὺς ἐπιτηδεύοντας φιλοσοφίαν, Ϲ   εἴτε χρηστοί εἰσιν εἴτε πονηροί, αὐτὸ τὸ πρᾶγμα βασανίσας καλῶς τε καὶ εὖ, ἐὰν μέν σοι φαίνηται φαῦλον ὄν, πάντ' ἄνδρα ἀπότρεπε, μὴ μόνον τοὺς υἱεῖς· ἐὰν δὲ φαίνηται οἷον οἶμαι αὐτὸ ἐγὼ εἶναι, θαρρῶν δίωκε καὶ ἄσκει, τὸ λεγόμενον δὴ τοῦτο αὐτός τε καὶ τὰ παιδία.

CRI. Certainly I do, of course.

SOC. Well then, in each of these, do you not see most men making a ridiculous show at their respective tasks?

CRI. Yes, I know: what you say is perfectly true.

SOC. Then will you yourself on this account eschew all these pursuits, and not let your son have anything to do with them?

CRI. No, there would be no good reason for that, Socrates.

SOC. Then avoid at least what is wrong, Crito: let those who practise philosophy have their way, whether they are helpful or mischievous; and when you have tested the matter itself, well and truly, if you find it to be a poor affair, turn everyone you can away from it, not only your sons: but if you find it to be such as I think it is, pursue and ply it without fear, both you, as they say, and yours.

INDEX OF NAMES

INDEX

INDEX

Printed in Great Britain by R. & R. CLARK, LIMITED, *Edinburgh*

THE LOEB CLASSICAL LIBRARY

VOLUMES ALREADY PUBLISHED

LATIN AUTHORS

AMMIANUS MARCELLINUS. J. C. Rolfe. 3 Vols.

APULEIUS: THE GOLDEN ASS (METAMORPHOSES). W. Adlington (1566). Revised by S. Gaselee.

ST. AUGUSTINE: CITY OF GOD. 7 Vols. Vol. I. G. E. McCracken. Vol. II. W. M. Green. Vol. III. D. Wiesen. Vol. IV. P. Levine. Vol. V. E. M. Sanford and W. M. Green. Vol. VI. W. C. Greene.

ST. AUGUSTINE, CONFESSIONS OF. W. Watts (1631). 2 Vols.

ST. AUGUSTINE: SELECT LETTERS. J. H. Baxter.

AUSONIUS. H. G. Evelyn White. 2 Vols.

BEDE. J. E. King. 2 Vols.

BOETHIUS: TRACTS AND DE CONSOLATIONE PHILOSOPHIAE. Rev. H. F. Stewart and E. K. Rand.

CAESAR: ALEXANDRIAN, AFRICAN AND SPANISH WARS. A. G. Way.

CAESAR: CIVIL WARS. A. G. Peskett.

CAESAR: GALLIC WAR. H. J. Edwards.

CATO AND VARRO: DE RE RUSTICA. H. B. Ash and W. D. Hooper.

CATULLUS. F. W. Cornish: TIBULLUS. J. B. Postgate; and PERVIGILIUM VENERIS. J. W. Mackail.

CELSUS: DE MEDICINA. W. G. Spencer. 3 Vols.

CICERO: BRUTUS AND ORATOR. G. L. Hendrickson and H. M. Hubbell.

CICERO: DE FINIBUS. H. Rackham.

CICERO: DE INVENTIONE, etc. H. M. Hubbell.

CICERO: DE NATURA DEORUM AND ACADEMICA. H. Rackham.

CICERO: DE OFFICIIS. Walter Miller.

CICERO: DE ORATORE, etc. 2 Vols. Vol. I: DE ORATORE, Books I and II. E. W. Sutton and H. Rackham. Vol. II: DE ORATORE, Book III; DE FATO; PARADOXA STOICORUM; DE PARTITIONE ORATORIA. H. Rackham.

CICERO: DE REPUBLICA, DE LEGIBUS, SOMNIUM SCIPIONIS. Clinton W. Keyes.

1

THE LOEB CLASSICAL LIBRARY

NEMESIANUS, AVIANUS, with "Aetna," "Phoenix" and other poems. J. Wight Duff and Arnold M. Duff.
OVID: THE ART OF LOVE AND OTHER POEMS. J. H. Mozley.
OVID: FASTI. Sir James G. Frazer.
OVID: HEROIDES AND AMORES. Grant Showerman.
OVID: METAMORPHOSES. F. J. Miller. 2 Vols.
OVID: TRISTIA AND EX PONTO. A. L. Wheeler.
PETRONIUS. M. Heseltine: SENECA: APOCOLOCYNTOSIS. W. H. D. Rouse.
PHAEDRUS AND BABRIUS (Greek). B. E. Perry.
PLAUTUS. Paul Nixon. 5 Vols.
PLINY: LETTERS. Melmoth's translation revised by W. M. L. Hutchinson. 2 Vols.
PLINY: NATURAL HISTORY. 10 Vols. Vols. I-V and IX. H. Rackham. Vols. VI-VIII. W. H. S. Jones. Vol. X. D. E. Eichholz.
PROPERTIUS. H. E. Butler.
PRUDENTIUS. H. J. Thomson. 2 Vols.
QUINTILIAN. H. E. Butler. 4 Vols.
REMAINS OF OLD LATIN. E. H. Warmington. 4 Vols. Vol. I (Ennius and Caecilius). Vol. II (Livius, Naevius, Pacuvius, Accius). Vol. III (Lucilius, Laws of the XII Tables). Vol. IV (Archaic Inscriptions).
SALLUST. J. C. Rolfe.
SCRIPTORES HISTORIAE AUGUSTAE. D. Magie. 3 Vols.
SENECA: APOCOLOCYNTOSIS. Cf. PETRONIUS.
SENECA: EPISTULAE MORALES. R. M. Gummere. 3 Vols.
SENECA: MORAL ESSAYS. J. W. Basore. 3 Vols.
SENECA: TRAGEDIES. F. J. Miller. 2 Vols.
SIDONIUS: POEMS AND LETTERS. W. B. Anderson. 2 Vols.
SILIUS ITALICUS. J. D. Duff. 2 Vols.
STATIUS. J. H. Mozley. 2 Vols.
SUETONIUS. J. C. Rolfe. 2 Vols.
TACITUS: DIALOGUS. Sir Wm. Peterson; and AGRICOLA AND GERMANIA. Maurice Hutton.
TACITUS: HISTORIES AND ANNALS. C. H. Moore and J. Jackson. 4 Vols.
TERENCE. John Sargeaunt. 2 Vols.
TERTULLIAN: APOLOGIA AND DE SPECTACULIS. T. R. Glover; MINUCIUS FELIX. G. H. Rendall.
VALERIUS FLACCUS. J. H. Mozley.
VARRO: DE LINGUA LATINA. R. G. Kent. 2 Vols.
VELLEIUS PATERCULUS AND RES GESTAE DIVI AUGUSTI. F. W. Shipley.

VIRGIL. H. R. Fairclough. 2 Vols.
VITRUVIUS: DE ARCHITECTURA. F. Granger. 2 Vols.

GREEK AUTHORS

ACHILLES TATIUS. S. Gaselee.
AELIAN: ON THE NATURE OF ANIMALS. A. F. Scholfield. 3 Vols.
AENEAS TACTICUS, ASCLEPIODOTUS AND ONASANDER. The Illinois Greek Club.
AESCHINES. C. D. Adams.
AESCHYLUS. H. Weir Smyth. 2 Vols.
ALCIPHRON, AELIAN AND PHILOSTRATUS: LETTERS. A. R. Benner and F. H. Fobes.
APOLLODORUS. Sir James G. Frazer. 2 Vols.
APOLLONIUS RHODIUS. R. C. Seaton.
THE APOSTOLIC FATHERS. Kirsopp Lake. 2 Vols.
APPIAN'S ROMAN HISTORY. Horace White. 4 Vols.
ARATUS. *Cf.* CALLIMACHUS.
ARISTOPHANES. Benjamin Bickley Rogers. 3 Vols. Verse trans.
ARISTOTLE: ART OF RHETORIC. J. H. Freese.
ARISTOTLE: ATHENIAN CONSTITUTION, EUDEMIAN ETHICS, VIRTUES AND VICES. H. Rackham.
ARISTOTLE: THE CATEGORIES. ON INTERPRETATION. H. P. Cooke; PRIOR ANALYTICS. H. Tredennick.
ARISTOTLE: GENERATION OF ANIMALS. A. L. Peck.
ARISTOTLE: HISTORIA ANIMALIUM. A. L. Peck. 3 Vols. Vol. I.
ARISTOTLE: METAPHYSICS. H. Tredennick. 2 Vols.
ARISTOTLE: METEOROLOGICA. H. D. P. Lee.
ARISTOTLE: MINOR WORKS. W. S. Hett. "On Colours," "On Things Heard," "Physiognomics," "On Plants," "On Marvellous Things Heard," "Mechanical Problems," "On Indivisible Lines," "Situations and Names of Winds," "On Melissus, Xenophanes, and Gorgias."
ARISTOTLE: NICOMACHEAN ETHICS. H. Rackham.
ARISTOTLE: OECONOMICA AND MAGNA MORALIA. G. C. Armstrong. (With Metaphysics, Vol. II.)
ARISTOTLE: ON THE HEAVENS. W. K. C. Guthrie.
ARISTOTLE: ON THE SOUL, PARVA NATURALIA. On Breath. W. S. Hett.

THE LOEB CLASSICAL LIBRARY

ARISTOTLE : PARTS OF ANIMALS. A. L. Peck ; MOTION AND PROGRESSION OF ANIMALS. E. S. Forster.

ARISTOTLE : PHYSICS. Rev. P. Wicksteed and F. M. Cornford. 2 Vols.

ARISTOTLE : POETICS ; LONGINUS ON THE SUBLIME. W. Hamilton Fyfe ; DEMETRIUS ON STYLE. W. Rhys Roberts.

ARISTOTLE : POLITICS. H. Rackham.

ARISTOTLE : POSTERIOR ANALYTICS. H. Tredennick ; TOPICS. E. S. Forster.

ARISTOTLE : PROBLEMS. W. S. Hett. 2 Vols.

ARISTOTLE : RHETORICA AD ALEXANDRUM. H. Rackham. (With Problems, Vol. II.)

ARISTOTLE : SOPHISTICAL REFUTATIONS. COMING-TO-BE AND PASSING-AWAY. E. S. Forster ; ON THE COSMOS. D. J. Furley.

ARRIAN : HISTORY OF ALEXANDER AND INDICA. Rev. E. Iliffe Robson. 2 Vols.

ATHENAEUS : DEIPNOSOPHISTAE. C. B. Gulick. 7 Vols.

BABRIUS AND PHAEDRUS (Latin). B. E. Perry.

ST. BASIL : LETTERS. R. J. Deferrari. 4 Vols.

CALLIMACHUS : FRAGMENTS. C. A. Trypanis.

CALLIMACHUS : HYMNS AND EPIGRAMS, AND LYCOPHRON. A. W. Mair ; ARATUS. G. R. Mair.

CLEMENT OF ALEXANDRIA. Rev. G. W. Butterworth.

COLLUTHUS. *Cf.* OPPIAN.

DAPHNIS AND CHLOE. *Cf.* LONGUS.

DEMOSTHENES I : OLYNTHIACS, PHILIPPICS AND MINOR ORATIONS : I-XVII AND XX. J. H. Vince.

DEMOSTHENES II : DE CORONA AND DE FALSA LEGATIONE, C. A. Vince and J. H. Vince.

DEMOSTHENES III : MEIDIAS, ANDROTION, ARISTOCRATES, TIMOCRATES, ARISTOGEITON. J. H. Vince.

DEMOSTHENES IV-VI : PRIVATE ORATIONS AND IN NEAERAM. A. T. Murray.

DEMOSTHENES VII : FUNERAL SPEECH, EROTIC ESSAY, EXORDIA AND LETTERS. N. W. and N. J. DeWitt.

DIO CASSIUS : ROMAN HISTORY. E. Cary. 9 Vols.

DIO CHRYSOSTOM. 5 Vols. Vols. I and II. J. W. Cohoon. Vol. III. J. W. Cohoon and H. Lamar Crosby. Vols IV and V. H. Lamar Crosby.

DIODORUS SICULUS. 12 Vols. Vols. I-VI. C. H. Oldfather. Vol. VII. C. L. Sherman. Vol. VIII. C. B. Welles. Vols. IX and X. Russel M. Geer. Vols. XI and XII. F. R. Walton. General Index. Russel M. Geer.

DIOGENES LAERTIUS. R. D. Hicks. 2 Vols.

DIONYSIUS OF HALICARNASSUS: ROMAN ANTIQUITIES. Spelman's translation revised by E. Cary. 7 Vols.

EPICTETUS. W. A. Oldfather. 2 Vols.

EURIPIDES. A. S. Way. 4 Vols. Verse trans.

EUSEBIUS: ECCLESIASTICAL HISTORY. Kirsopp Lake and J. E. L. Oulton. 2 Vols.

GALEN: ON THE NATURAL FACULTIES. A. J. Brock.

THE GREEK ANTHOLOGY. W. R. Paton. 5 Vols.

THE GREEK BUCOLIC POETS (THEOCRITUS, BION, MOSCHUS). J. M. Edmonds.

GREEK ELEGY AND IAMBUS WITH THE ANACREONTEA. J. M. Edmonds. 2 Vols.

GREEK MATHEMATICAL WORKS. Ivor Thomas. 2 Vols.

HERODES. Cf. THEOPHRASTUS: CHARACTERS.

HERODOTUS. A. D. Godley. 4 Vols.

HESIOD AND THE HOMERIC HYMNS. H. G. Evelyn White.

HIPPOCRATES AND THE FRAGMENTS OF HERACLEITUS. W. H. S. Jones and E. T. Withington. 4 Vols.

HOMER: ILIAD. A. T. Murray. 2 Vols.

HOMER: ODYSSEY. A. T. Murray. 2 Vols.

ISAEUS. E. S. Forster.

ISOCRATES. George Norlin and LaRue Van Hook. 3 Vols.

ST. JOHN DAMASCENE: BARLAAM AND IOASAPH. Rev. G. R. Woodward, Harold Mattingly and D. M. Lang.

JOSEPHUS. 9 Vols. Vols. I-IV. H. St. J. Thackeray. Vol. V. H. St. J. Thackeray and Ralph Marcus. Vols. VI and VII. Ralph Marcus. Vol. VIII. Ralph Marcus and Allen Wikgren. Vol. IX. L. H. Feldman.

JULIAN. Wilmer Cave Wright. 3 Vols.

LONGUS: DAPHNIS AND CHLOE. Thornley's translation revised by J. M. Edmonds; and PARTHENIUS. S. Gaselee.

LUCIAN. 8 Vols. Vols. I-V. A. M. Harmon. Vol. VI. K. Kilburn. Vols. VII and VIII. M. D. Macleod.

LYCOPHRON. Cf. CALLIMACHUS.

LYRA GRAECA. J. M. Edmonds. 3 Vols.

LYSIAS. W. R. M. Lamb.

MANETHO. W. G. Waddell; PTOLEMY: TETRABIBLOS. F. E. Robbins.

MARCUS AURELIUS. C. R. Haines.

MENANDER. F. G. Allinson.

MINOR ATTIC ORATORS. 2 Vols. K. J. Maidment and J. O. Burtt.

NONNOS: DIONYSIACA. W. H. D. Rouse. 3 Vols.

THE LOEB CLASSICAL LIBRARY

OPPIAN, COLLUTHUS, TRYPHIODORUS. A. W. Mair.

PAPYRI. NON-LITERARY SELECTIONS. A. S. Hunt and C. C. Edgar. 2 Vols. LITERARY SELECTIONS (Poetry). D. L. Page.

PARTHENIUS. *Cf.* LONGUS.

PAUSANIAS: DESCRIPTION OF GREECE. W. H. S. Jones. 5 Vols. and Companion Vol. arranged by R. E. Wycherley.

PHILO. 10 Vols. Vols. I-V. F. H. Colson and Rev. G. H. Whitaker. Vols. VI-X. F. H. Colson. General Index. Rev. J. W. Earp.
Two Supplementary Vols. Translation only from an Armenian Text. Ralph Marcus.

PHILOSTRATUS: THE LIFE OF APOLLONIUS OF TYANA. F. C. Conybeare. 2 Vols.

PHILOSTRATUS: IMAGINES: CALLISTRATUS: DESCRIPTIONS. A. Fairbanks.

PHILOSTRATUS AND EUNAPIUS: LIVES OF THE SOPHISTS. Wilmer Cave Wright.

PINDAR. Sir J. E. Sandys.

PLATO: CHARMIDES, ALCIBIADES, HIPPARCHUS, THE LOVERS, THEAGES, MINOS AND EPINOMIS. W. R. M. Lamb.

PLATO: CRATYLUS, PARMENIDES, GREATER HIPPIAS, LESSER HIPPIAS. H. N. Fowler.

PLATO: EUTHYPHRO, APOLOGY, CRITO, PHAEDO, PHAEDRUS. H. N. Fowler.

PLATO: LACHES, PROTAGORAS, MENO, EUTHYDEMUS. W. R. M. Lamb.

PLATO: LAWS. Rev. R. G. Bury. 2 Vols.

PLATO: LYSIS, SYMPOSIUM, GORGIAS. W. R. M. Lamb.

PLATO: REPUBLIC. Paul Shorey. 2 Vols.

PLATO: STATESMAN, PHILEBUS. H. N. Fowler; ION. W. R. M. Lamb.

PLATO: THEAETETUS AND SOPHIST. H. N. Fowler.

PLATO: TIMAEUS, CRITIAS, CLITOPHO, MENEXENUS, EPISTULAE. Rev. R. G. Bury.

PLOTINUS. A. H. Armstrong. 6 Vols. Vols. I-II.

PLUTARCH: MORALIA. 15 Vols. Vols. I-V. F. C. Babbitt. Vol. VI. W. C. Helmbold. Vol. VII. P. H. De Lacy and B. Einarson. Vol. IX. E. L. Minar, Jr., F. H. Sandbach, W. C. Helmbold. Vol. X. H. N. Fowler. Vol. XI. L. Pearson, F. H. Sandbach. Vol. XII. H. Cherniss, W. C. Helmbold. Vol. XIV. P. H. De Lacy and B. Einarson.

PLUTARCH: THE PARALLEL LIVES. B. Perrin. 11 Vols.

POLYBIUS. W. R. Paton. 6 Vols.

THE LOEB CLASSICAL LIBRARY

Procopius : History of the Wars. H. B. Dewing. 7 Vols.
Ptolemy : Tetrabiblos. *Cf.* Manetho.
Quintus Smyrnaeus. A. S. Way. Verse trans.
Sextus Empiricus. Rev. R. G. Bury. 4 Vols.
Sophocles. F. Storr. 2 Vols. Verse trans.
Strabo : Geography. Horace L. Jones. 8 Vols.
Theophrastus : Characters. J. M. Edmonds ; Herodes,
etc. A. D. Knox.
Theophrastus : Enquiry into Plants. Sir Arthur Hort.
2 Vols.
Thucydides. C. F. Smith. 4 Vols.
Tryphiodorus. *Cf.* Oppian.
Xenophon : Anabasis. C. L. Brownson.
Xenophon : Cyropaedia. Walter Miller. 2 Vols.
Xenophon : Hellenica. C. L. Brownson. 2 Vols.
Xenophon : Memorabilia and Oeconomicus. E. C. Marchant. Symposium and Apology. O. J Todd.
Xenophon : Scripta Minora. E. C. Marchant and G. W.
Bowersock.

VOLUMES IN PREPARATION

GREEK AUTHORS

Aristides : Orations. C. A. Behr.
Herodianus. C. R. Whittaker.
Libanius : Selected Works. A. F. Norman.
Musaeus : Hero and Leander. T. Gelzer and C. H.
Whitman.
Theophrastus : De Causis Plantarum. G. K. K. Link and
B. Einarson.

LATIN AUTHORS

Asconius : Commentaries on Cicero's Orations. G. W.
Bowersock.
Benedict : The Rule. P. Meyvaert.
Justin-Trogus. R. Moss.
Manilius. G. P. Gould.
Pliny : Letters. B. Radice.

DESCRIPTIVE PROSPECTUS ON APPLICATION

CAMBRIDGE, MASS.	LONDON
HARVARD UNIV. PRESS	WILLIAM HEINEMANN LTD